THE NORTH-WEST
MOUNTED
POLICE

1873 – 1885

JACK F. DUNN

The North-West Mounted Police, 1873–1885
Copyright © 2017 by Jack F. Dunn

PUBLISHER: Jack F. Dunn
6404 Norfolk Drive, N.W.
Calgary, Alberta, Canada.
T2K 5K2
jfdunn@telus.net

The Historical Resources Foundation (Alberta) provided a grant
to defray travel and photographic reproduction costs.

AUTHOR: Jack F. Dunn
EDITORS: Maureen Ranson and Alex Frazer Harrison
BOOK DESIGN/LAYOUT: Ghaile Pocock
PRINTING: Friesens

ISBN 978-0-9698596-1-1
Canadian Intellectual Property Office CIPO

Library and Archives Canada Cataloguing in Publication

Dunn, Jack F., author
The North-West Mounted Police: 1873–85/Jack Dunn
Includes bibliographical references and index.
ISBN 978-0-9698596-1-1 (hardback)

North West Mounted Police (Canada)–History.
2. Northwest, Canadian–History–1870–1905. 1. Title.

FC3216.2.D86 2016   971.2'02   C2016-906076-4

FIRST EDITION
Printed in Canada

My thanks to my wife, Maureen;

my daughter, Shawn; my son, David;

and my granddaughter, Ireland

for your patience, humour and support

CONTENTS

VISUAL REFERENCES

MAPS

CHARTS

ACKNOWLEDGEMENTS

Many dedicated archivists and librarians contributed to the research. I sincerely thank the staff at the Glenbow Museum Archives (Calgary), RCMP Museum (Regina), National Archives (Ottawa), Medicine Hat Museum, Royal BC Museum (Victoria), Athabasca Archives, Manitoba Provincial Archives (Winnipeg), Provincial Archives Alberta (Edmonton), Saskatchewan Archives Board (Regina and Saskatoon), Sir Alexander Galt Museum Archives (Lethbridge) Maple Creek Museum, Kootenai Pioneer Village (Pincher Creek), North Dakota Archives, South Dakota State Historical Society, Montana State Archives (Helena), University of Montana (Missoula), The British Library (London, England), North Battleford National Historic Site, Wood Mountain Historic Site, Fort Walsh Historic Site, Snake Creek Battle Site (Montana), Calgary Public Library, and the Bruce Peel Special Collections Archive, University of Alberta. Thank you to Jim Wallace for providing research information and to Bob Clay, Landis, Saskatchewan, for a historic photograph.

Six individuals have contributed immensely to the completion of this history project. Maureen Ranson edited the manuscript and launched the research. Alex Frazer-Harrison proofread and edited the final text. Ghaile Pocock did the design and layout for the book and the cover. Jodi Ann Eskritt, RCMP Museum, Regina, assisted with documentation of photographs. Robin van Eck completed the final reading. My friend, Arthur DePatie, supplied the maps.

PREFACE

THIS BOOK—*The North-West Mounted Police: 1873–85*—outlines the formative years of the Force in certainly the most momentous twelve-year period in Canadian Prairie History.

The arrival of the NWMP in 1874 established law and order in the western plains, opening the land for white settlement. Significant economic developments followed. River steamships and a transnational railway replaced the Red River carts in moving bulk goods and, second, effectively reduced the time spent on travel. Mail delivery, rudimentary telephone service, telegraph lines, and a dozen regional newspapers transformed communication. Agriculture and ranching underwent enormous growth: by 1885, more than one million bushels of both oats and wheat were exported while 70,000 range cattle grazed on the land that recently held great buffalo herds. Nascent industry emerged with lumber mills and coal mines. Towns rose overnight: the appearance of buildings, gardens, and trees altering the landscape. The region was surveyed in the largest such undertaking in history. The 1885 census listed a population of more than 50,000. Whites had become the largest ethnic group.

Settlement introduced important political and social features in the west. A territorial government administered policies through ordinances, elected municipal councils, imposed taxes and fines, and local police courts upheld the laws. Newly-constructed schools and hospitals provided literacy and healthcare while religious bodies maintained their important influence. Social associations improved frontier life and recreational facilities appeared in roller skating rinks, billiard halls, organized team competition in sporting events, and bicycle clubs. A number of official holidays were celebrated. Travelers now were able to find accommodation in hotels and competing merchants provided a variety of goods. In little more than a decade, it was a changed land.

At the same time, the Aboriginal lifestyle deteriorated. Treaty agreements in 1876 and 1877 dispossessed the Indians of their land. Teton Sioux under Sitting Bull and the battle-scarred Nez Percé brought an unwanted intrusion into Canada and the seemingly overnight disappearance of the buffalo brought starvation. In desperation, four thousand Canadian Indians left to hunt in Montana Territory. Within two years, the bands returned impoverished and distraught, leaving them no alternative other than accepting a confined reserve and the reliance on government rations. The historic nomadic Indian lifestyle was gone. An unsettling period of confrontation arose between the Natives and white newcomers.

A second aboriginal group, recent Métis settlers from Manitoba, pursued their grievances over land and linguistic rights. Their discontent erupted in an armed conflict in 1885 that ended with a decisive government military victory.

Three to five hundred men in the North-West Mounted Police policed this vast region. It was an exacting task, buffeted by often severe weather, a challenging environment, isolation and the lack of amenities. Most men made a commendable contribution to their chosen employment but there were, too, those who abandoned their wives, abused native women, and consumed excessive alcohol. The high desertion rate was troubling.

In his research, the author relied extensively on primary sources— diaries, letters, newspapers, official reports, and the NWMP personnel files. Four examples illustrate the fascinating scope of study:

1. In 1876, Assistant Commissioner A.G. Irvine escorted three prisoners from Fort Macleod to Winnipeg to face charges relating to the Cypress Hills Massacre. His police troop quickly found that they lacked the skills needed in running buffalo. Incredibly, the prisoners were given rifles to provide game for the party and only upon reaching the Manitoba border were the suspects handcuffed.

2. One jury trial at Fort Walsh in 1877 was exceptional. Colonel James Macleod, aware that local opinion prejudged Freeman Burnett (charged with forging a note) guilty, in turn, recruited a jury in Montana Territory. The court found the defendant guilty and Burnett was sentenced to two years imprisonment in Stony Mountain Penitentiary. This recruitment of a jury from another country is perhaps unparalleled in legal history.

3. A map printed in January 1875 (three months after the North-West Mounted Police reached Fort Macleod) precisely depicts the geographic features of the Canadian prairies. It even marks the new NWMP posts and the route taken

on the acclaimed march. The Mounted Police, on their 1874 March, did not enter a wilderness and many of the problems encountered were due to their own blunders. In fact, the following summer, the two sons of Inspector William Jarvis, aged 13 and 14, obtained a gun, and with the supplies they could carry, walked the same route as their father's column across the plains.

4. As part of the Alberta Field Force in the North-West Rebellion, Superintendent Bowen Perry led a twenty-man NWMP troop from Fort Macleod north to attack Big Bear's band in the Fort Pitt area. When the men returned to its base one hundred days later, the men had ridden 1,308 miles or more than 2,100 km. It was an arduous ride—matched by few, if any, military columns in history.

This book contributes immeasurably to Canadian Prairie history in the extent of information provided, the outline of the frontier experience, and its detailed survey of the lifestyle of the "Guardians of the Land." In all, *The North-West Mounted Police, 1873-85*, is an engaging account of Western Canadian history.

The text strives to be historically accurate, aware of historical distance, and avoids present-minded terms, using, for example, Indians and not First Nations. Words commonly expressed at that time, but today are sometimes regarded as offensive—such as savage, squaw, half-breed, nitchie—are occasionally used with no offense intended. Quotations used contain the original spellings. All illustrations are from the time period. Some of the photographs have never been published. The chapter content is arbitrary: horse stealing, for example, is in Chapter 9 (Horses of the Mounted Police) and not in Chapter 11 (*Maintiens le Droit*).

North-West Mounted Police rank designations were changed in 1879: constables to sergeants, inspectors to superintendents, and so on. In 1874, Sub-Constable Frederick Bagley rose in rank to become Sergeant Frederick Bagley by 1885. Numbers and distances are usually given in numerical form, such as 300 men, 128 km; dates follow the pattern of day, month, year (18 04 1876) or month, day (June 12); money is usually written $0.25, in preference to twenty-five cents. The International System of Units is preferred. Pounds most often written as lbs. Spelling is Canadian.

The author has chosen 31 December 1885 as the cutoff point. History moves on, valuable books dealing with the following years include:

Aitkin, Ronald. *Maintain the Right.*
Toronto: MacMillan, 1973.

Brendan, William and Stan Horrall, *Red Coats on the Prairies.*
Regina: Centex Books, 1998.

Macleod, R.C. *The NWMP and Law Enforcement 1873–1905.*
Toronto: University of Toronto Press, 1976.

Wallace, Jim. *Forty Mile to Bonanza.*
Calgary: Bunker to Bunker Publishing, 2000.

TIMELINE

Year	Month	Event
1870	August 24	Red River Expeditionary Force reaches Fort Garry.
	Oct. 24	William F. Butler begins his tour of The Great Lone Land.
1872	August 10	Robertson-Ross' reconnaissance of the North-West Territories (NWT).
1873	March 31	House of Commons provides a grant of money to organize a police force for the western plains.
	May 23	Royal assent given for an enabling bill providing money for the proposed North-West Mounted Police (NWMP).
	June 1	Cypress Hills Massacre.
	August 30	Order-in-Council officially constitutes the NWMP.
	Sept. 25	Order-in-Council appoints nine officers to recruit 300 men.
	Oct. 4–10	150 men in Divisions "A-B-C" leave Ontario by steamer for Thunder Bay. From this port, they crossed the Dawson Route to Fort Garry.
	Nov. 3	Osborne Smith swears in the troops at Fort Garry. This post is their base for the winter.
	Nov. 7	Federal election victory for the Liberals under Alexander Mackenzie.

Year	Month	Event
1874	June 6	Divisions "D-E-F" leave Toronto. The Force travels for twelve days in the USA.
	June 19	Set up of Dufferin camp.
	July 8	Column departs for Fort Whoop-Up.
	August 1	Roche Percée: "A" Troop is directed to Edmonton.
	Sept. 15	Treaty 4 signed at Fort Qu'Appelle.
	Sept. 19	Main column reaches the Sweet Grass Hills.
	Sept. 21	Commissioner French returns to Manitoba with "D-E" Divisions.
	Oct. 8	"B-C" Divisions arrive at Fort Whoop-Up.
	Oct. 11	North American Boundary Survey back in Dufferin.
	Oct. 13	NWMP reach what will be named Fort Macleod.
	Nov. 1	"A" troop arrives in Edmonton.
	Nov. 4	Divisions "D-E" arrive in Winnipeg.
1875	March	Desertion of eighteen men from Fort Macleod.
	July 7-24	Extradition trials in Helena. (Cypress Hills Massacre)
	July 22	River steamer *Northcote* arrives at Edmonton.
	Summer	NWMP posts built at Calgary and Fort Walsh.
	July/Aug.	Inspection tour by Major-General Selby Smyth.
1876	April	Telegraph line connected between Winnipeg and Battleford.
	June 19-22	Cypress Hills trials in Winnipeg.
	June 25	Battle of the Little Big Horn.
	July 4	US Centennial.
	July 21	Resignation of Commissioner French; J. F. Macleod succeeds.

YEAR	MONTH	EVENT
	July	NWMP Headquarters moved from Battleford to Fort Macleod.
	August 23	Treaty 6 signed at Fort Carlton.
	Oct. 7	David Laird appointed Lieutenant Governor.
1877	May 7	Sitting Bull enters Canada.
	Sept. 22	Treaty 7 signed at Blackfoot Crossing.
	Oct. 5	Nez Percé enter Canada after Battle of Bear Paw.
	Oct. 17	General Terry – Sitting Bull Conference at Fort Walsh.
1878		Widespread starvation forces more than 5,000 Canadian Indians to hunt in Montana Territory.
	Oct. 17	Federal election won by the Conservative Party led by John A. Macdonald. *Saskatchewan Herald* becomes the first prairie newspaper.
1879	July/Aug.	Lieutenant Governor, Edgar Dewdney, and Commissioner Macleod tour Blackfoot reserves.
	July	Colonel Nelson Miles fights Teton-Sioux in the Battle of Milk River.
	October	NWMP Headquarters moved to Fort Walsh.
	Nov. 17	Murder of Constable Marmaduke Graburn.
1880	Spring	Chief Beardy incident.
	Nov. 1	A.G. Irvine replaces Macleod as Commissioner.
1881	July 19	Sitting Bull returns to the US.
	Aug./Sept.	Marquis of Lorne Tour.
	October	Star Child trial.
		Westward extension of the Manitoba border.

YEAR	MONTH	EVENT
1882	January	Bull Elk confrontation on Blackfoot reserve.
	May 8	Division of North-West Territories into four Provisional Districts: Alberta, Athabasca, Assiniboia, Saskatchewan.
	Late 1882	Fort Walsh closed. Headquarters located in Regina.
	Dec. 8	Big Bear signs his adhesion to Treaty 6.
1883	March	Territorial Capital moved to Regina.
	August	Canadian Pacific Railway reaches Calgary.
1884	Feb. 24	Yellow Calf incident at the Crooked Lakes Reserve.
	April	Bear's Head confrontation.
	June	"Poundmaker Racket" near Battleford.
	July 8	Louis Riel returns to Canada.
	July	Blackfoot Indian chiefs taken on Winnipeg tour.
1885	March 26	Police and rebels clash at Duck Lake.
	April 2	Frog Lake Massacre involving Big Bear's Band results in nine white deaths and a number of hostages taken.
	April 24	Fish Creek skirmish.
	April 24	Relief of Battleford.
	May 2	Cut Knife Hill skirmish.
	May 9–12	Government victory at Batoche and the surrender of Louis Riel effectively ends the rebellion.
	May 28	Frenchman's Butte conflict.
	June 3	Loon Lake skirmish is the final military action of the NWR.

Year	Month	Event
	July 2	Surrender of Big Bear ends the North-West Rebellion.
	July 20	Trial of Louis Riel.
	Sept.	Marquis of Lansdowne—prairie tour.
	Aug./Sept.	Trials of the rebels—more than 55 captives are imprisoned.
	Nov. 7	Last Spike driven at Craigellachie.
	Nov. 16	Execution of Louis Riel creates widespread unrest in Quebec.
	Nov. 27	Hanging of eight Indians at Battleford.
1886	April 1	Lawrence Herchmer replaces A.G. Irvine as NWMP Commissioner.

Archives/Magazines/Government Publications

AH	Alberta History
AHR	Alberta Historical Review
B	Beaver
CC	Canadian Cattlemen
CHR	Canadian Historical Review
CS	Canada Sessional Papers
FCQ	Fort Calgary Quarterly
GA	Glenbow Archives
HCD	House of Commons Debates
MH	Manitoba History
MP	Manitoba Pageant
Mont. H.	Montana History
NAC	National Archives Canada
PAA	Provincial Archives Alberta
PAM	Provincial Archives Manitoba
PNQ	Pacific Northwest Quarterly
RC	Report of the Commissioner
RCMP Q	RCMP Quarterly
SAB	Saskatchewan Archives Board
Sask. H.	Saskatchewan History
SG	Scarlet and Gold

Newspapers

BS	Brandon Sun	*MHN*	Medicine Hat News
BT	Bismarck Tribune	*MHT*	Medicine Hat Times
CA	Calgary Albertan	*MG*	Montreal Gazette
CH	Calgary Herald	*MDS*	Montreal Daily Star
CN	Calgary Nor'Wester	*MJN*	Moose Jaw News
CTr	Calgary Tribune	*MC*	Moosomin Courier
CT	Chicago Times	*NNW*	New North-West
EB	Edmonton Bulletin	*NYH*	New York Herald
EJ	Edmonton Journal	*NYT*	New York Tribune
FBRP	Fort Benton River Press	*ODC*	Ottawa Daily Citizen
FBR	Fort Benton Record	*OFP*	Ottawa Free Press
FMG	Fort Macleod Gazette	*PAT*	Prince Albert Times
HDH	Helena Daily Herald	*PCE*	Pincher Creek Echo
HDI	Helena Daily Independent	*QV*	Qu'Appelle Vidette
HWH	Helena Weekly Herald	*RL*	Regina Leader
LAT	Los Angeles Times	*SH*	Saskatchewan Herald
LH	Lethbridge Herald	*SN*	Sherbrooke News
LN	Lethbridge News	*SPPP*	St. Paul Pioneer Press
LFP	London (Ont.) Free Press	*T*	Times (London, England)
MT	Macleod Times	*TG*	Toronto Globe
MFP	Manitoba Free Press	*TM*	Toronto Mail
MH	Manitoba Herald	*WDT*	Winnipeg Daily Times
M	Manitoban	*WS*	Winnipeg Standard
MCN	Maple Creek News		

THE NORTH-WEST
MOUNTED
POLICE

1873 – 1885

We wake the prairie echoes
With the ever-welcome sound.
Ring out the "Boots and Saddles"
Till the bugle notes resound.
The horses stand caparisoned
And chafe against the reins.
Ring out! Ring out! The march notes
For the Riders of the Plains.

– Thomas T.A. Boys, 1876

RIDERS OF THE PLAINS

1

RIDERS OF THE
PLAINS

NWMP Lancers at Fort Walsh

"I imagined that life in the NWMP would be one grand round of riding wild mustangs,
chasing whiskey traders and horse thieves, and hobnobbing with haughty Indian Princes
and lovely unsophisticated Indian Princesses."

– Frederick Bagley, "The '74 Mounties," *Canadian Cattlemen*, XIII, No.1, 23
  GA NA 2003 – 50

IN 1869, THE HUDSON'S BAY COMPANY transferred its territories
granted in the *Charter of 1670* to Canada. For the two-year-old nation
of 3.6 million people, this purchase of Rupert's Land was a momentous
decision. Canada, with four relatively small provinces, had its land area
increased by millions of square kilometres, unfolding the vision of a nation

from "sea unto sea." Second, this land acquisition thwarted northwestern expansion by the grasping American republic, now in its post-Civil War period of rapid western frontier settlement. Two years earlier, the United States, with a population of almost forty million, had purchased Alaska.

In the region west of the Red River, the Hudson's Bay Company's administration of Rupert's Land had brought only a handful of white traders who co-existed economically with the Native population. The Company maintained authority at its scattered outposts through Justices of the Peace and held criminal and civil courts at Fort Garry. The vast interior remained beyond official jurisprudence.

The Troubled Western Plains

In 1864-65, scarlet fever and measles ravaged the Saskatchewan area, taking the lives of an estimated 1,200 native people. A devastating smallpox epidemic on the northern plains followed in 1867-70, killing, in the Reverend George McDougall's estimation, one-quarter of the Canadian Plains Indians. One account numbered Indian and Métis deaths at 3,544.[1] In some of the isolated camps, no one survived. At the largest prairie settlement, the Roman Catholic community at St. Albert, 320 of the town's 800 residents died. On one day, ten deaths were recorded. This disease was incomprehensible; its mortality compared to a plague in medieval times.

Ghastly reports of smallpox deaths surfaced. In one account, when two traders were overtaken by a blizzard near present-day Regina, they made a windbreak for the night by stacking a dozen Indian corpses, victims of smallpox, that were found at a nearby abandoned campsite. "Next morning, the storm having abated, you may rest assured we lost no time in getting away from our gruesome camp," recalled one of the men.[2] William Butler, on his reconnaissance of the North-West Territories for the Canadian Government in 1870, vividly recounted the nightmarish reminder of smallpox at Fort Pitt:

> ... more than one hundred Crees had perished close to its stockades. The unburied lay for days by the road-side, till wolves approached and fought over the decaying bodies. From a spot many marches to the south the Indians had come to the fort in midsummer, leaving a long track of dead and dying men over the waste of distance.[3]

For the survivors of the smallpox epidemic, the arrival of whiskey traders and wolfers, who began in the late 1860s to cross into "British possessions" from Montana territory, compounded the misery. Many of the men had traumatic wartime experiences in the American Civil War, making them hard and reckless individuals. John La Mott and three companions, enraged that Indians had skinned 104 of the traders' poisoned wolves, followed the Indian trail to near present-day Red Deer, boldly entered an Assiniboine camp of seventy lodges, and through bluff and threats, recovered their lost pelts and seized another 600 wolf pelts that belonged to the band.[4]

Although reports exaggerated the number of Americans as high as 500 men, in fact, at any given time, only a few dozen traders peddled from wagons or small posts with colourful names—Slide Out, Fort Kipp, Spitzee Post, Robber's Roost, Whiskey Gap, and Standoff. When three Mounties were bringing "a cheering liquid not subject to frost" from Fort Macleod to the Pincher Creek police ranch, a sudden raging blizzard forced them to seek shelter in an abandoned shack—which they aptly named Freeze Out.[5]

The pre-eminent post was Fort Whoop-Up, located at the confluence of the St. Mary and Oldman rivers (then called the Belly). John Healy and Alfred B. Hamilton rebuilt the fort in 1871 near the burnt out ruins of an earlier post. It was an expensive undertaking. The palisade was about 45 m in length on all four sides. Inside the post were stables, shops, storage, and dwelling rooms, with all doors and windows facing the inner square. The roofs were covered with sod to thwart fire arrows and iron bars covered the chimney tops to prevent entry.

For defensive purposes, the post had loopholes in the palisade, several bastions, and two 3–pr. guns. Fluttering above the fort was a trader's flag that resembled the American Stars and Stripes.

Fort Whoop-Up gave the region its name. The *Helena Daily Herald* commented, "From Whoop-Up comes news of murder and violence. This place is inhabited by a class of persons whose sole occupation is trading whiskey to the Indians."[6]

One month later, under a heading "Some Recent Doings at Whoop-Up," the paper related a bloody incident where Blackfoot Indians entered a trading store, wounded three whites, and began helping themselves to the liquor. The proprietor, in the back room, charged out and shot three Indians while the others fled. The paper added that Whoop-Up was one of the toughest camps in the Rocky Mountains: "At this place congregate some of the worst characters from every source, many of whom engage in the traffic of whiskey to Indians, and rows which result in death are a frequent occurrence."[7] Only the enormous profits offset the dangers inherent in dealing in the whiskey trade. Healy and Hamilton netted $50,000 in one season's traffic.[8]

Since Indians were not allowed inside Fort Whoop-Up, trade was conducted through window openings in the walls. In exchange for furs, the traders bartered utility goods—guns and ammunition, blankets, clothing, hatchets, kettles, and consumables like tobacco, tea, and whiskey. Trade goods were valued by "skins."[9]

Whiskey adulterated with water, and with small amounts of molasses, tobacco, or Jamaica ginger added, was by far the most profitable exchange item for the white traders. It was estimated that $500 invested in "firewater" obtained as many robes as $5,000 worth of other merchandise.[10]

At his post at Bow River, Donald Graham would mix ten gallons of whiskey with forty gallons of water, and then add burnt sugar for colour to his "mountain dew."[11] A visitor to Fort Whoop-Up in 1871 stated: "the whiskey traders, whom I found to be very pleasant men, told me that they had come here to make money. They risked their lives among these warlike Indians. They traded everything to them, but made their money on whiskey."[12] David Akers described his whiskey trade at Fort Whoop-Up:

> Ye see I never used to get drunk myself when I used to be trading whiskey with the Indians. An' then of course I could watch the effects on them an' as soon as I saw one of 'em getting a little too much I'd put more water in his licker. I used to give it to the critters weak enough to begin with, but the second cup was allers weaker'n the furst, but I'd never kick 'em out or refuse to give 'em a drink as long as they had anything to trade.[13]

One trader boasted that, in one evening he obtained 200 robes worth more than $1,000 for ten gallons of whiskey—which cost about $50. He gave the Indians strong drinks until they were inebriated, then diluted his product with water. "At ten o'clock next morning," he boasted, "I had the robes, and they were all sober."[14]

Whiskey impoverished and demoralized Native society. Some addicted Indians traded their last possessions for a glass of "firewater." On their first contact with Indians near Old Wives Lake, the Mounties were so taken back by the squalor of the Sioux band that doubt arose over the existence of whiskey traders. One Mountie recalled: "Some men argued that if all the Indians were as poor as these, no whiskey trader could make a living out of dealing with them. Others advanced the idea that their poverty was caused by dealing with the whiskey traders."[15]

Excessive drinking by Native people often ended in violence. "Alcohol," one Mountie wrote, "transformed the Indians into wild beasts, and having obtained a quantity of it, they would keep themselves under its influence as long as the supply lasted."[16] In his official document to the Canadian Government, Patrick Robertson-Ross reported: "It is stated upon good authority that during the year 1871 eighty-eight Blackfeet Indians were murdered in drunken brawls amongst themselves."[17] A whiskey trader told John Craig, an early rancher near Fort Macleod, that, "if the Government had only let us alone a few years longer the Indian question would have been settled ... we would have had them all killed off with whiskey, or so few left that they would have been harmless."[18]

Fort Whoop-Up

"From Whoop-Up comes news of murder and violence. This place is inhabited by a class of persons whose sole occupation is trading whiskey to the Indians."

– *Helena Daily Herald*, 13 March 1872
  GA NA 550 – 18

Each winter, white American hunters, called "wolfers," came north for wolf pelts. Working in small "outfits" of two to six men, they would kill a buffalo, spread-eagle the animal on its back, cut the carcass open, and pour strychnine over the meat. Four vials of poison costing about $24 were required to bait a large bull. Since several wolves would devour the entire animal, the wolfers kept the predators away until the carcass was frozen and more difficult to consume.

John "Kootenai" Brown explained: "A quarter or half pound of poisoned meat was enough to kill a wolf and as strychnine was expensive we were careful not to waste any. It was a common thing to get twenty wolves dead the first morning after the poison had been put out."[19] Another wolfer recorded: "in some cases more than 100 wolves had been poisoned around a single bait, and as these skins were worth $2.50 to $3 each at [Fort] Benton it was quite a profitable and attractive business for adventurous spirits."[20]

But Indian dogs were also victims of the poisoned meat, a loss that angered the Indians toward the white intruders. In one confrontation, Indians attacked an outfit northeast of present-day Calgary, killed one man, and forced his partners to leave the area.

In some years, hunger brought misery to the Aboriginal people. Many outsiders viewed the Prairie Indian lifestyle as improvident, with periods of abundant food and comfort only to be followed by want. Even before the disappearance of the enormous buffalo herds, Native people often suffered from wretched hunger in winter. Trader Willie Trail wrote from Carlton House in April 1871: "We have had a long and tedious winter. Starvation has been general. Many of the poor Indians have starved to death."[21]

The winter before the arrival of the Mounted Police had been especially distressing. "Starvation again reigns over the Plains," wrote Traill, "there are no buffalo within three or four hundred miles."[22] Information in March 1874 from the Victoria Mission (east of Fort Edmonton) related that the lack of game had forced many Indians to eat their horses, dogs, buffalo robes and in some cases their moccasins.[23] A letter from Fort Pitt described the suffering: "Indians having been arriving here every day ... all starving. Several old men and old women died on the road coming in ... they were left when they were not able to walk."[24] That winter, rain falling on the snow cover had formed a hard crust, "making it almost impossible to hunt buffalo, the crust cutting the horse's legs."[25]

Ongoing tribal horse thefts and warfare destabilized the western plains. Four years before the arrival of the NWMP, near Fort Whoop-Up (Lethbridge), a Cree war party numbering perhaps 600 warriors attacked the Blood band, which had been ravaged by smallpox. Unknown to the Cree, the Blood camp had nearby Piegan allies, driven north from Montana Territory after the Baker Massacre in January, 1870.[26]

The four-hour battle, fought on 25 October 1870, and referred to as the Battle of the Belly (now Oldman) River, ranged through two coulees and in the river. The Blood alliance, armed with repeating rifles, overwhelmed the Cree who relied on musket loaders. The exact number of deaths is unknown but probably 200–300 Cree invaders were killed, compared to 40 Blood and Peigan deaths.[27] At one point in the fighting, a large number of Cree were forced into the river. From the high banks above, the Blood warriors shot down on them. It was a bloodbath. Jerry Potts, who later became a well-known NWMP scout, was with the Peigan. He told Police Surgeon George Kennedy, who wrote an account of the skirmish: "you could fire with your eyes shut and be sure to kill a Cree."[28] At his Touchwood Hills post in Saskatchewan, trader Isaac Cowie recorded that twenty Cree had debts, which he wrote off in his ledger, "Killed by Blackfeet."[29]

A second bloody Indian fight followed one year later in October 1871 when Red Crow led a Blood attack on a Crow camp in the upper Milk River area. A day later, trader George Houk counted sixty bodies with their scalps removed.[30] In the summer of 1874, the Boundary Survey Commission found and photographed corpses of dead Indians. One diary recorded: "They appear to be Crow Indians killed last winter in a fight with the Peigans. About twenty were riddled with bullets and everyone scalped."[31] Another observer wrote: "all had been shot, one body having no less than sixteen bullets in it ... they had dug small rifle pits with their knives and evidently had been butchered after running short of ammunition."[32]

Every year there were shootings and killings, most of them unreported. In 1874, surveyors in the North American Boundary Commission rescued a naked Métis they found tied to a tree beside the Frenchman (White Mud) River. His Indian captors in their "ingenious and barbarous" cruelty had cut all the branches from the tree to remove any shade. In a few days he would have perished from the effects of the sun's exposure, lack of water, and the myriads of mosquitoes biting his naked body.[33] And, as the police column approached what would become Fort Macleod, the riders saw the corpse of an Indian, shot through the head, and left beside the trail.[34] Captain C. Denny wrote: "He was an Assiniboine, and had been killed by the Blackfeet. The body had shriveled like a mummy's in the dry air; he was minus his scalp."[35] Several policemen buried the body.

Most shooting victims were left to rot. In a letter to Quebec, three months after the Force arrived at Fort Macleod, a Mountie wrote: "within a circuit of two miles from this Fort there are five dead bodies lying rotting on the Prairie."[36]

Whiskey and gunfire ruled this violent land. At Fort Whoop-Up, traders told a visitor that Indians were never allowed inside the post. In response to his observation that the roof did not seem an obstacle for intruders, they laughed and said that way had been tried, but the defenders, "lit the candles for them," and it was never tried again. "Lighting the candles," they explained, was shooting bullets through the ceiling whenever footsteps were heard above.[37]

Ten weeks before the Mounted Police left on their western march, the Department of the Interior had received a memorandum from a trader, a Mr. Johnstone, with information on the American posts in Canada. He believed that most American traders wanted law and order in the region for, as things were then "no man knows when he lies down at night whether he will have his hair on in the morning."[38]

The Transfer of Rupert's Land

The Hudson's Bay Company's transfer of land to the Dominion of Canada was scheduled for December 1, 1869. Prime Minister John A. Macdonald appointed William McDougall, the Minister of Public Works, as the Lieutenant Governor of this new territory. McDougall left Ottawa on September 1 to finalize the acquisition of land. One assignment was the organization of a police force.

The company's negotiations had been conducted in London, without consultation of the 12,000 inhabitants of the Red River settlement. In light of the expected influx of Ontario settlers, this population, mostly of mixed blood, expressed concerns for their land, language, religion, and culture. Fenian agitation in Minnesota and the arrival of government surveyors fueled the discontent. Led by twenty-four-year-old Louis Riel, a turbulent period of unrest began.

In November 1869, armed Métis horsemen had prevented William McDougall from entering the Red River region, effectively postponing Canadian sovereignty over the area. Highlighting the hectic events in the next six months were the seizure of Upper Fort Garry by Riel's followers, the formation of a Métis provisional government, and the suppression of political opposition. On 4 March 1870, a Métis firing squad executed Thomas Scott, an unruly Ontario Orangeman. News of this bloody and controversial killing incited Protestant antipathy for Riel across Canada.

The Canadian Government anticipated difficulties in the settlement and administration of the western plains. Most of all, the confrontational and very expensive American frontier experience was to be minimized. Hopefully, a paramilitary force that preceded settlement would buffer potential problems.

Prime Minister Macdonald envisioned a paramilitary force overseeing the Red River settlement. With the example in mind of British Imperial rule in India, where native troops augmented the British forces, Macdonald, who was also the Minister of Justice, proposed that half of the 200-man police force would be unmarried Métis—men skilled in horsemanship and knowledgeable of western life. The proposed three-year contract would

William Metzler, North-West Mounted Police

"Left home for the N.W.M.P. on the 24th May [1880]. Stopped at Ottawa over night on the 26th and took the train the next morning for Sarnia where I fell in with about fifty others bound for the same place."

– Diary of William Metzler, *GA* M 836
  GA NA 2252 – 1

pay fifty cents per diem and provide lodging, rations, medical care, clothing, and a land grant upon the completion of a term. The Eastern component would include French-Canadian troops. An officer in the Royal Artillery, Captain Donald Roderick Cameron, was tentatively recommended as the commander. Fort Garry would be the headquarters.[39]

Informal negotiations between Ottawa and provisional government representatives concluded with the *Manitoba Act* that paved the way for provincial status. The Métis community of 10,000 received certain linguistic, religious, and property rights. The date set for Manitoba becoming Canada's fifth province was 15 July 1870. But, while the Macdonald government drafted legislation for provincial status, it also dispatched a military force to Manitoba, ostensibly to oversee the peaceful transfer of the Hudson's Bay lands to Canada.

The Red River Expeditionary Force

In the spring of 1870, the 1,200-man Red River Expeditionary Force under Colonel Garnet Wolseley, a seasoned Imperial army officer, left central Canada for Manitoba.[40] Since the United States prohibited foreign troops on American territory, the expedition followed a more difficult all-Canadian route. The troops traveled west by lake steamers from Collingwood, Ontario to Prince Arthur's Landing where they disembarked on May 25. From this port, the men with their provisions and weaponry moved 80 km north over a partly corduroyed road to the waterway and portage connections (the North West Canoe Route) that led to Fort Garry.

On their three-month excursion from the Lakehead to Winnipeg, the soldier voyagers endured forty-five days of rain and unbearable hordes of insects. They made forty-seven portages and ran over 90 km of water rapids on the taxing journey. And, while the Expeditionary Force struggled through the wilderness, Manitoba had become Canada's fifth province.

The troops entered Fort Garry on 24 August 1870 without firing a shot. Riel was not in sight. As the expedition approached Winnipeg, he had fled to the United States. That winter, two militia battalions garrisoned the settlement. In the spring, this force was reduced to two companies under Major A.G. Irvine, who, in 1880, became the third Commissioner of the North-West Mounted Police.[41]

The so-called postage-stamp province of Manitoba—235 km wide and extending 185 km north of the international border—was a tiny part of the Rupert's Land purchase. The vast territory in the North West was to be governed as an unorganized tract by a Lieutenant Governor based in Manitoba. With military control affirmed in Manitoba, interest in a prairie police force waned.

One year later, in July 1871, British Columbia joined Canada. The commitment by Ottawa to construct a rail link to the Pacific Ocean renewed the focus of attention on the western plains, but it was not until 1873 that the plan for a police force re-emerged as part of John A. Macdonald's National Policy.

Official Reports on the NWT: Butler and Robertson-Ross

In October 1870, Lieutenant Governor Adam George Archibald of the newly created province of Manitoba commissioned a British army officer, William F. Butler, to observe the fur trade, the Native people, the havoc of smallpox, and the lawlessness prevalent in the North Saskatchewan area.

An Irishman, Butler had come to Canada at his own expense, hoping to join the Red River Expeditionary Force. All positions for the expedition were filled but Butler served by gathering intelligence in Minnesota and in Winnipeg where he met Louis Riel. He then traveled by canoe to Fort Frances to guide the advance of Garnet Wolseley's voyager-troops.

On October 24, thirty-one-year-old Butler left Winnipeg with a guide, a Hudson's Bay officer, five horses, a Red River cart, and smallpox medicine. The planned route was 380 km west to Fort Ellice, then northwest along the Carlton Trail to Fort Edmonton. It was an arduous assignment for someone inexperienced with the dangers of the prairie winter.

At the beginning of the trip, partly frozen rivers made travel hazardous. Boats ferried supplies across the South Saskatchewan River while the horses were forced to swim. Butler confessed that he cried like a baby after he shot his horse, Blackie, who was trapped in the floating ice. At Fort Carlton, the party had to wait five days for the North Saskatchewan River to freeze solid.

In late November, Butler reached Fort Edmonton. After a brief stop, he continued southwest to Rocky Mountain House, a distance of 300 km. Butler carried letters for the United States, but, as he was unable to hire a guide willing to escort him through Blackfoot country in the winter, he returned to Edmonton accompanied by Father Albert Lacombe, the well-known Oblate priest.

On his return to Fort Garry, Butler traveled alone by dog team over the frozen North Saskatchewan River. Other than a one-day stop on Christmas Day at George McDougall's Victoria mission, Butler pressed his lonely trip eastward. The temperatures were extremely cold and the land silent and empty. He was, therefore, astounded in this wilderness to meet a mail carrier at Fort-à-la-Corne who carried a package addressed to Butler with news on the Franco-Prussian War, a conflict that was of special personal interest.

At Cedar Lake, Butler turned south to cross Lake Winnipegosis and on to Fort Garry—which he reached in February 1871. On his 119-day journey he had traversed 6,150 km. It had been an engrossing accomplishment through a captivating land where "one may wander five hundred miles in a direct line without seeing a human being, or an animal larger than a wolf."[42]

The published account of his challenging journey—*The Great Lone Land*—was an instant success and an important document in Canadian history. In Butler's lifetime, seventeen editions were published and it remains a fascinating travel story and standard reference for the Canadian plains.[43]

Eighteen months after William Butler's return to Fort Garry, the Federal government assigned Patrick Robertson-Ross to report on the western interior. Robertson-Ross, born in Scotland, at age forty-four had military experience in the Kaffir Wars and Crimea. In 1869, he was appointed Adjutant-General of the Canadian militia. In this capacity, Robertson-Ross supplied 750 troops for Wolseley's Expeditionary Force, readied defensive positions in the event of Fenian attacks from the United States, and organized artillery batteries at Kingston and Quebec City.

Robertson-Ross traveled by steamer from Ontario to the Lakehead and then crossed the Dawson Route, reaching Fort Garry in late July 1872. At this garrison, he inspected the 243–member Red River detachment and made recommendations for the unit in his report.[44]

On 10 August 1872, accompanied by a guide, his sixteen-year-old son, and a young Indian, Robertson-Ross headed west with ten horses and two Red River carts. He rejected an offer to have six militia men accompany the expedition as only an added expense and ineffectual protection in the event of a resolute attack.

The company followed the route taken by Butler. Travel went well and they reached Rocky Mountain House, a distance of 2,000 km, thirty-one days after leaving Fort Garry. Unlike Butler, who returned east from this fur trade post, Robertson-Ross headed for the Crowsnest Pass, 500 km south. When a blizzard in the Porcupine Hills snowbound the party for six days, food supplies ran out. Fortunately, Robertson-Ross killed a large grizzly bear which they ate. And this time it was a real bear. In his official report, Robertson-Ross omitted that he paid damages at Fort Ellice for shooting a Hudson's Bay Company's ox that he had mistaken for a bear.

Once the storm abated, the company continued south, then turned west through the Crowsnest Pass to the gold diggings at Wild Horse Creek, and eventually they reached San Francisco, California. By December 1872, Robertson-Ross was in Ottawa where he personally reported his observations to Prime Minister Macdonald. His report was published in the *Canadian Sessional Papers*, 1873.

Although the two reconnaissance expeditions had skirted the central plains, information obtained from two missionary settlements and five Hudson's Bay trading posts furnished accurate details of the North-West Territories in terms of population, the number and distribution of Indian bands, the extent of the smallpox epidemic, and the immense agrarian potential of the vast region.[45]

It was agreed that lawlessness was unchecked throughout the region. Robertson-Ross watched Tahakooch, a vicious murderer, "swagger openly about Edmonton."[46] Butler wrote: "The region is without law, order or security for life or property; robbery and murder for years have gone unpunished; Indian massacres are unchecked ... and all civil and legal institutions are entirely unknown."[47] Robertson-Ross reiterated this point: "beyond the Province of Manitoba westward to the Rocky Mountains there is no kind of government at present whatever, and no security for life or property beyond what people can do for themselves."[48]

Both men advocated a police force for the region. Butler recommended a well-equipped force of 100 to 150 men, one-third mounted, carefully recruited and engaged for service in the Saskatchewan River basin. Robertson-Ross proposed 500 mounted riflemen garrisoned in detachments of fifty men at Hudson's Bay posts and 150 Mounted Riflemen at a combined military and customs post in the Porcupine Hills, northwest of Fort Macleod.

At Fort Garry, Robertson-Ross learned that the local Indians were unimpressed by the dark green uniforms of the Manitoba Provisional Battalion. He was told: "We know that the soldiers of our Great Mother wear red coats and are our friends."[49] Robertson-Ross recommended a red tunic for the proposed police force.

The choice of a scarlet coat won approval. *The Times* (London, England) commented: "A scarlet uniform has been adopted for the Police, in order that no misconception may exist in the minds of either Yankee ruffians or Indian warriors as to the nationality of the force, and it is, indeed, a glorious livery to fight in, if fighting has to be done."[50] Alexander Morris, Lieutenant Governor of Manitoba, had earlier recommended a police force under military discipline wearing a red coat, "as 50 in red coats are better than 100 of other colors."[51]

When news reached Fort Walsh in the spring of 1876 that Sitting Bull was in Canada, Colonel A.G. Irvine led a small eight-man party to the Teton camp. Paymaster Edmund Dalrymple Clark came as the recording secretary. He wrote: "It was felt, and with no ordinary pride, that our scarlet coats were far greater protection than any armed escort."[52] The bold entry of the troop into Sitting Bull's camp astounded the band.

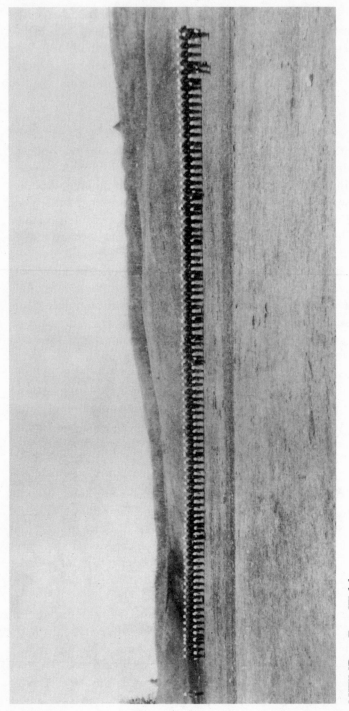

NWMP at Fort Walsh

"I am proud that I was a member of the Force that is honored for its wonderful service rendered to the Dominion of Canada, particular in the Wild North West in the early seventies."

– A.H. Scouten, "One of the Originals," SG, Twelfth Annual, 40
   GA PD 339 – 16

The authority of the red tunic extended beyond the NWMP. During the North-West Rebellion, the Alberta Field Force led by T.B. Strange, marched in three echelons from Calgary to Edmonton. At the troubled Battle River reserves (today Maskwacis), Strange learned the Indians were unimpressed when the 65th Battalion of Montreal soldiers marched past "as they did not wear red coats, and talked French like the half-breeds."[53]

Strange, therefore, ordered an ostentatious display for the following column, the red-coated Winnipeg Light Infantry. A member of the unit wrote of the march through the reserves: "With bayonets fixed and rifles at the slope, with band playing and every weapon exposed to view, we marched through, while the Indians gathered in the woods by the roadside and gazed wonderingly at the spectacle."[54]

During the three-month campaign, Indian Agent Cecil Denny wrote a memo that the black-coated Quebec Voltigeurs, garrisoned in southern Alberta, should not enter an Indian camp to make arrests without being accompanied by someone from the Indian Department. The Indians, Denny warned "didn't understand men in another color doing this duty."[55]

The red coat of Canada's national police force became recognized almost immediately throughout the world as a symbol of Canadian sovereignty.

Legal Establishment of the North-West Mounted Police

On 23 May 1873, an enabling bill (passed unopposed) providing for a police force in the North-West Territories received royal assent.[56] Unlike the earlier plan in 1871, there was no reference for the inclusion of Métis volunteers. This police force would have a commissioner, officers, a paymaster, veterinarian surgeon, and 150 men in the rank and file.

An Order-in-Council officially constituted the NWMP on 30 August 1873. Most important, the Federal Government, under the Department of Justice (headed by Prime Minister Macdonald) supervised the new Force. The NWMP would answer to Ottawa, not to local authorities. Deputy Minister Hewitt Bernard, Macdonald's brother-in-law, became responsible for the early organization. The Mounted Police were given significant legal authority, with every officer also a Justice of the Peace. They and three appointed Stipendiary Magistrates adjudicated all trials. After trying a case, Colonel James Macleod jested to an American trader: "We have only to wait for a wink from Ottawa to hang our man."[57]

Macdonald chose the Royal Irish Mounted Constabulary as the model for the proposed police force. The first name suggested for the new body, Mounted Rifles, was considered too militaristic for Americans living on their northwest frontier and was changed to Mounted Police.

The Cypress Hills Massacre

The organization of the NWMP was underway when frontiersmen from Montana Territory attacked an Indian camp in the Cypress Hills (*les montaignes des cyprès*) on 1 June 1873.[58] Ten days later, the *Helena Herald* reported the massacre: "Whites War Path Forty Lodges Wiped Out by Sixteen Kit Carsons."[59]

Another eleven weeks passed before Ottawa learned of this skirmish on Canadian territory and then it was only through the British Minister in Washington. And although five of the frontiersmen had Canadian backgrounds, Ottawa depicted the bloody incident as American freebooters violating Canadian jurisdiction. Obviously, a NWMP presence on the western plains was urgent. John A. Macdonald contacted Lord Dufferin, the Governor General: "This Indian massacre at Fort Benton shows the necessity of our losing no time in organizing the mounted police."[60]

Several weeks before the skirmish, Indians had stolen forty horses from a party of wolfers returning from Whoop-Up country to Fort Benton, the river terminus on the Missouri. The wolfers continued to Fort Benton where they formed a vigilante party led by John Evans and Tom Hardwick (the Green River Renegade) and set off after the Indian horse thieves.

For two weeks, the twelve-man troop trailed the Indians northward into Canada until they reached what would be named Battle Creek. Near this location in the Cypress Hills, where Fort Walsh was built two years later, independent traders Abe Farwell and Moses Solomon built trading posts several hundred paces apart. The two men traded in a violent area. That winter, Indians murdered Paul Rivers, a white trader, and, in recent days, were firing intermittently at Solomon's shack.

The wolfers rested and drank whiskey. An Assiniboine band of forty lodges under Hunkajunka (Little Soldier) was camped nearby. A hard winter had left the Natives destitute and, to compound their problems, many band members were drinking alcohol. Almost certainly they were not the Indians who had stolen the wolfers' horses weeks earlier.

Nevertheless, the issue over stolen horses arose when a French-Canadian trader, George Hammond, had a horse missing, returned, and then taken a second time. Hammond was enraged. He stalked about, loudly cursing the Indians in both English and French. His ranting incited the Benton men and, in spite of trader Abe Farwell and his assistant, Alexis Lombombard's attempts to prevent trouble, general firing erupted.

Conflicting accounts at the court trials in Helena and Winnipeg failed to ascertain whether the Benton men or the Indian band had started the shooting. There was, however, no doubt about the results. The Benton men, armed with repeating rifles, fired at the Indian camp from a sheltered coulee and then charged the camp on horseback. Possibly twenty Indians were killed while others fled into the bush. One account that the severed head of one Indian was attached to a lodgepole attested to the brutality of the skirmish. One whiteman, Edward Legrace, a Canadian, was killed. His companions placed his body under a shack which they torched to prevent his mutilation. Then the frontiersmen and the traders abruptly headed south to Fort Benton.

The First Contingent

On 25 September 1873, an Order-in-Council appointed nine commissioned officers to organize the new Force.[61] Recruitment of the rank and file began at once. Inspector Charles F. Young (assisted by Ephrem-A. Brisebois) was responsible for the Atlantic region; Inspector William Winder for Quebec; and Inspector J. Walsh for Ontario. The selection criteria recommended active and able-bodied men of good character, between the ages of 18 and 40 years, with a sound constitution and the ability to ride. Literacy could be in either French or English. The pay of one dollar a day for a constable was nominal, but food, clothing, weapons, and lodging were provided. And, upon the completion of their three-year assignment (with good behaviour), a land grant of 160 acres (66 hectares) was available in Western Canada. The urgent recruitment benefited from the Canadian militia providing men and funding.

Some applications were on hand. James Walsh, who had anticipated openings in the proposed force, had forwarded his interest. William Butler, author of *The Great Lone Land*, wrote that, although, he intended to join a military expedition to Africa, he would most likely be ready to participate early in the spring.

Applicants besieged the recruiting officers. News of the "massacre" had aroused great public interest. The anticipation of adventure was foremost. Sub-Inspector C. Denny wrote: "Looking back at the rate of pay and the work they performed, it seemed poor remuneration, but the lure of the unknown, and the prospect of a great adventure, brought thousands to apply for enlistment."[62] James Fullerton recalled that his friends "who wanted me in the cricket club, tried to dissuade me from joining, but that great adventure was too big an attraction to miss."[63]

Within a month, three fifty-man divisions ("A-B-C"), each with an Inspector and two Sub-Inspectors, had been organized. Added to the intense recruitment was a barrage of alarmist communication from Alexander Morris, Lieutenant Governor of Manitoba. Most critical, in his view, were concerns that native starvation would result in inter-tribal conflict. Morris urged immediate attention for the region. In late September, he contacted the Prime Minister, asking: "What have you done as to the Police Force? Their absence may lead to grave disaster."[64]

Time was uppermost. If the troops were to be posted that winter in Manitoba, they had to leave Ontario before the Great Lakes were frozen. James McKernan recorded this concern: "I joined the Mounted Police at Ottawa on September 29, 1873, and left Ottawa, along with a number of others, on October 2, 1873, for Manitoba."[65]

The departure port was Collingwood, located on Georgian Bay, 120 km north of Toronto. The recruits, in three contingents of forty-one, sixty-four, and fifty-six men (six officers and 155 men in all), took rail transport to the port. Along the route eight more men were added (including Sam Steele and his brothers, Richard and Godfrey), while several other men were dismissed. Sub-Constable J. Nelson missed the train in Toronto and T. O'Neil, a trumpeter, was sent back for drunken behaviour.

The units were billeted briefly in Collingwood, population 3,500, to await the arrival of the assigned vessel. Great coats and utensils were issued, and a memo warned the men to limit their use of intoxicating liquors. A Toronto newspaper praised the general behaviour of the recruits: "A more intelligent and finer body of men it would be difficult to find in the Dominion ... men in excellent health and spirits, and look with great pleasure to their trip across Georgian Bay."[66] There was one casualty: S. Todd accidentally shot himself in the forearm with his pistol. He joined the next group several days later. The contingents left within one week, on October 4, 8, and 10.[67] A guard was posted on each steamer to prevent any men from deserting at stops en route.

After reaching the Lakehead (Port Arthur–Fort William), each contingent moved west on the Dawson Route, a rugged 900-km wilderness passageway. Wagons transported the men and supplies for the first 80 km to waiting canoes. From this point, they moved by waterway or over corduroy roads that linked lakes and streams to Lake of the Woods. Fifty portages on the route made for heavy work. The diary of Inspector James Walsh for 10 October 1873 relates:

> Left Shebandowan at 6:30 a.m. arriving at Kashaboine Portage at 9:40, crossed the portage (¾ mile) and started on Kashaboine Lake at 10:30, arriving at Height of Land Portage at 12 noon. Crossed the portage (1¾ miles) and started on Lac des Milles Lake at 12:45. Arrived at Baril Portage at 5:30, crossed the

portage (¾ mile) and started on Baril Lake at 6:30. Arrived at Bruel Portage at 8:45 p.m., crossed the portage (½ mile) and halted for the night.[68]

In fourteen hours, the troops had crossed four portages, covering a total distance of 6 km. Each stop required the unloading and loading of supplies and carrying the canoes and supplies. And, even though a steamer transported the men 70 km across Lake Shebandowan, it had been a long and arduous day.

The first two contingents made steady progress. The leading group accompanied the last party of settlers going west and reached Winnipeg on October 22. While crossing the Dawson Route, James Fullerton, in the second contingent, recalled two "accidents" that undoubtedly relieved the onerous routine. In one, the men found their pork spoiled and the hardtack musty. While unloading a scow, some boxes of beef were "accidentally" broken. That night, the aroma of roasting beefsteaks filled the air. A second "accident" happened to an officer's keg of whiskey, said to be used for medicine, which "by magic" turned to water while in care of some men.[69]

The oncoming cold weather made the journey hazardous for the third contingent. Many became seasick from the high waves on Lake Superior. While on the Dawson Route, the hungry men broke into Hudson's Bay Company stopping (supply) houses and helped themselves to any food available. A snowstorm battered the men in their open boats (manned by Iroquoian paddlers) while crossing Rainy Lake and they reached Fort Francis looking, in one man's description, "like half-drowned rats."[70]

Unfortunately, the HBC winter supplies for the post had not arrived and, since the two earlier contingents had eaten all the hard biscuits, the HBC factor could only offer the hungry recruits two barrels of sugar cubes. The men opened a barrel taken from one stopping house only to find dried apples which were nevertheless quickly consumed. The nearby encampment of 400 Indians had no food.

Leaving Fort Francis, the contingent moved in boats down the Rainy River toward the Lake of the Woods. On the way, they encountered a Chipewyan camp on the United States side of the river and were able to purchase dried fish and corn. For J.H.G. Bray, never was a meal eaten in the Queens Hotel in Toronto so enjoyable. At Lake of the Woods, a steamer awaited the contingent, but a snowstorm delayed travel for three days. Fortunately, the vessel had an adequate food supply.

When the steamer reached the far shore (at a point called the North West Angle), the men had to break shore ice to disembark. They found the waiting carts frozen in mud and the ice-covered tents could not be unfolded.

This meant a discouraging walk to Winnipeg, a distance of 160 km, helped by two ox carts carrying the baggage. That night, the troop slept on the ground in the blowing snow and, in the morning, they continued west, frost-bitten and without breakfast. Harry Keenan recalled walking about half the distance before sleighs arrived to convey the troops to Winnipeg.

At St. Boniface, Archbishop Alexandre-Antonin Taché put the men up comfortably in the church facilities. There was supper with mutton chops, homemade bread, butter, and tea with cream. After the recent deprivations and recalling sleeping the previous night on the open prairie, the men welcomed towels, soap and a bath, beds with blankets—simply paradise. That night, the weather turned bitterly cold. The Red River froze solid, ending steamer transport to Fort Garry. In the morning, the men crossed the ice single-file to board sleighs that took them to Lower Fort Garry, 32 km north. This post would be the base for Divisions "A-B-C" until June 1875.

Lieutenant-Colonel W. Osborne Smith, the officer commanding the Winnipeg Military District, had been appointed Acting Commissioner of the North-West Mounted Police.[71] He informed the Prime Minister by telegraph on November 1 that all three contingents had arrived and that he was continuing with the organization of the Force.

It was a trying assignment for Smith. He leased the winter garrison at Lower Fort Garry (the Stone Fort) from the Hudson's Bay Company for $5,000. Another $3,363 was needed for additions, alterations, and repairs. The officers were quartered in the officer's mess, the troops in a renovated storehouse. A stable for fifty horses with equipment rooms and storage for hay and oats was rented, and thirty-three western broncos at $125 each were purchased. A contract with the HBC at $43,000 a month provided food, light, fuel, and forage.

Osborne Smith, in his acting capacity, on 3 November 1873, swore in the men for service. The paper they signed was headed *Mounted Police Force of Canada*. "We then realized," wrote Constable James McKernan, "that we were fully-fledged Mounted Police."[72]

Sixteen men (four French-Canadians and twelve recruits from New Brunswick) refused to sign the document. At issue was their understanding that they could resign from the NWMP by giving six months notice and now they faced a mandatory three-year term. The men drew pay for November and received subsistence until returning east in the spring. Their loss seriously affected the representation from east of Ontario.

Each man who signed received a regimental number. The rank number was of great personal pride, with a lower number signifying earlier service. The first numbers, 1 to 5, were, in order: A.H. Griesbach, James Walsh,

W. D. Jarvis, Sam Steele, and Percy Neale were all prominent North-West Mounted Policemen. Some of the first regimental numbers were referred to as the Old Series, as o.s. 421.

The detachment was supplied with fatigue uniforms, arms, and clothing from the Fort Garry military stores. Lieutenant-Colonel Smith appointed Superintendent W.D. Jarvis in temporary command, Inspector Walsh as adjutant, Sergt.-Major A.H. Griesbach in charge of discipline and foot drill, and Sergt.-Major Sam Steele responsible for breaking horses and riding instructions.

Riding training was held in two large warehouses. Twenty-two-year-old Sam Steele described the horse-riding training:

> Our work was unceasing from 6 a.m. until dark. I drilled five rides per day the whole winter in an open ménage, and the orders were that if the temperature were not lower than 36 below zero the riding and breaking should go on. The broncos repeatedly threw the men with great violence to the frozen ground; but no one lost his nerve ... when spring opened they were fine riders, laying the foundation of Canadian horsemanship in the wild and woolly west.[73]

Medical examinations in January revealed that the hasty recruitment had led to some unsuitable men being accepted. In Winnipeg, a local practitioner, Dr. David Young, examined the entire force. He found two men who were blind in one eye, five men with heart ailments, one man with tuberculosis, another with syphilis, and one man with a fractured leg. In all, nineteen men were released from the Force in the first two months.

The Force garrisoned Lower Fort Garry for eight months. The daily order book relates the repetitive and dull routine of stables, guard, and parade.[74] Another regulation dealt with their facial appearance, allowing mustaches and beards, but those who preferred to shave had to do so daily. There was a prohibition on liquor and card playing for money. Blankets had to be aired once a month.

There were problems with the work routine. The order book stipulated that any person connected with the Force could be assigned any work considered necessary. Those men on stable duty had to stay the full time assigned. Discipline was compromised because the only deterrent was fines. An argument with a non-commissioned officer cost $10, sleeping on duty two weeks lost pay, and, for drunkenness, an astounding $300 fine.

The rigid and austere police life quickly disillusioned some recruits. One man bitterly complained:

I'd as soon be in a penitentiary as with this corps. Our clothes are too large for us and they are made of inferior cloth. Thus far we have been treated more like brutes than men. We have to run like fury in an enclosure with horses that have never had a bridle on them before ... I'd give six months salary to be home once more ... we get dry bread and bad coffee for breakfast, boiled meat and worse potatoes for dinner and real bad tea and dry bread for supper—such grub![75]

Recreational activities were limited. The main activity that winter was ice skating on the river and the men enjoyed gymnastics and boxing. There was a grand ball in Winnipeg organized by sergeants in Lt.-Col. Irvine's Manitoba militia. On May 24, the detachment celebrated the Queen's birthday with a sports meet highlighted by a cricket match between the locals and the police.

The NWMP had one police undertaking during the eight-month stay at the Stone Fort. In December 1873, the Manitoba government requested that the NWMP investigate a whiskey operation located on the west shore of Lake Winnipeg. Major James Macleod, being skilled with snowshoes, selected nine men (three from each division), and Constable G.B. Hall. He trained his squad with snowshoes for one week and in mid-December, led by two Métis guiding two dog teams carrying supplies, the detail departed in extremely cold weather, headwinds, and deep snow.

On the first night, the men dug into a large snowdrift for their sleeping quarters. A second night was spent in a settler's cabin and a third on the ice in a large tent with pine boughs spread to comfort their sleep. On the fourth day, the police reached the whiskey trader's shack. Macleod led the rush on the building. The surprise was complete and six men were arrested. A search found ten gallons of whiskey, that was promptly dumped in the snow. Since it was impractical to escort the prisoners to the Stone Fort for trial, Macleod imposed a small fine on the traders. The next morning, the patrol left for home and, after a nine-day round trip, reached the Stone Fort on Christmas Eve. James McKernan recalled being, "tired and glad to get back to our own quarters, but none the less having enjoyed the trip and feeling proud that our first expedition had been carried out successfully."[76]

In mid-October 1873, Prime Minister John A. Macdonald appointed Lieutenant Colonel George French, Inspector of Artillery and Commandant of "C" School Gunnery in Kingston, as the first Commissioner of the North-West Mounted Police. His active command began upon his arrival at Lower Fort Garry two months later.

French faced an enormous task in the formation of his command. The logistics for the proposed journey were staggering—recruiting, ammunition, arms, uniforms, horse and oxen purchases, field guns, transportation, food supplies, and salaries. In his preparations, Commissioner French astutely approached officers in the Boundary Commission for information on prairie conditions. The previous summer, this joint Canadian-American undertaking had surveyed the 49th Parallel for 600 km west of Red River. Chief Commissioner Donald Roderick Cameron proved very helpful. French acknowledged: "I was fortunate enough to be able to obtain much reliable information concerning a portion of the country of which so little was known from senior officers of the Boundary Commission."[77] One thing was certain: it would require the 300 policemen first suggested by John A. Macdonald to establish law and order over this vast land. To address this concern, in February 1875, French left for Fargo, Dakota Territory, to make train connections to Ottawa. W.D. Jarvis took acting command of the base and the winter training.

By this time, a new government was in power. In the Federal election of November 1873, the Liberals, led by Alexander Mackenzie, bolstered by charges involving corruption (the Pacific Scandal), defeated Macdonald's Conservative party. There were concerns that Mackenzie's administration, handicapped by a severe economic downturn, would be reluctant to support the costs of an expanded police force. However, French succeeded in getting approval for the NWMP to add three additional Divisions, in effect doubling its manpower.

George Arthur French

George Arthur French (1841–1921) served as the first Commissioner of the North-West Mounted Police from October 1873 to July 1876—almost thirty-four months. Born in Ireland, French began his military career at Sandhurst and the Royal Artillery School at Woolwich, England. At age nineteen, he arrived in Canada and, in 1862, married Janet Clark Innes of Kingston. French served in Kingston and Quebec.

In 1870, Great Britain withdrew its Canadian garrisons, entrusting the three-year-old nation with the responsibility of its own defence. Prime Minister John A. Macdonald seconded French, appointing him Inspector of Artillery and Warlike Stores. In this capacity, as a Lieutenant-Colonel in the Canadian militia, French supervised the transfer of fortifications and armaments to Canada. Later, in the autumn of 1871, the Canadian government opposed a request by the British government to return French to his Imperial regiment. Ottawa informed London that the services of

Commissioner George Arthur French

The First Commissioner of the NWMP, French served from October 1873
to July 1876—almost thirty-four months.

– GA NA 23 – 1

Lieutenant-Colonel French, "are very urgently required at present by
the Dominion government in the interest of the militia and defence of
Canada."[78] The British government conceded to Canadian concerns.

French was thirty-two when he became Commissioner of the North-
West Mounted Police. With only eight months to prepare the column
for the western march, he was engrossed in organization. His logbook
details the varied and extensive preparations required for this task.[79]

The Mounted Police successfully crossed the plains, established permanent bases at Fort Macleod and Swan River, and within months, curtailed the whiskey trade. The following summer in 1875, posts constructed at Bow River, Fort Walsh, and Fort Saskatchewan consolidate police authority over the Canadian prairies. By 1877, NWMP detachments were in eleven locations.

In the late summer of 1875, Major-General Selby Smyth, Commanding General of the Canadian Militia, undertook an inspection tour of police posts with the purpose of providing Parliament a first-hand appraisal of the North-West Mounted Police. Smyth reported: "Lieut.-Colonel French's service to this Dominion have been valuable, his whole desire is concentrated in serving well the Government which employs him, in developing a powerful and useful force and so far, he has been, in my experience of it, very successful."[80] This positive endorsement of the NWMP countered what many of French's detractors in Ottawa wanted.

Commissioner G. French's forthright manner aggravated his abrasive relationship with his superiors in Ottawa. French acknowledged that his dissent opened him to charges of not concurring with government policy, but he frankly preferred taking the risk.[81] In a letter to the Minister of Justice, French had berated the government for denying any official recognition of the Force's accomplishments. Now that Major-General Smyth's favourable report was published, "the thanks of Parliament are now due to the officers and men of the Force."[82]

In March 1876, Edward Blake, the Minister of Justice, refused a request by French to come to Ottawa to discuss concerns. Even though French offered to pay the travel costs, several further requests were dismissed. Apparently, the government's mind was set. A committee of the Privy Council recommended that, "it will be absolutely necessary in order to maintain discipline and to introduce the necessary reforms in the management of the Force that a change must be made in command."[83]

The rank and file knew of the rift between Commissioner French and Ottawa. More than a year before French resigned, Surgeon R.B. Nevitt had written: "We have heard lately that an investigation is going on about the march across the prairies. The belief here is that Col. French will be dismissed."[84]

Opinion differed among the men over French's leadership. From the beginning of the '74 March, criticism mounted over his strict discipline. Commenting on French's retirement, Constable Jean d'Artigue wrote: "French, to the joy of about every member of the Mounted Police, resigned his commission ... just in time to save the Government from dismissing him."[85]

Sub-Constable Joseph Carscadden, likewise, was unimpressed: "From what I have seen of our commissioner I must say that I consider him wanting in human feeling and without honour."[86] But, conversely, French also had strong support. J.B. Mitchell wrote: "I had taken a course in 'A' Battery under him and he was the finest man I had ever met. It was he who put the Force on the right foundation."[87] Sam Steele agreed: "In July, Colonel French, our good and capable commissioner resigned."[88] Young Frederick Bagley blamed, "incompetents in Ottawa, supported by many a mean slander, eventually forced French to resign after less than three years as Commissioner."[89]

The company stationed with George French at the Swan River post grew to respect their commander. On his departure from the base, French shook hands with each man and looked sad. Sam Steele, on behalf of the detachment, presented French with a gold watch valued at $150 and an expensive solid silver tea set for his wife. William Parker wrote to his mother in England, "We are very sorry to lose him & we non-commissioned officers presented him with a splendid gold watch ... he made a splendid speech & at the latter part of it I was quite overcome."[90] Edward Maunsell thought French "devoid of human emotion, absolutely indifferent, apparently, to our opinions of him. So great to our surprise, when we made the presentation to find that he was a very human warm-hearted man."[91] French had served fifteen years in Canada.

French, only thirty-five, returned to his Imperial military career with postings in the Royal Artillery in England, Queensland, Bombay, and New South Wales.[92] He attained the rank of major-general two years before his retirement in 1902.

His interest in Western Canada remained. In 1878, French wrote to the *Manitoba Free Press* rejecting the proposed northern route of the C.P.R., based on his Swan River experience.[93] Shortly before World War One, French, now in his seventies, traveled across western Canada in a modern railway coach—a far cry from his 2,000 km ride in 1874. No doubt he marveled at the dramatic changes four decades had brought to the region. French died in London, England, in July 1921.

Divisions "D-E-F" Move West

Advertisements in eastern newspapers for 150 additional volunteers had a great response. In Toronto alone, 3,000 men applied for service. In his many interviews with candidates, Commissioner George A. French certainly never encountered anyone more determined to join this western adventure than fifteen-year-old Frederick Bagley.

Bagley's father and the Commissioner had served together in the Royal Artillery in the British Imperial Army. If young Bagley thought that this connection would guarantee his enlistment, he was surprised:

> The Colonel informed my father in downtown Toronto of my action and whereabouts. Father lost no time in coming post haste to interview the Colonel, with the view of preventing my enlistment, but after a rather stormy argument between us, (or in his father's words 'stupid stubbornness'), he arranged with the Colonel to take me on as Trumpeter for a period of not more than six months. I am now a member of the NWMP at the age of fifteen years.[94]

As soon as he was issued a uniform, young Bagley had his photograph taken to "satisfy my vanity and as a memento." Years later he could smile at the faded photograph of a "rather goofy-looking youth."[95]

Near Sarnia, William Parker, working as a farm labourer for $13 a month, read an announcement that Commissioner French would select twelve recruits in London on 4 April 1874. Parker arrived at Tecumseh House early, but was discouraged and thought his chances were poor when he saw two hundred strapping men waiting at the hotel. But, to his surprise, his interview with French went well and, after a character reference arrived by telegraph, he was accepted, conditional on passing a medical examination.

The three added Divisions, numbered "C-D-E," trained at the New Fort, a warehouse in Toronto. Inspector Thomas Jackson, an ex-officer of the Kingston battery, instructed rifle drills and organized an artillery unit. Commissioner French found the scores in target practice astonishing. Having 174 of the 300 recruits with previous military service no doubt contributed to the positive results.[96] Riding training was held in an arena with a sawdust-covered floor. Staff Constable T. Miles instructed the recruits, yelling derisively when a man fell from his bareback mount, "Who told you to dismount?"[97] Or, in the case of one recruit who banged heads with his horse, "that's right young fellow, me lad, kiss 'em and e'll be good to you."[98] But, in spite of the sarcasm, the Staff Constable's training proved effective and, within ten days, remembered William Parker, most of the men were capable riders.

In the evenings after the "wet'" canteen closed, the men indulged in horseplay that always wound up in a march around the parade ground led by piper Donald McAulay playing "Cock of the North, or The Barren Rocks of Aden." The procession continued until Last Post ordered everyone to bed. The recruits were mostly healthy, with only four men invalided.

William Parker, in a letter on April 15 to his relatives in England, excitedly recounted his new calling:

> At half past six we have to fall in & are marched to the stables, clean & feed the horses & finish them up, fall in again, marched back in front of our rooms & dismissed for breakfast at eight o'clock. At nine there is a general parade to drill, dismissed at half past ten, parade again at eleven for riding exercise, dinner at one & fall in for drill at two & again at five for stables, tea at six. We can go down town from six to ten so you see we have not bad times at all.[99]

At the end of May, French ordered a general parade intended to get rid of those who were not willing "to rough it."[100] Before the assembled, he highlighted the hardships and dangers ahead and advised anyone with second thoughts to leave the ranks. Almost everyone remained keen for this adventure. "It was true that we were not well trained, like regular soldiers," admitted Jean D'Artigue, "but certainly, courage and patriotism, qualities which every true soldier must possess were not wanting."[101]

On June 6, Divisions "D-E-F," with Commissioner G.A. French, his wife and children, sixteen officers, 201 men and 210 horses, paraded to the Grand Trunk Station before cheering onlookers. The crowded station buzzed with excitement. A band played the national Anthem, "Vive le Canadien," and "The Girl I left Behind Me." G.C. King remembered boarding the train "with mingled feeling of joy and anticipation."[102] For young Trumpeter Frederick Bagley, it was the happy day of departure from Toronto. He wrote:

> The tremendous excitement, the music of the bands, and the cheers of the mob rendered me almost heedless of my dear Mother's admonition to 'be a good boy; say your prayers regularly, and come back soon' as at the last minute she pressed into my hands a blank diary book and a watch and chain.[103]

It was fourteen years before Bagley was to see his family again and, as he admitted, "during the course of which much of my motherly advice was sometimes forgotten."[104]

Then, with final handshakes and farewells, the two trains pulled out of the station. They were on their way West! The men were boisterous in their cramped quarters and hardly anyone slept the first night.

As the two designated trains moved through Ontario, onlookers waved in recognition. At station stops juvenile boys were less hospitable, taunting the policemen, because of their shorn heads, as jailbirds. At every stop, policemen called "the dog robbers" kidnapped dogs, only to release them at the next station and raid the hapless canines of that place.

For Constable E.H. Maunsell, "it seemed to have become the ambition of nearly every member of the force to possess a dog, with the result that every town or village we stopped at found its canine population largely reduced when we left."[105]

Nine rail cars containing wagons and implements were attached at Sarnia, and, in Detroit, two more rail cars with thirty-four horses were added. Three times each day the horses were unloaded to be fed and watered.

Each man received one dollar a day for meals. This was an adequate amount at most stations, except in Chicago where the meals cost fifty cents. The arrangements for meals were telegraphed ahead to the selected station stops. Constable William Parker recalled having splendid meals happily served by pretty girls. Staff Constable J.B. Mitchell, who received several hundred dollars to feed his charges, used the ten per cent premium on Canadian money to purchase extra delicacies at stops in the United States.

Before entering the United States, all arms and ammunition had to be packed in sealed cases and placed in the freight cars. Further, those men not dressed in mufti had to don civilian clothing to comply with the American restriction on wearing foreign military uniforms on United States territory.

The trains reached Chicago at 5 p.m. on June 7. The city of 400,000 was undergoing a spectacular construction and rebuilding boom. Only three years earlier, the Great Chicago Fire of 1871 had destroyed one-third of the buildings, left 90,000 people homeless and caused 200–300 deaths. Before the end of the decade, the city would have over 500,000 residents.

A two-day stop was taken to rest, water and feed the 275 horses. For the two officers and thirty men in the stable detail, it was a miserable assignment, burdened by relentless rain and the overpowering stench coming from thousands of pigs held in mud-soaked pens at the nearby slaughterhouses. Rats overran the stock yard and brazenly drove the horses from the feed boxes. The men repeatedly used sticks to drive the rodents away.

Those men not on duty rested in hotels to enjoy, as Jean D'Artigue said "the comforts of civilization."[106] One sight to be seen was Frank James, brother of the outlaw Jesse James, smoking a cigar with his feet resting on the railing of the hotel's veranda. About one dozen men were recruited in Chicago and St. Paul. While in St. Paul, a city of 28,000, a large crowd waiting in the early morning to see the "red-Britishers" was disappointed that the men wore mufti.[107]

The NWMP rested one day (June 10), with the men put up in hotels or billeted mainly with Scandinavian families. Mowing machines were purchased along with supplies of oats, flour, and bacon. The men enjoyed the brief stop in a city they liked more than Chicago. One account related: "We were exceedingly well received here, and complimented on being the finest set of men which had ever appeared in the Queen city of Minnesota."[108]

On the morning of June 12, six days after leaving Toronto, the trains crossed the Red River to Fargo, Dakota Territory. This ended a rail journey of over 2,400 km that had gone remarkably well, with only two men requiring medical attention. The general behaviour of the company (other than the dog kidnappings) had been commendable. Surgeon Kittson lauded, "their neat appearance, sobriety and high spirits that won universal admiration where so ever they passed."[109] Commissioner French likewise was impressed. His report lauded: "the conduct of the men has been most exemplary, their general appearance and conduct invariably attracting the favourable notice of the railway officials and others en route."[110]

At Fargo, the horses, dissembled wagons, equipment, supplies, and baggage cluttered a field. This disarray, commented one recruit, "greatly pleased the inhabitants of Fargo, who thinking we would be detained several days, were figuring, like true Yankees, how many dollars they would make by our long stay."[111] However, any economic gain for the local merchants in the town of 2,500 was not forthcoming.

Early the following morning, Commissioner French assigned fatigue parties to specific tasks and, spurred by what Bagley called the "vocal assistance of the terrible sergeants," in the early afternoon "D" troop left with twenty-nine loaded wagons to set up a camp 10 km north.[112] At 7 p.m. "E" Division joined the camp and, by the next afternoon, "F" troop had completed the sorting and repacking of the supplies. Arrangements were made to send the machinery and heavy goods downriver by steamboat. The following day was spent in camp as a Sunday observance.

On June 15, the column departed for Canada following a 270-km trail that paralleled the west bank of the Red River. It was a hectic five-day trip. Many of the horses had never been harnessed and resisted pulling wagons. One recruit wrote: "The horses could not or would not haul their loads, some were balky, and there were two or three runaways, loads were upset, many got stuck in mud-holes, which had to be unloaded and we had to carry the stuff on our backs to dry land."[113] Sub-Inspector James Walker likened the harnessing of horses "to a circus every morning during the march to Fort Dufferin."[114] On the third day, at Grand Forks (about one-half the distance), Mounties from the Stone Fort brought the column twenty-five western horses. This was helpful as many eastern horses were unfit after the long rail journey. Four horses had died—two from sunstroke on the trail and two others had been trampled in the boxcars.

The campsites were marked by confusion. Sub-Constable Jean D'Artigue described the first evening as "the greatest tumult I ever witnessed reigned for a time among us. Constables were shouting for night sentries, cooks were calling for wood and water ... while just by them, was a flowing river, whose banks were covered with fuel."[115] Young Bagley could record on one occasion: "No supper. All cooks drunk."[116] For the Sunday dinner, the men had one soda biscuit, a piece of fat bacon, a seventeenth part of a small loaf of bread, and no sugar with the tea.

On the march north, the disorder and incessant complaints by the men won "cold comfort" from Sergt.-Major Joe Francis, a Crimea war veteran. He forewarned the recruits of the coming days: "You poor, miserable, molly-coddled mother's pets. If you consider you are badly used now, what will you think when some of these fine days before summer has ended you may have nothing to live on but the smell of an oily rag?"[117]

In the late afternoon on June 19, five days after leaving Fargo (and twelve days in the United States), the column crossed into Canada. Commissioner French wrote: "I felt a great responsibility taken off my shoulders to be again on Canadian soil."[118] Waiting was the newly appointed Assistant -Commissioner, James F. Macleod, with troops "A-B-C" from the Stone Fort. His men felt special being the first Mounted Police in the West and called themselves the '73 men and "Originals."

For the next forty-two days, the six Divisions of the NWMP remained as one body.

Dufferin: June 19–July 7, 1874

Fort Dufferin (today Emerson, Manitoba), named after Lord Dufferin, Governor General of Canada, 1872–78, was located on the west bank of the Red River, a short distance north of the international boundary. The tiny settlement consisted of a Hudson's Bay store and a collection of ramshackle dwellings. For the last two years, the North American Boundary Commission had used the settlement as its supply base for the joint Canadian-American survey of the 49th Parallel westward to the Rocky Mountains. When the police reached Dufferin, the surveyors were already far out on the plains.

The police camp was arranged in a square, with wagons on three sides and tents on a fourth. When not grazing nearby, most of the horses were tied to the wagons. The men spent the first day sorting the supplies.

At about midnight the first night, a thunderstorm struck the camp causing, in one Mountie's words, "a scene which will never be forgotten by those who witnessed it."[119] The violent winds ripped the canvas covers from the wagons, terrifying the horses, and then a lightning bolt struck nearby. The crazed animals broke from their fastenings and stampeded through the tents, trampling six men. It was a scene of havoc with the thunder, unceasing flashes of lightning, terrified horses, and shouting. Sam Steele wrote:

> I shall never forget that night. I had full view of the stampede, being not more than fifty yards from the horses as they rushed at the gate and attempting to pass it, scrambling and rolling over one another in a huge mass. This and the unceasing flashes of lightning, the rolling of thunder, and the loud shouts of the troopers … gave it a weird and romantic complexion, typically suggestive of the wild west.[120]

The hoof of a horse struck Sub-Constable William Latimer on his head, tearing his scalp open from ear to ear. Sub-Constable J. Coleman's team ran away while he was in the wagon box. Two hungry men, Sub-Constables Edward Maunsell and Jack Dunbar, were returning late to camp after unloading supplies from a river steamer and wanted some milk with their hardtack biscuits.

Maunsell was holding a cow by the horns while Dunbar milked into a fruit jar when the horses charged toward them. Dunbar ran one way to safety, but horses toppled Maunsell. In the confusion and darkness, the two men shouted and searched unsuccessfully for each other. Maunsell collapsed upon reaching the campsite. When he came to, Doctor Kittson was attending him. His body was badly bruised and, although there were no broken bones, he was unfit for duty for one week.

In the chaos, as one Constable put it, "human efforts were negligible against that tidal wave of terror-stricken animals."[121] The spooked herd stampeded across the rickety Pembina River bridge and south toward Dakota Territory.

Once he caught and saddled a horse, Superintendent James Walker trailed the herd. In the pitch black night, he could only see the fleeing horses when lightning flashed. "Fortunately," Walker recalled, "there were no wire fences in those days."[122] It was not until he reached Grand Forks, 100 km south, that Walker and troopers sent to help were able to turn the herd and drive the animals northward.

Walker returned to the Dufferin camp almost twenty-four hours after the storm began. He recalled: "During that time I had ridden five different horses, and had been wet through and dried out three different times, and had ridden 120 miles [200 km] by trail, besides many extra miles rounding up horses by the way."[123]

Fifteen-year-old Frederick Bagley, one of the troopers sent to help Walker, wrote about his return: "When the horse I was riding walked unchecked into camp about 12 midnight I was found to be fast asleep in the saddle and so fagged out that I had to be lifted off and put to bed."[124]

Thunderstorm at Dufferin (Henri Julien)

"I saw a terrifying sight. The two hundred and fifty horses, with their eyes like fire, tails straight up in the air, and what looked like steam coming from their nostrils, were charging down on top of us at breakneck speed."

– Constable William Parker in Dempsey, ed., *William Parker Mounted Policeman*, 6
GA NA 47 – 3

It was remarkable that only one horse, believed to have drowned in the Pembina River, was lost. The aftermath of the storm, however, lasted for months. Inspector Sam Steele pointed out, "for the remainder of the summer every thunderstorm brought us out of our tents at night, and in the daytime we had to be amongst them to calm the horses' fears."[125]

After the tumultuous introduction to Western Canada, the remaining sixteen days at Dufferin seemed rather uneventful. Commissioner French transferred fifty recruits to Divisions "A-B-C." Inspector A. Shurtliff left with ten men northwestward to Fort Ellice, an important Hudson's Bay post located near the confluence of the Assiniboine and Qu'Appelle Rivers (about 5 km east of the present Saskatchewan–Manitoba border). Their task was to prepare the site as the designated NWMP headquarters. The horses were shod and supplies unloaded off a river steamer from Fargo. Uniforms were issued and a pay parade gave each officer $24, each man $10 "on account." Much of this money found its way to whiskey joints and bordellos across the border.

Excessive drinking caused problems. Staff-Sergeant Tommy Lake was reduced in rank to Corporal for drunkenness. And, on the night before departure, George French dismissed Inspector Charles F. Young for "using grossly insubordinate language to the Commissioner when on duty."[126] The former British officer, who had served in the Maori Wars, "would not keep sober and he had to go," agreed Colonel Macleod.[127] Inspector Éphrem-A. Brisebois replaced Young in charge of Division "B."

The stay at Dufferin was a frustrating delay. Edward Maunsell spoke for his comrades: "We fretted much at being delayed at Dufferin as we were anxious to start on our crusade."[128] Most irksome were the poorly prepared and cooked meals, a concern that French noted in his official report. And the insects were troublesome: the Commissioner commiserated "to be worked hard all day and to be pestered all night by mosquitoes (was) not encouraging to an ordinary individual."[129]

James Finlayson's diary recorded: "Nothing of interest for one week except men deserting."[130] This comment on desertion pinpointed a serious concern. In the eighteen-day camp at Dufferin, thirty-one men deserted the Force, an easy matter with the border a few hundred paces to the south. This loss was substantial—more than ten per cent of the contingent. Most serious was the loss of men having skilled trades. For example, all the farriers deserted.

Commissioner French had anticipated losing a number of recruits and overstaffed the Force by twenty men. Still the desertions affected the camp's morale and, to address this concern, French ordered a full-dress parade. Young Bagley thought the scarlet tunics and white pugni bound helmets made an inspiring sight. It was the only NWMP parade with all six Divisions present.

Before the assembled, French told his command that any half-hearted individual could leave, but from those remaining he wanted the utmost loyalty. His challenge proved effective. A few men took their discharge, but the lure of adventure remained enticing. For Commissioner French, "the chicken-hearted rascals who deserted at Dufferin were a good riddance."[131] Everyone agreed. Henri Julien, an artist-journalist from Montreal who had been hired to draw pictures of the westward march, spoke for the men: "We all came to the conclusion that we were well rid of these cowardly fellows who have bred trouble at every turn."[132] Constable W. Grain assessed that, "most of the weaklings have been weeded out through desertions."[133]

There were two last-minute delays. First, the revolvers ordered from England did not arrive until the first week in July. During shipping, many of the weapons had been damaged, making repairs necessary. Second, the American army reported that a Sioux band had massacred a family in the Métis settlement at St. Joseph, Dakota Territory, and might be headed for Canada. French responded quickly. The grazing horses were brought in and, within thirty minutes, a mounted column was dispatched to the border. Now was a chance to fight Indians. One trooper described his fanciful excitement:

> I expected, at any moment, to see Indians, as I had read of them in novels, springing from the grass with their war-whoops, and charging us with their tomahawks; but I was disappointed in my expectations. We hunted the plain for miles around until sun-set, without the appearance of Indians, when to the great dissatisfaction of all, the order was given to return to camp.[134]

"We were," in Constable William Parker's words, "all disappointed in not being in a scrap with the Indians."[135]

Not all the men in the Dufferin camp participated in the famous march west. Forty-three men were stationed at Dufferin and Lower Fort Garry, four men required medical attention, and Inspector Albert Shurtliff earlier had taken ten men along to prepare Fort Ellice as the proposed NWMP headquarters.

Finally, on the afternoon of 8 July 1874, the North-West Mounted Police left for The Great Lone Land. The *Manitoba Free Press* ridiculed the departing column: "Colonel French left for Saskatchewan yesterday with four troops of police, the fifth having nearly all deserted."[136]

NOTES

1. *M*, 16 September 1871.

2. N.M.W.J. McKenzie, *The Men of the Hudson's Bay Company* (Times-Journal Presses, Fort William, 1921), 14. See James G. MacGregor, *Father Lacombe* (Edmonton: Hurtig, 1975), 206–7; *RCMP Q*, IX, No. 3, 318–9.

3. William Francis Butler, *The Great Lone Land* (London: Sampson Low, 1872), 250.

4. *LH*, 17 September 1927. See Hugh A. Dempsey, *Firewater* (Calgary: Fifth House, 2002).

5. *RCMP Q*, XV, No. 4, 329.

6. *HDH*, 13 March 1872. The newspaper named and gave the cause of death of four whites and three half-breeds killed at or near Fort Whoop-Up.

7. *HDH*, 8 April 1872.

8. *HDH*, 15 June 1870. For his visit to the fort, see John McDougall, *On Western Trails in the Early Seventies* (Toronto: William Briggs, 1911), Chapter XXIV. Also *LH*, 15 November 1924.

9. Butler, *The Great Lone Land,* 283. A horse traded for sixty skins, a gun was worth fifteen skins, and tobacco, ten. The term "skin" meant a beaver skin.

10. *HDH*, 5 January 1875.

11. Hugh A. Dempsey, ed., "Donald Graham's Narrative of 1872–73," *AHR*, IV, No. 1, 16. For the term "mountain dew", see *GA*, SARP M4561, Box 1, f. 4, 55.

12. *GA*, Tom Moore, M 3627.

13. *TG*, 30 December 1882. *MFP*, 20 January 1883.

14. *MG*, 4 November 1881. Also *GA*, D. McEachran, M 736.

15. E.H. Maunsell, "Maunsell's Story," *RCMP Q*, XLVIII, No. 1, 28.

16. Jean D'Artigue, *Six Years in the Canadian North-West* (Toronto: Hunter, Rose, 1882), 9.

17. P. Robertson-Ross, *Reconnaissance of the North West Provinces and Indian Territory of the Dominion of Canada, and Narrative of Journey Across the Continent Through Canadian Territory to British Columbia and Vancouver Island* (Ottawa: CSP, 1873, VI, No. 9), cxxiii.

18. John Craig, *Ranching with Lords and Commons* (Toronto: W. Briggs, 1903), 60.

19. William Rodney, *Kootenai Brown: his life and times*, 1839–1916 (Sidney, B.C.: Gray's Publishing, 1969), 115.

20. Dempsey, ed., "Donald Graham's Narrative of 1872–73," 18.

21. K. Douglas Munro, ed., *Fur Trade Letters* (Edmonton: Univ. of Alberta Press, 2006), 71.

22. Ibid.

23. *NAC*, Charles Bell, RG 10, Vol. 3609, f. 3229.

24. *GA*, Hardisty, M 477, Box 3 f. 68, 345. W. McKay to Hardisty, April 73.

25. *PAM*, Alex Morris Papers, MG 12 B1.

26. Major Eugene Baker's troops attacked a Piegan camp near the Marias River, killing 170 Indians. The American spelling is Piegan, the Canadian, Peigan.

27. *Lethbridge Historical Society,* The Last Great Indian Battle, Occasional Paper No. 30.

28. *LN,* 30 April 1890.

29. Isaac Cowie, *The Company of Adventurers* (Toronto: William Briggs, 1913), 414.

30. *LH,* 15 November 1924.

31. "Impressions of the West in the early Seventies from the Diary of the Assistant Surgeon of the B.N.A. Boundary Survey, Dr. Millman," *Woman's Canadian Historical Society of Toronto,* Transaction No. 26, 1927–28.

32. *PAM,* L.F. Hewgill, MG 1, B 23.

33. Ibid.

34. Hugh A. Dempsey, ed., *Frontier Life in the Mounted Police* (Calgary: Historical Society of Alberta, 2010), 17. Hereinafter, Nevitt, *Frontier Life in the Mounted Police.*

35. Cecil Denny, *The Law Marches West* (Toronto: J.M. Dent, 1939), 42.

36. *SN,* 14 January 1875.

37. Dempsey, ed., "Donald Graham's Narrative of 1872–73," 16.

38. *NAC,* RG 18, v. 1, f. 63–74. (21 April 1874). He added that an Indian life is not worth a cent if he gives the traders any trouble.

39. On the formation of the NWMP, see S.W. Horrall, "Sir John A. Macdonald and the Mounted Police Force for the Northwest Territories," *CHR,* LIII, No. 2, 1972, 179–200. Cameron was the son-in-law of Charles Tupper, a prominent Conservative politician. Another individual under consideration was Colonel J.C. McNeill, but he was in Africa. In Manitoba there was support for two French-Canadian officers.

40. Wolseley, aged thirty-seven, went on to an illustrious military career that culminated in 1895 as commander-in-chief of the British Imperial army. His account of the Red River Expedition is given in *Blackwood's Edinburgh Magazine:* CVIII, December 1870, CIX, January 1871, CIX, February 1871.

41. Other members of the Red River Expeditionary Force who joined the Mounted Police include Sam Steele, James F. Macleod (the second Commissioner of the NWMP), William Winder, Jack Bereford, Jack Allan, A.H. Griesbach, William Herchmer, William Blackby, William Buchanan, and Herbert Swinford.

42. Butler, *The Great Lone Land,* xv.

43. In 1873, Butler traveled to Peace River and west through the mountains to New Westminster, British Columbia. He recorded this journey in *The Wild North Land.*

44. Robertson-Ross, "Reconnaissance of the North West Provinces and Indian Territories of the Dominion of Canada," cvii–cxxvii. Also Hugh Dempsey, ed., "Robertson-Ross Diary," *AHR,* IX, No.3, 5–22.

45. For example, Robertson-Ross accurately details the Siksika or Blackfoot proper; this band numbers about 700 men, 1,000 women, 1,100 children, with about 3,000 horses and ponies, 400 dogs, and the following arms: 105 rifles, 260 revolvers, 436 flint guns, 286 bows, 48 spears, and 37 war axes. *Reconnaissance,* cxvi. Robertson-Ross assessed the Prairie Indian danger as overrated. He concluded the Indians were poorly armed, lacked cohesion, and were so scattered as to be an inept threat.

46. Hugh Dempsey, ed., "Robertson-Ross Diary," *AH,* IX, No. 3, 14.

47. Butler, *The Great Lone Land,* 367.

48. Robertson-Ross, *Reconnaissance of the North West Provinces and Indian Territories of the Dominion of Canada,* cxxii.

49. Ibid. cxi.

50. *The Times* (London), 1 July 1874.

51. *NAC,* Macdonald Papers, v. 252. Morris to Macdonald, 17 January 1873. See R.C. Macleod, *The NWMP and Law Enforcement 1873–1905* (Toronto: University Toronto Press, 1976), 14.

52. *RL*, 17 March 1885.

53. Thomas B. Strange, *Gunner Jingo's Jubilee*, 2nd ed. (London: Remington, 1894), 444.

54. R.G. MacBeth, *The Making of the Canadian West* (Toronto: Briggs, 1898), 163.

55. Cecil Denny, *The Riders of the Plains* (Calgary: Herald Co., c. 1905), 205.

56. Act of Parliament (36 Vic., Chap. 35). Earlier, on 31 March 1873, Prime Minister John A. Macdonald asked the House of Commons for a moderate grant of money to organize a mounted police force for the western plains. The collection of customs, installation of criminal courts and jails, and appointed magistrates would be included in its mandate.

57. Paul F. Sharp, *Whoop-Up Country* (Helena: Historical Society of Montana, 1960), 110. Source − James F. Macleod to W.F. Sanders, 10 August 1877, in W.F. Sanders papers, Historical Society of Montana Library.

58. See Philip Goldring, *Whiskey, Horses and Death: The Cypress Hills Massacre and its Sequel* (Ottawa: Canadian Historic Sites, Occasional Papers, No. 21, 1979).

59. *HH*, 11 June 1873.

60. *NAC*, MG 26, A1.

61. Colonel Osborne Smith, William Jarvis, Charles Young, James Macleod, William Winder, Jacob Carvell, James Walsh, Ephrem-A. Brisebois, and E. Dalrymple Clark.

62. Cecil Denny, *The Law Marches West* (Toronto: Dent, 1939), 5.

63. James Fullerton, "Toronto to Fort Garry," *SG*, Seventeenth Annual, 17.

64. *NAC*, John A. Macdonald papers A-41. Vol. 252A, 114204 MG 26.

65. James McKernan, "Expeditions Made in 1873," *SG*, Second Annual, 84.

66. *TM*, 6 October 1873.

67. The steamers were *The Cumberland, Chicora*, and *Frances Smith*.

68. James Walsh, "Old-Timers' Column," *RCMP Q*, XXVIII, No. 2, 134.

69. Fullerton, "Toronto to Fort Garry," 17.

70. Ibid.

71. William Osborne Smith arrived in Canada with a British regiment in 1856. He had fought in Crimea and against the Fenian incursions in 1866 and 1871 in Quebec and later in Manitoba. In 1871, Smith was placed in charge of Military District (no. 10) in Winnipeg. Smith served as the temporary Commissioner of the NWMP in 1873. In the 1885 North-West Rebellion, he raised and led the Winnipeg Light Infantry Battalion as part of the Alberta Field Force.

72. McKernan, "Expeditions Made in 1873," 84.

73. Steele, *Forty Years in Canada* (New York: Dodd, Mead & Company, 1915), 61.

74. Philip Goldring, "The First Contingent: The North-West Mounted Police, 1873−74. Appendix B. Daily Routines," *Canadian Historic Sites: Occasional Papers in Archaeology and History* (Ottawa: Parks Canada, 1979), 29−30.

75. *TG*, 2 January 1874. *OC*, 26 December 1873.

76. McKernan, "Expeditions Made in 1873," 85.

77. *RC*, NWMP, 1874, 5.

78. Howard Noble, "The Commissioner who almost wasn't," *RCMP Q*, XXX, No. 2, 10.

79. *NAC*, RCMP, RG 18, Series B3. Letter books of Commissioner G.A. French. Reel T-7131.

80. *A Chronicle of the Canadian West* (Calgary: Historical Society of Alberta, 1975), Appendix VI, Confidential Report of Major-General E. Selby-Smyth, 32.

81. *RCMP Q*, 1, No.3. Jim Wallace, *A Double Duty* (Winnipeg: Bunker to Bunker Books, 1997), 125–138.

82. *NAC*, RG 18, IX, f. 33–76.

83. *GA*, RCMP fonds, M 8380.

84. Hugh A. Dempsey, ed., *A Winter at Fort Macleod* (Calgary: Glenbow-Alberta Institute, 1974), 85.

85. D'Artigue, *Six Years in the Canadian North-West*, 102. Earlier, (page 51), D'Artigue wrote, "Other officers on the Force could have done a better job than he."

86. *GA,* Joseph Carscadden, M 6608.

87. *NAC,* J.B. Mitchell, f. o.s.156.

88. Steele, *Forty Years in Canada*, 100.

89. Fred A. Bagley, "The '74 Mounties," *CC*, XIII, No. 2, 28.

90. *GA*, William Parker, M 934. Also *MFP*, 24 August 1876; *TM*, 30 August 1876.

91. Maunsell, E.H. "With the North West Mounted Police from 1874 to 1877," *SG*, Second Annual, 57. French's relations with the local community appear troubled. One letter to the *Manitoba Free Press* states: "he is a sour despot who is not only hated by his own force but by others, with whose personal freedom he constantly interfered." *MFP*, 12 November 1875.

92. He was awarded a CMG in 1877 (Companion of the Order of St. Michael and St. George) and KCMG in 1902 (Knight Companion of St. Michael and St. George).

93. *MFP*, 26 September 1878.

94. *GA*, Fred Bagley, M 43.

95. Bagley, "The '74 Mounties," No. 1, 23.

96. In numbers: 41 men in Regular Service; 14 Royal Irish Constabulary and Civil Police; 32 Canadian Artillery; 87 Canadian militia.

97. Hugh Dempsey, ed., *William Parker Mounted Policeman* (Calgary: Glenbow-Alberta Institute, 1973), 4.

98. Bagley, "The '74 Mounties," No. 2, 28.

99. Dempsey, ed., *William Parker Mounted Policeman*, 102.

100. *RC*, NWMP, 1874, 9.

101. D'Artigue, *Six Years in the Canadian North-West*, 18.

102. *CH*, 4 July 1925.

103. Bagley, "The '74 Mounties," No. 2, 29.

104. Ibid.

105. Maunsell, "With the North West Mounted Police from 1874 to 1877," 51.

106. D'Artigue, *Six Years in the Canadian North-West*, 23.

107. *St. Paul Journal*, 10 June 1874.

108. Henri Julien, "Expedition to the North-West," *AHR*, IX, No. 1, 8.

109. *A Chronicle of the Canadian West,* Appendix IV, Report of Surgeon John Kittson, 19.

110. *RC*, NWMP, 1874, 7. James Macleod was delighted with the good behaviour of his troop when passing through Winnipeg on their way to meet French.

111. D'Artigue, *Six Years in the Canadian North-West*, 26. See *RC*, NWMP, 1874, 7. French wrote: "The Fargo people enjoyed the sight; they considered that it would take at least a week before we could get off."

112. *GA*, Frederick Bagley, M 43.

113. A.H. Scouten, "Way Back in '74," *SG*, Second Annual, 103.

114. *CH*, 15 March 1924.

115. D'Artigue, *Six Years in the Canadian North-West*, 27.

116. Bagley, "The '74 Mounties," No. 3, 32.

117. Ibid.

118. *RC*, NWMP, 1874, 7.

119. D'Artigue, *Six Years in the Canadian North-West*, 33.

120. Steele, *Forty Years in Canada*, 64. Also *NAC*, B. Welstead, f. o.s. 221.

121. William Grain, "Pioneers of a Glorious Future," *SG*, Twenty-ninth Annual, 62.

122. *CH*, 15 March 1924.

123. Ibid.

124. Bagley, "The '74 Mounties," No. 3, 33.

125. Steele, *Forty Years in Canada,* 64.

126. *NAC*, Charles F. Young, v. 3436, file 0–15.

127. *GA*, James Macleod, M 776. Young later became a Justice of the Peace. It was said, perhaps jocularly, that in one case when he ordered the destruction of illicit spirits, tears were running down his face. *GA*. Shaw, M 4166.

128. Maunsell, "Maunsell's Story," 26.

129. *RC*, NWMP, 1874, 9.

130. *NAC*, James Finlayson Diary, MG 29 E58. Fifteen men left the night before the Force began its famous march.

131. J.F.C., "First March of the NWMP," *Canadian Defence Quarterly*, Vol. 11, No. 4, July 1925, 385.

132. Julien, "Expedition to the North-West," 10.

133. Grain, "Pioneers of a Glorious Future," 62.

134. D'Artigue, *Six Years in the Canadian North-West*, 38–39.

135. Dempsey, ed., *William Parker Mounted Policeman*, 7.

136. *MFP*, 10 July 1874. French (*RC*, NWMP, 1874, 10) commented on his skeptics, "some of the Fort Garry croakers say we won't be back until Christmas, and experienced ones say we will lose forty per cent of our horses."

2

THE GREAT LONE
LAND

Sergeant G. Rolph (left) and Indian Grave

"When an Indian dies the custom in this Country They generly put the corps up in
a Tree on four poles. They don't bury them so the wolfs wont get at the body."

– S.J. Clarke, NWMP, Diary, 14 March 1879
  GA NA 936 – 36

IN THE PERIOD 1873-85, the North-West Mounted Police patrolled
an area north from the International Boundary to the North Saskatchewan
River and from the eastern slope of the Rocky Mountains to the province
of Manitoba.[1] This region encompassed approximately 600,000 km[2]—more
than two and a half times the area of the present-day United Kingdom.[2]

It was an immense land for 300 Mounties to police. In the first years, one assignment was escorting prisoners from Fort Macleod to Stony Mountain penitentiary, near Winnipeg. Constable George Boswell recalled:

> The prisoner sat on the horse all day and at night the policeman would get the pack off the packhorse, make a fire of buffalo chips and prepare the meal. The prisoner was fed while still sitting on his horse in irons. Two picket pins made of iron with a swivel were driven into the ground and two rawhide ropes made of twelve-strand buffalo hide were tied to each. The prisoner was ordered to lie on the ground, his head pointing at one pin, his feet at the other, and the ropes were passed through his leg chains and his arm chain out above his head. He was thus staked out for the night, not so comfortable, but reasonably safe as far as the possibility of escape was concerned.[3]

On his return to Fort Macleod two months later, Constable Boswell had ridden more than 2,280 km, farther than the direct air distance between London, England and Moscow.[4]

Superintendent A. Bowen Perry's log book in 1885 confirms the extraordinary distances that the Mounted Police often traveled. As part of the Alberta Field Force in the North-West Rebellion, Perry led a twenty man NWMP unit from Fort Macleod north to attack Big Bear's Cree band in the Frog Lake-Fort Pitt area. When the troop returned to its base 100 days later, the men had ridden 1,308 miles or over 2,100 km. It was an arduous ride—matched by few, if any, military columns in history.[5]

And even when not on special assignments, the men rode remarkable distances. Commissioner A.G. Irvine's Report for 1880 states: "The distance travelled by Constable Armour and his team from the first of April to the first November was 3,080 miles [5.130 km]."[6] Constable R.C. McLaren recorded that between September 1877 and August 1880 he had ridden an incredible 13,600 km (8,153 miles)! His trips in 1879 included:

> Jan. 1879 went to Foot of the Mountain and returned one hundred and forty miles. Jan. 1879 went to Ft. Benton and returned three hundred and twenty miles. Feb. 1879 started for Red Deer River had to turn back travelled eighty miles. Feb. 1879 went to Cree camp on mouth of Red Deer River and returned two hundred and forty miles. March 1879 went to Ft. Macleod and returned three hundred and fifty miles.

April 1879 went to Wood Mountain and returned four hundred miles. June 1879 went to line (border) and returned ninety miles. July 10 1879 left Ft. Walsh for Ft. Macleod arriving there July 13 one hundred and seventy miles. July 24 left Ft. Macleod for Ft. Calgary arriving there July 25 one hundred and ten miles. Aug 1 left Ft. Calgary for Ft. Edmonton arriving there Aug. 26 two hundred and twenty five miles. Aug. the 14 left Ft. Edmonton for Battleford arriving there Aug. 20 two hundred and fifty miles. Sept. 5 left Battleford for Cypress arriving there Sept. 11 three hundred miles. Sept. 15 left Ft. Walsh for Wood Mountain arriving there Sept. 20 two hundred miles.[7]

Anyone who has crossed the vast Canadian prairies, even in the comfort and speed of a motor vehicle, can only marvel at the incredible distances and accompanying hardships the early Mounties undertook on horseback.

Policemen on an extended trip lost communication with the outside world. Major A.G. Irvine, who left Winnipeg on 26 October 1875, knew nothing of his appointment to succeed Colonel Macleod as Assistant Commissioner until he arrived in Fort Macleod two months later. "He was of course immensely pleased," observed Surgeon Barrie Nevitt.[8]

Prairie Inhabitants

In 1874, the Canadian plains had an Indian (now First Nation) population numbering 27,000.[9] About 11,000 Plains Cree occupied the region north and east of the Red Deer River; the Blackfoot Confederacy—Blood (Kainai), Peigan (Pikuni), and Blackfoot (Siksika), numbering 14,000 Indians, had their home in southern Alberta. About 250 Sarcee (Tsuu-T'ina), allied to the Blackfoot, lived near the Bow and Red Deer rivers.

Stoney or Assiniboine (Assiniboin) bands of about 1,000 Indians were located in the foothills of the Rocky Mountains and east of the Cypress Hills. A small tribe of Saulteaux (Ojibwa) occupied the southeastern region of present-day Saskatchewan. This area also held a small band of Dakota (a Sioux sub-division), who had come to Canada after the Sioux Massacre in Minnesota in 1862.

In their hunt for buffalo, prairie Native people ranged over the Canadian plains and ventured into American territory, often infringing on other tribal hunting grounds. Some non-area Indians, such as the Kootenai from British Columbia, came to the plains each summer to hunt buffalo. In August 1877, a police patrol in the Crowsnest Pass met Kootenai Indians returning home with 600 horses loaded with dried buffalo meat.

Ottawa arranged for John McDougall, a Methodist missionary at Morleyville (west of Calgary), to apprise the Indians of the forthcoming police arrival. McDougall recalled: "I was to travel from camp to camp and inform the Mountain and Wood and Plains tribes of this action of the Government, and also to explain the full purpose thereof ... we had for years told the Indians this was coming."[10]

Blood Indian and Women (n.d.)

In 1874, there were 27,000 Indians on the Canadian prairies.

– Fort Macleod Museum
 FMP 81 150

But would the indigenous people welcome a column of armed whites? The summer before the arrival of the NWMP, a geological survey party had left the "Elbow" (the point where the South Saskatchewan turns north) to explore Swift Current Creek and the Cypress Hills. Robert Bell wrote: "We had only proceeded 45 miles, when we were met by a large number of Indians who compelled us to turn back."[11]

A second prairie group was a growing Métis population that numbered 4,000. This Métis element, at that time called half-breeds (or, by the police, "the moccasin aristocracy"[12]), distinguished itself from the Indians by having rather strong Christian religious influences, European surnames, a predominant French language base, purchasing manufactured clothing (with a distinctive red sash for males), European influenced music and dance, using superior technology (such as cart transport and agrarian skills), employment as freighters and interpreters, establishing permanent settlements with farming, and having political contact with Ottawa. Greater self-reliance and economic diversity buffeted the Métis communities from hunger and suffering once the buffalo herds were gone. The Indian-Métis interaction often was tenuous.[13]

Alexander Morris, Lieutenant Governor of Manitoba and the North-West Territories, categorized the Métis population into three groups.[14] First, he suggested, there were families who lived near Hudson's Bay Company posts along the North Saskatchewan River, in the Edmonton area and at Fort Qu'Appelle. St. Albert, with 800 Métis residents, was the largest community in the North-West Territories. The settlement grew cereal and root crops and caught fish at nearby Lac Ste. Anne. The Oblate mission at St. Albert acted as both an education and religious centre for the region. William Butler thought it was "a curious contrast to find in this distant and strange land, men of culture and high mental excellence devoting their lives to the task of civilizing the wild Indians of the forest and prairie."[15] Second, some Métis identified with the Indians, lived in their camps and understood their language. A third group, in Morris' opinion, followed the buffalo chase. As the herds diminished, the hunt moved farther west where some families, called *hivernants*, built small winter camps, such as near present-day Eastend, Saskatchewan. The largest Métis winter gathering was at Tail Creek, a tributary of Buffalo Lake that ran south to the Red Deer River. Inspector Sam Steele counted 400 lodges at this locale in 1876.

After the Red River troubles of 1869–70, many Manitoba Métis relocated in the Batoche area and at Wood Mountain in southern Saskatchewan. Three times on their westward match, the struggling NWMP column sent wagons to Wood Mountain to purchase oats and pemmican.

Fewer than 1,000 white people lived on the western plains in 1874. Almost one-half this number was in the Prince Albert area. Others resided at Hudson's Bay posts along the North Saskatchewan River and on the eastern plains at Fort Ellice and Fort Qu'Appelle. Missionary communities were found at Prince Albert, Morleyville, Victoria (now Pakan), and St. Albert. Individual priests visited and sometimes lived in the Indian camps. Fort Whoop-Up was the only permanent structure south of the Bow River. Most whiskey traders operated from makeshift camps on a seasonal basis. About fifteen miners panned gold on the North Saskatchewan.

At any given time, large areas of the Canadian plains were devoid of human life. When the NWMP column left Dufferin in July 1874, the men eagerly anticipated contacting Indians and seeing the legendary buffalo herds. Yet, it was thirty-five days before they met a Native band and not one buffalo had been sighted. By this time, some of the men were beginning to doubt the existence of both Indians and buffalo.

The following year, while traveling from Fort Carlton to Edmonton on his military inspection of Western Canada, Major-General E. Selby Smyth reported that, "along the entire distance of 400 miles [670 km] I met no living soul except one traveling half breed and the monthly postman."[16] For the Mounted Police contingent that left Toronto (population 70,000) in June 1874 and stopped briefly in Chicago (population 400,000), the North-West Territories was truly "The Great Lone Land."

Surface Features

Glacial and post-glacial geological forces had formed vast plains, cut by eroded river valleys, and pocketed with numerous sloughs, wetlands, and small lakes. Travelers frequently compared the grassland to an ocean. One account described the region as "a land sea, sometimes perfectly level, at other times abounding in hillocks and undulating ground, and occasional prominences from which a panoramic view can be obtained to a horizon ten or twelve miles distant."[17] Sub-Constable Frank Carruthers wrote to relatives in Toronto, "you can no more imagine its vastness than you can describe the limits of the ocean."[18] In August 1883, Brit Stephens wrote to England: "The country is one vast prairie for thousands of miles. It is the same as the ocean ... you can travel hundreds of miles and not see a house, human being, or even a tree."[19] The Marquis of Lorne, Governor General of Canada, described his prairie excursion in 1881 as through a "green sea."[20] A newspaper reporter with the tour observed that one looks out for a house here as one looks out for a ship at sea. A recruit wrote of the '74 march west: "It was monotonous to the extreme—nothing to be seen day after day but the rolling prairie. It reminded me of a long sea voyage, where nothing is in view morning after morning but the boundless ocean."[21] The Cree spoke of the prairies as "the bare land."[22]

The elevation slopes to the east and northeast. Fort Macleod's altitude is 950 m; Prince Albert 430 m; Fort Qu'Appelle 485 m; and Edmonton 667 m.[23] Uplands such as the Porcupine Hills, Cypress Hills, and Turtle Mountain rise several hundred metres above the surrounding plains. At an elevation reaching 1,466 m (4,816 ft.), the Cypress Hills is the highest point directly east of the Rocky Mountains to the Atlantic Ocean.

The level and sweeping landscape often disorientated travelers.[24] Constable Robert Patterson recalled that, near the Belly River, one of his companions, "thought he would take a 'short cut' and went up another hill and got hopelessly lost. He did not turn up for two or three days."[25] On the return journey in 1874 of Divisions "C-D" to Manitoba, two men disappeared. A scout sent out by Commissioner French found the men so confused that they were walking west. And, even with a mountain skyline to his left as a landmark, Constable S.G. Hogg was lost for two days while going from Fort Macleod to Fort Calgary.

Newcomers commented on the loneliness of this vast prairie expanse that made you, as the Métis said, "think long." One Mountie commented, "This sense of solitude is so overpowering that it towers above all other feelings … it is a strange, haunting silence;—a hush that may be felt."[26] After being lost and wandering for half the day with only his rifle and a few rounds of ammunition, Surgeon Barrie Nevitt wrote: "You can form no idea how intensely lonely one can feel out here, especially if he is alone on the prairies."[27]

An eerie silence compounded the loneliness. Captain Dalrymple Clark commented: "in crossing these plains the vastness and endless space oppresses one; there is nothing but sky and land, and an indescribable stillness reigns over all—a stillness such as one notices before the burst of a storm."[28] A recruit from England, stationed his first winter at Prince Albert, observed: "The stillness of the atmosphere here is intense; and strangely clear. You can hear sounds at immense distances."[29]

A NWMP recruit wrote of the boredom and silence in his journey across the plains in 1874:

> The eye dwells on vacancy, tired of glancing at the blue sky above, or at the brown earth below. A feeling of weariness creeps over you, interrupted at intervals by vague longings for something beyond the far low line of the horizon which is ever barred across your vision. The silence is oppressive. It is in vain that you attempt to relieve the tedium of conversation with your companions. Besides that, the stocking trade of chatter is soon exhausted in these wilds, whither nothing from the outer world reaches you, and the very labour of talking becomes irksome, and you fall to meditation. You throw the reins on your horse's neck and let him jog at will, while your eyes roam over the waste, and your thoughts wander as the winds. This truly has been called the Great Lone Land.[30]

A person could cross this empty land for weeks without seeing another human. In 1879, John Macoun, directing a small survey crew, moved westward on the open prairie for two months without once encountering any human life. He was, therefore, taken aback "when two policemen suddenly came up and wanted to know our business."[31]

Rudimentary trails linked the scattered Hudson's Bay trading posts. The most well-known route was the Carlton Trail that connected Fort Garry with forts Ellice, Carlton, Pitt, Victoria, and Edmonton. Inspector William D. Jarvis used this trail to take "A" Division from Roche Percée to Fort Edmonton on the '74 March. Rather than a single pathway, the Carlton Trail had as many as sixteen somewhat parallel wagon grooves. Signs attached to wooden poles gave information of directions or needs, as "L'eau, nord 2 milles." Trails without signposts could cause problems for newcomers. When the trail south of Edmonton bifurcated, Sub-Constable Jean D'Artigue and two police companions took the wrong pathway to Pigeon Lake, 90 km northwest of their intended destination at Buffalo Lake.

One moved on land by foot, horseback, and in wagons or Red River carts. In winter, because of problems in obtaining forage, the policemen sometimes replaced horses with dog teams. Sub-Constable Jean D'Artigue's first attempt to drive a dog team proved exasperating. The owner of the team told the young Mountie to resolutely discipline any uncooperative dogs, advice that D'Artigue was reluctant to enforce. He quickly realized that the owner was correct.

> The dogs soon perceiving that their master was no longer present, stopped, and notwithstanding my urgings, would go no farther ... I fastened them to a tree, and beat them unmercifully ... the plan succeeded; for, no sooner were they released than off they went with the speed of the wind.[32]

The policemen, living a spartan life far from their homes, craved contact with the outside world. Until the completion of rail and telegraph, there was only slow and unreliable mail service. At Fort Macleod, all mail went through Fort Benton, Montana Territory. A letter sent to Ontario requested that return mail be sent to "Fort Calgary, Montana, U.S." One card was addressed: "James Fullwood, North West Mounted Police, Fort McLeod, Porcupine Hills, via Benton, Montana Territory." W.H. Cox remembered:

> We had to use United States stamps which often sold at a premium as high as fifty cents for three-cent stamps. It was quite an amusement for the citizens the day the mail arrived. At the

highest point of vantage in the town there would be a half dozen or more watching the prairie to the south with spy glasses, looking for the Benton mail, and often giving false alarm by way of diversion.[33]

Plodding ox teams carried the mail between Fort Macleod and Fort Benton. When horsemen overtook the ox train, the riders routinely took delivery to the post where, as Colonel Walker remembered, their "arrival was heartedly welcomed."[34] Reverend John Maclean made sure to carry the mail with him when he left Fort Macleod to deliver a sermon at the Pincher Creek police ranch. The NWMP headquarters at Swan River had its mail base at Winnipeg. A relay of horses or dog teams stationed at posts every 70 km delivered the mail every three weeks.

In spite of the loneliness and unsophisticated lifestyle, this empty land held a magnetic charm in the sweep of the grasslands, the clear air, a bracing but healthful climate, aurora borealis, magnificent sunsets, winter sundogs, and the arrival of spring.

Newcomers were overwhelmed by the grandeur and immensity of the land. One visitor declared that Canadians who have not visited the northwest had little idea of the joyousness of prairie life. He wrote: "There is something in the boundlessness of the plains that tempts one to give 'a wild shriek of liberty,' as he bursts, for the first time, into the freedom of primitive nature."[35] Everyone recognized the potential that the Canadian prairies held for future white generations.[36]

A letter, published in the *Toronto Mail*, describing Christmas at "Fort Calgarry" in 1877, lamented that two-thirds of the troop would be discharged in the spring. Most of the men, the writer predicted, "would go back to Canada, blessing their stars to get out of this worthless waste—only to return again to it, so alluring are the charms of prairie life."[37]

Vegetation

The region is characterized by prairie, fringed to the north by aspen grove and brush parkland. Evergreens are found northward and at higher elevations. Every spring, wild flowers blanket the land.

Geographers classify the drier southern area as short-grass prairie, roughly that region known as Palliser's Triangle (The Palliser Triangle). Spreading outward in a semi-circle from this area, added moisture produces the mixed grass zone. A brown soil (podzol) top layer features the short -grass prairie; a dark brown or black (chernozemic) top soil, the mixed grass region. In years of abundant rainfall, the grass growth was luxuriant.

On a ride from Fort Macleod to the police ranch at Pincher Creek, Constable A.H. Lynch-Staunton rode through "a sea of grass reaching to our stirrups."[38]

On their '74 March, the Mounted Police rode through the driest and most inhospitable part of the prairies. The few trees and shrubs the men observed were beside waterways, in wind-sheltered valleys, and in distant uplands as the Cypress Hills. Surgeon Barrie Nevitt recorded: "One great drawback of this part of the world is the total absence of trees—for days and days we see no signs of them."[39] After leaving Wood End, so appropriately named, the column never saw a tree for weeks other than one "petrified tree about 1½ feet thick, standing by itself on the bald, flat prairie."[40] The ride west became tedious. Sergeant-Major J.B. Mitchell lamented: "There beneath us was the earth with the grass becoming brittle and there, day after day was the sky. That was all, Earth and Sky."[41]

The growing (frost-free) season ranges from 60 days at higher elevations to 100 days on the broad plains. Calgary, for example, has eight fewer frost-free days than Edmonton, which is 300 km north, but 385 metres lower in elevation. Even Prince Albert, much farther north than Calgary, has eleven more growing days. One reason given for abandoning the NWMP Headquarters at Fort Walsh (at 1,100 m) was because early frosts destroyed the garden and oat crop.

Long summer sunlight hours compensated for the short growing season. The fine gardens and cereal fields astonished outsiders. A sportsman from Liverpool in 1878 described Constable S. Tabor's garden at the Fort Saskatchewan post as "quite a sight. I never saw anything so luxuriant as the growth and size of the vegetables in his well-kept plot of ground of about four acres."[42] Still, many policemen were disappointed that the common products of Eastern Canada—apples, cherries, peaches, grapes, pears, tobacco—could not be grown. Wild strawberries, saskatoons, and raspberries were hardly a substitute.

Mounties used wood and coal for heat and cooking. There was abundant firewood in the parkland region and at higher elevations. On the '74 March, the column used coal from outcroppings at Roche Percée in the forges and fires. The police post at Fort Macleod purchased coal delivered by wagons from Fort Whoop-Up. By 1880, coal mines operated at Medicine Hat and Coal Banks (Lethbridge). The coal at Coal Banks was transported by barge to Medicine Hat or carted by ox train to Fort Macleod.

On the open prairie, the Mounties used buffalo chips (*le bois de vâche* —wood of the cow) for fuel. One of the first tasks upon reaching a campsite was filling gunny sacks with dried dung for the cook.

Sub-Constable William McQuarrie related that, "all you had to do was walk around and pick them up. They were round and about two inches thick, similar to what you find in cow meadows, only the chips were hard and dry."[43] Splinters of wood were burned to ignite the chips. Wet or frozen chips were difficult to burn. However, noted Surveyor George Dawson, buffalo chips, once taking fire, were difficult to extinguish and sometimes caused prairie fires.[44] Snow cover in winter made it necessary for police patrols to carry firewood.

Every summer and fall, numerous prairie fires, often caused by lightning, swept over the land. Some burnt areas were massive. A match carelessly discarded by a member of the Boundary Survey in 1873 started a blaze that burned 250 km eastward before turning south to reach the Missouri River.[45] Prairie fires in 1884 left the first 100 km north of Calgary without a blade of grass or stick of firewood. This meant the Alberta Field Force had to carry a fifteen-day supply of forage on their march to Edmonton in the spring of 1885.[46]

Prairie fires were awe-inspiring sights. Henri Julien, the artist assigned to the '74 March, wrote that, "the spectacle was sublime. The crackling flame, the heavy masses of smoke rolling low at first over the surface of the grass, then mounting higher and higher, till, caught in the stratum of breeze, they veered and floated rapidly to the east, formed a scene of impressive grandeur."[47] At night, fires would light the "whole sky red and as bright as day for miles around."[48] Constable John Donkin, awestruck by the roar and splendor of one fire, wrote: "No pyrotechnic display could equal this effort of nature."[49]

A strong wind quickly spread the flames. One Mountie observed that "within half an hour afterwards the plain was black behind us as far as we could see."[50] Constable Thomas B. Boys, riding in a troop from Fort Pitt to the Cypress Hills in 1876, wrote on the danger:

> A prairie fire sprang up before us just after the Col. had passed the spot. Advance galloped up and tried in vain to beat it out. It swept down on the train which was in some danger. Happily they got around it. I sprang through the wall of fire without harm. It followed us and chased us after dinner but we got off. The smoke filled the heavens.[51]

Safety measures were urgent if an advancing fire could not be avoided. When a large fire approached a Boundary Survey camp in 1873, the men removed the tents, placed the supplies in a nearby slough, and burned an area of grass to protect the oxen. However, the frightened animals left the safety area and "rushed about wildly in the flames and were badly singed about the legs. One of the men had the hair on his face burnt, and in the rush of wind accompanying the passage of fire, his hat went away adding fuel to the flames."[52]

If there was time, the men back-burned the grass for safety. When four Mounties, returning with a six-horse team from Stony Mountain Penitentiary to Fort Walsh, faced a dangerous approaching fire, the men wet gunny sacks in a slough and, by controlled burning, soon had a large half-circle burnt in front of their wagon, while the water body protected their rear. As the fire neared, the situation became desperate. Constable Edward Barnett recalled:

> There was much excitement to secure our horses from stampeding. A herd of deer passed with glaring eyes and distended nostrils, fear lending wings to their feet; prairie wolves shot past and the thundering hoofs of buffalo was heard. Would they go through our camp? Quickly we hung out blankets to divide them. This had the desired effect, but never could one forget the sight of those poor frightened beasts with lowered heads, frothing at the mouth, running in a blind frenzy. They passed and plunged into the lake.[53]

For these Mounties, it was a harrowing and unforgettable experience.

On several occasions, prairie fires threatened the police posts. Upon their arrival at Swan River in late 1874, Divisions "D-E" found a fire had burnt most of the winter hay supply. This loss forced one half of the column to move to Dufferin, their starting point five months earlier.

A prairie fire left the land scarred and unsightly. One wayfarer in 1878 wrote: "Nothing can be more dreary than passing over a burnt prairie, an unbroken black waste, and here and there a buffalo skull or bone; no animal life, and fine ash getting into the mouth and nose creating great thirst."[54] It took one troop of Mounties three days to cross a burnt-out area. One of the riders, F.C. Carruthers, marveled: "How the horses lived for those three days I don't know, but live they did and traveled from daylight to dark too."[55]

In late summer, the dry grassland was prone to fire. Throughout the prairies, a haze dulled the sky and obscured the landscape. In September 1885, a soldier at Prince Albert complained that the smoke was "so heavy that one could hardly breathe."[56]

The Territorial Government passed legislation that penalized anyone starting arson fires or leaving a campfire burning. There were several convictions, but the law proved ineffective. Although the Native people

Scouting Bow River, N.W.T., 1879

North-West Mounted Police scouting the Bow River in the North-West Territories.
William James Latimer is mounted on the horse.

– Photo courtesy of Bob Clay from Landis, Saskatchewan

routinely left their campsite fires burning, the police only advised them of
this danger. According to Inspector Sam Steele, the Indians deliberately,
"set the prairies on fire so that the bison would come to that part of the
country to get rich green grass which would follow in the spring."[57] After
the completion of the railway, Métis "bone-pickers" also deliberately fired
the prairie to expose buffalo bones which they sold for $6–$12 a ton.

The buffalo herds left the grassland bare. The Boundary Commission
recorded in 1874 that, for 170 km of longitude, the buffalo, "like an invasion
of locusts, had swept everything before them. The scant vegetation was
everywhere nibbled close, so that our own oxen and horses fared very
badly."[58] In the first summer at Fort Macleod (1875), a moving herd of
buffalo delayed a police patrol for an hour. After the animals passed,
Alfred Nedham noted, "not a blade of grass could be found erect, as they
cropped everything in sight."[59] Gopher and badger holes riddled some
fields. To a lesser extent, beavers had altered the landscape in parkland
regions by felling trees and damming waterways.

In 1874 and 1875, migrating locusts destroyed the prairie vegetation. On the fourth day of their famous western march, the police column watched in wonder at the sight of an approaching swarm of locusts. Inspector Sam Steele was incredulous:

> The air for the height of hundreds of yards was full of them, their wings shining in the sun, and the trees, grass, flowers, and in fact everything in sight, were covered by them … even the paint and woodwork of the wagons, and our carbines were not free from their attacks, and our tents had to be hurriedly packed away to save them from destruction.[60]

The locusts continued eastward toward Red River. Five weeks later, "A" troop, nearing Fort Ellice on its march to Edmonton, encountered another swarm. Inspector Sévèrn Gagnon wrote: "Again we found our friends, the grasshoppers; it was just like thick snow."[61] In two days, the locusts devoured the carefully planted garden at the Fort Ellice police post.

Locusts reappeared the following year. At Fort Macleod, an awestruck Police Surgeon Barrie Nevitt estimated 100 million grasshoppers were approaching Fort Macleod in "dense purplish masses in the shadows of the distant horizon … and looking up towards the sun the air is for miles up an immense mass of white wings … they start up in clouds from the earth as one walks. Our poor garden is gone."[62]

Locusts even ate William Parker's boots. The Mountie was chasing an escaped prisoner and took off his boots to run faster. Several days later, when he went to retrieve his boots, he found only shreds of leather remaining.[63]

Surface Water Flow

The Saskatchewan River basin contains the overwhelming volume of prairie water flow. Smaller drainage systems are the Qu'Appelle River flow into the Assiniboine River; the Souris following a path into the United States before returning to join the Assiniboine in Canada; and the Milk River and several small streams that are tributaries of the Missouri River. The river gradients are gradual and the water volume in prairie waterways is comparatively small.[64]

For more than a century, waterways had been the fur-trades entry into the northern regions. Traders built Fort Edmonton in 1790—eighty-four years before the arrival of the NWMP. The frozen rivers facilitated travel in winter. On his famous reconnaissance, William Butler used a dog team along the frozen North Saskatchewan to return to Fort Garry.

In the summer of 1875 (only three years after Butler's famous trip), the first river steamer reached Fort Edmonton, opening a new, but short-lived, transportation link into the interior. The police used steamers and barges to transport supplies to the Saskatchewan River police posts but, other than Commissioner Irvine moving by river steamer on one inspection tour of Battleford, Fort Pitt, and Prince Albert and Colonel W.D. Jarvis using an HBC York boat to travel from Fort Saskatchewan to Fort Pelly, river transport by the NWMP was minimal. The police used canoes and small boats for recreation. In one example, Inspectors Jackson, Walsh, Winder, and Surgeon Kennedy arranged to have their horses taken to Fort Kipp and then enjoyed a delightful journey down the Oldman River to the post.

The waterways were helpful in the construction of police posts at Fort Macleod, Battleford, and Fort Calgary. Work crews went upstream to wooded areas where they cut and floated logs to the site.

The last important use of waterways by the police and military was during the North-West Rebellion of 1885. In a controversial decision, the Fort Pitt NWMP detachment abandoned the post, leaving the civilian population at the mercy of hostile Indians, and fled in a scow downriver to Battleford. Later in the campaign, General Middleton's strategy used the *Northcote*, fortified with timber, in a quixotic attempt to co-ordinate the attack on Batoche. In the final month of the campaign, three steamers transported troops and supplies on the North Saskatchewan. In the final analysis, river transportation on the prairies was restricted by a short ice-free season, meandering river paths, fluctuating river flow, and sandbars. Completion of the rail line in 1885 abruptly ended steamboat transportation.

The waterways had an impact on NWMP travel. Inspector Walsh had to wait until the Oldman and St. Mary rivers were fordable before returning the police herd that wintered in Montana. He then left to build a police fort in the Cypress Hills. When possible, the police used the few ferries that crossed major rivers. At key river crossings, such as the Red Deer–South Saskatchewan confluence, the police cached boats to assist in their travel.

Crossing a large river was time consuming and sometimes difficult. After the signing of Treaty 6 in 1876, it took a police column moving south to Fort Walsh three days to cross the South Saskatchewan River. Constable Robert Patterson detailed the labour required:

> We took all the wagons apart, at least there must have been twenty, lashed two of the wagon beds or boxes together with a wagon sheet underneath and around them to keep some of the water out, we also made a raft of some dry cottonwood we

found along the river; in crossing, our unwieldy crafts would drift a considerable distance down the river, and would have to be towed up to the landing place, unloaded, then towed up the river again in order to make a landing near the camp. The river current was swift ... we had considerable trouble with the horses as the two half-breed guides could not or would not try to put them over. At last two of our men volunteered to cross them over. These men got them all safely over. I thought it was a wonderful feat.[65]

The two Mounties, Staff-Constable Billy Mitchell and Constable Charles Daley, swam the river, helped by holding the tail of a horse that was forced into the waterway. To celebrate the crossing, Dr. Kittson issued "hospital comforts" (whiskey) to the entire troop.

At river crossings, Constable George Guernsey related, the sweeps (oars) cut from poplar poles were ineffective from preventing the current drifting the makeshift scow downriver. Sometimes, the scow had to be returned a kilometre upstream to the crossing point.

An important crossing of the South Saskatchewan was Gabriel's Crossing, operated by Gabriel Dumont, who became the foremost Métis rebel in the North-West Rebellion. Since the crossing lacked a cable, horse teams pulled the clumsy 8x4-m scow to an upstream launch. From here the scow, propelled by four sweeps and the current, headed for the opposite bank. A licence issued by the Territorial Council granted Dumont 10 km of river front. Among his charges were: every horse and rider, 20 cents; single vehicle, 25 cents; sheep, hog, colt and calf, 5 cents; foot passenger, 10 cents; horse, mule, cow, 10 cents. In general, the limited ferry crossings hampered travel and commerce in the North-West Territories. Even in 1885, there was no ferry service across the Red Deer River.

Flooding can occur during spring runoff, after sustained heavy summer rains, and from ice jams. The rivers often rise quickly. In the spring of 1875, an ice jam near the Prince Albert settlement flooded an island and forced nine Indian women to climb trees for safety. Before help came the next evening, five of the women had fallen to their deaths. In Battleford, an ice barrier in April 1881 caused the river to rise five metres, forcing residents to scurry to higher ground. When the Alberta Field Force marched to Edmonton in late April 1885, the first echelon of troops crossed the Red Deer River with minor difficulties. Twenty-four hours later, rising waters delayed Inspector A. Bowen Perry's NWMP detachment for four and a half days as it was necessary for the men to build a scow to cross the waterway.

The problem of spring floods at Fort Macleod, then located on an island, led the local press to ridicule: "Each succeeding springtime the betting is almost even that the fort, town and inhabitants will form a stately procession on the watery road to Winnipeg."[66] The town was relocated to its present site in 1882.

Ice made the waterways dangerous. When he found that newly formed ice on the Belly River would not support the weight of his horse team, Constable R.N. Wilson chopped a pathway through the ice with an axe, freezing his hands in the process. Constable Alfred Nedham related how difficult it was crossing rivers that were not completely frozen:

> You had to break the ice out from the shore, then lead your horse into the current until you reached deep enough swimming water which was usually the swiftest. Only those who have been through zero weather on the prairie wilds can realize how almost instantly one becomes caked up with ice when coming out of a river after swimming across ... but it was all in a policeman's day's work. They had a right to say we were tough in those days. We had to be.[67]

The temperature and the force of the river's current determined the time needed for solid ice formation. A troop under Superintendent Sam Steele found that they could advance the freezing process and make a pathway strong enough to support a horse's weight by placing straw on the thin ice over which they poured water to freeze.

Thawing ice in the spring was deceptive and dangerous. In late March 1885, Constable William Parker delivered news to Edmonton area settlers announcing the outbreak of the North-West Rebellion. On his return, he broke through the ice on the North Saskatchewan. Parker—"for some reason unknown to me"—had taken his sword, which fortunately caught across the hole in the ice and prevented his total submergence.[68] The horse surfaced and Parker remounted and rode on to Fort Edmonton, 15 km away. When he reached Ross's Hotel, his clothes were frozen stiff and two men had to pull him from the saddle. Sergt.-Major J.H.G. Bray and Constable George Gamsby ended up in neck-deep water when their sleigh broke through ice on the Highwood River. The two men struggled to get the horses and sleigh on solid ground, after which they hurried to the only house between Fish Creek (Calgary) and Fort Macleod. The rancher had to chop the two Mounties out of the sleigh, as they were frozen to the seat. Surgeon Nevitt was up to his waist in ice water for an hour helping to free his wagon that had broken through the ice.

Between 1874 and 1885, seven policemen drowned. Constable Claudius Hooley died crossing the Belly River when the current swept his horses and wagon downstream. His three companions swam to safety, but Hooley was trapped under the overturned wagon. Several weeks later, his body was recovered 18 km downstream. Constable Adam Wahl, a member of a large contingent of recruits moving up the Missouri River on the *Red Cloud*, fell overboard while fishing. His body was never recovered. Constable Norman J. D'Arcy drowned in the Qu'Appelle Lakes. The men were amusing themselves in canvas skiffs. D'Arcy's boat collapsed and he never rose to the surface. William Gilroy of the Winnipeg NWMP detachment drowned when his boat capsized on the Assiniboine River in July 1885. The 20-year-old recruit from Ireland had only joined the Force two months earlier. It being Dominion Day, Inspector Frank Norman had given the detachment the day off for recreation. On their return to Ontario after the North-West Rebellion, soldiers from the Midland Battalion in Winnipeg, helped the search by firing cannon shots over where Gilroy had disappeared until the body surfaced.

Matthew Rice, nine days after his enlistment in the NWMP in 1882, disappeared from the steamer *Manitoba* traveling on the Assiniboine River westward to Fort Ellice. Rice was last seen sitting at the stern of the boat with his feet hanging over the water. He had previously complained of a bad headache and was reported to look dazed. Inspector Bowen Perry at Fort Ellice speculated that Rice had either jumped off the boat or was knocked off by a tree branch at a bend in the river. The NWMP report had charged Rice as a deserter, even though there was no conclusive evidence.

Quicksand claimed one Mountie's life. In June 1877, while crossing the South Saskatchewan, Sub-Constable George Mahoney and his half-breed companion, Goodwin Marchand, became trapped in quicksand. At the police hearing, Marchand explained that wearing moccasins had enabled his escape, while the heavy police boots encumbered Mahoney. Marchand was without a rope and he could only watch helplessly as Mahoney slowly submerged. Before he disappeared, Mahoney asked Marchand "to say goodbye to his wife and children in Battleford and that she was to have the farm in Manitoba and any other property that he owned."[69]

Seventy-one years after Mahoney's death, his daughter contacted the RCMP Headquarters requesting information on her father, whom she believed was a constable in the NWMP and had drowned near Battleford.[70]

There were other close calls in quicksand. While fording the Belly River, Constable McCarthy's horse was trapped in quicksand. McCarthy swam to shore, stripped, and swam back to the horse where he removed the saddle and then used a rope to pull the horse free. On "A" Division's '74 march to Edmonton, Sam Steele's horse plunged through soft sod into quicksand almost up to its neck. Steele threw himself face down and, using swimming motions, reached safety. The horse, which Steele thought must have been in quicksand before, did not struggle, but each time when called plunged ahead until extricated. Inspector Cecil Denny, riding alone, had his horse sink in quicksand until only the saddle and the animal's head could be seen. Denny had to walk 5 km to obtain a horse team to pull the animal out. His horse, remembered Denny, was none the worse for this experience and, for many years, carried him on many a hard ride.[71]

Potable Water

Flowing water and some western lakes provided drinking water and, in winter, the snow could be melted for water. Potable water was less available in the southern prairie regions where many of the sloughs and lakes had an unpleasant alkaline taste or were polluted by buffalo wastes. On the '74 March, the horses took one drink from Old Wives Lake and no more. A member of the Boundary Survey in 1874 noted, "the few pools of water available for camping purposes were generally taken possession of by buffalo so that the water was spoiled for drinking, and even the horses could not be induced to drink it."[72] The buffalo tramped the border of many water bodies into a mud hole and, unless very deep, the water was unfit for use. NWMP Constable Patterson had to "dig a hole on the edge of the lake and let the water seep in. We always strained it to keep the insects out."[73] And even when the water had been boiled, a nauseating smell and dirty colour remained. "Still," wrote one Constable, "when one is without water for perhaps twenty-four hours he will drink anything."[74]

Most recruits came west on a Missouri River steamer to Fort Benton and then walked north to Fort Walsh. This trek introduced the men to the difficulty of obtaining good drinking water on the plains. One recruit from Toronto vividly described his journey:

> The day was hot, and we had become extremely thirsty; this, in fact, had become our only thought. Our throats were parched and the dust was choking our nostrils. Suddenly we came in sight of a pond or sheet of water, about one mile to our right. So eagerly were we to reach this spot that, of one accord, we started to run. Imagine our chagrin and disappointment when we found, instead of clear water, a sheet of black, oily water, covered with scum, the odor of which was sufficient to nauseate any one.

But such is thirst that we attempted to drink some of the water by filtering it through our handkerchiefs, but the dose was impossible ... compelled to return to our path with our thirst unsatisfied, we felt the heat ten times worse. Traveling a few miles farther, we found that the wagon ruts of the trail had at one place caused so deep a cut that rain water was still in evidence. Here, with "kerchief" filters, we managed to squeeze a few drops of the water, which we drank, relieving our throats temporarily, getting them at the same time well coated with chalky mud.[75]

Sometimes, "the boys" resorted to ingenious methods to quench their thirst, such as dragging a cloth in the grass to collect the dew, which was then squeezed out of the cloth. This method provided insufficient moisture. In the disorder of a buffalo run, Constable William Parker found himself alone until an Indian guide rode up. In response to Parker's signs that he was parched, the guide led the young Mountie to a dead buffalo cow and, taking a knife, dug a hole in the sod, cut a piece of the hide, and pressed it into the hole to form a good basin. Parker related:

Then he stuck his knife into the cow's udder and a good two quarts of milk flowed into the basin. He had a good drink and said in Blackfoot, "Oxee" meaning good. The milk looked dreadful with blood streaking through it, but I was so parched that I went to it and found it as good as the Indian had said. On looking up, I found that Captain Dalrymple Clark had arrived on his pony Minnie and saw me drinking. "Captain" I said, "come and have a drink." "Parker," he replied, "I have always thought you were a beast, and I know it now." Then he put his spurs to Minnie and galloped off.[76]

The Captain referred to, E. Dalrymple Clark, died in 1881 at Fort Walsh from mountain (typhoid) fever carried in the polluted water in Battle Creek, the source of water for the post.

Weather and Climate

The northern latitude with defined seasons, a continental interior location, a western mountain barrier that inhibited the flow of mild maritime air, and an altitude between 2,000–4,000 feet (600–1,200 m) influenced the weather and climate. One classification for this climate (*Köppen*) designates mid-latitude semi-arid continental or steppe (*Bsk*) for that area called the

Palliser's Triangle and Humid Continental Cool Summer (*Dfb*) for the parkland region.[77] Large air masses decidedly affect the weather. Cyclonic storms with low pressure are associated with unstable air and precipitation. Anticyclonic storms with high pressure produce clear, dry weather. The track of the jet stream adds another factor determining the weather.

A significant aspect of the prairie weather is its variability in temperature and precipitation. Area residents spoke of the warm winter of 1877–78 and the cold winter of 1879–80.[78] There have been winter months (1931) with a temperature almost 15°C warmer than normal, and winter months (1936) having a temperature 15°C below normal. Most police posts recorded the daily temperature. As a measure of the temperature variability, Constable Price at Battleford recorded a reading of -40°C on 22 December 1876; on that date one year later, he recorded a temperature of -5°C.

N.W.M. Police in Winter, Calgary, 1883

"We don't envy the boys on their trip." (Calgary to Lethbridge)

– *Calgary Herald*, 20 February 1884
  PAA 8.1856

The variability in precipitation is critical to an agrarian region. Even in consecutive years, the range can be extreme. Maple Creek, for example, recorded 248 mm of precipitation in 1931 and 451 mm the following year. Two or more consecutive years with reduced rainfall will greatly contribute to drought conditions.

The region receives the most hours of bright sunshine in Canada, with all stations recording at least 2,100 hours of bright sunshine each year.[79] Estevan, with 2,537 hours of annual bright sunshine, ranks first among cities in Canada. The hours of bright sunshine follows a decided seasonal pattern: Regina has 329 hours in July, only 88 in December. The length of day changes dramatically with the season. At extremes, daylight in Winnipeg on December 21 is 8 hours and 5 minutes; this increases to 16 hours 23 minutes on June 20—eight additional hours of daylight. After a long winter at the isolated NWMP posts, the lengthening days of spring elevated moods and increased police activities. In one example, when Inspector Sam Steele attacked the Indian camp at Loon Lake on 3 June 1885 at ten o'clock in the morning, his sixty-two troopers had been in the saddle for seven hours.

Precipitation

Precipitation in the Western Interior Basin is light. The average annual amount of moisture at Swift Current is 378 mm; at Edmonton, 448 mm.[80] Almost 60 per cent of the moisture comes during four months—May to August, which fortunately corresponds with the warm growing season. Almost 75 per cent of the total precipitation is rainfall.

Spectacular thunderstorms often accompanied summer precipitation. The storm that struck the first night the Force assembled at Dufferin was remembered as a terrifying introduction to the West. Sub-Constable Jean D'Artigue, a native of France, observed: "In this country, storms rage with a fierceness and fury seldom witnessed in other countries and even the native animals are filled with fear at their approach."[81] One policeman described a storm:

> The rain came down in bucketfuls. We were compelled to rise and roll up our blankets and hold on to the tent pole and skirts of the tent to prevent it from blowing away. The level space outside was soon changed into a lake, and with every flash we could see our poor horses standing in this sheet of water, with their backs humped up and turned toward the pitiless storm.[82]

A thunderstorm for Sub-Constable John Donkin, from Ireland, was "indescribable in its grandeur."[83] He wrote:

The black darkness is illuminated by a ceaseless, quivering fire of
crimson and purple … every few minutes, sometimes seconds,
a bolt of steely blue comes down … thunder rattles and rolls,
and shakes the earth in awful bursts of sound. The wind roars
with an eldritch shriek, and rain splashes down in one sheet,
as though a sea were falling.

If heavy rains were expected, experience taught the men that a tent
pitched in a small land depression would fill with water. Surprisingly, even
in winter this could be a problem. When Mounted Policemen John Bray
and George Gamsby awoke wet in their tent, they were amazed to find that
a chinook had melted the snow around them while they slept.

On the open prairie, there was little shelter for the men. Angus McKay,
a police courier in the North-West Rebellion, prepared for an oncoming
thunderstorm by tethering his horse and removing the saddle for a pillow.
After covering himself with his waterproof tarp, he lay down to wait
until the storm passed.

Heavy rains delayed travel. One storm made a journey from Fort
Macleod to Fort Walsh for Sub-Inspector William Antrobus and three
constables four days longer than expected. The men, traveling in a light
rig, lost the trail and took a route that required lowering and then raising
the rig by ropes at each coulee. They slept on the wet ground and were
unable to light a fire. Constable Alfred Nedham recalled that the only
cheer on the trip was the discovery that drinkable water could be obtained
by wringing and squeezing the rain out of their coats.[84]

Any point in the prairies can expect forked lightning from twenty to
twenty-eight days each year. No Mounted Policemen were killed, but one
former policeman on the '74 March, Alexander MacKenzie, was struck
about 20 km south of Edmonton while employed as a teamster during
the North-West Rebellion. The *Edmonton Bulletin* described his death:

> He said to the cook this is worth a dollar, and raised his cup to his
> lips for a second drink … when there came a blinding flash of
> lightning and crash of thunder which stunned the men standing
> around. The air was filled with blue fire and the smell of
> electricity … MacKenzie was lying on his back near the fire quite
> dead with electric flames coming out of his mouth and nose.[85]

An approaching dark cloud portending hail was an acute concern.
The prairie hailstones, marveled one eastern soldier in 1885, were "of
inconceivable size."[86] On the fifth day of the western march, the hailstones

that hit the column were described by Commissioner French as large as walnuts. The men took refuge under the wagons. Anyone caught in the open resorted to ingenious methods for protection from hail.

One young man, reported the *Saskatchewan Herald*, imitating "partridges and prairie chickens, stuck his head in a badger hole but declares it afforded only partial protection."[87] More often the only alternative was to lie down and hold on to the grass. On the Governor General's tour of the North-West Territories in 1881, a reporter from Scotland, "where hailstorms of such violence are quite unknown," watched from the safety of Lord Lorne's covered wagon as the Mounted Police escort scrambled for cover and, "having no shelter to run into, the men had to lie down with their faces to the ground, and their bodies were bruised as if struck by heavy stones."[88] And the hailstorms were destructive to property. One storm broke ninety glass panes at the Battleford barracks.

In most months, the precipitation falls as snow. The average annual snowfall varies considerably throughout the region: for example, in Swift Current, 102 cm; in Edmonton, 134 cm (that fall on 50 and 57 days). Snowfall accumulation is an average depth of 30–50 cm and usually covers the ground for five consecutive months, except in southwestern Alberta where warm chinooks open the grassland.

A policeman who failed to take precautions against sun reflecting off the snow risked blindness. In mid-January 1876, a six-man party under Sub-Constable Parker left Swan River with eighteen horses and sleds on a twelve-day trip to bring back supplies from Shoal Lake. Cold weather and deep snow made the return journey difficult. The troop was without goggles and everyone, except Parker, who had rubbed charcoal around his eyes, was hospitalized for blindness. Two incidents in the North-West Rebellion illustrate the consequences of sun glare. In Alberta, eight men in a fifteen man troop of Steele's Scouts, who escorted settlers from Red Deer to Calgary, became snow-blind. And twenty-two police became snow-blind on the march from Fort Qu'Appelle to Prince Albert days before the outbreak of the North-West Rebellion. Hospital orderly E. Braithwaite positioned the men in a row. Each man's hand was placed on the shoulder of the next, and they marched north in what appeared a puzzling sight.

Air Temperatures
The policemen lived in an invigorating climate, with freezing temperatures on more than half the days in a year. Regina, for example, has 214 days (59 per cent) in this category; Edmonton, 196 (54 per cent). The annual mean temperature in Edmonton is 3°C and the monthly mean is below freezing

for 5 of 12 months. In winter, the air temperatures decrease to the north and east. Strong winds increase the wind chill and sometimes bring blizzards. Prairie winters are long, often with periods of intense cold once the polar continental air settles over the region. Edmonton has experienced a daily high temperature below freezing for eighty-four consecutive days. A temperature of -57°C (-70°F) has been recorded at Prince Albert. On New Year's Eve in Regina in 1884, Superintendent R. Burton Deane recorded a temperature of -50°C. The following day was slightly warmer (-45°C), but, with a wind blowing an estimated 55 miles per hour (90 km/h), outside conditions were dangerous.

The cold winter temperatures are modified somewhat by the low relative humidity (hygrometric state of atmosphere) making, many outsider observers claimed, a cold comparatively less penetrating. For example, a visitor from Nova Scotia in 1880, the Reverend George Roderick affirmed that "-10 degrees below zero in Pictou [Nova Scotia] was as severe on the human system as -40 degrees in the northwest."[89]

The temperature range between January and July is extreme. The daily mean temperature in Medicine Hat in January is -10.2°C (13.6°F); in July 19.5°C (66.4°F)—a difference of 29.7°C (53.4°F). Regina has reached a high temperature of 43°C and a low of -49°C—an incredible range of 92°C (165°F). Even after warm afternoons, the prairie nights can be cool. On the '74 March, the men needed blankets on the night of July 26 when the temperature dropped to 0°C. The following afternoon, the temperature reached a sweltering 30°C.

The police carefully prepared for winter by storing large supplies of wood or coal at each post. Buffalo coats were issued, and moccasins became the winter footwear. Adjustments had to be made to deal with the cold. Sergeant Frank Fitzpatrick, assigned to take notes while on winter tour of Indian reserves, had the ink bottle freeze in his saddle bag. Afterwards, he kept the ink bottle next to his body when riding.

Care had to be taken when traveling in winter. Even though it was snowing, a rash young Constable Kennedy, returning from Battleford in a buckboard, was so anxious to reach Fort Carlton that he moved ahead of his slower, heavily laden companions. The winds increased in severity and the Mountie became lost and spent the night on the open prairie without even food or a fire. When Hudson Bay traders rescued him the following day, Kennedy's horse was exhausted and hardly able to move. The Battleford newspaper warned: "It is hoped that this escapade will be a warning to others not to attempt to travel alone, even for a short distance, during a North-West snow storm."[90]

A constable working his trap line met a struggling American army deserter making for Fort Walsh. He helped the man to the base, but J.E. McEntyre, the camp cook, recalled, "the poor chap was so badly frozen that the doctor could not help him and he died and his body lay in a tent just outside my kitchen door, with the tent flapping and the winter wind howling, it gave one an eerie feeling."[91] Presumably, the detachment buried the unfortunate man once the ground thawed.

Three mounted policemen froze to death. Sub-Constables Frank Baxter and T.D. Wilson died in a blizzard near Fort Macleod on 31 December 1874, the NWMP's first winter in the west. Constable W.M. Ross died from exposure on 1 January 1885 in Kicking Horse Pass. Ross and police companion Ernest Percival were on leave to see a tailor at the Third Siding, about 15 km east of their camp at Golden City (Golden). The train never arrived and the two men began walking along the railway tracks. About halfway, Ross was exhausted and collapsed. Percival left his buffalo coat with Ross and hurried to the destination. A rescue party arrived by handcar at 6 a.m. and transported Ross to his camp but he died the following night.[92]

Severe frostbite sometimes required amputations. As a member of a hundred-man column traveling north from Regina to Prince Albert in 1885, a recruit with five months service, Roger Pocock, wet his boots, which froze and, when he was unable to obtain moccasins, severely chafed his feet. Hospital attendant E.A. Braithwaite wrote: "Pocock was riding in the back of a sleigh, reading a book and didn't change his footwear. Finally he couldn't get his boots off and we had to cut them off."[93] Afterwards, Braithwaite placed Pocock's frozen feet in a bucket of ice water until the column reached Humboldt Station eight hours later. Pocock apparently had dismissed advice from comrades to run occasionally beside the sleigh to stimulate circulation, retorting, "that he would rather freeze like a man than run behind like a dog."[94] At Prince Albert, a surgeon amputated all the toes on Pocock's right foot.[95]

Land promoters and the western press always downplayed the region's reputation for an inhospitable cold climate. A ninety-four-page business brochure published in 1885 promoted the Calgary area for its industries and natural assets that included exceptionally mild winters. Early settlers joked about the weather:

First Emigrant:
"Is there any summer in this country?"

Second Emigrant:
"I don't know. I've only been here ten months."[96]

Roger Pocock, North-West Mounted Police, 1885

"On April 10th … Dr. Miller removed five toes from my right foot. I was under influence of ether and was dosed five times unsuccessfully."

– Roger Pocock, Private Diary, 1885
GA NA 943 – 2

Summer, of course, always came. On the prairies, summers are warm with brief periods of hot temperatures. Yellow Grass, Saskatchewan, has reached a temperature of 45°C (113°F). Medicine Hat has 50–60 days every year with a high temperature above 27°C (80°F). The highest daily temperature usually occurs about 3 p.m. It is perhaps the months of September and early October with a period known as "Indian Summer" that are most enjoyable in the region.

Mirages

Atmospheric conditions sometimes produced mirages. This phenomenon fascinated the Mounted Policemen. While camped at Old Wives Lake on the '74 March, the men had seen a mirage in the form of an island floating down on them. A recruit walking from the Missouri River to join the Force at Fort Walsh wrote:

> We finally came to see what we thought was a beautiful lake. We could see the waves lapping on the shore. About half the party made for the lake, a few hundred yards away. I did not go. An old timer said, "Don't go, there's not a drop of water there,"—and he was right; it was a mirage. I would have bet anything that there was water there. You should have seen the look on those men's faces when they came back from that dust covered lake.[97]

Constable A.R. Dyre posted at Fort Calgary saw "the Red Deer River, 50 miles away, was laid out before us, the trees and a solitary horseman appearing right before us."[98] Constable William Parker, traveling west from Fort Carlton to the Red Deer River in 1876 wrote that: "we did see some wonderful mirages in the sky. One especially was like a large city upside down, showing houses, large buildings and churches, even the spires."[99] John Donkin described a mirage his patrol witnessed: "When we were twenty miles from the city, a huge windmill rose before us in the sky ... there it was magnified and lifted into the heavens, while the houses were invisible."[100]

Winds

One morning when the Fort Macleod detachment entered the parade square, the men were astounded to see two heavy cannon barrels dislodged from their wooden carriage mounts. For days there had been blustery winds, but still this damage seemed unbelievable. Soon the puzzle was solved: as a practical joke, two comrades had dismantled the guns during the night. The episode quickly spread as a tall tale of the velocity of the winds that swept this treeless land. An English recruit noted that in this land "there is always the wind."[101]

A storm hit the NWMP camp three weeks out from Dufferin on the march west. Sub-Inspector John McIllree recorded in his diary:

> The wind was blowing a hurricane. The first thing I knew was the curtain of the hut blew up and I nearly got smothered with a load of dust and gravel. The next thing was the tent went

bodily up into the air, followed by my helmet and sundry tin plates, blankets, etc. I grabbed my clothes and got some of them on and went about the camp. I could not help laughing. Nearly every tent was down, and the men were rushing round in their shirt tails or other equally classical costume trying to find their raiment.[102]

Henri Julien, the artist from Montreal, remembered that he had stood helplessly as his tent was blown away.

In winter, frontal systems bring bitterly cold temperatures and sometimes blizzards. The strong winds reduced visibility and increased the intensity of the cold, in what meteorologists now measure as wind chill.

All westerners knew that travel in a blizzard was hazardous, but these storms sometimes appeared with little warning. Anyone caught in the open had to take immediate safety measures. Such was the case when a blizzard caught Constable Edward Barnett on Nose Creek, a tributary of the Bow River north of Calgary. Barnett immediately made a shelter in a snow bank and gathered some wood, but was unable to light a fire. The only paper available was his diary which he had kept from the time he joined the Force. Barnett rationalized: "It was a precious record but when it came to a matter of life and death the diary must go. I lit the pages one at a time."[103]

The plains skills of scout Jerry Potts saved a five-man police troop overtaken by a blinding blizzard while on their way from Fort Macleod to Helena, Montana Territory. Potts had the men unsaddle the horses, use their saddles and packs as a windbreak, and, with hunting knives, cut a cave in the north bank of Milk River.

For the next thirty-six hours, the men huddled in the cave. Buffalo crowded in the river bottom and near the horses, tied with picket-ropes. One policeman, Cecil Denny, wrote:

> We took two-hour shifts at holding the halter ropes and keeping the buffalo from crowding in on our animals. This seems almost incredible, but the fierceness of the blizzard and intense cold had driven all fear from the beasts, and they huddled together for warmth and shelter. Our snow-cave was damp and chilled us to the bone. We slept little, but ate at intervals, and the bacon, bolted uncooked, no doubt helped us pull through.[104]

After two nights, the party decided to take their chances and continued south in the bitterly cold weather. Denny hoisted Ryan (whose frozen breeches made him unable to mount his horse) on his mount.

Fortunately, they met an American cavalry troop who guided them to Fort Shaw where General Gibbon, helped by the officer's wives, did everything to comfort the Mounted Policemen. It had been a dangerous trip. Two men required hospitalization for frostbite and three of the five horses had died.

In striking contrast to the perilous blizzards were the warm chinook winds in southwestern Alberta. In winter these winds buoyed spirits and provided an immediate respite from frigid temperatures. The sudden and remarkable rise in temperatures astounded the Mounties. In 1877, the Fort Macleod post measured an incredible temperature increase of 38°F (21°C) in five minutes.[105] At Fort Macleod, Surgeon Barrie Nevitt recorded in February 1875:

> ...still cold and the snow on the ground about 6 inches deep. At about 4:30 a strong wind from the west sprung up and in nine minutes the thermometer had risen 32°! ... The wind could be felt warm and balmy as the soft breezes that blow o'er Ceylon's Isle. As soon as it began a crowd of men appeared like magic with brooms on the roofs of their quarters, brushing the snow off to prevent it leaking through.[106]

Two days later, Nevitt's diary marveled, "the Chenook continues and the prairies are a series of lakes, running brooks and mud holes. You never saw such a change in your life. A few days ago, so white and cold and hard, now so black and brown and wet."[107] Nevitt's observation that this is the greatest country for winds and changeable weather is bolstered in Constable R.N. Wilson's remarkable diary entry for 3 December 1885:

> September-like weather up to today. Prairie fire last night burnt out Stand-Off & most of the Range between the two Rivers. The same wind which made the fire so destructive last night shifted this morning to the North & blew up a snow storm. The scene was changed in twelve hours, from the smoke & fire & roar of the burning dry prairie grass to the deep snow, cold wind & creaking of foot steps on the snow.[108]

One Mountie aptly complained: "There is always some sort of weather here."[109] Each year, an average of forty-four tornadoes strike Alberta and Saskatchewan. In this 1873–85 study, only one tornado is recorded. On 2 July 1883, a tornado struck Medicine Hat, blowing down houses and sinking two barges loaded with coal. The total damage was estimated at $5,000.[110]

ANIMAL LIFE:
(a) Small Annoying Pests

Written accounts by Mounted Policemen downplay the innumerable bees, wasps, butterflies, moths, lady bugs, innocuous insects, and spiders, but focus on annoying insect pests—black flies, locusts, horse flies, and mosquitoes.

Mosquitoes were the foremost "enemy." Every travel account of the period commented on their troublesome presence.[111] Constable William Parker, assigned to deliver mail from Winnipeg to Swan River, plastered his face, neck, and hands with mud to relieve "the torture."[112] He ended his ordeal by riding the final 235 km in 26 hours. At Swan River, he wrote to his family in England: "this is a dreadful country for mosquitoes in fact they are biting me so now I can hardly write. We have to keep smudges burning day and night so that the horses can go to the smoke whenever they like for sometimes they are nearly driven crazy by the flies and mosquitoes."[113]

"They are," exaggerated Constable Tom LaNauze in a letter to his mother in Ireland, "as big as daddy longlegs."[114] A second Mountie, perhaps with a zoological bent, classified mosquitoes as a species of hummingbird.[115] An American correspondent, riding with Major Walsh and four Mounties to Sitting Bull's camp at Wood Mountain, wrote:

> The ruthless mosquitoes, which are a positive plague during the summer months, swarmed by the millions, their venomous bites covering our hands, necks and faces with blotches, resembling smallpox pustules. We went at a gallop most of the time, but even the breeze created by rapid motion, did not free us from the winged tyrants.[116]

Although the night was hot, the men covered themselves with blankets to avoid the stinging pests. Long Dog, the Indian guide, spent most of the night slapping his face and neck and exclaiming the English swear words that he had learned.

Under ideal breeding conditions, mosquitoes swarmed in huge numbers. One of the first ranchers near Fort Macleod described the suffering of his horses: "The mosquitoes covered the poor animals so that, in many instances, it would be difficult to tell their colour."[117] When the Alberta Field Force pursued Big Bear's band north of Frenchman's Butte in May 1885, the police built smudges at each stop to protect their mounts. The horses could be seen with their noses poking into the dense smoke. Farther east, the men in a military column under General Middleton sported gauze veils, a gift from a Toronto women's organization. Nevertheless, General Middleton remembered "being torn to pieces by the mosquitoes and flies."[118]

Horseflies, called "bulldogs," viciously bit the horses, causing blood to flow. The suffering animals became frantic, running wildly about and rolling over to rid themselves of their tormentors. John Poett, the police veterinarian, while riding from Dufferin to Swan River in 1875, noted the problem: "When the bulldog bites a horse's abdominal veins which he frequently does, horses will bleed to a considerable extent ... Such numbers of them assembled that the horses would not feed but congregate together switching their tails and otherwise protecting themselves from the bites of these insects as best they could."[119]

Tiny blackflies (sandflies) were a plague in the northern wet areas. They appeared to rise in clouds. "The blackflies," wrote one Mountie on patrol, "nearly drove us crazy, getting so far into our ears that we could not get them out, occasioning some pain and a good deal of apprehension from the fear of evil consequences."[120] In the pursuit of Big Bear in 1885, members of Steele's Scouts insisted that blackflies deliberately followed the troop.

As outlined earlier, in 1874 and 1875 enormous swarms of locusts destroyed the vegetation. Reverend John McDougall watched a migrating swarm pass overhead for six hours. Dead locusts crusted the Lake Winnipeg shoreline three feet deep and some residents in the city used snow shovels to clean their doorsteps.[121] Constable Robert Patterson, traveling from Winnipeg to Swan River, could not sleep in his tent as the grasshoppers bit him so badly. He was forced to sleep in one of the covered wagons. Dead floating locusts covered the surface of a nearby stream.

On the '74 March, Constable Grain recalled the locusts "swooped down upon us like a malicious black cloud, blocking out the sun ... rose and fell upon us with a weird and tantalizing rhythm. It is almost impossible to describe the unbelievable density of this moving swarm."[122] Their bodies covered the grass, two to three inches deep. On uneven ground the wagons slid from the slime of the crushed grasshoppers. When on a steep decline, the wagon locks failed to stop the sliding and the men used ropes to safely lower the wagons.

Lice were an ever-present nuisance. The first contact with Indians on the '74 March left the entire column affected. Some men abandoned their tents to sleep on the ground and "as far apart to discourage the migratory instincts and sociable tendencies of these little pests. Everyone had enough of his own without acquiring any from his neighbour."[123]

Boiling or changing clothing proved ineffective and the Mounties copied the Métis example of placing their clothing on ant hills where the ants made short work of the "cooties." At halts along the route, men could be seen searching for ant hills. "We were," mused one Mountie, "the first nudist colony in the West."[124] William Metzler and several companions manned a small outpost on the St. Mary River that every passing Indian stopped to visit. Metzler had to throw all his clothes away several times on account of the crawlers.

Bed bugs infested many of the crudely constructed shacks. In one instance, a NWMP troop traveling west of Fort Benton stayed in an unoccupied cabin used by American soldiers. No sooner were the candles out then someone shouted "Bugs!" Corporal Alfred Nedham recalled: "Candles were hurriedly lighted. To our amazement the light showed bugs coming down the center of the room in platoons, apparently anticipating a great feed on us sleepers in the dark."[125] Everyone moved outside. Nedham slept under a wagon.

Prairie residents welcomed the first autumn frost as relief from the many insect tormentors.

James H. Schofield, NWMP, Fort Walsh, 1878

In a rare moment of battling the elements and managing the responsibilities of administering to such a large geographic area, NWMP Constable Schofield took time to pose for a photograph.

– Photo taken by NWMP photographer George Anderton
  GA NA 1602 – 5

(b) Fish, Birds, Reptiles

The Mounted Police were amazed at the abundance of fish in streams and lakes. In one month, three policemen at Turtle Lake caught 8,500 fish.[126] Fishermen supplied the Oblate Mission at St. Albert with 30,000 fish each year. Two white hostages in Big Bear's camp in the North-West Rebellion, using pitchforks, astonished their Indian captors by returning to camp with forty fish in less than one hour. The detachment stationed at Fort Brisebois (Calgary) needed only a piece of red rag for bait in the Bow and Elbow rivers. Waterton Lakes, where enormous trout weighing up to 40 lbs. (18 kg) were caught, at once became a recreational destination for policemen stationed at Fort Macleod.

Eating frogs was the furthest thing anyone imagined when the column left for Fort Whoop-Up, but, at a camp north of the Cypress Hills, Sub-Constable Jean D'Artigue, a schoolteacher from France, organized a frog hunt for his companions. He taught the men to hit the frog with a small whip, detach the legs, and place them in a pail. One of the men wrote: "We ate them ravenously three of us devouring 150 frogs and it was the most delicious meal we had on the march."[127] The meal was so tasty, Edward Maunsell recalled, that he lost his prejudice against the French for eating frogs.[128]

Garter snakes were the most common area snake. After hibernation, they congregated in enormous numbers. In their first spring at Swan River, the detachment held a snake-killing competition as part of the May 24 celebrations. The men were placed in fifteen-man teams, supplied with a pitchfork, wheelbarrow, and empty flour barrels. The results were incredible: in half-an-hour, the men killed 1,100 snakes.

The poisonous rattlesnake's habitat was the very southern parts of the plains. Recruits walking north from Fort Benton to Fort Walsh had to be cautious. Jack Clarke wrote: "They sure kept us busy watching them and from tramping on them. At this time their color was about the color of the grass. And they would kroll into our blankets at night for warm places and it kept us pretty busy. We killed quite a number and cut off the rattles and put them in our pockets."[129] Sergeant Frank Fitzpatrick remembered while on the trail, "we had with us quite a number of dogs, but lost a few of these through rattlesnakes when near Milk River."[130] On his walk northward from the Missouri, recruit William McQuarrie's blisters became so bothersome that he chose to walk in his bare feet. Cactus plants concealed in the grass was one problem but, when the bull whackers began lashing the grass and shouting about rattlesnakes, McQuarrie was not long getting into his boots.

Rattlesnakes fascinated the men. A Blood Indian (probably Calf Shirt) always attracted a wide-eyed audience of policemen to watch him handle a large rattlesnake. A Montana newspaper described a performance: "He would make him coil himself up and just make his rattles buzz; he put the snakes head in his mouth; he carries him coiled around his naked body. The boys [police] gave the exhibitor one dollar and fifty cents which pleased him wonderfully."[131]

The region abounded with song birds. Birds of prey included eagles, owls, and hawks. The police hunted prairie chickens and migratory birds. Migratory birds passed through the region in enormous numbers. On the journey west, the men killed and ate hundreds of molting ducks. Later, at the Bow–Belly junction, Commissioner French watched the flight paths of ducks to locate water sources. Canada geese were a nuisance. They completely destroyed the first crop of oats at the police farm at Pincher Creek. What one troop moving to Fort Walsh in October 1876 thought was snow on the ground near a lake turned out to be thousands of geese. A shotgun blast sent them skyward with a noise like thunder. One member of the troop recalled that migrating geese "made such a noise through the night that we got very little sleep."[132] Everyone found magpies to be cheeky and annoying birds.

(c) Smaller Prairie Mammals

Smaller prairie mammals included gophers, rabbits, porcupines, mice, and moles. Bobcats and lynx were occasionally seen. In the north beaver and muskrats abounded. The trade in muskrat pelts was considerable—240,000 pelts from northern regions were delivered to Cumberland House on the North Saskatchewan in one year.

Rabbit numbers appeared to follow a cycle and, in some years, rabbits appeared everywhere. Residents at the Victoria Mission, located east of Fort Edmonton, snared 300 rabbits in twelve days.

Badger holes riddled some fields and made horseback riding dangerous, especially when snow covered the ground. Constable James Steele wrote to his brother, Sam Steele:

> I was galloping along my horse put his foot in a badger hole about three feet deep & turned a somersault falling heels uppermost with his hole weight between my shoulders, the cantle of the saddle which was beech wood struck me so hard that it smashed to pieces, the horse bled freely after he got up & I of course felt pretty stiff.[133]

Sam Steele could relate to his brother's accident, having had his horse step into a badger hole. Steele wrote: "The poor animal rolled over my head … and when he staggered to his feet the blood poured from his nostrils, as his head had struck the gravel and stones, giving him a severe shock."[134] Even the Commissioner could take a tumble. French wrote in his diary on 30 July 1874: "I narrowly escaped a bad injury, my horse falling in one of the countless badger holes that are about, throwing me some distance over his head."[135]

Constable Poitevin never recovered from his injuries after his horse stepped in a badger hole and rolled on him. Poitevin was unconscious for a time and his broken arm failed to heal. In December 1884, more than two years after his accident, he was invalided out of the Force and then returned to Montreal.

Other predators included weasels, coyotes, foxes, skunks, and otters. Black bears were found in wooded areas to the north. For a short time, the Fort Saskatchewan post had three black bear cubs.

(d) Ungulates

Deer were common in the river valleys and moose found in water bodies. Wild herds of cattle, horses, and elk roamed the plains. The pronghorn (also called cabrie) were common and easily outdistanced any horseback pursuit. The Mounted Police learned to entice the swift animals into rifle range by attracting their curiosity. A letter from a Mountie stationed at Fort Macleod in 1875 related that, "cabrie abounds here, and affords excellent sport. It is inquisitive as a woman, and if you do not show too plainly, will work its way within shot to see what you are."[136]

(e) Large Predators

Two large predators, wolves and grizzly bears, no longer found on the Canadian prairies, are of special interest.

Prairie wolves abounded. On the '74 March, a rocket was fired at night to signal two lost men the location of the camp. The eerie response from hundreds of howling wolves surprised and thrilled the men who had not seen one wolf. Joseph Carcadden, with the column returning east in 1874, wrote of wolves at Wild Horse Camp: "They are here by the hundred and are no doubt hungry for they keep very near us, too near to be safe … it takes all our time to keep them off at night."[137] On his journey between Edmonton and Fort Calgary, the howling of wolves kept Constable D'Artigue from sleeping. Constables John Bray and George Gamsby lost twenty lbs. of beef from their jumper (sled). While the two men slept brazen wolves "gnawed a hole in the bottom of our sack and made away with the meat."[138] Mounties in Steele's Scouts pursuing Big Bear's band north to Beaver River in 1885 found the wolves aggressive and fascinating:

> Our pickets and sentries were troubled with wolves and coyotes at night who prowled constantly close to our camp yelping and howling, but not molesting anyone ... the wolves were quite large and seemed ferocious coming closer at dusk and waiting around in a circle and snarling like mad dogs.[139]

A chance encounter with a wolf was terrifying. One Mountie, walking alone and without a weapon, startled an immense wolf. He wrote: "Quick as a flash I spread my arms as wide as I could, and yelling like a Comanche I dashed toward the foe. It worked! The wolf turned tail and ran, and so did I—in the opposite direction."[140] After this close call, he vowed never again to be alone without his revolver.

Colonel James Walker encountered an aggressive pack of wolves:

> I was riding out west of the Cypress Hills one day looking for water and came across a band of eight or ten large timber wolves eating a half-grown buffalo they had just killed. I rode close to them and they showed fight and made as if they would attack my horse.[141]

Walker left the wolves to finish their meal and rode off to continue his search for water.

Wolf pelts were a prized fur. In winter, hunters called "wolfers" killed buffalo and poisoned the carcasses with strychnine. The results were truly astonishing. After Constable John Herron shot several buffalo from a window at the Fort Calgary barracks, he watched a hunter poison the carcasses. "The next morning," wrote Herron, "we counted seventy-five dead wolves on the flat."[142]

Under desperate circumstances, wolves could be shot and eaten for food. In December 1876, an eight-man police patrol left Battleford for Fort Walsh—a direct distance of 370 kilometres. On the second day, a blizzard struck with intense cold and caused limited visibility. Strong winds prevented building a fire and, with only cold pork to eat, the men walked most of the night to keep from freezing. In the meantime, the horses broke away and were only recovered the next day after a demanding search. Snow had obscured the trail, but the troop continued south, determined to reach the South Saskatchewan River to orientate themselves. The trip was now seven days over expectations and food ran out. A wolf in a large threatening pack that was trailing the troop was shot and its meat (along with a dead horse) sustained the men until they reached Fort Walsh. In shooting the wolf, Sergeant Frank Norman learned a practical (and painful) lesson not to touch a steel barrel with bare hands in frigid weather.[143]

Huge grizzly bears roamed the prairie land. They were fairly common. At his trading post in the Cypress Hills in the winter of 1871–72, Isaac Cowie purchased 750 grizzly pelts.[144]

The sight of one of the great lumbering animals was thrilling. A police troop riding from Battleford to Fort Walsh in 1876 chanced upon a grizzly bear with two cubs. Corporal Patterson watched a captivating chase:

> She started to run off in a heavy lumbering gait, while one of our guides was selecting a horse that would approach her. After a hard run of three or four miles, he killed her, but had to use three regulation cartridges to do it. Our French Canadian pony Billy was hitched to his cart and hauled her into camp. Her weight was estimated at 1100 pounds. She was skinned and her robe afterwards decorated our canteen and recreation room in Macleod.[145]

A second account of probably the same incident related that each time the pursuers got near, the bear would stop, turn around, stand on her hind legs with front paws extended, and show her enormous teeth. She was shot in the abdomen but ran off on three legs, "at the same time pushing the projecting entrails back into her body with her remaining front paw." A shot through her head at the next stop brought her down. On the advice of an Indian guide that it was "bad medicine" to kill the two cubs, they were not molested. The troop ate bear steak for supper and found it tasty.[146]

Constable William Maunsell described his exciting encounter with a grizzly bear:

> We came upon a grizzly and a cub. The bear had just killed a buffalo cow. A few of us gave chase. The horses could easily outrun the bear, but were afraid to approach near enough for us to shoot from off their backs. The halfbreed guide urged his horse within about fifty yards of the bear, then he jumped off his mount and shot, wounding the animal. This brought it to bay, but it did not charge. Some of us then dismounted while the others held their horses, and in a few seconds poor bruin was

riddled with Snider bullets. The cub, which was about a year and a half old, was let go. We examined the buffalo cow the bear had killed, and found its neck was broken, which showed the fearful strength of the bear.[147]

Constable N. DeTilly, in a three-man French-speaking horse guard near Fort Walsh, had a hair-raising encounter with a grizzly bear. While on his way to a nearby creek to get some water for the night, the young Mountie met a huge upright grizzly on the pathway. DeTilly threw the pail at the bear, turned and ran back to the camp for a rifle. In his fright, he smashed into the tent pole, knocking himself senseless. Once he was brought around to explain his panic, his companions, carrying rifles and lanterns, went along the pathway. The bear was gone, but massive footprints remained of its presence.[148]

(f) Buffalo

Most of all, one animal—the bison, commonly called buffalo, epitomized the Canadian prairies. In 1874, enormous herds roamed the land. As the NWMP moved west, the North American Boundary Commission was returning east along the international boundary. Dr. Thomas Millman with the Boundary Commission recorded on 2 September 1874:

> Buffaloes to-day were as thick as bees. It was a splendid sight. The prairies were black with them. I believe you could see about half a million at once. A large herd came (rushing?) over a hill and almost went through our train. The men opened fire and killed several. For fear they might make a rush on us during the night and stampede the horses, we corralled the wagons, put the tents close together and kept the horses inside. The howling of the wolves at night was almost deafening.[149]

It was incredible but, the next day, Millman saw only two or three buffalo—the last he ever saw.

A migrating buffalo herd was a breathtaking sight. While in Montana Territory, Sergt.-Major John "Turkey Legs" Bray watched buffalo crossing the Missouri River at a point that was over a kilometre wide. He wrote:

> They were coming over a twelve foot cutbank—the animals crowding the head ones, always forward over the cutbank, ever-continually ... we were watching them with our glasses ...

the river just one mass of black heads, many were drowned by others climbing on their backs ... we could see them floating away in the Missouri's muddy waters.[150]

Bray was told that this was the third day of the migration and the herd was expected to take another three days to cross the river.

Dr. Millman described the buffalo "as thick as bees" on 4 September 1874 and then saw only three animals the next day attests to the migratory movements of the buffalo. Even though millions of the animals ranged the plains, large areas were without the shaggy beasts at times. Butler had not seen one buffalo on his famous winter journey in 1873. That summer, on an eleven-week journey from Fort Garry to Rocky Mountain House, Alfred Selwyn and his geological survey company of six men did not sight a single buffalo on the entire 4,000 km.[151]

On their '74 March, the Mounted Police had eagerly anticipated seeing the legendary prairie animal, but it was not until September 2, fifty-six days into the journey, that the men met the first buffalo herd. Shortly after, Constables D. Gopsill and Edward Maunsell had a most remarkable unplanned encounter with buffalo when they were assigned to herd fifty oxen to a swamp for water. Once the oxen entered the water and appeared relieved, the two men (ignoring strict sentry policy), dozed off. They were awakened by a great racket. In the rising moonlight, the policemen could see that a large herd of buffalo had entered the swamp and mingled with the cattle. Maunsell described their dangerous predicament:

> We were in a deuce of a fix, being on foot, and about a thousand buffalo some fifty yards away, mixed with the cattle we were supposed to be herding. We couldn't very well cut the cattle out on foot, because if anything startled the buffalo they would stampede and take the cattle with them, and they might run over us, so we remained perfectly quiet, and soon the buffalo, having drank their fill, drifted leisurely out of the swamp.[152]

The Métis guides warned dismounted policemen to be ready to remount if a buffalo was wounded. Several men had close calls. Cecil Denny watched "one of our men chased by a bull he had wounded. The animal was close behind, and as he was swinging his carbine as he ran, by chance the butt struck the bull in the nose, when immediately he made off, to the relief of trumpeter [James] Pell".[153] At Fort Macleod, Surgeon Nevitt watched a buffalo bull chase one man to the fort. At Blackfoot Crossing, John Lauder recalled, "one old buffalo charged at me and chased me into camp, where one of our party shot him down."[154] William Parker recalled a guide running a buffalo into the police wagons (train) where "he charged us right and left and had about fifteen shots in him before he fell."[155] The men cut him up and carried the meat along.

A bullet had to hit a vital organ to kill the great beasts. "I fired eight shots into this buffalo's head without making much of an impression," one novice police marksman recalled. "He simply stood his ground and switched his tail at each shot. Our guide then advised me to aim at the rear of the shoulder and after the first shot at that spot, the beast tumbled over."[156]

No policeman ever forgot his first buffalo kill. William Parker was with a troop that sighted an unwary herd about a mile away. By riding in small depressions, the twelve men approached within 400 yards. Then topping a rise, the order to "charge" was given. Parker wrote:

> I noticed the bulls swing around the cows and calves, with their horns lowered. My pony went off like an arrow ahead of the other riders and made straight for the lowered horns. I was sure I was going to be killed, but when some of those behind me fired at the herd, they broke just as I landed in the thick of them. My pony brought me alongside a fat three-year-old cow and, firing just behind the shoulder, I killed my first buffalo.[157]

A buffalo run was both rousing and extremely dangerous. In one of the last buffalo runs on the Canadian prairies, Pierre Ouellette of St. Laurent (Batoche) shot a buffalo cow, but his horse stumbled and threw him upon the wounded animal. He was badly injured and died in a few hours.[158] One constable described his party approaching a small herd downwind to within fifty paces before charging at the herd, the men all riding on the same side to avoid crossfire. They cut the tongues and tenderloins from the dead animals. Since the remaining meat could not be collected until the next day, scouts told the police to gut the entrails as food for the wolves to gorge on, leaving the choice meat untouched.[159]

Colonel James Macleod quickly learned how very dangerous and yet unpredictable the buffalo were. Sub-Inspector Denny details the incident:

> During the morning the colonel took a fancy to test the speed of his horse in chasing one of the great brutes. He followed an old bull for a good mile before overhauling him, but had no idea of killing the animal. As he drew alongside the bull suddenly swung his massive head in a vicious lunge at the horse. The sharp horn caught the stirrup leather, ripping it clear from the saddle,

and almost unseating the colonel, missing his leg and horse by a hair. This was enough for Colonel Macleod. He dropped behind leaving the bull to lumber on unmolested ... "Colonel, I guess you leave dem ol buffalo bull alone after dis, hey?" said Jerry Potts.[160]

Even for a group of policemen, buffalo were intimidating. Facing the great beasts alone was even more daunting. North of Fort Macleod, Constable John Herron was driving a wagon by himself through a large herd that was peacefully feeding when a winter storm suddenly arose. The animals turned their backs to the strong cold winds and milled about with the rear animals pushing ahead. Herron became concerned that the animals might stampede but turned the team toward the advancing herd. He wrote: "I got out my rifle, and when the leaders were within fifty yards I fired and shouted. They swerved right and left, ample distance apart, which was lucky for me."[161]

In the first years in the West, the Mounties saw immense herds of buffalo. A '74 man, Edward Larkin, later told a reporter, "I saw the prairie black with buffalo."[162] One Mountie, traveling with a Métis guide from Fort Walsh to Fort Macleod, likened a herd to a wall: "We could not go around them, so I put my red coat out of sight and started through them. For forty miles to Chin Coulee we were riding through one vast sea of buffalo. They paid no attention to us, being too busy picking out the nice bunch grass."[163] He added they always gave an old lone bull a wide berth.

Inspector Cecil Denny recalled that, "sometimes we would travel over miles of country with nothing but buffalo in sight as far as the eye could reach. On other occasions we would ride at an easy lope and see a continuous stream of tens of thousands crossing not over a hundred yards ahead ... it is almost impossible to realize that they have been completely exterminated in such a few years."[164]

The killing was excessive. A party from Fort Victoria (Pakan) in 1874 killed 283 buffalo on the first day of their hunt. Sitting Bull's band killed 800 buffalo in one day. A Métis hunter from Tail Creek, Abraham Salois, alone killed 600 buffalo in the summer of 1874. In one remarkable run, he shot 37 animals. By 1879, only five years after the arrival of the NWMP, few buffalo remained on the Canadian plains. The following summer, George Moore, a member of an exploring expedition that covered 800 kilometres of prairie land, saw only two buffalo.[165]

The disappearance of the great beasts brought tragic consequences, altering the Indian lifestyle and bringing incredible hardships. The news of a handful of buffalo sent the starving Indians racing to the location. A visitor at an Indian camp that was waiting government emergency supplies wrote: "Before evening, however, word reached camp that buffalo were coming. It was a scene of excitement, noise and confusion that defies description. In a few minutes fifty Indians were in the saddle, fording the stream, and urging their still willing steeds to still greater exertions. In the evening six carcasses were brought into camp, and a feast followed."[166]

Serious international concerns arose when several thousand Canadian Indians entered Montana Territory to hunt the last great prairie range of an estimated million animals. Overkill quickly destroyed the herds and, within three years, the starving and destitute bands returned to Canada.

Shipping Buffalo Bones by C.P.R. Freight, Moose Jaw, c. 1885

"Sometimes we would travel over miles of country with nothing but buffalo in sight as far as the eye could reach … it is almost impossible to realize that they have been completely exterminated in such a few years."

– Inspector Cecil Denny, *Riders of the Plains*, 62
 GA NA 4967 – 10

The last noteworthy hunt on Canadian soil was near Wood Mountain in July 1881, when five hunters killed fourteen buffalo in a herd that had moved north from the United States.

For the police (or anyone) who had seen the great herds, it seemed implausible that in a few years the sighting or killing of a single animal had become a newspaper item. But it was true. The *Edmonton Bulletin* recorded on 4 November 1882: "W.R. Ord's survey party shot several buffalo north of Blackfoot Crossing." The *Regina Leader,* 28 June 1883 reported that a "herd of buffalo appeared on a ridge of a bluff and snorting took to their heels." The *Winnipeg Daily Times*, 23 July 1883, reported Indians had shot four buffalo twenty miles south of Swift Current. It was incredible that even seeing the tracks was now a newspaper item. One press account stated: "A trader named Marchand had seen a few fresh tracks of buffalo on the north side of the South Saskatchewan."[167]

The buffalo were ceaselessly hunted until they disappeared from the Canadian prairies. In 1883, when passengers on a train moving west of Medicine Hat saw a lone old bull running parallel to the train tracks, several men and ten Mounted Policemen grabbed carbines and opened fire from the moving train. A witness related that, "for two minutes at about 300 yards distance a perfect fusillade was kept up from the train until the buffalo sheered off and was lost to view."[168] One of the Mountie marksmen remembered that, although the old bull escaped, he was doomed: "Within two weeks afterward a halfbreed buffalo hunter took his horse and got this buffalo."[169]

NOTES

1. In 1884–85, a Mounted Police detachment policed the rail line under construction in British Columbia and there was a small recruiting depot in Winnipeg.

2. The Census of 1885 records Three Provisional Districts of the North-West Territories as 309,000 square miles or 800,000 km²—one constable for every 2,600 km².

3. *LAT*, 13 August 1933. Also in *FCQ*, VI, No. 4, 2–6.

4. This distance is the direct route between Fort Macleod and Stony Mountain Penitentiary. Boswell's trip, with detours (sloughs, lakes) was much farther.

5. *RC*, NWMP, 1885, 73.

6. *RC*, NWMP, 1880, 13.

7. *NAC*, R.C. McLaren, RG 18, v. 3321, f. 196. Hereinafter, all citations from the Personnel Files will omit RG 18 and volume number. For example, *NAC*, R.C. McLaren, f. 196.

8. Nevitt, *Frontier Life in the Mounted Police*, 111.

9. *HDI*, 19 October 1876.

10. MacDougall, *On Western Trails in the Early Seventies*, 174. Ottawa also commissioned HBC trader William McKay to visit the bands with presents of tobacco and tea and to inform them of the coming of police to the region.

11. Robert Bell, "Report on the Country between Red River and the South Saskatchewan," *Geological Survey of Canada, Report on Progress for 1873–74.* (Montreal: Dawson Brothers, 1874), 70.

12. John G. Donkin, *Trooper and Redskin in the Far Northwest*, (London: Sampson Low, Marston, Searle & Rivington, 1889), 93.

13. On this point, see B. Peyton Ward, *Roughing it in the North-West Territories of Canada* (London: Worrall and Robey, 1896), 94; Captain Samuel Anderson, "The North American Boundary from the Lake of the Woods to the Rocky Mountains," *Royal Geographical Society*, XL, 1876, 252; "Memorandum of Information Furnished by Mr. Johnstone," *NAC*, f. 63–74, 20 April 1874; *MFP*, 31 July 1876.

14. Alexander Morris, *The Treaties of Canada with the Indians of Manitoba and the North-West Territories* (Toronto: Belfords, Clarke, 1880), 293–94. The Métis, Morris maintained, exerted a strong influence on the Indians.

15. Butler, *The Great Lone Land*, 261.

16. *CSP*, "Annual Report on the State of Militia for 1875," 1876, (No. 7), xxxviii.

17. Samuel Anderson, "The North-American Boundary from the Lake of the Woods to the Rocky Mountains," *Journal of the Royal Geographical Society*, XLVI, 1876, 239.

18. *PAM*, Frank Carruthers, MG 6, A6.

19. *LH*, 11 July 1935.

20. The Dominion Annual Registry and Review (Montreal: Lovell, 1880–81), 458. Henri Julien's first sights of both the prairies and sea equally. Also Butler, *The Great Lone Land*, 199; Roger S. Pocock, *Frontiersman* (London: Methuen, 1903), 24.

21. *MDS*, 20 May 1885.

22. Robert Jefferson, *Fifty Years on the Saskatchewan* (Battleford: The Canadian North-West Historical Society, 1929), 25.

23. In feet, Fort Macleod is 3,116; Prince Albert, 1,413; Fort Qu'Appelle, 1,593; Edmonton, 2,185; Fort Walsh, 3,624; Calgary, 3,444.

24. *EB*, 4 August 1883, has a graphic account of the dangers of being lost: Chas. Imbloan was discharged from a survey party near Medicine Hat on the 5th of June. He was given six biscuits and a pound of ham and turned loose to find his way to that city as best he might. He was found on the 28th of June, about two miles above the mouth of the Bow River, with no clothing on but his trousers. He had subsisted all that time on grasshoppers, prickly pears, and young birds which he found in their nests but was nearly dead. The person who found him applied to the police at Medicine Hat and to a survey party working near there but was refused in both cases. A hotelkeeper in Medicine Hat finally took charge of him.

25. *GA*, Robert Patterson, M 2470. Assistant Commissioner A.G. Irvine was lost three times on his journey from Winnipeg to Fort Macleod in 1875.

26. John Donkin, *Trooper and Redskin*, 3 and 228.

27. Dempsey, ed., *A Winter at Fort Macleod*, 18.

28. *RL*, 17 March 1885.

29. Donkin, *Trooper and Redskin*, 89.

30. *Illustrated News*, 6 February 1875.

31. John Macoun, *Autobiography of John Macoun* (Ottawa: Ottawa Field-Naturalist Club, 1922), 140.

32. D'Artigue, *Six Years in the Canadian Northwest*, 83.

33. *LH*, 11 July 1935. W.H. Cox, "Diary of a Mountie from 1880 to '85."

34. *CA*, 22 March 1909.

35. Henry E. Clarke, "A Holiday Excursion to the Rocky Mountains," *The Canadian Methodist Magazine*, XXIII, January to June, 1886, 219.

36. Examples include: Henry Clarke, "A Holiday Excursion to the Rocky Mountains," 221; George M. Grant, *Ocean to Ocean* (Rutland, Vermont: Charles E. Tuttle, 1873), 112, 122, 124; John P. Pennefather, *Thirteen Years on the Prairies* (London: Kegan, Trench, Trubner, 1892), 22–23; *WDT*, 17 October 1881; *CH*, 22 January 1885; McDougall, *Western Trails in the Seventies*, 25.

37. *TM*, 19 February 1877.

38. A.H. Lynch-Staunton, "Scarlet Uniforms in 1874," *Prairie Grass to Mountain Pass* (Pincher Creek Historical Society, 1974), 1.

39. Dempsey, ed., *A Winter at Fort Macleod*, 18.

40. Grain, "Pioneers of a Glorious Future," 65.

41. GA, Kenneth Haig, 921. M681.

42. A.P. Percy and Mrs. H. Percy, *Journal of Two Excursions in the British North West Territory of North America* (Shropshire: Bennion & Horne, 1877 & 1878), 22.

43. *NAC*, William McQuarrie, f. 724. Superintendent McIllree, craving a cup of tea, used buffalo bone chips for a fire.

44. A.R. Turner, "Surveying the International Boundary, the Journal of George M. Dawson, 1873." *Sask. H*, XXI, No. 1, 1–23.

45. Anderson, *The North-American Boundary from the Lake of the Woods to the Rocky Mountains*, 246.

46. Jack Dunn, *The Alberta Field Force of 1885* (Calgary: Jack Dunn, 1994), 85.

47. Henri Julien, "Expedition to the North-West." 13.

48. Frederick U. Graham, *Notes of a Sporting Expedition in the Far West of Canada 1847* (London: Printed for Private Circulation), 62.

49. Donkin, *Trooper and Redskin*, 280. Also Dempsey, ed., *William Parker Mounted Policeman*, 123.

50. *PAM*, F.C. Carruthers, MG 6, A-1.

51. Maureen and Mike Mansfield Library, University of Montana, Missoula. Hereinafter *UMM*, Thomas B. Boys Diary.

52. Anderson, *The North-American Boundary from the Lake of the Woods to the Rocky Mountains*, 245.

53. *Stettler Independent*, 2 December 1937.

54. Percy, *Journal of Two Excursions in the British North West Territory of North America*, 5.

55. *PAM*, F.C. Carruthers, MG 6, A-1.

56. *GA*, Rutherford Diary, M 4843, file 67.

57. *Steele, Forty Years in Canada*, 69. Examples of convictions include: Jacob Fortier, $50 or one month; J.G. McKlintock, $20; P. Falcon $50, or two months imprisonment.

58. Anderson, *The North American Boundary from Lake of the Woods to the Rocky Mountains*, 251.

59. *LH*, 11 July 1935.

60. Steele, *Forty Years in Canada*, 65.

61. *GA*, R.A. McDougall, M 729. "A" Troop – An Eyewitness Account of the March West (hereinafter, *GA*, Diary of Sévère Gagnon, M 729).

62. Nevitt, *Frontier Life in the Mounted Police*, 83.

63. *GA*, Jessie DeGear, M 314, Scrapbook 11. Parker supposedly chased the prisoner for 40 km. The article does not say whether the policeman captured the prisoner.

64. The average discharge of the Bow river is 129 cubic metres per second; Oldman, 91 m³/s; Red Deer, 70 m³/s; Battle, 10 m³/s; South Saskatchewan, 249 m³/s; North Saskatchewan, 238 m³/s. Major rivers in northern Alberta are considerably larger: Peace, 2,100 m³/s; Athabasca, 623 m³/s.

65. *GA*, Robert Patterson Memoirs, M 2470. For river crossing, see *PAM*, F.C. Carruthers, MG 6, A-1.

66. *FMG*, 14 November 1882.

67. *LH*, 11 July 1935.

68. Dempsey, ed., *William Parker Mounted Policeman*, 68.

69. Ibid., 33.

70. *NAC*, George Mahoney, f. o.s. 409. Mahoney was married to Emma Ballendine, a Métis. The couple had two children.

71. Denny, *Riders of the Plains*, 40–41.

72. Anderson, "The North American Boundary from Lake of the Woods to the Rocky Mountains," 251.

73. *GA*, Robert Patterson, M 2470.

74. Maunsell, "With the North West Mounted Police from 1874 to 1877," 53.

75. Frank Fitzpatrick, *Sergeant 331* (New York: Published by the author, 1921), 17–18.

76. Dempsey, ed. *William Parker: Mounted Policeman*, 31. Whiskey trader Donald Graham, with two companions traveling south of High River, shot a newborn buffalo calf. The thirsty men cut out the stomach and removed a gallon of clear-looking milk

which they drank. Hugh Dempsey, ed., "Donald Graham's Narrative of 1872–73," *AHR*, IV, No. 1, 12.

77. Köppen classification examples: (Dfb) Edmonton; (Bsk) Medicine Hat.

78. *RC*, NWMP,1878, 20: "The winter was extremely mild ... was little or no snow ... countryside burnt over and buffalo herds didn't come into usual winter feeding ground"; William Parker describes winter of 1879–80: "the hardest I have seen since I have been in the country," Dempsey, ed., *William Parker Mounted Policeman*, 140.

79. Other examples (in hours): Halifax, 1,876; Quebec City, 1,714; Toronto, 2,043; Vancouver, 1,784.

80. In millimetres: Toronto, 875; Vancouver, 1,443; Halifax, 1,377; Montreal, 1,062. Swift Current has rain on 57 days, snow on 50; Edmonton, rain on 66 days, snow 57.

81. *D'Artigue, Six Years in the Canadian North-West*, 33. The thunderstorms could result from strong convectional heating or be associated with frontal systems.

82. *FMT*, 31 July 1924.

83. Donkin, *Trooper and Redskin*, 267.

84. *LH*, 11 July 1935.

85. *EB*, 20 June 1885.

86. Dunn, *The Alberta Field Force of 1885*, 195.

87. *SH*, 5 July 1880.

88. James MacGregor, "Lord Lorne in Canada," *AH*, XXII, No. 2, 11.

89. *MFP*, 9 March 1880. A visitor from Ottawa noted: "When the weather is 30 degrees below zero here, I do not feel it so much as I did when it was five degrees below in Ottawa." Also *MFP*, 11 April 1883.

90. *SH*, 4 November 1878.

91. *SAB*, J.E. McEntyre Diary, A 110.

92. *NAC*, W.M. Ross, f. 760.

93. Geoffrey Pocock, *Outrider of Empire* (Edmonton: University of Alberta Press, 2007), 27.

94. Roger Pocock, *Frontiersman* (London: Methuen, 1903), 36.

95. *NAC*, Roger Pocock, f. 1107. Pocock, *Outrider of Empire*, 297.

96. Dorothy Kamen-Kaye, "The Composite Pioneer," *Sask. H.*, VIII, No. 1, 7.

97. *NAC*, William McQuarrie, f. 724.

98. C.E. Rivett-Carnac, ed., "Letters from the North-West, *RCMP Q*, XVIII, No. 1, 17.

99. Dempsey, ed., *William Parker Mounted Policeman*, 29.

100. Donkin, *Trooper and Redskin*, 237.

101. Ibid. 89.

102. *GA*, John McIllree, AB McIllree, # 1.

103. *GA*, Edward Barnett, M 6458.

104. Cecil Denny, *The Law Marches West*, 68–69. For Macleod's account, see Michael Craufurd-Lewis, *Macleod of the Mounties* (Ottawa: Golden Dog Press, 1999), 255.

105. *MFP*, 1 June 1877. From 9 to 44 degrees Fahrenheit. Also *MFP*, 23 January 1879.

106. Nevitt, *Frontier Life in the Mounted Police*, 43.

107. Ibid., 49. Also 12–13.

108. *NAC*, R.N. Wilson Diary, MG 29, E – 47.

109. Donkin, *Trooper and Redskin*, 89.

110. *EB*, 4 August 1883. Also *WDT*, 4 July 1879, reported that at Saddle Lake a child died after being picked up by a whirlwind (tornado?) and carried into a lake.

111. For example, Rev. A. Sutherland, *A Summer in Prairie Land* (Toronto: Methodist Book and Publishing House, 1882), 38−39; W.H. Williams, *Manitoba and the North-West* (Toronto: Hunter, Rose, 1882), 55.

112. Dempsey, ed., *William Parker Mounted Policeman*, 19.

113. Ibid., 115.

114. C.D. LaNauze, "Echoes and Letters from Fort Walsh," *RCMP* Q, VIII, No. 1, 38. Tom LaNauze had ranched for ten years in Uruguay before joining the NWMP.

115. Donkin, *Trooper and Redskin*, 155.

116. John F. Finerty, *War-Path and Bivouac or Conquest of the Sioux* (Norman, Oklahoma: University of Oklahoma, 1994), 355.

117. *GA*, Duncan McEachran, 971.23 M141.

118. Middleton, *Suppression of the Northwest Rebellion in the North West of Canada*, 1885, ed. G.H. Needler (Toronto: Univ. of Toronto Press, 1948), 68. Also *MFP*, 5 August 1910.

119. *NAC*, VI, 335−75. Poett added: "I would mention that while marching this comparatively short distance to Swan River our horses suffered more from attacks of insects than they did on the whole route of our western march last year." Poett observed that bulldogs attacked the horse's underside; black flies, the ears, and neck; and mosquitoes, the chest and sides of the animals.

120. *UMM*, Thomas B. Boys, Diary. 4 September 1876. Flying ants were somewhat similar. One Mounted Police troop encountered a cloud of flying ants in 1886 that extended for ten miles and "nearly drove us crazy." Pox-o-nachie, "When the West was Young," *SG*, Ninth Annual, 72.

121. *LH*, 1 March 1924.

122. Grain, "Pioneers of a Glorious Future," 67.

123. Ibid., 65.

124. *GA*, Edward Barnett, M 6458.

125. *LH*, 11 July 1935.

126. *OFP*, 18 February 1880. That winter, the Indians caught more than 70,000 fish.

127. *GA*, Joseph Carscadden, M 6608.

128. Maunsell, "With the North West Mounted Police from 1874 to 1877," 55.

129. *GA*, Simon J. Clarke, M 228.

130. Fitzpatrick, *Sergeant 331*, 19.

131. *FBRP*, 20 July 1881. One recorded death from snake bite in Medicine Hat in 1883.

132. Dempsey, ed., *William Parker Mounted Policeman*, 32.

133. James Steele, PAA, 85.448 (16 August 1879).

134. Steele, *Forty Years in Canada*, 145.

135. *RC*, NWMP, 1874, 38.

136. *TM*, 8 March 1875.

137. *GA*, Joseph Carscadden, M 6608.

138. Gillett, "Interview of J.H.G. Bray," 18.

139. *MFP*, 24 June 1910.

140. Fitzpatrick, *Sergeant 331*, 95.

141. Col. James Walker, "My life in the North-West Mounted Police," *AHR*, VIII, No. 1, 7.

142. *LH*, 21 June 1924.

143. *WDT*, 3 February 1882.

144. Cowie, *The Company of Adventurers*, 436. He believed that traders and Métis, who were not his customers, got as many more.

145. *GA*, Robert Patterson, M 2470.

146. Dempsey, ed., *William Parker Mounted Policeman*, 32. Bear meat was eaten on rare occasions. At the first Christmas dinner at Swan River, the men found the meat palatable as long as ample buffalo fat was added. For Constable Fitzpatrick at the East End outpost, a grizzly bear meat was too oily and greasy to be appealing.

147. Maunsell, "With the North West Mounted Police from 1874 to 1877," 59.

148. Gillett, "Interview of J.H.G. Bray," 15–16.

149. Woman's Canadian Historical Society of Toronto, Transaction No. 26, 1927–1928. "Impressions of the West in the early Seventies from the Diary of the Assistant Surgeon of the B.N.A. Boundary Survey, Dr. Millman," 50.

150. Gillett, "Interview of J.H.G. Bray," 12.

151. Alfred Selwyn, "Observances in the North West Territory on a journey across the plains from Fort Garry to Rocky Mountain House, returning by the Saskatchewan River and Lake Winnipeg," Geological Survey of Canada—Report of Progress for 1873–74 (Montreal: Dawson Brothers, 1874), 61.

152. Maunsell, "With the North West Mounted Police from 1874 to 1877," 54.

153. Denny, *Riders of the Plains*, 64.

154. *CH*, 25 October 1930.

155. *GA*, William Parker M 934. *MFP*, 11 August 1876. Healy needed fifteen bullets to kill one cow.

156. Fitzpatrick, *Sergeant 331*, 33.

157. Dempsey, ed., *William Parker Mounted Policeman*, 31. Parker added, "I went on and wounded another. We must have chased them five or six miles until they came to a deep coulee and disappeared."

158. *MFP*, 6 October 1880 (from *Saskatchewan Herald*).

159. *TG*, 3 August 1876. Also *PAM*, Frank Carruthers, MG 6, A-1.

160. Denny, *The Law Marches West*, 68–69. For Macleod's account of the incident, see Michael Craufurd-Lewis, *Macleod of the Mounties* (Ottawa: Golden Dog, 1999), 254.

161. *GA*, E. Price, M 1000 f. 1.

162. *LH*, 25 June 1949.

163. Veteran, "The Buffalo Liar," SG, Tenth Annual, 76. Also *WDT*, 20 May 1882.

164. Denny, *Riders of the Plains*, 62.

165. *WDT*, 3 September 1880.

166. *SH*, 20 October 1879.

167. *WDT*, 3 August 1880.

168. Anonymous, "A Buffalo Hunt on the CPR in 1883," *AH*, L, No. 3, 27.

169. *LH*, 14 January 1954.

3

THE '74 MARCH WEST

Crossing The Dirt Hills (Henri Julien)

"The prairies over which we traveled presented the same undulating, monotonous appearance. Not one green bush of the most dwarfish size to relieve the eye. The effect of this loneliness upon the imagination is very singular ... the silence is oppressing."

– Henri Julien, *Expedition to the North-West*, 17
  GA NA 361 – 10

WRITERS HAVE GIVEN THE WESTWARD march of the North-West Mounted Police many titles: The March West, The Great Adventure, The Hardest March, The Amazing March, The First Patrol, The Big March, and The Famous March. For the men who participated in this adventure, it was simply the '74 March and they were the 74 Men or the Originals.[1]

Dufferin to Roche Percée

On the afternoon of 8 July 1874, the Mounted Police left the Dufferin camp for Fort Whoop-Up, home of the notorious whiskey traders. One troop would stay to garrison this fort while the main column continued north to establish the key post at Fort Edmonton. Logistics and travel delays, however, radically altered this initial plan.

The departure of the six troops of 275 men, wrote one participant, "was a splendid sight, but destined to last but a short time."[2] The men wore scarlet Norfolk jackets, white helmets, white gauntlets, grey or flesh-coloured Bedford cord riding breeches, long boots, and brown leather cartridge belts. For weapons, the troops had Snider-Enfield carbines and Adams revolvers. Each Division rode horses of one colour:

DIVISION	INSPECTOR	HORSES	SUPPLIES
A - 41 men	William D. Jarvis	56 dark bay	13 supply wagons
B - 40 men	Ephraim Brisebois	41 dark brown	10 wagons
C - 43 men	William Winder	50 bright chestnut	2 field guns, 2 mortars ammunition
D - 60 men	James M. Walsh	66 grey	
E - 48 men	E.J. Carvell	49 black	
F - 41 men	Theodore Richer	51 light bay	

The column departed by Division alphabetical order. Two 9-pr. M.L.R. guns and two mortars formed the artillery. These weapons were fired on several occasions to impress the Indians, but mostly they impeded movement. A supply train of 114 ox-drawn Red River carts, 73 wagons, portable forges, field kitchens, and mowing machines followed the horsemen. The carts, carrying supplies for six months, were driven by twenty half-breeds whom Commissioner George French thought had miraculously achieved a level of sobriety after their excesses the previous night. Horsemen driving a herd of 130 cattle ended the column.

Although the 275-man column (21 officers and 254 men) with 310 horses, 2 field guns, 2 mortars, and accompanying vehicles appeared most formidable, Commissioner George A. French had concerns. In a letter (written upon his return to Dufferin in November), French recalled: "My heart failed me somewhat as I saw the Train draw out … where was the fighting force? … when the drivers were deducted, [the Train] merely looked like an escort."[3] Moreover, French contended that to, a stranger, it appeared as an astonishing cavalcade with armed men and guns, but what could ploughs, harrows, mowing machines, cows, and calves be for?[4] And wasn't it unusual for a police column to have artillery? Nor was the order of advance an astute military tactic: even closed the column extended for 2 km but, once in motion, 7 km sometimes separated the lead from the rear troops. On several days, the rear wagons failed to reach the evening camp. Advancing in parallel columns apparently was never attempted. And, for troops entering a semi-arid region, not having individual water canteens and water barrels was a serious oversight.

There are no photographs of the famous march. There are, however, drawings in the *Canadian Illustrated News* by Henri Julien, a 22-year-old artist from Montreal. The newspaper, in response to Commissioner French's request, assigned Julien to provide drawings of the expedition. Julien immediately left Montreal to join the contingent about to leave Toronto. He traveled with the column to the Sweet Grass Hills and returned across the plains with the troops that had been assigned to Swan River. Julien drew forty illustrations, some appearing in the paper while the march was in progress. Both his drawings and diary are important historical records of the Mounted Police march that summer.[5]

Balky horses and stubborn oxen, unaccustomed to being harnessed, made the departure from Dufferin anything but orderly. Sub-Constable James Finlayson watched, "quite a number of runaways among horses and oxen. Many men were thrown from their saddles."[6] Once underway, in what was called a "Hudson's Bay start," the column moved only a few kilometres before setting up camp beside a small lake. At this stop, the men checked their supplies and made adjustments to the equipment and carts. Each man had a baggage allowance of 10 lbs. (4.5 kg), the officers, 50 lbs. (22.7 kg). In the morning, wagons with the men's extra clothing and luxuries (such as two wagon loads of syrup) were returned to Dufferin to be replaced by oats. The baggage kits were not returned for over a year and by then the men were in desperate need of clothing.

As the column prepared to leave camp in the afternoon, Commissioner French placed Inspector Theodore Richer under arrest. Richer was charged with using insubordinate language while refusing to supply saddle horses for the wagon teams. He further threatened to notify Ottawa of what Richer claimed was the deplorable mismanagement of the Force. This disciplinary action by the 32-year-old Commissioner was very important. Recruit Jean D'Artigue agreed: "Notwithstanding, his many faults, the Commissioner was a well-disciplined and experienced officer, and, knowing well that if this disobedience remained unpunished he would soon face revolts of a more serious character."[7] Sub-Inspector Leif Crozier replaced Richer in charge of Division "F".

Departure For Fort Whoop-Up (Henri Julien)

"There were quite a number of runaways among horses and oxen. Many men were thrown from their saddles."

– Sub-Constable James Finlayson, Diary, *NAC*, MG29, E58
GA NA 361 – 2

Throughout the western march, French enforced strict discipline. When biscuits were missing from a barrel, he assembled the sentries on guard that night and had their coats searched. No biscuits were found, but two men with crumbs in their pockets were shackled. Sub-Constable Joseph Carscadden was incredulous: "Those crumbs may have been in their pockets for several days as we were often served out biscuits during the march."[8] On the intervention of Assistant Commissioner James Macleod, the men were released after they each paid a $15 fine (half a month's salary) for not preventing the biscuit theft. The penalty for misbehaviour was a fine.

Some men were clearly not suited for police life. Sub-Constable J.W. Wheeler, "A" Division, received the following fines:

26 – 8 – 1874	absent from his duties as cook	fine $3
8 – 9 – 1874	profane language	fine $5
9 – 9 – 1874	sleeping at post on guard	fine $5
15 – 9 – 1874	neglect of duty on picquet	fine $3
30 – 3 – 1875	insolence to Corp. Carr, Fort Edmonton	admonished

Repeated offences by Sub-Constable G. Elliot led to the recommendation that he be dismissed from the Force as soon as possible.[9]

On several occasions, individuals openly challenged the authority of Commissioner French. A few days after the confrontation with Richer, one unhappy recruit donned civilian clothes, walked south of an iron stake that marked the International Boundary, and told Commissioner French "to go to hell."[10] In a second example, Sub-Constable M. Smyth disobeyed the order to walk every other hour to rest the horses and instead rode in a cook wagon. In response to the Commissioner's threat of arrest, Smyth rejoined: "I joined a mounted force, not a foot one, and as I am not feeling well today, I must ride on something."[11] French left him in the wagon.

Transportation difficulties quickly became obvious. Many recruits were untrained in driving teams of horses or oxen. To his dismay, 21-year-old William Parker found himself assigned to driving a team of oxen:

> I had no experience driving oxen but they told me there was nothing to it. If I wanted to go to the right, I was to shout "Gee," and to the left "Haw." They also gave me a stick with a small spike at one end to prod them. I had to sit on a cramped narrow seat in front just behind the oxen and there was no way to get off when moving.[12]

To the young Mountie's alarm, no sooner had he got the team underway than the animals ran away at a full gallop over the rough prairie. Fortunately, two Métis drivers stopped and returned the team to the column while a shaken Parker chose to walk back.

Weeks earlier, Young Bagley was a Toronto school boy. Now he was in charge of driving oxen westward on the vast Canadian prairie. He related that his first attempt at driving a cart was disastrous after he deemed the team was moving too slowly:

> I ventured to hit the lead ox a resounding thwack on the back with a stout stick, thereupon all three set off on a mad gallop across the prairie, scattering the various sacks which constituted their loads. As I could not stop them in their wild stampede, it almost seemed to me that only the barrier of the Rocky Mountains would prevent them from reaching the Pacific coast.[13]

It was, Bagley thought, a godsend when Colonel Macleod happened by on horseback, and, after a hearty laugh, halted the runaways and sent some men to help gather and reload the scattered cargo.

In response to seeing Edward H. Maunsell almost upsetting his horse-drawn wagon into a stream, Major James Walsh rode up and angrily asked Constable Maunsell whether he knew the difference between "haw and gee." When Maunsell responded negatively, Walsh retorted, "You won't be driving any more wagons of mine."[14] (Maunsell then rationalized: "I knew they meant right or left, but I didn't know which was which, and selected the wrong one").

Walsh assigned Maunsell to drive an ox cart, making the Sub-Constable the butt of his companion's jokes. Maunsell's troubles only continued. His ox continually left the trail to graze, forcing the young Mountie to lead the beast all day. At camp, he unhitched the animal and decided to take a short nap before dinner. Sub-Inspector John French (the Commissioner's brother) interrupted his slumber to tell him the ox was eating the harness collar. A furious struggle followed as Maunsell fought with the ox to extract the harness from its throat. He succeeded, but the harness was ruined.

The next day, Maunsell observed that each half-breed driver tied his ox to an advance cart, making the animals proceed in an orderly manner. This was too good to be true: Maunsell's cart carried bedding and he enjoyed a cozy sleep until awakened by none other than Commissioner French yelling that the ox had eaten a sack of flour in the attached cart. The hapless recruit, obviously inept in driving carts, was placed in a wagon ambulance and given a shotgun to kill ducks. In this task, he proved very capable and kept Inspector Walsh well supplied with the birds.[15]

The strident racket of the 114 Red River carts added to the frustration of driving a team. It was a din, one recruit complained, so dissonant that, "a den of wild beasts cannot be compared to it in hideousness. Combine all the discordant sounds ever heard in Ontario and they can not produce anything so horrid as a train of Red River carts."[16] A second recruit, an eyewitness in Swift's packing plant in Chicago during the slaughter of hogs, affirmed that the "clamour of protesting porkers was a mother's crooning lullaby compared to the squeals, grunts and groans of one Red River cart."[17] The noise of what the men labeled the "Red River Band" could be heard long before the cart train came into sight.

Commissioner French and the senior officers quickly became exasperated with the Métis cart drivers seeming indifferent to the morning departure and their troublesome penchant of stopping by for tea at inconvenient times. To increase the column's pace, rather than have the carts proceed as a unit, French interspersed riders in their midst. This, he hoped, would bring a sense of urgency. Some recruits, paid $0.75 daily, were annoyed when they learned that the Métis drivers earned $2–$5 per diem.

French was pleased with the keen rivalry the police showed in the morning preparations, the rule being that the six Divisions departed according to readiness. But the men knew that this order was not always an advantage. Each evening, Staff-Constable J.B. Mitchell in "E" Troop questioned the guides about the next day's route. He wrote that, "if a good trail was expected, 'E' troop made every effort to get out first, and having many farmer men generally succeeded; however, if it was expected to break trail, 'E' Troop was not so smart and came about fourth."[18]

The column followed the Boundary Commission Road, a trail made a year earlier by surveyors marking the International Border. On the second day there was a halt at a solitary log house where a Scotsman named Grant lived with his Indian wife and children. Henri Julien watched some officers buying milk and whiskey. This was, he criticized, counter to the orders restricting the drinking of whiskey. Grant's shack was the last occupied structure the men saw until they reached Fort Whoop-Up, ninety days later.

This first stage of the western march—Dufferin to Roche Percée—took sixteen days. Plodding cattle and the cumbersome machinery impeded the pace. Other than two dilapidated bridges that needed repair, all waterways had to be forded. As each cart crossed, the banks became increasingly muddy, often making it necessary to link added oxen to help a labouring team ascend the river bank. The delays at river crossings soon placed the front and rear wagons far apart. On several days the end wagons failed to reach the evening camp. On the morning of July 17, the ox teams left late and Commissioner French in the lead group did not see them all day. At the Turtle Head Creek camp that night, the exhausted men never bothered to pitch their tents but slept under the wagons.

Assistant Commissioner James Macleod, in a letter to his future wife, described the difficulties:

> I have not had a moment to myself ... I hardly know when a day ends or commences. Last night I was left behind to see everything off and as I came along the rear of the train a young officer came galloping up to say there were three ox teams stuck and could not pull an inch further, so off I had to go, sent my horse on to camp and took the oxen with my own hands ... it was long after dark when I arrived.[19]

It would be expected that the food provisions for this lengthy journey had been finalized and yet at the first camp there was no bread. The next morning Inspector John McIllree's diary recorded: "Great complaints among the men about rations. Say they are starved."[20]

On July 12, only the fourth day of the journey, the men broke camp without breakfast and no water was available. Three days later, each man was issued eight biscuits for the day. Frederick Bagley rashly ate five of his allotment for breakfast. The next day, James Finlayson recorded: "One Slap Jack per man for breakfast. Lucky to get that … arrived at Turtle Mountain after dark and camped near a small stream. Had supper as I had for dinner, namely Nothing."[21] At one camp, when a sentry challenged a man arriving with an oxcart at midnight, the reply "a famished man" admitted entry.

There were occasions when the men had to compensate for the absence of rations. When Sub-Constables Frederick Bagley and Jean Claustre strayed from the column, they found that Claustre's cart contained only flour while Bagley's had only sugar. That evening, the novice cooks satisfied their hunger by concocting a sugar-flour paste with water added from a stagnant slough. They rejoined the column in the morning.

On July 14, the column reached the Pembina River, a stream 12 m in width, less than waist-deep, and with good water. A dilapidated bridge was repaired and the column camped 10 km farther west. The first buffalo bones, of what became a common sight, were seen. That day, Pierre Léveille, a Métis plainsman and five companions joined the column. They brought six carts with gifts from Alexander Morris, the Lieutenant Governor of Manitoba, to be distributed to the Indians. Léveille, a large man weighing 300 lbs. (137 kg), was hired as a guide and interpreter. Interestingly, his father had fought in Napoleon's army at Waterloo.

On July 18, the tenth day of the march, the column reached the First Crossing of the Souris River, 290 km west of Dufferin. The campsite was surrounded by hills and had good grass, water and thick woods along the river bank. One officer recorded: "There was much dissatisfaction amongst our men on account of the scarcity of food."[22] A two-day rest was in order.

The men enjoyed this break. They bathed in the clear river, fished, and washed their clothing. The horses were washed, some shoed, and carts were repaired. Two oxen were butchered for fresh meat. A nearby passing prairie fire was a spectacular sight. On the second day the temperature reached 99°F (37.2°C).

At the camp, Sub-Constable Pierre Lucas rejoined the column after being absent for several days. He recited a fanciful story that he had lost his horse in a gunfight with five Indians. This was unusual: to date no Indians had been seen. "Everyone," wrote one man, "was convinced that his story was a fabrication."[23] Commissioner French dismissed Lucas' story as a lie but pursued no further investigation. That Lucas was later dismissed from the Force attests to his unstable character.[24]

The men discovered ducks in nearby sloughs that were molting and helpless. On the previous day, there were complaints to Sub-Inspector Gagnon about the lack of food and the men had refused to harness the horses until sufficient rations were provided. Now they had a vulnerable food source. Some enterprising men even added duck soup to their fare. The artist, Henri Julien, who ate four ducks at one sitting, wrote:

> The men would go down with big sticks, knock them over the head, and catch them by the leg in their feeble attempts to fly away ... it was butchery but one cannot afford to be sentimental on the plains when he is worn by constant riding and half-starved on government rations. We, therefore, made no scruples to devour as many ducks as we could kill.[25]

On the '74 March, the men augmented the column's food supply by shooting game birds, rabbits, antelope, and buffalo. By August, berries had ripened. They ate gooseberries, raspberries, and especially saskatoon berries, which they picked from bushes in ravines north of the Cypress Hills.

Men of the NWMP Killing Ducks With Sticks (Henri Julien)

"It was butchery but one cannot afford to be sentimental on the plains when he is worn by constant riding and half-starved on government rations."

– Henri Julien, *Expedition to the North-West*, 14
GA NA 47 – 15

Finding potable water for 300 men, their mounts, the cattle, oxen and weakened horses was a daily concern. On the second night, the horses had to be watered across the International Border. Two days later, the men dug in the mud of a dried slough for a few buckets of water that, even after being strained, was as black as ink. One known water source, St. Peter's Springs, resembled a dirty mud hole but after digging several shallow wells, shored by wooden barrels, abundant ice cold water issued. In commemoration of their success, the springs were renamed "Mounted Police Wells." The arrival of large numbers of birds in search of water was an interesting sight. Once the column entered "buffalo country," the search for fresh water became more demanding as many sources were alkaline or polluted by buffalo wastes. Stops without water were called "Dry Camps."

Tea was the preferred beverage. Surgeon John Kittson, whose later report recommended an increased tea ration, observed, "on the march the men constantly grumbled as to the insufficiency of tea."[26]

Insects pestered the men and animals. Those men who had visited other parts of the world agreed "that nowhere had they seen anything to rival the mosquito of the prairie."[27] As the twilight deepened, the mosquitoes rose in "clouds" and, as the swarms neared, the hum swelled into a roar. Henri Julien wrote:

> The attack is simply dreadful. Your eyes, your nose, your ears are invaded. If you open your mouth to curse them, they troop into it. They insinuate themselves under your clothes, down your shirt collar, up your sleeves cuff, between the buttons of your shirt bosom. And not one or a dozen, but a million at a time. You can brush them off your coat sleeves in layers.[28]

A "million" is the artist's exaggerated frustration, but still at times the only refuge was under blankets, even on hot, sultry evenings. The horses could be seen rearing, kicking, and pitching.

Early in the march, on the fifth day out from Dufferin, locusts appeared "against the sky like clouds of smoke."[29] One recruit wrote: "We could hardly see the sun."[30] As the airborne locusts neared, the sunlight reflecting off their wings made a dazzling sight. Joseph Carscadden recorded in his diary: "The grasshoppers fell about us like hailstones—so thickly that it was with difficulty we could keep our eyes open."[31] Once the swarm landed, they seemingly devoured everything not moving.

Another insect annoyance for a brief time in the late summer was flying ants. On August 19, Sub-Constable James Finlayson wrote: "Suffered much from flying ants today. We had all we could do to keep killing them."[32]

A second account of this pest related: "We were very much annoyed during the evening by swarms of flying ants which got underneath your clothes and stung."[33]

Adverse weather, not unexpected, was certain to impact the march. On the third day out, a violent storm with hail stones compared in size to walnuts struck the camp. On July 20, the thermometer recorded 36°C (96°F) and, on the following day, 38°C (101.4°F). Inspector Sévère Gagnon wrote: "We can hardly bear the heat."[34] Rest stops on hot afternoons were necessary. It was then surprising that most nights were cool. Everyone was amazed at the Roche Percée campsite on July 20 when ice formed on the brook and white frost coated the tents. On September 9, two months out from Dufferin, driving snow portended the coming winter.

The travel, heat, insects, poor forage, and water problems quickly weakened the horses, especially the saddle horses that were harnessed to pull wagons. At some stops hay, if available, was cut for the animals. Sub-Inspector Cecil Denny (called Texas Jack) herded a "sick list" of as many as twenty weakened horses that were placed at the end of the column.

On July 17, horses in the column kept dropping from fatigue all day and four animals were left on the trail. The Eastern horses, called "Canadian," although larger and more impressive in appearance than the western mounts, needed to adjust to prairie conditions. Veterinarian Surgeon John Poett concluded that, once a horse was run down, it was difficult for the animal to recover as the column was constantly on the move.

On three occasions Colonel Macleod left the column to obtain oats. French approved the purchase of 60,000 lbs. (27,500 kg) of oats and although the price was high, oats were essential for the stamina of the horses. Commissioner French estimated: "I really believe we would have lost 100 horses if we had not had these oats to supplement the scanty pasture."[35]

After a hard day of traveling, sentry duty was an unwanted assignment. At the beginning of the march, thirty mounted men acted as the camp guard. Each man would ride out a distance and, upon returning, call out to the sergeant, for example, "Number Five and all's well!" Sub-Constable E. Maunsell (who Walsh had berated for not knowing "gee from haw") ignored this routine and rode away in the dark. When he located the camp in the morning, only the cattle drivers remained. The officer in charge, Staff-Constable R. Betcher, who reported Maunsell deserted, rather than arresting the wayward sentry and as a lesson assigned him to drive cattle. The inept recruit further suffered by having nothing to eat for thirty-six hours.

On July 21, the column left the First Crossing Camp at 5:30 a.m. The men were ordered to walk every alternate hour to relieve the horses. During the day, Commissioner George French rode several times down the line to check this directive. Still, that day the pace was slow and at evening camp it was found there were six men remaining behind with nine horses who were unable to maintain the pace.

The following morning, departure was delayed until twelve missing horses were recovered. That day, the men rode across a flat barren country without wood or water. In the late afternoon, the column reached the Second Crossing of the Souris. The muddy banks delayed the teams and it took seven hours before the last wagon had crossed the river. It had been a difficult day. Two men were injured by horses—one man was kicked in the head, the second fell under a horse team that was descending a steep hill.

That night the column camped near a well-known landmark called the "Hill of the Murdered Scout." The 4-m rock formation, according to the legend, outlined a murdered Mandan Indian lying on his back, his legs spread out and arms stretched back of his head.[36]

On July 24, the column moved about 1 km west of Roche Percée, a prominent outcropping in a weathered irregular shape that was pierced by a large hole, giving the name "pierced rock." This sandstone landmark, located 18 km southeast of present-day Estevan, Saskatchewan, was an object of both Indian superstition and veneration. Markings on the rocks depicted Indian hieroglyphics of birds and animals, and the names or initials of white persons traveling through. One surprise sight was a flock of vultures scavenging on nearby buffalo carcasses. The men found one buffalo skull with the hair still attached.

For the third time, the column had crossed the Souris River, a stream with its source in Canada that entered the United States and then flowed northward into the Assiniboine River near Brandon. The campsite at Short Creek had excellent water, wood, and nearby grazing land. Commissioner French chose to rest the horses and oxen at this stop for five days. On a tall pole, a Union Jack marked the campsite.

The respite was needed. Jean D'Artigue described his comrades as, "a routed army corps. For a distance the road was strewn with broken carts and horses and oxen overcome with hunger and fatigue."[37] And many men were disappointed that no encounters with either Indians or whiskey traders had occurred.

The men relaxed and loafed about the camp. They enjoyed bathing and washed the horses and their clothes. Young Bagley likened the rest to the "Life of Riley." Letters were given to a passing Boundary Surveying party on its way to Dufferin. The rock formations were explored and the engravings observed. Some men added their names. Coal was found and used in the forges. Each evening there was a singsong with the favourite songs being, "Home Sweet Home" and "God Save the Queen" (to which

Sub-Constable Frank Norman paraphrased, "Get us out of this damned fix; God save all here"). Sub-Constable Bill Latimer, fully recovered from his terrible scalp wound suffered in the Dufferin horse stampede, with a fife, and trumpeter Frank Parks, hammering tent pegs on a tin dish, entertained their comrades as a makeshift band.

And there were Constable Frank Spicer's songs. From under a wagon, Spicer, with several sidekicks, would entertain the troop with their version of Italian opera. Spicer confessed: "The best thing about our singing was that if any one of the singers knew a word of Italian they kept the fact carefully to themselves, we made up our Italian as we went along."[38]

Church Parade at Roche Percée (Henri Julien)

Commissioner French enjoyed the hymns, in view of the fact that, "unfortunately, the language of a great many is by no means Scriptural."

– *RC*, NWMP, 1874, 37
  GA NA 361 – 7

On a very hot Sunday on July 26, the first church parade was held. Officers conducted four services: Roman Catholic, Presbyterian, Methodist, and Church of England. To Jean D'Artigue, it was a grand sight to see the men standing in the wilderness offering prayers to their Creator and singing the "Ave Marie Stella," even if they sung, in Inspector Sévère Gagnon's opinion, "rather badly."

Commissioner George French enjoyed the hymns, considering that, "unfortunately, the language of a great many is by no means Scriptural."[39] Later, he was shocked by the crude language and ribald songs—some of which fifteen-year-old Bagley thought were quite good.

Perhaps the only excitement during the Roche Percée stay was a near stampede after a careless bullet struck a horse. And, with so many disabled horses, the birth of a foal was a great boost. Several men were transferred to other Divisions and there was an inspection of the saddles and bits.

The general health of the men overall was quite poor. At a sick parade, almost 10 per cent of the men reported ill. For those men having cholera, Dr. Kittson prescribed 20–30 grains of trinitrate of bismuth and a one-grain dose of opium. Two men with pneumonia were sent to Bismarck, Dakota Territory, for treatment.

In what seems unconventional strategy, once the march was underway, there was no scheduled contact with Ottawa. Readers in Eastern Canada, however, received news on the general progress of the Force from letters and dispatches. Henri Julien's illustrations of the '74 March were featured in the weekly *Canadian Illustrated News* as early as July 25, two weeks after leaving Dufferin. The *Toronto Daily Mail* provided (on September 8) a critical account of the "somewhat romantic mission" and concluded that it needed no oracle to predict that this expedition will fail in the accomplishment of its objective. Another eastern newspaper reported the column's arrival at Roche Percée and that the men were in good health and spirits. The *Manitoba Free Press*, 29 September, "happily contradicted the dismal reports circulated about the Force," and related the powwows with the Sioux, the purchase of oats, and that the Cypress Hills had been reached one month earlier.[40] Upon the return of French to Winnipeg on November 4, the *Manitoba Free Press* gave a detailed account of the march.

At Roche Percée, the men welcomed courier C.S. Chapman (who had been a member of the Boundary Survey) and Assistant Surgeon R.B. Nevitt. They brought letters and newspapers. The men read with chagrin a report in an American newspaper that Sioux warriors had wiped out the column. Nevitt told the men that churches throughout Canada had held prayers for the safety of the expedition.

Another arrival was Sub-Inspector Albert Shurtliff who brought six replacement horses from a police camp located 15 km to the west. This small police detachment had been set up before the main column left Dufferin and was informed by a courier to provide the horses.

It had taken sixteen days to travel 450 km to Roche Percée. In one month, it would be September. To reach Whoop-Up country before winter, a much faster pace was imperative.

With this in mind, Commissioner French consulted his senior officers. The decision reached had "A" troop, under Inspector William D. Jarvis, leave the column to take the Carlton Trail to Fort Edmonton. Jarvis had traveled this route the previous summer. His troop would take the cattle and machinery, giving the main column greater mobility. Commissioner French wrote in his diary: "I have now broken the train and feel relieved."[41] Several days were spent distributing the supplies for "A" troop and for Sub-Inspector Shurtliff, who left with Quartermaster Charles Nicolle and seven constables to prepare Fort Ellice as the NWMP Headquarters.

Fort Ellice was an established Hudson Bay post near the junction of the Qu'Appelle and Assiniboine rivers, a distance of 175 km northeast of Roche Percée. In addition to preparing the future Headquarters, the detachment was to check carts passing on the Carlton Trail for alcohol. That fall and winter, the men inspected more than 1,000 carts without finding even one bottle of whiskey.

Roche Percée to the Sweet Grass Hills

At 6 p.m. on July 29, the main column left Roche Percée for Wood End Depot, about 15 km west. Sub-Inspector John McIllree remembered, "it was a lovely moonlight ride, and I rode most of the way alone thinking of things, past and future."[42]

The Wood End Depot had springs, wood, and grass. Preparations were made for the coming days. The troops gathered a supply of firewood to carry, the cooks baked a three-day supply of bread, and a muster checked the men and horses.

From Wood End, the column moved southwest for five days along the Boundary Survey road. Many men suffered from diarrhea. One water source that Surgeon B. Nevitt observed with his microscope revealed "animals in it that look like huge fleas."[43] Twenty-two men turned up at Sick Report on August 2, the largest daily number on the entire march. Five men were relieved from duty. That day more than 100 ducks were killed. Sub-Inspector Cecil Denny remembered shooting as many ducks as he cared.

On August 4, the column struck its own route northwest beside Long Creek, crossing the dry waterway four times. The land was treeless and the only water found was in pools which teamed with waterfowl. The men killed ducks with sticks, stones, or by gunfire. Commissioner French alone shot twenty-five birds.

After his inquiries, French found that the guides were not familiar with the route and he referred to earlier published sources. These, unfortunately, contained several flagrant errors. Captain Palliser's map (1859), for example, placed Old Wives Lake 70 km east of its correct location and the report of Robertson-Ross in 1873 incorrectly located Fort Whoop-Up at the conjunction of its Bow and Belly (now Oldman) rivers, 90 km east of the correct site near present-day Lethbridge.

French assigned Sub-Inspector James Walker to map the route. Walker attached an odometer to a wagon wheel for an approximate measure of mileage and determined directions with a compass. At each midday stop Commissioner French calculated the latitude and at night he measured the magnetic variations by the Pole Star. Altitude readings were taken at prominent elevations.

At midnight on August 3–4, a violent windstorm struck the camp, smothering the men with dust and toppling most of the tents. Sub-Inspector John McIllree's tent blew away with his helmet, tin plates, and blankets. The accompanying thunderstorm drenched everyone. When the moon reappeared, the destruction was apparent. Nearly every tent was down and the men could be seen running around in their shirt tails. Only Captain Carvell, who had rolled himself into a large oil canvas, never stirred and looked comfortable.

During the thunderstorm, the men had held the horses, still skittish from their terrifying experience while at the Dufferin camp weeks earlier. Fortunately, most of the animals were hobbled. When a rocket was fired several days later as a signal to guide two lost men, some of the horses stampeded. The men, Henri Julien and Sub-Constable A. Hare, turned up the next day, shaken at how easily one could become lost on the prairie.

There was excitement on August 5 at the sight of distant animals. They turned out not to be buffalo, but five antlered deer. As several men moved closer to shoot the prey, Sub-Inspector Cecil Denny's rash horseback approach frightened the animals out of range, much to the anger of John French, the Commissioner's brother.

The column, now almost four weeks from the Dufferin camp, needed supplies. While the march continued north beside Long Creek, Assistant Commissioner Colonel Macleod, in the first of three trips for supplies, left with four men and six carts to purchase pemmican and oats at the Wood Mountain Métis settlement, located 150 km directly west. He then rejoined the column six days later at Old Wives Lake.

While Macleod was gone, the column proceeded northwestward and, on August 6 reached the Dirt Hills or Cactus Mountain. The 300-m elevation was an arduous climb, especially for the teams pulling the gun carriages. Henri Julien questioned the need for the heavy guns that encumbered the advance, took up the time of several men and good horses, and were never fired at the enemy. He rationalized: "I suppose they looked military and therefore had to be dragged along with us, as much for show as anything else."[44] On the long ascent of the Dirt Hills, the front and rear troops became separated by almost 15 km, giving the column a disjointed and vulnerable appearance. At the summit the men slept in a dozen small camps. The field guns did not arrive until the next day. French ordered a one-day rest. To everyone's surprise there was wood, good pasture, a beautiful spring, and three dilapidated hunter's shacks. The altitude was measured at 885 m (2,900 ft.). It was sultry and hot with the thermometer reading 33°C (91°F).

At 5:30 a.m. on August 8, exactly one month after leaving Dufferin, the column began its descent from the Dirt Hills, following a buffalo trail that led to a point from where they could see Old Wives Lake (*Lac La Vieille*) 17 km to the northwest. Constable William Grain remembered: "we sighted the water about ten miles back, and what a glorious sight it was after the dry, dusty days of travel behind us."[45]

French was determined to reach the lake that day and it was a long and tiring trek before camp was set up on the southeast corner of the water body. Some of the wagons did not arrive until the following morning.

Camp at Old Wives Lake (Henri Julien)

"Stopped here for one day. The water being alkaline, was very bad for drinking; almost poisoning horses and men. Diarrhea very prevalent."

– Joseph Carscadden, Diary, *GA*, M 6608
  GA NA 361 – 14

At the lake, Sub-Constable William Grain remembered, "the horses and cattle were so overjoyed that they splashed in before we could stop them."[46] But, after one taste of the brackish water, the animals drank no more. The alkaline water caused dysentery and veterinarian John Poett was kept busy in the next days, administering anti-purgatives to the horses and oxen. He urged moving to a better water source.

The column rested for one day: Sunday, August 9. A break was needed. The men were covered with dust and burnt from the sun. Young Bagley's lips were so swollen that he couldn't sound a note on his trumpet. Many men had diarrhea which they blamed on the brackish water. The campsite was likened to the Dead Sea. Alkali stifled plant growth along the shoreline and a nauseating smell issued from the lake. Moreover, the large lake, 30 km in length and from 8 to 15 km in width, was so shallow that anyone who wanted to swim had to wade for half a km to reach shoulder-deep water. Those men who attempted to swim found the water was so clammy that they were glad to get out.

The men shot waterfowl and a skunk was stoned to death. Commissioner French shot a large pelican with a wing spread of 2.4 m. (8 ft.). Many men were fascinated by a mirage, described by John McIllree, "as a big island that was floating down on us and lasted some time."[47]

Disillusionment with this great adventure was growing. One Mountie complained:"All day we tramped over the endless prairie, suffering the pangs of hunger by day, devoured by parasites by night. This was very different from which we had pictured ourselves doing when we joined the Force."[48]

On August 10, the camp relocated 10 km west beside a small bay where the nearby grass was better. That day, Colonel Macleod returned from Wood Mountain with pemmican and 4,700 lbs. (2,140 kg) of oats.

Two days of steady travel brought the column to Old Wives Creek where there was fresh water, but little grass. Cracks in the ground were reminders of the hot, dry summer. At the campsite, the men saw carcasses of buffalo killed the previous fall. Commissioner French called a halt while Macleod left a second time to obtain supplies at Wood Mountain, 75 km south. He took sixteen carts, each with a driver and a police guard. And, most exciting, a Sioux scout came into the camp. Here at last was the anticipated encounter with the Prairie Indian. French invited him to bring band members for a meeting.

In the late morning of August 13, police trumpets heralded a powwow arranged in a double-sized tent. Some thirty Indians, under Raising Bull, chanting in a monotonous tone, approached in a line with the men followed by their wives and children. They were met by policemen, dressed in full uniform, obviously to impress the visitors. The police demonstrated a short arms drill and a squad fired a field piece which alarmed the band considerably. Inside the tent, the Native men squatted on one side, the women opposite, while Commissioner George French and his officers sat on the ground or in rough benches placed around a table. At the tent door, policemen jostled to view the proceedings. The interpreter was Pierre Léveille. Sub-Inspector John McIllree described the meeting:

> We sat and looked at each other for half an hour and smoked, when one of the braves got up and shook hands all around, saying how-how or something like it. He then proceeded to make a speech commencing by wanting to know why they were coming through their country, which was a beastly piece of cheek as they are Sioux who have been driven out of the States but they ended up by begging for flour and ammunition. Two or three made speeches that professed great love and esteem for us. We gave them some flour and calico and powder balls and flints, and after sitting and looking at each other for another half hour, they left.[49]

Henri Julien related Léveille's translation of one Native's impassioned address:

> The Great Spirit gave the land to all his children. We want to know why you come here and where are you going. All who have hair on their chins are rich; we have clean chins and are poor. I am telling no lies. We had horses and land on the other side, but the Yankees lied to us. They gave us drink and killed us and took our lands away. The Sioux wished to keep quiet, but the Yankees wronged them, drove them away with their big guns.[50]

Chief Raising Bull concluded that England never harmed her red children and now that the Sioux were poor, they needed guns and ammunition. French asked the interpreter what he had said and received a succinct answer: "He say he d—d glad my dear Kurnell."[51]

On the part of the NWMP, Commissioner French, called by the Sioux "Wachasta Sota" (The Man with Power), explained the police intrusion and their purpose to stop the whiskey trade. One statement certainly failed its intent. His Force, he told the listeners, represented Queen Victoria who had red, white, and black children. Laughter erupted when one Native rejoined, "something to the effect that the 'Great White Mother's' morals are not quite what they ought to be."[52] After a second Native spoke, the peace pipe was again smoked, hands again shaken, and the Indians returned to their camp.

The next day, Surgeon John Kittson examined nine band members. He diagnosed lung and eye ailments prevalent, aggravated, he believed, by the smoky teepees. Later that day, the Indians demonstrated bow and arrow shooting and performed a Snake Dance. The monotonous chanting and rigid movements soon bored most policemen.

The appearance of the impoverished Indians dispelled any positive images of the noble red man. "The sight of these Indians caused me great resentment against Fenimore Cooper and more especially Longfellow," wrote Sub-Constable Edward Maunsell, "No imagination could manufacture a Hiawatha or Minnehaha off such material as these Indians."[53] Artist Henri Julien described the men as dirty, ugly, low-browed, dull-eyed and brutish in appearance. The women were no better: "Even the budding girls, have not a single feminine grace. The man must be hard up indeed who takes such a wife."[54] Sub-Inspector John McIllree reiterated the overall impression: "They are a very plain, dirty looking lot. The women are very ugly."[55] To Sub-Inspector Denny "They were a very dirty looking lot and did not give us a high opinion of western Indians."[56]

First Meeting with a Prairie Band (Henri Julien)

"They come in and sit down in a tent, and they will not budge for hours. They are a nasty begging lot and will sell anything they got ... one of our men got a scalp for two plugs of tobacco."

– Sub-Inspector John McIllree, GA, AB McIllree #1
GA NA 361 – 12

Sub-Inspector John McIllree thought the band a nuisance. He grumbled: "They come in and sit down in a tent, and they will not budge for hours. They are a nasty begging lot and will sell anything they got ... one of our men got a scalp for two plugs of tobacco."[57] Young Bagley was happy to obtain two pairs of moccasins. Surgeon Kittson nicknamed the visitors the "Sooty Sons of the Plains."[58]

"This band," complained E.H. Maunsell, "left a lasting impression on us for in a week or ten days every man, from the Colonel down was infested with lice."[59] It was conceded that, "our midget friends play no favourites."[60] Boiling or turning the clothing inside out gave only temporary relief. The Métis example of placing the clothes on an ant hill where the ants made short work of the "cooties" proved more effective. In all, a six-day stop was taken to await Macleod's return.

On August 18, Macleod arrived from Wood Mountain with 15,000 lbs. (6,800 kg) of oats. With him was Lawrence Herchmer, a supply officer with the Boundary Commission and a brother of NWMP Inspector William Herchmer. Twelve years later, in a controversial Government appointment, Lawrence Herchmer, who had no NWMP background, became the fourth NWMP Commissioner.

The column moved that afternoon, and the following days contacted several traveling parties. One was a small Sioux band with women and naked boys leading horse and dog travois. A search of a wagon train under one Ouillette going to Winnipeg with dried meat found no alcohol. Traders with Ouillette sold seven horses and several carts to the police. A member of the Boundary Survey on his way to Winnipeg passed by and took the police mail with him. And a rough frontiersman, Frances Morreau (Morrin, Morriseau) rode into camp from Wood Mountain. Although Commissioner French hired him as a scout, it was with reservations. French wrote, "He is a hardlooking case, describing himself as a trapper and says he trapped on the Bow River three years ago. Many think him a spy for the outlaws."[61] Three weeks later, French called Morreau, "the greatest liar I have ever met."[62] His distrust of Morreau was supported on 30 November 1876 when Sergt. Major Belcher escorted Morreau by dog train from Fort Edmonton to Bow River (Calgary) to face charges for stealing NWMP horses.

On August 19, at a site with good grass, water, and wood, Commissioner French set up a camp, fittingly named Cripple Camp. Constable James Sutherland was left with six ill men, fourteen broken wagons, twenty-eight ailing horses, and provisions—including 20,000 lbs. (9,000 kg) of oats which Colonel Macleod had arranged at Wood Mountain for delivery. Sub-Constable W.H. Onzman was so critically ill that none of his friends ever expected to see him again. The men manned this post (5 km northeast of present-day Gravelbourg, Saskatchewan) until French picked them up seventy days later on his return with Divisions "D–E" to Manitoba.

That afternoon and the following day, the column moved 60 km farther west. There were signs of buffalo in fresh trails, cropped grass, bleached bones, skinned carcasses, and water holes contaminated by the animals. Each day, buffalo chips were gathered in gunny sacks for the cooks. Buffalo vertebrae were found to be ideal candle holders. One wagon, empty of oats and pulled by two weak horses, was sent back to Cripple Camp. It carried the box of a wagon which had its wheels dismantled to be used as spares.

On August 21, the column met a Métis brigade camped in a field of cactus. The waist-high height of some of the spiny plants astonished the Mounties. The Métis drivers reported that buffalo had eaten all the grass as far west as the Cypress Hills. French hired Louis Léveille, one of Pierre Léveille's six brothers, as a guide. A dust-covered, ragged priest, Père Joseph Lestanc, a cleric hardened by nineteen years on the plains, administered the brigade. One month later, the priest overtook "A" Division on the Carlton Trail and related news of this meeting with the main column.

Eight-year-old Gabe Léveille, son of Louis Léveille, was with the cart brigade. In 1956, an officer posted at the Maple Creek RCMP detachment interviewed the by-then 90-year-old pensioner. Gabe Léveille recalled that the Mounties had poor horses, thin and with half bobtails, which were useless in whipping off mosquitoes. The men, he thought, "looked terrible … they wore little bits of hats no bigger than a plate. No shade at all. Their faces were burned almost black and they were all bitten by mosquitoes."[63]

At this time, Macleod left the column for the third time with twenty-seven carts, each with a Métis driver and a policeman, to purchase supplies at the Boundary Survey Depot at White Mud River. Also accompanying the party was Sub-Inspector James Walker, assigned to purchase twenty-five horses, two of which, he hoped, would replace his private mounts that had been assigned to the gun team. The day after Macleod's departure, the column met a third Métis brigade. A search of the wagons found no alcohol. Commissioner French bargained to purchase some horses, but the asking price of $150–$200 a horse was unreasonable.

In the meetings with the Métis brigades, apprehensive policemen asked the cart drivers what perils whiskey traders presented. The picture given was ominous: the police would confront 500 whiskey traders (helped by Negro mercenaries) defending the forts with underground fortifications and even cannons. Commissioner George French dismissed these alarming warnings "as extraordinary."[64]

Bright moonlight guided the column to the Swift Current River (*Rivière à l'eau courant*) on August 24. A fatigue party with shovels and picks leveled the river bank to facilitate the crossing. Camp was set up beside a small slough despite the air reeking from buffalo carcasses rotting in the water. The advance guard reported that they may have sighted a buffalo herd that day. The column was about 1,000 km west of Dufferin. On the southern skyline, the Cypress Hills were visible, a reminder of the tragic massacre only fourteen months earlier. The hills, too, marked the approach to Blackfoot country. Accordingly, precautions added twelve men to the camp guard of fifteen sentries. Sub-Constable James Finlayson recorded: "Orders came out today to hold ourselves in readiness, to turn out at a moment's notice. We have to march in scarlet tunics with belts and carbine close at hand. We also got twenty rounds more ammunition"[65] At night, the horses were contained within a wagon compound and turned loose to graze at daybreak. And, from then on, a small advance guard led the column.

The Force moved to a better camp beside a cold creek where they waited three days for Macleod's return from the White Mud depot. During this time, a lancer company was organized (but said to be useless, other than in appearance), carts were repaired, and the blacksmiths shod twenty-two oxen.

Each night, signal rockets were fired to guide Macleod's return and the new scout, Morreau, left to meet the wagon train. He failed in this task, but shot a cabri (pronghorn), the first game killed other than birds. This animal and several other cabri killed in the following days somewhat compensated for the shortage of bacon. A skilled police marksman, G.W. or S. Taylor, left the train each day to shoot antelope.

Two days of rain turned the campsite into a quagmire. Three sick men were sent to Cripple Camp and courier C.S. Chapman and a companion left for Fort Garry with pay sheets and letters. Lightning frightened thirty grazing horses and, although hobbled, they managed to move several kilometres away. That it took two hours to recover the animals reinforced Commissioner French's concern that horse stampedes were the most detrimental happening to a marching column. He had been warned by American officers of the dangers of horse stampedes in time lost and he was now, "determined to keep all horses hobbled after dark, no matter how little chance they may have for feeding."[66] And tensions during the stay were rising: young Bagley watched a loud argument and near blows between men in "D and E" troops, each accusing the other of stealing frying pans.

At dusk on August 31, Sub-Inspector Walker returned with twenty horses he had purchased at the White Mud depot. Walker reported Macleod and the carts were about 30 km behind.

The following day, Macleod arrived to the cheers of the men and the westward march resumed. The immediate goal was to locate the South Saskatchewan River. Fort Whoop-Up, according to the Robertson-Ross map published two years earlier, would be located near its confluence with the Bow River. The column moved 15 km across a plain with little grass and sloughs contaminated by buffalo wastes. The guides were unfamiliar with the route.

This day, the first of September, was a date for reflection. They had left Dufferin almost eight weeks earlier and were still far from reaching Fort Whoop-Up. All day, a cold rain had made their travel miserable. One discouraged Mountie wrote:

> We were all young men inspired with the spirit of adventure. We had imagined ourselves mounted on spirited horses chasing desperadoes over the prairies. We had also thought that the Indians might not appreciate the motive of our coming and prove hostile. All of which would have been more exciting than fighting hunger and cooties. [67]

And where were the legendary buffalo herds? The answer came the next day, September 2, fifty-six days after leaving Dufferin, when the struggling column at last met its first herd of buffalo. At once, the men rode out to kill the wild animals.

The hunt was absurd. Sub-Inspector Cecil Denny watched one man riding alongside an old bull and hitting the animal with his rifle butt. James Walsh was so excited that he set off after the herd in a wagon. In a hectic chase after three bulls, Henri Julien fired three shots into one bull. The first hit was ineffective, a second brought the beast to one knee, but he arose and raced away. Julien described his chase:

> I pursued a considerable distance and had a third shot which proved fatal. The noble animal stopped, fell, quivered and died. My companions standing on a hill watched my chase in the prairie below and when they beheld my success sent up a cheer. When I got off my horse to survey my victim, I found that I was nearly half dead myself.[68]

Blood splattered his horse, Rooster's sides, Julien confessed: "I had spurred him unmercifully, and my rowels were all bent."[69] Commissioner French, riding his thoroughbred mare, outdistanced the other riders, and he and a guide shot three animals. Pierre Léveille killed the fifth buffalo.

The First Buffalo Hunt (Henri Julien)

"I pursued a considerable distance and had a third shot which proved fatal.
The noble animal stopped, fell, quivered and died."

– Henri Julien, *Expedition to the Northwest*, 24
GA NA 361 – 18

Two large buffalo provided 1,720 lbs. (780 kg) of dressed meat. The Métis
drivers cut chunks of meat from the other dead animals which they
voraciously ate raw or carried for later eating.

Since leaving Cripple Camp, the men had been on half-rations, sometimes
only an unappetizing lump of half-baked dough and a small piece of boiled
bacon. From this point in the westward march, food was never a problem
for the column. Sub-Inspector Cecil Denny remembered that, "many times
we killed buffalo from the saddle without going out of the line of march."[70]
Since the meat from the old bulls was tough, cows and younger animals
were preferred for food. On September 7, eight buffalo cows and calves
were shot. For sport, the men fired fusillades at herds of distant antelope.
In one instance, twenty-five shots were fired without hitting one animal.
Jackrabbits were everywhere. Orders forbade the unnecessary shooting of
wildlife as there was more food than needed.

The cooks boiled the buffalo meat. In the morning, each man placed
a supply of meat in his haversack. One Mountie wrote that, instead of a
regular time for meals, "it seemed as if we were eating all day long. In this

way we easily consumed ten lbs. [4.5 kg] each day. Even then we did not feel satisfied as our craving for vegetable food was intense."[71] The glut of buffalo meat caused diarrhea. Surgeon Kittson's health report recorded that diarrhea accompanied the excessive consumption of fresh meat. Written accounts give no information of how bodily wastes were disposed of by a marching column. Latrines were constructed, if at all, while at a camp. Military units often designated an area near the camp as a waste site.

Several scouts were sent to look for Fort Whoop-Up but their search proved futile. Their failure only increased doubts of this undertaking. Wild speculation had the search for Fort Whoop-Up being abandoned and the column going to the United States for railway connections to Ontario. Conjecture held that, "the government must have been hoaxed and that such a place [Whoop-Up] didn't exist."[72] Other than the small bands near Old Wives Lake, they had encountered no Indians. What would whiskey traders sell in this barren land? Some men even doubted the existence of the Rocky Mountains, calculating that, after eight weeks from Manitoba, they should have caught sight of the storied range. One man summed up the situation: "We have been dispatched on a fool's errand and would become the laughing stock of Canada."[73]

In the next days, the column moved through an area with little grass and no water. At one evening camp, tension arose when seven Sioux approached with pointed rifles. The threat was resolved when a French-speaking Sioux came forward and, explained that they had mistaken the police advance guard for Blackfoot. French gave the Indians tea, biscuits, buffalo meat, and ammunition. The Indians admired the lancers and after eating, they performed a dance. The following day, Sub-Constable W. Chamberlayn was nearly killed when driving two ox carts that tumbled into a deep ravine.

On September 6, near present-day Medicine Hat, the men finally sighted the South Saskatchewan River. It was in the words of Constable Finlayson's, "the finest water body seen."[74] The column then descended (probably via Seven Persons Coulee) and camped near the river bank. However, deep ravines leading to the river impeded movement beside the waterway and compelled the return of the carts to the level plateau south of the river. It was ironic, with fresh water so near and after covering 35 km the next day, camp was set up where there was no wood or grass. The water hole was likened to liquid mud.

On September 8, the column rode 30 km through a desolate region in miserable weather. Wet buffalo chips made camp fires impossible and the men retired that night wet and cold. Four horses died. The capture of a fine Indian pony wandering on the plains was perhaps the only encouraging incident that day.

September 9 brought snow and rain. The weakened horses suffered terribly. When some of them were driven down a ravine for water, five animals were unable to climb out. Orders had each man give one of his two blankets to cover the horses and to "double-up" for sleep. That night, another eight horses died, giving the stop the name Dead Horse Camp. Unknown to the troop, they had passed within 5 km of the Bow-Belly confluence, thought to be the site of Fort Whoop-Up.

The next day, Inspector James Walsh left for the previous camp to explore the area. His party lost their way but, guided by two rockets fired and a lantern attached to the top of a flag pole as a camp beacon, they returned to the campsite that night. Walsh had important news.

The search had located the sought-after confluence of the Bow-Belly rivers. However, three abandoned, roofless shanties that were found there, occupied not by the whiskey traders but by skunks, obviously was not Fort Whoop-Up. Commissioner French reflected on the disappointing news:

> … so we were at last at our journey's end, the Bow and Belly Rivers, where there was supposed to be such luxuriant pasturage … a perfect garden of Eden, climate milder than Toronto, etc … instead for seventy miles in every direction the land is little better than a desert, not a tree to be seen anywhere, ground parched and poor, and wherever there was a little swamp it was destroyed by buffalo.[75]

One recruit, who disliked French, noted that the Commissioner "who can fine any individual without the slightest change of countenance or features," was beginning to look downhearted.[76] There was a sense of urgency. The animals were exhausted and the supplies dwindling. The candles were giving out. Constable Finlayson's diary described the despair: "We are lost on the prairie. No one knows where we are … horses and oxen dying fast, provisions getting scarce, things look very dark."[77]

French knew that on September 20, one year earlier, a foot of snow had blanketed this land. If a night of cold rain killed eight horses, what would be the effect of a major snow storm on the animals? And what would the column have for fuel if snow covered the land, hiding the buffalo chips? French's diary entry for September 10 expressed his growing concerns: "I began to feel very much alarmed for the safety of the Force."[78]

That morning had been difficult. The horses had to be driven 5 km for water and "B" Troop, angered that they had no supper the previous day, refused to leave camp until they had breakfast. Only 10 km was covered that day. The night was cold with rain.

Everyone was glum and low-spirited. Breakfast had consisted only of buffalo meat. One man approached the Commissioner and demanded his immediate discharge, declaring, "My primary object in joining this Force was to fight the good fight for Queen and country; but the only battles I have engaged in so far have been against hunger, thirst, cold and—yes, Cooties."[79] French refused this entreaty and instructed Dr. Kittson to evaluate the man's mental state. The opinion of the troop judged their irate comrade insane and that he should be put in irons.

Officer John McIllree expressed the gloomy prospects of the current conditions in his diary:

> The country is a barren waste ... the horses are getting weaker every day from want of enough food, and a good many of them are worthless for work. The buffalo chips are getting soaked and as there is no wood it is hard to keep up a fire. All together our prospects are not very bright. Winter is fast approaching and we have nothing but our summer clothing with us.[80]

A letter from one recruit was printed in the *New York Times* under the heading, "The Mounted Police Expedition, and what has become of it?" The Mountie wrote:

> We are now burning buffalo chips for fuel. Starvation stares us in the face, and a cold, relentless fall before us. If we go to Fort Benton, eighty-four miles distant, we must walk there, jaded as we are, and then discard our arms and enter into an American fort for protection for the winter. A sorry spectacle. The horses on the wagons are dropping dead every day, and the poor brutes look more like hat-racks than horses.[81]

On September 11, the column moved up the Belly River 30 km until a ford was found. Two reconnaissance parties were sent out from this point. Sub-Inspector Vernon Welch took two scouts westward along the river valley to find the Whoop-Up Trail. A second troop under Sub-Inspector Denny and three Métis scouts was directed to move upriver along the Bow River. Later that day, French held a council with the officers. It was decided to turn the column south to regroup in the Sweet Grass Hills.

The Sweet Grass Hills lie in American territory, 3 to 6 km south of the International border. Three prominent peaks (The Trois Buttes) rising to 2,100 m (7,000 ft.) are visible far out across the plains. In his report, Commissioner French wrote that the column had sighted the prominent uprisings when near the confluence of the Bow-Belly (Oldman) rivers, a remarkable 105 km to the north. Available water and abundant grass were known to be at the site.

For two days, the column waited for information from the reconnaissance missions. The first day was spent in camp. The men fished in the Belly River and shot numerous jackrabbits. A short move was made the second day so the horses and oxen could graze.

Welch's party returned on September 13. They had ridden 50 km west without finding any signs of whiskey traders or the Whoop-Up Trail. Welch reported that there was hardly a blade of grass remaining and the massive buffalo herds were migrating south.

On September 14, Commissioner French ordered Inspector J. Walsh to take seventy men, fifty-seven horses and twenty-five days of supplies to Fort Edmonton where they would meet "A" Division, marching along the Carlton Trail. That day, the troop forded the river. French wrote in his diary: "A good many [animals] in camp look as if they have not much longer to live. Denny's party not in. I must leave this p.m., and strike south."[82] At 4 p.m., just as the main body started for the Western Butte, Denny's party was sighted, much to the relief of the Commissioner who was anxious for their safety.

Denny related a gripping story of their reconnaissance. In the afternoon, two Indians on foot were sighted but, as Denny approached, a line of fifty Indians, also on foot, suddenly appeared with pointed rifles. After his half-breed guides spoke in Cree to the warriors without success, Denny safely withdrew his detail as he thought the Indians appeared hesitant. It was only after persistent persuasion that Denny enticed his companions to continue north in a wide detour west of the earlier confrontation.[83] The men rode all night without finding a trail or habitation. They concluded that it would be impossible to get the horses across this dreadful country to Fort Edmonton. This information forced French's hand. A courier was sent after Walsh's troop with a counter order to return and follow the main column's trail to the West Butte. They were to collect any played-out horses and oxen abandoned along the trail.

The 80-km trip to the West Butte took five days. For the first three days, the only available water was in dirty mud holes that buffalo had trampled. Men could be seen lying spread-eagled, pressing their lips into the mud. There was only enough water for tea; the animals went without.

The column was a far cry from the proud departure from Dufferin ten weeks earlier. Tattered men shuffled along with their feet wrapped with gunny sacks or buffalo hide. Sub-Inspector John McIllree watched, "a man walking the whole of one cold rainy day with no stockings and an old pair of carpet slippers down at heel."[84] One man was seen leading seven or eight saddle horses so weak, they were tied together in a line. If one of the animals fell, sometimes the whole line would tumble—like a lot of bowling pins. Commissioner French candidly commented: "Line of march looked as if more of the men were dismounted than mounted."[85]

On every side, buffalo herds were migrating south. One Mountie wrote: "We were on a height and as far as the eye could see eastward there was a mass of buffalo, estimated at from eighty to one hundred thousand head, slowly drifting, their dark bodies showing in relief against the snow-covered ground."[86] The buffalo, in their pressing migration, took little notice of the men and carts.

The highlight of this five-day march was the first sighting of the legendary Rocky Mountains. For weeks, the men had strained their eyes westward, ever hoping to see the storied mountain range, but, on the second day, while the camp was still in darkness, unforeseen and spectacular the

Left Turn to the Sweet Grass Hills (Henri Julien)

"The line of march looked as if more of the men were dismounted than mounted."

– Commissioner French, *CR*, NWMP, 1874, 17
GA NA 361 – 22

sun illuminated the higher snow-covered peaks to the west. It was a sight that no one ever forgot. Maunsell recalled: "They looked unreal because we had seen nothing like this before."[87] He wrote in his diary:

> The whole scene was a marvelous panorama. Not only were the mountains visible to the west, but south of us rising out of the prairie stood the three buttes of the Sweet Grass Hills looking like giant sentinels guarding the unknown.[88]

One moment of amusement alleviated the dismal journey south. On the second day, the column reached a large body of water which the Métis drivers decided to name Commissioner's Lake. To celebrate the occasion, stones were heaped to make a crude cairn and a fourteen-round rifle salute fired, accompanied by shouts of "Hurray for le Colonel!" on each discharge.

The column reached Milk River on the fourth day, and camped in a dry coulee. Large nearby rock formations had Indian pictographs. Coal was found and used for fuel. The next day, September 19, the men camped in a hollow, appropriately named Dead Horse Valley (today Black Coulee), on the north side of the West Butte. It took little imagination to name this camp. Fifteen horses and four oxen had died on the five-day trip south. The troop under Walsh arrived on the second day of the camp. He reported passing nine dead horses on the trail. His mounts also had suffered trying conditions. Six of the fifty-seven horses taken north had died.

In the fifty-two days since leaving Roche Percée, probably one-sixth of the horses had died.[89] Commissioner French, in a letter in November, wrote that, between the Cypress Hills and Bow and Belly rivers, twelve of the hardy Red River oxen and about twenty-five of our horses died from the effects of hunger and cold.[90]

During the three-day stay, Veterinarian John Poett ministered to the weakened animals. A team of men would raise any prostrate animals. Those standing received medical treatment and extra oats and often recovered; the horses that fell usually died. Poett reported: "The debilitated state of the horses generally at this place was a sight that will not soon be forgotten."[91]

Dead Horse Valley (also called Death's Hollow) was a splendid camp, with buffalo chips, clear spring water, and excellent grass for the animals. Buffalo were grazing nearby. Coal was found and used for cooking. Also found were ten gallons of syrup and some sugar left by the Boundary Commission. This find, remembered Sub-Inspector Denny, "almost started a war."[92]

Some men marked their presence. Young Bagley wrote in his diary: "I and others carved our names in the sandstone walls of a cave."[93] Those men who climbed the West Butte, which reached a height of 2,150 m (6,980 ft.), had a magnificent view unfold of the surrounding plains. Two climbers were Sub-Inspector James Walker and Commissioner George Arthur French. At the summit, Walker asked French to estimate the number of buffalo in sight. Walker wrote: "After looking around for some time he said there were a million or more and I agreed with him."[94]

A contingency plan, should circumstances warrant, had the Sweet Grass Hills serve as an alternative winter base in place of Fort Whoop-Up and Fort Edmonton. Macleod and a scout rode out in search of a boundary marker. They found all Three Buttes were within American territory, ruling out any plans for winter quarters at the Western Butte.

The Force needed a rest. Young Constable Bagley (who turned sixteen at this camp) wrote:

> A glance around the camp revealed very little to remind us of the brilliant parade of the Force at Dufferin several months ago. See that sentry pacing back and forth in front of the Commissioner's quarters with gunny sacking around his feet, whiskers decorating his face, and his rags of clothing fluttering in the breeze?[95]

Bagley added that a visitor would mistake the tatterdemalion police mob for tough-looking armed bandits or outlaws.

There was good news when Constable Elliot Thornton stumbled into camp. He had become lost while hunting, left his weakened horse and, knowing the column's destination, started walking toward the buttes. After five days alone and without food he was, in Sub-Constable Grain's words, "next thing to a raving maniac. For several days he didn't even know his own name."[96]

A buffalo cow was killed for food. Her bawling calf caused a wild commotion, with Frank Spicer riding on its back and sawing the poor animal's throat, as it careened through the camp, scattering pots, pans, and kettles. Finally weakened from loss of blood, the calf died before the laughing and cheering onlookers.

On the hot afternoon of September 21, four Divisions marched out of the valley and back into Canada while Division "C" remained in camp. After an 8-km march, Divisions "B-F," led by Superintendent Winder, turned west and "D-E" east. In the moonlight, regretful farewells were waved. The men sensed that many of them would never meet again.

The following morning, Commissioner French, Assistant Commissioner James Macleod, and eight men left the Dead Horse Valley camp for Fort Benton to purchase supplies and to contact Ottawa by telegraph. They carried bags of letters from the men.

Dead Horse Valley (Henri Julien)

"If the people of Canada were to see us now, with bare feet, not one half clothed, half
starved, picking up fragments left by the American troops and hunting buffalo for meat
... I wonder, what would they say of Colonel French?"

– *NAC*, Jos Finlayson, MG 19, E 58
 GA NA 361 – 21

The detail rode the 135 km rapidly and, in spite of delays when forcing
their nervous horses through a buffalo herd estimated at 80,000 animals,
reached the Missouri River port at noon on September 24. Sub-Constable
Wilkins, who suffered from lung congestion, accompanied the troop. He
was discharged and left with acquaintances in Montana. He may have died.

As they neared Fort Benton, the troop met a trader who told French
that the Blackfoot had told him the police were coming from Bow River.
This news was surprising as not one Indian had been seen.

At Fort Benton, which Colonel Macleod described as a, "miserable hole,
nothing but two stores and a collection of whiskey shops," telegrams from
Ottawa were waiting.[97] Commissioner French was pleased at last to receive
some reliable information.

Most important, revised directions for the Force placed the NWMP
headquarters at Swan River (Livingstone), 160 km north of the earlier
proposed site at Fort Ellice. Commissioner French was to return east with
Divisions "D-E" to occupy this post; Assistant Commissioner Macleod
would continue with Divisions "B-C-F'" to Fort Whoop-Up. As planned,

Division "A" would establish a base at Fort Edmonton. On this day, "A" troop, which had left the main column at Roche Percée, was camped at Jackfish Creek, north of present-day Battleford, and still five weeks from its destination. French telegraphed information to Ottawa.

At Fort Benton, French learned that Fort Whoop-Up was located near the confluence of the St. Mary and Oldman rivers, near present-day Lethbridge. And, in what proved to be an astute move, the Commissioner hired Jerry Potts, a skilled plainsman, for a salary of $90 a month—three times that of a Sub-Constable. Potts (also called Ky-yo-kos, or Bear Child) began a legendary career with the Force that continued until his death twenty-two years later in 1896. Commissioner French also made enquiries about the Cypress Hills massacre. Ottawa planned to pursue this matter and a confidential agent was hired to collect information on the skirmish.

Fort Whoop-Up

Assistant Commissioner James F. Macleod now commanded the 150 men in "B-C-F" Divisions. This pleased most of the troop. One wrote: "Col. French is a perfect devil of an officer he will fine a man $20 for near nothing but we are all right know for he has gon back and we have Colonel McCloud for Commanding officer now & he is a fine man."[98]

A second man supported the choice of command: "Macleod was the favourite with us whereas the Comr was hated with a bitter hate."[99] On October 4, Colonel Macleod rejoined the column with Jerry Potts. That afternoon, the men were delighted to see that Potts was dressing a buffalo for the evening meal.

Constable Godfrey Steele updated his brother, Sam (who was with the Edmonton contingent), on his adventures to date:

> We have ben traveling for the last three months on the plains where there is nothing but buffalo & Indians this is a very poor country out here no grass no water for thirty of forty miles travel some days we are 40 miles from whoop up or smuggler's Fort … we have seen some of the smugglers and they are a very tough hard lot just what you read of them in novels … this is a great place for buffalo. You can see thousands of them here everyday.[100]

As they rode toward Fort Whoop-Up, the troop encountered a great herd of buffalo. It was a sight, recalled Sub-Constable William Grain, "that surprised and thrilled every one of us [and] created a never-ending argument as to the exact number in the herd."[101]

Jerry Potts warned against firing guns, as the noise might stampede the herd through the camp. The men were astonished that the buffalo ignored their presence—this is, until an old bull charged into the cook wagon, causing thousands of nearby frightened buffalo to stampede dangerously near. Later that day, migrating buffalo would check the troop's movement for two hours.

They met and searched several traders for alcohol. One enterprising trader, John Glenn, caught up to the column. He knew that the men were a ready market for canned fruit, sugar, and so on, and his wagon load was quickly emptied—even at prices of $20 for a sack of flour, $12 for a keg of syrup. "There's going to be a blow out tonight," anticipated one Mountie.[102]

The troop reached Fort Whoop-Up on October 8. It was, the men recalled, the first building sighted since they left Grant's cabin on the second day out from Dufferin. After ninety-three days, the NWMP had finally reached their destination. Would there be a skirmish tomorrow?

At daybreak the men readied the two 9-pr. guns and two brass mortars. One hundred men prepared for a skirmish; the remaining fifty men were assigned to guard the carts and horses in the camp. Now was the historic moment. One recruit remembered: "As we advanced not a sound was to be heard, except the rattle of rattlesnakes and the noise of some hogs the whiskey traders kept to destroy the snakes. All was quiet. The only sign of life was a woman going from building to building."[103] All eyes focused on Colonel Macleod as he approached the fort with his revolver ready. Macleod rapped on the door of the main gate.

Other than several Indian women and David Akers, a Civil War veteran with a wooden leg, the fort was deserted. The whiskey traders were long gone. The Reverend John McDougall later learned that they had known the police were coming before the column had reached the Wood Mountain area, two months earlier. Akers opened the door and greeted Macleod cordially: "Walk in, General, and make yourself at home."[104]

The less than heroic "capture" of the famous whiskey post was entirely anti-climatic. One Mountie wrote: "We had no fighting, much to the disappointment of some warlike members of the Force."[105] In fact, the unkempt Akers invited Macleod for dinner.

Charles Schafft, a Montana gold prospector, in a letter to the *New North-West*, a newspaper at Deer Lodge, Montana Territory, described the arrival of the "Manitoba Mounted Police." That first evening, he watched Macleod lead a detail "up stairs and down stairs, peeped into all kinds of holes and crevices, but their search was of no avail."[106] As for the appearance of the police, Schafft was unimpressed:

The boys after their 4 months' march looked hearty in physique, but wear a most abominable uniform—a short red coat, leather britches trucked into boots, all supplemented by a white cover that looks no more like a head cover than a coal scuttle.[107]

Macleod offered to purchase the fort for $10,000. The counter offer of $25,000 was far above NWMP means. The police would build their own post.[108]

For the next three days, the column moved to the northwest. Buffalo were everywhere. At times, the advance guard had to stop to allow animals to pass. One Mountie wrote to a Quebec newspaper:

We travelled all day through buffalo, nothing could be seen as far as the eye could distinguish, but dense moving masses of these animals, and on ascending an elevation on the prairie we discerned the dark lines mingling with clouds afar off in the horizon. No estimate could possibly be formed of their numbers, but there were certain a million Buffalo browsing within a space of 10 square miles. [109]

Surgeon Barrie Nevitt remarked: "All that was necessary was to shoot to either side, and then cut up your buffalo meat."[110] Along their route, they came across the exposed body of an Indian. A detail buried the man.

On October 13, the column overlooked the Oldman River. They would build their post on Gallagher's Island. Surgeon Nevitt wrote to his fiancée in Ontario: "We have come to our journey's end at last ... a beautiful place in the valley of the rivers."[111]

"A" Division to Fort Edmonton

At 5:30 a.m. on August 1, two days after the main column left Roche Percée, "A" Division headed for Fort Edmonton, a distance of 1,500 km. Inspector William D. Jarvis was selected to lead the troop, having traveled this route the previous year. He had thirty-two Mounties under his command, twelve Métis drivers, fifty-five weakened horses, sixty-two oxen, one hundred head of cattle, seventy-nine carts and wagons, and the agricultural implements. Troop morale was low: after they had watched the main column depart, the men were, in Sergt.-Major Sam Steele's words, "a disconsolate lot."[112]

The first leg of the march took the troop 175 km northeast to Fort Ellice, the proposed NWMP headquarters. Travel was slow: the footsore cattle had to be goaded along the trail as they stopped to forage. The depleted column was so understaffed that the officers helped herd the cattle—"very amusing indeed," complained Sub-Inspector Sévère Gagnon.[113] Three days of heavy rain drenched the miserable men. After a Sioux band was spotted moving parallel to the column, the night guard was doubled and everyone slept with his carbine ready. On August 8, Gagnon recorded: "We again found our friends, the grasshoppers; it was just like a thick snow."[114]

Inspector William Jarvis halted the column four or five times each day for the animals to graze. This practice contrasted with Commissioner French's urgent pace—who, in one opinion, "compared himself to conquerors like Alexander and Caesar, and wanted to leave in the shade the marches of these illustrious men."[115] Though many difficulties continued—three horses died, several were abandoned, and, at one creek, five animals collapsed and were pulled out of the mud—the slow recovery of the stock was apparent.

It took twelve days to reach Fort Ellice, an important Hudson's Bay Company trading post located near the confluence of the Assiniboine and Qu'Appelle rivers. The fort, almost 100 m above the Assiniboine floodplain, was unimpressive: a wooden palisade that enclosed the trading buildings, several company homes, and about a dozen nearby Indian wigwams. By this date in mid-August, the grass was sparse and the livestock had to be grazed a distant 8 km from the post.

The Indians flocked to the police camp. This was the first meeting between Mounted Police and prairie Natives. Sub-Inspector Sévère Gagnon wrote: "We had the visit of many Indian women; some are almost pretty. All the girls have their cheeks heavily painted in red, and the men have their head painted the same color. The Indians are very jolly and appear to be sociable."[116] Sub-Constable D'Artigue appraised the Indians as so effeminate that it was hard to see them as warriors in the bloody Sioux uprising in Minnesota twelve years earlier. A Mountie grumbled: "During our stay at Fort Ellice [the Indians] did nothing but encumber our camp with their squaws and papooses, and devour the remains of our meals."[117]

During the six-day stopover, the troop undertook an inventory and redistribution of the supplies. Two Mounties trailed and returned with a half-breed deserter who had been hired as a cart driver. He was fined $10.

On August 18, "A" Division resumed the march to Fort Edmonton on the Carlton Trail. The thirty-five man column (two officers, twenty policemen, and thirteen half-breeds) had thirty horses, thirty cattle, sixty-five wagons and carts, sixty-nine oxen, and now four dogs. Several water barrels reflected the practical awareness of prairie travel. Left behind were the farm implements, weakened horses, and seventy head of cattle. It would take seventy-four days to reach their destination.

The Carlton Trail was the main route to the Northwest and, not unexpectedly, the police troop met many travelers: a number of Métis traders in the Touchwood Hills from whom Jarvis purchased pemmican; a Cree band heading south to hunt buffalo; two missionary parties (one, including Rev. George McDougall and his wife); and Surgeon John Kittson's brother on his way to Winnipeg.

On September 25, Father Joseph Lestanc, in his tattered clerical garb, also going to Edmonton, passed "A" troop. He had captivating news that, on August 21, twenty-five days earlier, he had met the main column as it neared the Cypress Hills. The priest reported (incorrectly) the death of a policeman and that the horses were in such poor condition that many of them would die.

Communication with the main column was unreliable. While on the route, Inspector Jarvis had received a short note from Colonel Macleod that it was impossible to send the remainder of "A" troop to join Jarvis but it was not until his arrival at Fort Edmonton that the Superintendent learned of the revised deployment of the Force.

The lack of bridges often made river crossings a major delay. This was obvious on the first day when the banks of the Qu'Appelle River quickly became a mud slide and extra teams were hitched to help the carts onward. Once across this waterway, it was another 430 km to reach Gabriel's Crossing on the South Saskatchewan River.

It took the column three weeks to cross this treeless plain with its large burnt areas and alkali sloughs. One day, the men marched 35 km without wood or water. In his official report, Superintendent Jarvis reported after Fort Ellice he found, "pasture and water was so bad I had great difficulty in procuring enough to keep life in the horses and oxen."[118] Upon reaching the Touchwood Hills, about half-way on this stage of their journey, a noticeable improvement in the vegetation was helpful.

At the South Saskatchewan River, Gabriel Dumont, the Métis leader in the resistance of 1885, operated a ferry known as "Gabriel's Crossing." The horses were swum across the river, but it took two days before all the carts reached the opposite bank. Once the column reassembled, it was a relatively short 35-km to Fort Carlton located on the south bank of the North Saskatchewan. The weather became windy and cold.

Fort Carlton had been a fur trade post for eighty years. The men noted all the signs were written in English and French. The Hudson's Bay factor, Lawrence Clarke, lodged the men in the fort and stabled the stock in barns. During the stay, Jarvis purchased eighty bushels of barley for the horses and resolved problems with the half-breed drivers who threatened to quit.

Throughout the journey, Constable D'Artigue contended that, "perfect harmony never ceased to prevail in our ranks, officers and men were equal to the situation and felt mutual dependence upon each other."[119] Each evening a half-breed fiddler, standing on a flat door, played the "Red River Jig" and other reels. Inspector William Jarvis fascinated listeners by relating his Kaffir war experiences. According to D'Artigue, Jarvis was admired: "We performed our duties not only for our country's sake, but to please our commander ... if he asked us to follow him, even to the North Pole, not one of us would have refused."[120]

The supply of food had been satisfactory and now hunting game added to the fare. On August 12, twelve prairie chickens were shot. Several days later everyone was astounded when one spectacular shot by Sub-Constable E.H. Carr killed eleven geese. At the Victoria Mission, a large supply of fish taken from Whitefish Lake was available.

After a seven-day stay, "A" Troop left Fort Carlton on September 18. Carts and supplies crossed the North Saskatchewan by barge, while cattle and horses were forced to swim the river. It took three days to cross.

From the standpoint of progress, "A" troop had completed about half the distance to Fort Edmonton. With 700 km remaining to travel, the awareness that winter would soon arrive increased the sense of urgency. As early as September 2, the men had noted an ice cover on the water buckets.

In contrast to the first part of the trip, water was readily available. In some sections of the trail, heavy rains that summer made travel almost impassable and further weakened the already exhausted animals. At some points, the men were knee-deep in mud and had to unload and drag the wagons by hand. Once on firm ground, the supplies were then reloaded.

Each morning, some animals had difficulty rising; others fell as they moved along the trail and were dragged out of the mud with ropes or wooden poles thrust under the bellies to hoist them erect. Sam Steele recalled lifting the horses to their feet forty times a day: "We were up every night lifting horses and keeping them up and endeavoring to keep life in them."[121] On one day, Steele and Sub-Constable Carr lifted one horse out of the water twelve times. When an ox fractured its shoulder, it was shot and butchered. Gagnon's diary vividly relates the tragic end of some animals:

> No. 84, a grey horse left on the trail yesterday, was found in a state of insensibility and was shot through the head; horse No. 66 "C" Troop breaks its neck in the wheels of a wagon; left horse No. 297 at the foot of a hill near river; the morning we left No. 129, (a mare) dying at the camp.[122]

Debilitated horses and oxen were dying every day. Inspector William Jarvis commented that, had they "been my own property, I should have killed them as they were mere skeletons."[123]

Two months after leaving Fort Ellice, the column reached Victoria (now Pakan), a small Methodist Mission settlement founded by the Reverend George McDougall eleven years earlier. Here they enjoyed a two-day stopover. Nearby Cree Indians visited to "wonder at" the red-coated police. The police, in turn, must have been in awe of a Native visitor named "Sky-Blue-Horn-Sitting-Down-Turning-Round-On-A-Chair."

Superintendent Jarvis arranged to leave all the livestock at the mission for a cost of $15 a head for oxen, $10 for cows, and $5 for calves. Eleven feeble oxen and two wagons were left behind.

It was now October 21, and Fort Edmonton remained a distant 150 km. To expedite the final leg of the march, Sub-Inspector Gagnon took an advance party of six men to repair small bridges and build some corduroy (wooden) roads across swampy areas. This entailed cutting large numbers of trees, stripping their branches and placing the logs on the trail to facilitate their travel. One log-road section was 100 m in length. Jarvis estimated that, in total, the corduroyed roads were over 3 km in length.

Even with this preparation, the final stage of the march proved difficult. Some waterways could not be bridged and ice now coated the ponds. Flood waters made Sturgeon Creek, 30 km east of Fort Edmonton, impassable and forced a trying 3-km detour upstream in search of a ford. And, with the fort in sight, the animals were played out. A marquee was pitched as a shelter for the night. Steele remained in charge of the camp while the two senior officers, Jarvis and Gagnon, rode the final 6 km to Fort Edmonton where Richard Hardisty, the Hudson's Bay factor, welcomed them.

It had taken eighty-eight days (sixty of which were traveling) for "A" Division to cover the 1,500 km (900 miles) from Roche Percée to Fort Edmonton. In Sub-Inspector Sévère Gagnon's diary, he recorded: "Sunday November 1 – At last everyone has reached its destination ... we left Carlton with ten wagons drawn by oxen and arrived with four only, the rest having perished on the way."[124] Sub-Constable Jean D'Artigue watched four comrades unceremoniously entering the post with "each man holding his horse with both hands, one at the head and another at the shoulders, to keep the poor skeletons on their legs. And in this manner we entered the gates of Fort Edmonton."[125]

The Division had undergone a difficult march. At least, Sub-Constable Edward Carr thought so. He wrote: "I thought I'd have an easy ride to the Rockies, with a fine horse carrying me; instead I had a tough walk to Edmonton with me carrying the horse."[126]

Divisions "D-E" return to Dufferin

While Commissioner French visited Fort Benton, Divisions "D-E" had left the West Butte and set up camp 110 km eastward to Wild Horse Lake. "It makes us happy," wrote one recruit, "to see that we are retracing our steps. It is now two months since we received any letters."[127] At the Milk River crossing, an arrow-pierced and scalped body of a half-breed was a stark reminder of this savage land.

The campsite had good water and abundant grass. Food was plentiful during the four-day stay. Sub-Inspector John McIllree recounted:

> The swamp is full of ducks and geese and the men shot a good many. There are generally two or three antelopes shot every day too. We also got a couple of buffalo, so we have plenty of fresh meat. The wolves are very plentiful and getting quite bold. They sit in a heap about a mile from camp and make a hideous noise. We have tried to shoot some but they are too cute. The grass here is very good and the horses are getting a good rest and perking up.[128]

The men bathed and applied juniper oil to rid themselves of lice. Sub-Constable Edward Maunsell wrote: "Ever since leaving Old Wives Lake these loathsome pests had dealt us misery. I could see little chance of getting rid of them unless I could get to some kind of civilization where I could buy new raiment, and enjoy the keen pleasure in making a bonfire of all my old clothing and bedding."[129]

French arrived at the camp on the evening of September 29. The ride from Fort Benton had been difficult with only eight men to handle the wagons and thirty-one horses. He brought corn, boots, clothing, tobacco, syrup, cabbage, butter, and potatoes. The men were delighted with new footwear and to each receive a half pound of potatoes. There was a blanket for every horse and an ample supply of oats. Sixteen horses had been purchased. And the Force was adapting to western conditions: French had brought water barrels for the horses. With French, for some reason, were a handful of tough-looking "Yankees" and insolent Blackfoot Indians. These companions soon left.

At Fort Benton, French had notified Ottawa: "Force on way back—state of affairs on Bow and Belly Rivers has been greatly exaggerated."[130] He now wrote to James Macleod. Among the ten points in the *Memorandum of Instructions to the Assistant Commissioner* (delivered by courier), French ordered Macleod to establish a post (named Fort Macleod) on the Belly River near Fort Whoop-Up; arrange supplies from the Fort Benton traders;

stamp out the whiskey trade with fines and the seizure of robes; forward lists of horses, stores, and equipment; number any horses purchased; provide a monthly muster roll of men and horses; and keep French informed of the state of the Force.

At 8 a.m. the next morning, after a muster of men and horses, the column departed for Cripple Camp where sick men had been left six weeks earlier. At a noon halt the following day, French shot a buffalo, the last to be killed on the return journey.

The two divisions rode eastward near the boundary line in pleasant Indian summer weather, covering 200 km in five days. Sub-Inspector Walker had been sent ahead to get supplies and horses from Cripple Camp and, on October 4, the column met Constable J. Sutherland with wagons carrying 5,000 lbs. (2,300 kg) of oats. The previous night, thirteen of the sixteen horses that Walker was bringing to the column had strayed. Fortunately, French's men found the herd just before a Sioux band was about to take the animals.

After crossing the Frenchman River (White Mud), the column had a powwow with an Indian band of twenty-nine lodges camped nearby. The gifts provided apparently encouraged the Indians to trail the column and camp nearby that night. The following day (October 6), the police rode east for 20 km before turning north in the direction of Cripple Camp.

At this point, Commissioner French left in a wagon east to Wood Mountain depot. He purchased (for $100) the depot, two corrals, and eight tons of hay from the Boundary Commission. Then he rode north to reach Cripple Camp on the evening of October 8. On his ride, by chance, French met a half-breed carrying a large package of important letters for him. The main party reached Cripple Camp the next morning.

There was only good news. All the sick men and weakened horses had recovered. The men had dug a well and the oats delivered from the Boundary Survey camp had revived the horses. Friends of Sub-Constable W.H. Onzman were overjoyed to find him fully recovered. He was so ill when they had left seventy days earlier that no one ever expected to see him alive. In fact, Bagley thought the former "cripples" were impudent: "Their shouted challenges to us to compete in foot races were received with sour looks by our rag-tag and bobtail mob."[131]

Two men were missing. Sub-Constables Thomas Mooney (an Imperial soldier for fourteen years) and John Richardson had been sent to recover an ox that was left on the trail. They had become so disoriented that they were riding west when scout Louis Léveille found them. Perhaps as a punishment, French assigned the two men to the Wood Mountain depot for the winter to care for six horses and an ox. Mooney recalled the post was in an excellent buffalo range and was a favorite campsite for Indians and Métis hunters.[132]

At 4 p.m. on the same day as their arrival, the column left Cripple Camp for Fort Qu'Appelle. Those men who had spent two months at the camp wrote their names on a white parchment which they attached to a wooden post as a memento of their stay.

The troop rode east through "a bed a cinders" left by the numerous prairie fires.[133] The men were covered with black dust and finding good water and grass was a problem. Fortunately, they carried an adequate supply of oats and hay. On October 10, camp was set up at Old Wives Lake, the site of their earlier unpleasant stay. Farther east countless buffalo bones littered Moose Jaw Creek.

In the late evening of October 15, the column reached Fort Qu'Appelle. The barking of dogs and sound of horse hooves on wooden sidewalks were "cheerful and homelike sounds ... of back in civilization again."[134] The Hudson's Bay Factor, William McLean, welcomed the troop with the luxury of a ham dinner. And there were eastern newspapers available. The men read with chagrin that, the expedition was a failure, with only four horses alive and the men on the verge of starvation—that is, those men who had not been killed by whiskey traders and Indians.

No, they were alive, but ashamed of their ragged appearance. The troop collected parts of suitable clothing so that one man would be able to make a presentable appearance at the company store to purchase flour and other supplies. French sent dispatches east with news of the Force. Four weak horses were left to winter at the post. In turn, French purchased two oxen and exchanged six horses.

After one day at Fort Qu'Appelle, the column crossed the Qu'Appelle River in the afternoon and set up camp. On October 17, the march resumed northeast for Fort Pelly, a Hudson Bay trading post located beside the Assiniboine River. One officer and four men left for Fort Ellice to report to Sub-Inspector Albert Shurtliff.

For five days, the troops passed through burnt countryside. Fires raged in every direction and dense smoke obscured the northern landscape. Daytime temperatures were pleasant, but, as the nights were cool, the men built roaring fires. French wrote: "Whole trees were chopped down and placed in the fires, as if to make up in some measure for the deficiency in fuel for the last thousand miles we marched."[135] And the morale was good. Surgeon John Kittson visited the camp fires each evening where he listened to touching songs and watched the weary men dance to some merry tune of a flute and the roll of a drum made out of a cheese box.

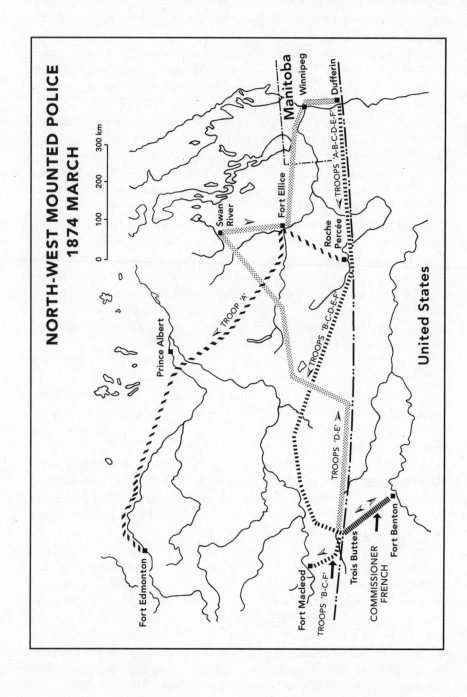

NORTH-WEST MOUNTED POLICE
1874 MARCH

0   100   200   300 km

Manitoba

United States

Dufferin
Winnipeg
Fort Ellice
Swan River
Prince Albert
Fort Edmonton
Roche Percée
Fort Macleod
Trois Buttes
Fort Benton

TROOPS 'A-B-C-D-E-F'
TROOP 'A'
TROOPS 'B-C-D-E-F'
TROOPS 'D-E'
TROOPS 'B-C-F'
COMMISSIONER FRENCH

On October 21, one day before Divisions "D–E" reached Fort Pelly, Comm. French rode ahead to inspect the assigned NWMP headquarters near the confluence of Snake Creek and Swan River. The post, called Swan River Barracks or Fort Livingstone (after the famous explorer), was selected for its location near the proposed telegraph and railway lines.

French was shocked. Rather than the substantial barracks expected, Fort Livingstone was an unfinished collection of half-built and poorly insulated buildings. A prairie fire had burnt to within eight paces of the barracks and destroyed half the stored hay. Only a quarter of the 400 tons of hay ordered from Fort Ellice had arrived.

The Government contractor, Hugh Sutherland, Superintendent of Public Works, had been paid the huge sum of $430,000 to prepare the base. Problems in transporting the machinery from distant Ontario for a shingle mill, sawmill, and boiler engine delayed construction. It was not until mid-July that the workforce of seventy-seven men with twenty carts left Winnipeg. It took twenty days to reach Swan River, meaning that work never began before mid-August. The eleven-hour work day and the worker's unsatisfactory living accommodations resulted in a brief strike. Some of the discontented men quit and returned to Winnipeg, a difficult 575-km walk. Clearly, as things stood, the Swan River barracks could not garrison both "D and E" Divisions.

French dispatched a messenger with orders for the column to halt at a place with good grass near Fort Pelly, 16 km south. Three senior officers, Surgeon Kittson, and Veterinary Surgeon Poett were to come to Swan River to review the situation. The meeting decided that Inspector Jacob Carvell, a Civil War Confederate campaigner, would stay at Swan River with six officers and thirty-two men from "E" Division. They would have thirty-six horses and the same number of cattle. Commissioner French would take "D" Division and the remainder of "E" troop to Fort Dufferin, likely to be near his family in Winnipeg.

On October 23, French returned to Fort Pelly. He selected the strongest horses and oxen for his command and left the next day with his troop for Fort Dufferin. The men left at Fort Pelly moved north to Swan River and set up a nearby "Harvest Camp" where they cut grass in the swamps for hay. In the next weeks, the increasingly cold weather made this task miserable as often they worked in ankle-deep cold water. Still, ninety tons of hay was cut for the winter ahead.

The immediate goal of French's troop was south to Fort Ellice. On the second day, they met teams going to Fort Pelly. Commissioner French purchased three oxen, carts, and harnesses for $256. The following day, rain and snow ended five weeks of Indian Summer. That evening, the horses were tied to the wagons and fed oats, hay, and hot bran before being blanketed for the night.

From Fort Ellice, the column moved east toward Winnipeg. Snow and winds made progress difficult. The Shoal Lake landscape impressed the police and the following year a small post was built beside the lake.

On November 1, "D" troop met a ten-man party under Paymaster Dalrymple Clark on its way to Swan River. One of the men was Constable William Parker, who was so critically ill on the '74 march that, at Roche Percée, he had been sent back to Dufferin. He had been unconscious for a week and was not expected to live. However, Parker was attended by both an American army doctor stationed at nearby Pembina and the wife of a Boundary Commission member. Slowly, he recovered. Constable Parker would serve in the NWMP for thirty-eight years and write an invaluable account of his career.

The physical appearance of "D" Division astonished the men in Paymaster Clark's command. William Parker wrote:

> Nearly every man was walking; horses were swaying and wobbling from side to side; an odd team of horses every once in a while fell down ... the men appeared rosy and in the best of health. But oh, what a sight! All were virtually in rags, no hats, most of them with no boots and several wearing their own makes of moccasins made from the rawhide of buffalo. Nearly all were growing beards.[136]

Clark's group joined the troops heading eastward. The evening camp was boisterous. French's troop had heard little of the outside world. The men made pancakes (using axle grease as a butter substitute). But best of all, Clark's troop had two bags of mail. That night the men sat around a roaring campfire and sang songs. The favourite songs were: "My Heart Still Bends to the Good Old Friends," "Tenting in the Old Camp Ground," and "'Tis Growing Very Dark, Mother."

Commissioner French, Paymaster Dalrymple Clark and a guide hurried ahead in a light buckboard to reach Winnipeg on November 4. The troup of sixty-two men with seventy horses arrived three days later. Lieutenant Governor Morris addressed troops with praise for the great march. The troops responded by presenting arms and giving three cheers. The *Manitoba Free Press* praised the column for a physique and military bearing that would hold its own with any other corps in the country and added that their tattered appearance after the hardships undergone was very satisfactory.[137]

After a short stay in Winnipeg, most of the column rode 90 km south to Dufferin, leaving the weak horses in Winnipeg with Veterinarian Surgeon John Poett. Three officers and twelve men were posted to Fort Garry. Also, several sick men stayed in Winnipeg under the care of Dr. Codd of the Manitoba Provisional Battalion. Sub-Constable Robert Tetu died; a autopsy linked his death to a blow or fall that injured his head. For several days before his death, Tetu had complained of headaches.

The Mounties were back in Dufferin where, 102 days earlier, they had set off on their great adventure across the vast northwest. In that time, they had ridden or walked 3,265 km (1,959 miles). Sub-Inspector James Walker had worn the soles off two pairs of his boots, discarded out a dozen pairs of moccasins, and his uniform had been replaced with whatever he could obtain along the way. He recalled, "We were a healthy but ragged lot on our arrival at Fort Dufferin."[138]

That winter the five officers and fifty-five men (with seventy-seven horses) occupied buildings belonging to the Boundary Commission. In the spring, on 20 May 1875, the men rode northwestward to rejoin their comrades at Swan River.

The North America Boundary Commission

Two Government-sanctioned bodies were also on the western plains in the summer of 1874. First, the North American Boundary Commission, a joint Canadian-American surveying expedition in its third year, completed its survey of the 49th Parallel from the Great Lakes to the Rocky Mountains. The men erected 388 boundary markers of iron, stone, timber, or sod. On the western plains, the surveyors usually built a mound of sod two metres in height, surrounded by a shallow circular ditch. These mounds, erected every 5 km along the boundary, left no question for Indians, the military, and travelers as to the country they were in.

In addition to determining an international boundary that disregarded natural geographic features, Boundary Commission scientists and engineers took meteorological readings, astronomical observations, and also made a topographical survey of the land 10 km north of the boundary line. Botanical and bird specimens were collected for the British Museum.

While there are no photographs documenting the '74 NWMP march, 234 photographs—(in one example, the scalped bodies of twenty-one dead Crow Indians)—illustrated both the journey and undertaking of the Boundary Commission. The boundary expedition was far better prepared for western conditions than the Mounted Police. Arrangements, for example, had been made with a Fort Benton contractor to deliver forage, oats,

North American Boundary Commission

"We were in advance of the Mounted Police and never lost a man."

– L.F. Hewgill, *PAM*, MG 1, B 23
    NAC C73304

cattle, and coal to Wood Mountain and depots spaced every 125 km farther west. The surveyors had five months of provisions, portable water barrels, a library wagon, and regular mail contact with Dufferin. The men read editions of the *Toronto Globe* one month after they were published.

In 1873, the Boundary Commission had completed the survey west to Wood (sometimes Woody) Mountain. From this base, 700 km west of Dufferin, the Canadian team, led by Captain Donald Roderick Cameron, moved west on June 22, two weeks before the NWMP began their march. The American delegation of 250 men, led by Commissioner Archibald Campbell, included two cavalry units and five companies of soldiers. A vote in Congress for survey appropriations delayed its start until late June. As a result, the American surveyors and military followed the Canadian contingent across the plains. In early August, the two contingents reunited at a camp in the Sweet Grass Hills. The concentration of 500 men was an impressive sight in the heart of Indian country.

On August 18, the surveyors located the boundary cairn built by Government surveyors working east from the Pacific Ocean in 1861. This finding in the eastern Rocky Mountains delineated the international border from the Great Lakes to the Pacific Ocean and completed the arduous, three-year survey.

When the NWMP camped at Dead Horse Valley at the base of the Western Butte, members of the North American Boundary Commission were returning east. The American surveyors traveled by boat down the Missouri, and the military component rode to the United States posts. The Canadian company retraced its route west and reached Dufferin on October 11, two days before the Mounted Police arrived at what would become Fort Macleod. The Canadian survey team had traveled 1,450 km (860 miles) in 43 days. All the horses were in good condition.

In light of the fanfare and praise the Mounted Police received for crossing the plains, some Boundary survey members felt their work was overlooked. L.F. Hewgill, in response to an article in *Scribner's Magazine* (reproduced in two issues of the *Regina Leader*) that praised the Mounted Police, wrote his account of the Boundary survey, noting that they "were in advance of the Mounted Police and never lost a man."[139] Also of interest, some Boundary men had even visited Fort Whoop-Up (a location that the NWMP was uncertain of), where they purchased brandied peaches and horses.

The second government party on the western plains that summer of 1874 was the 200-man Manitoba Militia. Led by Colonel Osborne Smith (the temporary acting NWMP Commissioner in 1873), this troop escorted Lieutenant Governor Alexander Morris from Winnipeg to Fort Qu'Appelle to sign Treaty Four. On their return to Winnipeg, the detail had covered a distance of 1,170 km (727 miles) in sixteen and a half days. They had crossed the same plains as the NWMP with no loss or injury to men and horses—and with little recognition. In fact, the Manitoba Militia traveled farther than Divisions "B-C-F" did on their famous trek to Fort Macleod.

The '74 March Reviewed

The 1874 march of the North-West Mounted Police garnered enormous popular interest. It did not matter that the NWMP never made one arrest nor even once encountered the terrible whiskey traders. Commissioner George A. French could officially report:

> Day after day on the march, night after night on picquet or guard, and working at high pressure during four months from daylight to dark … with little rest, not even on the day sacred to rest, the

Force ever pushed onward …with dogged determination, they carried through the service required of them, under difficulties which can only be appreciated by those who witnessed them … under such adverse circumstances all true Canadians may well be proud.[140]

The *Toronto Mail* extolled: "Canada may well be proud of its small band of soldiers who have carried out and enforced her laws to the base of the Rocky Mountains."[141] Frank Oliver, publisher of the *Edmonton Bulletin*, recounted: "No more widely impossible undertaking was ever staged than the establishment of Canadian authority and Canadian law throughout the western Prairies by a handful of mounted police."[142]

The expedition had plunged into a vast wilderness, carried its own supplies, traveled great distances, endured many hardships, and effectively established law and order. It was, in Superintendent Sam Steele's words, "the longest on record of a force carrying its supplies."[143] Constable F.W. Spicer bragged, "No new country in the world has there been less crime in the opening up of it."[144] A comrade wrote: "Considering the few men we had, the Indians being twenty to one, the traders quite numerous and as well armed, it is something to be proud to know that we have done all, and more, than was expected of us."[145] Frederick Bagley was very proud "that I was permitted to take part, however small, in the history-making march of the '74 Mounties."[146]

Six deaths, occurred on the '74 March. S.G. Marshall died in Dufferin of asthma shortly before the column left the camp. Three men died of typhoid fever. Sub-Constables A. McIntosh and William C. Brown had started with the column but were returned to Dufferin where they died; Sub-Constable Godfrey Parks died at Fort Macleod two weeks after the men reached that post. Sub-Constable Robert Tetu died after the return east in Winnipeg, possibly the result of a fall. Sub-Constable Wilkins, who had ridden with French to Fort Benton, may have died in Montana.

The often-asserted claim that the NWMP entered a yet-uncharted wilderness is false. That the NWMP relied on inaccurate maps overlooks the fact that the topography was precisely known. A remarkable map of the North West Territories, published by the Department of the Interior (dated 20 January 1875), only three months after the Mounties reached Fort Macleod, accurately pinpoints the landforms, lakes, and waterways of the region. The map even depicts the four NWMP posts (marked by a flag), Fort Hamilton (Whoop-Up), and correctly traces the route taken by the column west and the return of Divisions "D-E" east.[147]

Yes, there had been mistakes. It would have helped to have advance depots with supplies, water canteens for the men and water barrels, and perhaps, in some places, to advance in dual columns. Sub-Constable Edward Maunsell, who later became one of southern Alberta's first ranchers, wrote "Afterwards during my ranching days I often thought how completely ignorant the Colonel was in thinking that cattle could keep up with the troops."[148] Sub-Inspector Denny recalled that the men had only a vague idea of the journey before them and were ignorant of what they were to encounter. Second, he doubted that any expedition of importance had undertaken a journey without competent guides. And certainly the line of communication was poor. It was not until he reached Fort Benton in late September that Commissioner French received information by telegraph of the Government's revision of plans.

In the final analysis, the NWMP successfully established the government's presence and ended the whiskey trade. The memories of often adverse weather, hardships, lack of pay, unpredictable mail, lice, insects, shortage of food, and polluted water faded with time, and the men who took the journey remembered it as a wonderful experience in their youth. They were the '74 men—a bond that held them forever.

That summer, one hundred and forty years ago, these young men had observed wonderful sights: vast grasslands, enormous buffalo herds, native Indians in their primitive lifestyle, and the magnificent Rocky Mountains. On Cecil Denny's reconnoitering assignment, his party traveled up the Bow River where they witnessed "thousands of buffalo swimming the Bow, at this point a considerable stream, and very swift."[149] It was a sight that soon would never be seen again.

And the men were healthy for the journey. Surgeon John Kittson noted that, in spite of the hardships and sometimes shortage of food, "every man gained weight except one who was better for losing a little."[150] Upon his return to Montreal, (where he would raise seventeen children), Henri Julien evaluated his journey: "My trip has been worth a great deal to me in health, experience, and knowledge."[151]

At Fort Edmonton, Inspector William Jarvis was proud of "A" Division. He wrote: "I may state that looking back over our journey I wonder how we ever accomplished it with weak horses, little or no pasture, and for 500 miles with no grain, and the latter part of it over roads impassable until we made them."[152]

Crossing the Canadian plains was commonplace. That the small Fort Ellice detachment checked more than 1,000 carts for contraband whiskey the first winter and spring in the West attests to the extent of western travel.

William Metzler, NWMP in Frontier Dress

In 1874, 275 members of the NWMP marched west to establish a government presence. They endured many hardships on this journey. Their compensation was the adventure, amazing sights never before experienced, and an incredible bond they forged being one of the '74 "Originals."

– GA NA 2252 – 2

If Inspector Jarvis expected accolades for his achievement from the Reverend John McDougall, they were not forthcoming. In response, the minister countered that, each spring, a French half-breed near Edmonton loaded his carts with furs and with his family crossed the plains to Fort Garry. He returned to Edmonton to put up hay and prepare his winter quarters. He then moved several hundred kilometres south to the plains to run buffalo and make pemmican. McDougall summed up: "And still, it is not yet winter; and thus this native has traveled about three times the distance you and your party did, Colonel; and they had no government behind them, and what they have done is a common occurrence in this Western country."[153]

And, most telling, the following summer in 1875, Inspector Jarvis, while supervising the construction of Fort Saskatchewan, must have been thrilled at the sight of two young adventurers approaching the post. They were none other than his two sons, aged thirteen and fourteen. All by themselves, the youths had set off from Fort Pelly with a gun, the supplies they could carry, and walked and crossed rivers on the same route as their father and "A" Division on the celebrated western march.[154]

NOTES

1. *MFP*, 19 September 1883. Constable Frank W. Spicer wrote, *SAB* R – E 3291 Accession No. 21, "well the men of '74 went through much together and today when a '74 man meets another there is the grip of the hand, a look in the eye, which each gives to the other that means more than ordinary friends have met. They meet like men who have been tried and found not wanting."

2. D'Artigue, *Six Years in the Canadian North-West*, 40.

3. J.F.C., "The First March of the Mounties," 384–85.

4. *RC*, NWMP, 1874, 10.

5. Henri Julien, "Expedition to the North-West," 8–26. The Mounted Police provided Julien with transportation, a horse, rations and clothing. See George F.G. Stanley, "The Man Who Sketched the Great March," *Men in Scarlet*, Hugh A. Dempsey, ed., (Calgary: Historical Society of Alberta), 27–49.

6. *NAC*, Jas. Finlayson Diary, MG 29 E 58.

7. D'Artigue, *Six Years in the Canadian North-West*, 41. D'Artigue added: "We did not expect that French would dare do this, as the officer (Richer) was well known to be backed by men of high standing in the Government." The outcome of the incident is unclear. In three days French had dismissed two Inspectors.

8. *GA*, Joseph Carscadden, M 6608.

9. *NAC*, V 6, Defaulters List f. 305–75. Elliot's fines in 1874 included: $5 at Roche Percée for neglect of duty; 26 October 1874: fine $5 for neglect of duty on piquet; 25 December 1874: making a false report to Inspector Jarvis; 26 December 1874: fine $2 and costs for carelessly destroying a tin pail. In all cases, a police officer provided the evidence.

10. Maunsell, "With the North West Mounted Police Force from 1874 to 1877," 52. This person, with the same surname, may have been a relative of Richer.

11. D'Artigue, *Six Years in the Canadian North-West*, 13. Also Bagley, "The '74 Mounties," No. 4, 27.

12. Dempsey, ed., *William Parker: Mounted Policeman*, 9.

13. Bagley, "The '74 Mounties," No. 4, 26.

14. Maunsell, "The Great Trek of '74," 11.

15. The column had only six shotguns—one for each Division.

16. D'Artigue, *Six Years in the Canadian North-West*, 45. Often, one ox would pull three linked carts.

17. Bagley, "The '74 Mounties," No. 4, 26.

18. J.B. Mitchell, "Sir S.B. Steele, Major-General," *SG*, First Annual, 25.

19. *GA*, James Macleod, M 776.

20. *GA*, John McIllree, AB McIllree #1.

21. *NAC*, Jas. Finlayson, MG 29, E 58.

22. *GA*, John McIllree, AB McIllree #1.

23. D'Artigue, *Six Years in the Canadian North-West*, 50. Also Bagley, "The '74 Mounties," No. 3, 41; and French in *RC*, NWMP, 1874, 36.

24. In May 1878, Pierre Lucas made false accusations against Constable S.M. Hall and the food stores. Lucus was fined $27.50 and dismissed from the Force.

25. Julien, "Expedition to the North-West," 14.

26. *A Chronicle of the Canadian West*, Appendix IV, Report of Surgeon John Kittson, 27.

27. Julien, "Expedition to the North-West," 10–11.

28. Ibid.

29. *GA*, John McIllree, AB McIllree #1.

30. *NAC*, Jas. Finlayson, MG 29, E 58.

31. *GA*, Joseph Carscadden, M 6608.

32. *NAC*, Jas. Finlayson, MG 29, E 58.

33. *GA*, John McIllree, AB McIllree #1.

34. *GA*, Sévère Gagnon, M 729.

35. J.F.C., "The First March of the North West Mounted Police," 383.

36. For the legend, see Julien, "Expedition to the North-West," 15. Bagley, "The '74 Mounties," No. 4, 27.

37. D'Artigue, *Six Years in the North-West*, 50.

38. *SAB*, Frank Spicer, R-E 3291 accession No. 21.

39. *RC*, NWMP, 1874, 37. Membership of the first 150 men accepted was: 101 – Church of England, 29 – Roman Catholic, 25 – Presbyterian, 5 – Other. The 1881 Census at Wood Mountain gives: 49 – Church of England, 13 – Roman Catholic, 9 – Presbyterian, 4 – Methodist.

40. For additional newspaper accounts see the *Ottawa Times*, 15 October 1874; the *Toronto Globe*, 24 October 1874, for a letter written from the Sweet Grass Hills, 20 September 1874. Also *Toronto Daily Mail*, 8 September 1874 and 26 February 1875.

41. *RC*, NWMP, 1874, 38.

42. *GA*, John McIllree, AB McIllree #1.

43. Nevitt, *Frontier Life in the Mounted Police*, 7.

44. Julien, "Expedition to the North-West," 14.

45. Grain, "Pioneers of a Glorious Future," 66. Old Wives Lake was also called Johnson's Lake.

46. Ibid.

47. *GA*, John McIllree, AB McIllree # 1.

48. Maunsell, "Maunsell"s Story," 28.

49. *GA*, John McIllree, AB McIllree #1.

50. Julien, "Expedition to the North-West," 21.

51. Ibid.

52. Bagley, "The '74 Mounties," No. 5, 36.

53. Maunsell, "With the North West Mounted Police from 1874 to 1877," 54.

54. Julien, "Expedition to the North-West," 22.

55. *GA*, John McIllree, AB McIllree #1. See also Chapter 13.

56. Denny, *Riders of the Plains*, 35.

57. *GA*, John McIllree, AB McIllree #1.

58. *RC*, NWMP, 1874, 69.

59. Maunsell, *SG*, "With the North West Mounted Police from 1874 to 1877," 54.

60. Bagley, "The '74 Mounties," No. 3, 41.

61. *RC*, NWMP, 1874, 41.

62. Ibid., 46.

63. *GA*, Elenor Luxton, M 4561. Also *CH*, 25 April 1957. Gabe Léveille recalled that as the brigade moved north from Fort Benton the buffalo were so thick that one boy rode ahead of the carts to clear the trail and a second youth rode at the rear to keep the buffalo from closing around.

64. *RC*, NWMP, 1874, 22.

65. *NAC*, Jas. Finlayson, MG 29 E 58.

66. *RC*, NWMP, 1874, 13.

67. Maunsell, "Maunsell's Story," 28.

68. Julien, "Expedition to the North-West," 24.

69. Ibid.

70. Denny, *The Law Marches West*, 32.

71. Maunsell, "Maunsell's Story," 29.

72. Ibid.

73. Maunsell, "The Great Trek of '74," 29.

74. *NAC*, Jas. Finlayson, MG 19, E 58.

75. *RC*, NWMP, 1874, 15.

76. *GA*, Joseph Carscadden, M 6608.

77. *NAC*, Jas. Finlayson, MG 19, E 58.

78. *RC*, NWMP, 1874, 46.

79. Bagley, "The '74 Mounties," 24. Bagley added that the man recovered from his temporary insanity and served the Force well for many years.

80. *GA*, John McIllree, AB McIllree #1.

81. *TDM*, 24 October 1874

82. *RC*, NWMP, 1874, 48.

83. Denny later learned from a whiskey trader the war party was an Assiniboine band that had attacked white traders about 150 km north, killed one man and stole all the horses and supplies. In turn, a Blackfoot war party had attacked the Assiniboines and taken the horses which explained why the Assiniboine were on foot.

84. *GA*, AB McIllree #1.

85. *RC*, NWMP, 1874, 17.

86. Maunsell, "The Great Trek of '74," 7.

87. Ibid.

88. Maunsell, "Maunsell's Story," 30.

89. There is no official count of the number of horses that died. Julien said that eighteen horses died between September 9 and 17.

90. J.F.C., "The First March of the North West Mounted Police," 384.

91. *RC*, NWMP, 1874, 73.

92. Denny, *The Law Marches West*, 37.

93. *GA*, Frederick Bagley, M 43.

94. James Walker, "Police Experiences," 33.

95. Bagley, "The '74 Mounties," No. 6, 25.

96. Grain, "Pioneers of a Glorious Future," 70. Large fires, rockets, and search parties had been used to locate Thornton. He may have been fined $150 for the loss of his horse. Fifty-four years later, at age 78, Thornton sought compensation, claiming that his legs were never the same after the long walk. He was informed that, since he had deserted the NWMP, he was ineligible for any benefits.
NAC, Elliot Thornton, f. o.s. 392.

97. *GA*, James Macleod, M 776, 14a.

98. *PAA*, G.M. Steele, 85.448/13.

99. *GA*, Joseph Carscadden, M 6608.

100. *PAA*, G.M. Steele, 85.448/13. The letter was written four days before the column reached Fort Macleod.

101. Grain, "Pioneers of a Glorious Future," 70.

102. *NAC*, Jos. Finlayson, MG 18, E 58.

103. Frederick Bagley, "The Capture of Fort Whoop-Up," *SG*, Twenty-third Annual, 67.

104. John McDougall, *On Western Trails in the Early Seventies*, 77. Also *FBR*, 9 January 1880.

105. *MFP*, 17 October 1877.

106. Hugh A. Dempsey, "A Letter from Fort Whoop-Up," *AHR*, IV, No. 4, 28.
J.W. Schultz, *My Life as an Indian* (Forest and Stream, 1935), 144.

107. Ibid., Schafft's letter (10 October 1874) also described Fort Whoop-Up, the unattractive country, and the Indians.

108. Information is not clear to whom Macleod made this offer. It may have been Akers; the owner of the post, Alfred Hamilton, apparently was not at Fort Whoop-Up.

109. *SN*, 14 January 1875.

110. Nevitt, *Frontier Life in the Mounted Police*, 18.

111. Ibid.

112. Steele, *Forty Years in Canada*, 67. Included in the thirty-two Mounted Police was the small Fort Ellice detachment.

113. *GA*, Diary of Sévère Gagnon, M 729.

114. Ibid.

115. D'Artigue, *Six Years in the Canadian North-West*, 42.

116. *GA*, Diary of Sévère Gagnon, M 729.

117. D'Artigue, *Six Years in the Canadian North-West*, 66.

118. *RC*, NWMP, 1874, 68.

119. D'Artigue, *Six Years in the Canadian North-West*, 68.

120. Ibid., 61.

121. *MHT*, 29 March 1910.

122. *GA*, Diary of Sévère Gagnon, M 729.

123. *RC*, NWMP, 1874, 68.

124. *GA*, Diary of Sévère Gagnon, M 729.

125. D'Artigue, *Six Years in the Canadian North-West*, 77.

126. Colin Thomson, *Swift Runner* (Calgary: Detselig, 1984), 35.

127. *GA*, Joseph Carscadden M 6608.

128. *GA*, John McIllree, AB McIllree # 1.

129. Maunsell, "With the North West Mounted Police Force from 1874 to 1877," 56.

130. *PAM*, Morris Papers, Telegram Book No. 2, 24 September 1874. B.J. Mayfield, "The Interlude: The North-West Mounted Police and the Blackfoot Peoples, 1874–1919." See William M. Baker, ed., *The Mounted Police and Prairie Society, 1873–1919*, University of Regina: Canadian Plains Research Centre, 1998.

131. Bagley, "The '74 Mounties," 19.

132. The following summer, the men went to Fort Walsh where Mooney was assigned to carry the mail to Winnipeg. On one trip, he froze his feet so badly that he was forced to leave the NWMP.

133. *GA*, Joseph Carscadden, M 6608.

134. *GA*, Frederick Bagley, M 43.

135. *RC*, NWMP, 1874, 18.

136. Dempsey, ed., *William Parker: Mounted Policeman*, 10.

137. *MFP*, 10 November 1874.

138. James Walker, "Police Experiences," *SG*, First Annual, 33.

139. *PAM*, L.F. Hewgill, MG 1, B23. *RL*, 28 December 1893 and 4 January 1894.

140. *RC*, NWMP, 1874, 27. In private, Commissioner French said: "I was not sorry when it was over."

141. *TM*, 5 April 1875.

142. Thomson, *Swift Runner*, 34.

143. Steele, *Forty Years in Canada*, 83.

144. *SAB*, Frank Spicer, R–E, 3291 accession No. 21.

145. *TM*, 5 April 1875.

146. Bagley, "The '74 Mounties," (August 1950), 27.

147. Map of the North West Territories, including the Province of Manitoba and Tracts of Country ceded in Treaties 1, 2, 3, 4. Issued by the Department of the Interior, Dominion Land Branch, J. Johnson, Chief Draftsman, J. Dennis, Surveyor General, 20 January 1875.

148. *CH*, 23 October 1923. In his report, French maintained that his own freighting saved $70,000.

149. Denny, "The Law Marches West," 36.

150. *RC*, NWMP, 1874, 24.

151. Julien, "Expedition to the North-West," 26.

152. *RC*, NWMP, 1874, 69.

153. John McDougall, *On Western Trails in the Early Seventies*, 223. In 1873, McDougall had traveled from Edmonton to Fort Garry in fourteen days. Goodwin Marchand crossed the plains seven times in the summer of 1884 with freight carts. His largest brigade included one hundred and fifty carts. *SH*, 4 October 1884.

154. *NAC*, William Jarvis, RG 18, v. 3436, f. 2. The boys, William and Arthur, as adults joined the NWMP.

4

PIONEERS OF A GLORIOUS FUTURE

NWMP Parade, Fort Macleod, 1875

"When I was seventeen years of age, I became uneasy for a broader life than I could find in the Ontario town I was raised. The spirit of adventure took hold of me for there were plenty of openings in those days with the Canadian Mounted Police opening up."

– Edward Barnett, *GA* M 3875
  PAA P.2434

SIX MONTHS AFTER THE NWMP ARRIVED at Fort Macleod, a Mountie contacted a Helena paper declaring, "the Northwest Mounted Police are the pioneers of a great and glorious future. Our duties are to suppress the whiskey trade or die in the attempt."[1] This assertion implied a fixed presence in this dangerous land. Defensive bases were paramount.

Building Fort Macleod

On 13 October 1874, the column reached Gallagher's Island, a crossing point on the Oldman River, west of the Willow Creek confluence with the river. The island, about 1,600 m in length and 800 m wide, was large enough for the buildings and a small horse pasture.

The 150-man detachment was on its own, outnumbered by the Native people in the area and without any possibility of reinforcements. At once construction began on the fort. The men were placed in squads with their assigned tasks. Logs were cut upriver and then floated downstream to the island. Workers constructed a palisade, about seventy paces on each side, by placing and tamping upright poles in a trench. All doors of the inner buildings opened inward to the square compound. The horse stables were built first, then men's barracks, officers' quarters, blacksmith's shop, guard room, storehouses, latrines, and hospital. Flat roofs of the buildings were made of split logs and, although covered by ten centimetres of dirt, they did not stop water from leaking in. "If it rained, especially at night," recalled William Parker, "many a sleeping man got a daub of mud in his face."[2]

In the middle of each room, a small coal-burning stove (with an attached chimney pipe) dispensed poorly circulating heat. Windows, doors, and stoves were purchased from Fort Benton traders. The floors were bare, pounded earth; one could see the trace of a buffalo trail crossing the floor of the officers' mess. Wooden plank floors and room partitions had to wait until the construction of a sawmill the following summer.

On the elevated prairie south of the river, a small community of houses and trading buildings also was under construction. The I.G. Baker Company offered Colonel Macleod the use of its store for his temporary headquarters. But other relationships with the trading companies were less helpful. The detachment bitterly resented the merchants taking advantage of the police shortages by charging excessive prices. A jar of jam, for example, cost $1. And many prices were noticeably raised—such as, large blankets increased in price from $12 to $20.

Everyone worked with enthusiasm on the urgent construction of a fort. Colonel Macleod could be seen with his partner Cecil Denny splitting logs—that is, until he replaced Denny who was breaking too many axe handles. A letter from an acting constable lauded Macleod's efforts: "The gentleman in charge here has done all in his power for the men. He has not only done his duty here as commander, but has worked with the men in building huts and shelter … he is a general favorite among the men under his command."[3] Work on the fort and buildings continued incessantly, even on Sunday.

Frigid weather with temperatures recorded as low as -35°F (-37°C) impeded construction. The clay used to fill the gaps in the log walls had to be heated in hot water to become pliable. It was necessary to dig a pit for the cooks to prepare the meals out of the bitter winds. There was a ready supply of buffalo meat, but the meals lacked variety and were poorly cooked. Most men disliked a cooking assignment. Constable William Grain recalled, "They would stick it for a day or two and then quit."[4]

Everyone was dirty. One letter complained, "Not a day was allowed for the purpose of washing clothes, the men being in a state of most degrading filth, and covered with vermin."[5] Surgeon Barrie Nevitt summed up the situation aptly: "This is not the earthly paradise it was represented to be— far from it ... It is a howling wilderness & it remains to be seen whether civilization can do anything to turn it into a better country and make the wilderness blossom as a rose."[6]

The cold weather and hard work took its toll. Constable Godfrey Parks died of typhoid fever on October 26, two weeks after the arrival of the column. He had gone outside his tent without a coat or hat and returned complaining of cramps. Within hours, he was dead. His death from natural causes, it was observed, was the first of a white man in this wild region. Parks was buried with military honours near the post.[7] One week later, twenty-six men, one-sixth of the troop, reported sick. Nevitt reasoned, "I wonder that more of the men are not sick, what with tramping around in the snow and slush in moccasins full of holes or boots without soles and sleeping in cold tents."[8]

Each night, a ten-man guard was posted. James McKernan described how the first guard was selected: "The small men always fell in on the left, and it so happened that this night the guard numbered from the left, and I, being the smallest, became No. 1, so that I had the honor of being the first to mount guard at old Fort Macleod."[9] The countersign (password) that night was "Sweet Home."

The want of storage facilities and the expensive cost of hay, priced at $50 a ton, compelled Colonel Macleod to winter many of the horses and oxen in Montana Territory. While he carried mud to plaster the stable, McKernan was ordered to headquarters. Knowing that Colonel Macleod was a stickler about dress, he replaced his fatigue covers with a full uniform. The Sub-Constable gives a first-hand account of their conversation:

> When I arrived at headquarters tent I found Colonel Macleod and other officers ... the Colonel said: "Hello, McKernan, come in. Do you feel like taking another trip of about 200 miles?"

"Yes sir," I replied, "if I am ordered to." "Very well, then," he said,
"I have decided to send all the horses I can spare, together with
the cattle we have here, south to Montana. Major Walsh will take
charge of the party going south and will make arrangements for
you there. After he has done this he will return, leaving you there
to look after the stock for the winter. So now go to the tailor's
tent and leave your measure for a buffalo coat and a pair of
moose skin pants."[10]

McKernan thus proudly claimed another "first"—that being the first of
his detachment to wear the acclaimed buffalo coat.

At the end of October, Inspector Walsh left for Montana Territory with
twelve men driving sixty-four horses and thirty oxen. On the fourth day,
the diary of James Finlayson portended what was in store for the animals:
"Crossed the Boundary Line today. Had some words with Captn. Walsh
because I would not wade the river to assist in getting a horse out but rode
across first. Lost four oxen. Three horses died in camp."[11] As they continued
south, the raw weather took its toll on the livestock. Animals stuck in the
snow in ravines were shot. By the time the detail reached the Sun River
pasture (30 km west of Great Falls), fifteen horses and almost all the cattle
had died. The men built a large corral to hold the horses at night and
hopefully prevent them from being stolen.

There was no respite from the arctic weather on the return to Fort
Macleod. The Walsh party was stormbound on the trail for ten days and
barely moved on another two days. On November 28, the men finally
reached the fort. One man wrote of the trip: "Home once more. This is
the worst trip I have been on yet. The wagons often sank to the axles in
hard snow and had to be dug out ... Lost 25 oxen on this trip."[12]

At Sun River, McKernan boarded with a settler. Twice each day, the
young Mountie rounded up the stock to check that none had wandered.
In the spring, Walsh and six men arrived to herd the animals back to Fort
Macleod. McKernan was assigned to purchase twenty-seven steers for
the NWMP and, alone, he drove this herd to Fort Macleod.

On November 20, the men working on Gallagher's Island had moved
from their tents into the rough barracks. Three weeks later, the rudimentary
fort was completed. It was a proud achievement. A letter written in the
following January praised their efforts:

When the inclemency of the weather is considered, the cutting
and hauling of logs (in the former of which many of the men

employed had never before swung an axe), the dimensions of the buildings … it will surely be admitted that all parties were worthy of the highest encomiums.[13]

A visitor at this time was John McDougall, the well-known western Methodist minister. He commented on the worn clothing and the difficult conditions but noted, "All hands were cheerful and hardy, and glad to have finally reached their objective point."[14] It was estimated that building the post had cost $3,205.[15] Surgeon Barrie Nevitt sent a sketch of the post to Commissioner French.

The post had been completed, but troop morale was sinking and the discontent growing. There had been no mail or pay. The unrest peaked in December when most men refused to turn out for fatigue call. Assistant Commissioner J. Macleod visited each barrack to discuss the problem. He apparently had success as they cheered him most heartily when he left.

Two men, William Knowles and Jack Dunbar, were fingered as the chief malcontents. Knowles complained that he worked every day, not had a free Sunday off or time to wash his clothes, and was owed $125 in back pay—which forced him to borrow money from the traders at five-per cent interest. These grievances do not seem unreasonable, but Commissioner Macleod still reduced him in rank. The Assistant Commissioner berated Dunbar, "in the plainest and strongest English that I am capable of."[16] Nevertheless, tensions and discontent continued to mount and neither the troops nor the non-commissioned officers were willing to quickly reconcile their differences. In March 1875, eighteen men deserted the post and left for Montana Territory.

Celebrating Success

The first Christmas at Fort Macleod was momentous. Only six months earlier, the men were camped at Dufferin and anticipating a great adventure. Since then, the troop had crossed the great Canadian plains and built a base in the West. It had been a difficult, but enriching experience. And now, far from their families and friends, it was a day to celebrate.

The police were eager to display their weaponry—to convince the Indians that these red-coated men had formidable, almost supernatural power. Colonel Macleod sent Jerry Potts to invite the nearby Indians to the post for the purpose of an artillery demonstration.

In the morning, Captain Thomas Jackson positioned a field piece before a large group of curious Indians. Sergeant Frank Fitzpatrick described the spectacular results:

Sergeant Spicer, Sergeant O'Connor and myself were to shoot three or four rounds each, and we tossed a penny to see who would have the first shot. Spicer won. Right across the valley stood a lone, dead tree, midway up the bank. The tree had a large trunk, and Spicer decided that it would be an excellent target for a common shell which would explode on contact—as, in the case of a miss, it would in any event raise an immense cloud of earth, and would carry the same mental effect with it. He aimed carefully and fired. It was one shot in a hundred. He had cut the fork branch, and raised an enormous amount of earth ... the strongest impression had been made, and we would not spoil it with a second shot.[17]

The shot stunned the Indians. They sent several men to confirm if what they had seen was true. They returned to affirm the unbelievable.

Later, at two o'clock, the main body of Indians arrived. The Mounties showed the effect of the earlier artillery shot which greatly impressed them. Everyone then entered the fort where the Indian visitors were fed biscuits (with molasses), rice, and coffee while Colonel Macleod met with the prominent leaders. He told them that stealing horses was forbidden and all offenders would be punished. Second, a regulation would prohibit firearms. This declaration alarmed the Indians considerably until it was explained that a firearm ban only applied to anyone against the government.

That evening, the police had their own dinner. The hall was blazoned with banners painted in vermilion on white cloth: "Law and Order is Peace and Prosperity"; "Our Absent Friends—God Bless 'em"; and, most prominent, "Pioneers of a Glorious Future."[18] And for the men who months earlier had survived on half rations, the meal was a feast: buffalo, venison, antelope, canned fruit, plum pudding, and tea. The I.G. Baker Trading Company even provided a turkey to somehow be shared amongst the 150 men. Sub-Constable John Stuttaford remembered this first Christmas dinner as the best ever.

At dinner, with no alcohol available (or present), Colonel James Macleod used a glass of cold water to toast "absent friends." He then lauded the detachment's achievements, but also reminded everyone of their precarious situation. It was obvious, too, that many men were dissatisfied with their spartan and isolated life: to date, they had not received mail or pay, the weather was extremely cold, and their clothing in tatters. Men could be seen doing "sentry go," with a blanket wrapped around their body for warmth and raw buffalo hide substituting for shoes. The Colonel's speech, however, proved effective in "winning back hearts of the refractory ones."[19] The Assistant Commissioner, observed one Sub-Constable, "was one of the boys that night, as he joined the holiday spirit."[20]

What should they name their post? While the column had camped in the Sweet Grass Hills, Macleod had suggested to French that the western post should be named after the Commissioner. French rejected this idea and proposed instead that the forts take the name of their builder. A vote by the men unanimously "officially" chose the name Fort Macleod.

The officers, who later ate separately, had a small jar of whiskey (a present from Fort Benton merchants) to drink to their absent friends. It was also a time to reflect. Surgeon Barrie Nevitt wrote that they "sat and smoked and talked of Christmases gone by, of friends and home."[21]

About eleven o'clock, the firing of the two 9-pr. M.L.R. guns signaled everyone to "B" Troop barracks for a concert and a dance. At midnight, the detachment went to "F" barracks for supper and a dessert of oysters, canned fruit, pie, plum and rice pudding. But the evening was not over. At 2 a.m., an interpreter went to the Indian camp to invite the "squaws" to lively dancing (along with songs by Skiff Thompson) that lasted until 4 a.m. It was a great time, even though Constable William Grain observed, "a dirt surface isn't exactly an ideal dancing floor."[22] Nevitt commented:

> I guarantee that such a Christmas had never been seen in the Nor'West. Everyone expected to have a gloomy sad time but the united efforts of men and officers managed to dispel the gloom, and if Christmas was not exactly merry, it was at all events pleasant.[23]

Four hundred kilometres to the north, the twenty-two policemen at Fort Edmonton likewise celebrated Christmas with fervour. Inspector William Jarvis organized a dinner dance to repay the area hospitality his troop had received. In an exacting undertaking, the policemen delivered invitations to every settlement and hunter's camp within 150 km of the post. The men voted to contribute one month's salary (which they had not received) to defray the evening's expenses. Game birds and stacks of buffalo meat were purchased for the dinner and, for dessert, Sub-Constable S. Tabor headed a squad that made plum puddings and mince pies.

The Edmonton community shared in the festivities. Richard Hardisty, the Hudson's Bay Factor, arranged a large storehouse (with a fireplace) for the dance and provided tables, chairs, and eating utensils for the dinner. Townspeople offered overnight accommodation to distant arrivals.

The celebrations began with supper, followed by a dance that lasted until morning. After breakfast, there was a church service and another meal served by Superintendent W. Jarvis and Sub-Inspector Sévère Gagnon. The Queen's health was toasted with tea and dancing resumed to lively music. The favourite dance tunes were: "The Red River Jig," "Lord John Macdonald's Reel" and "The Eight Hand Reel." The dancing continued until yet another meal concluded the Christmas festivities.

At the NWMP headquarters at Swan River, Christmas featured a "grand dinner" and a dance that lasted three days and nights, except for brief intervals for refreshments. The post invited Hudson's Bay employees from nearby Fort Pelly and every Métis family living within 80 km. For this occasion, the detested "rattlesnake pork" from Montana was replaced with food purchased at Fort Pelly. Pemmican was available and, for venturesome souls, there was some tough bear meat that needed buffalo tallow to soften before chewing.

Conspicuous on the dance floor were Métis "dandies" dressed in coats of the finest blue broadcloth with highly polished buttons down the front and a rainbow sash around the waist from which hung a beaded "fire bag" containing kinnikinick (tobacco), flints, and steel. Moccasins and leggings were lavishly decorated and head gear was a round cap trimmed with fur, the flat top embroidered blue broadcloth, and set so high on the head it had to be secured by broad, black ribbons tied under the chin. The long-haired dancers, bobbing through reels and jigs and the floor-thumping fiddlers were, in young Bagley's words, "a sight never to be forgotten."[24]

Two tragic deaths marred the Fort Macleod celebrations for the New Year. On December 31, Acting Constable Frank Baxter and Sub-Constable T.D. Wilson, posted at Fort Kipp, a small outpost occupying a former whiskey post, were caught in a blizzard while returning after sundown from Fort Macleod.[25]

In the morning, a Native youth reported seeing two Indian horses with police saddles. Guided by two Indians, a search party under Captain Ephrem Brisebois found Wilson crawling on his hands and knees in a coulee about 3 km from Fort Kipp. He was taken to the post, but the young Mountie soon died. Baxter was not found until the next day. His body was located about halfway between Fort Macleod and Fort Kipp, but 5 km from the trail. Nearby was a rubber bag with three quarts of whiskey.[26] This explained the purpose of the two men's 50 km round trip to Fort Macleod.

The bodies were taken to Fort Macleod for burial. However, the corpses, frozen into unwieldy positions, would not fit into a coffin and had to be placed in a zinc-lined water trough to thaw out. In the afternoon, they were buried in wooden coffins beside the grave of Constable G. Parks, who had died of typhoid fever two months earlier. It was, a letter to the *Ottawa Citizen* related, "a sorry sight to see the military funeral, with the boys filing out of the square, on a bitter cold day, bearing the remains of their late comrades."[27] One companion wrote: "Poor fellows! So far from home, and after having gone through so much, to die in the wilderness."[28]

Their deaths were also a warning: the two men had not worn proper winter clothing. One policeman recorded: "It was a bitter lesson, and taught us never to go any distance without overcoats in spite of the promise of fair weather."[29] Sub-Inspector Cecil Denny remembered that, "These three deaths cast a gloom over us all, and our first New Year in the West."[30]

The Whiskey Traders

Two weeks after the column reached the Oldman River site, Three Bulls, a Blackfoot (Siksika) chief, informed the police that he had traded two horses for whiskey from a Mexican-Negro trader, William Bond, who operated from a cabin at Pine Coulee. Colonel Macleod acted at once.[31] To conceal his plans, he directed a ten-man patrol under Sub-Inspector Leif Crozier, with the best horses, to meet Three Bulls and scout Jerry Potts on the north trail after dark.

On their route to Pine Coulee, the detail met whiskey traders whom they searched. Five men were arrested when two wagons were discovered to carry whiskey. The patrol escorted these prisoners with three Indian women, three wagons of buffalo hides, and alcohol to Fort Macleod where Colonel James Macleod fined Bond and Harry "Kamoose" Taylor $200 each and three others $50 each. In addition, the police confiscated the horses, two wagons, weapons, alcohol, and 116 buffalo robes. The alcohol was emptied into the river, "to the great astonishment and regret of a number of Indians present, a few of whom plunged into the river and skimming the surface with their hands drank greedily the then diluted spirits."[32] Police tailors used the confiscated robes to make winter gloves and buffalo coats for the detachment.

The next day, J. D. "Old Waxey" Weatherwax, a Benton trader, paid the fines for everyone, except Bond, who he said could stay in jail for all he cared. For the fine payment, the police accepted cash, 326 lbs. of bacon, 5 gallons of syrup, a pitchfork, axe handles, and 105 buffalo robes. Even though the police sold his horse and rifle, Bond was unable to pay his fine. Macleod planned to investigate the prisoner's background. There were suspicions that Bond had murdered a number of Indians and possibly a family in Chatham, Ontario.

Several weeks later, while going to the latrine, Bond bolted from his guard and escaped. Although the sentries, Constables C. Uniacke and R. Killaly, fired at the prisoner, Macleod found both men guilty of negligence and reduced them in rank. In the spring, Bond's body, with a bullet in the back, was found 50 km south of the fort.

Only eight weeks after the Mounted Police arrival at the Oldman post, an overconfident Colonel Macleod wrote French: "I am happy to report the complete stoppage of the whiskey trade throughout the whole of this section of the country."[33] The *Helena Daily Herald* also acknowledged the NWMP success: "We learn that whiskey traders are entirely expelled from British possessions ... consequently the Bloods and other Indians are in better circumstances than for years before."[34] For a short time, merchandise sales to the natives increased and there was a surprising shortage of several items. Major James Walsh commented while visiting Helena: "Heretofore the traders have regularly 'swapped' cheap whiskey for robes and horses,

Donald W. Davis, former Whiskey Trader

Donald W. Davis was the first elected Federal Member of Parliament from the North-West Territories. In an opponent's opinion, "it seems incredible. He is the worst robber and scoundrel in the N.W.—and that is a big country to choose from."

– GA Strange-Lotbinière Correspondence, M 692
GA NA 659 – 58

while this winter the tables are turned ... and the Indians are resupplying themselves with horses ... ammunition and necessary articles of grub and clothing."[35] The Indian prosperity would be short-lived. Within two years the disappearance of the buffalo brought the most terrible hardships.

The whiskey trade, in spite of Colonel Macleod's optimism, was still in place. In January 1875, the Reverend John McDougall at Morleyville reported that Indians had purchased whiskey from traders at Sheep Creek (present-day Okotoks). Colonel Macleod prepared to act. However, cold weather and the necessity of obtaining horses delayed the mission until February 2. An eighteen-day account, written by Sergeant W.D. Antrobus, details the patrol's experience.[36]

The task for Inspector Leif Crozier, in charge of a thirteen-man patrol, was to investigate two whiskey posts—one at Sheep Creek and a second near the Highwood-Bow River confluence. Arrest warrants were prepared for known whiskey traders. Each trooper carried frozen "rattlesnake" pork, tea, hardtack, bedding, and thirty rounds of ammunition. The journey lasted longer than planned and it was fortunate that a deer and an antelope were shot to augment the food supply.

On the first night, penetrating cold made sleep impossible and the men tramped in the snow all night to keep from freezing. Hardly anyone spoke. William Grain recalled: "Never have I experienced such an endless night. Every minute seemed like an hour as we watched the morning star rise, and listened to the crunching steps of our fellow travelers."[37] An added anxiety for men watching the hours pass was that no one had a watch. Most of the wristwatches had been sent for cleaning at Helena following the westward '74 March.

In spite of their misery, in the morning, overriding the advice of Scout Jerry Potts to return to Fort Macleod, the patrol chose to continue to a whiskey shack at Pine Coulee, a distance 90 km north of Fort Macleod. This meant another night huddled in sub-zero temperatures. Strong winds blew the one tent down and the frozen buffalo chips provided little heat. Sergeant Antrobus described their suffering: "Imagine two or three men lying in snow behind a bush, shivering like leaves, with the coldest of winds and snow blowing over them and you see our small party."[38] The next day, the drifted snow forced the men to make their own trail. Only 7 km from Pine Coulee, the horses played out, making the troop spend a third night in the open, but fortunately there was a ready supply of firewood.

At Pine Coulee the patrol occupied a deserted two-room cabin. Sergeant William Antrobus noted that the whiskey traders, using pine logs rather than cottonwood trees, had better living quarters than the police did at

Fort Macleod. Sub-Constables Bob Scott and William Grain used wood from a counter to build (without a single nail) a sleigh to help transport the supplies. After several days at Pine Coulee, the troop headed for High River.

The weather remained extremely cold and the men had to lead their horses through the deep, crusted snow. Even though the temperature was -40°C, the Highwood River was not frozen, forcing the troop to wade the waterway. The campsite chosen had abundant wood and that night a roaring fire was kept burning: Sub-Constable Grain remembered that one side of the body would be cold and the other side warm, so the men kept turning all night like meat on a spit.

It was decided to first target Dick Berry's post near the Bow-Highwood confluence. Although supplies were cached to expedite their ride, the trip proved difficult, with the men having to lead the horses through the deep snow. Meeting whiskey trader Edward L. Smith proved helpful. He informed the patrol that the Bow-Highwood whiskey traders knew of the NWMP mission and had abandoned the post. Either they or the Indians had burned down the fort. The patrol took Smith with them on their return to High River.

Neil Campbell's fort on the Sheep River (about 18 km north) remained the final objective. Here they arrested whiskey trader Smith. At Fort Macleod, he would be fined $300 and given a six-month prison sentence. His incarceration was later suspended for providing evidence against John Weatherwax and on the condition that he would leave the country for one year.

Inclement weather confined the troop to Campbell's fort for three days. During this time, the arrival of three men for whom the police had arrest warrants proved fortunate. They were arrested and two loads of buffalo robes seized. A visitor to the post was the weather-beaten Oblate priest, Constantine Scollen. The twelve-year veteran of the plains captivated the police with his knowledge and personality.

On February 19, the detail escorting the four prisoners left for Fort Macleod. The pleasant weather soon turned into a blinding blizzard and the party, traveling in two groups, lost contact. They spent the night at High River in separate camps but, in the morning, the troop reunited and continued south to stay at Pine Coulee that evening. On the third day of their return trip, the men were unwilling to spend another night on the cold open prairie and rode the final 90 km to Fort Macleod in nineteen hours. William Antrobus wrote in his diary: "We put the prisoners in the guard house, sent the horses to the herd, and after a good meal and a smoke, went to bed and had a comfortable night's rest."[39]

Inspector W.D. Antrobus, NWMP

"We would think a man mad in Eastern Canada who would start out to make a journey of 200 miles on horseback in the middle of winter."

– Dempsey, ed., *A Mountie's Diary, 1875,* 10
 GA NA 944 – 5

The wanted suspect at the Highwood-Bow fort was Dick Berry, a known whiskey trader. He avoided arrest, but his alleged American supplier, John Weatherwax, was later arrested on flimsy "manufactured evidence."[40] His payment of earlier fines for "Kamoose" Taylor and the drivers seemed suspicious. Second, the trading firm of Wetzel & Weatherwax had been under surveillance for some months. One Mountie explained, "We had our Yankee detectives shadowing them since last fall."[41]

On 17 February 1875, Weatherwax was convicted of whiskey trading and sentenced to six months in the guardhouse, fined $500, and had 711 buffalo robes confiscated. This detention, in one Montana newspaper's opinion, had, "showed how the rights of an American citizen are trampled underfoot, without the application of law or justice, in her Majesty's dominions."[42] A second Montana paper referred to the NWMP seizure of the furs as the "mounted grabbers of the spoil."[43] But what justice was there for Americans in Western Canada? The *Fort Benton Record* criticized:

"We did not expect that the conduct of the Queen's Regulators would be according to law; in fact we knew from experience that wherever the English flag floats, might is right."[44]

A furious Weatherwax threatened to make the wires to Washington "hum" over the treatment of Americans. In turn, a Mountie wrote to the *Helena Daily Herald*:

> Old J.D. [Weatherwax], the chief of all the smugglers and desperadoes of the great Northwest was locked up in jail, while the Union Jack floats triumphantly over his place in solitary confinement ... Weatherwax is all the time growling about illegal and arbitrary proceedings, and threatening to bring the matter before his Government. What do we care for his Government? They can't reverse our decision, and they can't send troops to this distant region.[45]

Upon his release, Weatherwax headed for Fort Benton, helpfully taking the police mail to post.

Who were these vile whiskey traders who accommodated the police mail delivery after serving a jail sentence? According to one policeman, they were, "coarse, unpolished and uneducated, they are insulting in their conversation and disgusting to our sight. They call us Hinglish, Red coats, Yahoots, Fish's Fools and more apt to tell us to go to h–l than to give a civil answer to a civil question."[46] A letter from a Mountie, published in the *Sherbrooke News*, agreed: "To see them daily lying round the trading posts, neither too well dressed nor over clean, and to listen to their conversation which abounds with incomprehensible slang particular to the western prairies, one cannot imagine a more reckless and desperate class of men."[47] An I.G. Baker employee called the whiskey traders, "a desperate set of men, many of them being escaped murderers ... no friendship exists between Indians and the traders. The former are an intelligent race and quite aware of the evils of the whisky trade."[48]

Other opinions revealed the whiskey traders in a more positive light. Inspector Cecil Denny wrote: "We found them a very decent lot of men in spite of all we heard against them."[49] And L.F. Hewgill, with the Boundary Commission, recalled, "these desperadoes were not half such bad fellows as they were painted."[50]

The imprisonment of Weatherwax effectively curtailed the whiskey traffic. A Montana paper credited the Mounties: "To the scarlet uniform belongs the fame of destroying the whisky traffic, or at least checking it beyond restoration."[51] The I.G. Baker trading company reported: "The Americans in Montana are surprised at the success of the Mounted Police."[52] The Blackfoot, in their calendar system, later recorded the year 1875 as *itsixowatorpilnapiorki*—when it was finished.[53]

In all, the whiskey trade in Western Canada was relatively brief—not more than six years—but its exploitation of the Aboriginal population had been devastating.

Once their trade declined and came under steady scrutiny, many of the whiskey traders turned to follow other pursuits. Some of the Americans chose to live in Canada. Harry "Kamoose (Squaw Thief)" Taylor operated the Macleod Hotel, which gained attention because of the outlandish regulations.[54] Donald W. Davis was the first elected Federal Member of Parliament from the North-West Territories.[55]

The Whoop-Up Trail

Fort Benton, Montana Territory, the terminal port of river navigation on the Missouri, was the supply and communication base for the southwest Canadian prairies. The unrefined settlement, which called itself "the Chicago of the Plains," attracted the tough and transient—many of whose antecedents, one Canadian visitor suggested, "are better not to trace."[56]

With eighty whiskey outlets in a town of 1,500 (as of 1881), lawlessness and gambling thrived. The Reverend John Maclean, bringing his bride from Eastern Canada to Fort Macleod, wrote: "Benton was a revelation. Early in the morning the main street was literally covered with playing cards, swept from gambling saloons after the night's debauch, where a new pack was used in every game, as a precaution against marking."[57] Methodist minister John McDougall recalled being pulled into a saloon by a friend. McDougall, an abstainer, asked for an apple to eat while his friend smoked and drank. The bartender refused. McDougall wrote: "My friend grabbed his revolver and told him to pass it down."[58] McDougall got his apple.

One-third of the upriver cargo that reached Fort Benton went north to Canada. The 400 km trail northwest to Fort Macleod was called the Whoop-Up Trail. Plodding bull trains, driven by bull-whackers notorious for their "Montana language" (which one minister described as, "a torrent of the fanciest expletives of startling originality into which neither reiteration nor plagiarism ever creeps"[59]), carried the goods.

Six to eight yoked pairs of oxen pulled three wagons hitched in tandem. The "outfits" traveled in bull trains or brigades of up to thirty wagons followed by a cart. A bull train was an expensive investment—costing as much as $25,000.

Travel was slow. On steep inclines, the teams had to be doubled, which delayed travel time even more. Each day had two spells (travel periods) broken by a mid-day stop to water, rest, and allow the animals to graze. A team moved 13 to 20 km each day, making the journey from Fort Benton to Fort Macleod take from three to four weeks. Mule (called "string") teams hauled lighter loads and, although much faster, were used less.

Traffic on the Whoop-Up Trail often was crowded. In 1882, for example, the *Macleod Gazette* noted that one hundred teams of all kinds were on the road between Fort Macleod and Benton. A bull team hauled a substantial volume of freight. One delivery brought 70,000 lbs. of oats to the Fort Calgary detachment. The teams delivered a variety of items. In May 1884, the I.G. Baker list of goods charged to the Fort Macleod post included:

coal, prunes, calico, lye, tobacco, sugar, tea, castor oil, saws, chisels, augers, matches, currants, crackers, bacon, beans, tacks, pepper, oysters, tapioca, shingle nails, tape line, screws, nails, door jack, door, cross cut saw, window sash, files, hatchet, wash board, corn meal, socks, canned tomatoes, borax, ribbon, oil, Florida water, boots, spikes, oats, and carpenter pencils.[60]

Fort Benton traders dominated the economy of the southwest Canadian plains for ten years. As the buffalo-hide trade declined, delivering coal from new mines at Coal Banks helped defray the cost of returning with empty wagons to Fort Benton. This coal was priced in 1880 at $5 a ton and, although transportation costs increased the price fourfold, it was still a cheaper and preferable fuel to the local area cottonwood trees.

Fort Benton banks and merchants profited substantially by supplying the NWMP. In both 1875 and 1876, I.G. Baker (paymaster for the Force) delivered goods exceeding $120,000 to the Mounted Police, almost one third of the police budget.[61] Perhaps as a measure of gratitude, I.G. Baker Company launched a small Missouri stern wheeler in 1878, its name incorrectly spelled *The Colonel McLeod*.[62]

Canadian trading and business interests resented American commercial inroads. Commissioner A.G. Irvine complained a "large amount of money has been expended, in return for which there is little or nothing to show, our money is merely aiding to build up the town of Benton, U.S.A."[63] Economics dictated the direction of trade. Fort Benton merchants would deliver goods to Fort Macleod ten cents a pound cheaper than items from Winnipeg whose overland delivery line to southern Alberta was 800 km farther. Most items coming through Fort Benton sold for one-half the price charged by the Hudson's Bay Company.

Bull team on the main street of Fort Macleod

The 400 km dirt road linking Fort Benton and Fort Macleod was called the Whoop-Up Trail.

– GA NA 3321 – 8

Bull-whacker camp, Benton-Macleod Trail

Bull-whackers were known for their "Montana language"—which one minister described as, "a torrent of the fanciest expletives of startling originality into which neither reiteration nor plagiarism ever creeps."

– *Fort Macleod Gazette*, 29 July 1882
    GA NA 17 – 1

The American influence in Whoop-Up country was immense. The currency of both countries circulated freely across the international border until 1881.[64] All mail and telegraph communication from southern Alberta went through Fort Benton. In 1883, a stagecoach linked Fort Macleod and Fort Benton by a six-day trip. Before July 1882 (when the *Macleod Gazette* was launched), two Montana newspapers had correspondents at Fort Walsh and Fort Macleod who reported events in the region. The *Fort Benton Record* even printed a digest of debates in the Canadian House of Commons.[65]

American residents in Fort Macleod boisterously celebrated American Independence Day and George Washington's Birthday. The year 1876 was especially significant, being the 100th centennial of the Grand Republic.

For Washington's celebration, several citizens rented a hall that they decorated with trimmings and pictures. The *Fort Benton Record* related that the men sang patriotic ballads and described the dress and jewelry of the eight females present. Readers were informed that "Ms. J-m Cr-mp" wore jewelry worth at least two dollars and a half (including custom duties) and that "Miss K-y-se" had on a black silk dress, sailor collar, and a black eye.[66] Constable Jack Clarke's diary in 1881 stated, "the American Citizens gave a grand Ball in Honer of George Washington in (?) hall on the 22nd. Most of the Police and Citizens were drunk."[67]

In August 1883, the Canadian Pacific Railway (C.P.R.) reached Calgary. Already, Fort Benton commercial interests had foreseen the future. One month earlier, the last large shipment north departed for Fort Macleod, leaving Fort Benton to return to its sleepy self. The local press reported, "not even a dog fight relieved the monotony."[68] The Whoop-Up Trail, soon overgrown, left faint markings of this once-important travel route.

The Difficult First Winter: 1874–75
Several minor uprisings and widespread unrest featured in the first winter the NWMP spent in the West. Many of the once-eager men became upset with the isolation, poor amenities, unreliable mail, and lack of pay. At Swan River, Frederick Bagley looked at his threadbare clothes with the comment, "the glory has departed."[69] His comrades were dismayed by the bland food, stark living conditions, and cold weather. Each day, four cords of wood were burned to heat the poorly constructed buildings. Constable Carscadden commented, "We have six stoves and a large log fire going all the time and yet many a blue face can be seen."[70] One officer wrote: "The men don't know how cold it is when they are out working. But when they go to bed they should know it is cold enough to freeze their ears, as was the case with Sub-Constable McCrum."[71]

The police livestock at Swan River suffered dreadfully from the lack of forage and the cold temperatures. At the end of March, 1875, of the sixty horses and eighty head of cattle, only twenty-three horses and nine cattle had survived the winter.

Several confrontational incidents worsened the unrest in Swan River. On 23 November 1874, the men refused Inspector Jacob Carvell's order to complete the stocktaking that night. It took Sergt.-Major J.B. Mitchell's intervention (offering extra rations and a holiday the next day) before the men agreed to finish the work.

The second showdown was more serious. In January, 1875, Inspector Carvell ordered a cook, Sub-Constable W. McCarthy, to feed four Indians. McCarthy provided one meal, but refused further food, protesting he had only enough bread for the detachment's breakfast. Nevertheless, McCarthy was fined $10 for his insubordination and arrested when he threatened to appeal to a higher authority.[72] In response to his questioning what law he was being held under, an officer told him it was none of his business.

After two corporals unsuccessfully appealed for McCarthy's release, a number of men staged an attack on the sentries at the guardhouse and seized the prisoner. A search failed to find McCarthy, and Inspector Carvell ordered a troop parade at which he berated the assembled men for their mutinous conduct. When McCarthy suddenly appeared, Carvell ordered suspected ringleaders Sam Orr and Bill Onzman be imprisoned with McCarthy.

In the morning, calling themselves prisoners, Acting-Sergeant G.W. Crawford and Sub-Constable (J.H. or W.H.) Smith refused to take charge of the guard tent. At a subsequent hearing, Carvell fined the men thirty days pay or a reduction in rank. And, in Bagley's words, "to add insult to injury he also ordered the release, without punishment, of the cook—the cause of all the trouble."[73] The difficulties at Swan River continued. In early March, a letter notified an Ottawa newspaper that a member of the Swan River detachment was coming to that city and, "please have a reporter interview him closely on the mismanagement from which the Force is suffering from a bungling government."[74]

Inspector Jacob Carvell, a former American Civil War officer, had apparently enough of the NWMP. That summer, he took leave to arrange the move of his family from Boulder, Colorado, to Swan River. While in Colorado, he sent a letter of resignation to Commissioner French.

The remainder of Divisions "D and E" stationed at Dufferin also underwent a difficult first winter. By March 15, twenty men had applied for a discharge. A.E.A. Lowes wrote Sub-Inspector James Walker on 24 February 1875:

I respectfully do hereby tender my resignation as a member of the North West Mounted Police Force ... when I enlisted I was not aware that my duties would be of such a heavy and disagreeable nature as has been required of me since I have been in this country, and do not consider myself capable of enduring the work to the end of my term.[75]

Commissioner French, who resided with his family in the comfort of Winnipeg, did not recommend any discharge applications. Sub-Constable Lowes completed his term and years later, in 1931, explaining that he was living in poverty, applied for a NWMP pension. Lowes was informed that three years of service did not entitle him to any benefits.

A petition by the troop to Sub-Inspector Walker, the base commander, complained that excessive manual work was assigned. In March 1875, Chief Constable A.H. Griesbach informed NWMP Headquarters that the men quartered in Dufferin were disgruntled. He explained:

They are desirous to learn skills of policing but instead called upon duties uncalled for and foreign to the Articles under which they engaged. Complain they care for 77 horses and attend, feed, and water 137 oxen. Above the barrack duties they obtain hay nineteen miles across a bleak prairie.[76]

Griesbach warned that the growing "mutinous" feelings of the overworked men could result in wholesale desertion or the refusal to carry out extra duties. Four months later, the relocation of the Dufferin detachment to Swan River ameliorated some of the discontent.

At the other end of the plains, at Fort Macleod, unrest was widespread. One letter described the scarcity of necessities: "I have just offered ten dollars for a piece of paper and an envelope, without success. A comrade has shared his stock with me at the last moment."[77] The ragtag troop had not been paid since leaving Dufferin in July 1874 and most men owed money. An acting constable expressed the growing discontent in a letter written on 8 March 1875: "It is the opinion among the men here that if they are not paid soon, there will be few of them left to guard the prisoners ... it is very discouraging to men who have been on a hard march all summer, that they should be treated with so much neglect."[78]

Eastern Canadians were aware of the trying conditions. The *Ottawa Daily Citizen*, under the headline "The Great Neglected," published a letter from a policeman stationed at Fort Macleod. The recruit complained that the column had arrived at Fort Macleod in rags and without boots or socks.

While they still lived in tents with snow covering the ground, a Yankee trader arrived and they were all "forced either to buy at ruinous prices or freeze to death."[79]

The discontent culminated the first week in March when a roll call at 9:30 p.m. discovered that eighteen men "had shifted their residence to Benton, United States."[80] The report noted that, although they would have to travel on foot more than 300 miles (500 km) across a cold and bleak prairie to reach the next settlement, "they preferred this to staying here to be badly treated and ill-used again."[81] The deserters were led by George Frazier, an old British soldier, who had served in the Crimean War with an English Fusilier regiment. The men, subsisting on raw buffalo meat, suffered badly as they plunged through the snow. Frazier would beat those who fell and force them to continue with the group.[82]

Superintendent Crozier led a police detail to overtake the deserters. On a hill called Belly Butte, the deserters entrenched themselves and defied the police. Crozier was uncertain whether his men would support the use of force and withdrew, leaving the deserters to continue south. This loss of eighteen men only burdened the workload of the remaining troops.

To rectify the deteriorating situation, Macleod rode to Helena to have Ottawa forward supplies and money to the detachment. He also contacted Commissioner G. French in Winnipeg. French informed Col. Bernard, Department of Justice (the government department administering the NWMP) that Macleod was in Helena and wanted instructions regarding supplies. The remainder of the message was in cipher and it read:"He reported great dissatisfaction for want of pay and clothing. Eighteen have deserted. If not paid many more would doubtless desert."[83]

Macleod encountered some of the deserters in Helena. He reinstated six men and purchased police rifles from others. One Sub-Constable, S. Perreault, was taken on again, completed his term with his conduct on the discharge form marked "good." Sub-Constable Wright had promised to return to Fort Macleod if given clothing. At Fort Shaw on his return, Wright changed his mind. American authorities turned him over to a Justice of the Peace who sentenced Wright to twenty days confinement.

In the depleted detachment at Fort Macleod, many men remained dissatisfied with their lot. Constable J.A. Thom wrote on April 28:

It is very questionable whether the duties of a mounted policeman ought to include erecting log shanties, chopping, building bridges, teaming and bull driving. It is pretty hard, too, that we are obliged to buy our own clothing, and many of us had to purchase blankets during the past winter.[84]

He added that if the Canadian government wanted to keep a police force in the North-West, better treatment, clothing, and food was essential. His warning was correct. On May 12, Elliot Thornton, a butcher and S.C. Leonard, an old soldier who was heavily in debt from gambling, went out hunting and rode into the United States.

Signs of improvement were showing. On March 8, wild cheers greeted a wagon from Fort Benton carrying the first sizeable mail delivery. James Macleod granted an afternoon holiday for the men to read and answer their correspondence. John Bray received two letters, one sent ten months earlier from a young lady in England and a second with a receipt for $0.87 from a Chinese laundry in Toronto for a bill paid ten months earlier. A copy of the Illustrated News with many of Henri Julien's drawings of the '74 March was passed among the men. "Over-drawn" sketches by the "Special Artist," which portrayed the police as a ragged army of Falstaff, brought contempt and disgust.[85]

In May, Colonel Macleod sought to remedy the excessive local prices when he suggested to Commissioner French that the post open a canteen, where items would be sold at cost price and that spirits be made available under proper restrictions. He ordered $1,000 in canned fruit and vegetables from San Francisco, which were issued to men at cost price, a savings of one-half what they were paying in town.[86]

Spirits of the men would continue to improve as spring advanced. The Helena Daily Independent, under the headline "How the Glorious 24th was inaugurated in the North-West by the Mounted Police," described the first Queen's birthday celebration at the post.[87] And, even though the only refreshment was "oceans of lemonade," it was a lovely spring day, long to be remembered. The setting was spectacular with the brilliant scarlet tunics against the distant mountains, the flower-covered emerald prairie as level as a billiard table, and the waving flag of "Old Britannia." The day began with the first cricket match in the region—"F" troop led by Surgeon R.B. Nevitt against "C" troop under Inspector Winder. A baseball game followed between the civilians and the "Boys in Red," who won. There were sporting events and horse races. In the evening, "the boys" gathered in the barracks to sing patriotic songs.

A letter written on June 15, signed "One of the Boys," related that "our men are contented and happy now and show a good contrast to what they were last winter ... no one with greater interest in the welfare of the men than Col. Macleod."[88]

The tiny detachment at Fort Edmonton fared relatively well in their first winter. Having accommodations in cottages used by the Hudson's Bay workers was helpful. Constable J. D'Artigue found life monotonous, with little work other than looking after the animals, and this lessened as many of them died. An on-going grievance was not receiving pay and having to buy tobacco and other items from the Hudson's Bay store on credit.

Only one police action was undertaken that winter. The first week in January, Inspector William Jarvis took thirteen men to check for illicit whiskey at Buffalo Lake (Tail Creek). It was a determined effort—a return trip of over 300 km in the coldest temperatures measured in thirty years of Hudson's Bay records.

The Cypress Hills Massacre Trials

Canada pressed extradition charges against the so-called Evans-Hartwick gang, who were held responsible for the June 1873 Cypress Hills Massacre. While overlooking the fact that five of the accused men were Canadian, Ottawa portrayed the skirmish as lawless American frontiersmen who deliberately attacked Indians on Canadian soil.

White settlers on the rapidly expanding Montana frontier found it incomprehensible that Canada championed the arrest of Americans on hallowed United States soil.[89] Were not the wolfers rightfully protecting their property from thieving Indians? One of the wolfers had written: "we fought for our lives, as only men on the brink of eternity can fight."[90] The *Fort Benton Record* justified the killings: "There is but one way to punish and bring to account these savage perpetrators—that is, to pursue and punish according to their own method of warfare."[91]

Second, were the arrests a Canadian ploy to win the confidence of the Indians to facilitate the forthcoming Treaty negotiations? In the words of the *Helena Daily Herald*, "it looks very much like a job put up by the Canadians to conciliate the savages at the expense of the Americans."[92] Another Helena newspaper agreed with this: "Canadians will not hesitate to sacrifice these men if they get them into their possession, if for no other reason than to conciliate the Indians."[93]

Commercial interests in Fort Benton, anxious for business in the northwest, initially welcomed the NWMP arrival at Fort Macleod. With the buffalo trade foreseen to decline, merchants hoped to capitalize on a potential market in western Canada.

The Cypress Hills arrests by "Her Majesty's Mounted Ruffians" altered this view.[94] Were the police working to accommodate the Hudson's Bay Company's ambition to monopolize trade in the Northwest?[95]

Ottawa had carefully prepared its case against the Montana wolf hunters. On the '74 March, when Divisions "D and E" returned east, Commissioner French left the column to observe the massacre site. Six months later, in the spring of 1875, Lieutenant-Colonel A.G. Irvine resigned his command of the Manitoba militia to join the NWMP. His first assignment was to gather information on the massacre. Once the Missouri River ice broke, Irvine traveled by boat to Fort Benton. On his trip, he fortuitously met trader Alexis Lebompard, a witness to the Cypress Hills killings. Without revealing his mission, Irvine hired the frontiersman as a guide. Through this association he gained important information on the bloody skirmish. At Helena, Irvine helped Colonel James Macleod finalize the criminal charges against the American "vigilantes."

The federal government of the United States facilitated Canadian extradition efforts. On 7 May 1875, the British Minister in Washington requested warrants for the arrest and extradition of ten men that were wanted for murdering Assiniboine Indians.[96] Washington contacted the Montana territorial governor to have two United States marshals go and apprehend the alleged offenders.

Helena, Montana Territory, Main Street, 1873

The gold rush settlement, founded in 1864 (ten years before the arrival of the NWMP), had a population of 3,106 in 1870.

– Montana Historical Society, Helena Uncatalogued 'Streets–Main St.'

At Fort Benton, however, the county sheriff, accommodating public opinion, refused to implement this order. It required federal marshals (supported by army troops) to arrest five of the wanted men on 21 June 1875 in Fort Benton. They were then escorted 200 km to Helena for the extradition trial.

The American federal involvement incensed the local population and reinforced the western contention that Easterners and Washington were out of touch with life on the frontier. The Montana press ridiculed the Eastern humanitarian sympathy "over the poor Indian."[97]

These arrests triggered angry demonstrations in the Montana Territory. Petitions denounced the "British invasion" of American rights as being unwarranted and effected through purely selfish motives and British gold. At a public meeting in Fort Benton, "Colonel" John J. Donnelly, leader of a small local Fenian Brotherhood vilified both Canada and her British institutions. Resolutions passed denouncing the unnecessary and unjust arrests, the government policy in dealing with Indian affairs offered heartfelt sympathy for the accused in "their hour of trouble."[98]

Donnelly had a checkered past. He had participated in two abortive raids on Canada, the first from Vermont in 1870 and the second the following year entering into Manitoba from North Dakota. The one-day "invasion" of Manitoba captured an unoccupied Hudson's Bay post near the border.

The Montana press defended the frontiersmen charged in the Cypress Hills killings. It was, according to the *Fort Benton Record*, completely incomprehensible that, "whites are to be punished for protecting their lives against Indians."[99] A second newspaper questioned the evidence Canada used in this extradition. It asked: "Surely not that of Assiniboine savages? ... the lives of citizens of Montana are not so cheap that they can be sacrificed for a savage's oath, which can be purchased for a drink of whiskey."[100]

On 7 July 1875, United States Commissioner W.E. Cullen opened the "Extradition Trial" in a crowded Helena courtroom. The legal proceedings were fractured by bitter partisan politics—the prosecution led by the Republican supporter Colonel Wilbur F. Sanders, the defence directed by Joseph K. Toole, a Democrat. Outside, on the streets and in the saloons, miners and frontiersmen vented their anger.

Prosecutor Sanders denounced the accused as "Belly River wolfers, outlaws, smugglers, cutthroats, horse thieves and squaw men."[101] The cross-examination of the leading Crown witnesses, trader Abe Farwell and Alexis Lebompard (sometimes La Bompard), produced contradictory and inconclusive evidence. Local opinion vilified Farwell as a liar and personally maligned him as, "a Jew and squaw man."

The tenth day of the trial, July 17, had brought a dramatic twist in the proceedings when Elijah Deveraux, one of the accused, citing false arrest, had local officers arrest Colonel James Macleod. Deveraux claimed damages of $25,000 for false imprisonment.

It is not every day that the Assistant Commissioner of the North-West Mounted Police is thrown in jail. Macleod immediately posted the bail of $3,000, a large sum of money. Three days later, Chief Justice Wade dismissed the Deveraux claim, ruling that Macleod was acting according to his government's instructions and with the approval of the United States government and, therefore, could not be personally held responsible.

The Helena extradition trials concluded with Commissioner W.E. Cullen finding the defendants, as expected, not guilty. In his summary, he questioned the confusing evidence:

> The testimony on both sides is of the most conflicting and unsatisfactory character. The witnesses both for the prosecution and defense contradict each other in many important particulars, and not infrequently contradict themselves.[102]

The mining town celebrated the verdict with whiskey and a torchlight parade. The *Fort Benton Record* commented that the decision surprises no one: "We only wonder that it was not rendered at an earlier date."[103]

The vindicated wolf hunters returned to Fort Benton where they were welcomed with an escorted parade through the town. Cannon shots added to the excitement.[104] That evening, townspeople gathered in the town hall to celebrate the acquittals and to malign the United States and Canadian governments. Welcome slogans and posters decorated the room. Attached to the American flag were the words "Home Once More." A prominent sign read "Didn't Extradite" above a drawing of a British lion in full retreat while an American eagle bit its tail. The five former prisoners were escorted into the hall to cheers. There were speeches and a purse of money was given to Trevanion Hale (one of the Cypress Hills party) to benefit the acquitted frontiersmen. The revelry lasted all night.

John Evans soon opened a hotel, aptly named The Extradition Saloon. Trader Abe Farwell, scorned as a "hired witness" and physically threatened, moved to Fort Macleod where he found employment delivering mail. In June 1876, he again was the key crown witness at the trial held in Winnipeg for three more Cypress Hills "vigilantes."

The Canadian expenses for the Helena trial, paid in gold by Assistant Commissioner James F. Macleod (through I.G. Baker and Co), amounted to $5,777.[105] The largest expenditure was $1,500 to W.F. Sanders for his legal services. This amount included $250 for defending Colonel Macleod on the Deveraux charge of false imprisonment. U.S. Federal Marshall W.F. Wheeler received $921 for services, warrants, and prison guards. The Hotel St. Louis billed the NWMP $703 for lodging and meals. The two main witnesses were generously rewarded: Abe Farwell received $450; Alex Lebompard, $204 for guiding. Other costs were for livery service, telegraph, and even $2.50 for a road toll.

Extradition trial, Helena Court House, 1875

"It looks very much like a job put up by the Canadians to conciliate the savages at the expense of the Americans."

– *Helena Daily Independent*, 27 June 1875
Glenbow Museum, pencil collection, 74.7.47.15B

Within weeks of the Helena trial, the Canadian government, apparently undeterred by the acquittals and court expenses in Helena, charged three more frontiersmen for participation in the Cypress Hills Massacre. Philander Vogel and James Hughes were arrested at Fort Macleod and, after a cursory hearing, Major Irvine left with the men for trial in Winnipeg. On the route, the party detoured to Fort Walsh to study the skirmish area and to have Surgeon R.B. Nevitt draw sketches of the site for evidence in court.

While at Fort Walsh, the detail arrested young George Bell, a third "vigilante." The *Manitoba Free Press* was not deceived that the youthful looks of Bell precluded guilt, stating that, "as an American citizen [he] has probably been educated to believe that the killing of a few Indians is only what is expected of him."[106]

Guide Louis Léveille led the eastward party that included Assistant Commissioner Irvine, three Mounted Policemen, key witness Abe Farwell and his family, and the three prisoners. They rode through an empty wilderness. On some nights, shots had to be fired to keep the buffalo out of the camp. And, for men on their way to trial, it is incredible that they were given rifles to supply the party with food. None of the policemen knew how to run buffalo. The *Manitoba Free Press* described how this problem was solved:

> The prisoners being experienced buffalo hunters, did good service in supplying the party with steaks and were allowed considerable liberty, until the borders of this Province were approached, when it was deemed best to handcuff them.[107]

Canadian authorities hailed the three arrests as proof of the Queen's justice. Major Irvine, reported the *Manitoba Free Press*, "is of the opinion that there is not an Indian in the North-West who is not aware of the enterprise which he is engaged, as he was constantly meeting scouts from several encampments."[108] The newspaper concluded that the arrests did more to establish the confidence of the Indians in the government, than any amount of presents, promises, and powwowing. Needless to say, settlers on the Montana frontier again were infuriated on the news of the three arrests. Was this but a repeated insult to Americans? One newspaper asked: "If they couldn't defend themselves at Fort Macleod what kind of trial will they receive at [Fort] Garry?"[109]

Trevanion Hale, one of the five wolfers acquitted at Helena, wrote to Montana Governor B.F. Potts, disclaiming any involvement by the three men in the "so-called massacre." He maintained that, although Vogel worked for trader Solomon, he had frozen his feet that winter and needed crutches to walk; Bell who worked as a night watchman for Solomon, was at the trading post during the shootings; and, although Hughes was part of the wolfer party, he was not with them at the skirmish.[110]

In Winnipeg, on 13 October 1875, ten weeks after the Helena acquittals, Chief Justice C.J. Wood committed the three men for trial. Because the defendants had problems securing evidence, the Chief Justice postponed the trial for eight months. This delay, in Montana opinion, was another example of contemptible British injustice. It was, in the opinion of the press, "a revolting mockery of justice which characterizes the trial of the Fort Garry prisoners in Canada."[111] The *Fort Benton Record* demeaned the main crown witnesses as two scoundrels: "The notorious Farwell, whose perjured lips moved glibly in the self-imposed, paid task of convicting innocent men, by his false tales, and the long haired half-breed Lebompard, who a few months ago was unable to identify any of the accused parties."[112]

The prisoners were held in a military prison. They found themselves in a trying situation—penniless, far from their homes, on trial in a foreign country, unable to obtain favourable witnesses, and without local public support. In desperation, they turned to the local American Consul, James Wickes Taylor, for help. Although at first indifferent to the case, Taylor came to their aid. He hired an able Winnipeg barrister and, through correspondence, had John Evans in Fort Benton raise $400 for legal fees and provide a promise of further help. Evans placed calls for subscriptions in Montana newspapers. One appeal stressed that, "three fellow-citizens are to be tried before a foreign judge and jury for defending their lives and property and to be tried on the evidence of perjured informers."[113]

From his inquiries, Taylor concluded that the massacre was a frontier fight with both sides responsible. Second, Ottawa likely wanted convictions to influence the Indians at the coming treaty negotiations.

Three years after the "massacre," the trial convened in Winnipeg on 19 June 1876.[114] The charge was the wanton and atrocious slaughter of forty peaceful and inoffensive people who were shot down in cold blood without warning. Alexis Lebompard, a witness to the skirmish, when required, served as an interpreter. Attorney S.C. Biggs represented the accused.

The purpose of Canadian authorities remained in question. It was, in the *Helena Daily Independent's* view, an attempt to "establish in Indian minds an impression that no matter what the Indians do to the people of Montana they shall be protected by the Canadian government."[115]

Conflicting evidence clouded the five-day trial. The Crown relied on Farwell as the first of eight witnesses. The defence countered Farwell's testimony by admitting, although the three accused were near the killings, they were at Solomon's nearby post and took no part in the skirmish. Four Métis crown witnesses actually supported the accused by claiming that the Indians, who would rob, pillage and murder if they had the opportunity, planned to attack the wolfers for their whiskey.[116]

On June 22, His Lordship the Chief Justice C.J. Wood charged the jury stating there was no evidence that the men had murdered Indians. He added that whiskey was the real culprit and this fight was another of its fearful effects upon western Indians. After a short deliberation, the jury returned with a verdict of not guilty. The three accused were released on their own recognizance, even though two indictments remained. Two days later, they left by stagecoach for Grand Forks, Dakota Territory—the first step on their long way back to Montana Territory.

The exonerated men sought indemnities from the Canadian government. Legal delays interfered with their lawsuit and it was not until six years later, in 1882, that the government officially dismissed the indictments against the three Fort Benton wolfers, finally ending the tiresome affair.

New Posts

In the summer of 1875, the North-West Mounted Police consolidated its regional presence by building posts at Fort Saskatchewan, Fort Walsh, and Fort Brisebois (now Calgary). A post at Fort Battleford, constructed the following year, replaced the Swan River NWMP headquarters in 1877.

The most strategic post constructed was in the Cypress Hills. This 2,500 km^2 upland had springs and timber, making it a historic gathering point for Indian winter camps, and was used as a base to hunt in the surrounding buffalo range. Whiskey traders and rival Indian bands made the prominent elevation, in one Mountie's words, "as lawless a section as could be found in the territory."[117]

After returning to Fort Macleod in May 1875 with 116 horses that had wintered at Sun River, Major J. Walsh took thirty men from "B" troop to construct a fort in the Cypress Hills, 300 km east. The troop had a tattered appearance. Three men even wore purchased American blue cavalry tunics. On June 7, Walsh chose a site in a valley near the location of the skirmish two years earlier. Tall nearby pine trees were ideal for construction.

On the troop's third day in camp, a large Sioux band appeared. While Walsh sat at a table under a Union Jack flagpole explaining the purpose of the NWMP arrival, several Indians interrupted to say that he lied, drawing attention to the men wearing American tunics. Walsh pointed at the flag and asked: "Don't you know the Queen's flag?"[118] When they responded that it looked like the American flag, Walsh bellowed at the Métis interpreter in the Sioux band: "All right, try cleaning us out, and a lot of you will be killed too, and before many moons the redcoats will be as thick in these hills as the buffalo are on the plains."[119]

At this critical moment, a dust cloud appeared in the east, interrupting the argument. All watched as a large Cree band appeared, causing the Sioux to withdraw at once. In the time frame of a broader context, this encounter with Major Walsh predated the Custer battle by several weeks.

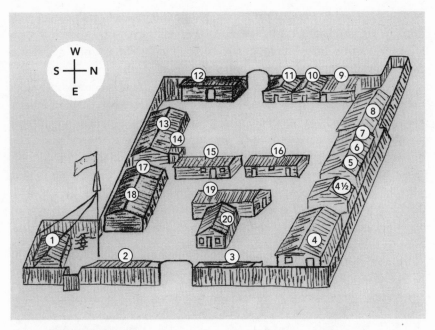

Fort Walsh: 1878–79

The fort underwent extensions and changes throughout its seven-year occupancy. Other drawings show a library, sick horse's stable, wood yard, harness maker shop, root cellar, orderly room, sundial, sentry box, water well, horse trough, and a nearby cemetery.

– GA, Stuart Wood, M 8065, f. 4. Sketch by Jim Schofield (not to scale)

1. Major's Quarters
2. Officer's Quarters
3. Hospital
4. Officer's Mess and Kitchen
4½ Sergeant's Mess
5. Men's Qtrs. "B" Troop
6. Harness, Tailor, Shoe Shop
7. Magazine
   (140,000 rounds ammunition)
8. Stable
9. Coal House
10. Blacksmith Shop

11. Carpenter Shop
12. "E" Troop Stable
13. "B" Troop Stable
14. Stable Sergeant's Office, Gunsmith
15. Canteen
16. "E" Troop Stable
17. Troop Kitchen "B" & "E"
18. Men's Quarters
19. Quartermaster's Stores
20. Guardroom

Not shown are bastions on the Southeast and Northwest corners, the latrine outside the east side, and a garden on the east side.

The Cree were delighted to see the police and insisted on shaking hands until, in the words of Constable Grain, "we were nearly dizzy and our arms felt as if they no longer belonged to us."[120] That night a strong guard was posted and the men slept with their weapons at hand.

Fort Walsh was built as a four-sided post with the north and south sides measuring 96 and 91 m, the east 73 m, and the western side 59 m in length. Five-metre poles were placed in a trench and tamped into an upright position, linked and stabilized by single plank to form the palisade. The one-storey inner log buildings with beaten clay floors and sod-covered roofs all faced the inner square. There were two large gates that, when closed, were braced by a strong wooden bar. The larger east gate had a small doorway for use when the gate was closed. Two corner bastions (later four) provided defensive protection.[121] These bastions, at times, fell into disuse, even to the point of being used only for grain storage. An 18-m flag pole in front of the Commissioner's residence marked the post.

Fort Walsh, NWT

For five years, the NWMP police post and its immediate area was the largest populated settlement in the North-West Territories.

– GA NA 2003 – 52

Archaeological excavations at Fort Walsh during the late 1970s examined 42 buildings and uncovered 150,000 artifacts.[122] In its seven-year lifetime (1876–82), Fort Walsh was occupied by an average of 112 men a year.

The post was built with materials available at hand. The men cut and skinned (removed the bark) 2,500 pine trees for the buildings and palisade. Logs were laid horizontally except for the privies and stables where upright logs were placed in a trench. The roofs were made from split poles, covered with 8–15 cm of clay, and then topped by overlapping planks.

Only the storage buildings had a pitched roof and pine shingles. Most floors were glaringly uneven and, in one building, sloped 30 cm. All the buildings were a single storey. The logs forming the palisade were of varying size. The untreated poles rotted in the acidic soil and, rather than a strong defensive barrier, the palisade became more a boundary than a deterrent.

Archaeologists identified lifestyles based on rank. Artifacts indicated the officers drank more expensive alcoholic beverages, had better medicines, ceramicware, and even better cuts of meat than the enlisted men. The officers and enlisted men lived in separate quarters, each with their own mess, kitchen, and privies. Alcoholic bottles were deposited in the outhouse wastes, prohibition legislation being in effect.

When Surgeon Barrie Nevitt arrived at the post three months after its completion, he was impressed: "After going through a deep defile the valley and the fort burst suddenly upon us ... the fort is built in a beautiful place and with excellent prime timber and is as pretty as Macleod is ugly."[123] For all its physical attractiveness, mountain fever (typhoid) made Fort Walsh an unhealthy post. Two Mounties and one former policeman died from typhoid. In 1879, eight per cent of the garrison contacted this disease.

From a military standpoint, the buildings and compound were within vulnerable rifle range from the surrounding hills. One military observer appraised that "if ever Fort Walsh were made the object of an attack by hostile Indians, not a man dare show himself in the barrack square."[124] At threatening moments, sentries were posted on the hills to warn the garrison of portending dangers. The Indians were not allowed inside the fort after sundown. Upon hearing the bugle signaling their exit, they would chant "*Kee-gally, Kee-gally*" which in Sioux meant, "Get out! Get out!"[125]

Fort Walsh set up small summer surveillance tent camps at Four Mile, Six Mile, Ten Mile (as measured from Fort Walsh), Kennedy's Crossing, and East End (southeast of Fort Walsh, but ironically located in southwestern Saskatchewan). Ten Mile, close to the Fort Benton Trail, had wood, water, and pasture. A sergeant supervising four to six men spent the summer surveying passing travelers.

In mid-August, an I.G. Baker bull train with fifteen wagons arrived, signaling the start of a settlement north of the fort. A town of fifty clapboard buildings quickly grew. Shops included trading stores of T.C. Power and the I.G. Baker Company, a barber shop, two billiard parlors, warehouses, and a hotel where you needed your own bedroll. Several former Mounties opened businesses. Jean Claustre, who had fought in the Franco-Prussian War, had a store and billiard hall. Ex-Constable George Anderton operated a photography studio. His photographs of the Mounties and Indians are very valuable historical records of that time.[126] A number of interesting persons such as—"Four Jack Bob," "Nigger Annie," (who called herself the first white lady at Fort Walsh)—added to the town's western character.[127] Bull teams brought supplies from Fort Benton. The cost of one cent per one hundred lbs. for each mile was expensive.

The Fort Walsh police post, town, winter Métis buffalo hunters' families and Indian encampments made (for five years) Fort Walsh the largest populated settlement in the Territories. In October 1877, Fort Walsh attracted international attention when Sitting Bull and Brigadier-General Alfred Terry of the United States unsuccessfully negotiated the return of the Sioux to the United States.

"A" Troop, under Inspector William D. Jarvis, lodged the first winter in the Hudson's Bay post in Edmonton. In the spring, Jarvis overrode many strenuous objections from Edmonton residents and moved his twenty-man detachment 30 km northeast to Fort Saskatchewan. This relocation would remain a contentious concern. Ten years later, during the North-West Rebellion, one leading Edmonton resident commented: "Having the police stationed at this distance and on the opposite bank of the river was perfectly useless."[128]

Constructing Fort Saskatchewan was a challenge. The lack of nails required attaching the boards and logs with wooden pegs. Morale was low. The men had not been paid and personal items had to be purchased at outrageous prices from the HBC store. A farming initiative lacked enthusiasm. It was necessary to place several refractory men under arrest.

A third post built in the summer of 1875 was Fort Brisebois, today Calgary. Colonel Macleod had taken fifty "F" Troop men from Fort Macleod to the Tail Creek Métis settlement to meet Major-General E. Selby Smyth, commander of the Canadian militia, on his tour of the western police posts. On the return to Fort Macleod, a small troop left the column to build a post beside the Bow River.

They approached the Bow River from the northeast. The sight, one Mountie wrote almost sixty years later, "of our new home looked like a veritable Garden of Eden."[129] A companion rider described the sight:

The view from the hill on the north side of the Bow amazed us. Before us lay a lovely valley, flanked on the south by rolling hills. Thick woods bordered the banks of both streams; to the west towered mountains with their snowy peaks ... buffalo in large bands grazed in the valleys, but of man we saw no sign ... our first sight of this enchanting spot was one never to be forgotten ... it was by far the most beautiful we had seen since our arrival in the West.[130]

The men in "F" Division crossed the Bow river near its confluence with the Elbow. The horses were forced to swim the river while the wagons were caulked and, held by roped tarpaulins, became makeshift rafts to float across the river.

They found a tent occupied by Father Leon Doucet, a native of France who had been sent from the St. Albert Mission to learn Blackfoot. He and his young Indian companion were ecstatic to see the police. The pair obviously lacked hunting skills and were famished, even though buffalo

Fort Calgary

"Our first sight of this enchanting spot was one never to be forgotten ... it was by far the most beautiful we had seen since our arrival in the West."

– Cecil Denny, *The Law Marches West*, 83
GA NA 354 – 23

were grazing nearby. A second find was a ghastly array of skulls and bones near an abandoned whiskey shack that the Blackfoot had attacked the previous summer. One body was identified as William Berry, a white man and an associate of whiskey trader John Weatherwax. Wolves had dug up and partly eaten his body. The police re-buried his remains.

Camp was set up near the confluence of the Elbow (also known as Elk) and Bow rivers. A courier was sent south to inform Fort Macleod of the location and, within a week, a bull train had arrived with small stoves, supplies and some winter clothing.

Superintendent Ephrem-A. Brisebois commanded the post, which he named after himself. Major-General Selby Smyth had ridden from the Red Deer River to the Bow River with Brisebois. His report to the Minister of Justice was extremely unfavourable: "Marched with him several days. Did not form a high opinion of him. He appeared little qualified for his position, and unreliable."[131]

The men set to building the post. A boom placed across the Elbow River trapped logs that were cut 3 km upstream. The construction followed the pattern used to build other police forts—logs placed upright in a trench to form a palisade, all buildings faced inward to the centre square, and sod-covered flat roofs. Added at Fort Brisebois were fireplaces built with field stones from the river and floors, doors, and window frames built from wood whipsawed by hired mixed-bloods from Edmonton. Within a month, the buildings, at a cost of $3,476, were ready for the men.

A small nearby settlement quickly rose. Harry "Kamoose" Taylor, the first whiskey trader arrested by the NWMP, brought a billiard table from Fort Benton. The I.G. Baker Company set up a store, run by ex-whiskey trader Donald Davis and former policeman Alex Kinghorn. The Hudson Bay Company floated its store by barge downriver from Ghost River and appointed John Bunn manager. A small Catholic chapel was built, and the Reverend John McDougall erected a church west of the fort. Two well-known settlers lived in the area. John Glenn had an irrigated farm on Fish Creek, 13 km south of the fort, and Sam Livingstone farmed 10 km west beside the Elbow River.

Brisebois's leadership quickly antagonized his troop.[132] In December, the 25-year-old Superintendent ordered the detachment to build a cabin for the Métis interpreters. When the men refused, Brisebois ordered arrests for insubordination, but no one obeyed the order. He enflamed the crisis by appropriating the barrack cook stove for his mixed-blood girlfriend. The irate detachment sent three men to report their grievances to Colonel J. Macleod. On their arrival at Fort Macleod, they were placed in the guardhouse, but released once the facts became known.

Inspector Ephrem-A. Brisebois

"This officer was in command of "B" Division as a Sub-Inspector, but there was so much crime and misconduct that I had to remove him … He is inclined to be insubordinate and to make difficulties about trifles." (Commissioner French to the Minister of Justice)

– *NAC*, RG 18, v. 3436, f. 0–8
  GA NA 828 – 1

Letters from the fort complained about the state of affairs. Added to the men's anger was the lack of winter clothing and pay. Surgeon Barrie Nevitt commented on Fort Brisebois: "The state of the troop has been bordering on mutiny for some time and the Col. will find his hands full endeavouring to sift matters and get the truth."[133]

Colonel J. Macleod, now a Stipendiary Magistrate, with his recently appointed replacement, A.G. Irvine, arrived in January 1877 by dog team to deal with the complaints. They brought an appreciative $6,000 in back pay for the detachment. Irvine informed Headquarters in Ottawa that Inspector Brisebois, without consulting superiors, issued an order that all public documents sent from the fort were to be headed "Fort Brisebois." Irvine cancelled the order at once and, at Colonel Macleod's suggestion, on April 5, had the post officially renamed Fort Calgary (often spelled Calgarry), although the old name, "the Elbow," clung for years.

Later that month, the Assistant Commissioner and Brisebois exchanged acrimonious correspondence over what Irvine perceived as inadequate punishment given to the detachment's offenders. On 25 April 1876, Irvine contacted the NWMP comptroller Col. Bernard: "I am sorry to say that I consider Inspector Brisebois utterly unfit to command them."[134] In July, Brisebois' earlier request in January for a four-month leave of absence was approved. He resigned from the Force in August.[135]

The turbulent beginning of the fort aside, the men posted to the base were proud of their service. R.W. Fletcher recalled:

> When I pass the site of the old fort, the memory of days long ago come surging over me. I see the old stockade ... the flag of Old England as I saw it in the old days, waving there, fair and free in the clear air and bright sunshine ... I see the courtyard and I see the ghosts of men since gone to their rest.[136]

Six Mounted Policemen were posted at Tail Creek, a Métis winter community located halfway between Fort Saskatchewan and Calgary. Each mid-October the population mushroomed to 500 with the arrival of carts with mix-blood hunter families from buffalo country and small Indian bands on foot or horseback. One Mountie recalled that the deafening powwows of the Indians and the discordant screeching violins of the Métis "turned a hitherto peaceful valley into a very bedlam."[137]

In 1876, the NWMP built an important fort at Battleford with logs that had floated down the North Saskatchewan. One day, the detachment halted construction to shoot at a herd of buffalo moving between the Battle and North Saskatchewan rivers. Within two years, buffalo were never seen again in the area. Although labeled by Lieutenant Governor Dewdney "the centre of nowhere," the Battleford River post quickly gained importance. In 1876, the telegraph link to Winnipeg was completed and, in the following summer, the town replaced Swan River (Fort Livingstone) as the capital of the North-West Territories.

Inspection Tour by Major-General E. Selby Smyth

In the late summer of 1875, Major-General E. Selby Smyth, commander of the Canadian Militia, undertook a military inspection of the NWMP posts in the North-West Territories. Alexander Mackenzie's Liberal government had instructed Smyth to conduct a special inquiry into the organization, equipment, distribution, and general efficiency of the Force. Commissioner George A. French's dealings with authorities in Ottawa were strained.

Smyth's prairie tour began at the Shoal Lake detachment the final week in July, moved northwest to the NWMP headquarters at Swan River, and then, with a fifty-man police escort, traveled west to Fort Carlton, Fort Pitt, Victoria (today Pakan), and the NWMP post under construction at Fort Saskatchewan.[138] From there, he was joined by Inspector Jarvis and they rode south toward Fort Macleod. At the Tail Creek settlement, a detachment from Fort Macleod waited to escort the party to their base. The important post at Fort Walsh, built earlier that summer, was not visited.

On the southward journey from Tail Creek, a troop left the column to construct Fort Brisebois (Calgary). Time commitments prevented Smyth from visiting Chief Crowfoot's gathering at Blackfoot Crossing. A number of Indians overtook the Smyth party and spent one night in the camp. Smyth gave them gifts of food and tobacco. The Indians spoke "in high terms of the mounted police, and the security and good order their presence had established throughout the country."[139] Smyth was impressed with the NWMP escort that accompanied him for the 2,500-km journey. He wrote that, "through all that long and toilsome march, day by day, this escort never flagged, always ready, willing, and obedient, untiring in their exertions, which sometimes called for much endurance. If I were to judge of the Mounted Police Force as a body, by that little escort, they deserve a very high character from me."[140] Moreover, he never met a more hard-working body of men.[141]

While Smyth went 400 km south to Fort Shaw, Montana Territory, to discuss border problems with American officers, his staff at Fort Macleod took time to rest or hunt. On his return, Smyth visited a Peigan camp of 170 lodges. The Indians, wrote Smyth, "were also loud in their praises of the

Mounted Police, and the great good which they had effected in suppressing the liquor traffic ... now they were much better off, whereas before the arrival of the Mounted Police they were every day getting poorer."[142]

From Fort Macleod, Smyth rode westward through the Crowsnest Pass into Washington State Territory and eventually reached Victoria, British Columbia. He returned to Ottawa by rail from San Francisco. In six months, Smyth had traversed almost 18,000 km (3,300 on horseback)—a distance reputed to be the longest tour undertaken by a British military officer.

The official report that Major-General Smyth submitted to Parliament at the end of November 1875 contained 154 points.[143] He reviewed the '74 March and made a number of recommendations for the NWMP including the location of posts, supplying field glasses (which he noted most Indians had), barracks, horse equipment, weapons, stoves, ferry scows, barrack canteens and reading rooms, uniform dress, pay, transport, and growing oats. Smyth suggested that, since there was no Territorial militia, a volunteer police be formed at future settlements to support the NWMP in case of serious troubles.

A key proposal advocated establishing a depot in Ontario to train recruits during the winter months in horsemanship and to instruct them on military and legal practices. This base would sift out "useless" men, thereby cutting transport and equipment expenses. Candidates with farming experience were suggested as best suited for the Force.

Smyth lauded the presence of the Mounted Police in the area: "Where formerly the Indians had bartered horses, clothing, buffalo robes, for the maddening fire-water, the result was drunkenness, squalor, murder and robbery, chaos let loose among all tribes. What a change has been the immediate result of the power of the law to repress crime."[144] In his assessment of Commissioner G. A. French, Smyth concluded, "his whole desire is concentrated in serving well the Government which employs him, in developing a powerful and useful force, and so far he has been, in my experience of it, very successful."[145] This was hardly the evaluation wanted by Ottawa.

Smyth castigated those Ontario newspapers that had denigrated the NWMP.[146] He countered: "I am now satisfied that the defamatory letters which from time to time appeared in the press were written by ill disposed persons, and did not give a true statement of this Force ... I congratulate Colonel French, the officers and men, on the excellent condition of this new Force."[147] Nevertheless, within a year, Commissioner George French would lose his command.

NOTES

1. *HDH*, 18 March 1875.

2. Dempsey, ed., *William Parker Mounted Policeman*, 36. Parker also describes the layout of the buildings.

3. *MFP*, 10 April 1875.

4. Grain, "Pioneers of a Glorious Future," 72.

5. *ODC*, 7 April 1875. The letter was dated 10 January 1875.

6. Nevitt, *Frontier Life in the Mounted Police*, 25.

7. Friends of Godfrey Parks in England wrote to the post for information on where he was buried. Surgeon Nevitt drew and sent them a sketch of the gravesite.

8. Nevitt, *Frontier Life in the Mounted Police*, 23. Colonel Macleod, in a letter to Commissioner French on 4 December 1874, reported that forty-five men were on the sick list. See *RC*, NWMP, 1874, 62.

9. McKernan, "Expeditions Made in 1873," 155.

10. Ibid.

11. *NAC*, Jos. Finlayson, MG 29 E58.

12. Ibid.

13. *ODC*, 7 April 1875.

14. McDougall, *On Western Trails in the Early Seventies*, 212.

15. *NAC*, RG 18, A-1, v.7, f. 306−375. Colonel Macleod, October 1875, estimated the costs: working pay Troops "B-C-F"−$1,710, 4,500 feet lumber−$225, window sashes−$84, glass−$24, nails−$32, other hardware−$95, freight of lumber−$294, freight hardware−$18, Baker & Co. hauling logs−$475, Jos. McMillan−$50, Chas. Thomas−$63, Jerry Potts−$63, John Glen (building chimneys)−$75.

16. *NAC*, RG18, A-1, v. 8, f. 475−80.

17. Fitzpatrick, *Sergeant 331*, 116. Mable Perkins, "Early Days at Fort Macleod," *SG*, Thirtieth Annual, 57, provided a second account of the firing: "Col. Macleod had gunners load the guns, and asked the Indians to stand away back of the guns. He told the chief to ask his people to watch the tops of some trees some two miles down the river. He asked the gunner to shoot at the trees and to the amazement of the Indians the tops of the trees were cut off, and dropped to the ground."

18. A letter written by a Mountie to the *Helena Daily Herald*, 15 March 1875, opened "the North-West Mounted Police are the pioneers of a great and glorious future." The phrase was also quoted in a letter written in January 1876. Seventy years later, Carell Grain interviewed her 90-year-old grandfather, William Grain, one of the last living '74 men. The elderly man related his thrilling police experiences and concluded: "We can look back to that motto which hung on the roughly hewn wall in Fort Macleod and realize that we, as Canadians, are still the 'Pioneers of a Glorious Future!'" *SG*, Twentieth-ninth Annual, 82. *MFP*, 26 June 1876.

19. *OC*, 7 April 1875.

20. Grain, "Pioneers of a Glorious Future," 74.

21. Nevitt, *Frontier Life in the Mounted Police*, 31. Also Hugh Dempsey, Christmas in the West (Saskatoon: Western Producer Prairie Books, 1982), 51.

22. Grain, "Pioneers of a Glorious Future," 74.

23. Nevitt, *Frontier Life in the Mounted* Police, 31.

24. Bagley, "The '74 Mounties," No. 8, 27. Also *MFP*, 16 January 1875.

25. Inspector E. Brisebois supervised thirteen men (with fourteen horses) at this outpost established only one month before the deaths of the two men.

26. *NAC*, RG 18, v. 4, f. 63−75. Colonel Macleod questioned the men (under oath) who had contact with Baxter and Wilson. All denied knowledge of the whiskey.

27. *ODC*, 7 April 1875.

28. *TM*, 5 April 1875.

29. Grain, "Pioneers of a Glorious Future," 75.

30. Denny, *The Law Marches West*, 56. Denny at Fort Edmonton, includes death of Godfrey Parks from typhoid fever on October 26, two weeks after reaching Fort Macleod.

31. *RC*, NWMP, 1874, 59−61.

32. *SN*, 14 January 1875.

33. *RC*, NWMP, 1874, 62.

34. *HDH*, 5 January 1875. Also see *HI*, 30 May 1876.

35. *HDH*, 5 January 1875.

36. *LH*, "A Policeman's Diary," 28 October 1921. "A Mid-Winter North West Mounted Police Patrol in 1875," *SG*, Ninth Annual, 44−47. Hugh A. Dempsey, ed., "A Mountie's Diary, 1875," *The Early West* (Edmonton: The Historical Society of Alberta, 1957), 8−13.

37. Grain, "Pioneers of a Glorious Future,"75.

38. Dempsey, ed., "A Mountie's Diary, 1875," 9.

39. Dempsey, ed., "A Mountie's Diary, 1875," 13. The column included: Inspector Crozier, Scout Jerry Potts, Sergeant W.D. Antrobus, Constables Grain, Scott, Dunbar, Bliss, Fraser, Patterson, Duncan, Shannon, Johnston, and Sharpe. William Grain described this action in Grain, "Pioneers of a Glorious Future," 61−82.

40. *FBR*, 15 March 1875.

41. *HWH*, 25 March 1875.

42. Ibid.

43. *FBR*, 15 March 1875.

44. Ibid.

45. *HWH*, 25 March 1875.

46. *HDH*, 15 March 1875. The letter was written 30 January 1875.

47. *SN*, 15 July 1875.

48. *NAC*, RG 18, v. 4, f. 98−75.

49. Denny, *Riders of the Plains*, 54.

50. *PAM*, L.F. Hewgill, MG1 B23.

51. *FBR*, 1 March 1875.

52. *NAC* RG 18, v. 4, f. 98−75.

53. Hugh A. Dempsey, *A Blackfoot Winter Count* (Calgary: Glenbow, 1965), 16.

54. Higinbotham, *When the West Was Young*, 79–81. When he was late in life, Fred Kanouse, a foremost whiskey trader in the NWT, was interviewed by a young reporter. "Is it

true, sir," queried the newsman, "that you were on the Canadian prairies before the coming of the North-West Mounted Police?" "Son," reflectively replied Kanouse, "I was the reason they came."

55. See Dempsey, *Firewater*, Chapter 16—"What Became of Them."

56. *GA*, Duncan McEachran, M 736. Also in *MG*, 4 November 1881.

57. *LH*, 21 June 1924.

58. John McDougall, *On Western Trails in the Early Seventies*, 262.

59. *FMG*, 29 July 1882. On bull trains, see Paul F. Sharp, *Whoop-Up Country*; A.C. Forster Boulton, *Adventures, Travels and Politics* (London, U.K.: Heath Cranton, 1939), 35–36; William Pearce, *Chronicles of the Old West*, 971.202 Pea, Calgary Public Library; Grain, "Pioneers of a Glorious Future," 73; *NAC*, William McQuarrie, f. 724; Nevitt, *Frontier Life in the Mounted Police*, 67–68; *WDT*, 29 August 1882. The *MFP*, 21 May 1880 relates: "each train consists of about eighteen wagons, usually three wagon hitched together drawn by 20 head of oxen. The manner in which these 'bull punchers' handle their enormous whips, with lashes 20 feet long, is really surprising to one not native of this rather too free land. They seldom strike the animals but bring the lash down with a crack like a rifle in close proximity ... with the help of their tongues, which will throw an oath as long and startling to the ear of an outsider as is the crack of the whip to the oxen ... they manage to make from ten to fifteen miles a day over the prairie. These men get from $60 to $80 a month and board, and upon their arrival from a trip every cent goes in a general debauch in Benton."

60. *Fort Macleod Archives*, 79 –1–18.

61. *CSP* 1879 xii, X, no. 188.

Year	Expenditure	Payment
1875–76	$370,000	$123,000
1876–77	$353,000	$126,000

One order (1 September 1875) to I.G. Baker for $15,034 contained 184 items. CSP, 1879, xii, X, no. 188. The first order was 15 October 1874 (only days after reaching Fort Macleod) paid $45 in gold for 1,000 lbs. of buffalo meat.

62. The small vessel had a short but busy "career" before sinking near Bismarck, Dakota Territory, in November 1879. See *HDI*, 28 July 1878; 2 December 1879.

63. *CSP*, No.18, 1882, 13; RC, NWMP, 1881, 13.

64. Sharp, *Whoop-Up Country*, 227.

65. Ibid., 205.

66. *FBR*, 4 March 1876.

67. *GA*, S.J. Clarke Diary, M 228.

68. *FBR*, 12 August 1883. That same year, Fort Benton received another economic blow when the US Northern railway reached Helena.

69. *GA*, Frederick Bagley, M 43.

70. *GA*, Joseph Carscadden, M 6608. A letter (*ODC*, 22 February 1875) bitterly complained of the mismanagement and affairs at the post.

71. Nora and William Kelly, *The Royal Canadian Mounted Police* (Edmonton: Hurtig, 1973), 50.

72. *MFP*, 30 March 1875. Also *ODC*, 5 May 1875.

73. *GA*, Frederick Bagley, M 43.

74. *ODC*, 5 May 1875.

75. *NAC*, A.E.A. Lowes, f. o.s. 363. Another example is *NAC*, Frances Parks, f. 55.

76. *NAC*, RG 18, v. 4, f. 84–75.

77. *TDM*, 26 February 1875.

78. *MFP*, 10 April 1875.

79. *ODC*, 24 April 1875.

80. Ibid., 7 April 1875.

81. Ibid., 24 April 1875.

82. *Benton Recorder*, n.d. October 1919.

83. *NAC*, RG 18, v. 4, f. 150–175. The telegram to Ottawa was sent 25 March 1875. A Slater Code form may have been used in which the contact people use chosen numbers to send and decipher a message. A selected number, for example twelve, would mean the correct word was twelve dictionary entries (same dictionary) before (or after) the word given. The beginning of the message read: iconoclast (HE), roach (REPORTED), heresy (GREAT), eighteen (DISSATISFACTION), gelatinous (FOR), everard (WANT), parallel (OF), piston (PAY), etc.

84. *ODC*, 1 June 1875.

85. *ODC*, 7 April 1875. Falstaff, a fictional character in three of Shakespeare's plays, depicted a fat, vain, and boastful comic figure.

86. *NAC*, RG 18, v. 6.

87. *HDH*, 3 June 1875. Also Nevitt, *Frontier Life in the Mounted Police*, 69.

88. *MFP*, 10 July 1875.

89. Between 1870 and 1890, the population in Montana Territory increased from 20,600 to 143,000.

90. *FBR*, 26 June 1875.

91. *Bozeman Times*, 6 July 1875.

92. *HDH*, 27 June 1875.

93. *HDI*, 27 June 1875.

94. Ibid., 8 May 1875.

95. *HDH*, 27 June 1875. Sharp, Whoop-Up Country, 70.

96. The five men charged were John Evans (age 29), Thomas Hartwick (The Green River Renegade) age 32, E.J. Deveraux (40), John Harper (27), and Trevanian Hale (35). All Canadian diplomacy went through the British Embassy.

97. *HDI*, 12 January 1878.

98. *HWH*, 1 July 1875.

99. *FBR*, 26 June 1875.

100. *HDI*, 27 June 1875.

101. Sharp, *Whoop-Up Country*, 71.

102. *HDI*, 25 July 1875. The Decision of the U.S. Commissioner W.E. Cullen. Also *HDH*, 24 July 1875.

103. *FBR*, 31 July 1875.

104. *MFP*, 11 September 1875.

105. *CSP*, Expenditure for the North-West Mounted Police, 1876-7-8 (Ottawa: MacLean, Roger, 1879).

106. *MFP*, 14 September 1875.

107. *MFP*, 11 September 1875.

108. *FBR*, 16 October 1875. (From *MFP*).

109. Ibid. 13 September 1875.

110. *HWH*, 7 October 1875.

111. *HDI*, 10 November 1875.

112. *FBR*, 9 October 1875.

113. *HDH*, 31 May 1876.

114. Court proceedings are detailed in the *MFP*, 20–24 June 1876.

115. *HDI*, 30 May 1876.

116. *MFP*, 23 June 1876.

117. Denny, *The Law Marches West*, 76.

118. Grain, "Pioneers of a Glorious Future," 77.

119. Ibid.

120. Ibid. "The Indians never shook hands with one another; they merely grunted in salutation, but they always wanted to shake hands with a white person whom they considered a friend." 78.

121. *GA*, Stuart Z. Wood, M 8065, Box 1, f. 4. James Schofield sketch. Also *MFP*, 21 May 1880.

122. Jeffrey Murray, "Archaeology at Fort Walsh, B, Outfit 311:3, 18–25. Jeffrey Murray, "The Mounties of Cypress Hills," *Archaeology*, XL, No. 1, 32–38.

123. Nevitt, *Frontier Life in the Mounted Police*, 91.

124. *MFP*, 11 February 1883.

125. Fitzpatrick, *Sergeant 331*, 21–22.

126. Brock Silversides, "The Face Puller", *TB*, v. 71:5, 22–31. T. George Anderton, *AH*, XXV, No. 4, 18–25.

127. William Parker, in a letter from Fort Macleod, 27 April 1877, wrote: "There are a number of hard cases knocking about who have extraordinary names, such as Slim Jim, Spanish Joe, Dutch Fred, and some squaws the same, such as The Double Barelled-Pair-Of-Scissors and The Good-Stealer."

128. *GA*, Letters of Thomas Anderson, *PAC* #636.081 .P976.

129. *CH*, 18 November 1933.

130. Denny, *The Law Marches West,* 83.

131. *NAC*, Smyth to the Minister of Justice, RG 18, v. 3436, f. 0–8.

132. Hugh A. Dempsey, "Mutiny at Fort Calgary," *AH,* L, No. 3, 9–12.

133. Nevitt, *Frontier Life in the Mounted Police*, 114.

134. Dempsey, "Mutiny at Fort Calgary," 11. Source: Correspondence Book, Fort Macleod, 1876, RCMP Museum, Regina.

135. Hugh A. Dempsey, "Brisebois: Calgary's Forgotten Founder," in *Frontier Calgary* (Calgary: McClelland and Stewart West, 1975), 28–40.

136. *CH*, 4 July 1925.

137. D'Artigue, *Six Years in the Canadian North-West*, 105. Also "Narrative of James Gibbons," *AHR*, VI, No. 4, 14. In this incident, prisoner Morin was handcuffed to interpreter Washington Brazeau for the night. In the morning, Brazeau awoke to find himself handcuffed and Morin sitting by the fire.

138. Smyth's staff included: Captain M. Stapleton (Coldstream Guards); Captain Ward, A.D.C. to the Governor General; Lieutenant T. Fitzwilliam (Royal Horse Guards); and E. Ellis, late Royal Navy.

139. *MFP*, 2 October 1875.

140. *NAC*, John Herron, o.s. 378.

141. Ibid.

142. *MFP*, 22 November 1875.

143. *CSP*, 1876 (No. 7), Annual Report on the State of the Militia for 1875, xx–xlvii. A Confidential Report of Major-General E. Selby Smyth that lists forty-four recommendations is found in *A Chronicle of the Canadian West*, 31–36.

144. *CSP,* 1876 (No. 7), Annual Report on the State of the Militia for 1875, xlii.

145. *A Chronicle of the Canadian West*, 32.

146. See *TM*, 26 February 1875.

147. *MFP*, 9 September 1875.

5

MEETING THE NEW ORDER

Corporal George Purches, Calgary, 1883

"The Mounted Police Force is the beginning of a new order of things in the North West Territories, prosperity and security will follow in its track."

– Maj. General E. Selby Smyth, 7 August 1875
RCMP Historical Collections Unit, "Depot" Division, Regina, SK. 1973.137.1

ON 1 DECEMBER 1874, SIX WEEKS after the police had reached the Oldman River site, Chief Crowfoot came to the fort to meet Colonel James F. Macleod. Through their remarkable communication—"the moccasin telegraph"—the prairie Indians knew of the approaching police column and the construction of the post. Although Macleod had already contacted and interviewed Blood and Peigan chiefs, the standard version portrays this "powwow" as the meeting that opened amicable relations between the NWMP and the Blackfoot Confederacy.[1]

On one side was the aquiline-featured Chief Crowfoot (Isapo-Muxika), aged forty-four, talking to a bearded Colonel Macleod, six years younger and named by the Indians Stamixotokan (Bull's Head). Through interpreter Father Constantine Scollen, Macleod informed the Indians that the police had come to stop the selling of "firewater" and that the Great Mother would treat Whites and Indians equally. Crowfoot replied that the police had arrived just in time as the whiskey trade had impoverished and disheartened his followers. Now the band was looking to better times. Other Blackfoot chiefs would visit the next week.[2]

Police–Indian Contact

The Police–Indian meetings followed a prescribed ceremony. After an interpreter introduced the parties, both sides shook hands. The Indians expressed pleasure at meeting Macleod. The interpreter would light a pipe and give it to a sitting chief, who, after several puffs, handed it to the next person. Everyone was silent until Macleod spoke. He explained why the government had sent the Force and outlined the laws to be enforced for both Whites and Indians. In response to Macleod's remarks, a chief would stand up, shake hands with everyone, and recount the present lawlessness. Now the Indians foresaw encouraging change, as one old chief told Macleod, "before you came the Indian crept along, now he is not afraid to walk erect."[3] After the meetings, Macleod gave presents of clothing and tobacco.[4]

In his official report for 1874, James Macleod assured Ottawa: "A number of traders are sedulously spreading reports amongst the Indians that we are to be here only for the winter, and will be off in the spring. All that have come to see me invariably ask how long we are going to stay. Their delight is unbounded when I tell them that I expect to remain with them always."[5] Four months after building the police post, Surgeon Barrie Nevitt declared, "Our presence here has had the most salutary effect upon them. They used to lay their hands upon anything that was carelessly lying around but now they pass them or return them to their owners ... now the worst the police have to fear was having their horses stolen."[6] Sergeant William Parker recorded in August 1877:

the Blackfoot nation have presented a wonderful bear skin robe to the Force in a token of their thanks for suppressing the liquor trade. The robe is painted all over in brilliant colours showing

where all the different tribes with their names are situated. There
are also paintings of Mounted Policemen on horseback riding up
& capturing the whiskey traders while in the act of trading it to
the Indians who are drunk & murdering each other.[7]

Constable Edward Larkin linked the early NWMP success with the
police keeping their word: "the Indians knew this and trusted the police."[8]
At a NWMP reunion fifty years later, John A. Lindsey recalled that "the
police were always on friendly terms with the Indians."[9]

Bull Back, Blood Chief, c. 1878

"The warlike tribe of Blackfeet were more than pleased with Comr. Macleod and
his men for putting out the whiskey trade."

– Sub-Constable J.A. Martin, *PAM*, MG 6 A8, Angus McLean file
  GA NA 5501 – 20

The Indians were anxious to cooperate with the police. In May 1876, Assistant Commissioner A.G. Irvine reported that Chief Little Black Bear had detained a fugitive in his camp (by holding a feast and dance), giving Sub-Inspector Welch time to come and arrest the accused man.[10]

A letter signed by an "American," written eighteen months after the Mounted Police had reached the region, commended the success of what the Indians called "police law."

> The presence of the North-West Mounted Police has been an incalculable benefit to the country. Working under great disadvantages, they have made human life safe, and that, too, with a mere handful of men scattered over a large tract of country, they have enforced law where heretofore no law was known, and they have the Indians under complete control.[11]

The clergy agreed that the NWMP presence had been an incalculable benefit to the country. The Reverend D.D. Wood was quoted: "they have accomplished a noble work. The whiskey trade has been broken up, the frontier rowdy has re-crossed the line, the bowie-knife and the six shooter are no longer flaunted about as formerly."[12] George McDougall at the Morley Mission stated: "The Mounted Police have done good work and we are grateful for their services."[13] Bishop Vital-Justin Grandin agreed: "Thanks to them, troubles caused by the whiskey traffic have ceased. The Indians have become more reasonable; they do not kill one another anymore and they respect even their brethren from other tribes. At the present time travelers may cross our plains without fear; they do not have to guard their horses and be alarmed about their scalps."[14]

The immediate and effective establishment of law and order by the NWMP was a remarkable achievement. Donald W. Davis, a whiskey trader, wrote to his mother in Vermont, 10 February 1876: "The Country is not quite as wild now as when I first came here there is some Mounted Police in the Country now so the red skins keep quiet now."[15]

Who are these Scarlet-Coated Men?

Indians in Southern Alberta were in contact with White people for more than a century, but these men were different. The red-coats wore clothing of the same colour, were without women and had formidable weaponry that they quickly demonstrated. The spectacular demonstration at Fort Macleod when their field piece hit a tree several kilometres away had stunned the Blackfoot. On their first contact with Kootenay Indians from

British Columbia in June 1875, the Fort Macleod detachment fired the field piece and, after dark, rocket fire "astonished them wonderfully."[16] These policemen appeared formidable. While the troop was constructing Fort Macleod, Colonel Macleod was puzzled to see Indians erecting nearby teepees. In response to his query, he was told, "that they had no fear near us, as the Government would protect them. Their enemies would be afraid to come near them."[17]

In February 1875, when his police patrol contacted sixty Indians near Sheep Creek, Sergeant William Antrobus related: "As soon as they saw us to be soldiers, as they called us, they scampered off like mad."[18] The next morning, Old Sun, head chief of the Blackfoot, led a party bearing a flag (an upside-down Union Jack with the Hudson's Bay Company initials) to the police camp. He kissed Captain Leif Crozier and Sergeant Antrobus, but not Constable Shannon, who ran into a trading shack and stood behind the counter where Indians were not allowed.

After Crozier provided a meal for the visitors, Old Sun explained, through interpreter Jerry Potts, the headlong flight the previous day was because, "they were very much afraid of us, thinking us great men, for they are afraid of the traders and know the traders are afraid of us, so in their eyes we are no common men."[19] In December 1875, William Leslie Wood, at the Hudson's Bay Spitzee post (High River), spoke of the NWMP presence: "The Indians are quiet and well behaved. I have had no trouble with them. They have a wholesome fear of the NWM Police Force."[20] Certainly, one bizarre incident added to the Indian's fearsome impression of the police. In this case, after an Indian prisoner had died in the Fort Saskatchewan jail, a hospital-sergeant began an autopsy in an adjoining shack built from rough timber. Through chinks in the planks, a Métis prisoner, Felix Plante, watched the incisions, then "emitted an unearthly shriek and, in spite of the ball and chain leaped the fence, and dashed into the dense brush surrounding the fort."[21] Plante was recaptured two days later, but not before he spread word that the policemen ate prisoners. This incident at Fort Saskatchewan, reasoned one Mountie, "certainly did much to increase the respect and fear of the Police held by the Indians."[22]

But there was uncertainty with the police presence. Surgeon R.B. Nevitt wrote that, when one Indian was arrested for maltreating his wife, band members were, "in a dreadful state of anxiety and think he is going to be hanged straight off."[23]

This initial Indian "fear" or, better, "apprehension," was not sustainable and the Mounted Police's continued prestige and authority hinged upon the Indian perception of fair treatment. The *Manitoba Free Press* noted:

"The trials of offenders are always held as openly as possible, in order to give the Indians every opportunity of observing that impartial justice is always meted out to all alike, without respect to race or color."[24]

The courts bypassed some cultural distinctions. Indians who left their campfires burning were admonished but, unlike white offenders, never imprisoned. Nor were the Indians charged with polygamy. "I met a chief," marveled Constable Thomas T.B. Boys, "with twenty wives."[25]

But challenges to Canadian law and order inevitably arose. The Mounted Police promoted Christian dogma and enforced many laws that were alien to Aboriginal lifestyle and traditions. Foremost, the theft of "pinto buffalo" (horses) was no longer a brazen and proud exploit, but a criminal offence.

Punishment for the theft of horses was understandable, but there were other Canadian legal restrictions that baffled the Indians. After former Mountie John Stuttaford, upset with Indians stealing from his vegetable garden near Fort Walsh, punched an Indian named Green Thing (who was sitting on his garden fence), band members went to the post where they complained bitterly about the assault. Colonel Macleod had Stuttaford arrested and fined him $3 for assault. Upset Indians vented their anger at Stuttaford's home. A witness described the commotion:

> In no time the garden was full of Indians firing their rifles and making havoc with the poor man's vegetables. Their yells were frightful. Colonel Irvine and Captain Cotton happened to come out of the fort on horseback. They were unarmed, but put their spurs to their horses and gallantly rode into the midst of the infuriated band. Immediately rifles on all sides were leveled at them, but when the Colonel, with his habitual coolness, spoke to the savages and ordered them to stop. They gradually withdrew and abandoned the spot.[26]

Captain Edmund Frechette explained the uproar: "The Indians could not understand how a man could escape imprisonment by paying money."[27]

Prison was an unfamiliar and dreaded concept to the Indians. A lengthy sentence in the closed confines could almost be considered terminal. Both Poundmaker and Big Bear died shortly after their release from Stony Mountain Penitentiary where they were imprisoned for their resistance in the 1885 Rebellion.

Indian prisoners abhorred having their heads shaved. One Indian, sentenced to three years imprisonment for horse stealing, refused to eat after having his hair cut "as if for the prize ring."[28] Band members reacted to the police cutting the hair of a Sarcee prisoner by knifing cattle and horses on ranches near Fort Calgary. Rancher John Glenn complained that the Indians had slashed the rump of a valuable horse.[29]

The Mounties brought six prison uniforms west. They were a sight to see. Perhaps to shame the victim, a uniform had one bright red sleeve, one blue; one blue leg and one red leg. In one case, this intent to humiliate had the opposite result. Sergeant Major J.B. Mitchell recalled one Indian, who was given a one-month sentence for beating his wife, asking at the completion of his sentence, whether he had to take off this suit. When he was told yes, he promised to be back soon. So, Mitchell related, "the harlequin suits were never used again."[30]

The scarlet-coated newcomers brought fascinating skills and technology. On several occasions, Chief Crowfoot arrived at Fort Macleod at reveille, sat in a chair and watched the post's routines until sunset. Once the Fort Macleod sawmill was completed in 1875, there was a constant parade of Indian visitors "gazing at the saw and engine by the hour."[31] Constable T. Boys watched Crowfoot and Red Feather having a heated argument over the source of the steam engine's whistle. Whenever he set up his easel, Surgeon R.B. Nevitt invariably expected Indians peering over his shoulder. The onlookers raptly watched each brush stroke and exclaimed aloud as the oils unfolded distinct distant landscape features. Nevitt wrote "I did a sketch of Crowfoot and he recognized it immediately as also did his squaws. Was that not a triumph of art?"[32] A policeman lathering and shaving, with a mirror tacked to a tree trunk, soon attracted curious bystanders. Watching Veterinarian Surgeon John Poett wash his false teeth was novel but, when he removed his glass eye and placed it in a water tumbler, the Indian spectators fled in fright.[33]

The Indians enjoyed watching police sporting events that were always part of holiday celebrations. It was not hard to understand horse races, throwing skills, running and jumping contests, the squaw race, and wrestling on horseback. But some novel events were puzzling. There was a tobacco race in which each contestant ran with a pipe and three matches (the pipe must remain lit at the finish line), a hundred-yard race with the contestant balancing a water bucket on his head (the winner being the participant with the least spilled water), and a greased pole climb for the prize of a pig. Certainly, the "nigger race" was bewildering. In the "nigger race," the contestants (who had the name of a neighbour on a placard attached to the back) moved continuously forward but as slowly as possible, with the winner being the person who finished last—a contest that exposed the contemporary racial stereotypes.[34]

At one field day at Fort Walsh, several Indians were invited to join a rugby match. The game took other dimensions, however, when a shoulder block by Constable George Adams sent one Indian opponent flying. When the downed man got up and drew a knife, Adams "made for the fort."[35]

Although the Indians embraced many white practices, others were avoided. For some reason, many Indians resisted being vaccinated. A group of Sioux refused to pose for a Moose Jaw photographer telling him that, if the pictures fell into the hands of their enemies, it could be perilous.[36]

There were misunderstandings with simple explanations. Upon hearing repeated gunshots from the Indian camp, the detachment at Fort Walsh prepared against an attack. But no signs of trouble ensued and all remained quiet. Later, it was explained that the gunfire was the Indians celebrating a full moon emerging from the clouds.

Mounted Police Impressions of Indian Society

A letter from a mounted policeman described the Blackfoot as "a warlike, dangerous lot of fellows, armed *cap a pie* with the most improved weapons ... well mounted, and many of them are owners of from fifty to sixty head of ponies ... they are a fine intelligent race of men, tall and slight, but wiry and muscular."[37] Cecil Denny described the tribe as "splendid looking men, well off ... and were the happiest people in the world."[38] Sam Steele assessed the Blackfoot as a "fine race of splendid physique; the men tall and well formed, pleasant in their bearing and very straightforward."[39]

Three months after reaching the Oldman River, James Macleod wrote French: "All the Indians I have so far met appear to be a very intelligent lot of men ... extremely hospitable to strangers."[40] In a later assessment, Macleod described the "Blackfeet are a splendid race physically, and endowed with considerable intelligence; some of their headmen exhibited on occasion an amount of astuteness and diplomatic capacity surprising in such a remote and savage tribe."[41] Commissioner French envisioned Blackfoot warriors, if organized and disciplined like the troops in India, and with white officers, as being the most formidable cavalry on the Great Plains.[42]

The Mounties admired the Indians' riding skills, their uncanny ability in finding directions, physical endurance, and remarkable talents. When his party ran out of matches, Constable Robert McCutcheon watched an Indian cleverly start a fire by cutting a small piece from his blanket, place gunpowder inside, and shoot the blanket wad from his shotgun into flame.[43] After a police troop had a futile search for their strayed horses, an Indian guide quickly found the herd (and received $1 for each horse), explaining that untethered horses always moved downwind. In April 1877, Major

Walsh hired Indians to search for the body of George Green with the promise of a horse for the finder. A Montana newspaper acknowledged: "this is a good move as only Indians can find anything in the badlands."[44] And no Mounted Policeman would ever dream of the ingenious Indian method for having fresh buffalo meat at a later date. An Indian would excise the eyes of a captured calf and leave the animal near a slough. Knowing that the buffalo would not wander from his water source, the Indians could return later to kill the animal.[45]

At the same time, the policemen applied European values that demeaned Indian society as dirty and uncivilized. The first meeting of Indians on the '74 March west shattered any notions of a carefree, pristine Native lifestyle. The small Sioux band was squalid and filthy and everyone in the police column soon had lice. Many policemen, often not models of hygiene themselves, described the Indians as dirty.[46] Tom LaNauze wrote: "I don't see much of the noble savage about them …their general appearance much resembles the pictures one sees of the distressed Irish."[47] Sub-Constable John Donkin used the analogy for an Indian to, "voluntarily to wash himself, is about as revolutionary as it would be for an archbishop to dance the can-can. The Sioux and Blackfeet bathe occasionally; the Crees never."[48] Surgeon Barrie Nevitt first described the Indians as a, "most pitiable object, first on account of his filthy habits and appearance, then his moral status is so low. He will steal, or murder for the slightest thing he covets and is the greatest and most unblushed beggar under the sun."[49] After sleeping and eating in an Indian camp for two days, Inspector Cecil Denny described his hosts as, "being very hospitable, freely and gladly giving him of their best, but they are filthy and that he never wishes to live with them."[50]

Most Mounties disdained the Indian campsites as filthy and overrun by hordes of barking vicious dogs. In warm weather, flies and excrement were everywhere. The Indian food, in some cases, was revolting. Denny was nauseated when given a portion of a buffalo embryo, a food his hosts relished as a delicacy. Nor was eating dog meat offensive to the Indians. A group of Mounties at a Sun Dance feast were aghast upon learning that the main ingredient in the soup was dog meat. On a New Year's visit to an Indian family, Sergeant Frank Fitzpatrick cautioned his companion that refusing food was an insult to the hosts. The two men were welcomed and ate stew offered from a pot. Fitzpatrick wrote:

> Our call at an end, we left by the usual porthole of the tepee, when I remarked to my friend: "That was not bad stew, was it? I wonder what it was.""No," he said, "it was quite tasty. I presume

it was rabbit." While asking the question, however, having suspicions of my own, my eyes had made a quick survey of the tepee surroundings. I replied to my friend that he was wrong, the unused portion of the stew was still hanging up on the tripod at back of the tepee, a good-sized half carcass of an Indian dog.[51]

The Indians seldom washed their dishes. Constable J.E. McEntyre abhorred "squaws sitting around our tents while we were at our meals and exploring each other's hair and any promising capture was inserted in their mouths, the result of which performance was to us, the loss of appetite."[52]

The Sun Dance ceremony, where young Indian men endured brutal initiating rites, reported one Mountie stationed at Fort Walsh, "was the most disgusting sight we ever saw."[53] At another Sun Dance, Frank Fitzpatrick, along with five companions, were invited to sit in the front row. They left before the dance concluded, "our stomachs rebelled at the brutal exhibition and we mounted our horses and departed, vowing that one Sun Dance was about sufficient for any white man."[54]

The policemen informally compared the tribes. John Donkin ranked the Wood Crees very much superior to Indians of the plains. He described the Sioux women, as a rule, as virtuous, "which was more than could be said of their sisters in other tribes."[55] William Parker instead rated the Blackfoot much superior to other Indians and with strict moral laws, such as cutting off the nose of woman who committed adultery. Cecil Denny thought the Sarcee were the most troublesome tribe on the plains. Joseph Carscadden at Swan River regarded the Saulteaux as the lowest order he have seen.

Many of "the boys" sought Indian artifacts and mementos. Captain E. Dalrymple Clark, in the first police party to Sitting Bull's Camp in May 1877, wanted to purchase General George Custer's watch as a gift for his widow but was disappointed to learn that it had been lost when the band crossed the flooded Missouri River. Inspector A.R. "Paper Collar Johnnie" Macdonell obtained forty items from Sitting Bull. His "collection" included arrows, leggings, quirts, moccasins, and a beautiful beaded dress for which he refused an offer of $1,200. Sergt.-Major Joseph Francis had dresses that once belonged to Sitting Bull's daughter and niece. Some policemen claimed artifacts of a questionable source. W. Ritchie had a war club which he alleged had killed Custer, the scalp of Crow Chief Iron Dog, and a pair of moccasins he said were personally given to him by Sitting Bull.[56]

Some quests for Aboriginal mementoes abandoned any decency. One policeman twisted the skull free from an Indian body and brought it back to Fort Walsh as a souvenir.[57] W. Parker climbed a tree to get carved images of animals that were placed with the body tied in the branches. His search ended when the remains dislodged, knocking him, in his words, "flat with the bones rattling around me ... I jumped to my feet and ran to the shanty as if the devil was after me. The men gave a great laugh."[58] The ghoulish episode was not over. For three days, dust in his mouth from the dead body made everything Parker ate or drank taste of the deceased.

To be given an "Indian" name was something special and worth writing home about. Cecil Denny was called Kis-sta-ke-ot-sokas (Beaver Coat); Superintendent James Walker, Pee-tee-quack-kee (Eagle that Protects); Superintendent Leif Crozier, Mahto Hoska (Long Bear); Inspector A.R. Macdonell, Boloka Seecha (Bad Stallion); and Major Walsh (Long Lance) and (Sitting Bull's Boss).

Dances at the police barracks bridged the two cultures. These well attended affairs routinely lasted all night and, on some occasions, for days. Métis fiddlers provided the music. The participants would sit on the floor, women on one side, the men on the opposite. Anyone wanting a dance would approach a chosen partner, bow, and lead that person by the hand to the dance floor. An unwritten rule forbade the refusal of a dance request.

Police medical services positively linked the two societies. Seven months after the building of Fort Macleod, R.B. Nevitt wrote that his "practice is quite an extensive one amongst the Indians, chiefly diseases of the eye ... aggravated by dirt and the irritating smoke of the lodge."[59] One outside observation related that surgical operations on warriors greatly astonished them and they placed great confidence in the power and skill of the surgeons. Indeed, the report concluded, "Colonel Macleod is of the opinion that much of the success that has attended the force is owing to the kindly attention the physicians of the force have bestowed on the Indians."[60]

Knowledge of the other's language enhanced communication. Some policemen learned Indian sign and spoken language. Major Walsh knew rudimentary Siouan; William Cox, fluent Blackfoot; and Sergt.-Major Spicer spoke Blackfoot "like a native." George Guernsey learned Cree. Surgeon Nevitt taught himself basic Blackfoot to aid his medical practice. Many Indians had a rudimentary knowledge of English trade terms and basic conversation. In a rare written account by an Indian, police scout Mike Oka commented on his introduction to English: "believe it or not the first English words I learned were swear words."[61]

The police employed Indian men as guides and hired women for the domestic chores and providing foods such as duck eggs and mushrooms. Some barracks hired Indian youths for chores. In Constable Thomas Boys' evaluation, "our adopted boy is a singularly active little fellow. He speaks

Blackfoot and Cree as well as English and seems to know a little of everything. He is a very good boy and has no bad ways only he smokes as much as a man."[62]

Contact between the two cultures brought inevitable changes. While, in the first years, members of the Force had visited Sun (Thirst) dances out of curiosity, by 1882 a new stipulation was in effect. "The Indians," observed the *Saskatchewan Herald*, "profiting by the example of their white brethren, had bills printed and imposed an admission fee."[63]

James Farquharson Macleod

James F. Macleod was born in 1836 on the Isle of Skye, Scotland. His family moved to Canada nine years later, settling north of Toronto. For his advanced education, Macleod attended Upper Canada College and Queen's College in Kingston, where he earned a BA, graduating with honours in classics and philosophy. After passing his bar exams at Osgoode Hall, Macleod practised law for ten years in Bowmanville, Ontario.

"Jim," as close associates called him, had a keen interest in the militia, and served in several companies. Active service in the 1861 Trent Affair and in the 1866 Fenian raids honed his military passion. Through the political patronage of Prime Minister John A. Macdonald and his former legal employer, Cabinet Minister Alexander Campbell, Macleod had obtained a commission as Brigade Major in the 1870 Red River Expedition. He remained with the militia at Lower Fort Garry until the spring of 1871.

His return to Ontario may have been linked to his failure to gain the appointment as commanding officer of the garrison. In late 1872, Macleod was in Scotland, possibly in search of employment. The following spring, Prime Minister Macdonald's offer of a senior position in the newly formed NWMP prompted his return to Canada.

A NWMP recruit described Major Macleod as a "man of magnificent stature, commanding in appearance, with keen and searching eyes, denoting seriousness and strength of purpose."[64] A full beard complemented his striking appearance. It was said in the barracks that a policeman at a hearing could gauge the severity of the punishment by the number of twists Macleod gave the long, curling ends of his mustache.

In October 1873, Macleod led the first contingent of 150 officers and men (Troops "A-B-C") from Ontario to garrison Lower Fort Garry. In December, in the first police action, he headed a patrol that arrested whiskey traders on the west shore of Lake Winnipeg. Five weeks before the '74 March, on 1 June 1874, Macleod became the Assistant Commissioner of the North-West Mounted Police.

Colonel James F. Macleod

"Colonel Macleod was everything that could be desired of a Commissioner. He was a handsome, rather stoutly built man, with heavy dark brown whiskers and mustache and eyes that pierced right through you."

– Constable William Grain, "Pioneers of a Glorious Future," *SG*, Twenty-ninth Annual, 82
   GA NA 354 – 1

On its famous westward march, after the camp in the Sweet Grass Hills, the column separated. Commissioner George French returned with two Divisions to Manitoba, while Macleod rode northwestward with Divisions "B-C-F" to build the post that bears his name. This placed the two senior officers of the Force at distant ends of the Canadian prairies, connected by poor communication.

Macleod selected the site and supervised the construction of Fort Macleod. His role was appreciated. An eastern newspaper wrote: "All credit is due to Colonel Macleod for the able manner in which the work was pushed along under the most trying circumstances."[65] A recruit wrote to a newspaper in Sherbrooke, Quebec: "I never saw an officer take so much interest in the welfare of his men as Colonel Macleod does. He has done all that lay in his power for our comforts the past winter."[66]

For fifteen months, J. Macleod remained in command of his new post. It was a very challenging time. He gained the respect of the area Indians, suppressed the whiskey trade, dealt with the desertion of eighteen men, and oversaw the extradition trials in Helena, Montana Territory. New posts at Fort Walsh and Fort Brisebois (Calgary) were erected, consolidating the NWMP presence in the region.

The Indians trusted Macleod. An eastern correspondent at the signing of Treaty 7 recorded that, when Macleod told the assembled Indians that every promise made on behalf of the Great Mother would be fulfilled, "as certain as the sun shines down upon us from the heavens, there was not one that felt that the colonel had spoken the simple truth."[67]

On 1 January 1876, James F. Macleod resigned from the Force to become a Stipendiary Magistrate in the Bow River Judicial District. Clearly, his relationship with Commissioner French was strained. In a letter to A.G. Irvine (Macleod's replacement), French criticized Macleod's indifferent financial responsibilities, the state of stores, and the incomplete data he forwarded on police and horses. The new Assistant Commissioner was to, "distinctly understand that after the first of January, he was in command at Fort Macleod, and that Lieutenant-Colonel Macleod's connection with the Force is at an end."[68]

Macleod's leave from the Force lasted six months. Then, in July 1876, Commissioner French resigned, ending his testy dealings with Ottawa. The Liberal government under Alexander Mackenzie, on 22 July 1876, appointed Macleod as the second Commissioner of the North-West Mounted Police. In a time rife with political patronage, this placement overlooked Macleod's conservative political leanings. One week later, Macleod, now forty, married Mary Drever. Their courtship had begun five years earlier when he was stationed in Winnipeg with the Red River Expeditionary Force. There was little time for a honeymoon, and the newlywed couple were soon on their way to Fort Carlton for the signing of Treaty 6.

Macleod served for four years (50 months) as Commissioner of the North-West Mounted Police. In addition to this position, he was a member of the North West Territorial Council. For some unknown reasons, he spent the winter of 1878–79 in eastern Canada and later returned in the spring with eighty recruits.

Important undertakings during his tenure as Commissioner included: the relocation of the North-West Mounted Police headquarters to Fort Macleod and then Fort Walsh; the signing of Treaties 6 and 7; facilitating the Sitting Bull–General Alfred Terry conference at Fort Walsh in 1877; and handling of both the Indian bewilderment and starvation that arose from the disappearance of the buffalo.

In September 1880, James Macleod resigned as Commissioner of the North-West Mounted Police. He had been struggling with several health concerns—rheumatism, stomach troubles, and weight loss. Macleod was re-appointed Stipendiary Magistrate with his own assize circuit. His influence on establishment of early Territorial law was pivotal.

There was widespread regret about his decision to leave the Force. "The news that the commissioner will leave the force," reflected the *Manitoba Free Press*, "has been received with feelings of universal regret ... his kind manners, and his readiness to hear a man's story, has endeared himself to one and all."[69]

Reverend John McDougall observed that, "the country was fortunate to have a man like Colonel Macleod at the helm in those early times. He fully believed in giving every man fair play."[70] Major Sam Steele wrote: "He was beloved by his officers and men and was a great loss to the service. His influence with the Indians was enormous, with whom he was fair dealing and truth personified."[71] Surgeon George Kennedy described J. Macleod as a, "man of action, the maker of history who made possible the Greater Canada and the splendid future that opened out before her."[72]

Until his death, James Macleod ranched near Pincher Creek with his wife and their five children. Macleod retained his position on the North-West Council, worked as a Stipendiary Magistrate, and was later appointed to the first Supreme Court of the North-West Territories. Macleod died from Bright's Disease (nephritis) in September 1894 at the age of fifty-eight. The family was left with few economic resources and his wife Mary sought employment as a seamstress.

Treaties with the Plains Indians

The Canadian Government wanted the settlement of the western interior without the costly American frontier wars or the Red River problems of the early 1870s. To implement this objective, Ottawa pressed the Aboriginal occupants to cede the "North West." In the years 1874–77, three numbered treaties were signed between Ottawa and the Plains Indian tribes. For cash annuities, medals and clothing, livestock, farm implements, and promises of assistance in adapting to a new way of life in enclosed land areas, the Indians acceded to the unfamiliar concept of a reserve.[73]

In 8 September 1874, Alexander Morris, the Lieutenant Governor of Manitoba and the North-West Territories, escorted by two companies from the Manitoba Militia under Lieutenant-Colonel Osborne Smith, met Cree and Saulteaux bands at Fort Qu'Appelle to negotiate Treaty 4, sometimes called the Qu'Appelle Treaty.

Ill will between the two tribes, delays in the meetings, Indian concerns over the proposed agreement, and what the government termed were "excessive demands" made the week-long negotiations trying. The Indians had wanted an explanation for the Hudson's Bay Company sale of Rupert's Land to Canada—"their land"—and demanded the money.[74]

Both time and monetary constraints, however, left Morris with little room to negotiate. He depicted a bleak Indian life without a treaty and urged the Indians to think of tomorrow—their future. He assured the Indians that the promises the government made would be carried out as long as the sun shines above and the water flows to the ocean. Lieutenant Governor Morris affirmed Ottawa's offer, and the Indians signed the agreement that surrendered the land areas south and east of the South Saskatchewan River from Medicine Hat to the present-day Manitoba border, about 75,000 square miles (200,000 km^2).

There were no Mounties at the negotiations. In the talks, Lieutenant Governor Morris alluded to their presence: "If a white man does wrong to an Indian, the Queen will punish them. The other day at Fort Ellice, a white man stole some furs from an Indian. The Queen's policemen took him at once; sent him down to Red River, and he is lying in jail now."[75]

On the date that the Treaty 4 was signed (15 September 1874), the '74 NWMP column was nearing the confluence of the Bow and Oldman (Belly) rivers. That day, Sub-Inspector John H. McIllree's diary recorded:

> Rouse at 6 A.M. Horses and oxen very weak and played out. All the men are walking now except those driving teams, and a good many of them have no boots … halted at 11:20 A.M. near

a lake about three miles long. It was not on the map, so the Colonel named it Commissioner's Lake. Went on again about 1:30 P.M. until nearly dark when we camped alongside a very small mud hole, where we got enough mud and water to make tea ... only made about 14¾ miles (24 km) today. Night quiet but raining a little.[76]

"A" Troop, en route from Roche Percée to Fort Edmonton, was at Fort Carlton. For four days, snow had stopped travel and delayed the crossing of the North Saskatchewan River.

The next treaty agreement in the North-West Territories came two years later at Fort Carlton. In the late August 1876 meetings, Plains and Wood Cree bands surrendered lands in the North Saskatchewan River basin. Earlier, to facilitate the Treaty 6 negotiations, Ottawa had Methodist missionary George McDougall visit the designated bands to outline the proposed terms and hopefully lessen some of the snags evident in the Qu'Appelle Treaty. McDougall distributed $3,000 in gifts to the bands. Superintendent Leif Crozier reported to Ottawa: "McDougall made everything right with the Indians about here and at Carlton."[77] At the same time, MacDougall observed the Indian distress over the rapid decline of the buffalo. Several confrontations with White people in 1875 reflected this anxiety.[78] And the response of Big Bear (Mistahimaskwa) to the enticements offered by McDougall indicated unease with the proposed meetings. The chief exclaimed: "We want none of the Queen's presents! When we set a fox trap we scatter pieces of meat all around but when the fox gets into the trap we knock him on the head. We want no baits. Let your chiefs come like men and talk to us."[79]

The proposed Treaty 6 negotiations appeared jeopardized when a rumor surfaced that Chief Beardy (Kamiyistowesit) of the Willow Cree band at Duck Lake planned to prevent Lieutenant Governor Alexander Morris, en route from Winnipeg, from crossing the South Saskatchewan River.

Superintendent James Walker had left Swan River with fifty mounted men to construct a police post at Battleford. On reaching Fort Carlton and learning of Beardy's threat, Walker rode with his detachment southeast to Duck Lake. Walker wrote: "I think they were the most surprised Indians I ever saw. It was the first time that they had seen 'mounted red coats' and apparently did not know we were in the country. The fact we had come behind them from the north bewildered them."[80] Walker's troop remained until the arrival of Lieutenant Governor Morris. Chief Beardy shook hands with Morris and welcomed him into the country.

Native and Non-Native Scouts with the Mounties

L–R, front row – Black Eagle, Elk Facing the Wind; middle row – Inspt. Cecil Denny, Staff-Sergt. Chris Hillaird, Sergt. George Cotter; back row – Scout Hunbury, Scout Jerry Potts.

– GA NA 556 – 1

It was planned to include the newly organized Swan River police band at the treaty ceremonies. Along their route to Fort Carlton, band members took every opportunity to practice and the men delighted in startling the Indians with loud outbursts of music. The drum was a great attraction and, at one stop, the Indians offered to trade two horses for the instrument. The band troop recognized signs of Indian uneasiness. When they reached one camp, William Parker watched "a number of squaws running into their tepees crying, we are losing our country."[81]

The government representatives made a grand entry at the Fort Carlton negotiations, aimed at awing the Indians. Not surprisingly, the police band with its booming drum led the procession, followed by the carriage of Lieutenant Governor Morris in full uniform along with a police escort. Métis interpreter Peter Erasmus observed that, "the police dressed in their smart scarlet uniforms and riding well trained horses made a big impression with the Indians."[82] He added, though few in number (108 officers and men with two field pieces), the police (*ke-manas-ko-motin*) established in the minds of the tribes the fairness and justice of government for all people.

Unskilled interpreters bogged down the talks. The Indians, to guard their interests, had prudently hired Erasmus as a principal interpreter in the discussions. Second, a handful of Saulteaux, unhappy with the Qu'Appelle Treaty (claiming white people were cheating the Indians), appeared bent on disrupting an agreement and left in a sullen mood.

Big Child (Mistawasis) and Star Blanket (Ahtahkakoop), the foremost Cree spokesmen, supported the proposed agreement. Both men would acknowledge that rapidly declining buffalo herds inevitably ushered in "another way of life." Big Child spoke favourably of the Mounted Police:

> The Great Queen Mother, hearing of the sorrows of her children, sent out the Red Coats. Though these were only of a number you could count on your fingers and toes, yet the cutthroats and criminals who recognized no authority but their guns, who killed each other on the slightest pretense and had murdered Indians without any fear of reprisal, immediately abandoned their forts ... and fled back to their own side of the line ... but ask yourself why the traders fled in fear from so few men ... it was the power that stands behind those few Red Coats that those men feared.[83]

Star Blanket, the next speaker, encouraged the assembly to accept the forthcoming White invasion: "They could not stop the power of the white man from spreading over the land like the grasshoppers that cloud the sky and then fall to consume every blade of grass and every leaf on the trees in their path."[84] Most important, the Queen would end the sale of "firewater" and stop the bloody fighting between the Indian tribes.

A small Cree faction, led by Poundmaker (Ptikwahanapiw yin) and The Badger, challenged the government proposals. Forceful denunciations by Poundmaker won support: "This is our land! It isn't a piece of pemmican to be cut off and given in little pieces back to us. It is ours and we will take what we want."[85] Interpreter Erasmus thought that the signing of an agreement was doubtful. However, Big Child (Mistawasis) downplayed the opposition. He asked the assembly: "I speak directly to Poundmaker and The Badger and those others who object to signing this treaty. Have you anything better to offer our people?"[86]

The Indians were astute in the talks and extremely apprehensive about their future. Treaty 6 included promises of assistance with food and health care in times of hardship. It must be remembered that the horrible smallpox epidemic was only six years earlier. After four days of negotiations, Treaty 6 was signed on 23 August 1876.

It took almost two days to complete the 1,800 Indian payments. Once this task was finished, it was time to celebrate. The Indians challenged the police to race their fastest horse against the best buffalo runner in the Indian camp. The betting was feverish—money, a rifle against a horse, Red River carts, harnesses, oxen, even clothing. Everyone, it appeared, moved to the level tract of land above the fort for this "great horse race" of about one mile. The police were delighted when Kangaroo, the police horse, won by four lengths. This was the first of horse races (with gambling) that lasted until sundown. "The Indians," one policeman concluded, "have a great craze for horse racing and gambling."[87]

On August 26, the Indians bid farewell to the Lieutenant Governor. After several brief speeches by Government representatives, the Indians, embracing White conventions, gave three cheers for the queen, three for Lieutenant Governor Morris, and one each for the Mounted Police and the Hudson's Bay Factor. Adhesions to Treaty 6 were signed in the weeks that followed with the Willow Cree bands under Beardy, One Arrow at Duck Lake and upriver at Fort Pitt with Indians led by Sweet Grass. In recognition of his status as a chief, Sweet Grass received a medal, uniform, and flag. At the conclusion of the signing, when the police band played "God Save the Queen," all Indians rose to their feet.

Seven Mounted Policemen signed Treaty 6: Commissioner J. F. Macleod, Inspectors J. Walker and W.D. Jarvis, Adjutant E. D. Clark, Hospital Steward J.H. Price, Inspector J. McIllree, and Constable J.B. Mitchell.

Leading Cree Negotiators at Treaty 6, 1876

L—R, front row – Star Blanket (Ahtahkakoop), Flying in a Circle (Kahkiwista),
Big Child (Mistawasis); back row – Louis O'Soup, Peter Hourie (interpreter).

– NAC C – 019258

Several Cree bands under Big Bear (Mistahimaskwa) and Little Pine
(Minahikosis) refused the Treaty and continued their nomadic lifestyle. Both
bands were regarded as a troublesome magnet for dissident Indians. It was
not until July 1879, after three difficult years for his followers, that Little
Pine signed his adhesion to Treaty 6. Big Bear remained "outside treaty"
for six years. Finally, in December 1882, the loss of followers and hunger
made the "contumacious" chief accept the Treaty.

On 22 September 1877, one year after the Treaty 6 agreement, the Blackfoot Confederacy signed the last of the numbered treaties relating to the Canadian plains. The report of the Commissioner viewed it was remarkable considering the large number of Indians from different bands that there was not a single casualty or a disturbance at the gathering. The area ceded was southern Alberta.

A government report said that, the Blackfoot Confederacy had "some of the most warlike and intelligent but intractable bands in the North-West."[88] However, a letter in 1876 from a missionary indicated that the tribe had showed a friendly disposition toward the White newcomers. With this in mind, Lieutenant Governor Morris urged negotiations with the Blackfoot at the earliest date. The Indians were notified. A visitor to the Morleyville Mission noted although the Stoney tribe, "anxiously awaited the coming of the commissioners next August ... they expressed the firm resolve to oppose the introduction of telegraph lines or the making of roads."[89]

The Government negotiators were NWMP Commissioner James F. Macleod and Lieutenant Governor of the North-West Territories David Laird.[90] The proposed meeting site was Blackfoot Crossing (*Si-she-pa-qui*— "ridge under the water") on the Bow River, 100 km east of Fort Calgary.

This location placed the Indians at odds: Blackfoot Chief Crowfoot was reluctant to meet at Fort Macleod (which he called a White Man's fort), but a convenient post for the Blood and Peigan bands. Colonel Macleod persuaded the two bands to travel 140 km northeast for the negotiations.[91]

Lieutenant Governor Laird's route took him 485 km from Swan River to Battleford where Assistant Commissioner Irvine, who had come north from Fort Macleod, was waiting. After a brief stop at Battleford, Laird with Irvine's four-man troop and an Indian guide, left on August 25 for Fort Macleod, 490 km southwest. On their journey, they encountered only small herds of buffalo and it was noted that there were few calves. As they approached the town Colonel Macleod with 100 policemen rode out to meet them while, in the distance, two field pieces fired a thirteen-gun salute.

Laird spoke highly of the local detachment: "The men, whose horses were in excellent condition, looked exceedingly well, and the officers performed their duties in a most efficient manner."[92] He praised the police patience with the "somewhat intrusive" Indians who, he observed, "always spoke of the officers of the police in the highest terms, and of the Commander of the Force, Lieutenant-Colonel Macleod, especially as their benefactor."[93]

The Fort Macleod detachment had carefully prepared for the coming treaty gatherings. Constable Patterson recalled the men underwent constant drills and the horses were accustomed to the noise of the field pieces.

"There was," Constable Nedham recalled, "excitement in the barracks in September 1877, when one hundred men from C and D troops were ordered out for duty and left for Blackfoot Crossing."[94]

The police moved in two groups to Blackfoot Crossing. On September 12, Commissioner Macleod left with eighty men, two field guns, and six supply wagons. The following day, Assistant Commissioner Irvine headed a second troop with the Lieutenant Governor who praised the splendid appearance of the body of men who formed his honour guard. After three days of travel on the 130-km route, the unabated barking of hundreds of dogs told the policemen they were nearing Blackfoot Crossing.

While the men set up camp, Sergt.-Major T. Lake positioned the two field pieces on a hill overlooking the river. The view was breathtaking:

> There must have been a thousand lodges ...They were plentifully supplied with meat, having only just left a large buffalo herd downstream to the east. Their horses covered uplands to the north and south of the camp in thousands. It was a stirring a picturesque scene; great bands of grazing horses, the mounted warriors threading their way among them and as far as the eye could reach the white Indian lodges glimmering among the trees along the river bottom. By night the valley echoed to the dismal howling of the camp's curs and from sun to sun drums boomed from the tents. Never before had such a concourse of Indians assembled on Canada's western plains.[95]

Constable James Stanford also felt an "element of menace and danger to us, a little body who had come as the representatives of law and order."[96] One policeman recalled their arrival:

> Once the Indians saw us making camp tom-toms began to beat, and excitement was noticed all through camp. Squaws and children could be seen in groups in the camp watching the police camp on the above butte. Young bucks mounted on their pet buffalo horses, painted over in fantastic colors, dressed only in a breechcloth, commenced to ride around the camp chanting their songs, and doing everything they could to show their fine horsemanship.[97]

The uproar was relentless. Doctor Barrie Nevitt bitterly complained that: "the monotonous sounds of the drum and the sharp voices of the squaws made the night hideous."[98]

The Blackfoot Confederacy camped on the south flats while the Stoneys with Reverend J. McDougall, their minister and interpreter, were across the river. Chief Bobtail with 432 Crees from Battle River were here to sign their adhesion to Treaty 6. They camped by themselves as a precaution against Blackfoot attacks. Wagons of traders sat anxious to profit from Indian payments. They had wanted to build log buildings to guard their stores, but complied with Indian objections to cutting timber.

Anyone fortunate to be at Blackfoot Crossing that autumn in 1877 sensed the historical occasion. There were Prairie Indians in the primitive splendor of a lifestyle soon to disappear. Perhaps that was why six police wives accompanied their husbands. Splendid autumn weather (even then called Indian Summer) added to the momentous experience.

At 1:30 p.m. on Monday, 17 September 1877, the boom of a field piece opened the Treaty negotiations. The chiefs sat in a circle in front of the Commissioner's tent and smoked the pipe of peace. Because of his gangling appearance, the Indians nicknamed Laird "the Crane." The introduction of the Indian speakers to Laird took on a humorous aspect when one Indian was introduced by interpreter Léveille, after a pause, as "Horse's Tail." This provoked Scout Jerry Potts to yell out, "You son of a bitch, you lie. I tell you it is Horse's Ass."[99] The refined and deeply religious Lieutenant Governor was visibly taken aback.

From his talk—"the Queen's message"—translated by interpreters, Lieutenant Governor Laird concluded that the attentive Indians were in a responsive frame of mind. But since the Peigan, Sarcee, and Blood bands were still en route, it was agreed to postpone the negotiations for another two days. To sustain the Indians, food, tobacco, tea, and sugar were made available. The Stoneys accepted the supplies, but the Blackfoot refused any provisions until there was a meeting, declaring: "Let us talk first, and if we agree then we will eat."[100]

On Wednesday afternoon, even though the Blood band had not arrived, the negotiations resumed. Band music, field-piece fire, and a fifty-man honour guard led by Assistant Commissioner Irvine, marked the opening of negotiations held in a council tent. Nearby, 4,000 Indians squatted on the grass. In his talk, Laird praised the Mounted Police:

A good Indian has nothing to fear from the Queen or her officers ... when bad white men brought you whiskey, robbed you and made you poor, she sent the mounted police to put an end to it. You know how they stopped this and punished the offenders, and how much good this has done. I have to tell you how much pleased the Queen is that you have taken the Mounted Police by the hand and helped them and obeyed her laws since their arrival.[101]

After Laird outlined the terms of the treaty, each tribe returned to its camp to discuss the government proposal. The Stoneys indicated approval while the Blackfoot, aware of the broken promises that followed the United States Blackfeet Treaty of 1855 and annoyed that other tribes and Métis were infringing on their hunting grounds, appeared to be wavering. From the stormy debate in the Blackfoot camp, one Mountie thought, "all chances of making a treaty would have to be abandoned."[102] On Thursday, Laird finalized the agreement details while Colonel Macleod interviewed Indian leaders on treaty issues and land choices for a reserve. He quickly reached an agreement on these concerns. On Friday, the large Blood tribe arrived. At once, Red Crow (Mekaisto) and Crowfoot held a council.

On Saturday, 22 September 1877, the final discussions were held. The prestige of the NWMP certainly bolstered the government's position. In a review of the Treaty three decades later, Laird attributed to the police a beneficial influence among the Blackfoot by suppressing the American whiskey trade and establishing law and order in the territory. This influence was exerted to secure the negotiations of the Treaty, which otherwise, he thought, could scarcely have been successfully concluded.[103]

Indian spokesmen praised the Mounted Police. Crowfoot's statement is well-known: "If the police had not come to this country, where would we be now? Bad men and whiskey were indeed killing us so fast that very few of us would have been left today. The Mounted Police have protected us as the feathers of the bird protect it from the frosts of winter."[104] Red Crow, leader of the Bloods, asserted:

> Three years ago when the mounted police came to this country, I met and shook hands with Stamix Otokan (Macleod) at Belly River. Since that time he made me many promises, he kept them all, not one has been broken. Everything that the Mounted Police has done has been good. I entirely trust Stamix Otokan, and will leave everything to him.[105]

Button Chief (who signed Treaty 7 under the name Medicine Calf) supported Red Crow: "The Great Mother sent Stamix Otokan and the police to put an end to the traffic in fire water. I can sleep now safely."[106] David Laird's report on Treaty 7 praised the police for their assistance:

Macleod my Associated Commissioner was indefatigable in his exertions to bring the negotiations to a successful termination … the same laudable efforts were put forth by Major Irvine and the other officers of the Force, and their kindness to me, personally, I shall never fail to remember. The volunteer band did much to enliven the whole proceedings.[107]

Several problems had interrupted the negotiations. One was a demand by a minor Blood chief for an individual cash payment for the wood used by the NWMP. Laird was unmoved and responded that, should there be any pay, the Indians should pay the Queen for sending them the police. The response by the Lieutenant Governor brought widespread laughter. Second, a deputation of Métis presented a petition that opposed the planned Buffalo Ordinance (limiting the killing of young buffalo) and also requested government assistance in farming.

Treaty 7 was signed Saturday, 22 September 1877. The band played "God Save the Queen" and the field pieces fired a salute. The document contained the signatures of Lieutenant Governor Laird and Commissioner James Macleod and fifty-one Indian marks. Eight other NWMP members had signed along with three police wives.[108]

Christian missionaries were to play a key role at Treaty 7. Both Father Constantine Scollen and his Methodist counterpart, John McDougall, urged their followers to accept the pact. The Indians, Constantine Scollen wrote later, signed the treaty as a provision for food and clothing in times of need and because previously they "had always been kindly dealt with by authorities and did not wish to offend them."[109] Chief Red Crow supported this stance: "The government said they would be good to us. We took what the government offered us."[110] A third authoritarian religious figure was Jean L'Heureux, a bogus priest and controversial individual. L'Heureux acted as an intermediary and interpretor for the Blackfoot and, in that role, exerted considerable influence on the tribe. [111]

The negotiations had been successfully concluded, but had they been fully understood? The money promised was an encouragement. Father Scollen, who had spent the past two decades on the western plains, earlier described the Blackfoot "as clothed in rags, without horses and without guns and utterly demoralized as a people."[112] However, in the three years since the arrival of the NWMP, the tribe's lifestyle had improved to the point where they had been able to purchase several thousand horses. But their understanding of the treaty they had signed was, in Scollen's opinion, "unhesitatingly negative."[113]

The Stoney tribe received lands in the upper Bow River hunting area, the Blackfoot Confederacy and Sarcee Indians accepted adjoining reserves on a narrow strip of land downriver from Blackfoot Crossing and running to the confluence of the Red Deer River.[114] Bobtail's Crees received the land they requested near Pigeon Lake and within the Treaty 6 boundary. The Stoneys were the only tribe that had made a request for agricultural implements and seed.

On Sunday morning, all was quiet. In front of the police tents, a single sentry paced back and forth when, suddenly, mounted Indians charged the camp. Hudson's Bay trader Richard Hardisty recorded:

At 8:30 a.m. without warning, not even the bark of a dog, the piercing war cries of some 3,000 braves led by their war chief rang out, followed by the deafening roar of the firing of hundreds of muzzle-loadings guns and pistols. There appeared on the skyline, the naked warriors in war paint mounted on ponies, bareback ... yelling their war cry and firing their guns. They made a mad dash down the hill, the leaders only drawing their horses to their haunches when their noses almost touched the first row of tents.[115]

The body paint on the warriors was captivating. One spectator wrote: "The squaws had painted the Indian warriors in the most hideous colors from head to foot. Some had yellow and black spots all over; others, white spots; still others, the body was half black and half white."[116] Steele observed warriors that, he thought, looked like zebras, others leopards. A spectacular sham battle followed. William Parker described the scene:

As they passed us at full gallop, they would lie along their horses on the opposite side with just their foreheads showing over the horse's mane. They would shoot off their rifles under the horse's necks right over our heads and after firing would come to an upright position on the horse. Then, as they galloped off, with hand to mouth they would yell out their shrill war cries.[117]

Everyone intently watched the Blood, divided in teams of fifty men (with one group representing the Cree), fight for half an hour in a masterful display of horsemanship. Men would fall from their horses, only to be attacked by an opponent who would fire a shot close to his head, pretend to scalp the fallen man, place an imaginary scalp under his belt, and let out a war cry. At the end, the Blackfoot team having the most imaginary scalps was declared victorious. The mock battle had enthralled the white spectators, although stray bullets came far too close for comfort. "It was," one Mountie wrote, "a hair-raising affair ... and we would not have missed it for the best farm in Manitoba."[118]

The next day, the treaty payments began. Inspector William Winder, Sub-Inspectors C. Denny and W.D. Antrobus, took three days to pay the 4,400 Blackfoot Confederacy, Sarcee, and the 430 Battle River Cree. There were delays in identifying the eligible Indians and determining their family members. It had to be explained to pregnant women that expectant babies were not entitled to money.

Lieutenant Governor David Laird, impressed by the distribution of payments, informed Prime Minister John A. Macdonald:

> I would urge that the Officers of the North-West Mounted
> Police be entrusted to make the annual payments to Indians ...
> the chiefs themselves had requested this ... The Indians have
> confidence in the Police, and it might be some time before they
> acquire the same respect for strangers.[119]

This suggestion became a NWMP responsibility on "Treaty Money Day." The Indians received almost $60,000 in cash. Waiting merchants were poised for the expected windfall. One American trader, William Hyde, related: "The money went into the hands of the storekeepers in a few hours. Conrad sold a band of horses at once ... every bottle of Pain Killer was sold ... I was offered $5 a pint for alcohol."[120]

Unscrupulous traders cheated the Indians of their new wealth. Many Indians did not understand the denominational values of currency, and the police "frequently found that the Indians had been given the labels off fruit jars or cans as money."[121] Some wary Indians approached policemen for help. "They would," wrote one constable, "come over to get us to count their money for them, as they did not trust the traders."[122] Constable Alfred Nedham recalled that they "would turn the money over to one of us and ask us to buy whatever they wanted."[123] Frank Fitzpatrick wrote: "I have seen many an Indian clutching a handful of bills, and make a beeline for the first Red Coat, saying '*Tonah*'—that is 'how much?'"[124]

To offset the problem of determining currency values, government payments afterwards were made in $1 bills. This was cumbersome. In Winnipeg in 1879, Superintendent James Walker was given $100,000 in $1 bills to deliver as treaty payments. This basic misunderstanding of rudimentary monetary denominations illustrates the differences between the negotiating parties.

Crowfoot and Red Crow: Leading Chiefs at Treaty 7, 1877

L—R, front row – Crowfoot (Blackfoot), Sitting on the Eagle Tail Feathers (Peigan),
Three Bulls (Blackfoot); back row – Jean L'Heureux, Red Crow (Blood),
Sergt. W. Piercy (NWMP).

– GA NA 13 – 1

For example, the Indians had no concept of private land ownership,
thereby making the apportionment of one section of land for each reserve
family of five a rather meaningless statistic. Language difficulties based
on construction and the need for translation caused further problems.
Since neither party had adequate knowledge of the other's customs and
laws, additional problems surfaced.

David Laird, Lieutenant Governor, NWT

Laird reported positively of his NWMP escort: "The men, whose horses were in excellent condition, looked exceedingly well, and the officers performed their duties in a most efficient manner."

– Alexander Morris, *The Treaties of Canada with the Indians of Manitoba and the North-West Territories*, 254

NAC PA-025478

White legal precedent emphasized written documentation; the Indians of southern Alberta relied on oral statements and tradition.[125] Also, the White people incorrectly believed that the Plains chiefs were autocratic spokesmen for their tribes, just as David Laird and James Macleod spoke for the Government of Canada. Therefore, the chief best known to the Mounted Police, Crowfoot, one of two Blackfoot head chiefs, received an elevated status while, in reality, two Bloods, Red Crow and Rainy Chief, had higher authority in the Confederacy and larger followings.[126]

There was an urgency to conclude the Treaty 7 negotiations. Ottawa and Washington, in an attempt to resolve the American Sioux influx into Canada, had arranged for an American Commission to meet with Sitting Bull at Fort Walsh in mid-October, only three weeks away. Therefore, on conclusion of the treaty payments, Lieutenant Governor Laird left for his new residence at Battleford. Laird had found five days of meetings taxing. Moreover, he had ridden 1,200 km to conduct the conference.

Commissioner Macleod rode with a troop for the conference scheduled at Fort Walsh, 260 km southeast. Three days later, the members of the Fort Macleod detachment departed for their base. The weather had turned very cold and snow blanketed the prairie.[127]

NOTES

1. The Blackfoot Nation (Confederacy) included the Blackfoot (Siksika), Bloods (Kainai) and Peigans (Pikuni). The term Blackfoot is preferred in Canada over Blackfeet.

2. An earlier Indian contact was Three Bulls. He reported a whiskey fort on the Highwood River.

3. *RC*, NWMP, 1874, 64.

4. White people have commented on the Indian penchant for shaking hands—which they never did with other Indians. Constable John Donkin in *Trooper and Redskin*, 243, wrote: "if one solitary redskin meets twenty policemen he must shake hands with every individual." Inspector Sam Steele, in the *Medicine Hat Times*, 29 March 1910, recalled Indians riding two or three miles out of their way to shake hands.

5. *RC*, NWMP, 1874, 67.

6. Dempsey, ed., *A Winter at Fort Macleod*, 38.

7. Dempsey, ed., *William Parker Mounted Policeman*, 129.

8. *LH*, 25 June 1949.

9. *LH*, 23 July 1924.

10. *RC*, NWMP, 1876, 23.

11. *TG*, 10 May 1876. He added that although the entire citizen population was American, they thrived under the Union Jack.

12. *MFP*, 3 January 1876.

13. *MFP*, 2 May 1876. At the same time, McDougall censured the NWMP. In a letter "The Last Letters of George McDougall," *AH*, XV, No. 2, 20, he wrote: "I have sometimes heard the Mounted Police swagger about what they would do with the natives in case of an insurrection, but my opinion is that if the good Lord had not predisposed the red man to look upon these troops as friends, very few of them would have gone back to tell the tale of their adventures in the North West."

14. "A Letter from Bishop Grandin," *AH*, XXI, No. 1, 21. Also C. Scollen in *WDT*, 20 March 1882.

15. Lewis Saum, "From Vermont to Whoop-Up Country," *Montana History*, XXXV, No. 3. 67.

16. *SN*, 29 July 1875.

17. *PAM*, Alexander Morris, MG6, B1, 962.

18. *LH*, 28 October 1921. Hugh A. Dempsey, ed., "A Mounties' Diary, 1875," *The Early West* (Edmonton: The Historical Society of Alberta, 1957), 8–13.

19. Ibid. This Indian view is supported in Cecil Denny, *The Riders of the Plains*, 52 and Constantine Scollen in Alexander Morris, *Treaties of Canada*, 247.

20. *GA*, Richard Hardisty, M 477, Box 4, f. 104.

21. *GA*, Frederick Bagley, Diary, M 44. Plante led a troubled life. The *MFP*, 15 November 1878, stated: "A half-breed named Felix Plante is under arrest at Fort Saskatchewan, charged with attempting to kill his father. Prisoner is undoubtedly insane, as he says that he is divinely commissioned to kill off the whole human race."

In 1879, Plante was charged as a dangerous lunatic and committed to prison. See Shelley Gavigan, *Hunger, Horses and Government Men* (Vancouver: University of British Columbia), 50–51.

22. *GA*, Frederick Bagley, Diary, M 43.

23. Nevitt, *Frontier Life in the Mounted Police*, 108.

24. *MFP*, 1 June 1877.

25. *UMM*, Thomas B. Boys Diary. Boys wrote: "Polygamy is universally practiced; every man has at least three wives. Colonel Macleod knew one old fellow who rejoiced in the possession of eleven dusky helpmates."

26. *MFP*, 28 February 1881.

27. Ibid.

28. *FBRP*, 9 November 1881.

29. *FMG*, 29 December 1882.

30. *CH*, 17 November 1945.

31. *UMM*, Thomas B. Boys Diary.

32. Nevitt, *Frontier Life in the Mounted Police*, 45.

33. John D. Higinbotham, *When the West was Young* (Toronto: Ryerson, 1933), 227.

34. *RL*, 9 July 1885.

35. LaNaunze, "Echoes and Letters from Fort Walsh," 35.

36. *MJN*, 23 May 1884.

37. *ODC*, 7 April 1875. The letter was written 10 January 1875.

38. Denny, *The Riders of the Plains*, 52. In a second account in the *Fort Macleod Times*, 3 July 1924, Denny related, "The Blackfeet never gave us much trouble. They were always loyal to us, and in fact helped us in our fight against the whiskey smugglers."

39. Steele, *Forty Years in Canada*, 80.

40. *RC*, NWMP, 1874, 65. Impressions of Indian women are given in Chapter 13 (Lovely Prairie Belles).

41. *MFP*, 1 June 1877.

42. *MFP*, 14 September 1876.

43. *CH*, 13 July 1935.

44. *FBR*, 13 April 1877.

45. *RL*, 27 May 1916.

46. *TG*, 19 August 1879.

47. LaNauze, "Echoes and Letters from Fort Walsh," 35.

48. Donkin, *Trooper and Redskin*, 210–11.

49. Nevitt, *Frontier Life in the Mounted Police*, 14. Surgeon's views later were less critical.

50. Ibid., 51.

51. Fitzpatrick, *Sergeant 331*, 82–83.

52. *SAB*, J.E. McEntyre Diary, A 110.

53. *OFP*, 19 December 1879. Also in *WDT*, 29 December 1879; *TG*, 19 August 1879; *MFP*, 22 August 1882, and Steele, *Forty Years in Canada*, 132–34.

54. Fitzpatrick, *Sergeant 331*, 38. See pages 35–38. Also Rivett-Carnac, ed., "Letters From the North-West," 324 and *SAB*, J.E. McIntyre, A 110.

55. Donkin, *Trooper and Redskin*, 227.

56. *WDT*, 8 August 1879.

57. George Guernsey, "Links with the Past – Memories of Fort Walsh," *SG*, Sixteenth Annual, 23.

58. Dempsey, ed., *William Parker Mounted Policeman*, 38.

59. Nevitt, *Frontier Life in the Mounted Police*, 53.

60. *MFP*, 1 June 1877.

61. Mike Oka, "A Blood Indian's Story," *AHR*, 111, No. 4, 16. Research on the Indian-White history of the Western Plains is decidedly unbalanced by the paucity of Indian written records.

62. *UMM*, Thomas B. Boys Diary.

63. *SH*, 2 August 1882.

64. Fitzpatrick, *Sergeant 331*, 3. Fitzpatrick's interview with Macleod is on pages 4–5.

65. *TM*, 5 April 1875.

66. *SN*, 20 May 1875.

67. *TG*, 30 October 1877. Also praise by Laird for the NWMP.

68. *NAC*, RG 18, A.G. Irvine, Volume 3437, f. 30.

69. *MFP*, 11 August 1880.

70. McDougall, *On Western Trails in the Early Seventies*, 243.

71. Steele, *Forty Years in Canada*, 156.

72. *CH*, 12 July 1924. Other positive comments are in Gillett, "Interview with J.H.G. Bray," D'Artigue, *Six Years in the Canadian North-West*, 102, and *GA*, Joseph Carscadden, M 6608.

73. Treaty 5 was signed in 1875. The territory covered central Manitoba and was outside NWMP jurisdiction.

74. Morris, *Treaties of Canada*. See Pis-qua, 102, and The Gambler, 106.

75. Ibid., 109.

76. *GA*, AB McIllree #1 Diary.

77. *NAC*, RG 18, v. 6.

78. In July 1875, Cree Indians stopped a party led by Andrew Bourke and ordered them back to Fort Carlton, telling him "they did not wish anyone to come into their country until the treaty had been made." *MFP*, 3 August 1875. Also that year near Fort Pitt, Indians blocked an eighteen-man crew under George Wright from building the telegraph line. Wright was told: "No treaty has been made with us and yet our land is invaded by white people ... if you go forward you may disappear forever." Wright temporarily withdrew. *OFP*, 26 November 1878.

79. *PAM*, Morris Papers, MG12/B1/1136. Hugh A. Dempsey, *Big Bear* (Vancouver: Douglas and McIntyre, 1984), 63.

80. Walker, "Police Experiences," 35. Also *CH*, 15 March 1924.

81. Dempsey, ed., *William Parker Mounted Policeman*, 23.

82. Peter Erasmus, *Buffalo Days and Nights* (Calgary: Glenbow-Alberta Institute, 1976), 239; Steele, *Forty Years in Canada*, 102–6; Constance Kerr Sissons, *John Kerr* (Toronto: University Oxford Press, 1946), 228–43.

83. Erasmus, *Buffalo Days and Nights*, 248.

84. Ibid., 249.

85. Ibid., 244.

86. Ibid., 247.

87. Dempsey, ed., *William Parker: Mounted Policeman*, 25. On Indian gambling, the *OFP,* 7 September 1876, commented "as a gambler, the Indian has no equal; he makes it his sole employment for days and nights." The continued gambling was accompanied by an Indian pounding on the drums.

88. *CSP*, 1878, V. 8, No. 10, Annual Report of the Department of the Interior Ending 30th June, 1877, xv.

89. *MFP*, 3 January 1876.

90. Lieutenant Governor (1876–81) David Laird was a member of a prominent Prince Edward Island family. He became a newspaper editor and a member of the House of Commons 1873–76. As Minister of the Interior, Laird attended Treaty 4. He replaced Morris as Lieutenant Governor in October 1876.

91. Morris, *Treaties of Canada*, 254–5. Also "The Annual Report Department of the Interior Year Ending 30th June, 1877," *Sessional Papers* 1878, Vol. 8, No. 10.

92. Morris, *Treaties of Canada*, 254.

93. Ibid.

94. *LH*, 11 July 1935; *CH*, 25 October 1930.

95. Denny, *The Law Marches West*, 106.

96. *University of Montana State Archives, Missoula*, James Stanford. (after *UMSA, Missoula*).

97. George Boswell, "Indian Treaties of 1877 and 1878," *SG*, Seventh Annual, 48–49.

98. Nevitt, *Frontier Life in the Mounted Police*, 14.

99. Dempsey, ed., *William Parker Mounted Policeman*, 41.

100. *MFP*, 8 November 1877.

101. Morris, *Treaties of Canada*, 267.

102. Denny, *Riders of the Plains*, 97.

103. David Laird, "Our Indian Treaties," *The Historical and Scientific Society of Manitoba*, Transaction 67, 1905, 7.

104. *TG*, 30 October 1877.

105. *TG*, 9 October 1877.

106. *TG*, 30 October 1877. Also George Boswell, *SG*, Seventh Annual, 83.

107. *CSP*, 1877, xlii. Also *TG*, 30 October 1877.

108. They were A.G. Irvine, W. Winder, L.N.F. Crozier, Dalrymple Clark, A. Shurtliff, C.E. Denny, W.D. Antrobus, and Frank Norman. The Mounted Police wives were Mary Macleod, Julia Winder, and Julia Shurtliff.

109. Hugh A. Dempsey, *Crowfoot – Chief of the Blackfeet* (Edmonton: Hurtig, 1972), 106.

110. *NAC*, RG 18, v. 19, f. 249. Hugh A. Dempsey, *Red Crow, Warrior Chief* (Saskatoon: Western Producer, 1980), 101.

111. Raymond Huel, "Jean L'Heureux," *AH*, LX, No. 4, 9–16. The *FBR*, 25 August 1881 comments on the Treaty payments: "The bogus priest L'Heureux is interpreting for the Government. He is as good an interpreter as he is an arrant knave."

112. Morris, *Treaties of Canada*, 248.

113. *GA*, 8038, b 5, f.1. Dempsey, *Crowfoot – Chief of the Blackfeet*, 106.

114. The reserve selections proved unsatisfactory. Within a few years, the Blood and Peigan moved southwest of Fort Macleod and, in 1883, the Sarcees accepted a reserve southwest of Calgary.

115. Richard Hardisty, "Blackfoot Treaty," *AHR*, V, No. 3, 21. Also *CH*, 18 November 1933.

116. Dempsey, ed., *William Parker Mounted Policeman*, 40.

117. Ibid.

118. Ibid. 41.

119. Morris, *Treaties of Canada*, 262.

120. *New North-West*, 19 October 1877.

121. Denny, *The Law Marches West*, 119. Also *CSP*, 1880, V. 3, No. 4, 92.

122. Dempsey, ed., *William Parker Mounted Policeman*, 130.

123. *LH*, 11 July 1935. Also *SH*, 15 August 1881.

124. Fitzpatrick, *Sergeant 331*, 72.

125. Father Lacombe, *WDT*, 20 July 1885, harshly commented that, "the Indians are mere children in matters of this kind. They don't attach the importance to a paper fixing a treaty as we do to the *Winnipeg Daily Times*."

126. Dempsey, *Crowfoot – Chief of the Blackfeet*, 95. *LH*, 22 November 1924.

127. Cree Adhesions to Treaty 6 were signed at Sounding Lake (located directly east of Red Deer, near the Saskatchewan border) in the spring of 1878. George Boswell, "Indian Treaties of 1877 and 1878," 85.

6

SITTING BULL AND
THE SIOUX

Sitting Bull (Ta-tanka I-yotank), Leader of the Teton Sioux

"I was particularly struck with Sitting Bull. He is a man of somewhat short stature, but with a pleasant face, a mouth showing great determination, and a fine high forehead. When he smiled, which he often did, his face brightened up wonderfully."

– A.G. Irvine, *Report of the Commissioner*, NWMP, 1877, 36
   GA NA 659 – 15

ON 25 JUNE 1876, SIOUX and Cheyenne warriors annihilated five companies of the 7th Cavalry, under General George A. Custer, at the Battle of the Little Big Horn. The outraged American army reacted forcefully against the "hostiles." From his headquarters in Chicago, General William T. Sherman directed "total war" against the Sioux. Military posts were built in buffalo country and army control exerted at the Indian agencies. After a two-day meeting in October 1876 between Sitting Bull and General Nelson A. (Bear Coat) Miles ended in disagreement, an arduous winter campaign ensued. American soldiers relentlessly attacked the Indian camps causing deaths, the destruction of provisions, and the loss of horses. The Sioux were left divided, demoralized, starving, and destitute. For band members unwilling to surrender, the only refuge was north of the border—a region they called "Grandmother's Land."[1]

One month before the Custer Massacre, Ottawa had informed Colonel Irvine that there was an impending incursion of Sioux Indians into the North-West Territories.[2] This movement was not unexpected. The *Manitoba Free Press* quoted Inspector E. Allen that, "the general feeling prevailing in the West was that Sitting Bull and his warriors would be compelled to cross the line."[3] If this proved true, a Sioux entry into Canada could have dangerous consequences. Alexander Morris, Lieut. Governor of Manitoba, warned Ottawa that the influx of Sioux "would be an event of the gravest possible character."[4]

White settlers living on the northwestern United States also foresaw the movement of the Sioux north. A Montana newspaper suggested that the NWMP increase its numbers, "as Sitting Bull and his savage host are more than probable to visit Her Majesty's Dominions before the close of this [U.S.] Centennial Year."[5]

Disquieting news arrived in July 1876 when Sub-Inspector Cecil Denny reported that, at a Blackfoot camp 400 km northeast of Fort Calgary, band leaders told him that the Sioux had sent a gift of tobacco to consummate a pact for warfare against the Crow Indians and American whites.[6] The Sioux promised mules and horses, "plenty" of white female captives, and support in attacking whites on this side of the border where the soldiers (NWMP) were weak.

The Blackfoot, who Denny described as in a "very unsettled state," had rejected this Sioux offer. A messenger had arrived shortly after the Sub-Inspector had entered the camp with the Sioux reply that, since no help was forthcoming, they would come over "to this side and show the Blackfeet that the white soldiers were nothing before them, and after they had exterminated the soldiers and taken their forts they would come against the Blackfeet."[7]

This was a disturbing threat. For his part, Denny assured the chiefs that the NWMP would confront any Sioux hostilities in Canada and that, as long as the Blackfoot were peaceful, the Mounted Police would remain their friends.

The Sioux Enter Canada

The Sioux-Blackfoot communication occurred only weeks after the Custer fight. Rumors followed that small parties of Sioux had crossed the border, which they called the "Long Road." This was alarming news, but there was little that ninety-five redcoats at Fort Walsh could do to prevent such forays. Colonel James Macleod acknowledged this fact in a letter to the Prime Minister, stating that "it would be impossible for the police to keep them in check over such an extended frontier."[8]

The constant American military harassment was making life unbearable for the Sioux. In August 1876, police scout Gabriel Solomon spoke to a Métis named Laframboise who had been in Sitting Bull's camp. Laframboise reported that the Sioux chief said he felt surrounded like an island in the middle of a sea and there were only two ways of escape—one to the country of the Great Mother, the other to the Spaniards.[9]

When reports placed some Sioux at Rock Creek, just south of the border, Inspector James Walsh sent a patrol under fifty-three-year-old Louis Léveille (who Walsh described as "the best scout I ever saw, faithful and efficient") to watch the boundary and to warn mobile traders of the likely danger.[10]

At this time, a handful of Sioux arrived at Fort Qu'Appelle during the Treaty Four Indian payments. They told M.G. Dickieson, the Indian Agent, that because life was perilous on the American side they wanted to come to Canada. "It is certainly gratifying," stated the agent, "to find that while the Indians look with distrust and suspicion on the United States Government, they have such faith in ours."[11]

This naive optimism aside, the Sioux were unwanted in Canada. Fourteen years earlier, after the Minnesota uprising in 1862, several Sioux bands had taken sanctuary in Canada. This precedent was not forgotten: upon contact with Canadian authorities every Sioux band claimed that they were King George Indians and they wanted to live in "Grandmother's Land."

The Canadian government was aware of the dangers that a Sioux movement into Canada would entail. Even before news of the "Custer Massacre," Lord Dufferin, Governor General of Canada, had contacted E. Thornton, the British minister in Washington, saying that the influx of these armed, warlike, and exasperated Indians would be anything but an agreeable addition to Canada and they could make the territory a base of operations for reprisals against their enemies and international complications of a difficult character may ensue.[12]

In early December 1876, Black Moon brought fifty-two Teton lodges into Canada to join an earlier American Sioux camp in the Wood Mountain area, 260 km east of Fort Walsh. There were now 109 lodges of Sioux refugees in Canada—about 500 warriors, 1,000 females, and 1,400 children. Observers counted 30 American army mules in the 3,500-horse herd.

Jean-Louis Légaré, a thirty-five-year-old French-Canadian, operated a nearby trading post. One day in mid-November, twelve warriors rode up to his trading shack, only to stay on their horses and look through the store window for thirty minutes. Then Little Knife, walked in, sat on the floor and called the others inside. No one spoke for two hours. Légaré wrote: "As for me I took care to say no word and make no gesture, but waited quietly to see what they would do."[13]

Suddenly, Little Knife jumped up, shook Légaré's hand, and returned to his place. One by one, each of the other warriors did the same. Then one Indian, named Crow, called in English to the north wind and the south wind and said: "We left the American side because we could not sleep, and had heard that the Big Woman was very good to her children, and we came to this country to sleep quiet."[14] Légaré gave his visitors ("to get rid of them") guns and ammunition for a promise they would trade furs. White people viewed some Indian behaviour as bizarre and unpredictable. Were more Sioux to come?

Mounted Police Contact the Sioux
On news of the Sioux arrival at Wood Mountain, Inspector James Walsh sent a small troop under Sub-Inspector Edmund Frechette to contact Black Moon. Most of the 320-km route from Fort Walsh passed through desolate prairie, with little shelter. The weather turned stormy and intensely cold.

When Frechette failed to return by December 13, a concerned Walsh took three scouts and twelve men to search for the earlier patrol. On the second day, they met Frechette's party. The fatigued men were in good spirits and able to return to Fort Walsh. In light of their ordeal (five horses had died and several times the men had to tramp all night to keep from freezing), they were given three days without duty. Meanwhile, Major James Walsh continued on to Wood Mountain.

Near Black Moon's camp there were 150 lodges under White Eagle, a Canadian Sioux (Santee) whose band had taken refuge in Canada after the Minnesota Massacre in 1862. Intimidated by the American Sioux arrivals, the Canadian band arranged a council between them and the North-West Mounted Police. Prominent American Sioux chiefs were Little Knife, Long Dog, Black Moon, and The Man Who Crawls.

At the council, with White Eagle acting as the interpreter, Walsh explicitly told the Sioux that they must obey the rules of Canada. He then asked: first, did they know that they were in the country of the Queen? Second, what had they come for? And third, had they taken refuge that winter only to raid the Americans in the spring? On this last point, Walsh was forceful: the White Mother would never allow them to attack Americans and return to Canada for safety. Any incursions into the United States opened American army retaliation against the band.

The Sioux responded that American soldiers had driven them from their homes and they were tired of continual warfare. Their grandfathers had told them that they would find peace in the land of the British. They implored the Queen to take pity on them and promised to obey the laws of Canada. A witness summarized the meeting: "The Major talked pretty plainly to them and told them if they remained in the British possessions they must obey the laws."[15]

The demoralized band was in desperate circumstances: they were hungry, their horses lean, and ammunition was so scarce that the hunters were even lassoing the calves and spearing buffalo with knives attached to poles. In response to Black Moon's request for ammunition, Walsh authorized trader Jean-Louis Légaré to issue a limited supply of cartridges. Before returning to Fort Walsh, Inspector Walsh posted Superintendent A.R. Macdonell, Constables T. Dunne and George B. Mills, and guide Joseph Morin at Wood Mountain to report Indian and Métis activities. Police patrols from Fort Walsh began watching the border for Indian movements.

In the first week of March 1877, four months after the Black Moon meeting (and ten months after the Custer battle) it was learned that Medicine Bear, a Middle (Yankton) Sioux, had crossed the Medicine line and camped beside the White Mud River (Frenchman River), 180 km southeast of Fort Walsh.

Walsh left to investigate, taking Constable B.H. Daniels and scouts Louis Léveille and Joe Morin. Near the Indian camp, the troop split into two parties. When Walsh and Morin reached the White Mud, a line of warriors on the opposite bank accused them of being Americans. At that critical moment, scouts Léveille and Daniels rode up, fueling the excitement. Walsh convinced the Indians that they were not Americans and led his troop across the waterway into the Indian camp. The police could not help but notice those Indians wearing American cavalry clothing taken from the dead at the Custer Massacre. While the police were in the camp, Four Horns arrived with fifty-seven Teton lodges from the United States and set up a nearby campsite.

Walsh requested a council with both Sioux bands. At the meeting, he repeated his earlier questions asked to Black Moon. In response, Four Horns and Medicine Bear complained that the Americans had driven them from their land and they had come searching for peace. Walsh emphasized that

Sitting Bull and Sioux Indians at Fort Walsh, 1877

"The Sioux invasion and their continued residence in our territory have entirely changed the Indian situation."

– *Report of the Commissioner*, NWMP, 1878, 23
PAA 3.1050

the newcomers must obey Canadian laws and never raid into the United States. Before he left, Walsh arranged a lookout post of three Mounties with six horses to report if more Sioux Indians arrived.

It was not "if," but when. Rumors were rife. One officer wrote on 30 April 1877: "reports Sitting Bull crossed line near White Mud ... if so, it looks bad for us ... as he is the worst Indian on the plains to white men."[16]

The rumors ended in May 1877 when information arrived that Sitting Bull was in Canada. Constable Tommy Aspdin witnessed their arrival:

> We were on routine patrol when our attention was attracted by a long column of rising dust moving swiftly in our direction. We reined up our horses and watched the strange panorama, keenly alert and prepared for any contingency, when Sitting Bull's mounted Hunkpapas emerged from the dust cloud and rode headlong in their flight to cross the 49th parallel to find asylum on Canadian soil. The women were astride the ponies with their papooses strapped to their backs and the children were lashed to the horses' backs. To say the least, we were dazzled by the barbaric splendor of their regalia and rich trappings.[17]

The American Western Sioux (Tetons) in Canada now numbered more than 3,000 Indians, about 600 lodges.[18] Would more Sioux come? The repercussions of the Teton presence were unpredictable and dangerous.

The NWMP attended at once to news of arriving Tetons. In May 1877, word came that Sitting Bull had camped with 135 lodges about 100 km north of the border at Pinto Horse Butte. Walsh immediately took a small force to that location. On the third day, the patrol, which included Sergeant Bob McCutcheon, scouts Louis Léveille and Gabriel Solomon, and three constables, discovered that they were being trailed. The redcoats continued to ride, displaying little concern. Suddenly, the hilly terrain opened to the outlying lodges of the Indian camp. The patrol dismounted, tethered the horses, and pitched their tents. The redcoats strolled about the lodges and talked to Sans Arcs (No Bows) band members. Spotted Eagle, a young Sans Arc chief, informed the police that they were in the camp of Sitting Bull. "Never," he declared, "had white men dared approach this close, as if they (the Indians) didn't exist."[19] As he spoke, a group of warriors approached. The short man with a limp was Sitting Bull. After handshaking, an afternoon council meeting was arranged.[20]

At the council, the chiefs took their seats with Sitting Bull at the head of the lodge. Walsh arrived and informed the Indians the purpose for his visit. After shaking hands, Sitting Bull launched into a history of his people, their broken treaties, and the cruel American army assaults upon the camp that murdered women and children. They were, Sitting Bull, said, "hunting me like wild animals, seeking for my blood, that he and his people had crossed the line seeking peace, the grass of Canada was not stained with blood ... I came to see the English, where we are going to raise a new life ... on the American side I saw they were running us in every direction. That is the reason I came to see you."[21]

After several speakers repeated the Sioux grievances, Walsh reiterated the point that Canadian laws were inviolable and that the Sioux forfeited asylum here if they used Canada for a base to attack across the border line. The Sioux requested ammunition and Walsh promised them a supply for hunting. That evening, Sitting Bull reflected (through an interpreter) on the events of that day:

> This is the most wonderful day of my life. Yesterday I was fleeing from the white men, cursing and reviling them. Today they enter my camp and pitch their lodges beside mine. Boldly and fearlessly they enter my camp. Their White Forehead [Walsh] walks to my lodge alone and unarmed. Alone and apart from his soldiers he quietly sits himself down cross-legged beside my lodge, giving me presents of tobacco and the hand of peace. It is a different world. What has happened? Is my reign at an end?[22]

The nonchalant entry into the camp by horsemen in scarlet tunics had astounded the Sioux. These redcoats acted fearlessly. That night the police party slept in the Indian camp.

As the police prepared to leave in the morning, White Dog, an American Assiniboine, rode into camp with two companions leading five horses. Scout Gabriel Soloman told Superintendent James Walsh that both he and Léveille had recognized three of the animals as stolen from Father Jules DeCorby, a priest in the Cypress Hills. Walsh had the two scouts check the horses again and, once confirmed they were unmistaken, Walsh said, "We shall give an observation lesson to the Sioux, show them how we treat horse thieves."[23]

He ordered Sergeant Bob McCutcheon to arrest White Dog and his companions, who were standing in a group of sixty Sioux warriors. When White Dog objected, insisting that he had found the horses on the prairies, Walsh approached carrying leg irons and resolutely declared: "You say that you will neither be arrested or surrender the horses. I arrest you for theft."[24]

The Sioux camp stood transfixed. Not a whisper was heard. White Dog repeated that he had found the horses wandering on the plains which by custom gave them to him. Major Walsh believed White Dog was lying, but knew the point had been made. As he released the accused, White Dog muttered words in his language. Walsh asked the interpreter to repeat White Dog's words—("I shall see you again")—and then boldly challenged White Dog to repeat his words. The Indian stood silent.

Again Walsh, using leg irons as a threat, told White Dog to withdraw his remarks or he would be taken to prison for threatening a police officer. The audacious police actions both dumbfounded and impressed the Sioux. The band had been in Canada only a few days and they had already witnessed a handful of redcoats (*Shaglashapi*) uphold the law and seize three horses—right in a large Indian camp.

Although this confrontation with the American Indians had auspicious results, serious concerns remained. Assistant Commissioner A.G. Irvine wrote to R.W. Scott, Secretary of State, that Walsh believed Sitting Bull was in a revengeful disposition and if he could get support would re-cross the line and make war on the Americans.[25] Commissioner James Macleod contacted Prime Minister Alexander Mackenzie: "The presence of these United States Sioux is a matter of very grave importance. There is not much reliance to be placed upon their promises, and they have not been on friendly terms with the Blackfeet or Crees for years back."[26] Macleod urged Ottawa to arrange the return of the Sioux to the United States. He warned that, if there were any delay, it would only make the movement more difficult to accomplish.

The Sioux faced a precarious future. A return to the United States meant certain attacks by the US army. The winter campaign by the United States army had left the band war-weary and poor. Added difficulties came that spring when a flood carried away most of the supplies in their camp beside the Missouri River. "They had," the *Bismarck Tribune* reported, "exchanged 280 horses for things absolutely needed but were quite destitute."[27] In the summer of 1877, a trader sold the Sioux $8,000 in stock for horses and buffalo robes in two days. One prized purchase was a beautiful white US cavalry horse with two bullet scars. Most of all, the Sioux depended on traders and Métis hunters for ammunition and supplies.

The ninety-five Mounties at Fort Walsh likewise were in a difficult position. They could not force the Sioux out of Canada and had to accept the present reality. For the time the best police policy was firmness, fair play, and readiness. Commissioner Macleod informed Ottawa that, rather than pressing the Sioux to leave the country, it was better to let matters take their course and perhaps time would teach them that they are not so well off on this side of the line. Still, Constable Sam Thurber recalled that the men slept with their arms nearby.

On May 29, three days after the Walsh-White Dog confrontation, six Hunkpapa warriors brought news to Fort Walsh that three Americans were in Sitting Bull's camp at The Holes, 230 km east of Fort Walsh. Assistant Commissioner A.G. Irvine regarded Sitting Bull's willingness to provide this information and to hold the men in camp until the police came "as indicative of his future conduct."[28]

Two days later, the Assistant Commissioner, Inspector Walsh, along with Sub-Inspectors Dalrymple Clark and J.B. Allen, three constables, two wagon drivers, and an interpreter left for the Sioux camp reported to hold 150 lodges under Sitting Bull and a nearby Yankton camp of 100 lodges.

After two days of hard riding, they reached the Indian camp. The police were met by "hundreds of savages so eager to shake us by the hand," wrote Dalrymple Clark, "that it was utterly impossible to move on ... we were objects of great curiosity, judging from the talk they carried on among themselves"[29] A tall Native led the police to Sitting Bull who warmly shook hands with the entire police troop. At the same time, the Indians began erecting a council tent.

While they waited for the meeting, the policemen walked about the camp or watched Indian boys playing a sham war game on horseback. The Mounties could not help but notice horses branded E7 (E Troop of the 7th Cavalry) and that many Indians carried carbines and wore clothing taken from dead soldiers of Custer's regiment. One difficulty came when Sergeant T. Dunne, a ventriloquist and skilled in sleight of hand, unnerved the Indians (when he fed a horse hay and then pulled six knives out of the animal's mouth) and he was told to leave the camp.[30]

The Hunkpapa camp impressed the redcoated visitors. Dalrymple Clark thought many of the women were very attractive in their beautiful dresses decorated with elk teeth, the number of teeth representing wealth and status. Constable Edward Warren was with the company:

> It was the finest sight I ever witnessed. We went down to the camp to release two U.S. Scouts ... and whom we afterwards brought up to Fort Walsh. Sitting Bull and Colonel Irvine had a great pow-wow. The camp of those Sioux was the largest I ever saw and you could see all kinds of people there from renegade white men to Nez Percé Indians ... the Sioux were the biggest men [Warren] ever saw, some of them over six and a half feet tall and of splendid physique. They had all kinds of fine animals in their camp—including U. S. transport mules and cavalry horses, some of which I bought for $10.00 ... on this

occasion the Sioux treated us well and gave us buffalo meat when ours ran out. They were very hospitable and offered to give us each a mule. Though, Major Walsh would not allow us to take the mules.[31]

Colonel A.G. Irvine was very impressed with the Hunkpapa camp and commented: "I never saw a happier lot of people."[32]

The three American prisoners, now in their sixth day in the camp, were the Reverend M. Marty, a Swiss Benedictine monk, John Howard, a scout for Colonel Nelson Miles, and William Halsey, an agency interpreter.

Abbot Martin Marty, in his first year in Dakota Territory, had taken on a personal goal to promote the peaceful return of the Sioux to the United States. The idealistic priest, through Catholic authorities, had his mission approved by the United States War Department and the Department of the Interior, conditional that it was at his own expense. He apparently made no contact with Canadian authorities.

The priest had taken a steamboat up the Missouri River to the Poplar Creek Agency and, from that point, rode nine days to Sitting Bull's camp where he and his companions were welcomed. Abbot Marty brought gifts, —coffee, sugar, and letters from the Commissioner of Indian Affairs in Washington and from Catholic authorities. However, his negotiations were stymied until the band heard from "Grandmother."

Two council meetings were held. Solemn rites opened the first session. A chief, Pretty Bear, his body painted a bright orange, lighted a peace pipe with a smoldering buffalo chip (the Indians refused to use a match which they regarded as deception), which was solemnly smoked by the leaders at the conference. Afterwards, the ashes were buried and the pipe broken into pieces that were placed over the buried ashes. Sub-Inspector Dalrymple Clark recorded the talks—which he found tiresome.[33] Walsh introduced Lieut.-Col. Irvine as the highest chief of the Great Mother. After several Indian speakers reviewed the tribe's British connections and their loathing of the Long Knives (Americans), Irvine addressed the assembled:

As long as you remain in the land of the Great White Mother, you must obey her laws. As long as you behave yourself you have nothing to fear. The Great White Mother, the Queen, takes care of everyone in her land in every part of the world ... you must not cross the line to fight the Americans and return to this country. We will allow you enough ammunition to hunt buffalo for food, but not one round of that ammunition is to be used against White men or Indians.[34]

He reminded the Indians that the Queen was powerful and punished any wrongdoing. Irvine praised the band for informing Major J. Walsh that three white men were in the camp and waiting for authorities. By remaining in Canada, Irvine assured the assembly, "the Americans cannot cross the line after you. You and your families can sleep sound and be not afraid."[35]

Sitting Bull spoke next. He asked Marty: "You tell me that you are a messenger of God. I hardly believe you, for God raised me on a horse, and you want me to give my horses to the Americans?"[36] The proposal that the Tetons give up their horses and ammunition was incomprehensible. Second, Marty had warned that, if the band stayed in Canada, they would live badly, while life on the other side offered promise. Sitting Bull rejected the priest's opinion: "What am I going there for? For the Americans to come after me again? My God will give me prosperity [plenty of beef]."[37]

No doubt, Sitting Bull's "intractable" hostility made any accommodation with the Americans unlikely. A reporter for the *Ottawa Citizen* recorded his translated statement: "I hate them; I was born an Indian and want to live and die an Indian. They shall not take my horse, and my gun and my knife from me."[38] Following another Indian speaker, Irvine ended the meeting by saying he would go and find out what the three Americans wanted.

Abbot Marty attended the second council later that day. After Irvine stated that the priest had come to hear their decision, Sitting Bull delivered a lengthy speech that reiterated his suspicion and grievances. Captain Clark's transcript recorded the concluding statements of the meeting:

> The Father:
> I am not sent by the Government, but I am assured that what I promise will be carried out. Do you intend to return to the other side or remain?

> Sitting Bull (turning to Col. Irvine):
> If I remain here will you protect me?

> Lieut.-Col. Irvine:
> I told you the White Mother would, as long as you behave yourself.

> Sitting Bull:
> What would I return for? To have my horses and arms taken away? What have the Americans to give me? They have no lands. Once I was rich, plenty of money, but the Americans stole it all in the Black Hills. I have come to remain with the White Mother's children.[39]

No, the Teton Sioux would stay in Canada. That night, a surprise visitor opened Assistant Commissioner Irvine's tent flap and sat down. He was none other than Sitting Bull. After an interpreter arrived, the chief spoke for hours of American duplicity and detailed the Custer battle. His account of the renowned battle was not recorded.[40]

The three Americans returned to Bismarck, Dakota Territory. Scout Howard and Abbot Marty told the local press that they both believed the Indians were thoroughly subdued. As for Sitting Bull, Marty expressed the opinion that the medicine man, "possesses the cunning of the redskin in the highest degree and, if civilized, would without doubt have become an astute diplomat and a sly demagogue."[41]

Commissioner James Macleod reported: "The Sioux invasion and their continued residence in our territory have entirely changed the Indian situation."[42] Most serious, the Tetons further depleted the declining buffalo herds. One morning, Louis Goulet, trading from a casement dug into a hillside at Wood Mountain, climbed a nearby hill to observe the plains. He wrote: "We couldn't see the plain at all, it was so completely covered with buffalo ... the Sioux killed one thousand that day. The day after, we bought at least six or seven hundred tongues."[43] Second, the Western Sioux (Tetons) were hostile to the Canadian tribes and prevented them from hunting in the lands they now occupied. This compelled Canadian Indians to hunt south in Montana Territory.

A quarrel between Assiniboine and Saulteaux bands encumbered the critical NWMP–Sioux negotiations that May in 1877. On May 26, three days before the Tetons reported the Americans in their camp, Little Child, a Saulteaux chief, arrived at Fort Walsh charging that two days earlier Assiniboine warriors, led by Crow's Dance, had intimidated his 15 lodges when they were leaving a large camp of 250 Assiniboine lodges. The Assiniboine warriors, he alleged, had recklessly fired bullets and arrows at the terrified Saulteaux women and children, cut lodge canvas, and killed nineteen dogs. When Little Child said he would report the harassment to the police, Crow's Dance struck him and declared: "We will do the same to the Police when they come."[44]

This threat was like waving a red flag at a bull. Within the hour, Walsh was headed for the Indian camp with Dr. John Kittson, fifteen men, and Little Child as the guide. By nine o'clock in the evening, after riding an arduous 65 km, the party reached the site of the disturbance only to find that the band had moved. The men rested and, once the predawn light broke, rode 12 km along a trail until lead scouts Louis Léveille and Little Child raced back with news that the Assiniboine camp was less than 2 km away. The men inspected their weapons and fed the horses oats (which they had carried) before ascending a hill from where they surveyed an idyllic camp of several hundred lodges resting in a green valley fringed by cottonwood trees and with a winding stream flowing through. The tents were arranged as a war camp with the war lodge in the centre. Their task, Walsh ordered, was to arrest those in the war lodge while the Indians were still sleeping.

A low butte overlooking a small lake was selected as the police base and point to withdraw should problems arise. Surgeon Kittson, two men, and the scouts were to stay at this point (Kittson's Butte) to build a breastwork from nearby rocks and, if the police attack encountered problems, send a rider to Fort Walsh for reinforcements. Kittson prepared a field hospital. Walsh's troop rode in a ravine to mask their approach:

> The silence and suspense while crossing this piece of prairie from the hill to camp was painful in the extreme. The neigh of a horse, the rattle of a curb would be sufficient to alarm these wily men that we wished so strongly to surprise, but our good horses seemed to respond to their master's feelings and moved gently along without being prompted by either rein or spur. One by one, we passed through the line of lodges. Dogs bark, but the war lodge is reached and surrounded.[45]

Ten dismounted policemen rushed the war lodge and seized the weapons before the occupants could rise. Crow's Dance and nineteen warriors were quickly escorted to Kittson's Butte, about 1 km away.[46] A trooper described the early morning arrests:

> Trotting briskly into camp we surrounded the war lodge ... Crow's Dance and a dozen sleepy-eyed warriors were soon under arrest and taken to a spot a mile away before the rest of the tribe were awake enough to realize what had happened... the powwow which followed was long and impressive, with much talk and waving of hands ... two hours later we started back for the fort.[47]

While the prisoners sat shackled in pairs at Kittson's Butte, the troops completed the breastwork of rocks and dirt over which they placed their saddles. Instructions were given for defence in the event of an attack. It was five o'clock in the morning and, while the men ate breakfast, Walsh sent a scout to the camp to request an immediate meeting with the chiefs.

At the council, Inspector James Walsh defended his raid, and informed the gathering that the prisoners would be tried by the law of the White Mother, and he berated the Assiniboine for earlier blocking the Saulteaux departure.[48] The band provided horses for the Indian prisoners, and the troop left for Fort Walsh, which they reached before midnight after a rather strenuous 80-km ride.

Walsh was proud of his men. His report stated: "From the replies and the way they acted during the whole time, I am of the opinion that every man of this detachment would have boldly stood their ground if the Indians had made any resistance."[49]

Assistant Commissioner Irvine and Walsh adjudicated the Assiniboine trials. They sentenced Crow's Dance to six months imprisonment with hard labour, a second man to two months' imprisonment, and released the remaining prisoners.[50] The Assistant Commissioner's report praised Walsh for effectively resolving a potentially dangerous confrontation:

> I cannot too highly write of Inspector Walsh's prompt conduct in this matter, and it must be a matter of congratulations to feel that fifteen of our men can ride into an enormous camp of Indians and take out of it as prisoners thirteen of the head men. The action of this detachment will have a great effect on all Indians throughout the country.[51]

The news that a handful of redcoats had fearlessly arrested warriors in the centre of a large Indian encampment was, as Irvine claimed, far-reaching. The *Fort Benton Record* commented that the thirty-seven-year-old Walsh was "evidently the right man in the right place, and deserves great credit for his energy and pluck displayed in subduing the belligerent reds."[52] At Fort Macleod, Surgeon R.B. Nevitt wrote: "It seems strange that fifteen men could go into a camp of 700 lodges with about 4,000 people in it and take prisoners and not shed a drop of blood."[53] The arrests, in Walsh's words, "established an influence, a prestige that made them [NWMP] respected through the length and breadth of the country."[54]

James Morrow Walsh

In the summer of 1882, the Canadian Press Association organized a special train to visit the North-West Territories. As the engine puffed up a grade near Fort Qu'Appelle, riders broke from cover and galloped alongside the cars in a wild welcome, saluted by the shrieks of the engine, the cheers of the men, and the waving of the ladies' handkerchiefs. Who would have concealed a troop in the bush and launched such an outlandish attack? People in the know recognized the leading rider in frontier dress as James Walsh, acting "in a spirited manner peculiar to him."[55]

Once the locomotive stopped to take on water, swashbuckling Inspector Walsh climbed on board and, until the train reached the last siding west of Regina, entertained the reporters and passengers with his comments. Before the surprised onlookers, he even christened an Indian baby "Climie Pense," after the surnames of both the secretary and president of the Canadian Press Association. [56] Above all, James Walsh craved attention.

The eldest of nine children, James Morrow "Bub" Walsh was born in Prescott, Upper Canada, in 1840. His education and early work career lacked dedication and he failed in a number of occupations before entering Kingston Military School, from which he graduated at age twenty-five in 1865. Five years later, he married nineteen-year-old Mary Elizabeth Mowat. They had one daughter, Cora, to whom Walsh wrote (in 1890) an important historical letter that recounted his Sioux experiences.

Walsh joined the NWMP in September 1873. His first responsibility involved recruiting fifty men from Ontario for the new Force. Soon after, in the fall of 1873, he traveled with Divisions "A-B-C" to Fort Garry and, that winter, as acting veterinarian surgeon, instructed the recruits in horsemanship. On the '74 March, he commanded "D Division" and spent the winter at Fort Macleod. In the spring of 1875, Walsh returned the horses that were wintered in Montana and then took a troop eastward to build the fort in the Cypress Hills that bears his name.

In June 1876, Walsh was in Hot Springs, Arkansas, taking treatment for erysipelas (a contagious skin infection), when a telegram ordered his urgent return to Fort Walsh to deal with the expected American Sioux influx. Upon his arrival on 22 August 1876, the detachment greeted him with three hearty cheers. A triumphal arch of evergreens and small flags decorated the post's gate along with mottos of "Welcome" and "Long Life to our Inspector." Walsh thanked the men and praised the favourable conduct report he had received from Captain Crozier, in charge during his absence. Walsh gave the men the remainder of the day to play sports.

Walsh was a popular and influential officer. Sergt.-Major Joseph Francis, in response to a Winnipeg newspaper reporter's question, described Walsh as "energetic, brave, active and well-liked by both the police and Indians."[57] A subordinate described Major Walsh "somewhat pompous and proud but a born leader of men."[58] A visitor to the region attributed the pacific behaviour of the Sioux "to the presence of Major Walsh at Wood Mountain although he has only twenty-five men. He has acquired a reputation, which prevails amongst the Indians, half-breeds, whites and outlaws, that he is a man not to be trifled with and that if any harm or anything wrong is done, someone will have to suffer for it."[59]

Profanity, according to Constable Barnett, was Major Walsh's "greatest characteristic." When one Métis annoyed James Walsh, Constable George Guernsey related that the "amount of profanity directed at the unfortunate breed was amazing."[60] A teamster added that he thought he was pretty good "at cussin" but the Major had him skinned by a mile.[61] A constable described Walsh's appearance:

> ... as about five feet nine inches, well-built man, with dark hair, moustache and imperial. He affected rather a bizarre style of uniform, a straight peaked cap like an infantry officer's of that period, but with a heavy gold band, or else a wide-brimmed light fawn sombrero, and a cavalry patrol jacket, Bedford cord breeches and U.S. Cavalry boots with the fronts reaching above the knee ... a man of undoubted pluck, he loved to advertise, and nothing pleased him more than to be referred to in the American newspapers as "Sitting Bull's Boss."[62]

This appellation—"Sitting Bull's Boss"—was one of many given to Walsh. Others were "White Forehead"; the Assiniboines called him "The One That Ties" (from the incident when he shackled White Dog); the Sioux called him "Long Lance" because, at the first meeting, his troops carried lances with red-and-white pennons and later, because of his sexual exploits with Sioux women, the ridiculing term "Squaw Man" was given to Walsh.

Walsh decidedly swayed the Sioux refugees—who were derided south of the line as "Walsh's pets." Jerome Stillson, reporting for the *New York Herald* at the Sitting Bull–General Terry conference, was impressed:

> Nobody would think of doubting Major Walsh's control over his savage wards after one hour at this post ... I must characterize him as one of the bravest and most remarkable diplomats of his day. He unites with a tact absolutely essential in diplomacy, the courage and presence of mind required in all intercourse with a savage and superstitious people.[63]

The *Chicago Times* agreed: "The officer has already shown a marvelous capacity in dealing with the Indians and possibly there is no man in either the American or Canadian service better acquainted with all the methods and characteristics of the savages."[64]

Major James Morrow Walsh

One constable described Superintendent James Walsh "as a dark, powerfully built man, sporting a Van Dyke beard, which all of his troops emulated. Profanity was his greatest characteristic—his most driving ambition was to get things done. Skilful in his handling of the Indians, he was responsible for keeping the Sioux, Cree and Blackfoot at peace."

– Edward Barnett, *GA*, M 6142
  NAC PA 204295

Sitting Bull found Walsh to be the first white man he could trust and counted on the police officer for help. Early in his stay in Canada, Sitting Bull sent a message to Walsh: "I am informed the Americans are coming after me and my people to fight us. I am tired of blood and will move close to the Police fort to avoid any fight ... I wish you to speak well to the White Mother for me and my people."[65] Observers felt Major Walsh exercised an influence over Sitting Bull that American soldiers thought was impossible.[66] NWMP Captain Edwin Allen, interviewed by the *Bismarck Tribune*, stated:

> Sitting Bull is a great friend of Walsh. The Major tells him the truth for one thing and he shows him that the Canadian government as personated by him means business if the old warrior doesn't stand up to scratch and keep the peace. Besides his respect for Walsh's veracity, Sitting Bull is physically afraid of him.[67]

Walsh was not a man to intimidate. On one occasion, Sitting Bull's demands for provisions at Wood Mountain opened a verbal exchange that nearly resulted in bloodshed. A witness described the scene:

> Sitting Bull stood up and said to Walsh: "Well, I'll make you give me what I want. No White man can talk to me and get away with it ... with these words Sitting Bull drew his pistol. Walsh told Morin to open the door, which he did. Sitting Bull made as if to shoot at Walsh, who was ready for it and, quick as lightning, hit the Indian chief a heavy blow on the fist making him drop the pistol at his feet. Seizing his adversary by the hair, Walsh gave him a mighty shove through the wide open door. Sitting Bull landed on his hands and knees at least ten feet outside the house. Before he had time to get up, Walsh gave him a few kicks in the rear.[68]

Walsh readily expressed his opinions. He relished being interviewed and wrote to newspapers. He praised William Van Horne for the speed of track-laying in 1882. Often his opinions were at odds with the prevailing frontier viewpoint, especially when related to the Sioux. In an interview with the *Chicago Tribune*, he described the Sioux: "I have found them the most noble, moral, hospitable, truthful, and tractable red men I have ever come in contact with. The character of their women would be a credit to any nation. As a people they are affectionate, and family ties among them are stronger than they are among white people."[69] In a letter written to the *Manitoba Free Press*, for example, Walsh accused Crow Indians, not Sioux, for the murders at Fort Peck of interpreter Lambert and his family and that many charges against the Sioux refugees, if properly traced, would be found to be the crime of other Indians.[70]

The Canadian government blamed Walsh for obstructing efforts to return the Sioux to the United States. To reduce Walsh's negative impact, Headquarters extended Walsh's leave in Ontario and then transferred his command to Fort Qu'Appelle, 235 km north of Wood Mountain.

Walsh resigned from the North-West Mounted Police on 1 October 1883 with a retirement gratuity for ten years' service of $1,166. His post presented him with an expensive ring. Regret for his departure appeared to be truly genuine. The *Regina Leader* lauded his courage and magnetism that influenced the Indians. He was "the soul of the Mounted Police ... the poetry of the Mounted Police is gone."[71] A Winnipeg newspaper added that, by his force of character, moral suasion and subsequent knowledge of the Sioux language, Major Walsh had obtained complete command over Sitting Bull and the Tetons, and so much did they respect him that they would sacrifice their lives in his defence.[72]

In the North-West Rebellion eighteen months after Major Walsh's retirement, some westerners clamored for the recruitment of James Walsh and James Macleod to fight the insurgency. Neither man was called. The *Regina Leader* viewed this as a mistake, citing their prestige and command experience, knowledge of the country, success with Indians, and describing both men as "brave as lions."[73]

But not everyone agreed. The *Fort Macleod Gazette* countered on 23 May 1885 that the country could do very well without Walsh's services as he was too self-laudatory and fond of blowing his own trumpet to be of any real solid worth to the country.

After his police career, Walsh attempted several business ventures in the coal industry. He kept in the limelight. In 1896, he wrote to Prime Minister Wilfrid Laurier questioning the NWMP reduction in manpower.

In 1897, helped by political connections and over opposition in the Force, Walsh was appointed to command the NWMP in the Yukon Territory. He remained his unconventional self. His communication with Ottawa from the Klondike would bypass the police headquarters in Regina. His administration in the Yukon was troubled by mismanagement, scandal, and problems with mining regulations. Walsh resigned in 1898. He died in Brockville, Ontario in 1905 at age sixty-five.[74]

Diplomacy

The influx of Sioux into Canada had immense military, economic, and political implications. Their presence taxed the already overstretched NWMP and shifted the deployment of staff. Fort Walsh was reinforced, making it the largest police post from 1878 to 1882. In 1880, 112 men at Fort Walsh and 30 at Wood Mountain made up 48 per cent of the NWMP manpower. Second, the Teton Sioux arrival destabilized the region. One Mountie wrote: "The Sioux were hostile to all the Indians in the country ... our Indians were much dissatisfied and uneasy with their presence."[75] The Sioux blockage of Canadian Indians from the last buffalo range in Canada forced starving Blackfoot and Cree bands to hunt in Montana Territory, much to the anger of American settlers.

The United States government and army regarded the Sioux presence across the border as an ongoing threat to the northern American frontier. In turn, Ottawa denied the Sioux any sense of permanency by the steadfast refusal of rations or a reserve. One thing was certain: both nations wanted the American Sioux returned to the United States.

The ten-year-old Dominion had not yet established any diplomatic representation in Washington. This entailed directing all the Canadian communication through Frederick Plunkett, the chargé d'affaires of the British legation in the American capital. Testy British relations with the United States in the aftermath of the American Civil War and over Fenian raids into Canada in 1870 compounded the difficulties. In British eyes the status of a few thousand Indians in the far North-West, although important, was subordinate to diplomatic rapprochement with Washington. James W. Taylor, the American consul in Winnipeg, was instrumental in pressing the issue of the Sioux presence in Canada.

During the summer of 1877, diplomatic exchanges involving Canada, Britain, and Washington focused on the political status of the Sioux refugees.[76] Were the Sioux, in the view of William Evarts, the American Secretary of State, political offenders seeking asylum which, based on the treaties with Great Britain, left the situation static? Or were the Sioux, in British representative Plunkett's opinion, not political refugees since they were wards, not citizens of the United States? On the northwestern frontier, American military commanders urged strong action, even invading Canada, to resolve the unsettled situation.

On June 23, Frederick Plunkett met the American Secretary of State with a request that the Americans encourage the Sioux to return home to the United States. Further negotiations followed.[77] Canada circumvented conventional diplomatic protocol when D. Mills, the Canadian Minister

Officers at Fort Walsh, 1879

L–R, front row – Dalrymple Clark; middle row – A.G. Irvine, James McLeod, Surgeon John Kittson; back row – Percy R. Neale, Francis Dickens, William Antrobus, John McIllree, Edmund Frechette, Cecil Denny.

– GA NA 98 – 15

of the Interior, had traveled to Washington in August 1877 and made an unannounced visit to the British ambassador's home in order to express Ottawa's concerns over the Sitting Bull question. Plunkett was taken back by Mill's intrusiveness as a "dangerous precedent" but agreed to accompany Mills to the United States State Department.

Meetings were arranged with the United States Department of the Interior.[78] Leading government officials—President Rutherford Hayes, Carl Schurz (Secretary of the Interior), George W. McCrary (Secretary of War)—participated. Schurz probed an interesting question: "How do you keep your whites in order?"[79]

The proposal by David Mills to have a commission contact the Sioux exiles to arrange their return to the United States won approval from President Rutherford B. Hayes and his cabinet. Mills conceded that the American demand for the Sioux to surrender their horses and weapons upon entering the United States made any talks certain to fail.

In 1877, the United States was beset by the disputed Presidential election of 1876 and the lingering turmoil in Reconstruction. A compromise to remove Federal troops from Louisiana and South Carolina was a priority. The Sioux in Canada were an important but lesser concern.

On August 24, David Mills, the Minister of the Interior, contacted Commissioner Macleod to escort the American delegation from the border to Fort Walsh. Mills added that Ottawa was most anxious that the United States Commission succeed in inducing the hostile Sioux return to the United States. Should they remain in Canada, the Sioux would become a considerable expense and, not improbably, be disposed to make warring incursions across the border and to get embroiled in hostile conflicts with Canadian Indians. It was in Canada's interest that Commissioner James Macleod use his influence to encourage the return of the Sioux Indians to their own reserves.[80]

The Nez Percé Cross the Medicine Line

On the morning of 30 September 1877, only seventeen days before the proposed Terry-Sitting Bull Conference at Fort Walsh, the American army attacked the Nez Percé (Nimiipuu) Indians at Snake Creek, Montana Territory. The Oregon Indian band, moving to refuge in Canada, was 60 km south of the Canadian border.

The American–Nez Percé troubles had begun in the early 1870s when white settlement encroached on the bands' lands in the Wallowa Valley in Oregon. Land negotiations failed and fighting erupted in May 1877. This led to a remarkable eastward trek by 800 Nez Percé to join Crow allies in Montana Territory, a trek that was unsuccessful.

For three months, the Nez Percé had outfought American soldiers in a series of highly publicized skirmishes. When most of the band finally surrendered near the Canadian border, their journey had covered 2,000 km, much over difficult terrain. The 115-day trek had been bloody: 180 white people (127 soldiers) had been killed and another 127 wounded; Indian losses ranged from 120–150 dead (60 women and children) and perhaps 90 band members were wounded. After the Battle of Canyon Creek (near present-day Billings, Montana), the tribe turned northward for sanctuary in Canada, a distance of almost 400 km.

Once the tribe crossed the Missouri River, the new headman, Looking Glass, chose to hunt buffalo and rest the horses, knowing that the border was within easy reach and that a pursuing army under Brigadier-General Oliver O. Howard was several days behind.[81] Unknown to the band, however, Howard had contacted Colonel N. Miles at Tongue River Cantonment on Yellowstone River with orders to intercept the fleeing Nez Percé. In a rigorous twelve-day, 500-km march, Miles' 380-man column attacked the Nez Percé at Snake Creek in what was known as the Battle of Bear Paw.[82]

The Indian defenders repulsed four frontal cavalry attacks, killing twenty-four soldiers and wounding another forty-three men. A flanking cavalry movement separated the band from its large horse herd and forced the Nez Percé to dig defensive rifle pits. In turn, the army cordoned the Indian camp and began a five-day siege on the entrenched Indian positions. The continued shelling killed twenty-five Indians and wounded another fifty tribesmen. In turn, several soldiers were killed and wounded.

An early winter blizzard, hunger, the loss of the band's horses, and the harassing shelling from field pieces broke the Nez Percé resistance. After a meeting negotiating the terms of surrender, Miles reneged on his guarantee of safety forcibly detaining Chief Joseph until an exchange for a white soldier was arranged. On October 4, Brigadier-General Oliver Howard reached the battle site. His troops followed only 50 km behind making further resistance for the starving Indians futile. The next day Chief Joseph surrendered 418 band members. His speech, ending—"I will fight no more forever"—won admiration for wisdom and eloquence and became an often quoted historical document of the "Indian Wars."[83]

Some Nez Percé escaped the battle site. Perhaps 150 band members had fled in the opening days of the fighting and, at the end of the battle, a second group under Chief White Bird, aged sixty, eluded the army cordon and headed north. Walsh gave the number of Nez Percé that reached the Sioux camp as 90 warriors and 200 women and children. He anticipated forty more band members to arrive.

Although the first refugees from the Battle of Bear Paw had evaded pursuing army patrols, Assiniboine and Gros Ventre Indians responded to Nelson Miles' offer of three blankets for each male Nez Percé captured by savagely attacking the Nez Percé. In one case of betrayal, a Nez Percé party of nine (five men, two women, and two children) reached an Assiniboine camp where they were well treated and given food and clothing. The following morning, they were betrayed. The Assiniboines took the guns from the men and told them to go north to Canada while they cared for the women and children. An hour later, Assiniboine warriors killed the men and brought their bodies back to camp. Here they killed one papoose and threw all the bodies into a lodge where two women were already held hostage. After three days of torture and rape, the women were given to a Gros Ventres band who took them to their camp just north of the border. One woman escaped from her drunken guards and, after a terrible ordeal, she reached Fort Benton; the second woman remained held in captivity. A "half-breed" brought word to Fort Walsh of her ordeal.[84]

Major Walsh would never tolerate such injustice. With Captain Allen and one constable, he rode to the Gros Ventre camp, disregarded claims that the captive was not a Canadian and none of his business and, while his companions stood guard, freed the wretched woman. Walsh reprimanded the lodge owner and chief Lame Bull for ignoring the law of the White Mother against holding captives. He further rejected Indian excuses that the abused woman was too ill to travel and took her to Fort Walsh.[85] Dr. Kittson took care of the woman, who was described as a pretty "squaw," but utterly broken from sexual assaults and hot iron brands on her back.

The Teton camp at Wood Mountain, fully updated by scouts on the Bear Paw fight 300 km away, debated sending warriors to join the Nez Percé fight against Colonel Miles. Walsh wrote of the indecision:

> The warriors were clamouring to move ... the camp was almost unanimous in favor of sending assistance to the Nez Percés and the council fully so—but we explained to the chiefs that this could not and must not be, or the asylum that they were engaged north of the line would cease and Canada would no more be a place of safety for them. The day passed. No Indians left the camp ... Grey dawn was appearing on the second day before the council adjourned ... at the end of that day the Indians concluded that it would be suicidal for them to render any help to the Nez Percés.[86]

Walsh was at the border with Teton warriors when the Nez Percés approached. How would Sitting Bull's camp treat the battered refugees? There were even Sioux and Cheyenne scouts in Miles' command. One prominent Nez Percé warrior named Yellow Wolf, recalled "We were never friends to the Sioux Indians."[87] When the two tribes met, the Nez Percés apprehensively formed a line of defence.

The Tetons proved friendly and hospitable. They shared tobacco and, using sign language, escorted the Nez Percés to the main camp. Here they took them in, fed and nursed the wounded, and soon provided the refugees with their own lodges. Yellow Wolf appraised his time in Canada: "They gave me everything I asked, just as if I was one of their children ...

we got along fine with the Sioux, who remained camped in the same place all the time we were there."[88] The Idaho Indians grouped together inside the main camp.

In May 1878, seven months after the Nez Percés had entered Canada, Commissioner James Macleod approved a US mission to meet the band. Lieutenant C.W. Baird, with three Nez Percés, arrived to encourage the Nez Percé to join Chief Joseph and the band's proposed move to Indian Territory in Oklahoma. The distrust of Washington remained overriding and learning that Chief Joseph was detained Fort Leavenworth dissuaded any agreement. White Bird concluded: "Our country is over here. Joseph is in the wrong direction, why should I go with him?"[89] Lieutenant Baird believed that, had he the authority to guarantee a return to Idaho, the entire band of twenty-five lodges would have accepted his offer.[90]

Preparations for the Sioux-American Summit

Would the Sioux meet with the American delegates? Superintendent James Walsh rode to Wood Mountain to encourage their participation. He met strong objections. Americans had murdered and traumatized the band. They had repeatedly given false promises. How could they be trusted? Only weeks before the proposed meeting, Father Jean Baptiste Marie Genin had visited the Teton camp. Sitting Bull had told the priest: "The Americans are liars and thieves, and I will not treat with them."[91] It was only after persistent persuasion by Walsh that Sitting Bull and the head chiefs agreed to meet the Commission at Fort Walsh.

On October 8, 1877, as the delegates prepared to leave, a scout rode up with news that a large party was coming from the boundary line. A second scout's report that they were white enemies threw the camp into a frenzy. Though Walsh reassured the camp that no white men would harm them, he had to ride ahead of 200 Sioux warriors to meet the approaching party.

The enemy turned out to be Nez Percé—fifty men, forty women, and a number of children who had escaped from the Battle of Bear Paw with 300 horses. Walsh and Sioux warriors conducted the refugees to the Sioux camp, which now appeared abandoned as most of the tents and supplies were packed and readied for flight.

The appalling sight of little children with their bodies bloodstained by bullets was heartrending. One woman was shot through the breast. The ball entered below the nipple and passed out her back. Walsh was asked: "Why do you come and seek us to go and talk with men who are killing our race? You see these men, women and children wounded and bleeding? We cannot talk to men who have blood on their hands."[92]

The Nez Percé suffering reinforced the Sioux hatred of Americans. Although Walsh now felt his mission was jeopardized, he continued his entreaties. He spoke before the assembled:

> I came here and asked you to come to one of the White Mother's forts to meet a commission sent to talk to you about returning to your own country. You need not accept their offer … you will not be forced to do so, but if you refuse to come to the fort of the White Mother you will be the first people who have ever done so. After a silence for two minutes and low talk to each other they asked me to remain one more night and they would go with me. I consented.[93]

A widely held belief in camp alleged that the American army would entrap the delegates or even that the NWMP would hand them over to the Americans. Certainly the band knew that, only one month earlier, Crazy Horse, a prominent Sioux chief at the Custer battle, was mortally bayoneted while in army custody. Moreover, the proposed meeting site was distant—a return journey of over 600 km across stretches of barren land. And, for Sitting Bull, it was time of personal grieving over the death of his nine-year-old son. As a sign of mourning, he wore a red head handkerchief.

In the morning at council, after persistent urging, promises of safe conduct, and assurances that American soldiers would not cross the line, Walsh succeeded in getting twenty Sioux delegates to move before noon. Travel was slow in the next days as the Indians continued to stop to smoke and review their decision. Nevertheless, Walsh had the delegates en route to Fort Walsh. He was, reported the *New York Herald*, "the only man in the Dominion of Canada who could, in the first place, have induced such determined enemies of the white man as Sitting Bull and his followers to come on and interview the United States Commission."[94]

Three weeks earlier, on September 22, Treaty 7 had been signed at Blackfoot Crossing. After the agreement, Commissioner Macleod rode to Fort Walsh and, after a brief stop, left to meet the oncoming Sitting Bull–Walsh party, then about 100 km east of the post. Upon contacting the Sioux delegates, Macleod realized how the shocking sight of the Nez Percé victims had affected the Tetons. He told the delegates not to fear the Americans for, when the Sioux crossed the border, there was a wall raised up behind them that their enemies dare not cross.

At Fort Walsh, although the Indians shook hands with all the men stationed there, they refused to enter the post, and set up camp on the north side. Sitting Bull said he had never been inside a stockade before

Fort Walsh

"No more romantic spot, no wilder scene, could impress a traveller at the end of a monotonous journey than the one that met our eyes."

– Jerome Stillson, *New York Herald*, 22 October 1877
  PAA B.2239

and would not now either. Moreover, the Indian delegates adamantly opposed reconciliation with the Americans. Walsh was told: "They had come up, as they understood the Queen had desired them to come, but that there was no use in their seeing the Americans, as they could not believe anything they said; that no matter what terms were offered they would not accept them."[95] The meeting appeared doomed to fail.

On the night before the scheduled conference, the Teton Sioux held a war dance. Curious police observers watched hideously ornamented and painted dancers circle a huge bonfire. One chief, Rain-in-the-Face, stood out. He wore only a breech cloth and his blackened body, with white-painted ribs, looked grotesque. His head had a long feathered head dress with a pair of buffalo horns on each side. Rain-in-the-Face brandished a coup stick embellished with scalps and, "as he recounted his deeds of valour, he pointed to the gruesome trophies and told how he had used this stick upon American soldiers at the Custer fight, knocking them from their horses and then dispatching them."[96] It was alleged that he had been the one that had killed Custer. The frenzied dancing around a bonfire in the moonlight heightened the excitement anticipated at the conference the next day. The American contingent arrived at Fort Walsh that evening, but whether they attended the Indian war dance is not known.

The American Commission, headed by Brigadier-General Alfred H. "One Star" Terry, had met in St. Paul, Minnesota on September 11, five weeks before the intended conference, for their schedule and negotiating instructions. The proposed terms were unyielding: on entering the United States, the Sioux were to surrender all firearms, ammunition, and horses. American representatives, moreover, were to "insist upon this condition to its full extent. In case the Indians refuse to return upon such terms, you will break off all communication with them."[97]

Rail and stage lines transported the Commission from St. Paul, to Fort Benton. From this river port, three companies of cavalry and one infantry unit escorted the American delegates and two news reporters north to the border. The correspondents, Jerome Stillson for the *New York Herald* and Charles Diehl of the *Chicago Times*, forwarded full-page details of the conference to a fascinated North American reading public.

The delegates had to wait one day at Wild Horse Lakes, the border point, for the North-West Mounted Police escort. Couriers between the Americans and Fort Walsh kept both sides abreast of developments. Brigadier-General Terry sent one message apprising Sitting Bull of his progress. On October 15, Commissioner James Macleod arrived with fifty men at the border. The waiting Americans at the Wild Horse camp first observed the approaching column as a dot in the dreary expanse but, as the police drew near, "their red uniforms and red and white pennants affixed to their lances contrasted beautifully with the monotonous dun color of the plains."[98]

Terry rode out to meet the approaching police and pleasant greetings followed. After a short talk between the officers, the American wagons were granted permission to proceed beyond the border and the twelve accompanying infantrymen "were disarmed before coming to the British soil so not to intimidate the Sioux."[99] The American military contingent remained at the campsite south of the sod border marker.

An official ceremony followed. The NWMP horsemen formed two lines and crossed their lances as the Commission passed under them. A trumpet sounded and the Canadian horsemen joined the column that was moving north at a lively trot, headed by Macleod and Terry.

That night the party camped 65 km south of their destination. Pickets were posted and newspaper correspondent Stillson, although he thought the danger decreased north of the line, reported, "the reassuring call of 'All's well!' rang musically through the dark hours."[100]

From a hill at sundown on October 16, the column overlooked Fort Walsh. Below them was the stockade with white-washed log buildings, an unfurled Union Jack, and the brilliant scarlet tunics of a small squad showed conspicuously. For the New York newspaper correspondent, "No more romantic spot, no wilder scene, could impress a traveler at the end of a monotonous journey than the one that met our eyes." [101]

Fort Walsh received the Commission warmly. The Americans camped in tents already pitched south of the stockade. One American observer thought the arrival of Brigadier-General Terry had alarmed the Indians badly and Major Walsh had all he could do to keep them camped at the fort until the morning.[102]

Brigadier-General Alfred Terry–Sitting Bull Conference

On 17 October 1877, five months after Sitting Bull had entered Canada, Fort Walsh hosted a meeting between an American Commission and the refugee American Sioux. Here, in the western wilderness of Canada, the Indians responsible for Custer's death were now negotiating their political status with American military authorities.

Heading the American delegation was Brigadier-General Alfred H. "One Star" Terry, a Yale-educated lawyer and Civil War veteran. As the commander of the Military Department of Dakota, Terry had directed the harassing military attacks on the Sioux the previous year. His stance would be firm. In an interview in late August, 1877, he told the newspaper reporter: "if Sitting Bull was discovered to be on this side of the line he would be pursued to the bitter end by the entire available force of troops in the Yellowstone country."[103] At 1.98 m (six feet six inches), his towering appearance in full uniform did not make him the best United States representative—but did the Americans care?

The two sides met in the Officers' Mess room. The American delegation ("Sitting Bull Commission") sat around a table. The representatives (besides Brigadier-General A. Terry), included Secretary-Captain H.S. Corbin, Recorder Jay Stone, and A.G. Lawrence (a former general in the United States army). Mounted Policemen and three interpreters had positioned themselves along the walls.[104]

At three o'clock, Major Walsh led the Sioux representatives (who had been searched for hidden arms) into the room. At once, the Indians made an ostentatious display of handshaking with Mounted Policemen while, at the same time, openly ignoring the Americans. Commissioner J. Macleod reported to David Mills, Canada's Department of the Interior: "Sitting Bull shook hands warmly with me, and then passed the Commissioners in the most disdainful manner ... it was evident from the manner and tone of speeches that they had come to believe nothing that was told to them."[105] Sitting Bull asked the Americans to sit in front of the tables. Terry responded that it was the habit of whites to sit in chairs. In turn, the Indians spread buffalo robes and sat on the floor in front of the American delegation.[106]

General Terry opened the conference without the customary Indian pipe ceremony by reading the President's "Message" line by line. The Great Father (President Rutherford Hayes), Terry began, desired a lasting peace and wanted all hostilities to cease. He wanted all the people of the United States to live in harmony for the sake of white and Indian people. Too much white and Indian blood has already been lost. It was time that bloodshed should cease. Of all bands at war with the United States, the Teton Sioux were the only one which had not surrendered. Each of the returning Sioux would be granted a full pardon with the past forgiven provided that, upon entering the United States, they surrendered their weapons and horses and went peaceably to the assigned Agency.

Money from the sale of arms and the Indian horses could buy the tribe cattle, and clothing and provisions would be made available. This proposal envisioned a belief that the best hope for the future welfare of the Sioux people and their children was to abandon their present mode of life for raising cattle. However, if they returned with their weapons, the United States would treat them as enemies.

The Brigadier-General Terry – Sitting Bull Conference, 17 October 1877

"You came to tell us stories, and we do not want to hear them; I will say no more; you can go back home."

– Sitting Bull, RC, NWMP, 1877, 48
  GA NA 5091 – 1

Terry concluded his speech by asking the Indians to consult on these proposals, after which he would hear from them. As Brigadier-General Terry spoke, the Indians impassively smoked and soon the room reeked with the smell of tobacco. The faces of the assembled Indians, thought correspondent Stillson, looked as impenetrable as granite. When Terry claimed that the Indians had been treated kindly, Sitting Bull, (described by Stillson, as "silent, stately, and impassive") smiled. The Sans Arc war chief, Spotted Eagle, naked to the waist and with a belt of Winchester rifle cartridges strung over his shoulder, his chest and arms covered with white paint, his hair knotted in front with an eagle's feather thrust through and armed with a war club of fixed knife blades, fondled his knife and winked at Colonel Macleod. Johnny Healy, reporting for the *Helena Weekly Herald*, observed that, "the policemen did not speak at all, but they looked for all the world like the masters of the situation."[107]

After Terry finished his address, the Indians sat silent. Sitting Bull then walked to the police officers and shook hands while other Indians exclaimed "How! How!" As first speaker, Sitting Bull set the mood:

> For 64 years you have kept and treated my people bad; what have we done that caused us to depart from our country? We could go nowhere, so we have taken refuge here ... we did not give you the country you took it from us ... you came to tell us stories, and we do not want to hear them; I will say no more; you can go back home.[108]

Twice during his talk, he stopped to shake hands with nearby NWMP officers. Four of the five other Indian speakers were chiefs. Each orator first made a point of shaking hands with policemen. They all deplored their miserable treatment, the stolen land, and the unending American lies.[109] The fifth speaker was a surprise. The-One-that-Speaks-Once, a wife of chief The-Man-that-Scatters-the-Bears, spoke as a deliberate insult to the Americans. One account explained: "A squaw's position in an Indian tribe is so abject that it is impossible to doubt that she was let to play orator by way of emphasizing the insult to the commissioners."[110] A Montana paper, in its report of the meeting, informed: "To allow a squaw to speak in council is one of the worst insults an Indian can offer."[111] A constable described this astonishing occurrence:

> At one stage of the proceedings Sitting Bull offered the greatest insult to the general that an Indian could to a white man. He introduced a squaw in council! She hadn't a great lot to say,

though one utterance seemed to puzzle Old Provost [interpreter] as to how he should put it. After a little thinking, however, he turned to the general and, in his thin, high-pitched voice, addressed him: "She says, general, you won't give us time to 'breed!' Probably your interpretation of what she meant agrees with mine."[112]

The American delegates appeared indifferent as the woman and the other Teton speakers recounted their grievances. As the Indians stood to leave, Alfred Terry asked: "Are we to say to the President that you all refuse the offers made to you?"[113]

Sitting Bull replied, "I have told you all I have to tell you. This part of the country does not belong to you, all on this side belongs to these people [police]."[114] A tribesman, The Crow, embraced the police and added, "You can go back to where you came from and stay there."[115]

Terry smiled and said to Macleod, "I think we have nothing more to say to them, Colonel." Macleod responded, "Well, I suppose you are right."[116]

The conference ended with yet another overdone Teton handshaking with the police while again openly spurning the Americans. A reporter from Montana derided Sitting Bull's actions: "He completed his insult by rising at the end of the conference, shaking hands with the Dominion officers and addressing to them terms of affection and respect, while at the same time he slighted all Americans present by not even saying the Indian 'how' or goodbye."[117] Correspondent Jerome Stillson succinctly assessed the conference in the *New York Herald*:

In short, the commission has met Sitting Bull and Sitting Bull has dismissed it abruptly and disdainfully. The expedition has failed in its purpose and the Sioux question is as far from a satisfactory situation as when General Terry and his brother commissioners first set out on their long journey to the Northwest.[118]

The newspaper commented (perhaps sarcastically): "We wish the Great Mother joy of her new subjects."[119]

That evening, General Terry asked Colonel Macleod to question the Sioux if they had grasped the implications of their refusal. In response, Macleod reported that he had impressed upon them the consequences of their decision, not only for themselves, but for their children, and, second, he reminded them that, although they claimed to be British Indians, the Queen's Government looked upon them as American Indians who had taken refuge in Canada.

Under this status, the Queen offered nothing other than protection and only if they would behave themselves. Commissioner Macleod concluded that the Sioux were unwavering and unanimous in their rejection of what they called "Sweet Talk."[120]

Both negotiating parties left Fort Walsh the next day. A NWMP column escorted the American Commission to the waiting companies of American cavalry at the border. From this point, the American delegation continued to Washington where, on November 28, they submitted their report.[121] One Mountie wrote: "the Americans thoroughly appreciated our work for them and again expressed astonishment that so small a force could control such a vast country and the thousands of warlike red men who roamed its plains and valleys."[122]

Walsh returned with the Tetons to Wood Mountain. He left Fort Walsh in his flamboyant way:

> Major Walsh mounted on his horse Barney, himself attired in boots, corduroys, a slouched hat and buckskin hunting shirt, saying 'farewell' and galloping away across the prairie, all the dogs of the two camps following his heels.[123]

The Teton camp was overjoyed to welcome the delegates. Walsh received a passionate kiss from a pretty young woman who ran out from her teepee and threw her arms around his neck. An old man stalked the camp shouting praise for Walsh, and haranguing the tribe for questioning that they would be deceived by the Great White Mother.

Walsh agreed to a Nez Percé request for a council. He was told that they were anxious to let him know (so that he could inform the White Mother) how badly they had been treated by the Americans. Second, the tribe was uncertain whether to stay in the Sioux camp or move to the Cypress Hills.

On October 16, while the Teton delegates were at Fort Walsh, Colonel Nelson Miles had sent a white man and a Nez Percé Indian to persuade the Nez Percés to surrender. Band members, however, accused the two emissaries of killing Nez Percés in the Bear Paw skirmish ten days earlier and threatened to kill them. The Teton Sioux intervened, declaring that the White Mother's law prohibited bloodshed in their camp. It was agreed to hold the men as prisoners until the NWMP were contacted. However, that night both of the men escaped. Major Walsh was certain that the Tetons had arranged their escape.

The outcome of the General Terry–Sitting Bull Conference changed very little. In the following years, there were several individual attempts to entice the Teton Sioux to return to the United States, but no further official meetings were arranged. This left the Sioux in "Grandmother's Land" for four more years, until July 1881. The Canadian government's refusal of land and economic aid thwarted any plans the band entertained for remaining in Canada. As the buffalo herds quickly disappeared, life for the Sioux became increasingly desperate. In the end, an unwavering Ottawa, hunger, and privation, not conferences, broke the Sioux resolve and forced their return to the hated United States.

NOTES

1. American soldiers and correspondents referred to Canada as "Europe" or "John Bull's Frontier." When the Mounted Police spoke to the Sioux, Queen Victoria was called the "Great White Mother."

2. *NAC*, G 21 series no. 2001, v. 3, H. Richardson to A.G. Irvine, 26 May 1876; Irvine to Richardson, 1 July 1876.

3. *MFP*, 30 May 1876. Rumors abounded. One hearsay on June 19 (before the Little Big Horn battle) had the Sioux about to attack Fort Walsh. The nearby Indians and Métis left the post area, but Superintendent Crozier believed the story had little substance. *NAC*, RG 18, v. 11, f. 59–76.

4. *PAM*, Morris Papers, MG 12, B-2, 177.

5. *FBR*, 28 July 1876.

6. *NAC*, RC, NWMP, 1876, 21–22. The Blackfoot were concerned with the disappearance of the buffalo and intrusions into their land by the Cree from the north and white men from the south and east. The Governor General relayed Denny's report to Queen Victoria. She expressed satisfaction with the Blackfoot loyalty and forwarded her concerns for the tribe's welfare.

7. *MFP*, 2 October 1876. The newspaper, on 25 September 1876, resented that the source of important prairie news was the American press. For some reason, Denny had sent his letter to the Chicago military headquarters and it appeared in the *New York Times* on 20 September 1876—almost two weeks before officials in Manitoba were aware of the problem.

8. *NAC*, G 21 James Macleod to Alexander Mackenzie, 30 May 1877.

9. *RC*, NWMP, 1877, 25.

10. *PAM*, James M. Walsh, MG 6, A-1. Letter to Cora (daughter), 28 May 1890. Walsh had met a band of Sioux earlier during the construction of Fort Walsh in 1875.

11. *CSP*, 1877, VII, Number 11, Annual Report Department of the Interior Ending 30th June, 1876, xxxvi.

12. Gary Pennanen, "Sitting Bull Indian without a Country," *CHR*, LI, No. 2, 123.

13. Norman F. Black, *History of Saskatchewan and the North West Territories*. 2 vols. (Regina: Historical Co., 1913), 1047.

14. F.C. Wade, "The Surrender of Sitting Bull—Jean Louis Légaré's Story," *Canadian Magazine*, XXIV, No. 4, 1905, 335–44.

15. *MFP*, 12 February 1877. The writer expressed the opinion that "the entire lot are not to be trusted; they have none of the virtues usually attributed to Indians, and are entirely different from the Indians about here." For Walsh's account see *RC*, NWMP, 1877, 28.

16. *GA*, John McIllree, AB McIllree # 1. Sitting Bull, although neither a chief nor a warrior, as a medicine man had a strong influence upon the tribe.

17. *GA*, Jessie DeGear, M 314.

18. The Sioux (also Dakota) tribal structure had three major divisions based on geography and language: Eastern (Santee), Middle (Yankton) and Western (Teton). Each division has its dialect: Eastern – Dakota, Middle – Western Dakota (sometimes Nakota), Western – Lakota. Most of the Sioux refugees in Canada were Western

Sioux or Tetons. The Tetons had seven large bands: the Hunkpapa, Minneconjou, Sans Arc, Oglala, Brulé, Two Kettle, and Sioux Blackfoot (Sihasapa).

19. *PAM*, James M. Walsh, MG 6, A-1.

20. *MFP*, 5 June 1881. A police sergeant described Sitting Bull "as a wild untutored, but very sharp and shrewd Indian, having all the quick perceptive powers of a white man, but entirely without education. He cannot speak English, though he understands a good deal of conversation in this language." Also *MFP*, 23 May 1879, describes Sitting Bull as "swarthy, with dark eyes and aquiline nose, stoutly built, and a head so large that a hatter would have some difficulty to fit it."

21. Ibid.

22. Ibid.

23. Ibid. Also *MFP*, 23 July 1877; *BT*, 11 July 1877.

24. Ibid. Other accounts are *MFP*, 23 July 1877 and *BT*, 22 July 1977.

25. *RC*, NWMP, 1877, 33.

26. *RC*, NWMP, 1877, 35.

27. *BT*, 18 June 1877. Also *NYH*, 23 October 1877.

28. *RC*, NWMP, 1877, 36. Surgeon R.B. Nevitt was skeptical: "Sitting Bull said he didn't know what to do … if he were on the American side he would know very well—which meant their scalps would adorn some lodge pole." Nevitt, *Frontier Life in the Mounted Police*, 175.

29. *RL*, 17 March 1885. Also, Captain E.D. Clark, "In the North-West with 'Sitting Bull'," *Rose-Belford's Canadian Monthly and National Review*, V, 69.

30. *NAC*, Edward Warren, f. 57. Whether Dunne left camp as ordered is not known. A surveyor visiting the camp wrote: "We found all the Indians were dressed in uniforms taken from soldiers in the Custer massacre but, as a matter of convenience, each had cut out a large round hole in the seat of the pants." Charles Shaw, *Tales of a Pioneer Surveyor* (Don Mills, Ontario, 1970), 85.

31. Edward Warren, *RCMP Q*, VIII, No. 2, 220. Also *NAC*, Edward Warren, f. 57.

32. *RC*, NWMP, 1877, 37.

33. *RC*, NWMP, 1877, p. 37–41. Also *RL*, 17 March 1885; *HDH*, 30 June 1877.

34. *RC*, NWMP, 1877, 39.

35. *RC*, NWMP, 1877, 39.

36. *RL*, 17 March 1885.

37. *RC*, NWMP, 1877, 40.

38. *GA*, Stuart Z. Wood, M 8065, Box 2, f.11.

39. *RC*, NWMP, 1877, 41.

40. Sitting Bull gave an account of this famous battle to Major Crozier. *WDT*, 10 May 1881.

41. Robert F. Karolevitz, *Bishop Martin Marty* (Yankton, South Dakota: Privately Printed, 1980), 68. BT, 22 June 1877. Abbot Martin Marty continued to encourage the exiled Sioux to return to the United States. In the summer of 1878, he visited government officials in Ottawa and Washington and, in 1879, he went to Fort Walsh where he met with Spotted Eagle, rather than Sitting Bull, whom the priest thought had little power among the Sioux. This mission also failed.

42. *RC*, NWMP, 1878, 26.

43. Guillaume Charette, ed., *Vanishing Spaces* – *Memoirs of Louis Goulet*, Trans. Ray Ellenwood (Winnipeg: Editions Bois-Brules, 1980), 81.

44. *RC*, NWMP, 1877, 54. The sources give three names for the leading Assiniboine instigator. Walsh, in his report (*RC*, NWMP, 1877, 53–54), uses the name Crow's Dance. In his report, Assistant A.G. Irvine writes that Crooked Arm, the ringleader, received six months' imprisonment. In his letter to his daughter, Cora, in 1890 (thirteen years afterwards), Walsh refers to the Assiniboine leader as Broken Arm.

45. *PAM*, James M. Walsh, MG 6, A-1.

46. *RC*, NWMP, 1877, 54.

47. *GA*, Edward Barnett, M 6142.

48. Walsh gave a different version of the events in his letter (1890) to his daughter. He wrote that the chiefs with hundreds of Indians had threatened to destroy the improvised barricades and demanded an explanation of the NWMP actions. Walsh responded that, in British Territory, the police protected the rights of man. The NWMP rejected further protests, leaving the band to provide horses for the prisoners to ride to Fort Walsh.

49. *RC*, NWMP, 1877, 55.

50. Two letters to the *TM* (31 July 1877 and 4 August 1877) are of interest. The first, a letter from "Saskatchewan" living in Winnipeg criticized the "rash provocative actions of Major Walsh" and the trial verdict based on the evidence of one man. In turn, Fred Geddes, living at Fort Walsh, countered that the actions were justified and that "the red-coated troopers are not afraid to go among any Indians, however numerous, when they have right on their side."

51. *RC*, NWMP, 1877, 53.

52. *MFP*, 5 July 1877.

53. Nevitt, *Frontier Life in the Mounted Police*, 175. Nevitt's numbers are excessive.

54. *PAM*, James M. Walsh, MG 6, A-1.

55. Steele, *Forty Years in Canada*, 166.

56. *GA*, Stuart Z. Wood, M 8065 Box 2, f. 11. *MFP*, 1 September 1882.

57. *MFP*, 25 May 1880.

58. *GA*, Edward Barnett, M 6142.

59. *MFP*, 21 January 1880. Interview with George H. Young.

60. George Guernsey (Waseecha Hoska), "Links with the Past – Memoirs of Fort Walsh," *SG*, Sixteenth Annual, 23.

61. Ibid. Also *NAC*, RG, vol. 1, f. 72–74.

62. Guernsey (Waseecha Hoska), "Links with the Past – Memoirs of Fort Walsh," 23. Also *MFP*, 14 June 1878.

63. *Recorder and Times*, Brockville, 4 September 1897. *NYH*, 22 October 1877.

64. *GA*, Stuart Z. Wood, M 8065, Box 2, f. 11.

65. *HDI*, 30 January 1878.

66. *NYH*, 22 October 1877.

67. *BT*, date unknown.

68. Goulet, *Vanishing Spaces*, 86.

69. *WDT*, 23 July 1879. Good example of a reporter interviewing Walsh is found in *WFP*, 30 July 1880.

70. *MFP*, 12 December 1879.

71. *RL*, 22 March 1883. Also *MFP* 24 March 1883.

72. *MFP*, 26 March 1883.

73. *RL*, 23 May 85.

74. *FMG*, 23 May 1885.

75. Denny, *Riders of the Plains*, 104.

76. *NAC*, RG 7, f. 2001. Plunkett was the ranking officer as ambassador Edward Thornton was on vacation in Britain. For the negotiations, see Gary Pennanen, "Sitting Bull Indian without a Country," 123–40.

77. *NAC*, RG 7, f. 2001.

78. Plunkett contacted Ottawa over the "dangerous precedent." *NAC*, G 21, no. 2001, v.3 Plunkett to W.B. Richards, 11 August 1877.

79. Sharp, *Whoop-Up Country*, 263. *NAC*, RG 21, No. 2001, v. 3.

80. *RC*, NWMP, 1877, 43.

81. The Nez Percé rotated the position of head chief. Other prominent leaders were Chief Joseph and White Bird. Howard deliberately slowed his pursuit to give Miles time to intercept the band.

82. This battle also is called the Battle of Bears Paw and the Battle of Bears Paw Mountains. The U.S. National Registry of Historic Places calls the site the Chief Joseph Battleground of the Bear's Paw.

83. Chief Joseph's speech is quoted in Jerome Greene, *Nez Percé Summer, 1877* (Helena: Montana Historical Society Press, 2000), 309.

84. *MFP*, 10 January 1878. Also *TG*, 9 December 1877.

85. *FBR*, 17 December 1877.

86. *PAM*, James M. Walsh, MG 6, A-1. An Account of the Sioux Indians 1876–1879. Letter to Cora Walsh, 28 May 1890.

87. L.V. McWhorter, *Yellow Wolf* (Caldwell, Idaho: Caxton Printers, 1955), 234.

88. McWhorter, *Yellow Wolf*, 238.

89. Jerome Greene, *Beyond Bear's Paw* (Norman: University of Oklahoma, 2010), 145. Also *NAC*, RG 7, G 21, v.323, f. 2000-1.

90. Merrill Beal, *I Will Fight No More Forever* (New York: Ballantine, 1993), 372. After Baird's mission, small groups of Nez Percé returned to Oregon. The journey was marred by cattle thefts and clashes with reservation Indians, miners, settlers, and a skirmish with American soldiers. White Bird remained in Canada where, in 1892, he was brutally murdered by band members who accused him of witchcraft. Hugh Dempsey, "The Tragedy of White Bird," *The Beaver*, February/March 1993, 23–29.

91. *NYT*, 25 September 1877.

92. *NYH*, 22 October 1877. See Joseph Manzione, *I am Looking to the North for My Life* (Salt Lake City: University of Utah Press, 1991), 133.

93. *NYH*, 22 October 1877.

94. Ibid.

95. *RC*, NWMP, 1877, 46.

96. Denny, *The Law Marches West*, 125. *BT*, 3 September 1880.

97. Manzione, *I am Looking to the North for My Life*, 79.

98. *NYH,* 22 October 1877.

99. William Zimmer, *Frontier Scout* (Helena: Montana Historical Society Press, 1998), 135. Zimmer had to remain in camp.

100. *NYH,* 22 October 1877.

101. Ibid.

102. *NNW,* 26 October 1877.

103. *CT,* 28 August 1877.

104. Baptiste Shane of Fort Benton (hired by the Commission) was to interpret; Provost (Fort Walsh) and Joe Lanaval (at the request of the Sioux) were to listen and check any mistakes. Two other Americans were Colonel Smith (aid to Corbin) and Major Freeman (commander of U.S. escort). Among the Mounted Policemen were Colonel Macleod, Captain Crozier, Captain Frechette, Surgeon Nevitt, Captain Allen, Doctor Kittson, Captain McIllree, and Major Walsh.

105. *RC,* NWMP, 1877, 46. A Sioux account of the conference is given by Harry Anderson, "A Sioux Pictorial Account of General Terry's Council at Fort Walsh, October 17, 1877," *North Dakota History,* XXII, No. 3, 93–116. The American document is: *Report of the Sitting Bull Indian Commission* (Washington: Government Printing Office, 1877).

106. Indian headmen were Sitting Bull, Bear's Cap (Head), Spotted Eagle, Flying Bird, Whirlwind Bear, Medicine-turns-around (Twinround), Iron Dog, Bear's that Scatters (The-Man-Who-Scatters-the-Bears), Little Knife, The Crow, and Yellow Dog. Sitting Bull requested all outsiders be excluded. The newspaper correspondents witnessed the proceedings through a hole in the wall.

107. *HWH,* 25 October 1877.

108. *RC,* NWMP, 1877, 48.

109. They were Hunkpapas—Runs the Roe, Nine, and The Crow along with Flying Bird, a Minneconjou.

110. *GA,* Stuart Wood, M8065. Also on insult see *MFP,* 2 June 1880.

111. *HDI,* 24 October 1877.

112. James Fullwood, "An Echo of the Past," *SG,* Seventeenth Annual, 51. See also *NYH,* 28 October 1877. Regina Mettler, Johnny Healy's daughter, wrote: "When my father saw the woman he knew there was trouble brewing … that her presence was intended only as an insult." Gordon Tolton, *Healy's West* (Victoria: Heritage House, 2014), 152.

113. *RC,* NWMP, 1877, 48.

114. *NYH,* 28 October 1877.

115. Ibid.

116. Ibid.

117. *HDI,* 4 November 1877. From *NYH,* 23 October 1877. The *HDI* commented on 30 October 1877: "The dignity of the Commission was fully maintained by Generals Terry and Lawrence and all the other members of it, who sat quietly and sedately and received the insults of the barbaric coterie."

118. *NYH,* 22 October 1877. The newspaper had hired Johnny Healy (the builder of Fort Whoop-Up) to relay Jerome Stillson's report to the telegraph office at Helena, almost 600 km southwest. Healy had boasted that, if the conference failed, he would carry news to the press that he had shot Sitting Bull. His murder plot, however, was foiled. Healy reached Helena in a remarkable forty-three-hour ride.

119. Ibid. 23 October 1877.

120. *HDI*, 6 November 1877. Macleod commented on the difficulty of Indians giving a precise statement of fact, as they always deal in generalities. *RC*, NWMP, 1877, 46.

121. The Commission, ordered to assess what danger there was of hostile invasions by the refugee Sioux on United States territory, concluded that they would not return at present. The Sioux, they felt were restrained by the recollection of the hostile pursuit that ended with them on foreign soil. Any incursions south of the border would make them enemies of both governments. Still, considering the Indians were bitterly hostile to the Americans, their close proximity to the frontier made them a continuing menace to the peace of the United States.

122. Denny, *The Law Marches West*, 127.

123. *NYH*, 23 October 1877.

7

UPHOLDING THE FORCE

"F" Troop on Parade at Fort Walsh

"The men were all adventurous souls. That is why, in the first place, they had joined the Mounties and come west to face dangers, privations and meet the demand for unlimited courage."

– Constable Alfred Nedham, *Lethbridge Herald*, 11 July 1935
  GA NA 2446 – 14

THE NORTH-WEST MOUNTED POLICE never had any problem in attracting recruits. In answer to his inquiry in 1878, Ottawa informed Ike Forbes, a nineteen-year-old shoemaker, that his application would be placed among the 2,200 on file. The following year, there were 1,700 applicants for seventy-six openings. Thirty-one men applied for the nine positions allotted to Montreal. Nineteen-year-old William Cox was so eager to join the NWMP that he filled his pockets with rocks to increase his weight. Most men, like John "Doc" Lauder, saw themselves as "lucky" to be accepted.[1]

Advertisements in newspapers informed interested young men of the dates and locations of recruiting stations. One such notice attracted William Parker to a one-day recruiting session in London, Ontario, in 1874. On his arrival, he was discouraged to see there was more than 200 applicants, all large, strapping men, lined up for the twelve openings. Parker judged that his prospects were poor, but his interview with Commissioner French went well and, to his delight, he was accepted. He proudly wrote his mother in England: "And I have some news to tell you; your dear old son Willie is a North-West Mounted Policeman ... everyone in Toronto thinks it is a splendid thing for a young man to go into."[2]

It was exciting to become a "Rider of the Plains." For Frank Fitzpatrick, an eighteen-year-old member of the Mounted Royal Rifles, "Visions of battles with the Indians ... awakened in me an inward call which I did not try very hard to resist. The field of adventures which lay before me, in the wonderful and trackless, great, lone land, finally brought me to my decision."[3] After Jean D'Artigue, a schoolteacher from France, read over a recruiting announcement in a Montreal newspaper, he had a friend point out the North-West on a map of Canada and explain the proposed trek. Twenty-year-old D'Artigue envisioned:

> Comrades riding days and nights together, over the vast plains of the North-West, fighting the Indians and the whiskey traders. I saw settlements destroyed by the red men, the ladies carried away to worse than slavery; husbands and fathers calling upon us to rescue their wives and daughters; ourselves rushing immediately to horse and over the plains *pêle-mêle*, in hot pursuit; and, after a long day's ride, coming upon the Indians at night, when a brief but fierce struggle would ensue and we would rescue the captives, and carry them back in triumph to desolated homes.[4]

Sweeping horse stables with a broom that he fashioned from willow branches quickly tarnished D'Artigue's fanciful imaginings.

Life in the North-West Mounted Police was austere, physically rigorous, and often boring—certainly a far cry from the image of a leisurely ride on a favourite mount across vast prairie expanses, always in summer. What recruit ever dreamed that police duty would entail crossing an avalanche area? But when Corporal A.E.C. McDonald (or McDonell) and Constables

Alexander Davidson and William Robert McMinn left the Second Crossing of the Columbia to escort two prisoners to Calgary, massive avalanches (that had fatally buried four railway workers) forced the men to cross the Selkirk Range on foot. It was only after considerable risk that they reached the rail line near the point where, six weeks earlier, Constable W. Ross had froze to death while walking along the tracks.[5]

Administration of the NWMP

The North-West Mounted Police initially answered to the Department of Justice, under Prime Minister John A. Macdonald. Following the election of Alexander Mackenzie's Liberal government in November 1874, Hugh Richardson, chief clerk in the Department of Justice, administered the newly created police force.[6] In April 1876, the government transferred supervision of the NWMP to the Department of the Secretary of State.

The Privy Council (a body appointed by the Governor General), through Orders-in-Council, oversaw NWMP expenses and made all of the administrative decisions relating to financial matters, construction tenders, and supplies. These directives covered an extensive range of management. Examples include: purchasing four 7-pr. guns for $6,250; the appointment of Robert Miller as a surgeon for an annual salary of $1,000; granting Constable Isaac Forbes a pension for life of $448.50 per annum; approving Commissioner A.G. Irvine's gratuity of one month's salary for each year of his service; terminating services—as in the case of Inspector H.R. Provost, who was absent without leave for four months; monetary compensation to the mother of murdered Constable Marmaduke Graburn, along with $200 for information leading to the conviction of his killer, an award of $30 to Constable G.Mowatt for meritorious service in extinguishing a fire in the barracks; communication with Washington to transport some ammunition through American territory; providing a land grant to the brother of Constable Nash (who died in a logging accident); and contacting men eligible for the Federal Rebellion Grant.

The Comptroller of the NWMP oversaw everyday issues. He approved all promotions, transfers, leaves, and internal matters. All official contact with the public went through his office. The parents of Constable M. Graburn were notified that their son had been murdered in the far northwest. In finalizing matters in the death of Constable Ralph Sleigh, killed at the Cut Knife Hill skirmish, Comptroller Fred White had extensive correspondence (by registered mail) with the constable's father in England to settle Sleigh's pay and bank accounts and to forward the constable's possessions.[7] William Pilcher, in Dublin, anxious about his son's sobriety, was assured that, "he is steady and well conducted in Barracks, a good rider, well accustomed to prairie life having a good knowledge of the country. There are no entries against him in the defaulter sheet, and I have never heard his sobriety called in question."[8] James Smith wrote from Dundee, Scotland, hoping to hear from his son who had joined the Mounted Police. The reply was curt: "Your Son is stationed at Prince Albert."[9] Comptroller White sent a $10 cheque to reimburse Hanford Crozier, invalided, who had paid his rail fare to Ontario from Fort Benton. W. Kelly needed advance funds to get from Montreal to Winnipeg. The recruit had $18; the fare was $32. A ticket solved the problem and the amount was later deducted from Kelly's wages. The recruit assured White: "I feel sure you will have no cause to regret taking me into your service as I will endeavor to perform my duties to your satisfaction."[10]

Some individuals contacted the Comptroller's office years after their service had ended. Alfred Arcane requested his regimental number and date of service to prove his age for his Old Age Pension. Other men requested proof that they had served in the North-West Rebellion to qualify for a $300 grant given in 1932. Thomas Thompson in 1910 wanted a copy of his lost discharge, valued to him because it had Superintendent Francis Dickens' signature. H.J. LeCain (Le Quesne), "one of old 'F' troop," wrote White asking for $22.50 compensation for the cost of the field glasses he lost in the North-West Rebellion eleven years earlier while chasing the rebel Indian Whitecap.

Isabella Moody requested a copy of her deceased husband's discharge certificate. Mrs. Prongua also wanted a copy of the discharge papers for her husband. It would be included in the petition she was organizing for the release of her husband, Anthony Prongua, who was serving a five-year term in prison for rustling. Sarah Foster, "in need," asked for information on a brother who had left for the Mounted Police "a good many years ago." She heard he was dead and left some property and money.[11] Thirty years after he deserted from the NWMP, William Clarke wrote from Seattle in 1916 asking for a copy of his lost discharge "that may be of good use to me now that I am growing old." White replied: "How could you lose such a thing as you never received it."[12]

Employers contacted the comptroller for information. Two letters from a Chicago firm in 1897, organizing travel excursions to the Klondike gold fields asked for verification of A. Welch's eighteen-year police career and his Yukon experience. The firm was informed that Welch had served three years in the NWMP and that "during this time he certainly would have no means of ascertaining anything about the Yukon country."[13]

Frederick White, Comptroller, NWMP

Frederick White, appointed in 1880, held this important position for
forty years. His imprint on the Force was enormous.

– NAC PA – 7437

The Inspector of Indian Agencies, Vernon, B.C., wanted information
on James Christie, a former policeman and "a squawman who is causing
trouble among the Indians."[14] A letter from a town office in England wanted
to help S. Gregory—("who was badly down on his luck, unpopular and
lives in a miserable hovel.")—asked for confirmation that he had served in
the NWMP. The reply informed the town office that Gregory deserted the
Force after 222 days.[15]

Many requests were from those studying genealogy or searching their family tree. The Crowsnest–Pincher Creek History Society wanted some information on F.R. (Baldy) Morris, a former Mountie who had settled in the area. The son of Alfred Stanton asked for his deceased father's unit and date of enlistment. Gordon Hall wrote from California in 1928 asking for a copy of his recently deceased father's discharge certificate. In 1967, E.C. Fowler, a descendant of Samuel Armour, wanted the NWMP member's service record. In 1933, Muriel Leonhardt asked for a copy of her father's discharge papers, where he was born, and the names of his parents.

The son of Fred Brown wrote from the United States in 1964 asking if he was entitled to any claims or benefits as a Canadian Indian since his father had married a Native woman. The Commissioner replied that there was no concrete evidence that Fred Brown was an Indian or that he had married an Indian woman.

Fifty-seven years after Terrence Fitzpatrick was invalided from the Force (May 1880), his daughter wrote for particulars on a father she had never known. She had found upon her mother's death that her father had not died before her birth (as she had been told), but that her pregnant mother had left him in Montreal and moved to California where she raised her daughter under her mother's maiden name of Edwards.

In some cases, the Comptroller's information may have dismayed the inquirer. A letter from Montana seeking information on the family's history was told that their grandfather, Leonard Fuller, had served in the North-West Mounted Police for fifty-seven days in 1881, followed by six months in the guardhouse for an attempted desertion.

Descendants, like Douglas Fyffe, regretted they had not paid more close attention to their father's NWMP career. In asking the Comptroller's Office in 1948 for information on his father's twenty-two-year career, Fyffe lamented: "Each day I live the greater is my regret that I did not think more of asking my Father for details of the many things which must have occurred during his period with the force."[16]

The NWMP Headquarters maintained contact with some of the early policemen. Commissioner S.T. Woods, on 6 April 1943, sent a telegram to Robert McCutcheon, Calgary: "Best wishes and many happy returns on your ninetieth birthday on April Seventh."[17] In February 1935, the Comptroller notified a Prince Albert probate lawyer that they held a Long Service medal for Harry Keenan who had died two months earlier. The lawyer responded: "The late Harry Keenan left his estate to his two boys who followed his runaway wife when he was in the Yukon and as yet we have not located them."[18]

Expenditures

In the first years, the annual expenditure for the Mounted Police exceeded $300,000—an amount that was frequently criticized by newspapers and Members of Parliament as unduly exorbitant.[19] Yet, the expenditure in 1877 of $352,750 (about $1,000 per man) was one-third the amount spent on an American frontier cavalryman. By 1884, the NWMP expenditure for 557 men had reached $470,000.[20] Accounts included:

$160,000	Pay of Force
80,000	Subsistence
73,000	Forage
47,000	Repairs, renewals, horses, arms and ammunition
45,000	Transport/freight charges, guides, mail carriers
37,000	Clothing
15,000	Fuel and light
7,000	Medicine, medical comforts, hospital expenses
4,000	Contingencies
2,000	Books and stationery

Each detachment submitted a monthly Paymaster's Requisition. For thirty-one days ending 31 December 1875, the Swan River post required $4,586.28. Among the costs were Commissioner French, $216.26; 107 Sub-Constables, $2,487.05; guide/interpreter, $40; two herders, $50; and one boy drawing water, $10.

NWMP Headquarters

In the years 1874–1885, four posts functioned as the NWMP prairie headquarters. Their first location at Swan River (Livingstone), close to proposed railway and telegraph lines, was a poor choice. Even before the '74 column had reached what would become Fort Macleod, the *Manitoba Free Press* quoted the Reverend George McDougall, "that it was better to select some point on the Bow River—where the whiskey is."[21] Second, Swan River was an unsuitable site for farming and military operations. One visitor had mordantly commented: "If the object was to pitch upon the most barren spot in the whole North-West, the genius who recommended this location has been admirably successful, for there is scarcely cultivatable land in the neighborhood to make a garden patch."[22] Sam Steele supported this assessment of the post: "How on earth any person in his senses could have selected such a situation it is difficult to imagine."[23] Steele may have been referring to the boulder-strewn parade square. In order to level the ground, the men built large fires and then poured cold water over heated rocks to split them. The barracks sat on a rocky point, so exposed that men would go outside and watch the buildings as they swayed in strong winds. Inadequate insulation had made the living accommodations stifling-hot in summer and unbearably cold in winter. Swan River remained the NWMP headquarters for less than two years. During that time, the post functioned as the capital of the North-West Territories, with the annual Council meeting being held in the Police Commissioner's residence.

In one of his first decisions after replacing George Arthur French as Commissioner in July 1876, Colonel James F. Macleod transferred the NWMP headquarters to Fort Macleod. The move of the Territorial capital to Battleford left Swan River to quickly fall to ruin. One observer described the post having "a sorrowful appearance ... and a large quantity of debris scattered about the barracks."[24]

The location of Fort Macleod on an island may have met defensive purposes, but otherwise the site had little to offer. "Our first question," inquired rancher Duncan McEachran, "was why on earth this low water surrounded, mosquito-eaten location has been chosen for a fort when there are so many commanding high airy points at hand?"[25] A visitor reinforced this opinion, describing Fort Macleod as "one of the most wretched places I have seen. It is a spit of sand, where the wind appears to be perpetually blowing a hurricane."[26] Spring flooding was a continuing problem and a new fort was built on higher ground in 1880. Fort Macleod served as the police headquarters until October 1879.

The incursion of American Sioux to the Wood Mountain area in the winter and spring of 1876–77 had drastically altered the regional security. Deployment of Mounted Policemen reflected the many potential dangers. In 1879, 175 men garrisoned Fort Walsh and its outposts at Chimney Coulee (just 10 km north of present-day Eastend, Saskatchewan) and Wood Mountain——almost one-half of the 362 men in the Force. Fort Walsh was the NWMP headquarters for three years.

By 1882, the strategic importance of Fort Walsh was outdated. The Sioux were returned to the United States, the transcontinental railway passed north of the post, and all Indian bands had been moved north of the Cypress Hills. In the spring of 1883, the men demolished all of the buildings and then moved to a new police depot at Maple Creek, located 40 km north on the newly constructed railway line. In August 1882, four months after the C.P.R. reached Regina, the town became the NWMP headquarters and training base. In March the following year, the transfer of the Territorial government from Battleford consolidated the importance of the site that had been a barren plain with few natural assets.

Widespread criticism arose over the selection of Pile of Bones (renamed Regina in 1882) as both the legislative capital and police headquarters of the North-West Territories. The *Winnipeg Daily Times* quoted Major James Walsh's observation that he had never seen Pile of Bones Creek flowing in August.[27] The *Manitoba Free Press* derided a choice that was in the "midst of a vast plain of inferior soil ... with about as much water in the miserable creek to wash a sheep."[28] The *Edmonton Bulletin*, which had ridiculed Pile of Bones Creek (now Wascana) as having so little current that it is hard to tell which way it was running, informed readers that the men at the police post were melting snow for the horses and their personal use as water could not be stored in the houses because of the stench being so bad.[29] Perhaps the most belittling observation came in 1885 when three visiting Indian chiefs from Battle River in Alberta reasoned that "the white man must be very strong to live in a place like Regina."[30]

Strength and Distribution of NWMP

At its inception in 1874, the NWMP had six divisions of 50 men each. The numbers changed through transfers and posting of recruits, mainly to Fort Walsh. In 1884 the men in "F" Division were attached to another division.

DISTRIBUTION	1878	1881	1884
"A" Division	22	41	48
"B" Division	73	54	129
"C" Division	51	64	68
"D" Division	29	57	200
"E" Division	88	56	112
"F" Division	66	20	–
TOTAL	329	293	557

Between the years 1875 and 1881, the number of Mounted Policemen (see chart—Deployment of the NWMP) averaged 318 men, with a range between 362 and 293 men. After 1882, a sharp rise in enlistment increased the number of men to 550 prior to the North-West Rebellion.

The increase of 181 men in 1882 primarily affected the new base at Regina (56 men) and southern Alberta where an additional 102 men were posted. The *Fort Benton Daily Herald* approved: "The Bow River country Indians give more trouble than all the other tribes in the North-West combined."[31] In 1884, in response to the Indian troubles on Poundmaker's reserve and the arrival of Louis Riel at Batoche, more than 200 NWMP manned posts in the Battleford-Fort Carlton-Prince Albert area. Fort Carlton was rented from the Hudson's Bay Company as a new post.

The North-West difficulties in 1885 confirmed the need for a larger police presence in Western Canada. During and following the revolt, 608 additional recruits brought the Force to 1,039 officers and rank and file. Four new Divisions—"G-H-K and Depot"—were then formed, giving the Force 10 divisions.[32]

Where did the recruits come from? Of the 241 birthplaces given for the first 300 men, 167 men (69 per cent) were Canadian (Ontario, 115, Quebec, 34, Nova Scotia, 10, New Brunswick, 4, Manitoba, 4). Other birthplaces were Great Britain, 43, Ireland, 20, United States, 7, and France, Germany, Jamaica, Channel Islands one each.

French-speaking recruits were underrepresented in the Force. The province of Quebec contributed 21 per cent of the recruits while having 32 per cent of Canada's population. And a number of the Quebec recruits were of English background and may not have spoken French. Prime Minister Macdonald was aware of the problem. He contacted Comptroller White: "Recommend DeQuoy. We have not enough French in Force."[33]

Superintendent Sam Steele asserted "the sentiments of the Force were always military."[34] Of the original 300 recruits, 174 Mounties had previous military service.[35] Canadian militia routines were evident in drill, target shooting, guard changes, oath of allegiance, signaling with flags, when a troop enters a post, all eyes turn to the right, and so on. Each post had a guardhouse and an orderly (batman) was assigned to each officer. The funeral of murdered policeman Marmaduke Graburn carefully observed established military traditions and routines. Informal militia practices were followed, with three cheers for departing troops and effusive welcomes for arriving comrades. Identification with a troop or post developed into a keen spirit of rivalry. This maintained discipline in the Force as an individual's misdeed could disgrace the entire troop and they made his life miserable for a few days.

The system of ranking copied the Canadian militia. In 1879, there was a revision of titles as indicated by the slash mark—for example, Constables had become Sergeants, Inspectors were now called Superintendents and the Sub-Constable rank was abolished. The policemen often referred to Superintendents as Major, Inspectors as Captain, Commissioner as Colonel, and Constables often called each other Private. Altogether, the mainstay of the Force, sub-constables and constables, always accounted for more than 75 per cent of the manpower.

RANK	1878	*1881	1884
Commissioner	1	3	1
Assistant Commissioner	1	–	1
Inspectors/Superintendents	25	4	8
Sub-Inspectors/Inspectors	–	11	14
Staff Constables/Staff-Sergeants	17	13	25
Constables/Sergeants	21	23	30
Acting-Constables/Corporals	22	16	33
Sub-Constables/Constables	244	223	433
Surgeons	3	–	3
TOTAL	329	293	557

*1881, the top two positions were called Staff Officers; Surgeons not listed.

STAFF TURNOVER	*1876-84
Discharged	430
Dismissed	21
Invalided	105
Purchased	12
Deserted	92
Deaths	8
Recruits	943

* The numbers do not include 1878, 1882, and 1885.

There was a substantial annual turnover of men. In 1883, only nine men re-engaged and the NWMP lost seventy-five men—15 per cent of its members. However, 110 recruits offset this loss and increased the total numbers. With the newcomers representing 20 per cent of the 518-man Force, concerns relating to inexperience were expected.

Outside opportunities, such as ranching or farming a land warrant, were becoming attractive alternatives to re-enlistment. Second, another term with its arduous and often boring routine, the lack of amenities, isolation, and rigid discipline, was no longer appealing. The excessive number of men who deserted in the years 1874–85 was astounding. A tally, exclusive of 1878 and 1882, indicates that at least 266 men deserted the North-West Mounted Police.[36]

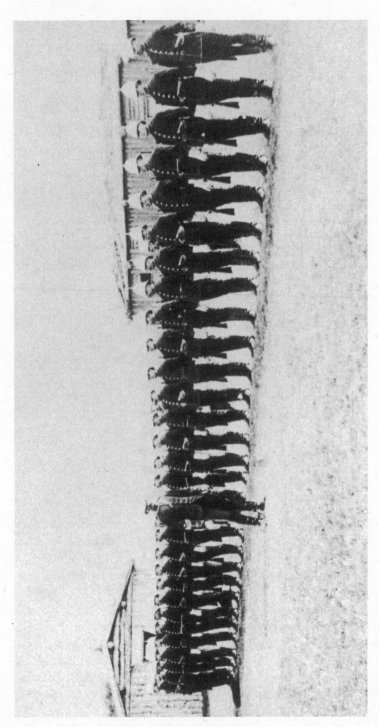

"F" Troop, NWMP, Fort Calgary, 1876

In the years 1873–85, the NWMP had six Divisions, named "A–F".

– GA NA 354 – 10

Joining the NWMP

A senior officer interviewed the applicants. Commissioner James Macleod went east several times to facilitate recruitment. In the winter of 1879–80, for unknown reasons, Macleod remained in Ontario from October until the following spring.

The selection process valued a military background. An ideal candidate, Edward Larkin, had served three years in the Irish Constabulary and two more years with the British army in India. An officer's recommendation letter for William Morgan, Quebec Hussards, bolstered his application: "He was a most attentive and active member of the troop, in fact one of my best men."[37] Kenneth Miller, officer commanding "D" Co., Queens Own Rifles, recommended J.C. Gordon:

> He is a honest, sober and industrious young man, has been a member of my Co in the Queens Own Rifles for some time, is well up in his drill, has obtained a Sergeants certificate by examination, is a member of the Signal corps and Telegraph corps connected with the Regiment and is one of our best Rifle shots. I am sorry to lose him & am sure that you will find in him a very valuable man.[38]

Another candidate for the Force, James Barwis, in his application in May 1877 to Lieutenant-Colonel Charles E. Panet, Deputy Minister of Militia and Defence, wrote detailing his military experience:

> I have the honor to offer myself to serve in the Mounted Police for the North West. I have served one year in "B" Battery and two years and two months in the Dominion Artillery at Manitoba, from which I was discharged on the reduction of that force in 1884. I am in my twenty-third year and sound. I have my certificate of Infantry and Gunnery. I also went through a regular course of riding and driving. I speak and write both languages. I have also certificate of discharge and character during my service in B Battery and at Manitoba I acted as sergeant to Battery Sergeant Major. I have the honor to be, Sir ... Your most obedient servant ... James Barwis.[39]

After nineteen-year-old Ike Forbes (whose motive for enlisting had come from reading Butler's *The Great Lone Land*) was rejected, he joined the local militia and contacted his Member of Parliament. Forbes was accepted into the Mounted Police the next year.

Some ambitious youths contacted senior officers to enhance their chances of being accepted into the Force. George Guernsey wrote to Commissioner A.G. Irvine in May 1880:

> I am desirous of joining the force & would have applied last Spring but unfortunately though big enough, lacked age. I am eighteen and six months old, measure 36 inches around the chest and am six feet in height and weigh 155 lbs, my eyesight is good and I am sound in body. I belong to No. 3 Coy 46th Battn & can refer you to Captn H.A. Ward or Lieut. Robertson for any particulars concerning my character &c. I am a total abstainer from all spirituous liquors. My Father is a retired officer of H.M. Regulars. I enclose an envelope addressed and stamped and hope that you will be kind enough to answer my troublesome questions. For the past three years I have been employed in an office in Town and have a slight knowledge of law.[40]

The aspiring recruit arranged to have his Member of Parliament forward the application to the North-West Mounted Police. Two candidates could be recommended by a member each year.

The application by John Loring from Barrie, Ontario, had the coveted experience of military training and horsemanship. On 23 March 1877, he wrote to the Honorable R. Scott, Secretary of State, Ottawa.

> Sir:
>
> I have the honor to apply to be admitted into the N.W. mounted police as a constable and submit in connection therewith the following personal particulars.
>
> 1. My age is 23 height 6 ft 1½ in weight 182 lbs, am healthy and strong – a good rider and know how to groom and take care of a horse.
>
> 2. Am well educated including a knowledge of French and can speak the language – further I have had some military training as a cadet at the Royal Military Academy Woolwich.
>
> If accepted I will be glad to engage at the earliest period.
>
> I have the honor to be, sir, yr obedient servant
> – John Loring[41]

In a time of widespread political patronage, personal connections were important. Vernon Welch, an unstable and erratic youth, would be accepted into the NWMP; his father supervised the Queen's yacht. Henry Penton wrote to the Secretary of State: "I beg respectfully to offer myself as a Candidate for a member of the North West Mounted Police Force. I am nineteen years of age single five feet nine in height and am son of the Chief of Police of Montreal."[42] William Carroll, a former page in the House of Commons, included twenty-six signatures of recommendation in his application.[43] Some applicants mentioned their family's political affiliation. David Craig's letter to R.W. Scott, Secretary of State, stated that "his parents worked hard for the party."[44] In Ireland, Norman D'Arcy, late of the 4th West-York Militia, promoted his application through the Earl of Langford's connections with Prime Minister J. A. Macdonald, who was currently visiting the United Kingdom.

Many appeals for entry in the Force were sent directly to the Prime Minister and Cabinet Ministers. S.A. Cameron wrote the Prime Minister:

> I beg respectfully to make an application in the Dominion Mounted Police Force. I am about 20 years of age and am familiar with both the French and English languages and if appointed I shall endeavor to prove myself worthy of the position. I beg to submit herewith testimonials which I trust will be considered satisfactory.[45]

Within nine months, Cameron was invalided as unfit from syphilis that he contacted more than two years earlier.

Years after he entered the Force, E.H. Maunsell reflected: "I didn't know what to do and my parents didn't know what to do with me."[46] Some parents, concerned with the direction (or lack of direction) in the life of a son, contacted authorities. The mother of twenty-eight-year-old Charles Ermatinger wrote R.W. Scott, Secretary of State, asking, "any chance for her son in the Mounted Police? He speaks English, French, and German and belongs to one of the best families in Quebec."[47] The father of John G. MacLeod pressed his own son's appointment through his Member of Parliament to Scott: "I am most anxious for his engagement because I have reason to hope he will prove himself deserving of the approval of his superior officer."[48]

Family members contacted authorities to promote their siblings. Bank employee J.F. Feilde wrote: "I have two young brothers at home in Prescott who have not as yet done much good for themselves and are not likely to, if they remain at home. They talk about going to Manitoba and if they can go with some object in view and under strict discipline it will be all the better for them."[49] Both brothers were accepted into the NWMP. Benjamin Daniels, to improve his chances of entry, wrote: "I may state that my brother Lewis has already joined the Force having gone up with Major Walsh's party."[50]

In some cases, family involvement met frustration and disappointment. After Charles Thompson failed in a Manitoba farm undertaking financed by his family, his father, J. Thompson, a retired Surgeon-General in the Imperial Army, arranged a NWMP placement for his son. The youth again proved unreliable, never corresponding with his parents, and receiving a nine-month prison sentence for stealing horses to abet "mutineers." His exasperated father used connections with the Prime Minister to purchase his son's discharge "as a special case." He apologized to Macdonald: "I regret more than I can express that he should have given you so much trouble, but I hope that his experiences may be of service to him in the future."[51]

The father of W. Stratton, angered that his son had joined the Force in Toronto only to leave the next day, contacted the base that he wanted his son to remain in the NWMP. Three Mounties went to his home, brought young Stratton to the barracks, and placed him in the cells. The base commander, Alex McKenzie, wrote to Comptroller White asking, "What should I do with him? He is likely to desert while traveling in the United States. Or should I make an example of him?"[52]

Previous personal contacts, as expected, were helpful in the selection process. In Winnipeg, aspiring recruit Frank Dobbs was delighted to be interviewed by Inspector Frank Norman, a former schoolmate in Ireland. Commissioner French came across the application of James Walker in a stack of 300 letters. He had commanded Walker in the Royal School of Gunnery. French appointed Walker as a Sub-Inspector.

A standard typewritten form replaced the first handwritten applications for engagement in the NWMP. Seven questions were asked.[53] The answers given by John Bushby are in parentheses:[54]

1. What has been your occupation during the last five years?

   (Four years cattle driving in N.S. Wales. 1 year shooting kangaroos in Queensland.)

2. Do you understand the care and management of horses, and do you ride well? (yes)

3. Have you ever served in the Canadian Militia, or have you in any other way received military instruction? (no)

4. Have you previously served in the N.W. Mounted Police,
   if so, when, and why were you discharged? (no)

5. Have you at any time applied for engagement in the Mounted
   Police and been ejected by the Medical Examiner? (no)

6. What is your Age? Height? Weight? Chest Measurement?
   (27, 5 feet 7½ inches, 163 lbs in ordinary dress, 40 inches)

7. Are you married or single? (single)

Most applications included a "certificate of character." Charles Perks, Tool Maker and Jobbing Smith, provided a reference for an employee, stating: "The bearer of this, Thomas Drinkwater, worked for me about five years and at the time of his leaving me was a competent hand, honest, sober and attentive to his work."[55] George Hough wrote: "I the undersigned certify that I have known William Strong for the last five years and always found him to be a steady, honest and laborious man. And also I may testify that he is thoroughly acquainted with the handling and caring of horses."[56]

The poor literacy of the time is reflected in many recommendations, as in the case of J. McArdle:

> 1876/Ottawa City June 4/Col Richanison, (Richardson)/Der sir/The beaner James Mc/Ardle I no him since/He came from the/Country about tow/Years to be a sober/Honest industers young/Man and i would/Be glad he would/Be appointed to the/Manotaba mountain/Police believing he would/Do his duty./Yours truly/John McLaughlin, NH. Walkr(?), D.J. Donoghue(?)[57]

Recruit, Stanislas Bond, marked his Enlistment Form with an "x."—which ran counter to the form requirement of literacy in French or English.

Candidates bolstered their character reference with the signatures of leading local citizens. William Allen's application had nine supporting names—surgeons, merchants, a minister, a justice of the peace—from his hometown of Odessa, Ontario. E.B. Cooke's application had fifteen names. The County of Lanark sent fourteen names of local youths—"all strong, hardy, active young men"—to Richard W. Scott, Secretary of State.[58]

One reason to enlist in the NWMP was the perception that there would be an improvement in health. The North-West was lauded for its bracing, but salubrious climate which with the vigorous physical exercise entailed

Group of NWMP, 1870s

"The class of comrades with whom my lot was cast were truly all sorts and conditions of men."

– John Donkin, *Trooper and Redskin in the far Northwest*, 38–39
RCMP Historical Collections Unit, "Depot" Division, Regina SK., 938–18–3

in police work would be beneficial. George C. King, who had several family members die in England of consumption, enlisted in Toronto on the advice of his physician. Still, there were other motives for joining the NWMP than seeking great adventure or improving health. John Retallack was heavily in debt and the NWMP offered an opportunity to gain a livelihood. John Donkin, employed by a farmer near Brandon, was fed up with breaking sod for petty wages.

Some men chose to enlist as a means to sever family ties. In June 1890, Commissioner Lawrence Herchmer received a letter from Benjamin Rolph of Quebec City:

Would you please be kind enough to inform me if there is in your service a person named Gordon Rolph? He entered the service some fifteen years ago since which time we have not heard from him. I am his father an old man 88 years of age and past labor. I am living with daughter who has lately ben left a widow with nine children and is not very able to support me.

Herchmer replied that Rolph had been discharged three years earlier and was believed living in the Battleford area.[59]

Others joined the NWMP to shirk responsibilities. The obituary of William Sanders of Swift Current in 1932, a man described in the local press as "a pioneer of southwestern Saskatchewan since 1882," triggered a response from Mrs. Ellen Edwards of Regina. She asked for information on Mr. Sanders who had come to Canada in 1882 and joined the NWMP. "My reason," she wrote, "is that a William Sanders married my mother and deserted her in London, England in 1882, leaving her with a baby girl (myself). She never heard any more of him and died four years ago."[60]

In another case, Ann Dann of London, England contacted NWMP Headquarters asking for the whereabouts of Frederick Dann who had abandoned her and joined the Force five years before in 1882. She claimed he "had left me totally unprovided for, also my child who is with Sergt.-Major Dann's parents."[61] The answer was of little help. Dann had been rejected for a second term and left the area.

A medical examination completed the selection process. There were minimum standards for height, weight, and chest-measurement; in several cases, they were overlooked. The doctor recommended James Thomson although his stature of 5 feet 4½ inches was 1½ inches below the stated requirement; George Service was taken on as a good candidate, despite being below the height and chest-measurement requirements. Cursory medical examinations were the rule. An example is S.J. Clarke:

> I have examined S.J. Clarke for the N.W.M. Police.
> He is in every respect a first-class man for the service.
>
> Height: 5 ft. 11 in.
> Weight: 175 lbs.
> Chest: 39 in.
>
> Swettend MD
> July 13/76[62]

It was found that the medical examinations accepted an astonishing number of men with serious health afflictions. After Augustus Jukes became the Senior Surgeon in 1882, all recruits were given a second physical examination upon their arrival at Fort Walsh.

Once accepted into the NWMP, a recruit—informally called "a buck"—signed an "Oath of Allegiance to Her Majesty Queen Victoria" and an "Oath of Office to the Mounted Police." These declarations were on printed stationery (except in a few cases when handwritten copies were signed once the post, usually Fort Walsh, was reached).⁶³ On several occasions, the Oath of Allegiance was a joint declaration with "I" replaced by "We." In one case at Fort Walsh, it had thirty-seven signatures. The third document was the "Engagement Form," for the length of term and signed, with the date, place and witness. For some men the date of engagement began upon their arrival at Fort Walsh rather than at the Toronto depot.

The term of engagement was three years. This was extended to five years in the Police Act of 1879. In special cases, the length of service was negotiated. David Lavalley, a talented blacksmith, had signed a one-year term in 1884. He continued in the Force for six more years until confined in the guardhouse for insanity.

Each recruit received an enlistment number that corresponded with the order of recruitment. George Guernsey, for example, was No. 463; William McQuarrie No. 729; R.N. Wilson No. 583. A low number indicated an early recruitment and was a source of pride and recognition. When Bobbie Belcher re-engaged, he was assigned No. 1023. He arranged to receive his original No. 3—the third man to join the Force. A file prepared on each man provided basic information. In 1880, the file included:

Engaged at _____ _____ day of _____ 188 __

Height, Age, Weight, Chest Measurement, Colour of – hair, eyes, complexion.

Marks (if any), Occupation, Former Residence, Previous Service (military), Religion, Next of Kin (name and address), Remarks.

Taking on recruits in a short time frame resulted in the terms expiring within days, causing a temporary staff shortage until replacements came. To stagger the retirement dates, the Force opened a recruitment depot under Inspector Frank Norman in Winnipeg. In 1882, forty-nine men were engaged in Winnipeg. Rather than the Missouri route west, these recruits moved by river steamer up the Assiniboine and walked overland to Fort Ellice or Fort Qu'Appelle. Once rail travel became available, Tom Clarke recalled detraining at Brandon from where teamsters transported his group to the Shoal Lake barracks. One-half the men rode in the wagons while the others walked, changing positions every thirty minutes. It was estimated that recruitment in Winnipeg saved $60 in transportation costs.

The NWMP and the Winnipeg city police often were at odds. One Mountie had written: "Superintendent Steele always impressed on us that we were North-West Mounted Police and that we must never let a pot policeman arrest us—no matter what the offence may be—and advised us always to go about in pairs or threes."[64] When three city policemen attempted to arrest one Mountie named Armstrong in Whalen's saloon, he knocked all three men out. After this incident, the city police contacted the barracks to handle any "problem" Mounties.

Recruits in the NWMP brought both valuable skills and interesting experiences. Both William McNair and George Martin participated in the Imperial Army's Nile Expedition. T.S. LaNauze had ranched for eight years in Uruguay; E. Brisebois had fought in the Papal Zouave in Italy; Edward Drinkwater worked in Bellini's circus; Seymore Jones had served eighteen years in the Royal Navy. Several of the men had fought in the American Civil War. Inspector F. Dickens had completed seven years in the Bengal Police and J.H.G. Bray ten years in the British Imperial Army. Hermann Des Barres and William Kost served in the Prussian army. John Donkin commented, "The class of comrades whom my lot was cast ... were truly all sorts and conditions of men."[65] Recruit Roger Pocock, in a letter to his mother, described his bunkmates:

> Winnipeg sewer hand – Jamaican plantation clerk – an old soldier – an ex-Constable rejoined – a law clerk – an Ontario Farmers son – an English parsons son – silk designer – A Bank Clerk of Paris – a Western "Tough" – a medical student – an Anglo-Indian – a brakesman – another "Tough" Irish – a farmers son – a French Canadian – Bossange (my Austrian chum) – a barber – a bar tender, & me. Don't you think we are a queer crowd? Yet we are all good friends indeed and never quarrel.[66]

A survey in 1877 of previous occupations of recruits shows that skilled workers were the largest category followed by clerks, farmers, and police/military.[67] Commissioner A.G. Irvine valued men with a rural background as most suited for policing. His report stated: "I consider the best class of men to recruit from are farmers ... or young men from rural districts, accustomed to perform hard manual labour, who understand the care and treatment of horses."[68] There were, he suggested, too many recruits "physically unfit for the manual work required—mere lads, to perform duties. I would recommend that the minimum age at which a recruit be accepted for service be fixed at twenty-one years of age."[69] Surgeon Jukes agreed. Colonel Macleod also advocated that men, "who have been brought up to farming, and who did not need to learn, after enlistment, how to either manage horses or endure fatigue ... and who are by principal and voluntary habit abstainers."[70]

Some recruits had a "cloudy" past. Several joined under false names. A fascinating case is Sergeant-Major Joseph Francis, age forty-three on his discharge from the Force in 1880, who proudly wore the Crimean and Turkish medals for military service in the Crimean campaign. He claimed to have participated in the heroic "Charge of Light Brigade" at Balaklava in 1854. The question of his service arose when research in 1956 failed to find his name in the Musters of the 13th Light Dragoons in the period 1853–74. Subsequent research linked Frances to a Joseph Lane who served in the Crimea and at the Battle of Balaklava. Although the RCMP Crime Detection Laboratories examined copies of the handwriting of both men, the results were inconclusive. In 1971, S.W. Horrall, RCMP historian, clarified, saying: "We believe that the two men, Joseph Lane and Joseph Francis are one and the same man."[71] One can only speculate on why Francis adopted a new identity.

Sergeant-Major Joseph Francis with Crimean and Turkish medals

"We believe that the two men, Joseph Lane and Joseph Francis are one and the same man."

– S.W. Horrall, RCMP Historian
  GA NA 98 – 16

Staff-Sergeant John A. Martin of Charlottetown, P.E.I. is listed in the NWMP Personal Files as Martin. He used this name in his correspondence with the comptroller (asking in 1925 how many original veterans were still alive, and in 1931 regarding the $300 grant given to veterans of the North-West Rebellion). The name, however, used in his will, obituary in the *Charlottetown Patriot*, and on his tombstone is one Malcolm Martin MacIntosh.[72] The explanation may be that Martin was married at the time of his engagement and took his mother's family name.

For some unexplained reason, when Charles B. Shepherd re-joined the NWMP in 1884, he used an alias to conceal his previous engagement in the Force and discharge at Fort Walsh five years earlier. Commissioner Irvine informed the comptroller they were dealing with the same person.

In addition to cases involving identity, the ranks, not unexpectedly, had a number of less than upright individuals. One Ontario paper reported:

> Woodstock, Nov. 22. – Tom Hardy, who went some years ago to join the Northwest mounted police, and was reported dead, returned unexpectedly a few days ago and reconsumed his old tricks of abusing his wife. For this he was taken in charge by the police. The police magistrate gave him an hour to leave town and he left.[73]

Commissioner Lawrence Herchmer replied convincingly to a New York employer's request for information on Peter A. Higgins who served five years in the Force:

> ... ex-Const. Higgins is a first class club swinger and should get employment in a circus. He had a very indifferent character while in the Mounted Police, and when he left Battleford last June, over a year after leaving the police, he deserted his wife there, and it would not be advisable for him to return.[74]

In response to accusations in the House of Commons of police misconduct, Prime Minister John A. Macdonald rationalized: "it was impossible to have a body of three hundred soldiers all saints."[75]

There was an option for re-engagement at the expiry of a term. The number of men who re-engaged varied considerably by year: 30 men of the 46 discharged in 1879 signed on; the following year, after wage reductions, only 22 of 136 time-expired men rejoined the Force. Younger men were preferred. Daniel Wilson, who re-applied at forty, was told "age is against you."[76] Hiring married men was discouraged. After his marriage, George Grogan, who had graduated from Oxford University, had his application for a third term rejected. His Superintendent, A.H. Griesbach, contacted the Commissioner: "Married men do not attend to their duties and shift the workload to those living in the barracks."[77]

Promoters of prairie development encouraged any time-expired men to remain in the region. The *Saskatchewan Herald*, a strong advocate of prairie growth, commented that three men who returned to Ontario found the region they left years ago very different from what they expected and were on their way back. Jarvis rejoined the Force, Lavalley opened a blacksmith shop in the town, and Davis planned to go into business.[78]

After a stint in private life proved unfulfilling, some men sought a re-engagement in the NWMP. Frank Blight purchased his discharge for $66, changed his mind, and then re-engaged. Sergeant Frank Fitzpatrick found employment in Massachusetts but, after six months in "civilization," he wrote to Commissioner Irvine saying that he was "frankly lonesome" for the West and that, if he were accepted, would leave for Winnipeg for a medical examination. In response, Commissioner A. G. Irvine notified Fitzpatrick that he must re-enter the Force as a constable, a reduced rank that dissuaded the former sergeant from rejoining. As a stipulation to his re-engagement, William McQuarrie agreed to have his transportation cost of $26.50 from Ottawa deducted from his pay.

Financial problems compelled some men to rejoin the Mounted Police. In 1889, three years after he left the Force, Stephen Warden applied for re-engagement. Warden explained: "of late, I have been very unfortunate, having lost all my horses and crop last year and the other day a wind storm destroyed my crop for this season."[79] Moreover, while he served in the Force, his wife would attend to the homestead. Warden had served nine years from 1876–86, received a land grant, his Defaulter's Sheet read nil, and conduct on his discharge certificate was marked "very good." With his record, he appeared an ideal candidate, but was not taken on.

Heading West

Recruits assembled in Toronto for the journey west. Rail travel took the contingent north to Collingwood, Ontario, for steamer connections across the Great Lakes to Duluth, Minnesota. From this port, they moved by rail to Bismarck, Dakota Territory, where they boarded a river steamer to take them up the Missouri River to Fort Benton. The final stage of the trip was the walk overland to Fort Walsh. The completion of the C.P.R. and the opening of a small recruiting depot in Winnipeg ended travel through the United States.

Departure from Toronto was always rousing. A band led the recruits from the warehouse training post past large crowds lining the route to the rail station. Favourite songs by the marching men were "The Girl I Left Behind Me" and the stirring "John Brown's Body." Most contingents took a number of horses with them. In 1879, the ninety recruits brought eighty horses.

The station was a frenzy of excitement and final farewells. There, too, were somber moments. A press reporter commented: "A noticeable feature was the number of very young lads who seemed at the last moment to wish that they might stay behind, and even tears were seen to roll down the cheeks of some as they bade their friends adieu."[80]

Their excitement was unabated as the train moved north through Ontario to the port of Collingwood. One recruit remembered: "We were feted and given a send-off at every eating point; the girls kissing us good-bye and crowds shouting hurrahs. In return, we kept singing songs, such as 'The Girl I Left Behind Me' among others that befitted the occasion."[81]

The voyage across the Great Lakes took five to six days. For many of the Canadian-born recruits, this was their first lengthy water voyage and, on several occasions, it was a stressful voyage. One storm that tossed a passenger overboard brought the captain on deck with the comment that he might as well look for a needle in a haystack as to stop the vessel to find the lost man. One recruit reflected that the death "cast a damper on the spirits of the rest on board, but it had the effect of making us all more careful afterwards."[82]

As one of thirty recruits in July 1876, Jack Clarke, aboard "an old wash tub," was in a storm that the captain described as the worst in thirty years. "Everything," recalled Clarke, "was broke on the boat. All hands sick."[83] R.N. Wilson described his five-day trip across the Great Lakes as "misery and semi-starvation."[84] Writing of his lake trip in 1880, Harry Ross recalled that, with half the men seasick, onlookers in Duluth found "it was a difficult matter to tell who were seasick and who were intoxicated."[85]

Once the contingent entered American territory, the men wore either mufti or covered their red tunic with blue denim. Scotch caps replaced the police hats. While waiting for train connections, one Mountie recalled that his troop, "entertained the citizens of Duluth with a demonstration of our efficiency in drill and marched up and down the hills of the city."[86]

From Duluth, Minnesota, the troops traveled by rail west to Bismarck, Dakota Territory. Telegraph contacts on this 670-km journey arranged for food service at the next stopping station. However, sometimes this plan was unreliable. Ike Forbes complained that the only food provided until reaching Fargo, Dakota Territory (about halfway by rail), was soda biscuits, cheese, and milk.

Bismarck introduced "the boys" to the American West. This frontier town on the Missouri River was an eye-opener. One recruit wrote:

> They work on Sundays as well as week days … a young fellow got into a row and was killed. The law took no notice of it. Every person seen was armed to the teeth with revolvers and knives. Went to the Opera. Everybody drank and smoked just as they pleased and the people were all armed there, too.[87]

Tom LaNauze, born in Ireland and for eight years a rancher in Uruguay, thought Bismarck was the toughest place he had ever seen:

> The Sioux had broken out and all the settlers had taken refuge in town. Most of them were drinking and gambling. A settler had a grievance against one of the card dealers and followed him and knocked him down twice. The card dealer then lost his temper, knocked the settler down and kicked him in the head till he was insensible. A local policeman came to interfere but a bystander pulled a gun on the policeman and told him the settler was only getting what was coming to him. The settler was finally carried into a saloon, laid on a billiard table and died shortly afterwards.[88]

Gambling was a popular pastime. In the words of one Mountie: "A number of us went into a gambling joint where there were all sorts of games of chance. In front of the players were stacks of chips, representing anywhere from ten dollars to ten thousand, with a six-shooter on the right side of each man … we were all glad to leave Bismarck."[89]

Bismarck was the transfer point for the men, horses and supplies to a steamboat bound upriver to Fort Benton, a trip that could last from ten to fourteen days. The men insisted that a third of the time was spent in "backward progress" or reversing the vessel in order to bypass over the sand bars or travel through shallow water.

Stops were needed to graze and exercise the horses, take on ice, and load wood. Men called "woodhawks," operating out of small cabins, sold the wood for $3 a cord ("no cash–no wood"). The recruits watched in disbelief as Negro deckhands loaded twenty to thirty cords at a furious pace of one cord a minute. The steamboat was moored to the river bank each night and the recruits slept out on the open deck.

They shared the crowded steamboat with settlers, machinery, crew, American soldiers, farm animals, and cargo. D.A. Fraser recalled:

The boat was exceptionally crowded there being in addition to our detachment of 210 men, 175 more including passengers and crew with many sheep and cattle. The nights were damp, often wet and cold, and the men lying everywhere about the deck were much exposed to the weather—a large percentage requiring daily medical treatment.[90]

As it moved west, the steamer picked up passengers. On one trip, the men recognized one boarder as Louis Riel. His stay was short. There were Orangemen in the North-West Mounted Police and Riel judiciously disembarked at the first wood stop 15 km upriver to wait for the next vessel.[91] Men on the *Red Cloud*, observing the number of American army reinforcements that were headed to "Indian country," grasped the perils that policing might entail.

The American Indians sighted were described as "degraded and spiritless."[92] At Fort Buford, Frank Fitzpatrick unkindly compared 400 Sioux——the younger children stark naked, the warrior's faces painted in bright vermilion, and wearing blue and red blankets, breech cloths, and eagle feathers—to a troop of baboons. He, too, realized that his unit was a long way from home. For himself, Fitzpatrick was delighted that his boyhood dreams had come true, that he was on the brink of such adventures as James Fenimore Cooper described.[93]

The river journey was a fascinating experience. As the boat moved slowly westward, beautiful landforms unfolded beneath the sweep of the open sky. The distances were vast. The men watched the pilot on the bow as he plaintively called out the depths. They watched the countryside. Wildlife sometimes suddenly appeared in enormous numbers. The recruits shot at buffalo and antelope who were feeding close to the river. Other targets were beavers and ducks. One small herd of buffalo swam so close to one steamer that men hit some animals with sticks. Another sighting was thirty buffalo standing stuck in the mud on one island. At one landing, the men mistook a pile of buffalo hides (sold for $2 each) for a wood pile. Tom LaNauze wrote of his upriver trip:

> We passed and shot at a large herd of buffalo that were feeding close to the river but with no effect, shot some antelope which came in well for the fresh meat ... one day some trappers and hunters came on board the steamer with a lot of deer skins and buffalo hides, and an Indian scalp. They shot him when stealing their horses, so were clearing out in case his friends should scalp them.[94]

William McQuarrie likened the Missouri River to the colour of pea soup. When he asked for a drink of water, a deck hand grabbed a rope with an old tomato can attached and threw it over the side. He pulled it in and handed the can to the policeman. McQuarrie was aghast. He wrote: "Is that what you drink on this boat?" I enquired. 'Yes' he said, and that was what we drank the whole trip."[95]

This source of drinking water was not reassuring to Ike Forbes, on the *Red Cloud* in 1878, when he watched buffalo carcasses floating down the river. McQuarrie remembered one island littered with rotting carcasses of buffalo. The smell was so noxious that everyone held their noses until the steamer had moved past. Henry Head recalled: "Some places the banks lined up with pelts ... hills and riverbanks were thickly strewn with the decaying corpses for miles, and the flavor of the atmosphere can be better imagined than described."[96] Still, the river trip was a marvelous experience. McQuarrie recalled:

> Every day was a picnic with us. Nothing to do but eat. We used to average about five fights a day. All this was just for exercise. The meals on the boats were fine but they could only feed fifty at one time so if you were the first fifty for breakfast, you would be the second fifty for dinner. That did not please Scotty, who was one of the boys who loved fighting. He wanted to be at first table all the time. So they sentenced him to eat with the coloured men. So we had great fun seeing Scotty with his big dish going to the cook and then sitting down on the deck.[97]

All the deck hands were Negroes. The captain disciplined unruly or lazy workers by leaving them on the river bank with a gun and a few supplies to wait until the downriver return of the steamboat picked them up, sometimes a week later. One angry man fired his gun at the departing steamer, narrowly missing the captain and recruit Jack Clarke. In another incident, when one policeman had an altercation with a Negro waiter, a laxative was allegedly put in the police coffee. The men persuaded the captain to put the waiter ashore with some hardtack to wait until the vessel returned.

Constable R.N. Wilson recalled his trip on the *Red Cloud* in 1881 as "one of interest & pleasure to us Pilgrims (so called by Western men because we are from the East). We had good board ... & were as comfortable as could reasonably be expected, & when we at last received orders to go ashore, many did so with feelings of regret."[98] The Canadians on board had even celebrated May 24 with passion. The men were ordered to the

Steamer *Rosebud*

The Missouri trip upriver from Bismarck to Fort Benton took ten to fourteen days; the downriver return only four days. The photo shows Mounted Policemen talking to American soldiers.

– NAC C – 004855

hurricane deck where they gave three cheers and sang "God Save the Queen." Those men with revolvers fired a volley. The newspaper account failed to relate how the Americans reacted on an American vessel in American territory.[99]

Newly appointed Surgeon A. Jukes' journey from Ontario to Fort Walsh in 1882 took thirty-two days, of which thirteen days were spent on the Missouri.[100] On board were 212 recruits and three officers. They shared the *Red Cloud*, a vessel 180 feet (55 m) long and 40 feet (12.2 m) wide, with horses, sheep, cattle, American settlers, and crew—in all, 382 people.

The weather was cold and wet and many men became ill from sleeping out on the exposed deck and from the unsanitary conditions. Surgeon Jukes was overworked attending to all the cases of fever, diphtheria, measles, and diarrhea. One recruit, Adam Wahl, fell overboard while fishing, and was never seen again. At Fort Benton Jukes converted one supply wagon into a hospital van for the trip northward to Fort Walsh.

Fort Benton was the last stop of the river journey. Here was a town one recruit described as being "even more wild and woolly than Bismarck."[101] The Reverend John Maclean, bringing his bride from Ontario to Fort Macleod, watched cowboys "riding at a mad pace through the main street, apparently under the influence of liquor as they kept shooting revolvers and yelling in a wild Western fashion."[102] Town prisoners could be seen working off their fines at $1 a day, encumbered by a ball and chain attached to an ankle. Always nearby was a guard holding a carbine.[103]

Many of the police recruits were not models of good behaviour. One unruly group seized a wagon loaded with beer and drank every bottle. Commissioner A.G. Irvine later settled the costs. Sub-Constable W.H. Metzler remembered that his contingent left for Fort Walsh "with four of our chaps in the jug in Fort Benton."[104]

An overland walk north to Fort Walsh was the final stage of the trip west. The 335-km journey usually took six days. By now it was June, which was often stifling hot. If there had been heavy rains, the trail became ankle deep in mud. One contingent had to wait nine days for the trail to be passable. The recruits were tired, miserable, wet through, and many had colds. William McQuarrie was footsore and removed his boots. His barefoot walk ended when the bull whackers began lashing the grass with whips and shouting "rattlesnakes." McQuarrie was "not long in getting back to the wagon and getting into those long boots. No more bare feet for me."[105] Jack Clarke wrote: "They sure kept us busy watching them and from tramping on them. At this time their color was about the color of the grass."[106]

Several times, the American Cavalry escorted a contingent to the border, where a Mounted Police mule or bull teams arrived with arms, ammunition, and scarlet tunics to replace their civilian clothes. Sometimes, the welcome was less than expected:

> The officer sent from Fort Walsh to guide the recruits north from Fort Benton was drunk most of the time, and acted like a ruffian, swearing at and abusing the men with most engaging freedom and impartiality. Once when he saw a man on horseback, he ordered him, with an oath, to come down as horses were more valuable than men in that country.[107]

One group went north accompanied by 150 Cree as a safeguard (for both parties) against Blackfoot depredations. A camp guard was posted each night. Some contingents had tents that held eight men; otherwise, the men slept in the open on the ground.

After a week to twelve days on the trail, everyone was happy to see Fort Walsh. The post had been described as "a pretty sight, down in the valley, and freshly whitewashed with white clay dug up from the banks of the creek."[108] Sometimes, the weary recruits were given three days to rest before the daily scheduled training sessions began:

> Since we were all fresh from the East, timbermen, labourers clerks … it was no easy task to train us. The first weeks consisted of drill, marching, horsemanship, target practice and guard duty. Then followed training in posting duties and charging persons caught violating the law. We were taught how to chain people to wagon wheels at night and how to tie them astride a cayuse when travelling with them during the day.[109]

And, for the next three or five years these young and eager recruits would be responsible for policing the plains.

Promotions, Transfers, and Leave

The Comptroller approved all transfers, promotions, and leaves of absence. Individual Mounties could request a transfer. Superintendent Shurtliff had asked for a posting at Maple Creek "to arrange affairs" and exchange locations with Superintendent John McIllree. The arrival of a body of recruits at Fort Walsh often necessitated the transfer of "old hands." For Constable Edward Barnett, this would mean a move to Fort Macleod. On leaving, he wrote: "We pulled out the last of September. 'F' troop band played 'Goodbye Mavourneen'—and we vanished, most of us never to see Fort Walsh again."[110]

The opening of a new detachment entailed the transfer of men for staffing. Fifty-seven men were assigned to the newly established Regina Headquarters in 1882. In 1883, twenty-seven men were posted to the new base at Maple Creek.

The abrupt dismissal of Inspector Theodore Richer at the beginning of the '74 trek west, although an isolated incident, nevertheless caused immediate rank adjustments with Sub-Inspector Leif Crozier promoted to command "F" Division. Most promotions, however, were based on recommendations from senior officers. Commissioner Macleod informed

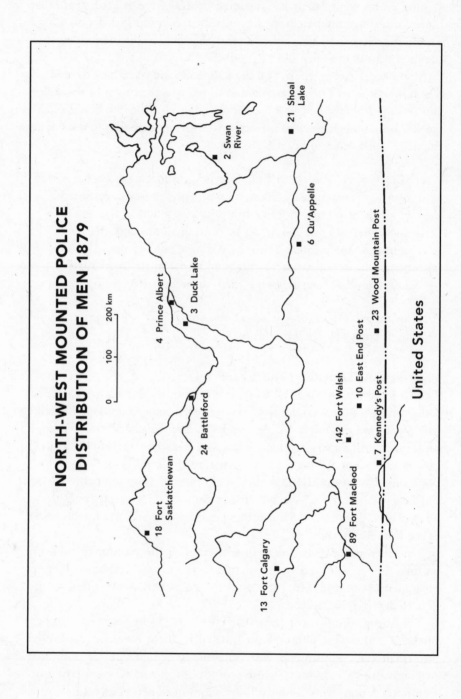

NORTH-WEST MOUNTED POLICE
DISTRIBUTION OF MEN 1879

0   100   200 km

18 Fort Saskatchewan

24 Battleford

13 Fort Calgary

89 Fort Macleod

142 Fort Walsh

4 Prince Albert

3 Duck Lake

10 East End Post

7 Kennedy's Post

23 Wood Mountain Post

2 Swan River

6 Qu'Appelle

21 Shoal Lake

United States

Ottawa that officers D. Clarke and J. McIllree had shown exceptional skills at crossing the South Saskatchewan River. Inspector William Jarvis' report in 1874 related to the Edmonton march. He suggested:

> I wish to bring to your notice the names of Troop Sergeant-Major Steele and Constable Labelle. Sergeant-Major Steele has been undeviating in his efforts to assist me, and has done the manual labor of at least two men. The attention paid by Constable Labelle to the horses has saved many of them.[111]

Commissioner A.G. Irvine recommended to Comptroller Frank White (January 1882) that Frank Norman be promoted to Inspector. That year, two hundred and fifty recruits opened many new positions and transfers.

A resignation or retirement of an officer launched a chain of promotions. In March 1875, the Department of Justice granted Inspector Jacob Carvell, an American Civil War veteran, a leave of absence to arrange his family's transportation from Boulder, Colorado, to Swan River. In October, however, rather than return, Carvell sent his resignation to Commissioner French. French recommended to the Minister of Justice that Sub-Inspector James Walker replace Carvell and Frank Norman assume Walker's position. H. Bernard, the Minister of Justice, asked Assistant Commissioner Macleod for some placement recommendations. In response, Macleod suggested Sub-Inspector T.R. Jackson, an artillery officer, and Constable Antrobus for vacant Sub-Inspector positions and that Constables T. Clyde, "F" Division, and H. Homan "richly deserve promotion."[112] In July 1880, a rotation of officer postings resulted after Ottawa, annoyed with James Walsh's obstruction of government efforts to return Sitting Bull to the United States, transferred him from Wood Mountain to Fort Qu'Appelle, 235 km from the Sioux camp.[113]

Confidential evaluations of officers informed Ottawa of men who were deserving of advancement. Commissioner Macleod's negative assessment of Sub-Inspector Albert Shurtliff was detrimental to that officer's career. Macleod wrote: "I have not a very high opinion of Sub-Inspector Shurtliff as a Police Officer, and I don't think he is well suited for the Force."[114] In sharp contrast, Macleod's assessment of Surgeon R.B. Nevitt was that it would be difficult to find a better medical officer.

Citations for impressive service indicated candidates worthy of a promotion. Assistant Commissioner Irvine wrote the Secretary of State in Ottawa: "I have much pleasure in bringing to your notice the satisfactory manner in which Inspector Crozier performed his duties and the tact and discretion he exhibited while temporarily in command of Fort Walsh."[115] Superintendent William Herchmer contacted Commissioner Irvine that Sergt.-Major Thomas Wattam's distinguished gallantry at the Cut Knife Hill skirmish deserved a promotion with a pay raise as a "tangible way of recognizing his services."[116] The leadership of twenty-four-year-old Inspector A. Bowen Perry, heading the Fort Macleod detachment north to fight Big Bear in the North-West campaign, marked a promising officer and he was rewarded with a promotion to Superintendent in command of "F" Division at Prince Albert. Bowen Perry served as the Commissioner of the RCMP for twenty-three years, 1900 to 1923.

Outside input into rank placement had to be carefully considered. Family members lobbied Prime Minister Macdonald for a promotion of Sergeant Maurice Duchesnay to replace a resigned Inspector. At a later date, Commissioner L. Herchmer evaluated Duchesnay as being of unsteady habits and incapable of doing duties.[117]

Some promotions were short-lived. Constable James Whipps had been promoted to Corporal in November 1885. Eleven days afterwards, he was reduced to Constable for being asleep while on duty.

An application for a leave of absence or a furlough (with the reasons and dates) was sent to the Commissioner to forward with his recommendation to the Comptroller. Staffing needs affected his decision. In May 1876, Col. Macleod rejected Albert Shurtliff's application for three months leave to visit an ill family member because Inspector Winder was on leave and Sub-Inspector Thomas Jackson had submitted an earlier application. Six months later, A.G. Irvine informed Justice Minister H. Bernard that there was a marked improvement in the Division under Shurtliff's command since replacing Sub-Inspector Jackson and he received a furlough. In December, Shurtliff requested a two-month extension, informing the Honorable R.W. Scott, Secretary of State, since two women were also accompanying him west it was unwise to cross the prairies in December.

All approved furloughs were subject to cancellation. Leave requested by Leif Crozier and W.D. Antrobus were placed on hold when important issues surfaced. Some men on furlough requested an extension of time. Constable Bagley, for example, received an additional two months' leave.

A policeman granted a furlough forfeited all pay and claims for rations during his leave. Some "extended" their time by arranging to carry the mail or escort a prisoner to Winnipeg from where the date of leave would begin. Sergeant Warden, headed for Scotland, escorted Snake-Man to Stony Mountain Penitentiary; Shurtliff, while on his way to Ontario to bring his wife west, took a prisoner to the same prison.

The post commander granted short-term leaves of absence (passes) with forfeiture of pay and rations. The policeman was issued a pass stating his name, number, permission to be absent from quarters, and purpose:

> W.A. Antrobus, Inspector to # 383 Const. H Ross. Permission to be absent from quarters from 6 a.m., March 18, 1884 to 12 (noon) on 9 June purpose of working in Prince Albert.[118]

Anyone considered incompetent or difficult was shuffled to another post. In October 1885, Superintendent William Herchmer wrote critically of Constable John Ballendine:

> He was bought down here by me last autumn. He was perfectly useless here. I sent him to the mountains. There he was even worse. Supt. Steele took him with him North and finding him useless left him at Fort Saskatchewan. He also reported that Ballendine who is a half-breed openly expressed his sympathies with the rebels ... I may add that Const. Ballendine is used up with syphilis and recommend that he be discharged as a useless man ... want Const. E.H. Brown sent in place.[119]

Two months later, Ballendine applied for discharge by purchase. Assistant Commissioner Leif Crozier recommended acceptance.

Leaving the Force

On completion of a term, a policeman appeared before a board of officers who verified service dates and calculated any coming pay. Personal items were checked against a list of issue and any usable police articles returned.[120] If there were no salary claims, the departing man signed a statement forfeiting further pay, clothing or compensation from the NWMP:

> Battleford, 5 June 1880
>
> I certify that I have been settled with to date and that I have no further claim against the Government either for pay or for clothing.
>
> W.L. Armstrong #262[121]

There were relatively few claims for wage or clothing compensation. Thomas Aspdin sought $456, claiming that, in his work as a farrier, his back had been injured by a horse. After extended correspondence between the

Commissioner and Comptroller Fred White in Ottawa, Aspdin received $106. In another claim, S.J. Clarke claimed $6.75 ($1.25 for stable trousers; $5.50 for a pair of blankets). W. Chamberlayne wanted $19.70 (for two buffalo robes — $12, two shirts — $4, six towels — $1.20, and one stable suit — $2.50). S. Henderson's claim for transportation costs to his home in Sarnia was refused. Sergt.-Major Joseph Francis claimed expenses of $140 relating to the '74 March, six years earlier.

Arthur Murray sought $2,000 for having been accidentally shot while on duty. Even though the bullet had never been extracted, Surgeon Jukes concluded that Murray was perfectly recovered, never on sick report, and ready to do his duty. Twelve years after the injury, Murray wrote to Prime Minister Wilfrid Laurier that he was now married with three children and employed as a railway fireman but all his attempts to get life insurance were rejected because of the bullet wound. Murray tenaciously pursued his claim and, ten years later (1904), a medical board approved a daily compensation of twenty-three cents.[122]

A Discharge Certificate finalized the proceedings. The document gave the years of service and the man's conduct record while with the Force. Usually, the conduct was marked "satisfactory." Other examples include: Richard Wyld — "bad," G. Casault — "indifferent," T. Baker — "very good," and James Beattie (who was dismissed) — "very bad."

Conduct rated "indifferent, fair, or bad" had important implications for pension benefits, land grants, and future police service. John O'Keefe, rated "indifferent character" on his discharge in 1879, applied to rejoin the Mounted Police in 1885. Commissioner Irvine rejected him on this fact alone, no doubt the correct decision. O'Keefe was destitute and had been living an unsettled lifestyle in San Francisco, Mexico, and Minnesota. In his application, he brazenly asked if he could borrow $5.[123] James Ritchie, living in Guelph, was informed: "No land grant. Fair conduct."[124]

In response to Constable David Joyal's (conduct fair) request to re-engage, Commissioner Herchmer sent a terse telegram: "Will not re-engage Joyal."[125] Charles Bowes, applied to re-list. His discharge form omitted his conduct. Commissioner Lawrence Herchmer wrote to the Comptroller: "Constable Charles Bowes was useless while he was in the Force and was in very bad health during the latter part of his service … I do not wish him to be re-engaged."[126]

Conduct infractions listed on the Defaulter's Sheet would effect one's eligibility for re-engagement with the Force. In answer to H.N. William Shaw's application to re-engage, the Commissioner L. Herchmer wrote that: "Considering the length of his defaulter's sheet, I do not propose to re-engage him."[127] Joseph Chabot, likewise, was rejected. Superintendent A.H. Griesbach wrote: "I cannot recommend re-engagement of this man, owing to a bad defaulter's sheet."[128]

Most Discharge Certificates included the Intended Place of Residence. We learn Angus McGillis was hired by the Cochrane Ranch; Henry Walker – Fort Benton; David Grier – Fort Macleod; Harold Ross – Prince Albert.

The NWMP requested an acknowledgement of the discharge. Joseph Percival answered, simply: "Received from Supt & Adjt R. Burton Deane my discharge from the North-West Mounted Police."[129]

Most men left the Force at the expiration of one term. Some returned "to Canada"—or what they referred to as the eastern provinces. Others remained in the West to start their own enterprises. Many of the early ranchers in Alberta had a NWMP background. Superintendent Walker left to manage the Cochrane Ranch. His annual salary of $2,400 was $1,000 more than what he earned in the North-West Mounted Police.

Before the 1879 *Police Act*, a policeman on completion of his term (with good conduct) was then eligible for a land warrant of 160 acres. Frederick Bourke, at Battleford, NWT, replied in December 1880:

> Sir – I have the honer to acnoladge the receipt of my discharge and certificate for land grant.
>
> Your obedient servant.
> Fredck Bourke.[130]

Complaints arose over the location of the land grant. The *Manitoba Free Press* noted "much dissatisfaction is felt among the men that they were not able to locate their 160 acres ... within 100 miles of the railway ... it is hoped that the Government will change the rule in that respect."[131]

In addition to expiry of term, men left the Force by being invalided, through purchase, by providing a substitute, for family or personal reasons, or being discharged for undesirable behaviour. A surgeon's note would recommend whether or not a man should be invalided. August Jukes, Senior Surgeon, wrote on April 1883:

> I certify that Reg. No 824 Const McClelland of B. Division is unfit for further service in the N.W.M.P. for the following reasons
>
> 1. Constitutional Syphilis – attended with disease of the Bones and recommend that he be invalided forthwith.[132]

Group of North-West Mounted Police, Medicine Hat, 1885

"It was strange, but our Force seemed to possess men who could do almost anything when the occasion demanded it."

– Frank Fitzpatrick, *Sergeant 331*, 111

GA NA 3409 – 4

In the case of T. McCutcheon, who had three epileptic seizures in a month, Jukes recommended that he be invalided "the sooner the better ... and never be trusted with a loaded weapon in his hand."[133] Six years later, McCutcheon unsuccessfully sought a pension, claiming he was invalided on account of injuries sustained during his service. Hanford Crozier was discharged when a medical examination revealed that he was blind in one eye. He had served on the Force for one year. Surgeon Robert Miller discharged Andrew Jones as a "confirmed hypochondriac."

Men purchased a discharge through negotiations with the comptroller. Opportunities for economic advancement was one reason to leave the Mounted Police. August Miller wrote:

> I honorably request that you forward to the Commissioner my application for discharge from the North West Mounted Police. The reasons for asking for my discharge are as follows. I have been offered a very good situation in Prince Albert, to work at my trade, that of a butcher, if I can obtain my discharge will accept the offer as I would be enabled to better myself very considerably so doing. Hoping that you will see fit to recommend this application.[134]

Although Superintendent A. Bowen Perry did recommend approval, Comptroller White requested a purchase of $3 for each month of service remaining, at a cost to Miller of $50. Campbell Young also purchased his discharge for $50. He cited an opportunity to work for R. Hardisty at the HBC at a wage much better than his police salary. D. Thomson purchased his discharge to work as a surveyor for the C.P.R. The family of Francis Mansfield, through contact with the Prime Minister, were able to purchase his discharge so he could start a cattle ranch in Manitoba. Albert Ozanne bought his discharge after he inherited some property on the island of Guernsey in the United Kingdom. He was eighty-three in 1939 when Nazi troops occupied his land.

The buyout amounts varied. Colin Genge asked for a discharge after four years and six months of service, six months short of his term, to attend to his ranch. Irvine approved his request at no cost since Genge planned to settle in the country.[135] James Fullwood left the NWMP after fourteen months because of severe eye problems. He paid $125 in gold— a questionable amount for a recruit earning $30 a month. In addition to paying for fifty months at $3 each, John Hutchinson had to pay $67 for his transportation East. M.H. Meredith bought his discharge for $3 for each month of unexpired time. James Carroll paid $100.

Patrick Curran paid $50. In his case, the Commissioner commented that he a married man with a large family, was discontented and useless, and better out of the Force. For some odd reason, Frank Blight chose to purchase his discharge for $66—then rejoined the Force. Joseph Fraser did even better by purchasing his discharge twice.

Charles Loscombe arranged to have his term reduced from three to two years. Const. Harold Smith claimed he was needed for urgent family business. His service was commendable without any defaults in three and one-half years. Comptroller White set his discharge at $3 a month for half a year, and $2 a month for the final year. J.S. Nicholas' application stated that a small legacy received that winter positioned him to marry and settle down. He sent $39 for his buyout. A reply informed him that the minimum cost for discharge was $50 and that his commanding officer at Wood Mountain was to collect $11 more from Nicholas.

Correspondence between Commissioner Lawrence Herchmer and Comptroller White agreed that Sergt-Major T. Kempster's application for purchase should be approved since he didn't get along with other members of the Force and, second, although he was married, he was "very nearly committing bigamy with a girl named Evans who followed him to his posting at Calgary. His running after the girl was neglecting of his work and detrimental to the division."[136]

James Shea created a messy situation after he paid $81 for his discharge. At the same time, on the recommendation of Father Albert Lacombe to the comptroller, Shea was given free discharge as he had promised to enter the Oblate Order and work at an Indian Industrial school. However, Shea was in Ottawa and had changed his mind. What should Lacombe do now? The priest wrote: "Am I to return the cheque to your office, or send it to Shea, or to have Shea endorse it and give that money for the benefit of the industrial school?"[137]

Staff-Sergt. George Fraser wanted to bring his long-separated family west and paid $100 for his discharge. He then rejoined the NWMP and served another twenty-three years.[138] J.J. Raymore asked for a discharge for personal reasons to attend to the family business because his ill father was unable to manage, his brother, suffered from consumption, and the health of his mother was failing.[139]

R.N. Wilson applied twice for a discharge, citing his mother's health. Comptroller White responded negatively to his requests, stating only in special cases of family bereavement and winding up of an estate were discharges permitted. After two more applications failed, Wilson was able to purchase his discharge for $63. He left Battleford for Fort Macleod, where he found work and apparently never went East to see his mother.

George Callaghan wrote to Major Crozier, Fort Macleod, 6 March 1882:

> ... i respectfully request that you will recommend this my application for Discharge from the N.W.M. Police by Paying the Sum of $100.00 i have served in the Force for 2 yrs & 9 mns & my reasons for wishing to obtain it are 1st that i have chronic Cattarch & Lung Disease 2nd that i feel that i am getting worse & i wish to Purchase my Discharge ... Hoping that you will be kind enough to forward this application.[140]

A doctor confirmed his illness and stated that the hardships of duties only aggravated his problems. Callaghan, incidentally, lived into his nineties.

Ottawa replied to G. Casault's letter that to purchase his discharge he would pay $10 for each of his five remaining months for a total of $50. Casault refused this offer and found another way out by being invalided on three counts: short-sighted, unable to ride because of a rupture, and having chronic bronchitis. Doctor Augustus Jukes' medical exam concluded, "He is unable to see it [target] clearly enough to distinguish a bull's eye from an outer ring and is incapable of either riding or shooting. I think he had better be invalided."[141]

A discharge by providing a substitute was infrequent. Whether or not the arrangement involved cash between the two men is not known. Charles Daley received his discharge through an approved substitute, ex-Constable C.F. Boyle. Sub-Constable Robert Whitney had a former Sub-Constable, E.C. Miller, complete his term. After James Sutherland, in charge of Cripple Camp on the '74 March west, arranged for a substitute to finish his term, Sutherland rejoined the Force one year later and went on to complete a second term of service.

After eleven months of service, William Davis provided a replacement. Then, only three months later, Davis signed on for a second three-year term. Charles Palmer, obliged to return home to Ireland for urgent business, paid three months salary for a substitute to finish his time. Thirty years later he contacted the comptroller that he was thinking of moving to Canada and asked if he was entitled to a land grant. He was informed that he was three months short of the required three years continuous service.

Commissioner James Macleod accepted John Graham, a blacksmith, as a replacement for Constable James Bell who, "altho a very good man is not particularly smart. He has commenced farming near Fort Macleod."[142] Graham proved a poor substitute, leaving the Force in fourteen months. His medical exam, in which the doctor observed, "this afternoon he had been drinking but I believe under proper discipline will be a good man for the service,"[143] should have indicated future difficulties. In unusual circumstances, an Order-in-Council could grant a discharge at the man's request. One case permitted the transfer of M.B. Hetherington to the Department of Indian Affairs.

The Force expelled men for contumacy and excessive drinking. In a seven-year period, there were twenty-one men who fell into this category. James Montgomery was found guilty of collusion by warning J. Beaudouin, a whiskey trader, of police raids. Montgomery was sentenced to eight months' imprisonment in the guard house and dismissed from the Force. His forthcoming $6 owed in pay was sent to the Receiver General.

There was occasional leeway. Peter Coutts, dismissed after his service of fourteen years, asked the Commissioner to reconsider his expulsion in view that Coutts had a wife and two children and promised to swear off alcohol. He was re-engaged.

Overt homosexual acts were abhorred. Anyone guilty of a homosexual offence was immediately dismissed from the Force without a prison term. At the hearing of Sergeant Charles Power Thomson, a Board of Officers heard statements given under oath from two constables that detailed the sergeant's "beastly designs" (homosexual advances) while they were sleeping. Commissioner Irvine dismissed Thomson "for grossly immoral conduct."[144] Louis Fontaine, found guilty of "committing an unnatural offence," on evidence of H.D. Jackson, was dismissed from the Force "with ignominy."[145]

Did anyone have a shorter NWMP career than J.W. Jones? Surgeon Jukes, annoyed for recommending him, reported to Comptroller White that Jones was:

> ... continually complaining of being unable to drill, or to do anything useful ... he has never left his mother before & has been badly coddled. He is very desirous to leave the Service & is a very useless, weak-minded, troublesome man in it. I regret much that I recommended him & I fear he will prove unreliable in every way ... recommend he be allowed to go ... he is decidedly the worst man admitted.[146]

Immediately upon his release, Jones demanded money for his service of thirty-five days.

Throughout the early years of the NWMP, the problem of retaining staff was a major concern. Completion of the term (with a land grant) offered the men an independent lifestyle. Others left the Force because of wage reduction, as invalids, or were expelled for unwanted behaviour. An inordinate number of desertions added to the loss of policemen.

Desertion

In response to a *Toronto Globe* reporter in 1883, Superintendent Sam Steele affirmed that "only about forty men have deserted since the Force was organized. We have fewer cases of desertion than any other force of the same number in the world."[147] His comparison with other military forces may have been correct, but Steele's number of forty men in nine years is clearly understated. He should have recalled that, during the eighteen-day camp at Dufferin, preparatory to the westward march, thirty-one men took what was called "French leave" and, in the first winter at Fort Macleod, eighteen men left for Montana Territory. Twenty-five men deserted from the NWMP in 1883, a considerable 5 per cent of the Force. Moreover, this high rate of desertions continued, with thirty-one men deserting in 1884 and an astounding 127 of the 880 policemen who had fought in the 1885 North-West campaign deserting within two years.[148]

Why would a man abandon this world-famous organization? Money was one reason. When nine men left Fort Walsh in 1880, the *Manitoba Free Press* speculated that "it is supposed that a craze about newly-found gold digging in Montana led them to commit this foolish act."[149] For policemen earning $30 a month, the prospect of making $10 a day in mining was an enticement. And anyone with a trade could expect attractive wages in Montana Territory.[150] But it is a puzzle why James Swift deserted when he was only twenty days short of completing a five-year term.

Second, some recruits resented the work, discipline, boredom, and isolation of their new police calling. A solution was to pick up and leave an unwanted situation. Commissioner Irvine observed that, when men are engaged in large numbers, they would form cliques that tended not to integrate quickly in the barracks. All the deserters in 1882, he noted, "have, without exception, been men of but a few months' service."[151] One western newspaper blamed the deserters themselves: "Many had never been out in the world and got homesick, while others foolishly thought that the mounted police service was only a prolonged picnic."[152]

There were recruits who had a "change of mind" while en route to Western Canada. As his contingent neared Fort Assiniboine, Montana Territory, R.N. Wilson recalled: "Ten of the fellows became discontented or homesick and left, walking back to the Missouri."[153] Jack Clarke, in a company walking from the Missouri River to Fort Walsh, resented Major Walsh's autocratic command and turned back with a companion named Mills. Walsh and an assistant trailed the two men and warned them, that in hostile country, it would be wise to rejoin the troop. They agreed but as Clarke wrote: "We went back under certain conditions. At this time we had the best of Major Walsh. We were on the American side of the line."[154]

Most deserters headed for the American border. At the Dufferin camp in 1874, it was a few paces to Minnesota. A man with a horse at Fort Macleod or Fort Walsh had a good start for the Medicine Line before he was even missed. The *Fort Benton River Press* commented: "It is only forty miles to the line from this post [Fort Walsh] and anyone who doesn't like the country can skip without much trouble."[155]

For men stationed at the police posts along the North Saskatchewan River, desertion meant traveling considerable distances to avoid arrest. If the route taken was south, a man crossing the plains needed a good horse, rifle, and supplies for a ride that would last many days. An eastward route usually required river transport. Constable Leonard Hatcher, facing charges in Battleford, left the Prince Albert detachment; it was assumed that he had gone northeast to Fort à la Corne to board the steamer *Marquis*. A policeman was sent downriver after him, but without success.

Summer and early fall was the opportune time to leave, and, the best time to "head out" was at night. At Battleford, constables Knight, Taylor and Duncan left at 2:00 a.m. with rifles and three swift horses. A patrol sent in pursuit failed to contact the men. At Fort Saskatchewan, W.H. Lovett and Fenty (?) left at 9 p.m., and it was six hours before their absence was noticed. Both men were described as worthless and good riddance. Lovett recently spent three months in the guard room for threatening to desert.

It was often easy to "skip out" while on patrol. Corporal M. Kenney, in charge of a five-man patrol, told his detail their ride was over as he and Gilbert were heading for the American border. On news of the incident at Fort Walsh, a party was sent in pursuit. They sighted the two deserters about 25 km "on this side of the line" and began a hectic chase.

> all parties ran their horses till they dropped. Corp. Kenney's horse stumbled and threw him. He left the horse and took to his legs and got away. They found his horse lying where he fell but could see nothing of him. Gilbert when he found his horse played out, cut off the road, left his horse behind him and took to his legs. The party returned today, the 18th, with the two horses and all their own played out. [156]

Kenney gave himself up four years later, time he had spent in the British army. He was reduced in rank, and served six months in the guardhouse. Surprisingly, he was taken on, likely because of his skill as a blacksmith.

An activity opened an opportunity to desert. Constables Elliot Thornton (who had been lost for days on the '74 March), and S.C. Leonard went out shooting and continued to the border. Constables Graham and Webster left with a four-horse team for Whoop-Up to get vegetables for the Fort Macleod mess. Instead, they picked up constables Kelsey and Ranton at the Stand-Off detachment and all four men crossed the border with six horses and anything of value from the Stand-Off quarters.

Anyone stationed at an outpost could leave at any time. Thomas Garland and William Morrow left the police ranch to scout up Pincher Creek, but instead crossed the line. James McCann, in charge of Peigan reserve post, told the constable on duty he was going to the Kootenay post on business and would return in three days. Instead, he rode across the border.

Some policemen did not return from leave. William Clark and Wallace Brownlaw left the Force in Winnipeg, M. Turnball in Brandon. F. Williams took a furlough to Ontario where he deserted. While on assignment to bring the son of Superintendent W. Herchmer from school in Winnipeg to Shoal Lake, Walter Long, trusted as a first-rate Mountie, astonished his superiors by deserting. It was later learned that Long, carrying a large amount of money from his barrack mates to purchase whiskey, had fallen into bad company and lost the money gambling. He was then ashamed to return to the base and deserted.

Some deserters were thoughtless or ill-prepared for their escape. P.H. Hawkins, J. Wright, and E.F. Davies left Fort Saskatchewan by skiff without coats or blankets and, when arrested, "were so reduced with exposure and hunger that they were rather glad to be taken."[157]

The first *Police Act* contained no specific charge for desertion. Justice, therefore, was upheld through a criminal charge of theft of government property—the horse, saddle, and carbine taken. When eight men who had left for gold-mining opportunities in Montana Territory were arrested, Stipendiary Magistrate James F. Macleod and Colonel A.G. Irvine found five men guilty of horse stealing and sentenced them from ten to twelve months in prison, while three others, charged with theft of government property, were confined for only three months. All sentences included hard labour which meant a daily work commitment.[158]

A charge could be laid for attempting to escape. A search of Leonard Fuller found extra socks and mitts concealed in his tunic. He was found guilty of attempting to desert and was sentenced to six months in the guardhouse. Constable Joseph McDonald was sentenced to loss of pay, six months' imprisonment, and dismissal from the Force for intending to desert. Instead of going as ordered with a troop of nineteen men under Superintendent E. Frechette to Battleford, he stayed overnight at a nearby Indian camp. While in prison, J. McDonald wrote to Comptroller Fred White, explaining that he had been ill for some time and the substitutes he offered had not been accepted. He thought disappearing until the troop moved out and returning to face the consequences was his solution. He never expected to be charged with attempted desertion for staying overnight in an Indian tent. His plea to White for "friendly mercy and a favourable reply for which you will never be forgotten" went unheeded.[159]

Upon completion of his prison term, a deserter was usually dismissed from the Force. One memo reports:

> The following constables of "B" Division are hereby struck off the strength of the Force from the dates set opposite their names respectfully:

Reg. No. 823	McCardia, T.	20/6/82
805	Buse, G.	22/6/82
811	Cornell, A.	22/6/82
839	White, L.	22/6/82
838	Weldon, C.C.	18/7/82
820	Dornan, W.	28/7/82
512	Campbell, A.	15/8/82
847	Austin, M.A.	23/8/82
849	Denningson, T.	23/8/82
804	Birch, S.	29/8/82

> A. Shurtliff, Supdt Commdy.[160]

Once it was ascertained there was a desertion, a three-man Board of Officers inquired into the illegal absence of the man. In the case of George Sinclair, who deserted while on a pass, the Board, aware he had collected mess fees and not paid the creditors, also charged him with embezzling from his barrack mates. Usually, written reports detailing the desertion were part of the hearing. In the case of Andrew Galvin, Sergeant Bray wrote:

> On the morning of the 14th June last, about 8:45, the Orderly Sergeant, Sergt. Martin came and reported to me that Constable A. Galvin was absent and he believed that he had deserted. I immediately sent two men to the herd of horses and reported the matter to the officer commanding, who took steps at once to pursue him. I at once took possession of his kit and found it complete with the exception of the articles enumerated in the schedule … Constable Galvin rode away on horse (can't decipher) which was afterwards recovered on the American side of the line by Inspector Dickens.[161]

The Board ruled that Constable A. Galvin had illegally absented himself from his duties and recommended he be struck off the strength of the Force.

In the early 1880s, a typewritten form had replaced the handwritten account of a desertion. The Force was getting more efficient:

I the undersigned *John Cotton of Fort Macleod*
a *Superintendent* of the North-West Mounted Police Force,
do hereby and in pursuance of Vic., ch. 36, sec.19,
as amended by 45 Vic., ch. 29,
certify that Regt *1203 Const. W. Blackley*
is a member of the North-West Mounted Police Force,
and that he was engaged for service in this Force
on the *22nd* day of *April 1885*
for a period of five years from that date,
and subsequently on the *5th* day of *May 1886*,
deserted from the same while
on duty at Fort *Macleod*

John Cotton, Supr.[162]

The post would sell the kit left by a deserter. After James Taylor deserted from Battleford on 9 July 1884, the following items of his kit were sold:

No.	Article	By whom purchased	Amt	Remarks
2	Towels	Const Storer	.40	
1	Ankle Boots	Const Simons	1.75	
1	Fur Cap	Const Potter	1.05	
1	Sheet	Sgt Fraser	1.25	
1	Tunic	Const McQuarrie	.10	
1	Serge	Const Bingham	.30	
2	Pr Breeches	No purchaser		worn out
1	Kit Bag	Returned to Stores		
2	Prs Blankets	Returned to Stores		
1	Cloak & Cape	Returned to Stores		
			$4.85[163]	

The money from the sale of kit and any unpaid salary was forwarded to the Receiver General of Canada.

The punishment for desertion in the years 1874–85 was inconsistent and arbitrary. Two men who left the Dufferin camp days before the '74 March were later arrested and imprisoned. One man received two months hard labour while Sub-Constable Thomas Mooney got four months, leaving his wife and large family destitute. Mooney's police comrades collected $150 to help the family. When Colonel Macleod was in Helena in the late spring of 1875, he encountered some of the eighteen men who had deserted in late March. He even purchased police rifles in their possession. One man with Macleod observed that "most of them, much ashamed, came to see Colonel Macleod, and endeavored to be taken back. A few of the best men returned with us to Fort Macleod."[164]

It was unusual for a deserter not to be charged. A letter from Dr. Young, the Medical Superintendent at the Manitoba Asylum, asked that George Bycroft be pardoned since his fear of arrest apparently impeded his recovery. Comptroller White agreed that no steps were to be taken against Bycroft. White added that the only deserter who had not been charged was Owens who had been so badly frozen, it necessitated the amputation of both feet.[165]

Long after his service, Charles Orr provided a "vivid" account of his life in the North-West Mounted Police for a reporter from *The Evening Times-Globe*, St. John, New Brunswick. Headquarters in Ottawa informed Acting Supt. E.C.P. Salt, Fredericton, 31 May 1933:

> We were greatly interested to read the press clipping from St. John, indicating the stirring experiences of fifty years ago as depicted by Mr. Orr. It may interest you to know that Mr. Orr enlisted in 1882 and after serving 157 days he decided he had enough and promptly beat it. This of course is for your own personal information.[166]

It appears, since Charles Orr was not arrested, that after fifty-one years the incident was overlooked.

Joseph Blackhall was arrested in Toronto three months after he deserted while on leave. He received a $50 fine or six months in prison—much less than expected in Western Canada. Commissioner Irvine advocated consistency in the punishment for desertion. Those men captured in the North-West Territories, he noted, invariably received a prison sentence while others who were able to reach "Canada" had the option of a fine or imprisonment. Irvine advocated a prison term in all cases.[167]

On several occasions, citizens informed Ottawa where to find NWMP deserters. John Smith wrote to Comptroller White: "Sir, about two years ago a young man of Ingersoll [P.Q.] named McGrath enlisted in the Mounted Police force and it was reported that he deserted on his way to the N W he is now in Ingersoll and little short of a public nuisance ... and there will be no difficulty in getting him."[168]

Justice for deserters could be incredibly harsh and swift. When two deserters from the Calgary detachment, Chris Carson and George Dequoy, were captured at Blackfoot Crossing, a four-horse team transported them to Fort Macleod. Stipendiary Magistrate Lt.-Col. James Macleod heard the evidence at 8 p.m. and sentenced each man to six years in the penitentiary. The magistrate "spoke in the strongest terms ... that the crime of desertion and horse stealing were most disgraceful, especially in the case of men who were in the country to prevent these very crimes."[169] The *Fort Macleod Gazette* commented these men were sent after and brought in, a distance of 300 km, tried and sentenced inside of forty-eight hours.

In contrast to the harsh sentences given to Carson and Dequoy, Silas Cheval and Horace McKenny received only thirty days imprisonment for desertion because of a delay in their trials and their cooperation in prison by escorting Indian prisoners from Wood Mountain to Fort Qu'Appelle.

Mounties sent to apprehend a deserter were in no mood for trouble. James Walker, riding a racehorse, overtook a deserter who refused to halt. Walker reached over, caught the man by the coat collar, pulled him from his horse, and jumped on him on the river ice. Walker wrote: "I searched my prisoner and put him on his horse, tied his feet in the stirrups, and gave him a lively ride back to the barracks. In Winnipeg he was given six months for horse stealing."[170]

George Gustin provides a rare written account by a deserter. He related that, as his company walked north from the Missouri River to Canada, Gustin became discouraged with the desolate wilderness, the insects, the stifling heat, lack of shelter and food—which each day consisted of one biscuit and salt pork. The officer sent from Fort Walsh as their guide was drunk and a ruffian.

While still in American territory, Gustin and several companions left the column. The men suffered terribly as they walked 650 km to reach an American fort, probably Fort Keogh. Upon his return to Ontario, Gustin had lost 40 lbs. (18 kg).

American army deserters on their northwestern frontier sometimes sought refuge in Canada. In several instances, they were charged with having stolen United States government property.[171] In one case, Captain Williams of the United States army attended a trial in Fort Macleod involving two of his men caught with stolen articles in their possession. One report from Fort Walsh stated that American soldiers "continue to arrive at this post ... they talk of pushing their way to Winnipeg."[172]

Several Mounties while working their trap line met an American army deserter making for Fort Walsh and brought the man in. Constable J.E. McEntyre, the camp cook, recalled, "the poor chap was so badly frozen that the doctor could not help him, and he died and his body lay in a tent just outside my kitchen door, with the tent flapping and the winter wind howling, it gave one an eerie feeling."[173]

A serious international situation arose in 1883 when American soldiers arrested three American army deserters inside Canadian territory. In June, A.H. (James?) Ellsworth, Franklin Switzer, and Henry Watson deserted Fort Assiniboine and crossed into Canada. A pursuing American cavalry troop arrested the men 50 km north of the line and returned them to Fort Assiniboine where they were each sentenced to two years imprisonment in Leavenworth military prison. Ellsworth, however, slipped his shackles and escaped from the guard house without his coat or shoes. A patrol found his body in October, "stretched out on the lonesome prairie."[174] Wolves had eaten his face and he was only identified by his clothing.

The Canadian press vigorously protested the arrests which occurred in Canadian Territory. Canadian government demands pressed the United States Secretary of War in January 1884 to telegraph General Terry and order the release of both Watson and Switzer, two Canadians who were serving in the United States army.

Some deserters who regretted their decision contacted Headquarters, asking for redress. In all cases reviewed, Ottawa refused to comply with their requests. William Bottrall and Charles Bairington inquired whether the Queen Victoria Jubilee Proclamation (that pardoned army deserters) applied to the Mounted Police. While Joseph Murdock, whose glowing references—efficient, reliable, prompt, good character, industrious, honest, sober—faded after only forty-one days with his desertion, wrote ten years later; "I do not like the United States and wish to return to the Canadian Northwest ... I want a discharge from NWMP."[175]

Thomas Kerr wrote from Buffalo, New York: "In the first place i am a Deserter having deserted from Fort Calgary on the 8th day of June 1884 ... now sir i am anxious to go out and put in my time i would gladly give $100 if i had it to be out there."[176] Kerr rationalized his actions stating he was on the sick list every other day for a month, but Dr. Kennedy thought he was trying to get out of duty. When he was sent with a "scum of troop" to Fort MacLeod it was more than he could take and, when Constable Barnes asked him to desert with him, on the impulse of the moment, he agreed. White replied, if Kerr desired, he could return to the NWMP and surrender at Regina where the Commissioner would deal with the case.

William Bliss deserted after one year of service in 1881. Five years later, he wrote the comptroller from Fort Benton, offering to pay a fine to allow him to return to Canada. In 1890, through the influence of prominent politicians, his brother again unsuccessfully offered money for a pardon.

Certainly, the most intriguing NWMP deserter was Charles Thompson, who joined Sitting Bull's camp where he had a pivotal influence on the Hunkpapa medicine man. Thompson had gone "Indian"—even to the point of wearing a breech cloth. Apparently, there was no effort made to arrest Thompson at that time. Three months before Sitting Bull returned to the United States, however, "the renegade Thompson" was in irons in the guard house at Wood Mountain for forging the name of a policeman on an order to a trader for $22.

Who, of all people, wrote to the Commissioner in 1914 concerning the organization in Winnipeg of a NWMP Veterans' Association? It was none other than Charles Thompson, the North-West Mounted Police "renegade" who, thirty-three years earlier, had dressed in Indian clothing and lived as a deserter in the Sioux camp.[177]

Deployment of the NWMP

	1875*	1876	1877	1878	1879	1880	1881	1882	1883	1884
Battleford		12	14	33	24	26	43	58	42	103
Blackfoot Crossing							15			
Dufferin	60									
East End Post				***	10					
Fort Calgary		37	27	***	13	4	8	64	76	66
Fort Carlton										49
Fort Edmonton	22									
Fort Ellice	6									
Fort Macleod	150	112	113	106	89	63	40	86	78	57
Fort Pitt									26	20
Fort Saskatchewan		22	23	22	18	10	12	16	26	19
Fort Walsh		102	89	139	142	112	97	103		
Maple Creek									55	35
Medicine Hat									17	10
Pinto Horse Butte			6							
Prince Albert				8	4	8	2	3	11	23
Qu'Appelle		5	6		6	39	47	17	5	2
Regina								56	140	96
Shoal Lake		8	7	21	21	4	4		2	1

Deployment of the NWMP

	1875*	1876	1877	1878	1879	1880	1881	1882	1883	1884
Swan River	38	33	24		2	3	3			
Winnipeg	15									
Wood Mountain	2		17	***	23	30	20	9	1	67
On Command****					10		2	59	39	
Other		4**	3**					3		9
TOTAL	295	322	329	329	362	299	293	474	518	557

* 1875 – 5 February, also 2 men in Ontario and before the desertions from Fort Macleod.

** 1876 – Beautiful Plains, 4 men; 1877 – Milk River, 3 men.

*** 1878 – Fort Macleod included Fort Calgary; Fort Walsh included Wood Mountain and East End Post.

**** 1882 – The 59 men "On Command" were stationed in small detachments at Shoal Lake, Broadview, Moosomin, Troy, Moose Jaw, Rosetta's Crossing, Fort Pelly, End of C.P.R. Track, Maple Creek, Ten-Mile Crossing, Crowsnest Pass, Whoop-Up, Stand-Off, Winnipeg, and along the Boundary Line.

Some years had small summer detachments: Kennedy's Crossing on Milk River; Stand-Off, south of Fort Macleod.

In 1885, (not given on chart), small detachments of NWMP were stationed at a number of rail-line stops: Laggan (3) men, Third Siding (2), Golden City (8), First Crossing (4), Beaver Creek (2), Summit of Selkirks (2), and Second Crossing (4). These postings changed as rail construction moved west.

NOTES

1. Elizabeth Price, "Doc Lauder," *AH*, XXXVII, No. 4, 28.

2. Dempsey, ed., *William Parker Mounted Policeman*, 101. Also *TG*, 11 May, 1877.

3. Fitzpatrick, *Sergeant 331*, 2.

4. D'Artigue, *Six Years in the Canadian North-West*, 13.

5. *CH*, 19 February 1885. See C.E. Rivett-Carnac, ed., "Letters from the North-West," 15.

6. Hugh Richardson held this post until he became a Stipendiary Magistrate in the North-West Territories in July 1876. He was the judge at the trial of Louis Riel in 1885.

7. Possessions included pipe, watch and chain, letters, diary, and money from auction of effects ($31.25) and bank accounts ($304). Sleigh's father was grateful to receive the chain which he had given his son for his twenty-first birthday. It was a consolation, too, that Sleigh died quickly and was spared a lingering death like his schoolmate William Lowry, who died in the same battle. White comforted: "It will, I am sure, be gratifying to you, to know that poor Sleigh's record in the Police Force was without a blot." *NAC*, Ralph Sleigh, f. 565.

8. *NAC*, W.J. Pilcher, f. 982.

9. *NAC*, William Smith, f. 1087.

10. *NAC*, W. Kelly, f. 1228.

11. *NAC*, W. Johnston, f. 273.

12. *NAC*, William Clarke, f. 638.

13. *NAC*, A. Welch, f. 208.

14. *NAC*, James Christie, f. 118.

15. *NAC*, S. Gregory, f. 674.

16. *NAC*, Jeremiah Fyffe, f. 530.

17. *NAC*, Robert McCutcheon, f. o.s. 458.

18. *NAC*, Harry Keegan, f. 301.

19. *TG*, 14 September 1883. The *Toronto Globe*, for example, pointed out that, in the past ten years, more than $3 million dollars had been spent on the NWMP.

20. *HCD*, 1884, 1294 (3 April). See *RC*, NWMP, 1877, 23. The NWMP received income from other Government Departments for services. In 1879, for example, Indian Affairs paid the police $250 a month for herding cattle and the Department of the Interior gave funds for providing food to Indians.

21. *MFP*, 10 September 1874. Earlier, on August 18, the paper wondered, "Why Swan River should be selected as headquarters for the peelers does not at once strike a person. In fact, it don't strike a person after some thought."

22. *TG*, 2 September 1876. Also Rev. G. Young in *MFP*, 24 July 1875. J.F. Klaus, "Fort Livingstone," *SH*, XV, No. 3, 93–110.

23. Steele, *Forty Years in Canada*, 96.

24. *OFP*, 14 October 1876.

25. *GA*, Duncan McEachran, M 736. Also *MG*, 4 November 1881.

26. John Brydges, *The Letters of Charles John Brydges, 1879–1882* (Winnipeg: Hudson's Bay Record Society, XXXI, 1977), 267. In a letter to a friend in 1883, Mary Inderwick, wife of a rancher near Pincher Creek, described Fort Macleod as "one of the last places to live in all the world." "A Lady and her Ranch," *AH*, XV, No. 4, 5.

27. *WDT*, 5 October 1882. Dr. Orton, *WDT*, 21 March 1883, refuted criticism of an inadequate water supply for the city by suggesting deep wells and the Qu'Appelle River, 27 km distant as future sources.

28. *RL*, 17 April 1883. Quoted from the *MFP*. Also *MFP*, 9 February 1883.

29. *EB*, 30 September 1882.

30. *RL*, 10 December 1885.

31. *MFP*, 15 July 1882.

32.
Division	Men	Main Base
Depot	121	Regina
A	102	Maple Creek, Medicine Hat
B	103	Regina
C	112	Fort Macleod
D	94	Battleford
E	101	Calgary
F	96	Prince Albert
G	99	Edmonton, Fort Saskatchewan
H	104	Fort Macleod
K	107	Battleford

33. *NAC*. George DeQuoy, f. 524. DeQuoy proved a poor choice. He deserted, was sentenced to six years in Stoney Mountain penitentiary from where he escaped and fled to the U.S.A. Also recommended as a French-Canadian was Godfrey Casault, *NAC*, f. 517.

34. *GA*, Steele, M 3462. Steele wrote Prime Minister Robert Borden in 1917: "If the police had not a military imprint the Force would not have been the success it was."

35. *RC*, NWMP, 1874, 33. Numbers were: Regular Service (41), Royal Irish Constabulary/Civil Police (14), Canadian Artillery (32), Canadian Militia (84).

36. Other desertions – 32 men from the Dufferin camp; 18 from Fort Macleod in March 1875; 127 of the men who served in 1885 North-West Rebellion.

37. *NAC*, William Morgan, f. 191.

38. *NAC*, J.C. Gordon, f. 670.

39. *NAC*, James Barwis, f. 17.

40. *NAC*, George Guernsey, f. 460. Arthur Williams, M.P., forwarded this application to the Department of the Interior with a strong recommendation of support.

41. *NAC*, John Loring, f. 187. Other positive applications are *NAC*, Henry F. McKain, o.s. 198; *NAC*, F. Butler, f. 114.

42. *NAC*, Henry Penton, f. 277. Another example is *NAC*, Samuel Cooke, f. 103.

43. *NAC*, William Carroll, f. 408.

44. *NAC*, David Craig, f. 119. In David Byers application, "the parents are politically with us." *NAC*, f. 117.

45. *NAC*, S.A. Cameron, f. 456. Also *NAC*, William Shaw, f. 502, *NAC*, Charles Zivack, f. 397, *NAC*, Frederick Shaw, f. 439, *NAC*, Alexander Duffy, f. 412.

46. Maunsell, "With the North West Mounted Police Force from 1874 to 1877," 50.

47. *NAC*, Charles Ermatinger, f. 127. He was accepted in June 1878. For parental efforts, see *NAC*, S. Armour, f. 306.

48. *NAC*, John G. McLeod, f. 197.

49. *NAC*, F. Feilde, f. 222.

50. *NAC*, B. Daniels, f. 73.

51. *NAC*, Charles Thompson, f. 957.

52. *NAC*, W. Stratton, f. o.s. 1091. The letter is incomplete and the results not known.

53. *NAC*, Gerald Thomas Bishop, f. 860. Also *NAC*, A. Dyre, f. 653.

54. *NAC*, John Bushby, f. 603. Bushby was invalided within seventeen months because of an earlier muscle injury and constitutional and nervous debility relating to syphilis. Also *NAC*, James Armstrong, f. 1190.

55. *NAC*, Thomas Drinkwater, f. 1233. Another example is *NAC*, Thomas Wattam, f. 0-75. July 18/80, Sergeant Wattam: "I have much pleasure in testifying to your character as being good in every way. Ever since I have known you, you have proved yourself to be thoroughly honest, sober & clean & since you have been under my command here you have given me every satisfaction. I believe you also to be a good scholar. Regretting the regiment is losing you & wishing you every success in the future. Believe me. Your sincere friend & well wisher, Walter J. Stewart, XII Royal Lancers, Canterbury Depot." Also *NAC*, Alexander Dyre, f. 653.

56. *NAC*, William Strong, f. 1194.

57. *NAC*, J. McArdle, o.s. 498. Also *NAC*, Samuel Cooke, f. o.s. 103.

58. *NAC*, McEwan, f. 233. Also *NAC*, W.H. Grey, f. 675.

59. *NAC*, G. Rolph, f. 963. See Chapter 2, Great Lone Land, Introduction page for a photograph of Rolph.

60. *NAC*, William Sanders, f. 831.

61. *NAC*, F. Dann, f. 649.

62. *NAC*, S.J. Clarke, f. 175.

63. An example would be *NAC*, Donald McAuley, f. 139. Also *NAC*, Chas. Sinclair, f. 204. Skilful penmanship often is noteworthy in NWMP documents and correspondence.

64. Rookie #2, "Remembrances of a Tenderfoot Rookie # 2," *SG*, Third Annual, 59.

65. Donkin, *Trooper and Redskin*, 38–39. The *Toronto Globe*, 26 May 1877, observed: "The applicants are very numerous and include men from all ranks of society."

66. Geoffrey Pocock, *Outrider of Empire* (Edmonton: University of Alberta Press, 2007), 20. In *A Frontiersman* (London: Methuen, 1903), 25, Roger Pocock has another description of the same bunkmates: "Every man in the barracks-room was a hero, fool, or villain, generally all three ... the man who slept next to me on the right was a waif raised in some wandering circus as a contortionist. The man on my left was eldest son of a marquis ... Tom the whiskey runner was a larrikin in an Australian mining-camp, then a tramp and sailor, before he became a whiskey runner and soldier—his bed was in the corner of the room."

67. *NAC*, RG 18, B-8. Another survey, *NAC*, RG, v. 10, f. 361–75, 7 July 1875 of the Swan River detachment lists: Farmer – 15; Clerk – 10; Labourer – 5; Soldier – 3; Blacksmith – 2; and Shoemaker; Dentist; Telegraph Operator; Surveyor; Painter; Sawyer; Baker; Tin Smith; Cheese Maker; Carpenter; Post Office – all 1.

68. *RC*, NWMP, 1880, 4.

69. *RC*, NWMP, 1882, 15. In 1881, he had also recommended the age of twenty-one.

70. *MFP*, 23 January 1879. For Jukes, *RC*, NWMP, 1882, 28.

71. *NAC*, Joseph Francis, f. 7. Harwood Steele, son of Sam Steele, found a reference in 1955 to Frances in the manuscript to his father's book *Forty Years in Canada*: "Joe, as he was known by the men, when his back was turned, was a good, rough and ready sort. His right name was Lane, which for domestic reasons he kept to himself. Francis left the NWMP in 1880 and shortly after died tragically in a house fire while attempting to rescue trapped people."

72. *NAC*, J.A. Martin, f. 41.

73. *NAC*, T. Hardy, f. 49. *The Morning Call*, 23 November 1888.

74. *NAC*, Peter Higgins, f. 1112.

75. Debates in the House of Commons, 11 April 1882.

76. *NAC*, Daniel Wilson, f. 43.

77. *NAC*, George Grogan, f. 459.

78. *SH*, 9 August 1884.

79. *NAC*, Stephen Warden, f. 507.

80. *TG*, 18 May 1882.

81. Fitzpatrick, *Sergeant 331*, 7.

82. *NAC*, Henry Head, f. 688.

83. *GA*, S.J. Clarke, M 229.

84. *NAC*, Robert N. Wilson, MG 29, E-47.

85. Rookie #2, "Remembrances of a Tenderfoot, 58. Also Thirty-Second Annual, 107–8.

86. Pax-o-nachie (Little Soldier), "When the West was Young," *SG*, Ninth Annual, 70. Duluth underwent rapid expansion between 1880 and 1890, with its population growing from 3,480 to 33,115.

87. *GA*, William Metzler, M 836. The permanent population of Bismarck in 1880 was 1,800 but a floating (transient) population of up to 5,000 at times occupied the frontier town.

88. C.D. LaNauze, "From the Pampas to the Prairies, 1872–1885," *Canadian Cattlemen*, XI, No. 1, 35.

89. Rookie # 2, "Remembrances of a Tenderfoot," 58. Also *SG*, Thirty-second Annual, 107–9.

90. *NAC*, D.A. Fraser, f. 663.

91. *NAC*, Robert N. Wilson, MG 29, E-47.

92. "A Trip up the Missouri," *WDT*, 1 July 1879. Also "A Trip to Fort Walsh," *WDT*, 22 July 1881.

93. Fitzpatrick, *Sergeant 331*, 13.

94. LaNauze, "From the Pampas to the Prairies, 1872–1885," 38.

95. *NAC*, William McQuarrie, f. 724.

96. *NAC*, Henry Head, f. 688.

97. *NAC*, William McQuarrie, f. 724. As a protest Scotty left the boat, had second thoughts and frantically waved for help. The captain, against the protests of some men, returned to pick him up.

98. *NAC*, R.N. Wilson, MG 29, E-47.

99. *WDT*, 22 July 1881.

100. *RC*, NWMP, 1882, 24–25.

101. Rookie #2, "Remembrances of a Tenderfoot," 58. Also in Thirty-Second Annual, 107–9. Some river journeys ended at Coal Banks, about 40 kilometres northeast of Fort Benton. This landing was the most northerly point of the Missouri River and directly south of Fort Walsh.

102. *LH*, 21 June 1924.

103. Fitzpatrick, *Sergeant 331*, 15–16. A correspondent in the *TG*, 3 August 1883, described the dissipation and immortality in Helena, Montana Territory, but contended, "the amount of liquor drunk here is not equal to that of almost any Canadian town of half its size."

104. *GA*, William Metzler, M 836.

105. *NAC*, William McQuarrie, f. 724.

106. *GA*, Simon J. Clarke, M 228.

107. *MFP*, 27 July 1881.

108. *RL*, 16 June 1928. *TG*, 13 May 1882.

109. *GA*, Edward Barnett, M 6142.

110. Ibid.

111. *RC*, NWMP, 1874, 69.

112. *NAC*, RG 18, v.9, 30–16.

113. Superintendents moved include: Jarvis – Fort Saskatchewan to Fort Macleod; Winder – Fort Macleod to Fort Walsh; Walker – Battleford to Fort Walsh; Herchmer – Shoal Lake to Battleford; Crozier – Fort Walsh to Wood Mountain; Walsh – Wood Mountain to Fort Qu'Appelle; Shoal Lake – non-commissioned officer.

114. *NAC*, RG 18, RCMP, Series A-1, v. 8, f. 230-276.

115. *RC*, NWMP, 1877, 25. Also *RC*, NWMP, 1881, 26.

116. *NAC*, T. Wattam, f. 594.

117. *NAC*, Maurice Duchesnay, f. 326.

118. *NAC*, H.E. Ross, f. 383.

119. *NAC*, John Ballendine, f. 1088.

120. For example, see *NAC*, B. Ryan, f. 354.

121. *NAC*, W.L. Armstrong, f. 262. Also *NAC*, Henry Penton, f. 277; *NAC*, P. McEwan, f. 233; *NAC*, Joseph Percival, f. 558.

122. *NAC*, Arthur Murray, f. 425. Like so many of the early men, Murray died destitute and alone. Public officials in San Francisco were unable to locate any next of kin.

123. *NAC*, John O'Keefe, f. 149.

124. *NAC*, James Ritchie, f. o.s. 170.

125. *NAC*, David Joyal, f. 972.

126. *NAC*, Charles Bowes, f. 403.

127. *NAC*, William Shaw, f. 1077.

128. *NAC*, Joseph Chabot, f. 474.

129. *NAC*, Joseph Percival, f. 558.

130. *NAC*, Frederick Bourke, f. 263. Also *NAC*, Edward Allen, f. 62; *NAC*, J. Daley, f. 266; *NAC*, C.D. Hutchins, f. 228; *NAC*, W.S. Grant, f. 305; *NAC*, A. Westwood, f. 61.

131. *MFP*, 21 April 1880.

132. *NAC*, T.G. McCelland, f. 141. Also *NAC*, C.W. Darland, f. 842.

133. *NAC*, T. McCutcheon, f. 965.

134. *NAC*, August Miller, f. 935. Miller suffered a scalp wound at the Duck Lake skirmish.

135. *NAC*, Colin Genge, f. 338. Genge was determined to obtain a discharge. Six months before his application, his mother contacted Prime Minister John A. Macdonald requesting a discharge for her son. Macdonald tactfully replied that the Rules of Police Service did not permit compliance. Also *NAC*, W. Newton, f. 826 for an example for a purchase discharge.

136. *NAC*, T. Kempster, f. 1120.

137. *NAC*, James Shea, f. 564. The file omits the final result.

138. Upon his retirement Fraser received a letter from Commissioner A. Bowen Perry: "I cannot allow you to sever your connection with the N.W.M. Police without placing on record my appreciation of your services... the Force can ill afford to lose the services of men of your experiences."

139. *NAC*, J.J. Raymore, f. 830.

140. *NAC*, George Callaghan, f. 323.

141. *NAC*, G. Casault, f. 517. Casault was responsible for the shooting death of George Johnston at Fort Walsh.

142. *NAC*, J. Graham, f. 178.

143. Ibid.

144. *NAC*, Charles Power Thomson, f. 388.

145. *NAC*, Louis Fontaine, f. 484. Comptroller White contacted W. Herchmer that offences not under statutes and in beastly cases surely way punished, not in books. Herchmer indicated Fontaine was to be tried in Civil Court. No charges are shown in Criminal statistics in the following two years. *NAC*, H.D. Jackson, f. 1460.

146. *NAC*, J.W. Jones, f. o.s. 932.

147. *TG*, 10 September 1883.

148. Donald Klancher, *The North West Mounted Police and the North West Rebellion* (Kamloops: Goss Publishing, 1999) 74–101. This rate of desertion was 14.5 per cent.

149. *MFP*, 27 December 1880.

150. *TG*, 23 December 1882. *FBRP*, 15 March 1882, lists the following daily wages in Fort Benton: bricklayers, $7; painters, $2–$2.50; plasterers, $6–7; labourers, $2–$2.50. *TG*, 23 December 1882.

151. *RC*, NWMP, 1882, 15.

152. *SH*, 15 August 1881.

153. *NAC*, R.N. Wilson, MG 29, E-47.

154. *GA*, S.J. Clarke, M 228.

155. *FBRP*, 9 November 1881.

156. *GA*, William Metzler, M 836. Deserting on patrol, see *NAC*, William Morrow, f. 553.

157. *SH*, 26 July 1884.

158. *RC*, NWMP, 1881, 35. R.M. Morton, G.J. Convery, and W.A. Cooper were sentenced to twelve months; D.H. Thompson and George Scott, ten months; Geo. Mills, P.H. Wilbur, and M. McDonald, three months. The Governor General, Lord Lorne, on his western tour, pardoned the men still in jail in September 1881. George Mills repeatedly asked to be re-engaged. Commissioner Irvine supported his application in a letter to Comptroller Fred White: "Mills is a first class prairie man and clean fellow. I would give the poor fellow another chance." Mills was taken on again. In April 1886 he suffered a severe blow to head in a fall from horse that resulted in the loss of sight in one eye. He was invalided in 1887. *NAC*, Geo. Mills, f. 1259.

159. *NAC*, Joseph McDonald, f. 428.

160. RCMP Museum Archives, 104–105.

161. *NAC*, Andrew Galvin, f. 478. Other examples are *NAC*, Thomas Garland, f. 531; Robert Blake, f. 471.

162. *NAC*, W. Blackley, f. 1203. Also *NAC*, J. Graham, f. 669; *NAC*, James Douglas, f. 1113.

163. *NAC*, James Taylor, f. 974. Also *NAC*, Jacob Clark, f. o.s. 499. *NAC*, S. Gregory f. 674.

164. *Denny, Riders of the Plains*, 71. Jean Claustre, a veteran of the Franco-Prussian War, rejoined the Force.

165. *NAC*, George Bycroft, f. o.s.1214. No file on Owens was found.

166. *NAC*, Charles Orr, f. 827.

167. Francis Kirkpatrick deserted twice. In 1882, he received a one year sentence in the NWT; his second sentence in Ontario was for six months.

168. *NAC*, J. McGrath, f. o.s. 1048.

169. *FMG*, 15 July 1882. Also *GA*, William Metzler, M 836.

170. *CH*, 15 March 1924.

171. *FBR*, 21 September 1877.

172. *FBR*, 9 June 1881, 21 September 1877.

173. *SAB*, J.E. McEntyre papers, A 110.

174. *FBRP*, 17 October 1883.

175. *NAC*, Joseph Murdock, f. 488.

176. *NAC*, Thomas Kerr, f. 702.

177. *NAC*, Charles Thompson, f. 106. Also *BT*, 22 April 1881. *NAC*, Fred Shindler, f.856 successfully deserted and became a Deputy United States Marshall.

8

POLICING THE
PLAINS

NWMP Detachment at Donald, BC, 1884-85

"I shall never forget my first sight of the Scarlet Riders of the plains. Just as the sun was setting, a bugle rang out, and about a mile away coming toward us ... was ... about fifty riders resplendent in scarlet and gold, coming to welcome us."

– "Pox-o-Nachie," *Scarlet and Gold*, Ninth Annual, 70
   GA NA 782 – 1

THE "RIDERS OF THE PLAINS" PATROLLED a vast western plain that had few permanent shelters. In winter, travel was often perilous and carrying a supply of firewood was advisable. One nine-man troop going from Fort Walsh to Wood Mountain used their broken sleds for firewood. About halfway into their trip, at Pinto Horse Butte, the last sled broke down.

The two officers went ahead for help, leaving the men with only tea and tobacco. Constable W.H. Cox remembered being "good and hungry" when a relief party arrived three days later.

Understandably, travel in winter, as one Mountie wrote, was "looked upon with horror by those who had to go out in it, and little wonder, as the cold is generally intense, and the danger of being lost on the plains during a storm is always present to the mind."[1] Watching his comrades preparing to leave on a winter trip, John Donkin heard "much growling and the atmosphere was generally blue with cuss words."[2] The local Calgary paper, commenting that constables Davidson and McCarty had left for Fort Macleod in mid-February, commiserated: "We don't envy the boys on their trip."[3] In very cold weather, a saddle was uncomfortable and the men preferred using horses or dogs to pull small wooden sleds called jumpers. On winter trips, few men bothered to carry a change of clothing. John Donkin recalled wearing the same uniform, day and night, for two weeks.

Constable R. Sinton was part of a five-man detail driving supply teams from Regina to Prince Albert in forty-degree-below-zero temperatures. During the day, it was uppermost for the men to keep moving to stimulate circulation. At the approach of night, they would make for a sheltered bluff, unhitch and double-blanket the horses, shovel the snow to make a windbreak, and clear a ground area so that the horses could find grass and lie down. The horses had to be watered: if there was a nearby slough, a hole was chopped through the ice, otherwise, snow was melted in a large iron kettle. The men then made supper of dried bannock, pork, beans, and tea. Sleeping "spots" were dug in the snow.[4]

Summer patrols, in contrast, were quite "fine fun, full of adventure and continued excitement. A party of men will start out in June and traveled all summer, going over thousands of miles of country … these trips are what the men love, and what keeps them in the Force."[5] The warming temperatures, lengthening days, migrating birds, and green growth uplifted everyone's spirits. In his medical report for 1881, Surgeon George Kennedy affirmed: "It is a well-known and noteworthy fact that a man is never, or very rarely, sick while on a trip."[6]

Duties and Responsibilities

Each morning a squad at the post raised the Union Jack. Bugle calls for reveille, boots and saddle, meals, mail, stables, lights out, and so on signaled the daily routine. One call at Fort Macleod alerted men at the townsite to return immediately to the fort. Once a month, the detachment held a muster parade where the roll call was taken of the men and the horses.

Most bases posted a daily bulletin. The Local Order applied to the post; the General Order pinpointed the Force. An example from Fort Walsh on 4 September 1882 stated:

Local Order No. 1
Detail for tomorrow
Orderly Officer of the day – Supdt Shurtliff
Next for duty – Inspt Norman

Local Order No. 2
Reg. No. 698 Constable Jones, A.D.
of "A" Divn was this day fined two dollars by the Officer Commanding for having absented himself from Stable Parade at noon on above date.

General Order No. 574
The following constables having completed their term of imprisonment for "Desertion" are hereby dismissed from the Force.

Reg. No. 518 Const. Cheval Silas
Reg. No. 548 Const. McKenny Horace E
Reg. No. 555 Const. Paquette F X

A Shurtliff, Supd. Commdy.[7]

The daily routine, regimented by the post timetables, was a far cry from the romantic image of scarlet-coated riders fearlessly patrolling the rolling Canadian prairie—always in summer. An outline of the varied activities appears in a Winnipeg newspaper:

Reveille sounds at six o'clock in the morning. All hands must get up then, dress, wash and make beds. Any man who fails in any of these things is put under arrest. We then fall in for stables, that is to say, we have to go to the stables to feed and groom our horses. After that we go to breakfast which is generally followed by drill for an hour and a half. A portion of each troop has then to engage in "fatigue duty," that is to say, hard work, of the kind that is performed by day laborers. For instance, we have to "mud up" the buildings; that is put a coating of mud from time to time on the low log buildings of the fort. Another task is unloading and storing goods ... from the American firm of I.G. Baker & Co.[8]

Many tasks were monotonous. For George Guernsey, herding police horses was a dull interminable assignment, and not having a watch only added to his boredom. A solution was to borrow a watch to make a crude sundial, giving the young trooper at least an approximate estimate of the time. One account evaluated: "The amount of police duty done, aside from work incidental to the force—which in itself is greater than at any military post I have ever seen—is almost incredible."[9]

Many men detested the compulsory Sunday church service. Stephen Yarwood no doubt felt this way, after he was charged with being absent from Divine Service and sentenced to twenty days confinement to the barracks. The bugle signal for the church assembly, one Mountie wrote, "was generally greeted with a groan."[10] At one post with only a Protestant clergyman, the Roman Catholics were ordered to step to the rear and leave. "It was amusing," wryly noted Constable J.E. McEntyre, "to watch and count the number of Roman Catholics who would fall out, even agnostics and rabid Orangemen."[11]

The officers were aware of the widespread dislike of the religious observances. Upon his arrival at Fort Macleod, an enthusiastic Reverend John Maclean offered a church service every Sunday. Colonel Macleod deferred, telling the minister that a compulsory worship would not be acceptable by all the men.

At Fort Walsh, after six men disregarded the church summons and continued their "studhorse" poker game, the Sergeant of the Guard arrested the card players. In turn, they protested to Commissioner Irvine over the compulsory religious service. Irvine released the men and ordered church attendance to become a voluntary commitment at the post. The Rev. Alexander Sutherland, determined to spread Christianity in the region, had complained that: "One great hindrance to the spread of religion in the North-West is the general disregard for the Sabbath by white men, and this is especially conspicuous in the case of the Mounted Police and Government agents."[12]

The foremost responsibility of the NWMP was to maintain law and order. This involved many difficult and dangerous assignments. Constable M.H. Meredith trailed horse thieves from Medicine Hat to the American border south of Fort Macleod only to find that his suspects had crossed into Montana Territory. His only alternative was a long return ride to his base. Corporal Denny and two constables rode from Fort Saskatchewan to Lac la Biche to arrest R. Berard for wife desertion. "Nosey" Berard was released after he promised good behaviour. The round trip covered 500 km and had taken eight days.

Constable Alexander Dyre related that even a routine patrol had dangers: "The boys got back from Blackfoot Crossing all right [to Calgary], only one shot being fired at them which came near enough Private Hutchinson's nose to smell unpleasant though."[13] There, too, were uneasy situations. When meeting Indians, Tom Clarke always had his revolver ready and, "never felt happy for the first couple of hundred yards after leaving them. I couldn't look back and let them think I was afraid."[14] Late in his life at his homestead near Lacombe, Constable Edward Barnett told a reporter that "very few people today understand the dangers that were on every turn, night and day."[15] The old-timer reflected:

> There were dangerous and exciting duties. We had to learn to ride long distances in all kinds of weather and find our way. Often we were chilled to the bone by rains, plagued by swarming mosquitoes and flies, and soaked when fording rivers and streams. We faced cold weather and prairie blizzards. Often we had to get out logs and put up buildings, dig wells, build corrals, and put up hay for the horses.[16]

Written instructions were given to assigned patrols. At Battleford in June 1884, for example, Inspector Antrobus ordered Sergeant Bagley— the same Bagley who, ten years earlier, was the fifteen-year-old boy bugler:

> You will leave this afternoon for Fort Pitt in charge of the following party.
>
> | Reg. No. | 515 | Carroll, J.W. |
> |---|---|---|
> | | 678 | Gavins, D. |
> | | 865 | Robertson, B.H. |
> | and horses | 224 | Dundar (in a cart) |
> | | 424 | Jack Bob |
>
> The carts are to be handed over to Sub. Indn. Agt. Quinn and the harness is to be brought back to this Post. You will remain at Pitt until someone (or the mail) is coming down with whom arrangements will be made for the transport of your bedding, camp equipment & the two sets cart harness. Insp. Dickens will detail a man to return with you in place of Robertson. Return as soon as possible.
>
> W.D. Antrobus Insp.[17]

NWMP Camp in the Cypress Hills in the '70s

"Unless a person has travelled through the country, he can have no idea of the amount of work there is to do. The men are kept constantly moving; they are required to go out in all sorts of weathers, and at all hours; yet they do so without a murmur."

– Commissioner A.G. Irvine, *Toronto Mail*, 4 November 1881
 RCMP Museum, Regina – 1977.99.10

These instructions were for a routine assignment. Travel arrangements for major tours (such as escorting Governor General Marquis of Lorne in 1881) involved extensive logistics.

There were accidents and suicides to investigate. The Frog Lake post inspected a nearby lumber mill in the industrial death of a young man. Colonel Irvine chaired a six-man jury that ruled the death of Thomas Clinton was from a self-inflicted dose of strychnine while in a "state of mental distraction."[18] Captain Joseph Howe and Doctor L.G. DeVeber rode to the Belly River where a cowboy was reported dead with a bullet in his head. They determined the death a suicide and, ever practical, the two officers buried the man beside his tent.[19] A police detail verified that William Oliver, a former member of the Mounted Police found dead in his stable, had died of heart disease. Sergeant Harry Keenan took an inventory of the deceased's assets for a brother in Toronto. Superintendents William Herchmer, John McIllree, and John Cotton were among the Territorial coroner appointments in 1884.

The Mounted Police delivered money to the annual Indian Treaty sites. Constable Jack Clarke remembered carrying $40,000 for the Indian Department, all in $1 bills. In 1879, Superintendent Leif Crozier took thirty-two men from Fort Walsh to help facilitate the Fort Qu'Appelle Treaty payments. The troop rode for nine days and spent fourteen days assisting the paymaster. One of their tasks was identifying eligible Indians for payment. A letter to the *New York Tribune* described a police officer having to use "all his detective powers to ascertain the truth as to the number of souls in each family."[20]

Greedy traders and self-serving individuals complicated the Treaty payments. Troubles seemed impending at the 1881 payments at Fort Walsh when "half-breeds" urged the Indians to make exorbitant demands.[21] At the 1877 Cree payment at Fort Carlton, Superintendent J. Walker arrived to find over 1,000 waiting Indians, but not the expected money, supplies or food. The officer purchased a two-day food supply from the Hudson's Bay Company for the Indians and then rode to Battleford to get Lieutenant Governor David Laird's approval of his actions. He later returned to Fort Carlton within forty-eight hours and placated the restless band until the money and supplies arrived.

Two years later, at a treaty payment, Walker again found himself in a dilemma when a river steamer transporting the money did not arrive. It was only after his determined persuasion that band members reluctantly accepted cheques. At another Treaty payment, police scout Jerry Potts informed Indian Agent J.J. McHugh that the American Indians (South Piegans) were posing as band members. McHugh told the gathering that all Treaty money was withheld until the police escorted the American Indians across the border. His offer of food, tobacco, and tea on their journey was refused and a stalemate followed. The Indian Agent recalled: "For two days the Indians bluffed in every way, shape, and form as to what we were going to do. I stood pat, and finally two hundred Indians lined up and with an escort of six Mounted Policemen, and with promised provisions for the trip they returned across the boundary."[22] To lessen the problems of ineligible Indians and those attempting to receive multiple payments, the government issued each family identification tags and held the Treaty payments on the same day at different reserves.

A very important NWMP responsibility was the collection of customs. The duty charged was a designated percentage of the value of goods. For example, twenty-three mules valued at $1,955 were charged 20 per cent, a duty of $391; eleven wagons valued at $385 were charged 35 per cent for $134.[23] As settlements grew, customs revenues would increase significantly. By 1882, revenues were $35,525 at Fort Macleod, $15,135 at Fort Walsh, $2,784 at Wood Mountain, and $1,075 at Qu'Appelle—a grand total of $52,522.36.[24] Anyone caught evading payment was arrested and fined. When Sergeant Blight apprehended two men without papers showing payment of duty, he sent them to Regina for trial. The suspects' mules and equipment were auctioned off even before guilt was determined.

Other federal responsibilities for the NWMP were assisting in the 1885 North-West Territories census and issuing contracts for the delivery of mail. The police provided security and were a visual presence at official functions such as the Governor General's tours of the NWT and special trains arranged to bring speculators to view the region.

The police fought prairie fires that threatened settlements. A small detachment stationed in the Crowsnest Pass used back-burning to save their shack and stored hay. When fighting a prairie fire, one policeman secured the horses while his companions and citizen volunteers moved ahead on foot to pound the flames with wet gunny sacks. If the fire endangered their lives, a prearranged signal alerted everyone to run to the horses.

Fighting prairie fires was tiring and dangerous work. Sergeant Frank Fitzpatrick described his ordeal: "We finally got the best of the fire and came back to the fort about 5 a.m. a sorry-looking lot—eyes red, faces blackened and the soles of our shoes nearly burned off. At 5:30 reveille sounded and we answered the call as usual."[25] One Mountie courageously carried three Native children, abandoned in a burning lodge by adult males, to safety.[26] Carelessness caused fires that destroyed Fort Carlton, a stable and some buildings at Fort Macleod, and the stables at Battleford.

Railway construction brought a new source of prairie fires when sparks from the trains ignited the nearby dry prairie grass. Police patrols were assigned to monitor the rail line.

The police organized searches for people reported lost. The Battleford detachment unsuccessfully searched for a thirteen-year-old Indian girl who disappeared while egg-hunting. The police had men scour the countryside for: M.B. Dickson, who was reported wandering out of his mind near Moosomin; J. Thompson, lost while returning to a survey camp near Red Deer, and an Englishman named Parkhurst, who had gone to search for his land claim. At Fort Qu'Appelle, Mr. Freeman was found frozen to death on the prairies and his effects were given to Inspector Griesbach to allocate. In June 1882, the police searched for the body of Nick Sheron, owner of the Coal Banks mine, who had drowned in the Oldman River.

A search party from Fort Walsh found the bodies of Richard Holt and John McMillan, dead from exposure while walking south from Maple Creek in a February blizzard. Holt, age twenty-two, from London, England, was a novice settler, but McMillan, a former Mountie, should have been aware of the risk. A police fatigue team dug a single grave in the frozen ground. Surgeon A. Jukes wrote in his diary:

> The bodies were decently interred by the NWMP, a number of citizens being in attendance. It was a bitterly cold day … there being no clergyman of any denomination here and the commandant, Captain Shurtliff, not caring to undertake it, asked me to perform the necessary duty which I did as well as able, reading over them the burial service of the Church of England.[27]

In January 1876, the disappearance of the Methodist missionary (and Treaty 6 and 7 negotiator), George McDougall in a blizzard on Nose Hill (part of Calgary today), attracted national attention. The local detachment undertook an extensive area search. After nine days, Inspector Antrobus wrote that he feared the body would not be found until spring.[28]

Many policing tasks needed strenuous physical effort. In the fall of 1876, five men from Fort Macleod cut and floated 2,000 pine logs down the Oldman River for the new sawmill at the post. There were complaints about the physical duties the police were assigned. One man wrote:

> We are not supposed to be hewers of wood and drawers of water for private mercantile firms but we are all the same … one thing that makes the boys mad about the "fatigue duty" is that there are so many loafers who, under pretext of being higher in rank

than ordinary troops, do nothing. Now for instance we are about eighty all told at Fort Walsh. Out of that number there were five officers … three sergeant-majors, four staff-sergeants and three sergeants. Each one of these has a servant, one of the troop, and the officers two of them, who had practically nothing to do.[29]

Recruit Jack Clarke resented being "put under arrest for not cutting wood while on fatigue. I said I had not joined the police for that purpose."[30] Acting Constable Beaudieu must have thought himself a cowboy. With the help of a Métis companion, he drove twenty-five wild steers 500 km from Battle River to the Swan River barracks. A letter from Fort Walsh suggested a good name for the Force would be the "Mounted Navvies."[31]

There was a variety of duties. One task assigned the Calgary detachment to rid the town of stray dogs. The men saw a solution in empty tin cans, provided by the cook, which, when attached to the animal's tail, made enough noise to hopefully frighten the canine far and away. The police delivered summonses. While Major Crozier issued matrimonial licences. Inspector A.H. Griesbach supervised billiard licences for the North-West Territories. Sergeant-Major F.G. Dann erected finger-posts (directional signs) on the trails to guide travelers. The Battleford detachment cut and stored blocks of river ice which they sold for $5 a ton.

Each post cut a large firewood supply for the coming winter. There were on going building and maintenance requirements. Fences had to be built, buildings painted, and trees and gardens planted. A squad at Calgary fired the field piece daily at twelve o'clock noon (C.P.R. time). Most posts recorded meteorological information. At Battleford, Staff-Constable J.H. Price provided weather data for publication in the local paper. Sergeant E.H. Carr was the auctioneer at a sheriff's sale at Fort Saskatchewan. There were a number of community activities involving the local detachment.

The detachments captured stray horses and then sold any unclaimed animals after three months. Advertisements placed in the local newspaper described the horses being held by the police. One onerous police task was collaring and escorting Indians from the town back to their reserve. And the police attempted to keep the rival tribes apart. Sergeant Fitzpatrick, seeing that two hostile bands might meet, compelled his group to change course and successfully avoided problems.

Some tasks exceeded the call of duty. In 1885, friends in England of Corporal Lowry (killed at Cut Knife Hill) sent violets to Calgary to be placed on his grave. Their knowledge of geography certainly was hazy, but Sergeant William Parker rode more than 500 km to Battleford to fulfill their request.[32] Days before his execution, convicted murderer Jesse Williams asked the Calgary detachment to provide him with decent clothing as he did not want to be hanged in rags.

One nineteen-year-old recruit, with less than three months of service, wrote to his father about his new vocation:

> Life here is curiously varied as a record of the past few days will show. Friday last I was in the stables from 6:30 am to 6 pm working cutting hay carting manure cleaning stables &tc, and sewed rents in my buffalo coat in the evening Saturday. Three hours at stables as usual & an hour's riding exercise. In the evening drawing & reading the Iliad. Sunday Stables and cleaning myself all day. Too cold for church. Escorting prisoners for 7½ hours while they cleaned the parade ground, picked potatoes, & moved a piano all in a blizzard ... Today washing dishes four hours & grooming horses three hours & Reading Dante's "Inferno."[33]

Sergeant Frank Fitzpatrick listed the duties of the Mounted Police: "We acted as magistrates, sheriffs, constables, collectors of Customs, postmasters, undertakers, issuers of licences. We married people and we buried people. We acted as health inspectors, weather bureau officials, Indian treaty makers; but above all as diplomats when it came to dealing with either Indians or half-breeds."[34]

The number and variety of tasks both bored and challenged the "Riders of the Plains"—yet, looking back years later, all the hardships lessened. Constable Francis Dobbs wrote:

> I always look back with pleasure at the good and happy old days I spent in her Majesty's uniform. It certainly was a great and healthy experience for a young fellow ... the Mounties' life was a fine and healthy one, lots of hard riding and outside work in wet or snowy weather. Sleeping wherever night overtook us and living on salt pork, hardtack and dried apples. We in fact often went for over six months never seeing butter, eggs or fresh vegetables. However, the majority of us grew strong and healthy.[35]

Most of "the boys" (those who did not desert) would agree with Dobbs. They were young and there were many fond memories of their days in the North-West Mounted Police.

Salaries and Benefits

The pay scale in 1874 gave the Commissioner $2,000–$2,600 a year and Superintendents $1,000–$1,400. Other ranks were on a daily pay rate. Constables received $1 per day, sub-constables, $0.75, surgeons, $3.84, and veterinarian surgeons, $1.92. Clothing, accommodations, and food were provided. A man with a special skill—horseshoeing, carpentry, tailoring, saddler, or blacksmith—received an additional $0.15 per day. At the completion of the three-year term, a policeman could apply for a land warrant (grant) of 160 acres. To be eligible for this grant, the applicant's discharge paper under "Conduct during Service" had to record good conduct (or better). In response to Henry Oldham's inquiry, Ottawa had informed the former Mountie that, since his discharge certificate stated "indifferent," the *Police Act* ruled him ineligible for the quarter section. The land grant was eliminated in 1880.[36]

Some policemen were granted leave for outside employment with the understanding that during this time they forfeited pay and rations. An example is Form No. 33:

North-West Mounted Police
Fort *Battleford. March 18th 1884. "D"* Division.
The bearer Regt. No. *383 Const. H. Ross* has permission to
be absent from quarters from *6 am.* of the above date
to *12 (noon)* of the *9th June* for the purpose
of working in Prince Albert.

Approved *W.D. Antrobus*

On Constable Ross's return from Prince Albert to his quarters in Fort Battleford, he would show this pass to the Officer on Guard.[37]

The monthly wages for the police force bolstered the depressed prairie economy. A letter from Prince Albert in 1881 contended that the entire community of 800 didn't have "over $1,000 cash at this present moment."[38] Father J. Hugonard recalled that most business was done by exchange as there was practically no money in the West. The North-West Mounted Police, stated the priest, "were the only ones who had cash."[39] In the early years, the money denominations came in large sheets which the police paymaster cut with scissors.

After expenses, a $30 monthly police salary left very little for savings. And the men often purchased their own meals and personal needs in town. A pair of Wellington boots would cost between $10 and $15, half a month's salary. Another expense was subscriptions (collections) for entertainment, gifts, and mess fees. The sergeants paid a $4.50 monthly mess fee for extra food delicacies and laundry expenses. Fines deducted from the monthly pay for misconduct crippled the men's income. The *Fort Battleford Post Journal* lists some penalties: Constable O. Worthington fined $10 and confined to barracks ten days for being drunk in barracks; Constable J. Tector was fined fifteen days pay for insolent language to Corporal H. Des Barres; Constable W. Grogan was fined ten days pay for loitering while on fatigue.[40]

The fines outraged the men. The *Edmonton Bulletin* informed its readers: "the long expected pay for the police at Fort Saskatchewan was dished out Monday last and proved to be a source of much profanity ... because of 'extravagant' fines the men received little ... one has his room decorated with a cheque for the large sum of five cents."[41]

A second newspaper criticized: "for some months past the police at Fort Saskatchewan have been unpaid and as no funds seemed forthcoming Captain Herchmer hit upon the expedient of fining them, with one or two exceptions, from $15 to $75 apiece all around."[42] A policeman who was confined to the hospital or had to be placed on the sick list (unless the injury occurred in the line of work) had a pay deduction of $0.25 per diem. Constable James Livingstone made a complaint: "For 237 days in hospital I got fifteen cents a day, which was just about enough to pay for my washing."[43]

Any delays in the monthly pay were annoying. Not having been paid since the column left Fort Dufferin eight months earlier certainly provoked the desertion of eighteen men from Fort Macleod in March 1875. Cheques for the Fort Saskatchewan detachment in March 1881 were not only three months in arrears, but devalued in the local economy. The *Edmonton Bulletin* commented: "The Mounted Police pay cheques, which used to pass here at face value, are below par now."[44]

In April 1880, in a controversial fiscal decision, Ottawa reduced police salaries and eliminated the land grant. Sub-Constables had their daily pay cut from $0.75 to $0.40 a day, making $12 the monthly pay. Resentment and morale problems immediately flared. The *Saskatchewan Herald* declared that: "No Mounted Police at this post whose term expires this season will re-engage."[45] Constable James Steele agreed. In a letter from the Fort Saskatchewan barracks, he wrote: "None of the old hands took on again ... it is very small pay for this country where everything is so dear."[46] The *Edmonton Bulletin*, noting that sub-constables Von Cortlandt, Smith, Fletcher, and Gilmore, about to get their discharges, all chose to enter the cattle business, caustically commented: "so much for starvation pay."[47]

Concerns arose when experienced policemen refused taking another term. The *Manitoba Free Press* commented: "The loss will be felt in the force as they have become well acquainted with the country, and it will require years for new men to acquire the same knowledge."[48]

The value of those men who understood what was called the "Indian character" was unquestioned. In one example, Constable Edward Barnett, part of a four-man detail, recalled entering an Indian camp where yelling naked and painted "savages" surrounded their wagon. The policemen sat in silence and watched the uproar until the head chief arrived, raised his hand for silence and opened the dialogue.[49] Less-experienced men might have responded rashly to the Indian protests.

Senior NWMP officers realized the folly of Ottawa's pay cutbacks. Commissioner Irvine wrote Comptroller White that $0.40 per day was too small a rate to pay new men.[50] In his autobiography, Inspector Sam Steele criticized that the wage cuts were "a blow from which it took some years to recover."[51] The decline in re-enlistments forced Ottawa to introduce a good conduct bonus of $0.05 per diem which was increased each year for five years, but the pay was still less than the former wage.

Mounted policemen augmented their salaries in several ways. There was the lucrative reward of receiving half the fine for making an arrest for having illegal liquor. Cutting firewood also provided an opportunity for earning extra money. At Battleford, Superintendent Walker paid men fifty cents a cord to supply wood for the post. Some men found temporary employment working for farmers. In one case, only six of the thirty men at the Battleford detachment were on duty, the remainder working for the fall harvest. Individual policemen could bid on government tenders but this competition rankled the local population. William Parker had contracted to supply Fort Macleod with 400 cords of wood. Three constables (with two horse teams) were assigned to chop and haul the wood over to the post. The men worked from a shack they built on a river bottom about 10 km west on the Oldman River.

A policeman received fiscal compensation if he suffered a debilitating injury. Sergeant J.H. Ward, shot at the Cut Knife Hill skirmish, was granted the maximum pension of ninety cents per day for the remainder of his natural life. A medical board awarded John Hayes, incapacitated by a broken leg in service, thirty cents per diem. Forty-two years later, this amount was increased to sixty-four cents. Another payout was a retirement gratuity for the officers based on one month's salary for each year of service. Major James Walsh, for example, left the Force in September 1883 with a payment of $1,166 for ten years' service.

S/Sgt Robert Riddle, NWMP

"The best years of my life were spent in the old force."

– Edward Warren, *NAC*, T. Warren, f. 57
RCMP Historical Collections Unit, Regina, SK. 1963.31.1

Twenty years of service was required to receive a NWMP pension, a commitment that was made by few men. After twenty-five years in the Force, Fred Bagley received ninety cents a day, which was two-thirds of his daily wage.[52] The pension ended upon the death of the recipient and, if married, his widow received only the amount of money outstanding during the last month that he was living. In the case of A. MacKenzie, a cheque for $18.81 (the outstanding pension of her deceased husband) was forwarded to her.

Some members of the Force invested their money wisely. In November 1882, Captain Denny sold his land claim at Calgary for $10,000, a sizeable sum at that time. His problems with alcohol, however, left him to die destitute. William Parker speculated in Winnipeg city lots during the Manitoba land boom by purchasing two city lots for $70. Two weeks later he refused a $150 offer. Captain Winder operated a store in Fort Macleod. Inspector Jarvis inherited some mining shares worth $15,000. He also sold a farm for $900, perhaps to meet expenses. The inspector was having marital problems and pay garnishees to support the boarding of two sons left him with a sparse monthly salary of $46.

Discipline

The first disciplinary punishments were rather inconsistent. One refractory constable had his wrists tied to the stirrup of a horse as punishment. When the horse bolted, he was dragged, fracturing his right clavicle. Surgeon Kittson, although acknowledging that this punishment was an authorized military practice, suggested that its practice be forbidden. While other infractions had only a fine. Commissioner French bemoaned the fact that many men were not deterred by a monetary punishment.

Anyone charged with an infraction appeared before a senior officer whose verdict was final and without appeal. Penalties could include fines, reduction in rank, incarceration in the guard room, confinement to the barracks, and infrequently (never more than three men a year) dismissal from the NWMP. A Defaulter's Sheet listed a policeman's infractions. Between 1882 and 1885 (when he was discharged because of poor eyesight), the Defaulter Sheet for Godfrey Casault included:

22 May 1882: neglect of duty for not unloading carbine before bringing it into barrack room
one month confined to barracks
(Commissioner Irvine)

29 Oct. 1882: reported (falsely) that he was sick
one month confined to barracks,
(Commissioner Irvine)

15 Feb. 1883: appropriating beef intended for the troop mess
one month's imprisonment at hard labour,
(Inspector Antrobus)

14 Nov. 1883: refused to sign his month's pay account
one month imprisonment at hard labour,
(Inspector Antrobus)

1 Dec. 1884: absent from stables when watering order sounded, using threatening language to orderly,
fined ten days pay, ten days confined to barracks
(Superintendent Crozier)

25 Jan. 1885: sitting in the stable when he should have been grooming his horse and impertinence to Superintendent Fraser who gave him an order
ten days pay, confined to barracks for ten day
(Superintendent Crozier[53])

The Defaulter's Sheet was a key reference when a policeman applied for re-engagement in the Force. Examples from Defaulter Sheets illustrate the broad range of charges. Confined to barracks is listed as "CB":

Name	Offence	Penalty
Oscar Dubreuil	Bed in a dirty condition	8 days CB (Crozier)
Joseph Chabot	Fell in with R.C. party instead of Methodists	7 days pay (Antrobus)
Michael Regan	Drunk in town (Fort Walsh)	fine $20 (McIllree)
Robert Walsh	Disobeying an order	14 days CB (Steele)
E. Percival	Absent without leave from watch	admonished (Herchmer)
John Hickey	Talking in ranks during drill instructions	admonished (Moffat)
Andrew Galvin	Drunk in barracks, used threatening language to Sergt. Spicer	fine $10 and 14 days CB (Jarvis)
George Miles	Late from Stable Parade	fine $1 (Irvine)
J.T. Labelle	Asleep on his Post on Stable Piquet (duty)	fine $10 and 14 days CB (Irvine)
Chris Carson	Assaulting a prisoner while on Duty	fine $10 (Crozier)

Each post forwarded a Monthly Defaulters' Sheet to Ottawa listing the disciplinary offences. An early example is at the Swan River post: October 1875—Boswell, neglect of duty $3, absent from Roll Call, admonished. Cookhouse dirty—Sub-Constables Wallace and Berry, fine $3. Emeri Leprohan, in charge of stores, charged $10 for missing stores, namely serges, four cups, boots, and forage.[54]

Some fines were ridiculous. One man at Fort Macleod was fined $5 for whistling "Yankee Doodle."[55] His excuse that he had fought in the American Civil War went unheeded. It cost Const. George Boswell $3 for taking a frying pan from the kitchen without permission. Other fines lacked consideration. R.N. Wilson lost three days pay and was given three days confinement in the barracks for neglect of guard duty while warming himself in the barrack room on a bitter February night. An inflexible application of the rules brought one dubious charge. In 1876, while riding from Fort Walsh to Fort Macleod, James A. Christie left the column to shoot a large bull buffalo grazing 500 m away. The shot startled his horse to stop short and threw Christy over its head. The wounded buffalo charged at Christie who was sitting and trying to reload his single shot carbine. A member of the troop observed:

> When the animal was within eight or ten yards of him, coming with his head lowered, Christie fired and the big brute fell dead right at the constable's feet. The whole column whipped off their helmets and cheered him to an echo. This was short-lived as the Sergt. Major rode out and placed him under arrest for disobedience of orders, as no buffalo were to be shot without permission.[56]

However, after a review of the incident, the arrest ended with a verbal "calling down."

Reduction in their rank was another disciplinary penalty. One diary commented: "Frank Pennock was reduced to the ranks and fined fifty dollars for not telling where he got his whiskey."[57] Surgeon Nevitt regretted that his likeable servant, William "Grizzly" Adams, was ordered to general duty, fined a month's pay, and confined to barracks for two months for being drunk. "He is a man that cannot stand drink at all," lamented Nevitt.[58] Superintendent W. Herchmer reduced Sergeant Alfred Stewart to corporal for leaving the barracks without permission and returning the next day under the influence of alcohol.

The "boys" had little recourse other than to grumble among themselves over the imposed penalties. One policeman went even further. Using a pseudonym "Battleford Barracks," he wrote to the *London Free Press* in Ontario: "Inspector Walker is not a fit man to be in charge of men, as he can hardly write his own name, and has to get his non-commissioned officers to make out his reports … he would do better on a farm driving a yoke of oxen."[59] Nor did Walker win any accolades from the detachment when he tore up a list of complaints without even looking at the contents.

Minor mutinies arose on several occasions. In 1875, the men at Fort Brisebois revolted against the commanding officer and had him removed. A more serious confrontation occurred in September 1883 when "C" troop at Fort Macleod, angered at "hard and unpleasant, if not unbearable duty," gave their complaints to newly arrived Sergt.-Major Ernest Bradley to present them to Commanding Officer L.N.F. Crozier.[60] When no response came, the troops refused guard duty, signed a letter exonerating Bradley, and pinpointed their concerns. Tedious arguments followed at an arranged meeting in the Orderly Room. Crozier admitted overlooking some issues and being ignorant of the existing conditions. Most requests were granted and the grievances eased. Crozier blamed Bradley by maintaining the troops were all right before his arrival.

The ranks enforced their own code of behaviour. Constable George Boswell was kicked out of the poker game at Fort Macleod for running debts. Startled onlookers in Calgary, watching policemen leading Constable John Edward Taylor by rope to the newly-constructed railway bridge, suspected a lynching was about to happen. Their excited cries were quelled when Taylor was thrown into the river, quickly pulled out and allowed to return to the barracks. On the incident, the local newspaper reported that barrack mates had seized Taylor while he was playing cards, put a rope around him, and marched him to the railway bridge because he was warning bootleggers of police raids, and thereby stifling possible revenue for the arresting constables.[61] Several days later, Constables Taylor, Pennyfather, and Montgomery were transferred to Regina to defuse further problems.

Fist fights among the men were frequent, especially when alcohol was involved. An entry in Jack Clarke's diary 13 August 1879 relates: "Const. B. Fields and Const. Battersbay had a fight over a bet in a shooting match. A good many Police Boys are drunk. constable Conroy and Const. Harland Had a fight. Conroy got the worst of it."[62] Even fifteen-year-old Frederick Bagley was quick with his fists:

> This evening an overgrown lout named McHamish threatened to kill me after I smacked him in the mouth with my small fist for stealing my drinking cup. But that red headed Irishman "The Leaping Goat" McKibbon seized him by the throat and promised to knock his head off if he did not "lave the boy alone."[63]

William McQuarrie remembered his steamboat trip up the Missouri River: "We used to average about five fights a day. All this was for exercise."[64] In 1885, the deployment of large numbers of recruits to Regina kept the local hospital busy attending to their injuries from fights. No doubt there was a tough element among the men. The local press reported: "On Tuesday the mounted police had a row among themselves at the station and even threatened to use their rifles."[65]

The *Fort Walsh Daily Post Journal*, on 24 July 1882, under General Order No. 520, gives an example of disciplinary punishment:

> Reg No 624 Acting Corporal Blackhall, Joseph was this day fined fifteen days pay and suspended from his duties as an Acting Corporal for "Having committed a breach of discipline in that he did create a disturbance by fighting on the morning of the 23rd inst."

Nor was being an indifferent spectator sanctioned. Three constables had been fined $2 each, "in that they witnessed a fight on the morning of the 23rd inst and did not interfere to prevent a breach of peace or to make an arrest."[66]

Living Accommodations

In the first years, the men occupied crude log buildings built within the stockade. Workmanship of the buildings was basic. During the construction of Fort Battleford in 1876, Superintendent James Walker complained that few men had building skills. Added to the problems was the interruption of work one day when a herd of buffalo lumbered through the site.

Rainwater seeped (at times, it poured) through the sod-covered roofs. The diary of Superintendent McIllree's tersely records: "Roof of 'B' mess room fell in. Fortunately only two men were in the room and they got out all right."[67] Dr. Nevitt complained that it was too wet to write with the rain leaking through every imaginable place in the ceiling.

The log walls of the buildings, chinked with mud, often failed to block the wind and cold. On winter mornings at Fort Qu'Appelle, Sergeant Frank Fitzpatrick used a shovel to remove snow that had drifted in during the night. Some men, he remembered, preferred sleeping in tents, even on one ghoulish occasion when two surveyors, dead from poisoned wild turnips, lay beside them until the next morning.[68] In summer, fine dirt drifted into the buildings. A visitor to Fort Macleod measured a layer of dirt 1 m wide and 5 cm deep. There was a draft in most of the buildings. It amused Surgeon Nevitt to watch tiny whirlwinds of dust flicker the lamps. In some buildings, the men tacked white cotton sheets to the walls to contain the dust. Until a sawmill was built at Fort Macleod, the floors were beaten earth. In the officer's quarters, a buffalo trail remained visible.

Although two central stoves heated each barrack, it was hard to keep the room warm in cold weather. With an outside temperature of minus-forty degrees, Surgeon Augustus Jukes kept a roaring fire going until he retired at midnight. In the morning, he found "everything liquid in my room frozen and though covered with three pairs of blankets and a buffalo robe, I was very cold."[69] Superintendent James Walker woke up one morning to find a water container frozen on top of his stove and yet the embers were still warm enough to rekindle the fire.

Huge stacks of firewood were cut by prisoners or policemen (paid an extra fifteen cents a day) for a post's winter supply. By the end of fall, 200 cords of wood dwarfed the tiny police hovel at Wood Mountain. The first headquarters at Swan River, where ninety stoves burned five cords of wood each day, was likened to a sooty English factory town. Coal mined near Fort Whoop-Up provided an alternate fuel for Fort Macleod.

Until glass windows became readily available, the first windows were a thin cloth covering. Train dogs (described by young Bagley "as more like wolves than dogs") tore and ate the dressed buffalo hide windows on the cook shack at Fort Edmonton. Lanterns and candles furnished the night light. The first Edmonton barracks used lighted rags (called bitches) hanging over the edge of tin dishes filled with grease. The eating tables and benches were made of rough wood. Hard benches used for beds had a buffalo robe and two blankets covering a thin straw or sawdust mattress (paillasse). There are few references to the latrines other than they were outside buildings with separate buildings for the officers and men.

Fire was always a hazard in the wooden structures. A fire killed seven horses and destroyed the stables and ancillary buildings at Battleford. At most posts, the lack of available water hindered all attempts to stop a fire from spreading. When a drinking party at Fort Macleod caused a fire in winter, the men frantically saved the horses but, with snow melted by the fire the only source of water, were unable to prevent the shoemaker's shop, storehouses, and horse stables from being destroyed. A bugle call signalled the fort to assemble for a bucket brigade. In a fire in the Fort Whoop-Up smokehouse, a bucket brigade was ineffective in bringing enough water from the Oldman River.

No one could expect privacy in the crowded barracks. In a letter to Ireland, one policeman wrote: "I scribble to you now in the long room containing fifty beds, the fellows on each side of me playing cards and further on a fellow at a flute, others singing and talking so it is not easy to write proper."[70] The teeming quarters tested patience. Even in the more spacious officer's building, Surgeon Nevitt tired of companions Winder and Jackson and moved to "B" Troop's officer's cabin. "Winder," the surgeon wrote, "is a very changeable man—one moment he is your best friend the next he turns around and abuses you like a pickpocket."[71]

Married men were solely responsible for their family's accommodation. Inspector William Winder arranged to have his wife come to Fort Macleod and had a house built near the post. Police workmanship was again suspect when the roof collapsed three months after its completion. It was February and repairs were imperative.

At several postings, the shortage of accommodations required renting nearby buildings. In 1879, the detachment at Battleford leased a church building for $12 a month and, at Duck Lake, a local merchant was paid $5 a month for a house. A two-storey building rented by the police at Prince Albert had a store, seven occupants, the mounted police kitchen, a dining room, store room, three police sleeping rooms, a guard house for prisoners, and a small space under the stairs where Sergeant Harry Keenan slept.

Eight Mounties lodged at East End post (Chimney Coulee) in 1878–79, located 76 km east of Fort Walsh and 8 km north of the present village of Eastend, Saskatchewan. Their building had an earth floor and was split into two rooms, one for the horses and one for the men. Frank Fitzpatrick remembered life as a dull routine of drills and riding but he enjoyed learning Sioux and Indian sign language from an Indian named Antelope.

East End Post, NWMP, 1879

"We were not downhearted in our solitude … on the contrary, we were ready to, and did, go to great trouble to make the most of it."

– Frank Fitzpatrick, *Sergeant 331*, 50
    GA NA 2446 – 17

Camp – Ten Mile Patrol N.W.M.P.

Ten Mile Patrol, a summer station, was named for its distance from Fort Walsh.

– GA, Stuart Wood
M 8065, f. 4.

Some outposts were summer camps. Kennedy's Post at Milk River Crossing had two shacks, one for the horses and a second that Robert McCutcheon called "our clubhouse, kitchen and bedroom."[72] Men at the tiny three-man post on the St. Mary River complained that every passing Indian dropped by as "if we are keeping lodging for them."[73] Ten Mile Patrol (named for its location ten miles from Fort Walsh) had several tents near the trail that went south to Fort Benton. One officer and six men manned the outpost camp.

Living at an isolated outpost tested the men. One account related the anguish they experienced:

> On top of Pinto Horse Butte and pretty close to the clouds, there is a police stopping place with good stabling, and stored with hay and firewood. From pencil notes scribbled on the doors of these buildings the reminiscences of some members of the police who had been weather-bound at this point appear to be anything but pleasant; for instance, "arrived on 7th February, left on 3rd of March; snowing and storming for over three weeks. Can't stand dried meat straight any longer."[74]

The small detachment was concerned about its vulnerability. One Mountie recorded: "I had a pretty hard time at Pinto Horse Butte for abut five Months. The Sioux would Come up in band and demand food and of cours we had to Make them Tea and give them alittle."[75]

Each police post could expect an annual inspection visit. At Shoal Lake in October 1879, Commissioner Irvine expressed his satisfaction with the appearance of the twelve-man detachment (under Superintendent William Herchmer) and the condition of the buildings and outer fence.

The policemen informally compared the police posts. Fort Calgary, called "the queen city of the far west," was a desired first choice and Fort Macleod was acceptable.[76] Constable Donkin called Battleford the "abomination of desolation with all sorts of dodges, sick–lists, etc. adopted to avoid being banished there."[77] Outbreaks of mountain fever dispirited anyone who was posted to Fort Walsh.

Most police accommodations were suspect. A rancher in the area, Duncan McEachran, described the "dilapidated condition of these so–called forts, McLeod and Calgarry, is neither creditable to the force nor the Government, consisting as they do, of rough log huts, mud-plastered and earth roofed, little better than the Missouri River woodman's shack."[78] John A. Macdonald, Prime Minister and Minister of the Interior, admitted in 1879 that the buildings occupied by the NWMP in the Territories were in a very unsatisfactory condition. Added awareness of this problem came later in the 1881 tour by the Governor General Marquis of Lorne. He and the five accompanying journalists praised the work of the police, especially in light of their living arrangements which were far inferior to Fort Shaw, the American base in northern Montana. The negative assessment likely stimulated NWMP building improvements in the next years.

The Battleford post, for example, received $20,000 for alterations. The Commanding officer's residence had a foundation of substantial masonry, dining room, a parlour, three bedrooms, kitchen, summer kitchen, pantry, stone cellar, guardhouse, large storehouse, and a shingled roof. They also built the barracks, a hospital, officer's quarters, two buildings for married men, workshops, non-commissioned officers' quarters, and stables large enough for 160 horses.

In 1883, prefabricated buildings, delivered by railway from Ontario, facilitated the construction of the new NWMP headquarters at Regina. The base rose quickly, with luxuries such as wooden sidewalks and a large cellar to store vegetables. Forty-nine buildings were assembled and twelve others received additions. The sewage and garbage previously deposited into Pile of Bones Creek was now transported to a distant dump. That year, $30,000 was spent on the new barracks at Fort Macleod. More than one million feet of lumber was cut in the Porcupine Hills and delivered by ox teams to the fort. All buildings had to be braced because of the strong winds in the area. Hardware, doors, and windows were sent by railway from Winnipeg to Medicine Hat and overland to the fort. Peter O'Leary, a visiting London, England, journalist suggested they generate electricity by burning coal to light the new barracks and a forty-foot tower to act as a beacon for travelers far out on the plains.[79]

Work at Fort Calgary included a new stable, quarters for thirty men, Sergeant's quarters, lavatory, hospital, artisan's building, magazine, latrines, hospital, and root house. The older buildings were replastered and their ceilings raised. New police posts were constructed at Maple Creek and Medicine Hat. The Report of the Commissioner for 1883 concluded, "most comfortable and commodious quarters have been provided for the greater part of the Force."[80]

Food and Drink

The men stationed at Swan River called it "Rattlesnake pork." Streaks of yellow, red and shades of green looked nauseating and its source, pigs in Montana that had been fed rattlesnakes, made the meat unappealing. No one objected when an Appeal Board in 1875 condemned the food as unfit for consumption.

Food at the police posts was often sparse, badly cooked, and of poor quality. In response to a Winnipeg reporter asking how the men were fed, Joseph Francis tersely replied "not very sumptuously."[81] Constable George Guernsey recalled: "Our diet was not remarkable for variety: bacon, hardtack and tea for breakfast and dinner; in the evening we mixed up pemmican, pounded hardtack and some compressed vegetables and made a royal stew."[82] F.A.D. Bourke, at Prince Albert, wrote: "For breakfast we got bread and tea, for dinner bread, tea, soup and beef hardly an appetizing fare."[83] A recruit described the food at Fort Walsh "Our grub is not the most refined, but a good appetite does wonders in getting down dry bread, tea, and coffee without milk and sugar … vegetables and such luxuries are not to be got."[84] If there was no food, as when on patrol, the men called their imaginary meal "wind pudding." A camp without water was called a dry camp.

Attempts were made to improve their diet. A "mess" was an agreement whereby the men would contribute a daily sum (often ten cents) to their appointed caterer for the purchase of special treats—milk, butter, pies, plum pudding, and so on.[85] Matthew Meredith recalled his companions loved Eagle Brand Condensed Milk spread like jam over their bread. Although, these "luxuries" were expensive: at Fort Macleod, rancher Joe

McFarland sold butter to the detachment for $0.75 a lb. The policemen resented the town merchants charging what was termed "visionary prices," for food and basic needs.[86]

Each post planted a garden (some with individual plots) and cereal crops. In 1879, the police farm at Battleford harvested 500 bushels of oats, 110 bushels of barley, 600 bushels of potatoes, and 64 bushels of turnips along with garden vegetables adaptable to Western Canada. The post also kept a fine lot of Bantam chickens. Anticipation of the first egg of the year from one of twenty-eight hens was such that the *Winnipeg Daily Times* informed its readers of the event happening in distant Battleford.[87] At Fort Macleod, the men bought a milk cow that was, in Constable Metzler's words, "too wild and we had to let her go as we could not handle her."[88]

The men hunted and fished for food, sometimes with astounding success. Three men at Fort Macleod caught 900 trout by fly reel in three days. In the first years, buffalo were even shot without leaving the fort. When food ran low, three constables stationed at a shack beside the St. Mary River shot thirty-one prairie chickens in two days—more than enough to eat until supplies arrived ten days later.

At the tiny East End outpost the ten men shot deer, prairie chickens, rabbits, and once an enormous grizzly bear—which they agreed was too oily and greasy when eaten. Bacon, pemmican, and buffalo meat were soaked in water to soften. The men caught whitefish with nets in nearby lakes, and they baked bread, adding raisins "as a luxury."

East End was an isolated outpost, yet Sergeant Frank Fitzpatrick recalled that, "We were not downhearted in our solitude ... on the contrary we were ready to, and did, go to great trouble to make the most of it."[89] And what was Christmas without plum pudding? Every police post had lavish dinners for the holidays. It was decided to send three men to Fort Walsh—a return distance of 160 km—just to get the ingredients for this treat.

A blizzard, however, foiled their return trip and, instead of eating plum pudding, Fitzpatrick and a companion spent Christmas Eve chasing two horses that had escaped from the horse room inside the building. That night, the temperature was -30°C and it was a 3-km chase before the policemen collared the mounts. "We were," Fitzpatrick recalled, "like two icicles when we got through, but we built a chimney fire ... and discussed Christmas and wondered what our folks at home would have thought if they could have seen us."[90]

Food was purchased from the Indians. At Fort Edmonton, Inspector Steele exchanged tea and flour for game from an old Indian hunter. The police particularly enjoyed roasted beaver. Indian women sold mushrooms (sometimes in wagon loads) and wild berries—saskatoons, cranberries, gooseberries, raspberries, and strawberries—at fifty cents a pail. At Fort Walsh, the men paid ten cents for a duck and five cents for each duck egg. They threw aside eggs found with developing chicks, and later watched in disgust as starving Indians ate the remains.

At Fort Walsh, the men in "B" Troop ate in a 12 x 18-m room. Rough tables extended along the room and side benches served as chairs. Beds backing against the wall cluttered the crowded building. Dishes and cups were made of tin, and knives and forks of iron. The men took turns to cook and serve the food. Robert McCutcheon reminisced, "and how we fellows could eat … we made a variety of dishes from buffalo meat, venison, beans, hard tack, dried apples, tea, coffee, sugar, each shift tried to excel in the culinary art."[91]

Cooking Facilities

"For breakfast we got bread and tea, for dinner bread, tea, soup and beef—hardly an appetizing fare."

– F.A.D. Bourke, NWMP, "Recollections and Reminiscences," *SH*, XXXV, No. 2, 55
RCMP Historical Collections Unit, "Depot" Division, Regina, SK., 1946.3.7

"C" Troop Mess, Fort Macleod

"Our diet was not remarkable for variety: bacon, hardtack and tea for breakfast and dinner; in the evening we mixed up pemmican, pounded hardtack and some compressed vegetables and made a royal stew."

– George Guernsey, "The Passing of the Great Lone Land," SG, Ninth Annual, 35
GA NA 98 – 27

Finding competent cooks was an ongoing problem. It was hardly appetizing to watch Jack Symonds toss beef on the floor and jump on it with his boots before placing it in the frying pan.[92] One cook named Si, without fuel for his flapjacks, lit the dry prairie and could be seen in constant motion trying to contain the fire. He was blackened and perspiring, but, by adding pork and beans and hard tack, provided a meal.[93] After his visit, a correspondent for a Toronto newspaper described the cooks at Fort Walsh as usually the dirtiest men in the fort. Moreover, they cooked in the easiest way they could by throwing the food into large pans—resulting in a mess that a dog could hardly eat.[94]

A post was lucky to have William Parker as a cook. He enjoyed making bread and his prairie chicken pies were a special treat. Constable McEntyre chose cooking to exempt himself from guard, stable, and outdoor work. He obtained a cook book and his efforts soon found favour with the fellow comrades. Recruit John Donkin at Fort Osbourne in Winnipeg described the police food as excellent.

The beverages, besides whiskey, were water and tea. Dr. John Kittson thought men had a natural craving for tea. He noted that, "on the march the men constantly grumbled as to the insufficiency of tea." Kittson urged the ration be increased from half to three-quarters of an ounce on the march or when doing hard fatigue work. And accepting the fact that many men craved alcohol, the doctor recommended in his 1879 annual report that beer and spirits be made available in the canteens under strict regulation, as practised in the army. This would add materially to the comfort, morals, and efficiency of the mounted police.[95]

Clothing and Kit

Each man received a clothing and kit issue as shown on page 367.[96] In the first years, the quality and delivery of dress was a problem. Commissioner Macleod, in 1878, criticized an English supplier for both the quality of material and workmanship. The delivery and distribution of clothing were also unreliable. Items that left Collingwood, Ontario, in August 1880 only arrived in late January. Supplies sent to Battleford in 1882 remained at Duck Lake all winter. Moreover, as one newspaper commented, "The articles most wanted were left behind ... this time winter underclothing."[97] Sergt.-Major Joseph Francis, in 1880, complained that the men had not had a tunic in three years, nor pants or boots; no new blankets in two years; and last winter's mitts came in mid-March. One Mountie recalled the Fort Walsh detachment lined up for a kit inspection: "I don't think any of us had more than half his original uniform or kit, and that in the last stage of despair or discoloration. We had made ourselves elegant buckskin shirts, breeches and leggings, and moccasins we would obtain from the trading store."[98] When apparel arrived on time, it was worth a newspaper comment: "the police goods have, for once, been received in the season in which they are supposed to be used."[99]

The early problems with the kit apparently improved. By 1882, the annual report rated the new clothing excellent. Constable John Donkin, who joined the Force in 1884, thought that "no other corps in the world supplies a better kit."[100]

The men wore a pillbox hat (forage hat) or a white helmet that was mainly reserved for full dress, scarlet tunic (serge) with yellow facing, and flesh-coloured (later dark-blue) breeches with yellow stripes, brown leather belt, and white gauntlets. For winter wear, the issue added buffalo coats (purchased for $20), mittens, blanket leggings called chaps, fur hats ($3), toques and moccasins. Balaclavas provided full face protection. Buckskin mitts had a forefinger to facilitate pulling the rifle trigger. An oil sheet with a hole cut for the head had the dual purpose of a ground cover and raincoat.

The boots and clothing, made in Kingston Penitentiary, had suspect workmanship. Men found wet boots difficult to remove. Their tunic or serge was often too tight and found unsuitable for everyday work. Blue overalls for fatigue wear made the men, in one newspaper's opinion, "look like a cross between the Confederate army and Mennonites."[101]

Other issue included: ammunition pouches, haversacks, carbine buckets, revolver holsters, cross belts of ammunition, binoculars, smoked goggles, and two blankets. The first spurs were tin-plated and of poor quality, and called by the men "Mackenzie's (the Prime Minister) spurs." These were replaced by solid silver German spurs.

The men hated the pillbox hat, even blaming it for causing baldness. A white cork helmet with a leather chin strap was hardly better. Constable Edward Barnett suggested the helmets, "served better for holding oats, when feeding your horse, getting a drink of water from a slough, or carrying your tobacco pouch when riding trail ... the greater part of the time they were carried in the wagons ... mostly we wore felt hats."[102] Col. Macleod admitted that unless obliged to, few men wore the pillbox hat or helmet.

The scarlet Norfolk tunic was an instant symbol of the North-West Mounted Police—so much so, that it is difficult to imagine the "Riders of the Plains" wearing any other colour. The sudden appearance of a troop was a thrilling sight. Little Kitty McLean was making pebble designs in her backyard when she heard an approaching brass band. Suddenly 200 Mounties entered the Qu'Appelle Valley, where her father was factor of the HBC post. Years later she recalled:

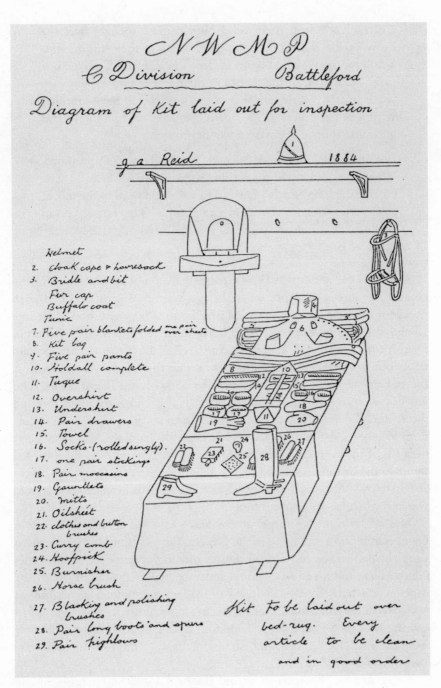

N W M P

C Division   Battleford

Diagram of Kit laid out for inspection

J a Reid   1884

Helmet
2. Cloak cape & havresock
3. Bridle and bit
   Fur cap
   Buffalo coat
   Tunic
7. Five pair blankets folded one pair over sheets
8. Kit bag
9. Five pair pants
10. Holdall complete
11. Tuque
12. Overshirt
13. Undershirt
14. Pair drawers
15. Towel
16. Socks (rolled singly)
17. one pair stockings
18. Pair moccasins
19. Gauntlets
20. mitts
21. Oilsheet
22. clothes and button brushes
23. Curry comb
24. Hoofpick
25. Burnisher
26. Horse brush
27. Blacking and polishing brushes
28. Pair long boots and spurs
29. Pair highlows

Kit to be laid out over bed-rug. Every article to be clean and in good order

North-West Mounted Police Kit

– RCMP Historical Collections Unit, "Depot" Division, Regina, SK.

I can see and hear them yet as they came into sight over the brow of the hill. The music grew softer as they dipped into a hollow, then swelled again as they came into full view. They came riding out of the woods in their scarlet tunics, their caps worn smartly on the left side of the head, black knee breeches with a broad yellow stripe down the sides, shining boots, and gleaming spurs. They were a wonderful sight.

But the horses! They glistened and shone, so beautifully groomed. What love and attention had been given those horses as they crossed the long, lonely prairies. How they pranced to the music, and no wonder, for the band was playing "The Flying Cloud Schottische." The instruments seemed as though they were made of gold.[103]

At a fifty-year reunion in 1924, George B. Hall related, while crossing the country, he entered a teepee where he was warmly welcomed. The Indian owner produced a large silver medal bearing an 1760 impression of George III and, through an interpreter, said it had been given to his grandfather in Detroit and, "whenever a soldier wearing a red coat was met that man would be an Indian's friend and protector."[104] During the North-West Rebellion, the Indians were not impressed when the 65th Mount Royal Rifles, who did not wear red coats and talked like "half-breeds," marched through the reserves at Battle River. Second, the Indians called the 9th Voltigeurs from Quebec City, then garrisoned at Fort Macleod, the "black soldiers" because of their green uniforms. At times, the Mounties gave discarded tunics to the Indians. It startled Francis Roe, the wife of an American officer at Fort Shaw, Montana Territory, when Cree Indians from Canada arrived wearing worn scarlet police tunics.

The scarlet tunic (or serge) always was a focus of attention. American newspaper reporters, coming to the General Terry-Sitting Bull Conference, were thrilled to see red-coated figures moving about Fort Walsh. James Clinkskill (a town resident) noted how the red coats, mixing with the dancers at a Battleford Bachelor's ball made a picturesque scene. Lovissa McDougall, moving from Ontario to her new home in Edmonton, first saw the Mounted Police at the Sounding Lake Treaty payments. The forty men, she said, "looked splendid although," adding, "most of the police are a set of rowdies."[105]

Every one of the recruits prized his new look. Seventeen-year-old William McQuarrie remembered, "We thought we were quite smart as we walked down Yonge and Queen Streets [Toronto] in the evenings."[106]

Officer's Dress

The officers wore a more elaborate tunic with gold braids on the front
and rank badges on the sleeves.

– PAA B.1853

Matthew Mededith recalled "the uniforms were often ill-fitting but for the
recruits there was an intense feeling of pride when we paraded the streets
in Toronto."[107] Roger Pocock, "was choked with sheer glory at wearing the
Imperial scarlet, faint with pride when I first walked into town [Regina]."[108]

Most men had a beard or mustache, a personal feature evident for the
first four Commissioners. All thirteen men in the group photograph at
Maple Creek in 1884 (see page 489) have facial hair.[109]

Weapons

The Mounties were armed with revolvers and carbines. The officers and
sergeants also had swords in a scabbard, more for appearance than utility.
Major-General E. Selby Smyth, in his 1875 report, suggested that the officers
wear swords, which have a "great effect upon the Indian mind."[110] Although
limited sword drill was practised both mounted and on foot, the weapon
was considered an encumbrance while on patrol and was kept in storage,
for the most part, except for formal occasions.

Revolvers were carried in a holster on the man's left side. The first sidearm was the Adams Revolver, First Model Mark 11, caliber .450, holding 6 bullets in its cylinder. Many of the 330 weapons, purchased in England for $15 each, were damaged during shipping and the necessary repairs delayed the '74 March several days. The 50,000 rounds purchased were of poor quality. Most of these handguns soon became unserviceable and, by 1876, they were replaced by the "Second Model," a double-action revolver that could be cocked and fired by pulling the trigger. In 1883, 200 Enfield revolvers Mark 11 were ordered as an improved handgun. In September 1885, an additional 600 Enfield revolvers were purchased along with 100,000 rounds of ammunition.

The Force came to the West with Snider-Enfield carbines, an outdated, breech-loaded single-shot carbine. Because of the large ammunition supply purchased that was not interchangeable, the Snider-Enfield carbines were only gradually replaced by the Winchester repeating carbine, a favourite rifle among westerners. In 1878, 50 Winchesters, at $33 each, and 10,000 cartridges, at $35 per 1,000, were purchased.

By 1880, "A" and "D" Divisions had been armed with the new repeating rifles. In his 1882 report, Commissioner A.G. Irvine had recommended Winchester rifles as the standard carbine of the Force and the forty recruits leaving Toronto that year had these carbines. The outbreak of hostilities in 1885 brought the Winchester into universal service and 1,050 carbines were ordered in the first six months of that year. The Winchester repeating rifle (holding eight cartridges in its magazine) was a decided improvement over the Snider-Enfield. Inspector Crozier spoke to a Toronto reporter:

I was standing outside the stockade talking with Sitting Bull. He looked up towards the loop holes where the muzzles of several rifles were to be seen, and pointing to them said, "You've got repeaters." He noticed the magazine under the barrels of the rifles, and the fact of our being able to fire without having to reload gave the savage a better opinion of our capabilities for offence or defence.[111]

On horseback, a Mountie placed his carbine in a case (bucket) strapped to rings on the right side of the saddle. This proved awkward in mounting the horse and the men preferred placing the carbine in a sling which passed across the rider's chest. The bucket was used on long trips where action was unlikely and the sling preferred for patrol duty. Shotguns were supplied as a unit weapon. With only six shotguns issued on the '74 March (one for each Division), it was hardly an effective weapon.

Target practice in 1874, at 100 to 500 yards range, was limited annually to sixty rounds per man. This with thirty revolver shots at a shorter distance was decidedly insufficient for men involved in police duty. Later, Ottawa recommended 120 rounds of target practice with both carbines and pistols for each man. Commissioner Macleod suggested that target practice be spread throughout the year, with ten rounds fired each month.

The horses had to be accustomed to rifle fire and the roar of the field piece: this took patience and time. When the men practised firing from horseback, Surgeon Nevitt recalled that his mount, named "Old Satan," was fractious and badly scared.

Defective ammunition was a concern. The annual report in 1878 noted that the cartridges lost powder from shaking in the men's pouches which caused the ball to become stuck in the barrel or fall short of the target.

Munitions were stored at a central location in the fort. Fort Macleod had an underground magazine 6 x 4 m and 2.5 m deep. The eight cm concrete roof was covered by 1 m of earth. There was a ventilator and thick doors. The magazine held 150,000 rounds of Winchester bullets, 25,000 rounds revolver, and 10 kegs of gunpowder.

Lances were more for ceremonial purposes than for use as a weapon. The twenty-five lances requisitioned for the '74 March had a bamboo staff and were held in a leather bucket attached to the right stirrup and held by a sling looped over the rider's arm. As the column approached Blackfoot country in September 1874, Sergeant R. Belcher, a former 9th Lancer, formed a troop of lancers to support the advance guard.

The Force brought two 9-pr. guns and two mortars on their march west. The weapons were part of a purchase from the Imperial Ordnance stores for $22,767. A four-horse team was needed to transport the heavy 9-pr. field pieces. Sub-Inspector Cecil Denny complained that the artillery pieces "gave us more trouble and crippled more horses than all the rest of transport."[112] Rockets were fired to impress the Indians and to signal the camp location.

The expected influx of Sioux Indians into Canada after the Custer Massacre pressed the Force to purchase four 7-pr. bronze guns (mountain guns) from the Canadian Militia for $4,500. These weapons, manufactured in Great Britain in 1809, had been brought to Manitoba by the Red River Expedition in 1870. Sub-Inspector Percy Neale transported the four field pieces to Fort Walsh in October 1876. With the closure of Fort Walsh in 1883, these field pieces were sent to Calgary and Regina. As a response to Indian unrest in the fall of 1884, one of the Regina field pieces was relocated in Battleford. This field piece was moved in March 1885 to Fort Carlton and, shortly after, was used ineffectively in the Duck Lake skirmish.

Field Pieces, Fort Walsh

The recruits had a reputation for recklessness with their weapons. Constable William Cox commented: "The old hands were more scared of them than the Indians. Rifles were popping in all directions."

– *Lethbridge Herald*, 11 July 1935
GA NA 98 – 13

At the onset of the North-West Rebellion in 1885, the NWMP had the same artillery as in 1876—two 9-pr. field pieces, four 7-pr. "mountain guns," and two mortars. Once in combat, the aged artillery pieces broke down and proved unserviceable. Only the 9-pr. "Macleod gun" was effective. When the Alberta Field Force attacked Big Bear's band at Frenchman's Butte on 28 May 1885, shells directed toward the concealed enemy rifle pits killed one Indian and wounded five men. More important, the firing demoralized the Indian camp located to the rear. Soldiers arrived bent on killing the Natives. Several days later, the Cree band fragmented into small groups seeking refuge in the northern wilderness.[113]

Accidental gunfire was an ever-present danger. On the '74 March west, Percy Robinson lost one finger when his shotgun burst. Scout Jerry Potts wounded a Blackfoot child held by her mother. He was arrested and temporarily placed in the guardhouse. While showing a pistol to an Indian, R.N. Wilson shot him in the leg. Wilson wrote: "He raised a considerable row about it although I paid him for the injury and he had promised to say nothing about it. He reported me to the Indian Agent. I went down & made him confess before Red Crow & the Agent that I had paid him & that he had broken his promise to me."[114] The recruits had a reputation for being reckless with their weapons. Constable William Cox commented: "The old hands were more scared of them than the Indians. Rifles were popping in all directions."[115]

Two men were killed as the result of accidental gunfire. In the Fort Walsh barrack room Constable Godfrey Casault's rifle discharged as he attempted to remove a jammed cartridge. The bullet hit Constable George Johnston in the forearm and passed into his chest. Frantic barrack mates carried Johnston outside and sent for Dr. Kennedy. Johnston died while the surgeon attended to him.

Inspector Frank Norman chaired a six-man coroner's inquest that included two policemen. The coroners viewed the body and barrack room and heard evidence from Dr. Kennedy and the five policemen, including Constable Casault. The only question they asked concerned the personal fellowship between Casault and Johnston. The inquest ruled that the accidental discharge of a rifle in the hands of Constable Godfrey Casault was the cause of death. Dr. Kennedy wrote a death certificate and then forwarded a written report on the incident to the Commissioner.[116]

Three days after the death, the post had a sale of the kit and effects of George Johnston, "F" Division. Members of the troop purchased in total twenty-eight items—blankets, five pairs of socks, tunic, hair brush and comb, pair of braces, spurs, silk handkerchiefs—for $33.40.

Inspector Norman finalized the career service of George Johnston, No. 347, with the completion of two forms: "Proceedings of the Discharge Board" (marking the intended place of residence as "dead") and a "Final Account of Assets" from the sale of the kit, cash, twenty-three days pay due, and $4.25 extra pay for cutting firewood—in all, the deceased worldly wealth of $64.85. Johnston was buried in the cemetery north of the fort. He left a widow and one child.

In a second gunshot death, Constable Alfred Coulson, Surgeon Jukes' servant, was shot by a companion at Long Lake, just north of Regina. According to George Service, Coulson's companion in the boat, the two men had crossed the lake to visit a farmer and while leaving the boat a loaded rifle belonging to Service discharged, killing Coulson. A coroner's verdict ruled the incident was an accidental shooting death.

In settling the deceased's effects for his father in England, thirteen I.O.U. notes for a total of $644.50 were discovered. This substantial amount of money apparently came from a "loan shark operation" that charged an excessive interest rate of 20 per cent. More intriguing was finding that Coulson was an alias and his real name was Samuel Joseph Earl. In spite of these irregularities, NWMP Headquarters in Ottawa supported the estate and aggressively collected money from the men with outstanding I.O.U's. Incidentally, George Service owed Coulson $20.[117]

NOTES

1. *MFP*, 21 April 1880. Also Fitzpatrick, *Sergeant 331*, 91–93.

2. Donkin, *Trooper and Redskin*, 57.

3. *CH*, 20 February 1884. In *RC*, 1880, 14–15. Commissioner Irvine described a winter trip between Wood Mountain and Fort Walsh "in order that some slight idea may be formed as to the hardships encountered by the Mounted Police in the winter trips they were forced to make over the plains." Sam Steele provides a revealing account of a trip in winter in *Forty Years in Canada*, 134–5.

4. *GA*, Jessie DeGear, M 314 f. 27, Scrapbook 7.

5. *MFP*, 21 April 1880. Also *TG*, 17 April 1880.

6. *RC*, NWMP, 1881, 28.

7. RCMP Museum Archives, Regina.

8. *MFP*, 20 July 1881. Also Fitzpatrick, *Sergeant 331*, 23–24; Craufurd-Lewis, *Macleod of the Mounties*, gives an account of the routine of Commissioner Macleod, 274. Also Dempsey, ed., *William Parker Mounted Policeman*, 142.

9. *TG*, 10 May 1876.

10. "Reminiscences of a Tenderfoot," *SG*, Third Annual, 59. Also see *TG*, 17 April 1880.

11. *SAB*, J.E. McEntyre, A 110.

12. Sutherland, *A Summer in Prairie Land*, 110. Also on the "disgusting unbearable profanity of the police," see Sutherland, 153–4.

13. Rivett-Carnac, ed., "Letters from the North-West," 327.

14. *CH*, 31 August 1936.

15. *GA*, Edward Barnett, M 6142.

16. Ibid.

17. *GA*, Fred Bagley, M 2111, f.1.

18. *RL*, 8 November 1883.

19. *MFP*, 4 February 1884.

20. *MFP*, 28 February 1881.

21. *RC*, NWMP, 1881, 23.

22. J.J. McHugh, "Paying Treaty Money in 1882," *SG*, Seventh Annual, 81. The American spelling is Piegan.

23. *GA*, Supt. A. Shurtliff, M 1140.

24. *RC*, NWMP, 1882, 22. For 1883 to November: Port of Fort Macleod, $50,501, Port of Maple Creek, $28,417, a total $78,917.

25. Fitzpatrick, *Sergeant 331*, 117–18.

26. *RC*, NWMP, 1879, 13.

27. *GA*, Augustus Jukes, M 607.

28. McDougall's remains were found 6 February 1876. See letter from his wife, "The Last Letters of Rev. George McDougall," ed. Hugh Dempsey, *AH*, XV, No. 2, 29–30.

29. *MFP*, 20 July 1881.

30. *GA*, S.J. Clarke, M 228.

31. *MFP,* 20 December 1880.

32. *SH,* 28 September 1885.

33. Pocock, *Outriders of Empire*, 19–20.

34. Fitzpatrick, *Sergeant 331*, 22.

35. *GA*, Francis Dobbs, Pam 364.971 D632r.

36. Policemen were not allowed a homestead entry in addition to their land warrant. M. Kennedy wrote to England on 11 January 1878: "I have engaged for a term of three years service, at the expiration of which I am entitled to a free grant of 160 acres ... I know plenty of people who came with me to Canada are starving and would like to get home and cannot; America is one of the hardest countries in the world if a man does not happen to be lucky." *NAC*, M. Kennedy, f. 35. Other examples of land grants include: *NAC*, Oldham, f. o.s. 38, *NAC*, Spotten, f. o.s. 75.

37. *NAC*, Ross, f. 383.

38. *WDT*, 8 July 1881.

39. *RL*, 27 May 1916.

40. *Fort Battleford Post Daily Journal*, 1885.

41. *EB*, 7 February 1881.

42. *MFP*, 9 February 1881.

43. *MFP*, 20 July 1881.

44. *EB*, 14 March 1881.

45. *SH,* 26 April 1880. Also *MFP*, 20 January 1881.

46. *PAA*, James Steele, 85.448/24. Also *MFP*, 20 January 1881.

47. *EB*, 4 April 1881.

48. *MFP*, 21 April 1880; 7 September 1880.

49. *GA*, Edward Barnett, M 6142.

50. *GA*, RCMP fonds, M 8380.

51. Steele, *Forty Years in Canada*, 144.

52. Alfred Stewart received $0.91 per diem after twenty-three years' service. An additional bonus of one-fiftieth of the annual salary was given for each year above twenty-five years. *NAC*, Harry Keenan, f. 301.

53. *NAC*, Godfrey Casault, f. 517.

54. *NAC*, V 8, f. 470–81.

55. *HDH*, 15 March 1875.

56. Dempsey, ed., *William Parker Mounted Policeman*, 34.

57. *GA*, Simon J. Clarke, M 228.

58. Nevitt, *Frontier Life in the Mounted Police*, 159.

59. *London* (Ontario) *Free Press*, 13 November 1879.

60. *NAC*, R.N. Wilson, MG 29, E-47. Also Bruce Dawson, "Mutiny at Fort Macleod," *AH*, XL111, No. 3, 21–25. Complaints included inadequate and sometimes unfit food, delay in the issue of clothing, increased garrison duty because of understaffing, unbroken horses, and, counter to the *Police Act*, the men were assigned as bootblacks and grooms for visitors.

61. *CH*, 23 November 1883. Also L.V. Kelly in *The Range Men*, 161. Taylor received a six-month sentence for informing the whiskey traders.

62. *GA*, Simon J. Clarke, M 228.

63. *GA*, Frederick Bagley, M 43. On that date the '74 column was camped in the Sweet Grass Hills.

64. *NAC*, William McQuarrie, f. 724.

65. *RL*, 8 October 1885.

66. RCMP Museum Archives, Regina.

67. *GA*, John McIllree, AB McIllree # 1.

68. Fitzpatrick, *Sergeant 331*, 63.

69. *GA*, Augustus Jukes, M 607.

70. C.D. LaNauze, "From the Pampas to the Prairies, 1872–1885," *Canadian Cattleman*, December 1947, XI, No. 1, 35.

71. Nevitt, *Frontier Life in the Mounted Police*, 30.

72. *CH*, 13 July 1935.

73. *GA*, William Metzler, M 836.

74. *MFP*, 23 May 1878.

75. *GA*, Simon J. Clarke, M 228.

76. Donkin, *Trooper and Redskin*, 198.

77. Ibid. 181. For Wood Mountain see Chapter 16 (Problem-Solving).

78. *GA*, Duncan McEachran, M 736. Calgary was often spelled "Calgarry" in the early years.

79. *WDT*, 17 October 1884.

80. *RC*, NWMP, 1883, 29. Walter Hildebrandt, "Fort Battleford and the Architecture of the North-West Mounted Police," (Regina: Canadian Plains Research Centre, William Baker, ed., *The Mounted Police in Prairie Society*, 1873 –1919), 231–41.

81. *MFP*, 24 May 1880.

82. Guernsey, "The Passing of 'The Great Lone Land," *SG*, Ninth Annual, 35.

83. F.A.D. Bourke, "Recollections and Reminiscences," *SH*, XXXV, No. 2, 55. The daily ration was one and a half lb. of bread.

84. LaNauze, "From the Pampas to the Prairies, 1872–1885," 18.

85. Donkin, *Trooper and Redskin*, 40.

86. Ibid., 39.

87. *WDT*, 8 May 1879.

88. *GA*, William Metzler, M 836.

89. Fitzpatrick, *Sergeant 331*, 47–51.

90. Ibid.

91. *CH*, 13 July 1935.

92. Higenbotham, *When the West was Young*, 260–261.

93. *LH*, 23 June 1949.

94. *MFP*, 28 May 1881.

95. *RC*, NWMP, 1879, 32.

96. A list of the clothing kit is given in Donkin, *Trooper and Redskin*, 30–31.

97. *MFP*, 5 March 1880.

98. *CH*, 4 July 1925.

99. *MFP*, 6 October 1880.

100. Donkin, *Trooper and Redskin*, 30–31.

101. *MFP*, 21 May 1875.

102. *GA*, Edward Barnett, M 6142.

103. *Nor'Wester*, Vol. 100, No. 1, 15 July 1970.

104. *CH*, 3 September 1912.

105. Lovissa McDougall, *PAA*, #1 Occasional Papers, 12.

106. *NAC*, William McQuarrie, f. 724.

107. *Saskatoon Daily Star*, 31 March 1925.

108. Roger Pocock, *A Frontiersman*, 24.

109. Chapter 12, "A" Division, Maple Creek, 1884, FMP 80 153. Other examples: Chapter 6, Officers at Fort Walsh, *GA*, NA 98 – 15; Chapter 17, Non-commissioned Officers at Fort Walsh, *GA*, NA 659 – 30.

110. Smyth, *A Chronicle of the Canadian West*, 35.

111. *TM*, 2 February 1884.

112. Denny, *The Law Marches West*, 27.

113. Dunn, *The Alberta Field Force of 1885*, 159–171.

114. *NAC*, MG 29, E-47. Other members of the Force wounded were Constable Harrison in Regina (September 1885) and Sergeant Fletcher in Winnipeg (August 1874).

115. *LH*, 11 July 1935.

116. *NAC*, G.H. Johnston, f. 345.

117. *NAC*, Alfred Coulson, f. 641.

9

HORSES OF THE
MOUNTIES

Staff-Sergt. George Fraser, NWMP, with Old Buck

Old Buck became a great favourite of the Mounties as the last surviving horse of
the '74 journey. For all the men, it was a sad day in 1898 when Captain Richard
Deane shot the frail, thirty-two-year-old horse.

– GA NA 3173 – 11

CERTAINLY THE MOST REVERED POLICE HORSE was Old Buck.
At the Dufferin camp just prior to the western march, fifteen-year-old
Frederick Bagley had bought the mustang for fifty cents from a trooper
badly in need of grog. While the policeman drank, Bagley had Major Walsh
muster in the horse and assign it to Bagley. The young recruit rode Old

Buck across the plains.[1] As Old Buck aged, he became a great favourite of the Mounties as the last surviving horse of the '74 March. For all the men, it was a sad day in 1898 when Captain R. Deane shot the frail animal, aged thirty-two. Deane sent Bagley the last photo of the horse, one horseshoe, and his fore hoof with his last troop number (K 1) stamped thereon.

The men were amazed by their mounts. Among a group of horses that stampeded at Fort Battleford was Superintendent James Walker's Sport. When the horse was not found with the herd, it was assumed he was either dead or taken by Indians. However, six months later, in an extremely cold January, the horse appeared at Fort Walsh, almost 400 km south, and, as the astounded stable crew watched, Sport quietly walked into his former stall.[2]

Had not Charles Parker's horse, Custer, saved his life? In April 1883. the Mountie had left Stand Off with dispatches, but became snow-blind and lost his way. After five days with nothing to eat, a delirious Parker would have shot himself had he a pencil and paper to explain his death. His horse proved most helpful, standing near the sleeping Parker all night long, occasionally licking his face and, in the morning, coming up to be saddled. He was carrying Parker along the Benton Trail when they met up with the Macleod coach. A passenger described Custer as "almost human."[3]

On several occasions horses had guided their rider to shelter. On 31 December 1874, Inspector Cecil Denny left Fort Macleod for Fort Kipp to pick up the first mail delivered to the troop since they left the Dufferin camp six months earlier on their march west. When he was about halfway to his destination, a blizzard struck and night soon set in. Denny fastened the reins to the saddle's pommel and let the horse "have its head." Several hours later, the Mountie found himself surrounded by lighted windows. Without his realizing it, the horse had walked through the open gate at Fort Kipp and stopped in the middle of the square.[4] Constables Frank Baxter and T.D. Wilson died from exposure in this storm.

Young Constable William Metzler also had his horse carry him to safety. He was in a troop tracking horse thieves in the Crowsnest Pass when nightfall stopped their pursuit. The return to camp meant taking a narrow trail, less than a metre wide, overlooking a 30 metre cliff drop. Metzler related: "so I gave the mare her head to follow the trail and she followed the trail and I kept hollering to the others so they could follow me."[5]

And, in starving conditions, a horse could be shot and eaten. In December 1876, Major Walsh led a fifteen-man troop from Fort Walsh eastward in search of Sub-Inspector Edmund Frechette who had not returned from his mission to contact the Sioux Indians camped near Wood Mountain. Walsh wrote: "The weather was intensely cold, the snow deep, every day stormy and rations short. A band of buffalo we fortunately came across on our seventh day saved us from being forced to eat horse flesh."[6] However, by 1881, there were no buffalo to be had when Constable McDonald and his companion became lost while escorting an Indian horse thief suspect to Fort Battleford. The Mounties released their prisoner and shot one horse for food. This sustained the men until they reached the post.[7]

The value of having strong, healthy horses was truly indispensable for a mounted force. This was made evident to recruits arriving in 1881 at Fort Benton when they were met by an officer sent from Fort Walsh to guide them north. The man was described as a drunk and a ruffian who swore and abused the recruits with most engaging freedom and impartially. Once, when he saw a man on horseback, he ordered him with an oath to come down as horses were more valuable than men in that country.[8]

Attachment

The men spoke fondly of their favourite mount. Surgeon Barrie Nevitt's letters to his fiancée in Ontario routinely mention his horse. On the return of his horse from wintering in Montana Territory, Nevitt wrote: "He looks well, not very fat but in good order. He knew his old name and came up to me at once and ate some salt from my hand."[9]

Henri Julien, in spite of several trying incidents, praised the horse that carried him across the plains and back to Manitoba: "Old Rooster was not much to look at, but for the jog on the prairie, I could not ask for a better horse. I kept him to the end, and when I left the force at the end of my mission, I can honestly say that I parted from him with genuine regret."[10]

John Donkin reminisced about his horse as a game little fellow with whom he had many lonely winter rides over the plains. Bummer was obedient, intelligent, docile, and his head was pretty as a deer's. Donkin recalled: "He would lift his foreleg the moment you asked him to shake hands and no distance, and no continued hard riding ever played him out."[11] Donkin later mused about whatever happened to poor little Bummer:

Where are you now? Have you been "cast" I wonder, and sold to some sordid mossback? Or has your brave heart given way at last, and do your bones bleach on those great dreary plains you knew so well, and has your flesh formed food for the cowardly coyotes? Wherever you may be, Waes hael![12]

While serving in the Irish Constabulary, Commissioner George French had purchased Silver Blaze, a chestnut-coloured horse with a white blaze and white socks. He brought the horse to Canada and rode him during the '74 March. After leaving the NWMP in 1876, Commissioner French organized the New South Wales military police. He took Silver Blaze with him to Australia, making the horse, according to the *American Cavalry Journal*, one of the most traveled chargers in horse history.[13]

Police Horses

The Mounties branded the police horses "MP", most often on the left shoulder. A police farrier would shod the horses and stamp the animal's regimental number on the wall of the hoof. Due to the shortage of shoes for horses in the early years, a debilitated horse had its shoes removed before it was abandoned on the trail.[14] The men bobbed the tails for appearance which made police horses distinguishable from a distance. On this point, Constable W. Cox related that his camp on the Fort Walsh—Fort Macleod trail failed to recognize an approaching police courier. The rider, Sergeant Frank Spicer, explained that he had exchanged his tired police horse for a western horse.[15]

Police reports usually included the regimental number of a horse. The *Fort Battleford Post Journal*, for example, recorded that "Superintendent Crozier, Sergeant Fraser, Constable Worthington and Guide Laronde, with horses Nos. 14, 50, 210, 30, 199, 266, 269, and 408 arrived from Carlton this evening."[16] In addition to a regimental number, most mounts had an individual name as Horse No. 72, "Grizzly." In his diary, Constable R.N. Wilson routinely named the horse that he was riding, whether Tommy Colt, George, Grey Charlie, Snort, Curly, Baby, Dick, Billy, Cockney Coyote or Toby .[17] Colonel Macleod proudly rode Blackfoot. The monthly muster assembly included a parade and roll call of all the post's horses. A report—"Numerical Return of Horses"—was later forwarded to Headquarters. At Swan River in October 1875, "E" Division listed fifty horses, each with a comment. For example:

Reg. No. 471 lost
140 sent to Winnipeg to be cast
93 with General Smyth's escort
16 at Fort Qu'Appelle[18]

The men disliked the first saddles, the Universal Pattern.[19] While the Force was stationed at the Stone Fort in the winter of 1873—74, fifty saddles of this model had been purchased from the Canadian militia in Winnipeg. In Toronto Commissioner French purchased an additional 300 Universal saddles (known as a Driver's Saddle) from England giving the NWMP

NWMP Corporal with Horse, Fort Macleod

The police horses were usually branded "MP" on the left shoulder.

– GA NA 1385 – 3

enough saddles for the '74 March. The order, however, arrived too late for rider training in Toronto, and the saddles were not assembled until the Force reached Fargo, Dakota Territory. The twenty-three officers purchased their own choice of saddle. It was later suggested that the officers use the same saddle type for a consistent appearance at mounted parades.

A general complaint held that the Universal saddles needed continual repair and were awkward for work. In 1878, thirty California saddles, a lighter saddle with a pommel and higher seat—similar to the modern cowboy saddle—were purchased for trial use at Fort Walsh. By 1881, most of the Universal saddles were no longer serviceable and Commissioner A.G. Irvine added another one hundred California saddles. The men preferred the California model as a more durable and a better working saddle, especially when breaking broncos. It had no buckles, was better when rain-soaked, and its wooden stirrups were more practical for prairie work. With the purchase in 1884, of another 250 California saddles (at $24.50 each), this model became the standard saddle of the Force until well into the twentieth century. A leather bucket was attached to the saddle to hold a carbine.

The *Report of the Commissioner* each year recorded in detail the horses and accoutrements. In addition to the saddles, efforts were made to improve the equipment. The numnahs (saddle blankets) were of good appearance but wore poorly and were replaced by recommended English felt. The first halter-bridle broke too easily and was replaced by the Pelham bit until 1884, when it was discarded for the Whitman bit. The wagons and harness equipment were evaluated. The NWMP used four types of wagons:

1. Heavy Spring Wagon (Murphy wagon): for four horses
   It could carry one-and-a-half tons, was easy in running,
   and its high body made it suitable for crossing rivers.

2. Light Spring Wagon: for two horses

3. Heavy Buckboard: for two horses
   Suitable for a long trip for a party carrying
   bedding, rations, and forage.

4. Light Buckboard: for a single horse
   Suitable for work around the post.

Hobbles were indispensable when traveling. Rope hobbles were found inadequate and were replaced with two metal rings, hinged and connected by a metal link that was locked by a key, effectively preventing theft of the horse by Indians. A horse was picketed by a band around the fetlock connected by a rope to a 45 centimetres iron picket pin driven into the ground. The top of the picket pin had a swivel ring that allowed the horse to graze within the area of a circle.

Failure to secure a horse could be a serious mistake, a lesson that the artist Henri Julien learned on the western march. When Julien dismounted to pick up a dead duck, his horse scooted away. Each time Julien moved near, Old Rooster would move a few steps farther. This "teasing" went on for a frustrating 14 km. By then Julien had discarded the duck and, finding swearing ineffective, he tried a different strategy. "I promised him all sorts of things," Julien related, "and talked to him like a father. He was actually fooled. He turned his head to see that I was earnest, when I made a desperate plunge and seized the bridle."[20] Julien's problems were not over. While he was pursuing Old Rooster across the prairie, the column took a turn and Julien was lost. He prepared for the night in a sheltered hollow.

Julian tied Old Rooster's bridle to his pastern (above hoof) and, using the saddle for a pillow, had a restless sleep with the mosquitoes pestering him "beyond endurance." At sunrise, he woke to find that Old Rooster had broken loose. A second chase of 7 km followed before Julien caught his horse. Shortly after, a police search party arrived.

After Surgeon Barrie Nevitt unsuccessfully chased his own packhorse for 7 km, he commented: "I was not so much afraid of losing my scalp as the horse—if they are stolen our provisions would also go and we should starve."[21] The loss of his horse left the rider with no choice other than walking back to the base or camp.

When William Metzler's horse broke free from a feeding stake and héaded for the St. Mary post, it meant that the young Mountie had to cross a waist-deep river with flowing ice. William Parker described his unhappy situation: "Went for a ride on a bronco horse in the afternoon ... when six miles from the fort, I dismounted and he broke away from me so I had to walk home."[22] The day was December 27, a time of the year that could be life-threatening.

One account relates the dangers of the icy cold in winter:

> Tony LaChappelle and Ed Maunsell and a indian boy were going to Fort Benton And on the South Forks at Night There horses Stamp And While outlooking for them A bad Storm Came up. They were Eighty Miles From the Fort and walked in. Ed Maunsell got both [h]is feet frozen. LaChapelle [h]is face or chin pretty badly frozen. They had to kick the indian boy to keep him from sleeping. If not he would have frozen to death.[23]

At the tiny East End Post, the lone building was partitioned into two rooms—one for the men, the second for the two horses. When the wind blew the horse door open, the horses ran off. Hearing the slamming door, two half-dressed Mounties ran after their mounts in the bitterly cold December weather. It was a risky 3 km pursuit, but they returned like "two icicles" with the valuable animals.[24]

Number and Source of Police Mounts

The North-West Mounted Police began their western march with 310 horses. The loss of one-fourth of the mounts on the journey entailed purchasing horses en route and later in Montana Territory. The American purchases were very expensive: the cost of eleven horses in March 1875 was $4,970.[25] The Force required at least 300 horses to operate effectively.

The horses were assigned to one of the six Divisions. This distribution varied considerably. The number of mares, stallions, and gelded is not given. Below is a chart outlining the distribution of NWMP horses in 1879.[26] Some forts shared a Division such as Fort Macleod, Calgary, and Battleford that shared Division "E," while others were part of two Divisions such as Fort Walsh being part of Division "B" and "F," and Fort Macleod being part of Division "C" and "E."

DIVISION		HORSES	COLTS	TOTAL
"A"	Fort Saskatchewan	11	3	14
"B"	Fort Walsh/Outposts	76	2	78
"C"	Fort Macleod	78	38	116
"D"	Shoal Lake	32	1	33
"E"	Fort Macleod/Calgary	49	11	60
"E"	Battleford	27	–	27
"F"	Fort Walsh/Outposts	61	–	61
COMBINED TOTAL		334	55	389

YEAR	MEN	HORSES
1877	329	315
1880	299	354
1882	472	361
1884	557	349

Each detachment wanted the best horses available. W.D. Jarvis, at Fort Saskatchewan, complained that only three of his eleven "wretched" horses were fit for the saddle. Four of the horses had been left at his base by other divisions because they were unfit. The Fort Walsh detachment complained in 1882 that few of the horses (supplied at $150 each) were worthy. Blame focused on officials in Ottawa who tendered contracts without knowledge of what the police required.

There was a considerable turnover of horses each year. In 1881, 135 remounts (with five colts) were taken on, while twenty-four horses were cast, sold, or transferred to the Indian Department, and fifty-eight horses died. Most remounts came from the Western region. Of the 133 remounts added in 1882, 89 were purchased from the Stewart Ranch Company and four others from within the Territories. Seven western colts were added to the herd. Forty horses were brought from Ontario. The horses came west with the recruits each spring. Constable Royce, part of a seventy-five man party in 1881, remembered bringing thirty horses on an arduous rail, river boat, and overland trip to Fort Walsh. Along the way the animals required care, water, forage, and stops for exercise.

E.C. Oliver, just graduated from the Ontario Veterinarian College, related bringing horses west in 1879. His professor, Andrew Smith, invited Oliver to lunch with Commissioner James Macleod. This meeting resulted in Oliver gaining employment as a veterinarian surgeon in the NWMP. The twenty-three-year-old recruit was anxious to do well and, therefore, was upset a few days later when a hundred horses selected for the trip were paraded in Toronto.

Commissioner Macleod asked how many would make it West and Smith, the founder of the Ontario Veterinarian College, replied that he thought they would be lucky if half survived. Oliver wrote: "Colonel Macleod, seeing that I looked worried turned to me and said 'Oliver, you do the best for these horses as you can and if they die we know what to do with them.' I never forgot these words. It gave me courage and I did work hard to save them."[27]

On the thirty-day journey from Toronto to Fort Walsh, only two horses of the seventy-nine died—one with a broken neck on the Missouri River steamer, the second from sunstroke while on the trail north of Fort Benton. Oliver was, of course, pleased with his success.

Captured stray horses were turned over to the police. If they were not claimed, the detachment advertised the horses in the local paper. A column in the Fort Macleod Gazette listed twenty horses in police possession. Number 13, for example, was described "as a Chestnut mare, six years old. No brand, two near white feet, stripe on face. Owners obtain by proving property and paying expenses. L.N.F. Crozier."[28]

A two-day sale at Fort Macleod disposed of eighty-three horses. One auction in Regina, certainly had "shady" dealings when the police put up a notice before dusk and sold all the horses to policemen before breakfast. The local press complained that some citizens woke up to find the sale over and that the six town horse dealers knew nothing of the auction. The police buyers did well. Horses bought for $20 later sold for $120.[29]

At first, the NWMP horses deemed unfit were sold at public auction, usually for a modest sum. Since many of the animals were judged still capable for agriculture work, after 1879 it was arranged that the horses be assigned to the Indian Department to be used for farm animals on the newly created Indian reserves.

In 1879, the NWMP started a horse-breeding ranch at Pincher Creek. The location in the foothills, 50 km west of Fort Macleod, had ideal water and grazing conditions. Inspector A. Shurtliff along with a seven-man detachment built the log shacks and cut 28,000 rails for fences to contain the 200 horses.[30] A large 50 by 70 metres corral was built with pine poles 4 metre high. That year, the men harvested 2,300 bushels of oats and 325 tons of hay that provided ample forage. The oat crop was valuable as the previous year oats were purchased from St. Louis at $1.70 a bushel. One Mountie describes the task of the detachment: "To police the country from the boundary line to the Porcupine Hills and west to the Rockies, to raise horses for the force, start a farm and keep our buttons shined."[31]

In the late summer of 1881, four Métis brazenly stole 130 brood mares and young stock and drove this herd and 60 horses belonging to settlers south into Montana Territory. Several weeks later, they were arrested and most of the herd was returned to Pincher Creek. A second setback came when migrating geese, downed by a heavy snow storm, destroyed the 320-acre oat crop in three days. After four years, the police ranching venture was abandoned, the ranch was closed, and the NWMP contracted the care of fifty-two brood mares and sixty two-year olds to the nearby Stewart Ranch Company.

One persistent argument pitted the Ontario horses against their Western counterparts. That most horses on the '74 march from Eastern Canada had experienced difficulties opened up a comparison to the hardy western broncos, called cayuses. The larger Canadian horses appeared superior, but were not conditioned for the tough western life and quickly played out. In his report for 1874, Commissioner French reported that almost all Canadian horses fail during the first season they are fed on prairie grass.[32] Artist Henri Julien commented: "Government horses, like government men, being used to feed well, are apt to become too dainty."[33] Captain Denny judged the eastern horses, unaccustomed to grazing and looking out for themselves, as unable to stand the hardship. A trader who met "A" Division, which had left the main column for Fort Edmonton, noted that the fine-looking horses from Eastern Canada, "were not acclimatized and soon played out. We had cayuses which actually fattened up on the trip, so we pushed on and left the police behind."[34]

The *Manitoba Free Press* praised the tough, smaller Indian (western) ponies that cost nothing to feed, but herd together and live on prairie grass, winter and summer, as having more endurance than grain-fed Canadian horses. The paper added that it was surprising how they safely passed over ground thickly perforated with badger holes, while a Canadian horse would certainly break its rider's neck or its own neck.[35]

This initial negative assessment of the Ontario horses would soon change. The Canadian horses, in Commissioner French's opinion, had very good recuperative powers and, within months of completing the march west, they "were in good condition, and full of life and spirit, the ponies being still poor, though getting the same rations of the horses. I notice also that the extra cold has so stimulated the growth of hair that the horses have now nearly as heavy and dense coats as the ponies."[36] The Ontario horses adapted quickly to prairie life. Sub-Constable Grain observed the horses in the snow: "At first they would watch the broncos pawing for grass and when a spot had been cleared, would drive them away and eat the grass themselves."[37] In no time, they were foraging for their own grass.

Eastern horses were judged far superior when harnessed for hauling. At Swan River in March 1876, Commissioner French had Chief Constable Arthur Griesbach prepare a report on the horses for the Deputy Minister of Justice. Griesbach contended that, if more than five years of age, the Canadian horses, fulfilled every condition when well fed. "They were docile, easily trained, and will prove to be the cheapest and most efficient."[38] Supt. Winder agreed: "Canadian horses are, in my opinion, far more serviceable and preferable for police work to the native stock of Montana."[39] At Battleford, Superintendent Walker found, "the Bronco horses are not so good for all purposes as the Canadian horses and would recommend that Canadian horses be sent here when the division is increased."[40] Commissioner A.G. Irvine reported: "Experience has taught us that the best class of horses for the Force is to be had about the rural districts of Canada."[41] Eastern stallions were preferred as the breeding stock.

In the 1885 North-West Rebellion, the performance of western horses upgraded their value. Superintendent Herchmer observed that Canadian horses all gave out while not one native horse from the Alberta ranges failed: "this speaks volumes for our Alberta horses and very little for the police to bring in horses from lower provinces."[42] The *Calgary Nor'Wester*, commenting on the movement of the Alberta Field Force, recommended that military horses be native: "A western horse could rustle for itself, the eastern horse has been accustomed to have food brought to him three times a day and until he is acclimatized has a hard time generally. In short he would have starved where the western horses would pick a good living."[43] In the final military action in the Rebellion, troopers pursued Cree into the wilderness north of the North Saskatchewan River. John Donkin related, "the majority of the Ontario horses died off, after the Green Lake expedition; thus demonstrating the superiority of the native bred bronco for these climates."[44] It appears that a decisive consensus was never reached over the controversial merits of the two horse sources.

NWMP Constables Learning to Ride, 1880

"A man who cannot ride is useless for service in the police, in fact a mere encumbrance."

– A. G. Irvine, *Report of the Commissioner*, NWMP, 1880, 5

RCMP Historical Collections Unit, "Depot" Division, Regina, SK., 52–20–17

Horsemanship

In Commissioner A.G. Irvine's words, "a man who cannot ride is useless for service in the police, in fact, a mere encumbrance."[45] Quite simply put, skilled horsemanship was essential for a mounted force. Surgeon Kennedy invalided Charles Walsh because of a hernia, with the explanation: "He is totally unfit to ride, therefore unfit for service."[46]

A rider's failure to control his horse brought derision. During the troubles at the Big Bear-Poundmaker gathering near Battleford in 1884, mounted Indian warriors taunted the Mounties by charging the police line, stopping abruptly, and unfolding umbrellas to spook the police mounts. The Indians mocked Antrobus when the Inspector's horse shied, causing the officer to lose his helmet, and raced wildly away. Twenty-four years after he had left the Force, former Commissioner Irvine adamantly refuted a newspaper article that he had been pulled off his horse by Indians, asserting, "No man, white or red, ever pulled me off my horse."[47]

Riding training was strict. At the New Fort in Toronto, while preparing for the western trek, recruit William Parker remembered the "Sergt.-Major standing in the centre of the circle with his long whip driving us around bareback and when the command to trot was given, quite a few would tumble off into the sawdust."[48] Always the Sergt.-Major would shout out: "Who told you to dismount?" In spite of the early difficulties, however, within ten days most men could ride fairly well. In addition to riding skills, instruction included harnessing horses, saddling and bridling their mounts, and driving wagons.

Some horses balked when being harnessed. On the first days of the journey west, there was a commotion every morning hitching the uneasy horses to wagons. At times, the powerful animals were hard to control. William Parker's horse charged into a 4 metre embankment, smashing the cutter to smithereens, and ran off. As Parker cursed the fleeing horse, his riding companion, Bishop Machray, reproached him for swearing.

In the first two weeks of riding drill at Fort Walsh, the recruits rode bareback. The horses were well-trained and immediately followed all commands. On the order "Halt!" every horse would stop while most riders kept going. The Sergeant-Major would always yell (in what appeared to be a standard remark), "Who in hell told you to dismount?" For the next two weeks, the men trained using a saddle and, after a month's time, were competent riders. Recruits insisted that some horses were chosen to torment them. Sergeant Spicer's Charlie was one cayuse whose every step was intended "to split you in two."[49] As a final test, Corporal LaNaunce would lead the recruits for a wild ride through the timber, coulees, and hills. Those riders who failed to keep up were sent back for more training.

Most officers felt men with a rural background were the best candidates for managing the horses. An urgency to quickly add 600 recruits for the North-West Rebellion brought many unsuitable men into the Force. The Commissioner's report admitted: "A large population are unable to ride, and are unaccustomed to horses."[50] These qualifications were hardly suitable for the famous Riders of the Plains.

The men worked with and rode powerful animals that caused difficulties and recurring injuries. Trooper R.N. Wilson found his mount so stubborn that it took one hour to cross a stream near Pincher Creek. There were many injuries. At Fort Walsh, Constable Holtorf had his jaw broken from a kick while taking horses to water. C.E.D. Wood was invalided when a horse rolled over him. He then co-founded the *Fort Macleod Gazette*.

Constable Parker had his horse rear up and fall back, knocking the Mountie out. He awoke while an attendant was pouring water on his face. Parker had Fox brought out of the stable and rode him at a gallop for 20 km. Parker wrote: "I found my spurs covered with blood. We understood each other better after that."[51] Veterinarian John Poett required a cane for some time after being kicked by a horse. At the Dufferin thunderstorm stampede in June 1874, Sub-Constable William Latimer had his scalp torn from ear to ear. The Sick Report for 1885 lists seven cases of contusions caused by horse kicks, leaving the men off duty for eighty-eight days.

The presence of buffalo unnerved the horses. In July 1877, Major Walsh led a party 150 km from Fort Walsh to meet recruits at Fort Benton. The party experienced the utmost difficulty in making their way through the wild, restless herds that in some places were "so closely wedged together that the plain itself appeared to be swaying to and fro."[52] Buffalo stampedes terrified the horses, and the riders had to remain on constant alert.

West of Battleford, John "Doc" Lauder remembered buffalo "terribly frightened our horses and we spent most of the night holding them."[53] Even the smell of buffalo disquieted a horse. Trooper John Donkin wrote:

> Woe to anyone who suddenly approaches one of these youthful steeds, in an overcoat of shaggy buffalo skin. They have a shuddering horror of this, and will snort and strike out in abject fear. I saw a recruit nearly get his brains knocked out, by rushing into the stall of an unbroken bronco.[54]

Constable William Grain had his horse panic at the smell of a buffalo hide. He had left the column with his ox cart to help transport the meat and hide of a buffalo shot by Sergt.-Major Joseph Francis. When the two men lost contact with the column, it meant camping on the prairie for the night.

Group of Sergeants in 1880s

The horseshoe on the Sergeant's stripes indicates a riding instructor.

– Maple Creek Museum, P.2.4.

They tied Francis' horse and the ox to the cart and climbed under to sleep, using the newly skinned buffalo hide as a blanket. At once the frenzied horse broke from his restraint, inciting the ox to also break free. The animals were caught and again tied to the cart while the two men slept in the open a short distance way. In the morning, a search party found and returned the two lost men to the column.

The Mounties broke the tough western broncos. When one mare proved intractable, her rider raced her 23 km across the prairie, which "took the buck out of her for a while."[55] There were even instances when a bronco would throw a rider and then bite the prostate man. The Hospital Report for 1885 lists one man hospitalized for two days from the bite of a horse.

The "old hands" at Fort Walsh enjoyed watching the newly-arrived recruits break the wild broncos. Sergt.-Major Tommy Lake was the riding master. He would tell the recruits: "I won't give the details for mounting; just climb on and stay with it. The old hands had the poor kids filled up with what the broncs would do to them."[56] The arrival of twenty-five broncos at Regina led the local press to comment, "Some good sport may be anticipated from the combination of fresh men and fresh horses."[57]

Some injuries from the horses ended a police career. In August 1885, Constable John W. Boyd was thrown and trampled "by a vicious Bronco horse." Both bones in his left leg were badly shattered, severely limiting his mobility. An operation proved ineffective and, finally, a medical board in Ottawa in 1888 recommended a pension of thirty cents per diem for life.[58] In October 1876, Constable H. "Paddy" Homan was preparing for a horse race when his mount threw him so hard that onlookers thought he was dead. Homan was taken to the hospital where he remained insensible for five days. The effects of his injury were still evident nine days later. A comrade wrote on October 22: "Paddy Homan wanders around next to crazy—does not know what he is doing."[59] His excessive drinking further impeded Homan's recovery. A diary entry dated December 28 related: "Homan who has been dead drunk off and on for 14 days is now sober."[60] He had to be invalided from the Force.

There were also several riding fatalities. Albert Montgomery, a ten-year veteran of the Force, died in 1890 when his horse stumbled during a riding drill and threw him to the ground. He was unconscious for three days before his death. In May 1882, Constable W.G. Hillier died in the Fort Calgary post hospital from septicemia. Two months earlier, a kick from his horse had opened up a large, deep wound on the inner side of his knee. Although this was carefully dressed, blood poisoning developed soon after, leading to his death.

Three months later, Hillier's sister in Ontario wrote to the base that she had received a letter from a member of the troop, "saying that my brother was dead and buried."[61] She inquired if he had left any photographs and money from his wages. In the letters that followed, the property of Hillier appears as a primary concern, as she wrote: "for we (she and her brother) are in great need of it at present and I am sure that my brother was not married."[62] They received $82 from the sale of Hillier's kit and a Dominion Savings Bank account.

Care of the Horses

The police horses required daily attention. There were stables to clean, and grooming, exercising, watering and feeding of the mounts. Hay had to be cut and stored for winter. In cold weather, snow was melted for water or the horses were driven to a hole chopped in the ice of a nearby slough. It is noteworthy that, when the column reached Fort Macleod on the '74 March westward, the men built stables for the horses before their own accommodations. The Force provided a small pay bonus for men with skills as a farrier or saddler.

The NWMP departed for the West with one veterinarian, John Poett. He was trained in Scotland and spent a brief period in the Imperial army before practising at Stratford, Ontario. Being a married man with five children made Poett an atypical member of the Mounted Police.

During his three years of service, Staff-Sergeant Poett had considerable influence on the Force. He introduced up-to-date ideas such as having a veterinarian field wagon, and offered suggestions regarding saddlery, the care and use of remounts, and nutrition. Poett pointed out that, once an extensive trip was underway (as on the '74 March), without a complete rest, a debilitated horse never recovered. Moreover, after any lengthy trip, the horses needed sufficient rest before any further service. And better care of the horses, in Poett's opinion, would follow if each man was assigned a horse of his own—but this suggestion was never actualized.

Oats were essential in maintaining a horse's stamina. On the '74 March, Colonel Macleod left the column on three occasions to purchase oats from the Boundary Commission. The price was high, but Commissioner George French approved. "Oats, at any price," he wrote, "is a Godsend to the poor horses."[63] Poett recommended a saddle horse be given 10 lbs. of oats daily and a draught horse 12 lbs. One order alone at Fort Walsh in 1875 was for 210,000 lbs. of oats at a cost of $15,400. To facilitate the Governor General's tour in 1881, the Mounted Police had stores of oats and fresh horses waiting along the proposed route.

The need of the horses for rest, forage, and water impacted on the mobility of the Force. On the '74 train excursion west, it was necessary to stop for two days in Chicago to feed and exercise the 300 horses. Horses traveling with recruits by steamer up the Missouri River had to be taken ashore several times each day for exercise and grazing. On a trip from Fort Walsh to Winnipeg in August 1876, Sergt.-Major Joseph Francis covered 90 km one day. That evening, mare number 134 had a foal, which delayed travel the next day. To make up time, Francis exchanged four weakened horses for sturdy animals at Fort Qu'Appelle.

The horses suffered from many ailments. On the '74 journey westward, drinking alkaline water weakened many horses with diarrhea. Veterinarian Poett treated any debilitated animals with a mixture of starch, flour, and carbolic acid. Colonel Macleod used a cumbersome sling along with a block-and-tackle to hoist weakened horses off the ground and give their legs a much-needed rest.

A deadly and very highly contagious disease for the horses was glanders, marked by coughing, fever, swollen lymph nodes, and a nasal discharge. There was no effective treatment for this disease and, when eight horses at the Battleford post were diagnosed with glanders, they were immediately shot. The NWMP also shot other horses with glanders that belonged to settlers. According to the *Moosomin Courier* on 23 July 1885, Veterinarian Poett ordered two horses belonging to settler J.D. Murray be shot. The carcasses were hauled away to rot or sometimes be eaten by starving Indians.

Two other serious afflictions for horses were mange and foot rot. Mange was indicated by itching, scratching, and accompanying hair loss. In winter this proved fatal. Foot rot, a contagious and painful bacterial infection, damaged the hoof, crippling the horse.

Functional and warm stables helped in the care of horses. The two stables at Fort Macleod each had thirty-eight stalls, two by three metres, partitioned by two-inch planks. Three large ventilators on each roof helped remove stagnant air. The buildings were lighted by a window in each stall and lights over the doors. The flooring in the stalls was sloped for drainage. Manure was regularly removed. At Fort Walsh, the stable crew isolated sick horses in a nearby "sick barn" that contained six stalls. The post also had a shed with a water well and two elevated water troughs to keep the horses hydrated.

The police posts had inadequate means of fighting fires. When a raging fire was spotted at two o'clock in the morning in the Battleford barracks, the detachment could do little other than protect the nearby buildings. The large stable, along with six adjacent work and storage rooms, had been completely destroyed. Some horses were rescued, but six of the best North-West Mounted Police horses and Inspector Herchmer's fine mount were lost in the fire. One witness wrote of the conflagration: "It was agonizing to stand by and hear the poor horses burnt to death, they were neighing, snorting & kicking at a frightful rate."[64]

A Hard Life

The police horses led a hard life. Commissioner Irvine conceded: "Few people understand the extraordinary amount of work that the police horses perform ... the distance traveled by Constable Armour and his team from the 1st April to the 1st November last was 3,080 miles [5130 km]."[65] In an urgent situation, a horse could be pressed to cover great distances. During the North-West Rebellion, Staff-Sergeant Sam Horner rode Caesar from Fort Macleod to Calgary in one day, a distance of 165 km. In another example, a NWMP constable brought the mail for Governor General Marquis of Lorne (on his western tour) by riding 170 km in twelve hours.

Upon his return to Fort Macleod from the General Terry-Sitting Bull conference, Surgeon Barrie Nevitt wrote in his journal: "On one day we had to travel from sunrise to sunset without stopping and without water. This was extremely tiresome and hard on the horses."[66] It took one police troop three days to cross a massive burnt-out area. The horses suffered terribly. At the tiny St. Mary outpost, having nothing to feed the horses, the men turned them loose. The hungry animals did not stray far and broke into a storage tent and ate the flour. On the '74 March, at least eighty-three horses died or were abandoned. "Dead Horse Coulee" was an accepted name for the column's three-day camp in the Sweet Grass Hills.

A significant number of horses died each year. In 1881, there were fifty-eight deaths—one in every seven mounts. And the end could come quickly. Constable W. Metzler's diary states: "Started for Whoop-Up this morning ... the horse I was riding fell and broke his leg and we had to shoot him on the spot."[67] Constable Parker had horse No. 417 throw himself backward and die in two minutes.

Badger holes were troublesome. Only two months before Metzler's horse broke his leg, another of his mounts, Old Bob, stepped in a badger hole and had to be shot. Constable Bottrell's horse, rising from a fall in a badger hole, rolled upon the prostrate rider, the saddle catching Bottrell in the small of the back and injuring his spine. Sam Steele recounted a horse-injury experience: "The poor animal rolled over my head ... and when he staggered to his feet the blood poured from his nostrils, as his head had struck gravel and stones, giving him a severe shock."[68]

Sergt.-Major Breadon, NWMP

"Summer patrols were fine fun, full of adventure and continued excitement. A party of men will start out in June and travelled all summer, going over thousands of miles of country ... these trips are what the men love, and what keeps them in the Force."

– *MFP*, 21 April 1880
  RCMP, Regina 72–82–5

In summer, mosquitoes and horseflies (called bulldogs) plagued the horses. Riding from Fort Brisebois (Calgary) westward to the Morley Mission, Surgeon Nevitt was bothered by clouds of mosquitoes penetrating his eyes, nostrils, ears and mouth. "The horses," he wrote, "were grey with the swarms clustering on them."[69] Constable Tom Clarke found herding horses at night taxing as the animals were unable to withstand the savage attacks of sand flies and the swarming droves of mosquitoes:

> At such times a white colored animal could not be distinguished from his darker colored mates ... rub a hand down the neck or back of an animal and it came away with a massed pulp of broken and crushed insects ... smudges had to be kept burning and in this smoked-filled surroundings the horses would stand, shifting their positions as the wind changed its direction.[70]

Frantic to escape the insect bites, some tormented horses would roll in the ashes of the smudges, sometimes severely burning themselves. William Parker, delivering the mail to Swan River, had clouds of mosquitoes drive his mount desperate: "The horse would stop about every fifteen minutes and would refuse to go on unless I got out of the buckboard and rubbed my hand all over her ... blood would be dripping from off my hand from the numbers I had brushed off."[71]

In June 1885, a troop of sixty-two cowboys and Mounties under the direction of Sam Steele joined the Alberta Field Force assigned to attack Big Bear. At Edmonton, the men used a two-week stay to accustom the skittish horses to noisy cannon fire by gradually moving them closer to the shelling. Further training conditioned the mounts to remain stationary when a trooper fired his rifle while it was placed across the animal's back.

After traveling east to a skirmish at Frenchman's Butte, Steele's Scouts pursued Big Bear's band through the difficult bush country north of Fort Pitt. Mosquitoes and horseflies tormented the horses and the only forage available was tough slough grass. Each night, the men would build smudges to protect their tethered horses from the myriads of mosquitoes flying about. The harassed animals could be seen with their noses buried in the smoke to escape the insect hordes.

In spite of these difficulties, on June 3 the troop rode 85 km in just thirty-one hours to attack the Indians at Loon Lake. After this skirmish, Steele's Scouts, short of supplies, returned to Fort Pitt. A measure of the suffering of the horses was evident from the numbers—only twenty-six of the seventy-five horses that began the pursuit returned to the fort.

If a police horse's life was difficult, it became intolerable when his rider ate the oats. But that is what Constable William Metzler did when he and his mount were immobilized for three days by a blizzard.

Horse Stealing

The theft of horses continually disrupted policing efforts in the North-West Territories. Warnings to the Indians to stop stealing "pinto buffalo" went unheeded. In 1880, Superintendent Leif Crozier reported 5,000 Indians in the Fort Walsh–Wood Mountain area "all stealing," and he feared there would be bloodshed between the tribes. It was, he maintained, only by prompt police action and mediation that the trouble was minimized. A visiting correspondent for the *Toronto Globe* observed that the Mounted Police "are kept in hot water by the persistent efforts of the Indians to steal all the horses they can lay their hands on. Every day during the last week expeditions have been sent out in search of the thieves."[72]

Bold Indian horse thieves even targeted the police horses. At Wood Mountain in 1878, "Peaches" Davis was assigned to guard a police herd of forty horses, with orders to shoot anyone wearing a blanket or hovering around the animals. Davis picketed his horse behind a small butte from where he could watch the Teton camp. For three weeks, his guard was uneventful. Then two war-whooping Indians drove about twenty horses beside the grazing police herd and collected four police horses as they rode away. Davis fired wide to scare the thieves. His rifle report alerted Major Walsh at the police camp. Davis recalled:

> The major asked me what all the shooting was about. I told him all that had happened. Then he asked me why I had not carried out his orders. Replying, I told him I thought it better not to shoot to kill ... the major told me that I was not paid for thinking, and threatened to give me six months for direct disobedience of orders, but owing to my youth and inexperience he would forgive me and that "the next time you fire at an Indian get him, or he'll get you."[73]

Big Bear's band executed an even more defiant theft of police horses. One Mountie recalled "the air was blue with unprintable words" when Commissioner Irvine learned that Indians had told a police guard that they were short of horses and galloped off with the police herd.[74] Irvine chose to respond personally to this "insolence" and selected a troop of one officer and twenty-two men to accompany him. They were issued extra ammunition and told to clean their uniforms to impress the Indians.

The troop unexpectedly met the band on a long ridge. The Indians looked formidable in their war paint and feathers. The chief, Big Bear, fully decked out and carrying a large Hudson's Bay knife, was astride a horse with the police brand.

The policemen dismounted and formed a circle around Big Bear, Irvine, and Jerry Potts, the interpreter. A spirited talk followed while, on the outside, Indian braves glowered and threatened the police. Irvine told Big Bear to return all stolen horses within a week. He would give the one he was riding (with the police brand) immediately. Edward Barnett recalled:

> All hell had broke loose amongst a violent mob of half-naked, red-painted heathens. They danced around us ferociously while brandishing their weapons—their tempers intense. We stood back to back in fours for mutual protection with revolvers drawn ... one act of violence would set off a human volcano.[75]

Shooting was avoided when Big Bear raised his hand and, at once, the braves quieted down. The order to mount was given and the police rode sedately through the large Indian camp. Barnett recalled: "Once out of sight our pace changed to a gallop—we weren't taking any chances on them changing their minds."[76] And as instructed, a week later, several Indians brought the stolen police horses to Fort Walsh.

Most police searches of the Indian horse herds were uneventful but, as the encounter with Big Bear showed, potential bloodshed could never be ruled out. In one case, Inspector Dickens, Sergeant Spicer, and Constable Callaghan escorted several Americans searching for stolen horses to the Blood reserve where, after discussions with Chief Red Crow, fourteen horses were recovered.[77] While the party waited at a corral for yet another horse, a minor chief, Many Spotted Horses, implored the Indians not to give up horses and a second Indian accused the Americans of stealing horses belonging to a band member. Although this allegation was denied, the situation deteriorated. White Cap, with some young men now "yelling and howling," attempted to seize the Americans. Inspector Dickens, finding it impossible to get a word in, placed himself between the parties. Sergeant Spicer coolly distracted the Indians, allowing Dickens to leave with the stolen horses to Fort Macleod. The party was unmolested, but learned afterwards that a war party had attempted to intercept their passage.

At Stand-Off on the Blood Reserve, corporals R.N. Wilson and Tom LaNauze recognized a horse that was stolen in the Cypress Hills. They drove the animal into a corral only to have an Indian rope and claim the horse. LaNauze choked the Indian into submission and the two Mounties rode away, leading the horse. However, angry Indians stopped them at the Reserve agency. Two minor chiefs, White Calf and Wolf Collar, told warriors not to allow the Mounties to take the horse. Wilson recalled,

> The Indians sent for their rifles & cartridge belts, a movement which was quite uncalled for as Tom & I were both unarmed. While the Indians were talking we suddenly wheeled our horses and made a run for it, of course taking the captured horse with us. We were riding old nags "George and Grey Charlie" that could not go fast enough to keep themselves warm.[78]

In no time, the Indians overtook the two Mounties and a second long discussion began. Wilson using his "most eloquent" Blackfoot convinced One Spot that the Indians were only getting themselves into trouble. The chief ordered his band members back to their lodges, leaving the two policemen to return to Fort Macleod with the stolen horse.

Not all police searches for stolen horses in Indian camps were successful. Albert Harrison from Montana Territory was annoyed when Inspector Crozier refused to search for forty-eight stolen horses believed on the Blood Reserve. When later pressed by a reporter to explain his inaction, the Superintendent responded, perhaps flippantly, that there were more Indians than white men.[79]

As prairie settlement grew, white rustlers from the United States added to the horse-stealing problem. One police report labeled the American horse thief "a desperado of the worst description, who holds the life of a man as cheaply as that of an animal."[80] Superintendent Crozier reported: "I very much fear that killing and stealing will increase to such an extent that the country along the border will scarcely be habitable."[81] A letter written in 1882 from Fort Macleod suggested that "horse stealing might become the leading industry of this place this summer."[82] The situation had failed to improve. The *Report of the Commissioner* in 1884 stated that theft of horses "is the marked feature of this year's annals of crime."[83]

Legal differences between the countries contributed to the increasing problem. Montana Territory, unlike Canada, had no law that prohibited bringing in stolen horses, although the animals were sometimes recovered. The *Fort Macleod Gazette* editorialized: "At present the law regulating stolen horses is very one-sided. While our laws will punish the Indian who steals a horse and brings him to this country ... the American Indian can steal from us with impunity and return to his country scot-free."[84] Commissioner Irvine, while acknowledging that American troops had eagerly assisted in the recovery of stolen property, commented: "A large proportion of the horses stolen in US territory have eventually been recovered by the police and returned, horses stolen by American Indians are almost never returned."[85] Irvine advocated that horse stealing become an extraditable offence between the two nations.

American settlers voiced complaints when Canadian Indians raided their frontier. In October 1881, a party of American ranchers arrived at Fort Macleod with a letter from Sheriff Johnny Healy over the loss of fifty horses stolen by Canadian Blood Indians. Healy warned that "the people of Montana have tired of being harassed by the marauding hordes of the north, and will wreak vengeance upon all war parties caught this side of the line."[86] Canadians, in turn, claimed that they received unfair treatment in retrieving stolen horses. Superintendent Shurtliff at Maple Creek commented:

> Anyone not familiar with the circumstances would think, on
> reading of reported raids in the Montana press, that our Indians
> were the only guilty ones and that their people were the only

sufferers. On the contrary ... their Indians and white thieves were constantly stealing from settlers and railway contractors on this side ... this horse stealing has become a very serious matter, as nearly every settler along the line of road in this section of the country has lost horses during the past season.[87]

Canada pursued an effective deterrent to crime through the *Vagrant Act* whereby loitering, indolent, or suspicious characters could be arrested. In 1884, there were twenty-four arrests for vagrancy with penalties that ranged from court dismissal to six months' imprisonment.

Canadian settlers censured the NWMP for failing to protect property. John Glenn told the Rev. Alexander Sutherland (who, in 1881, was touring the region for the Methodist church) that "we have no protection from the police. Indians may steal our cattle ... but we can get no redress. In that respect we would be better off if there were no police in the country at all."[88] A letter (exasperated over the theft of fifty horses from Red Deer Forks and Maple Creek) proposed that the government "will be required to do something, as the Mounted Police have long ceased to protect the country from horse thieves."[89] Broadview, Saskatchewan, was described as "infested" with horse thieves. A newspaper railed: "The absence of police protection being at the bottom of this state of things. How could two constables near the Manitoba border be considered protection for the whole eastern part of the country?"[90] Settlers at nearby Wolseley wanted the overstretched police to be stationed all along the line to curtail horse thieves. Commissioner Irvine regarded settler demands as unreasonable, in that, right after reporting a theft, they expected that the police would immediately scour the entire countryside.

In fairness to the NWMP, a 900-km border between the North-West Territories and the United States made policing difficult. Commissioner Irvine maintained that, his Force exerted the utmost effort to prevent horse theft "but I question if any force, however strong, could successfully bring about such a prevention."[91] The American horse thieves could choose the target place and escape route and, knowing the whereabouts of the police, pick the time for theft. Some horse thieves, it was claimed, even received information from paid contacts or agents in Canada.

It was a twelve-hour ride from the C.P.R. line to the border. The rustlers drove a stolen herd at top speed, switching mounts, and abandoning any lagging animals on the trail. When eight valuable horses, in training for the Dominion Day races, were stolen at Moosomin, a telegraph message had the police come by a special train from Regina, but pursuit was useless as the thieves were well on their way to the border. Farther west, horse

Crowsnest Pass Horse Thieves at Fish Creek (south of Calgary), 1884

"The prevalence of horse stealing by white men, half-breeds and Indians, indiscriminately throughout the Territories, is a marked feature of this year's annals of crime."

– A. G. Irvine, *Report of the Commissioner*, NWMP, 1884, 14
GA PD 262 – 37

thieves had hidden locations in the Cypress Hills from where, in one day, they could reach the Missouri River. Indian horse thieves left camp on foot individually or in small parties to later rendezvous at a pre-arranged point. They usually stole horses at night or during times of inclement weather and took a route that was difficult to track.

Some arduous police pursuits of horse thieves were successful. In the summer of 1884, three "Missouri Marauders" stole horses near Swift Current. Led by scout Léveille, a police party trailed the horses to a wooded area in the Cypress Hills. As the rustlers prepared a mid-day meal, the pursuers approached noiselessly and arrested the men without a struggle. They were returned to the barracks and imprisoned: Moise Racette to seven years and J.H. Brady (or Bradley) to three years in the penitentiary.[92] And, in another case, Jean Baptiste Robillard, a noted horse thief who bragged that there were not enough police in the country to catch him, found himself arrested and sentenced to three years in the penitentiary.[93]

Canadian courts dealt harshly with convicted horse thieves, making the lengthy sentences given to Racette and Brady not exceptional. In the first recorded case of a horse conviction, James Brooks (known as "Slim Jim") was sentenced to five years in the Stony Mountain Penitentiary. He drove the wagon with his police guard across the prairies to Manitoba. Ironically, upon Slim Jim's release, he found employment as a prison guard. Examples of strict sentences include: Ka-kah-wask, five years (1881); Little Fisher, five years (1881); and, in 1883, a group of eleven Indians each received two years for bringing stolen property (horses) into Canada.

The severe sentences failed to foil some horse thieves. As soon as he was released from prison, Pete Matt, accompanied by two young willing Métis women, ran off with five horses and six saddles stolen at Fort Macleod. The NWMP made a determined effort to arrest the well-known horse thief by sending a patrol into Montana Territory and posting a $500 reward. Matt evaded all pursuit.

South to Montana Territory was the wrong direction for a horse thief to take. The *Butte Miner* commented on the lynching of Pete Matt: "Matte [sic] was a professional horse thief, a man whose removal was necessary to the safety of his fellow citizens ... when a man's life is such that he has shown conclusively to be a dangerous enemy of his fellow men, the sooner he is called upon to give up that life the better."[94]

The horse thieves were rough and dangerous men. When Inspector A.R. Macdonell met a horse herd being driven toward the United States, the riders pulled off the trail and signaled Macdonell and his companion to pass, at the same time covering the police with their rifles. Under the circumstances, Macdonell knew that he was powerless and, after a few words they moved on, leaving the suspected horse thieves to continue on their journey to Dakota Territory.

In August 1885 near Moose Mountain, a horse thief named Frank Wilson (alias Williams) shot Constable Frank Sayers in the thigh. Relays of horses rushed a doctor to treat Sayers. A detail led by Sergeant Kempster, with interpreter Léveille, Constable LeQuesne, and eight hired Indians, unsuccessfully searched for Wilson.

Two murders were attributed to horse thieves. In late May 1884, 16 km southwest of Maple Creek, Indians shot a rancher, Saul Pollock, who had gone to the corral in the dark to investigate noises. Ranch hands carried the twice-wounded victim to the ranch house, but he soon died. Superintendent Norman at Maple Creek was certain that the murderers,

Constable Victor J. St. George, Fort Walsh 1882

In addition to a regimental number, most mounts had an individual name as Horse No. 72, "Grizzly." Mounties would routinely name the horse they were riding, whether it was Tommy Colt, Toby, Grey Charlie, Snort, Curly, Baby Dick, Billy, or Cockney Coyote.

– RCMP Museum, Regina, SK. 1933–20–49

were marauding South Piegans from Montana, whom he believed had stolen 106 area horses the previous year. He detailed Sergeant Paterson with six Mounties to follow the trail of five Indians, but the police party failed to overtake the mobile killers. The murder unnerved area settlers, reminding them of their isolation and vulnerability.

Six months later, a second murder occurred after Blood Indians ran off horses near the mouth of the Red Deer River. Four men started after the stolen horses but they became separated and one, a Métis named Charles Paul, was shot and killed. His companions reconstructed the death scene by observing his wounds and the horse tracks. They concluded that Paul had seen his stolen horses tied in the brush and, as he approached, was shot in the shoulder. He crouched down and a second shot grazed his stomach, forcing him up a pathway where he was fatally shot. The Indians had left fresh beef and a hide, evidence of a cattle killing.

Paul's companions notified the police in Maple Creek but, after waiting unsuccessfully for a coroner to conduct an inquest, they sent his body to Manitoba by rail. The *Fort Macleod Gazette* commented that here was a poor man shot down in cold blood while trying to recover his property. The paper harshly condemned the Indians:

> a lot of sentimental trash is written about the "Poor Indian," and the hard time he is having in the face of advancing civilization. Those who know them better have no such pity for them and it is by such outrages as this that they turn the country against them. No western man loves an Indian, and the reason is plain —they know them too well.[95]

No one was arrested in either murder.

NOTES

1. Bagley, "The '74 Mounties," No. 3, 33. When Fred P. (Pace?) re-assessed his exchange, he declared "That boy is a natural damned horse thief, and he'll come to a bad end at the hands of Vigilantes." The two men, at reunions years later, amiably recounted the "theft."

2. *SH*, 10 January 1881. Temperatures recorded that week: Fort Pelly -50°C; Fort Edmonton -40°C.

3. *FMG*, 14 April 1883. Parker suffered from frost bite and surgeons excised part of both ears. Higenbotham, *When the West was Young*, 181−85, contains a thirty-four-verse poem on the incident.

4. Denny, *The Law Marches West*, 54−55.

5. *GA*, William Metzler, M 836.

6. *PAM*, James A. Walsh, MG 6, A-1. Letter to Cora.

7. *RC*, NWMP, 1878, 26. The prisoner was later apprehended and sentenced to a five-year prison term.

8. *MFP*, 27 July 1881.

9. Nevitt, *Frontier Life in the Mounted Police*," 65−66; and 125, "Old Satan is looking perfectly magnificent, not too fat but sleek & well put together."

10. Julien, "Expedition to the North-West," 18.

11. Donkin, *Trooper and Redskin*, 282−83.

12. Ibid. A mossback was a backwoods settler or rustic. *Waes hael!* is a drinking toast "be well."

13. The Boundary Commission NWMP Trail Association, *An Astonishing Cavalcade −The 1874 Route of the North West Mounted Police Across Manitoba* (Winnipeg: Soaring Eagle Enterprise), 1995.

14. These abandoned horses often survived. Five horses left on the Governor General's 1882 tour were found the following year, 150 km from where they had been left.

15. *CH*, 25 April 1957. Gabriel Léveille remembered, as an eight-year-old observer of the '74 March, that the police horse tails were bobbed right to the bone and were of no use to keep off the mosquitoes and flies.

16. *Fort Battleford Post Journal*, 9 January 1885.

17. *NAC*, R.N. Wilson, MG 29, E-47.

18. *NAC*, RG, v. 7, f. 413−75.

19. For more about saddles, see William and Nora Kelly, *The Horses of the Royal Canadian Mounted Police* (Toronto: Doubleday, 1984), 181−188. Franklin M. Loew and Edward H. Wood, *Vet in the Saddle* (Saskatoon, Saskatchewan: Western Prairie Books, 1978), 34−44.

20. Julien, "Expedition to the North-West," 18.

21. *GA*, Richard Nevitt, M 892.

22. *GA*, William Parker, M 934.

23. *GA*, Simon J. Clarke, M 228.

24. Fitzpatrick, *Sergeant 331*, 51.

25. *CSP*, (No.188) A. 1879, *Expenditure for the North-West Mounted Police*, 1876–78, 187.

26. *RC*, NWMP, 1879, 5. Also *RC*, NWMP, 1876, 24; *RC*, NWMP, 1880, 12; *RC*, NWMP, 1882, 17; *RC*, NWMP, 1884, 67.

27. *NAC*, E.C. Oliver, f. 373.

28. *FMG*, 14 August 1883.

29. *RL*, 17 May 1883.

30. Sergeant Parker, Constables David Grier, Charlie Kettles, Jack Johnson, J. Bruneau, Peter McEwan, Bill Reid, A.H. Lynch-Staunton.

31. Lynch-Staunton, *Prairie Grass to Mountain Pass*, 1.

32. *RC*, NWMP, 1874, 11.

33. Julien, "Expedition to the North-West," 12.

34. "Narrative of James Gibbons," W.A. Griesbach, ed., *AHR*, VI, No. 4, 14.

35. *MFP*, 21 May 1880. *TG*, 17 May 1880.

36. *RC*, NWMP, 1874, 23.

37. Grain, "Pioneers of a Glorious Future," 73.

38. *NAC*, VIII, 29-1876.

39. *RC*, NWMP, 1879, 10.

40. *RC*, NWMP, 1883, 23.

41. *RC*, NWMP, 1880, 13.

42. *FMG*, 11 August 1885. Herchmer furthers this claim in *RC*, NWMP, 1885, 54.

43. *CN*, 14 May 1885.

44. Donkin, *Trooper and Redskin*, 165.

45. *RC*, NWMP, 1880, 5.

46. *NAC*, Charles Walsh, f. 573.

47. *LH*, 7 January 1909.

48. Dempsey, ed., *William Parker Mounted Policeman*, 4. On training also *LH*, 11 July 1935.

49. Rookie #2, "Remembrances of a Tenderfoot," 58.

50. *CSP*, 1885, Vol. XIII, No. 153, 13.

51. Dempsey, ed., *William Parker Mounted Policeman*, 39. Also see George McKay, *Fighting Parson* (Kelowna, B.C., 1978), 99-101.

52. *HDI*, 10 July 1877.

53. John (Doc) Lauder, *AH*, XXXVII, No. 4, 28.

54. Donkin, *Trooper and Redskin*, 35

55. *GA*, William Metzler, M 836.

56. Parks Canada, *Fort Walsh National Historic Park*, 39.

57. *RL*, 27 November 1884.

58. *GA*, RCMP fonds, M 8380.

59. James Stanford Diary, UMSA, Missoula.

60. Ibid.

61. *NAC*, W.G. Hillier, f. 685. Apparently, the information on Hillier's death reached his sister from non-official sources.

62. Ibid.

63. *RC*, NWMP, 1874, 42.

64. *GA*, William Parker, M 934, f. 18.

65. *RC*, NWMP, 1880, 13.

66. Nevitt, *Frontier Life in the Mounted Police*, 190.

67. *GA*, William Metzler, M 836.

68. Steele, *Forty Years in Canada*, 145.

69. Nevitt, *Frontier Life in the Mounted Police*, 130. Also Duncan McEachran, *GA*, M 736.

70. *LH*, 12 January 1944.

71. *GA*, William Parker, M 934, f. 11.

72. *TG*, 4 June 1880. An interesting account of stolen horses is given by an unidentified Mountie in "Recovering Stolen Horses," *SG*, Second Annual, 101.

73. Davis, "Peaches," "Chasing Horse Thieves," *SG*, Fifteenth Annual, 46.

74. *GA*, Edward Barnett, M 6142.

75. Ibid. In what was mostly likely the same confrontation, Commissioner Irvine wrote that he returned to Fort Walsh with thirty-two stolen horses. *RC*, NWMP, 1882, 10.

76. *GA*, Edward Barnett, M 6142.

77. Dickens told the Indians that, if they had a claim or complaint, they could come and speak to Superintendent Crozier at Fort Macleod.

78. *NAC*, R. N. Wilson, MG 29, E-47. Also see account by Wilson that involved rifle fire on 28 July 1882.

79. *TG*, 6 May 1882.

80. *RC*, NWMP, 1884, 15.

81. *RC*, NWMP, 1880, 33.

82. *FBR*, 22 June 1882. *MFP*, 5 August 1882.

83. *RC*, NWMP, 1884, 14. The following year (1885), military patrols during the North-West Rebellion completely eliminated horse stealing.

84. *FMG*, 24 November 1885.

85. *RC*, NWMP, 1883, 17. *FBRP*, 4 April 1885. *WDT*, 7 December 1881.

86. *RC*, NWMP, 1881, 15-16.

87. *RC*, NWMP, 1883, 17-18.

88. Sutherland, *A Summer in Prairie Land*, 52.

89. *SH*, 7 July 1883.

90. *MFP*, 16 July 1884.

91. *RC*, NWMP, 1883, 18.

92. *MFP*, 10 July 1884. Another successful pursuit and arrest of horse thieves by Constable Lewis Hooper is recounted in Chapter 11 – *Maintien le Droit*.

93. *FBRP*, 5 July 1882. Robillard escaped from the Fort Walsh guardhouse and apparently left the country.

94. *New North West*, 22 March 1878.

95. *FMG*, 7 November 1884. *FBR*, 15 June 1877.

10

PASS THE TEA AND LET US DRINK

S.J. "Jack" Clarke, NWMP, in Plainsman Costume, Fort Walsh, 1876

"At Moose Jaw, a literary looking character, carrying a valise did not fool Corporal Fyffe who upon investigation of the valise found that two beautiful bound volumes of 'History of England' were made of tin, and ... he found them full of alcohol."

– *Regina Leader*, 16 October 1885
GA NA 644 – 1

LEGISLATION PROHIBITED THE IMPORTING of alcohol into the North-West Territories. A legal loophole for obtaining spirits, however, was a permit signed by the Lieutenant Governor. A typical permit (marked not transferable), issued on 17 December 1878 to John Stuttaford, stationed at Fort Walsh, authorized two gallons of brandy and two gallons of port wine for "medicinal or sacramental purposes." Commenting on the point of "medicinal purposes,"[1] the local newspaper suggested, with tongue in cheek, that "Calgary must be a very unhealthy place."[2]

The glut of alcohol that entered the Territories served to reinforce the widely held opinion that the permit system flouted the law. In 1884, for example, approval had been given for more than 10,000 gallons of spirits for an adult white population (the natives received no permits) of 7,000 people—more than one gallon of alcohol for each adult.[3] It was said, one policeman noted, that after the arrival of the alcohol the life of a permit never exceeded twenty-four hours.[4]

The permit system was roundly criticized. The *Moosomin Courier* declared that this "whole system is a huge farce leaving the matter in hands of the Lieutenant Governor who can grant a permit to whom he pleases or refuse it when he sees fit without any reason being given for his actions."[5] At issue were several liquor applications that Stipendiary Magistrate Colonel James Macleod had supported, but were rejected and with no reason given.

Prohibition

The Mounted Police effectively stopped the "fire water" trade to the Indians. On 4 December 1874, less than nine weeks after arriving at their western post, Macleod proudly informed Commissioner French: "I am happy to be able to report the complete stoppage of the whiskey trade throughout the whole of this section of the country."[6] The Montana press acknowledged the success of this northern force. In early January 1875, the *Helena Daily Herald* also confirmed: "We learn that the whiskey traders have been entirely expelled from British Possessions bordering on Montana."[7] And a second American newspaper lauded: "To the scarlet uniform belongs the fame of destroying the whiskey trade, or at least checking it beyond restoration."[8]

The early success in ending the whiskey trade was, however, short-lived. In the following years, the sale of illegal spirits found a ready market as settlements grew. An observer at Battleford wrote the *London* (Ontario) *Free Press*: "Only a few days ago one hundred gallons of whiskey passed here for Edmonton … just think of it! One hundred gallons about to be turned loose among a semi-barbarous people."[9] In 1884, Commissioner A.G. Irvine outwardly admitted: "The traffic in illicit liquor cannot, I regret to say, to be said on the decline."[10]

In 1882, the construction of the railroad opened a new avenue for importing illegal intoxicants. Moosomin, the first rail station inside the North-West Territories, was the focal checkpoint for smuggled alcohol. At this and other rail stations, Mounted Police (who would, on occasion, attire in plainclothes) searched the trains, sometimes with success. The *Moose Jaw News* trumpeted: "F.F. Fyffe still on warpath—ten galloons in a trunk."[11] It was more likely, however, that a search failed.

One traveler recalled: "We were visited by a dozen or so Mounted Police in search of liquor. Fortunately they passed our valises … the fine is seldom imposed. Any liquor is emptied right on the spot."[12] A newspaper man from Toronto, traveling to End of Track in 1883, noted that, "from time to time, after passing the boundary between Manitoba and the North-West Territory, the train was boarded by members of the Mounted Police [who] extracted bottles of the forbidden 'firewater' and quietly walked outside the car and smashed the bottles on the track."[13]

The spillage of the "pocket pistol" flasks was not always on the ground. Take the case of Michael Brennan. The Regina press had reported that, "no Constable was ever more zealous in searching valises of passengers for whiskey, his hatred for such was so great that he always destroyed it instantly, and poured it where it would never do harm to the traveling public again—namely down the whiskey canon of Mike's enormous gullet."[14] Such excesses as this had consequences when a drunken Brennan dropped by Monsieur LaFrance's restaurant and swore at the proprietress. Mrs. LaFrance promptly used a chair "to annihilate the inspirited policeman."[15]

The construction of the C.P.R. employed 5,000 workers (called navvies). Many of these men had a previous dependency on alcohol, which added to the difficulty of policing prohibition. However, accounts credit the NWMP with skillfully minimizing problems and upholding law and order. A correspondent from Winnipeg traveled the rail line to End of Track in 1883 and reported "the good results of sobriety were seen everywhere."[16]

In 1884, 133 criminal charges connected to the sale or illegal possession of intoxicating liquor and yet another 63 convictions related to drunk and disorderly conduct. These court cases confirm that Western Canada was far from the dry paradise intended by legislation. A rancher living east of Calgary, General Thomas Bland Strange, commented that in the town, "the evils of drunkenness were greater than in any community which it has been my lot to live."[17] Criminal statistics in 1885 supported his opinion: of the 87 cases before Calgary courts that year, 53 had involved alcohol. When the Calgary NWMP detachment was deployed to Regina in March 1885 as a strategic move in the event of a Métis revolt, an Indian told a hardware merchant: "Police gone, plenty whiskey now."[18]

Three thousand eastern soldiers arrived in the Territories to combat the insurgents. The troops faced a unique military directive. Although General Frederick D. Middleton, Commander-in-Chief of Canada's Militia, did acknowledge that "most men in the militia were in the habit of having a certain amount of stimulants daily," he chose to adhere to the prohibition restrictions legislated in the North-West Territories.[19]

Most officers agreed with Middleton's "bold step." Lieutenant Preston wrote that: "Our Battalion had been recruited largely from towns on the Lake Ontario waterfront, from hard-bitten sailors and dockworkers, who, if liquor had been generally available, would sometimes have been in trouble."[20] Middleton's prohibition directive, however, proved impossible to enforce and, throughout the campaign, most of the soldiers took every opportunity to obtain liquor. In Calgary, Lieutenant-Colonel Guillaume Amyot, Commander of the 9th Voltigeurs, complained to Police Inspector Tom Dowling about the excessive sale of intoxicants to his troops.

The fine for drunk and disorderly conduct was $20, or one month in jail; convicted smugglers of spirits received a $200 fine, or six months' hard labour. The enormous profits from the sale of whiskey, however, clearly offset the cost of these penalties. A gallon of whiskey purchased for $4 in Fort Benton was poured into small bottles that sold for $10 each in Fort Macleod. A Montana paper reported that seventy-three cases of Jamaica Ginger, distributed at $1 for a small bottle, were consumed in two months at Fort Macleod.[21]

It is not surprising that many convicted whiskey traders resumed their trade. Tony Lachapelle, a Fort Macleod resident, was fined $400 on four occasions; a $250 fine issued by Superintendent William Winder in 1879 apparently did not deter Fred Pace, who received fines of $50 (1882) and $200 (1884). Pace complained, in a letter to the Fort Macleod Gazette, that the fines were bad enough without the police adding in the court costs. In his latest fine, he asked, "Just where did the $15.25 for costs go?"[22]

The court imposed fines for alcohol (and gambling) convictions that gave one-half of the money to either the informer or the person making the arrest. For the poorly paid policemen, this monetary reward helped compensate the unwanted task of liquor regulation. One trooper at Fort Qu'Appelle wrote: "I arrested a man for bringing liquor into the Territories without a permit. He was fined $50.00 and $11.00 costs, or six months imprisonment; he paid the fine and I received half of it and one dollar and a half of the costs. Paying business for me, eh?"[23] Another constable, who monitored construction camps along the railway line in British Columbia, also agreed: "I live well and make plenty of money capturing the festive whisky trader and maudlin drunk."[24] An American newspaper correctly gauged the motives of some of these men at Fort Walsh: "The policemen are on the lookout to make a few dollars for themselves as they cannot keep with the excitement of the camp on forty cents a day."[25] The second half of the fine went to the community. Fort Qu'Appelle used its share of the payment for the improvement of roads and bridges.

The "Riders of the Plains" detested the enforcement of prohibition as an onerous and unrewarding assignment. A well-known rhyme, written by Constable Sam Carruthers, recounted the feelings of the men.

> *Pass the tea*
> *And let us drink*
> *To the guardians of the land*
> *You can bet your life*
> *It's not our fault*
> *That whiskeys contraband*

Constable John Donkin expressed the viewpoint of the rank and file: "Whiskey hunting is not popular in the corps, and a man who persistently prosecutes for this offence is looked upon with contempt."[26] Commissioner A.G. Irvine's report for 1884 conceded: "The suppression of this traffic is the most disagreeable duty which the Police are called on to perform."[27]

One resident in Moosomin lamented: "We are honored with the presence of two of the Mounted Police. Thanks to the energetic and paternal care of the energetic officer in charge, Mr. Baker, we are left without stimulants these cold days, and the result is that most of us are afflicted with weak action of the heart."[28] Irvine acknowledged: "I may safely say that the majority of the people living in the North-West do not respect and do not hesitate to break the prohibitory liquor law ... men who were law abiding citizens in the old provinces think it no crime to evade the liquor law and do so on every opportunity."[29]

Corporal J.W. Fyffe's discovery that two volumes entitled *The History of England* concealed a tin container containing whiskey illustrated one of the many ingenuous methods that had been used to circumvent the law. In December 1883, the Calgary detachment found forty gallons of whiskey sealed in barrels marked oatmeal. Another search revealed coal oil (kerosene) containers delivered to railway workers had compartments soldered inside that were filled with whiskey.[30] There seemed endless clever ways to smuggle intoxicants into the region.

The police also dealt with alcohol "substitutes." Victor Beaupre, former acting Minister of Agriculture in Manitoba, was charged in a Calgary court for possession of a bottle of Ford's Extract of Peppermint, which surgeon George Kennedy analyzed as ninety per cent alcohol.[31] At Fort Macleod, Constable Jack Clarke related:

The General drink in this Country are patented Medicines with a large percentage of alcohol … [they] sell four ounce bottles one dolar Each. Extracts of Lemon and Vanilla sell for fifty and seventy-five Cents per bottle. These were favorites drinks and also Hot drops. Anything to make a person feel good and drunk.[32]

While visiting Winnipeg, Sergt.-Major Joseph Francis was asked by a newspaper reporter how did the Mounted Police manage out there for spirits, and what did they drink. His answer was most revealing: "At Wood Mountain they drink Florida water, cologne, pain killer, bay rum, and even muster liniment … they display great ingenuity in concocting drinks, which are fearfully and wonderfully made."[33] Edward Maunsell remembered one substitute (called "Number 6") that was prized for its quick effects.[34] The Indians concocted intoxicating drinks by mixing tea and tobacco.

On special public occasions, the police overlooked the liquor restrictions. The final event in the 1883 NWMP Dominion Day field day was a tug of war between the barracks and the town. The civilians won the contest and its prize of five gallons of beer.

Superintendent Sam Steele thought that, although the prohibition law preserved peace on the railway construction and kept the Indians from harm, it should not have been forced upon white settlement. He wrote: "The officers and men hated this detestable duty, which gave them much trouble … we soon learned that compulsion will not make people sober and made more drunkards than if there had been an open bar and free drinks at every street corner."[35]

For most policemen the search for illegal alcohol was an unwanted task that was both tiring and futile. Sub-Inspector E. Dalrymple Clark wrote:

Few people out of these territories have any conception of the hardships and privations that have been undergone by the police in their endeavors to break up the whiskey traffic. Day after day on horseback; night after night sleeping out with but one blanket; your provisions generally a buffalo tongue and a hard biscuit … Canada has good reason to be proud of the stuff of which her hardy sons are made.[36]

And the searches were frustrating. When the police stopped one wagon train, the drivers all maintained that they were temperate fellows and never drank—to which a policeman questioned: "Nearly every man on the road was temperate but still lots of liquor was being smuggled across the line into the North West."[37] Corporal Donkin watched his companions make

Constable Thomas Clarke

The constable was assigned to break confiscated whiskey bottles on rocks beside the Bow River. Once in a while, when the officer was not looking, Clarke admitted, "I would let one slither down the bank and get it after dark."

– *CH*, 31 August 1936
   GA NA 3251 – 15

an indifferent search by merely promenading with clinking spurs down the aisles of the train cars. Peyton Ward, as part of a hunting party, had police examine their permits at Shoal Lake "while we had drinks all round with the officers on duty."[38] Ward added, "The police fellows complain that they were worse off than the half-breeds, as they cannot get a 'permit' to have spirits."[39] At this same post, Sergeant White used a fencing foil to search stacks of furs in a fifty-cart train. He struck no hidden liquor, but angered the traders by piercing a dozen fine felt hats.

To accommodate complaints by Bishop Vital Grandin, Oblates of Mary Immaculate, at St. Albert that illicit liquor was being stilled near the town, two policemen spent two nights in the steeple of a church, watching for lights in the surrounding forest. Their efforts were unsuccessful but, on their return to Fort Saskatchewan, they met a party of drunken revellers who, on orders to stop, jeered the constables and drove on in their sleigh. This could not be allowed. Constable P.J. Curran overtook the party and, "when they did not stop on his first order, he put a revolver to the driver's head, which had the desired effect."[40] Six men were arrested and, after forceful demands by the police, they revealed their liquor source in Edmonton. As a result, hundreds of bottles were seized and destroyed.

One search baffled the Regina detachment. They found a still and a rather large quantity of alcohol at Long Lake, north of the post. But there was no evidence or complaints of the sale of whiskey in the area. A careful search explained the puzzle. An elderly man had steeped his brew over grain which migrating water birds stopped to consume. While the birds staggered in a drunken stupor, he snared them for sale to his neigbours.[41]

It delighted many westerners when they learned of evasions of the law. Who wouldn't be amused when the name of a prize bull obtained a liquor permit?[42] Residents of Fort Macleod laughed at how William Lawrence had outwitted the local detachment. In this case, Sergeant John Kirk, with two constables, had entered a suspected drinking establishment, where they observed three intoxicated men. The homeowner, Lawrence, who was in bed, told the officers that he would be with them in a minute. He rose, poured the contents of a jug into a basin, washed his face and hands, combed his hair, and then threw the contents of the washbasin outside. Although there were three intoxicated men and the cabin reeked of whiskey, a search failed to find any alcohol. Of course, the evidence had disappeared with the emptied washbasin.

And, when the Reverend John Maclean held a Temperance Meeting in a log church at Fort Macleod, he was pleased to see, not only the police and civilians present, but several Indians and a surprising number of rather tough characters. At the end of the sermon, Chief Manistakos (Father of Many Children) rose and, through an interpreter, suggested that everyone should listen to the preacher as whiskey was evil—but still a little would not hurt occasionally, except that the Mounted Police had drank it all. From the audience's laughter, Maclean realized that a ruse had been prepared and quickly ended the meeting. It was soon unearthed that some of the whiskey traders had paid the interpreter to falsify the Indian's speech. Colonel James Macleod was furious and was going to press charges against the interpreter for disturbing a public meeting, but instead fired him.[43]

The Mounties dumped the confiscated alcohol. One observer remarked, "It was much to the disgust of the men and Indians when men under Inspector Crozier dumped confiscated whiskey into a river."[44] After one large seizure of eighty gallons of whiskey was spilled on the prairie in front of Fort Macleod, "a guard had to be put on it to prevent the Indians from sifting the muddy stuff up and drinking it."[45]

The lawmen made light of the unwanted assignment of dumping alcohol. One officer discarded twenty barrels of beer near Swan River in 1876, he told Superintendent Herchmer: "May God forgive me for committing so awful a sin."[46] The *Regina Leader* described the disposal of this whiskey: "The countenances of the spectators who witnessed the spilling of the liquor outside the barracks was a sight to behold, something very like tears running down the cheeks of the majority. Our reporter was visibly affected."[47]

Skeptical westerners doubted that the police spilled the whiskey. One account claimed the Mounties, "always pour it in the same spot where they have a bucket buried to receive the precious fluid and which afterwards make merry with."[48] This allegation had truth. Constable Edward Barnett admitted that his comrades placed a straw-covered tub in a hole which they had dug in the ground. "The seized whiskey," Barnett later divulged, "was poured on the straw under the watchful eye of an officer. Once he left the liquor was gleefully recovered by the men and the evening was a happy and hilarious event."[49]

The Fort Calgary detachment carted the confiscated alcohol to the Bow River where, under the supervision of an officer, the bottles were smashed on rocks. Constable Tom Clarke, who felt he was trusted because of his youth, disclosed that, "once in a while when he wasn't looking, I would let one slither down the bank and go for it after dark."[50] And, in a most desperate occasion, after they had poured fifty gallons of whiskey into a snow bank, one Mountie confessed that, "The boys soon gathered it up and took it into the kitchen and made a punch of it and before night there was hardly a sober man in the fort."[51]

Border Whiskey Patrols

The NWMP kept a vigilant watch for whiskey traders entering Canada. A Toronto newspaper correspondent informed his readers that "the red coat of mounted policemen was visible on every butte and eminence within fifty miles of the fort [Walsh], armed with revolver, carbine and spy glass."[52]

In one police scheme, Major Walsh had three constables hide on the American side of the line to follow any suspected smugglers crossing into Canada. This plan proved successful and thirty gallons of alcohol were seized and spilled on the prairie. A Mr. Everson was fined $200, or given the alternative of six months imprisonment. He paid the fine and left "a sadder but wiser man."[53]

At Fort Macleod, the whiskey traders were well known to the law, and a careful watch was kept on their activities. Everyone in town knew the absence of a known trader meant he had gone to Montana to purchase a load of whiskey. "It was easy to calculate," one Mountie related, "how long he would take to make the trip, and when it came near time for his return, patrols were sent out to try and intercept him. This was an exciting game and, of course, the police were heavily handicapped."[54]

The open border had many entry points. A whiskey trader could pick his time for traveling and where and when he would return. Once in Canada, the alcohol was sometimes cached for a later pickup and sale. Townspeople ridiculed that the same policemen who a few days earlier were trying to capture the trader, now purchased liquor from him.

Some of the caches were found by chance. In late 1882, fifteen gallons of whiskey was found in a dry lake near the St. Mary River, and the police sent a wagon to bring the stash to Fort Macleod. In another example, a policeman hunting jackrabbits found thirty-five gallons beside the Belly River near Standoff.

It is not surprising that most police patrols were fruitless. One paper commented that: "Corporal Lauder and a detachment of ten men returned from a scouting expedition on the 26th. They had been as far south as Milk River in search of a band of American whiskey traders ... but did not succeed in finding whiskey, traders or Indians."[55] Once the smuggler safely returned to the town, the police acknowledged defeat and dropped all efforts to make an arrest.

Rather than patrolling the open countryside for whiskey traders, the police found a more effective tactic was to wait near a trail known to be used by the traffickers. Sergeant Frank Fitzpatrick was in a mounted detail that left Fort Macleod at midnight, showing no lights and using only whispered commands. Once they neared their objective (a ford on the Oldman River), one man remained with the horses while his companions moved ahead on foot to hide in the grass on either side of the ford. At about 2 a.m., the men heard the tell-tale noise of a horse fording the river and arrested the rider.[56]

The diary of R.N. Wilson contains a vivid anecdote of policing the border. In February 1882, Jerry Potts led three Mounties to the Boundary Line where they hid their horses in a coulee. From a nearby small hill, they watched the gap in the Milk River Ridge through which the Sun River Trail ran. In the afternoon, through field glasses, they observed two approaching riders. The police remained hidden until the lead man rode past them. Constable Wilson relates:

> We at once rode out & made him a prisoner, we then waited a few minutes longer & a man with a team and wagon rode up, this man was also made a prisoner of, & searching the wagon found over twenty gallons of pure alcohol in five gallon coal-oil cans. The owner was an old ex-policeman Cochrane who had been smuggling for some time, but always manages to avoid the men who were watching for him. The mounted prisoner was an American named Davis who was riding ahead to "scout" for Cochrane.[57]

The night was bitterly cold and the men, with only saddle blankets for warmth, began drinking the evidence. In no time, the two prisoners and Jerry Potts were "howling drunk" and incapacitated. The three Mounties continued to down the alcohol diluted with water—which Jerry called "mix." A priest from a nearby camp heard the ruckus and came over, only to be persuaded to take a drink for his stomach's sake. This offer induced further drinking:

> It was not long before he and Tom [LaNauze)] became very jolly and were toasting each other drinking out of two old fruit cans & touching them together every sip. Callighan had long retired, crawling in between Davis & Cochrane who were too drunk to prevent him & before morning I had the honour of being the only sober man in camp although I must admit that I took enough to keep the cold out.[58]

Everyone had a cup of whiskey for breakfast. Later, at Fort Macleod, Inspector Crozier fined his comrade, David Cochrane, $200 and confiscated his wagon and three horses. The "scout," Donald W. Davis, who five years later was the first elected NWT Member of Parliament, was fined $100.

E. Flint, NWMP, Maple Creek, Saskatchewan

"Only a few days ago one hundred gallons of whïskey passed here [Battleford] or Edmonton ... just think of it! One hundred gallons about to be turned loose among a semi-barbarous people."

– *London* (Ontario) *Free Press*, 5 September 1878
  GA NA 3811 – 114

Mounted Inebriated Asylum

When a detachment made a punch from alcohol dumped into a snow bank, it strongly suggests that many of "the boys" had drinking problems. James Stanford's letter to his mother in Nova Scotia supports this contention: "We came here to stop the whiskey trade and instead of doing so most of the fellows are drunk half the time."[59] Perhaps Stanford was referring to Percy G.H. Robinson. One diary related: "Dock Robertson [Percy G.H. Robinson] has been drunk this last six weeks back. He is drinking Bay Rum and ginger. He drinks five or six bottles a day."[60] Two weeks later, in spite of his claim of illness, Robinson was fined $5 and given ten days in the guard room for refusing to draw water. Robinson's chronic addiction came to a head when he purchased carpenter's levels, emptied the glass tubes into a cup, and consumed the contents. A comrade reasoned, "Doc was very ill after that, a fact which prevented carpenter's levels from becoming a popular beverage."[61]

After the death of George McCrum at Fort Carlton, a search of his room revealed more than 800 bottles of Perry-Davis Painkiller, which, one barrack mate reasoned, "no doubt accounted for his demise.[62] At Swan River, Constable John Wymerskirch was assigned to stable work. Any of the sick horses received a daily dose of sweet spirits of nitre. Sub-Constable E.H. Maunsell recalled:

> John, no doubt, to encourage his patients, always took the first dose himself, and those who had the privilege of seeing him do so, declared that he played more than fair, by taking a larger dose than he asked any horse to down. John was still alive when we left Swan River and seemed none the worse for his indulgence.[63]

And Wymerskirch was still alive to serve as a Special Constable with the Prince Albert Volunteers during the 1885 North-West Rebellion.

The geographical location of a post impacted the availability of alcohol. Detachments near the American border had the easiest access to liquor; more distant posts—Edmonton, Battleford, Swan River—relied on traders and returning comrades for their alcohol. Upon his transfer from Swan River over to Fort Macleod, Constable Edward Maunsell discovered that the conditions were very different. On the first night in his new quarters, a man from "C" Troop came in and offered the nine men a drink. As soon as the bottle was emptied a subscription was taken and two more bottles were bought.[64] For the first time in his life, Maunsell felt the effects of whiskey. He reflected that the unavailability of alcohol at Swan River had bolstered the detachment's health and improved their bank accounts.

Many policemen returning to the "dry" North-West Territories, aware that they would soon experience an uncertain alcohol supply, imbibed excessively. Such was the case in June 1875 when the Dufferin detachment left to help garrison Swan River. One rider observed "some of the boys who, knowing it would be their last chance for tippling, went into it pretty heavy and caused us a little trouble."[65] Constable Maunsell rode west from Winnipeg with several policemen whose friends had "thought the best way to show their friendship was to fill them up with liquor before they left for the North-West Territories."[66]

Any Mountie returning to the North-West Territories had a required "duty." John Donkin wrote of this task: "Each member of the Force is expected by his comrades when entering the territories to bring a libation of 'old rye' or 'bourbon' with him."[67] Constable W. Grain recounted the time he and two comrades had been sent to Fort Benton for the mail. Some of the boys, Grain related, had asked us to bring back a wee drop. The trio, returning in a four-team wagon, covered the bottles with the mail and a blanket. As they left for Fort Walsh, for some reason, American soldiers gave chase. "Imagine," recalled Grain, "the law chasing the law—what a crazy situation to get ourselves into."[68] Grain's team easily outdistanced their pursuers, certainly earning the thanks of the boys waiting at Fort Walsh.

Some Mounted Policemen had experimented, often dangerously, with alcohol substitutes, some with "a sufficient stimulating power to succeed admirably in stealing away the brain."[69] Ether added to a punch at the 1882 Christmas NCO's mess at Battleford was, in Superintendent William Herchmer words, "most disastrous, Sergeant Waltham for a time being was a regular lunatic."[70] As a punishment, Waltham was demoted to a lower rank. And, for a Christmas dance, hospital orderlies Acting-Sergeant Alex Bethune and Constable Charles Scott broke into the medicine cabinet and stole nine gallons of alcohol that they happily shared with others. The two policemen were sentenced to four months hard labour, and five citizens were fined to pay for the cost of the stolen alcohol.[71] Nor was cleanliness always paramount. On his return from Oregon to Fort Macleod, Tim Lynch mixed his painkiller cocktails in a wash tub.

At times, drinking bouts involved the entire barracks. In a letter, written seven weeks after establishing Fort Macleod, one policeman commented: "The laws are strict against the use of whiskey, yet our Fort often gets beastly drunk."[72] Corporal Clarke's diary confirms the alcohol overindulgence:

> The Police Boys are drunk again. Tony Lachapelle arrived from Benton with quite a load of Jamaica Ginger and Whiskey ...

Corporal Heney returned from Benton with a cargo of whiskey and there was a great drunk in the barracks ... most of the boys are drunk & kept it up till morning.[73]

One gathering involved all of the ranks. Constable Jim Stanford described the occasion: "Great times in the Fort all hands drunk Officers and Men together ... two days later Col Macleod had all Sergts up to try and find where they got the whiskey but they would not tell him & of course he could not push the matter being drunk himself."[74]

Not to be undone by the rank and file, some officers also engaged in prolonged drinking bouts. Jack Clarke's diary relates that, on 15 November 1879, "Capt Trechette [Frechette] and Capt McIllree and Dr Kennedy were drunk today. Three days later the drinking continued ... Capt Winder and Inspt. McIllree and Capt Frechette were drunk all day and night."[75] Archaeological excavations at Fort Walsh in the early 1980s uncovered large numbers of bottles deposited in the latrines, obviously to hide evidence of drinking. It was noted that the bottles retrieved from the officer's latrines contained more expensive alcohol.[76]

The NWMP officers were hardly models of temperance. One policeman accused a doctor and several officers of diluting the brandy given to invalids and saving the pure alcohol for themselves.[77] At his store at Fort Shaw, Montana Territory, J.H. McNight counted officers in the NWMP among his best customers. One of his agents wrote from Fort Macleod: "Captain Crozier wants three gals your best whiskey. Send it to him with bill, packed securely and marked 'c'. He is all right on the pay."[78] Another Montana trader wrote: "Every time the mail went north, by special arrangement, I put two gallons of whiskey in the mail sack, one for Col. Macleod, one for Captain Windsor [Winder]."[79] Inspector F. Dickens had a chronic drinking problem. He arranged for packages of spirits to be mailed to his post. The *Edmonton Bulletin* commented : "The Police mail for Fort Saskatchewan came in the Edmonton bag. This would seem to indicate that the liquor laws in the North-West should be more stringently enforced."[80]

Colonel Macleod's reputation for an enormous capacity of whiskey was legendary. One story, perhaps apocryphal, related that, while he was at Fort Assiniboine, Montana Territory, the American officers colluded to test him through a relay of drinkers. But, as the evening wore on and the bottle circulated freely, man after man disappeared under the table or fell into an armchair. In the end, as Colonel Macleod assisted the last "competitor" up the stairs to his bed, the man stopped short on the first landing and said, "By God Colonel, where d'you put it?"[81]

When whiskey was in short supply, it sold for $12 to $20 a gallon at Fort Macleod. Anyone having spirits ran the risk of theft from a barrack mate since it was deemed fair game to steal alcohol. Still, it was understandable that Surgeon Nevitt was annoyed when Inspectors Crozier and Jackson, knowing Nevitt had several bottles, continued to linger around his room.

Shortly after he left the Force, James Macleod wrote of his friend and replacement A.G. Irvine: "Irvine arrived last night and we did not get to bed till about 4 in the morning. After I turned in—sometime after he had gone to his room he appeared in his night shirt with a bottle of W & a glass, dancing about like the Lord Chancellor."[82] Was this the same A.G. Irvine who, two years earlier, had issued a General Order: "It has come to the knowledge of the Commissioner that liquor and intoxicating medicine have in the past been freely used at various Police Posts ... for the future it is to be distinctly understood that most rigid steps are to be taken for the stoppage of the liquor traffic, and the punishment of offenders?"[83]

Some westerners censured Mounted Police conduct and drinking. One visitor to Fort Macleod denounced the "Mounted Inebriated Asylum":

Mounted police at this post are a fraud of the worst description, and their drill consists entirely of devising means to swindle the Government, steal whiskey from the civilians or seduce squaws. The conduct of the officers and men has been such that any honest man would blush to be called a Mounted Policeman. The Force out here are properly called the Mounted Inebriated Asylum ... whiskey and other drinks are sold openly to the officers, men and Indians by men who the police favor. A two-ounce bottle of Jamaica ginger is sold for a dollar although it only costs wholesale delivered at Macleod 16½ cents.[84]

George Machon, employed in a government work party traveling to Battleford in 1876, was disgusted when the two Mounted Policemen who checked his party for illegal spirits later got so drunk, they had to be taken to the post in a dump car. He commented: "So much for the mounted police that are stationed in this country to keep the cussed whiskey out of it."[85] Excessive drinking certainly affected discipline and effective policing. After a pay day in Calgary, the men detailed to travel to Regina by train were so drunk that "they had to be loaded like cattle."[86]

Alcoholic abuse tragically ruined some NWMP careers. Inspector Frank Norman, a thirteen-year veteran, was dismissed at age forty-nine for being "unreliable and too fond of stimulants."[87] Michael Kirk joined the NWMP in 1877 after serving in the Irish Constabulary where he had the amazing

Inspector Frank Norman

Inspector Frank Norman, a thirteen-year veteran of the Force, was dismissed at age forty-nine for being "unreliable and too fond of stimulants."

– *NAC*, Frank Norman, f. 5.
RCMP Historical Collections Unit, "Depot" Division, Regina, SK., 72–68–3

ability to name the date and place of engagement of every man on the 13,000-man force. Years of drinking destroyed him. In 1890, Kirk came to Battleford, begging for a stimulant, but the post refused help. Kirk soon entered a state of delirium tremens. His temperature rose to 106°F. and he died in agony. The medical report attributed his death to complications from "protracted use of alcohol." Kirk left his wife destitute.[88]

In those days, Canada had both strong political and social temperance organizations. Many Mounties were abstainers; the number is unknown. But, for many men, the hard work, isolation and boredom only encouraged drinking, especially if they had a previous drinking problem. One man wrote: "I have discovered that a sojourn of two winters and two summers in the Nor'West, without stimulants, is quite enough to try the constitution of any white man who has not carefully been brought up under the protective wings of temperance and similar societies."[89]

Dr. Kittson recommended moderate alcohol usage in his 1879 report: "Last summer I wrote a special report on the advisability of introducing beer and spirits into the force … the introduction of a canteen, under strict regulations, as practiced in the regular army, would add materially to the comforts, morals and efficiency of the force."[90] It was not until 1891 that the North-West Territories repealed prohibition.

NOTES

1. *GA*, J. Stuttaford Fonds, M 2750 CB. N879. Stuttaford also required approval from the United States military post at Fort Benton to transport this liquor across the Gros Ventre Reservation. New regulations in 1882 allowed a maximum of two gallons per permit, one permit at a time, and police officers to forward a return every three months that listed the number of permits and quantity of liquor entering the region.

2. *CH*, 7 May 1884.

3. Alcohol in gallons: whiskey − 3,850; brandy − 1,250; beer − 3,565; wine − 938; gin, rum, other − 400.

4. Fitzpatrick, *Sergeant 331*, 30.

5. *MC*, 27 November 1884. In the 18 December issue, the paper commented that, "Surely if Colonel Macleod is not capable of judgment who is worthy of permits and who is not, there is no one here who is."

6. *RC*, NWMP, 1874, 62.

7. *HDH*, 5 January 1875.

8. *FBR*, 1 March 1875.

9. *LFP*, 5 September 1878.

10. *RC*, NWMP, 1885, 14. Irvine recommended trading whiskey with the Indians be made a penitentiary offence with no option of a fine.

11. *MJN*, 7 November 1884.

12. "Robert Martin Diary," *Sask. H*, VL, No. 2, 60. Also P.B. Waite, "Across the Rockies and Selkirks with G.M. Grant in 1883," *Canada − A Historical Magazine*, 1, No. 1, 42.

13. *TG*, 1 August 1883. Also Chapter 11, Maintien le Droit, 2.

14. *RL*, 24 September 1885. "Zealous Constable Succumbs in Arduous Discharge of Duty."

15. Ibid.

16. *WDT*, 27 August 1883.

17. Strange, *Gunner Jingo's Jubilee*, 423.

18. *WDT*, 27 March 1885.

19. Middleton, *Suppression of the Rebellion in the North West Territories of Canada*, 18.

20. J.A.V. Preston, "The Diary of Lieut. J.A.V. Preston," *Sask. H*, VIII, No. 3, 107.

21. *NNW*, 2 April 1880.

22. *FMG*, 14 November 1884.

23. Dempsey, ed., *William Parker Mounted Policeman*, 138.

24. Rivett-Carnac, ed., "Letters from the North-West," *RCMPQ*, Vol. XVIII. No. 1, 14.

25. *FBRP*, 9 February 1881.

26. Donkin, *Trooper and Redskin*, 90.

27. *RC*, NWMP, 1884, 20. Irvine wrote: "We are condemned on all sides for whatever action we take; settlers refuse to give information to assist in the laying of charges … detective or undercover work by police was widely believed to be an underhanded and dishonourable means of employment; local magistrates are reluctant to hear

liquor cases because it makes them unpopular. On the other hand, interestingly enough, the Mounted Police policy did receive the support of many of the Indians, who were still anxious to keep liquor off the reserves."

28. Gilbert McKay, *Moosomin and the Mounted*, (Moosomin: Saskatchewan, 1974), 5. Also *TG*, 24 July 1876.

29. *RC*, NWMP, 1885, 14.

30. *CH*, 19 February 1885. A. Anderson received a $200 fine; B. McCallum, $50.

31. *CN*, 13 May 1884, details the trial. Also, *WDT*, 2 May 1884.

32. *GA*, Simon J. Clarke, M228.

33. *MFP*, 25 May 1880. See also *MFP*, 10 February 1880.

34. *CH*, 13 October 1923.

35. Steele, *Forty Years in Canada*, 176–77.

36. *RL*, 17 March 1883.

37. Edward J. Brooks Letters, *Sask. H*, X, No. 3, 105.

38. B. Peyton Ward, *Roughing it in the North-West Territories of Canada*, 30–31.

39. Ibid., 120–21.

40. Dempsey, ed., *William Parker Mounted Policeman*, 66.

41. Henry Somers-Cocks, *Trials of a Tenderfoot* (Instow, England: s.n, 1936), 61–62.

42. *CH*, 18 November 1933.

43. *LH*, 21 June 1924.

44. *TM*, 5 April 1875.

45. Nevitt, *Frontier Life in the Mounted Police*, 167.

46. Ward, *Roughing it in the North-West Territories of Canada*, 121.

47. *RL*, 1 January 1885.

48. Ward, *Roughing in the North-West Territories of Canada*, 31.

49. *GA*, Edward Barnett, M 58.

50. *CH*, 31 August 1936.

51. *GA*, William Metzler, M 836.

52. *TG*, 19 October 1876.

53. *MFP*, 27 October 1876.

54. *CH*, 11 October 1923.

55. *FMG*, date unknown.

56. Fitzpatrick, *Sergeant 331*, 28.

57. *NAC*, R.N. Wilson, MG 29, E-47.

58. Ibid.

59. *TUMSA*, Missoula, James Stanford Letter.

60. *GA*, Clarke, M 228.

61. *CH*, 13 October 1923.

62. Ibid.

63. *CH*, 13 October 1923. Military service in *Edmonton Bulletin*, 1 August 1885. Not surprisingly, after he left the Force, Wymerskirch opened a non-alcohol (under 4 per cent) establishment.

64. *CH*, 11 October 1923.

65. Dempsey, ed., *William Parker Mounted Policeman*, 115.

66. *CH*, 13 October 1923.

67. Donkin, *Trooper and Redskin*, 14.

68. Grain, "Pioneers of a Glorious Future," 78.

69. *MFP*, 19 February 1880.

70. Aitken, *Maintain the Right*, 195. *NAC*, RG 18, B-1, 1, f.5.

71. Ibid. f. 52.

72. *HDN*, 15 March 1875. Letter was written 5 December 1874.

73. *GA*, S.J. Clarke, M 228. The dates of the diary entries are: 24 April 1879, 13 November 1879, and 10 January 1880.

74. *UMSA*, *Missoula*, James Stanford Diary.

75. *GA*, Simon J. Clarke, M 228.

76. Jeffrey Murray, "Archaeology at Fort Walsh," *The Beaver*, Outfit 311:3, 18–25; Jeffrey Murray "The Mounties of Cypress Hills," *Archaeology, XI*, No. 1, 32–38.

77. *MFP*, 20 July 1881.

78. Sharp, *Whoop-Up Country*, 129.

79. John Willard Schultz, *Blackfeet and Buffalo: Memories of Life among the Indians* (Norman: University of Oklahoma Press, 1962), 64. MG, 10 March 1885.

80. *EB*, 21 February 1881.

81. Burton Deane, *Mounted Police Life in Canada* (London: Cassell, 1916), 71.

82. *GA*, Macleod, M 776 f.14.

83. *NAC*, RG 18 B4, Vol. 8, General Order No. 28, 20 December 1880. E. Morgan, "The North-West Mounted Police: Internal Problems and Public Criticism, 1874–1883," *SH, XXVI*, No. 2, 57.

84. Hawkes, *The Story of Saskatchewan and Its People*, 3 vols. (Regina and Chicago: S.J. Clarke, 1924), vol. 2, 534.

85. *GA*, *Diary of George Machon*, 1876, M 745.

86. *GA*, G.E. Saunders, M 1093, f. 38.

87. *NAC*, Frank Norman, f. 5. Frank Norman, BA Trinity College, Ireland, had signed Treaty 7. He was dismissed from the Force in 1895 because of his drinking problems. The Commissioner wrote: "His tardiness in answering correspondence has given consistent trouble ... I have little confidence in his veracity." His retirement allowance was $329 per annum.

88. *NAC*, Michael Kirk, f. 27.

89. *MFP*, 31 July 1876.

90. *RC*, NWMP, 1879, 32.

11

MAINTIENS LE
DROIT

Swift Runner

"The Indians are generally adverse to hanging—they say it is a death only fit for a dog—but in this case the crime was so atrocious in character that they did not object to this mode of execution."

– *Saskatchewan Herald*, 12 January 1880
  GA NA 504 – 1

A MOUNTED POLICEMAN RECEIVED ONE-HALF the fine for the arrest and subsequent conviction of an offender. This amount could exceed his monthly police salary and, according to a Montana newspaper, likely directed policing: "The policemen are on the lookout to make a few dollars for themselves as they can not keep up with the excitement of the camp on forty cents a day. Citizens who conducted that little game known as poker were run in for $50 and costs; one half went to the informer."[1] In this matter, the *Winnipeg Daily Times* disparaged: "How is it that a peace officer in the government service should be allowed fees in such cases ... it is a garden of plunder for government officials with fines imposed divided among powers imposing the fines and securing the conviction."[2]

Egregious examples of injustice arose over this aspect of law. Hospital-Sergeant W.R. Abbott gave a glass of whiskey to Mr. Casey, a citizen who was having his teeth removed, to blunt the pain. He later brought Casey to trial for possession of whiskey and received one-half the court fine of $42.50.[3] In Swift Current, McKinney Burke sold alcohol to townspeople and then informed the police who was in possession of liquor. However, Superintendent J. McIllree was not fooled by this action. He fined Burke $200 or six months in jail (which he accepted)—much to the acclaim of the citizens. And, in Edmonton, Daniel Dagnon, scheming to get one-half of the fine, informed the police that J.C. Cameron had given him a drink of intoxicating liquor. In court, however, Cameron proved that he was away from the town at the time of the alleged offence and the case was dismissed, with the judge reprimanding Dagnon for having perjured himself. One week later, when Dagnon was charged for being drunk, the court sentenced him to two months hard labour, with no option of a fine.[4] That Constable Asprey had his friends deliver whiskey to people who were then arrested led the *Regina Leader* to demand: "It is surely time someone else was employed to prosecute the illicit whiskey dealer."[5]

As western settlement grew, the NWMP's right to arrest and then adjudicate the case at hand increasingly became questioned.[6] The 1883 arrest and $50 fine to N.F. Davin for illegally importing liquor heightened the issue. Davin had been found with a flask (pocket pistol) of whiskey that, he alleged, under an understood custom would have been spilled and the bottle thrown out the train window. However, on the train's arrival in Regina, Colonel W. Herchmer had him charged for having liquor in his possession without a permit. No doubt the open animosity between the publisher and the local police factored in this case of what Davin called "revenge." As news publisher of the *Regina Leader*, Davin censured both prohibition and the police authority.[7] In October 1883, he successfully had Sergeant E.A. Braithwaite charged with assault on his person.

Citizens at two well-attended town meetings in Calgary disputed the NWMP's authority regarding prohibition. The *Calgary Herald* of 3 December 1884, under "The Mass Meeting," reported a citizen's assembly unanimously passed several resolutions that would empower local officials to appoint Civil Magistrates, censured policemen for unjustly searching private homes

Nicholas Flood Davin—lawyer, politician and newspaperman

"A policeman's life in the North-West is not likely to be a 'happy one' hereafter, unless
he so manages it as to keep out of range of the *Leader's* long guns."

– *Regina Leader,* 23 August 1883
   GA NA 2883 – 23

without a warrant and refuted the policy that gave policemen one-half
the fine. Mr. H.M. Bleecker, a lawyer, commented (to loud applause) that
police combined, in liquor cases, five outrageous functions: informer, captor,
witness, judge, and jailer.[8] A Fort Macleod town hall meeting likewise passed
a resolution that questioned the unfettered police powers. In Regina, a
petition signed by the mayor and citizens protested the "monstrous" $200
fine given to a farmer. Local press commented "time has come to deprive
Mounted Police officers of magisterial jurisdiction."[9] Clearly, the NWMP
was facing growing scrutiny.

The Medicine Line

The NWMP's jurisdiction embraced the North-West Territories and a twenty-mile (33 km) belt on each side of the railway line under construction in eastern British Columbia. Along the southern international boundary, earth mounds built every three to five km clearly delineated the border, commonly called "the Medicine Line." These survey markers, completed weeks before the 1874 arrival of the Mounted Police, gave the refugee American Sioux a rough gauge of the distance that they could safely infringe into American territory on buffalo hunts.

Superintendent L.N.F. Crozier explained that the Indians called the boundary the "Medicine Line" because no matter what they have done on one side they feel perfectly secure after having arrived on the other.[10] Robert Higheagle, a youth in Sitting Bull's camp, recalled that the band members "believed things are different when you cross from one side to another. On one side [Canada] you are perfectly free to do as you please. On the other you are in danger."[11] Commissioner A.G. Irvine reasoned that American Indians and white desperadoes preferred the Canadian side of the Medicine Line to avoid the "contingency by bullet or rope which attends the exercise of their calling in the United States."[12]

An extradition agreement was not yet finalized between the United States and the nascent Canadian nation. This meant anyone crossing the border avoided arrest or further pursuit. When a horse-race dispute between two cattle herding camps caused "Al" to draw his revolver, two Mounted Police onlookers attempted to arrest the gun-wielder. "Al," however, jumped on his horse and headed for the border, 18 km distance. The police followed in what can only be imagined as a breathtaking Hollywood movie scene.

The cowboy successfully crossed over the boundary and was dismounted when his pursuers rode up. Even though the Mounted Police assured him that he would get off easy, "Al" chose to stay in the "Land of Liberty." Ever accommodating, the two policemen returned to the herding camps with a message to forward the cowboy's unpaid wages to Fort Benton.[13]

In July 1885 at Medicine Hat, Ben Hale shot Robert Casey in a drunken argument over a horse race. Hale at once left for the border. After Casey died the next morning, Sergeant Jones was dispatched to Fort Benton to have American lawmen arrest Hale. Sheriff Johnny Healy, although he knew where Ben Hale was staying, refused to co-operate unless he received a reward. Hale was never arrested.

Justice extended across the border on limited occasions. American army deserters were imprisoned at Fort Walsh and returned to the United States. Captain William Winder posted warrants in Helena, Montana Territory, for the arrest of Pete Matt, a notorious horse thief who had run stolen North-West Mounted Police horses into the United States. Constable Wilson acknowledged that his troop trailed whiskey traders 20 km into American territory. A determined Constable R.C. Lewis Hooper donned western wear and, with the owner of fifteen horses stolen at Indian Head, Assiniboia, trailed five horse thieves for several days into the United States. They arrested the desperadoes at gunpoint at night, knowing the thieves would be inattentive, and returned the men for trial in Regina.[14] American army mules were seized from Blood bands near Fort Macleod and held for American officers to retrieve.

The most serious infringement of the border was the pursuit and later arrest of three United States army deserters just 30 km inside Canada. This incident (recounted earlier in Chapter 7 – Upholding the Force), had international repercussions.

Administration of Justice

In 1879, only seven NWMP officers and three Stipendiary Magistrates adjudicated all the court trials. The police officers tried the case at their post; the Stipendiary Magistrates—Colonel Hugh Richardson, Matthew Ryan, and Macleod—had an arduous travel schedule. Colonel Richardson calculated that, in 1883, he rode over 5,000 km through largely uninhabited country. Colonel James Macleod's circuit ranged from his own bailiwick at Fort Macleod to Regina on the east and north to Edmonton. Within four years, the increasing number of criminal charges required the additional services of six police officers and five Justices of the Peace.

Since the Stipendiary Magistrates held court only twice a year, there were unwanted delays in administering justice. One man, awaiting his trial, remained incarcerated for four months over an offence involving $1.[15] A Mr. Kidd, arrested in Edmonton in 1877, spent nine months in custody before his trial and subsequent acquittal—"pretty hard lines," commented the *Manitoba Free Press*.[16] At the Pincher Creek police ranch, Constable Pickard was charged with maliciously wounding three cattle. His warning to ranchers to keep their animals out of his turnip patch obviously was not to go unheeded.[17] Magistrate L.N.F. Crozier heard conflicting evidence from thirteen witnesses (three were Mounted Policemen) and assigned the case to the next Court of Assize eight months away. At that session, Magistrate Macleod dismissed the case because of insufficient evidence.

Court proceedings were usually held in the police barracks. However, Inspector Steele held one trial in a tent and once even used a plank on a Red River cart as his bench. All trials were open to the public as it was important to demonstrate, especially to the Aboriginals, that impartial justice was meted out.[18] In one case, Staff-Sergeant MacKay went to the Red Pheasant Reserve to examine an Indian boy who was reported to have been badly beaten by the schoolmaster. The police followed with a summons against Charles Cunningham, the accused. The teacher was tried and fined $28 by Judge C.B. Rouleau.[19]

Most defendants appeared in court without legal counsel and few appeals of a verdict are recorded.[20] When one lawyer began arguing a point of law before Magistrate Macleod, he was curtly dismissed: "Mr., we want justice in this country, not law."[21]

While on a visit to Fort Macleod, Dr. Sweetland of Ottawa was favourably impressed by the ability and good judgment shown by the officer and men. He wrote: "I attended court, where sixteen cases, the offenses ranging all the way up from petty larceny to horse thieving were disposed of in a manner which surprised spectators, and I doubt if justice is better dealt out in any court in the Dominion."[22]

Jury trials were infrequent: of the 384 cases held in a one-year period following 1 December 1882 only nine charges involved a jury. It appears that most juries had been recruited by magistrates rather than selected by the legal sides. One jury trial at Fort Walsh in 1877 was exceptional. Colonel Macleod, aware that local opinion prejudged Freeman Burnett (charged with forging a note) guilty, then recruited a jury from Montana Territory who found Burnett guilty. One American observer "spoke highly of the Mounted Police and their just and impartial manner in conducting the trial."[23] This recruitment of a jury from another country is perhaps unparalleled in legal history.

What could a guilty person expect for a sentence? The subjective range of punishments is evident. Colonel A.G. Irvine gave W. Adshead, a young surveyor, two years in the penitentiary for shooting a cow; William Adams, charged with threatening to kill his wife, received a $10 fine and was bound to keep the peace for six months. Superintendent William Herchmer told Frank Webber, the "Crooked Kid," charged with vagrancy, to get out of Calgary—which he did. But later on farther west on the rail line, Superintendent Sam Steele gave the "Crooked Kid" a $10 fine and two months' imprisonment for vagrancy.

The NWMP arrest of the "Crooked Kid" in Calgary opened a legal issue with the municipal government charging the NWMP with "meddling." The town council recently passed an ordinance regulating vagrancy and hired a town constable to enforce the by-law. Mayor George Murdoch regarded the arrest of the "Crooked Kid" as an unwarranted interference into the affairs of the municipality. Town council forwarded a letter to Ottawa requesting legislation to divest the North-West Mounted Police of all judiciary powers within chartered municipalities.[24]

Having no consistent regulatory body to govern the law, many minor acts received a lengthy sentence or a hefty fine while more serious crimes were mildly consequented. Below is a chart of criminal offences in the 1880s and their accompanying sentence or fine.

Year	Name	Criminal Offence	Sentence/Fine
'78	Mary Foster	Assault on Anne Harris	$5
'80	L. Cobel	Using threatening language	$1
'80	C.J. Wheelen	Billiard hall without licence	$20 and costs
'80	M. Claustre	Contempt of court	$2
'81	James Folster	Selling liquor to the Indians	$50
'81	Jean Marie	Striking his wife with a knife	Dismissed
'81	L. Léveille	Assault	$1
'81	Léon Mayette	Assaulting wife	$2
'81	Thos. Wilton	Gambling	$50
'82	J. Nolan	Disturbing the peace	$5
'82	J. Fitzpatrick	Abusive & immoral language	$3
'82	J. Bowman	Setting fire to the prairie	$12
'83	W. Greig	Larceny	2 months prison
'83	Ellen Swift	Prostitution	$50 or 1 month
'83	W. Collins	Drunk & Disorderly conduct	$10
'84	Fred Pace	Illegal possession of alcohol	$200 & costs
'84	H. Nanny	Vagrancy	6 months prison
'84	W. Shepard	Business open on Sunday	$10
'84	Moise Racette	Horse stealing	7 years prison
'84	Hugh Bean★	Frequenter of a bawdy house	$10
'84	Ely Francis	Deserting his employment	1 month or $25
'84	P. Belanger	Shooting a dog	$3 and costs
'84	L. Jacobson	Peddling without a licence	$25 and costs
'85	Elmer Decker	Forged pass on C.P.R.	1 month prison
'85	W.P. Walsh	Dangerous lunatic	Imprisoned
'85	H. Wentworth★★	Firing revolver in streets	2 months prison

★ Nina Dow, madam of a house of ill-fame, was given a choice: six months in prison or leave Calgary on the first train. She was on the first train.

★★ Wentworth was unable to pay a $50 fine.

Offences involving horse-stealing, vagrancy, and alcohol-gambling received harsh sentences. A five-year sentence was given to Slim Jim and Little Fisher for horse theft, for example. Vagrancy netted four men in each Maple Creek six months imprisonment. Sherman and Gluck were both fined $500 and sentenced to three months imprisonment in 1876. The police had seen Sherman hanging around Fort Walsh and followed him south on the Fort Benton trail for 50 km where they arrested a gang of nine men with forty gallons of alcohol.[25] Even the refusal to give evidence on whiskey trading cost S. Alexander $100.

The most frequent criminal activity involved alcohol. In 1883–84 the number of cases (by grouping) included:

233	Selling intoxicants, related alcohol offences
169	Non-payment of wages
83	Drunk/disorderly conduct
75	Horse-stealing/bringing stolen horses into Canada
69	Larceny
64	Gambling
46	Assault and battery
25	Vagrancy
20	House of ill fame/inmates

The number of criminal cases that were listed in the Annual Report of the Commissioner, NWMP, grew from 43 in 1879 to 575 in 1884. This striking increase corresponded with a two-fold growth in population (mostly white) and added criminal charges. In Edmonton, in January 1883, for example, both Wright and McLaughlin each received twenty-five days imprisonment for desertion of employment and then an additional ten days in jail for refusing to return to work. Males faced far more criminal charges: in 1878 the male/female ratio was 14 to 1; in 1883, 383 to 1.

The growing number of court appearances burdened the already busy police officers. In twelve months following December 1882, they handled 308 cases. Supt. A. Shurtliff alone adjudicated 123 cases.[26]

The data given in the Annual North-West Mounted Police Reports is incomplete. In 1874–77, court charges are lacking and only fragmentary information on criminal activity is available. In 1877, a Montana paper listed the names of seven men the NWMP arrested for whiskey trading and related a trial at Fort Walsh where a Mr. Arnold was sentenced to two years hard labour for forgery.[27] Six convictions in Battleford by Stipendiary Magistrate H. Richardson in 1878, are omitted. The 1881 Annual NWMP

Report omits criminal cases from Fort Macleod and Fort Qu'Appelle. The 1883 Battleford and Edmonton statistics are incomplete. There is no record in 1885 of individuals sentenced at Beaver River for alcohol offences or the railway strike confrontations.

Since each North-West Mounted Police detachment disciplined its men, most criminal charges involving policemen have been omitted in the Annual NWMP Criminal Report. Some examples of police sentences include: for the theft of a parcel, Commissioner Irvine sentenced Constable McMillan to fourteen days in the guardroom, followed by dismissal from the Force; Christopher Rogers was convicted of stealing money from another member of the barracks, sentenced to six months in the guardroom and dismissed from the Force; in Edmonton, Inspector Griesbach sentenced Constable Smith to three months detention for stealing regimental spurs; at Fort Saskatchewan, Corporal Walwyn was reduced to private and given three months' imprisonment for tampering with a note; J. Dunbar received eight months incarceration for drawing a revolver in a most threatening manner on Sergeant Sam Horner.

The assertion that Aboriginal crime, based on newspaper reporting and criminal statistics, was proportionally less than that of whites overlooks the number of charges specific to whites.[28] In 1883–84, for example, there were 169 charges for the non-payment of wages. In 1883, these employment charges made up 24.8 per cent of the 386 total criminal cases. Second, the police routinely ignored many Indian crimes. While Jacob Fortier was fined $50 and J. Hamilton given one month with hard labour for causing a prairie fire, Colonel Irvine only admonished Indians who had left their campfires burning. Superintendent W. Herchmer was more forceful, making one party return to extinguish the smoldering embers. The Mounties overlooked Indian bigamy and gambling activities. Usually, officers ignored male Indians using a cane to beat their wives.[29] And many Indian disputes were settled by dialogue. One diary relates: "Two Indians got fighting in the fort to day one of the Indians was stealing anothers squaw. He was going to Shoot him when Major Irvine come up and settled it."[30] On the question of Indian disputes, Commissioner Irvine affirmed: "An immense number of cases of assault amongst the Indians, generally arising out of disputes about women, were settled by sending an officer to camp."[31]

Arrests
Sitting Bull's band was stunned when redcoated riders entered their camp and stayed for the night. In the morning, everyone stood transfixed as Inspector James Walsh shackled a suspected horse thief before their eyes.

It was an incredibly resolute act, but the determination in the NWMP to uphold justice was never in question. The awareness that a handful of policemen would enter a hostile Indian camp and make arrests was widely acknowledged. A letter in the *New York Tribune* related: "The officers and men of the police go singly into an Indian camp and make arrests."[32]

Policing sometimes required physical force. When a young Indian at Hay Lake drew a knife on Constable James McKernan, the policeman used his rifle butt to knock his assailant down. While making four arrests, Constable Parker watched his partner holding an Indian by the throat with his left hand while pounding him with his free fist.

Constable Clarke twisted one Native's pigtails around his neck to choke him into submission. Constable William Metzler watched Sergeant Ashe threaten and arrest a Stony Indian by placing a shooting iron in the man's mouth. In Gladstone, Constable Herron broke his baton in two while subduing an unruly McKinnon for disorderly conduct. He then drew his revolver for personal protection from a threatening group that had been inciting McKinnon's belligerence.[33]

A detail under Sergeant Frank Fitzpatrick circled an Indian camp for hours with drawn revolvers until daylight allowed the men to arrest the guilty parties. Corporals Fyffe and Davidson ignored threats from three Montana cowboys and confiscated twelve horses from their camp. When they returned to arrest Sam James, the cowboy jumped on his horse and headed south. After a chase lasting nearly an hour, Corporal Fyffe overtook and arrested James.[34] Inspector William Winder caught James "Slim Jim" Brooks, a tough horse thief and escapee from Montana, "after an exciting horse race of five miles, and had it not been for the superior swiftness of our horses he would have escaped across the line."[35] It was a second bullet by Constable Wilson that passed between Brooks' bridle arm and body that brought the fugitive to a halt. One police rider recorded:

> He then halted his horse and said, "Well, I guess you got me, but who is that policeman away back there?" Wilson replied, "That is Supt. Winder."
>
> "I thought so," said Slim. "I wish he had been up here so I could have had a shot at that old baldheaded son-of-a-bitch, just to see how he would have acted." When the Superintendent rode up, Slim cussed him in dreadful language.[36]

Being subjected to verbal abuse was part of the job. Winder had supervised "Slim Jim's" earlier six-month imprisonment.

There were many demanding missions to uphold justice. In the summer of 1876, Officers Leif Crozier and Cecil Denny led an eleven-man troop to arrest an Indian accused of murder. They rode northeast from Fort Macleod to the confluence of the Red Deer and South Saskatchewan rivers, an arduous trip of more than 270 km. At this point, they spotted a large Indian band moving towards them. The police selected a stand where the river bordered a high bank. Constable John Herron was in the troop:

> When the whole camp was within about half a mile of us they stopped. Fifty warriors came dashing towards us as fast as their horses could carry them. They rode at full speed until they came within 100 yards of us and then pulled up suddenly … one man came forward and shook hands with us. After the excitement was over, we had a little bit to eat and went down to the big camp and arrested our man.[37]

The police rode a short distance westward and then split into two groups, the two officers taking the prisoner (probably Nataya) to Fort Macleod while the remaining troop rode on to Fort Calgary.

In a time without standard identification cards, some arrests had to be made when there was little information about the suspects. Sergeant Frank Fitzpatrick received orders to arrest "a crazy man" in the File Hills, 35 km northeast of his post at Fort Qu'Appelle. He left with a buckboard, supplies, shackles, and handcuffs. At his destination, the police officer asked people he contacted if they had seen a crazy man who Fitzpatrick could not even name. All responses were negative. Then by chance, Fitzpatrick encountered a wild-eyed individual. Surely this was the crazy man.

The suspect was a huge man, but friendly. Fitzpatrick engaged him in diversionary conversation and suggested that they go for a ride. The police officer related: "As he took his seat, I pulled out the shackles and handcuffs, and asked him if he knew what they were for. He replied in the negative, and I told him I would show him."[38]

Once he had the suspect secured in the buckboard, Fitzpatrick carried on chatting as a distraction until they reached the Fort Qu'Appelle guard house. "There's your prisoner," Fitzpatrick told the sergeant.[39]

And no one was outside the clutches of the NWMP. Even Reverend William Newton of Edmonton found himself in jail on a charge of stealing cattle. The minister was released on bail of $800, a substantial sum at that time. He was acquitted when it was revealed there had been a mistake over the ownership of the animal.[40] Perhaps the local detachment was overly eager to imprison the parson. Two years earlier, Dr. Newton had publicly announced that "B" troop "was composed of a lot of scoundrels, from the colonel down."[41] The parson's humble apology ended police threats of court action for slander.

Discretion was needed in making arrests. Near Fort Walsh, trader Louis Watson entered a Sioux camp and seized two horses he claimed were stolen from him the previous night. The North-West Mounted Police overlooked his bold undertaking and, in Watson's words, "were amazed that I came back at all to tell the tale."[42] At one poker game, the police arrested everyone except Father C. Scollen, who was described as only an "onlooker." Captain A.H. Griesbach rode from Edmonton to Battle River to check on Donald Todd, who was reported to be a dangerous lunatic. Upon meeting with him, Griesbach decided the man was sane. But, ten days later, a warrant placed Todd in the Fort Saskatchewan guardhouse as a lunatic, pending the pleasure of the Lieutenant Governor.

Compromise, too, was prudent. Constable James McKernan arranged for Indians who had occupied and damaged a house to pay the owner three horses. Stipendiary Magistrate H. Richardson had Beardy return a horse the chief had taken from a settler and make a promise to behave better.

Policemen had to contend with bribes. When Constable Blake found contraband in a house, he was offered $10 to say nothing. The local paper reported that: "He indignantly rejected this and reported to headquarters. Major Dowling answered T. Blake would be given a favorable report on conduct to Regina."[43]

Did this famous Force, as the saying goes, always get their man? Well, mostly—but not always. When Constable Blake took a warrant (on a charge of selling whiskey) to John McGuire, he was greeted by McGuire holding a revolver and ordering him to depart. McGuire rode away and a search for the fugitive was unsuccessful.[44] McGuire's reckless confrontation may have been to avoid arrest. Two months earlier, he had received fines of $10 for being drunk and $200 for possessing illegal intoxicants. In their search for another wanted man, Constable Edward Barnett and a companion had stopped for a smoke when suddenly the armed suspect appeared from behind some willow bushes. He took their guns and horses and headed south. Barnett recalled: "'Better luck next time' he chided us, as he rode away."[45] Constable Barnett and his companion walked back to the fort.

Incarceration

Prisoners were confined in cramped guard houses. The tiny five-by-four-metre building at Fort Walsh had three cells on one side holding five or six prisoners, both male and female; four guards crowded the other side.

The arrest of nine Mounties for desertion at Fort Walsh overwhelmed the post's prison capacity and entailed their transfer to Fort Macleod. Conditions at that fort were hardly better:

> We had from two to six or more prisoners in a guard room not larger than fourteen feet square, in which there were two cells, and on one side a long platform about ten feet, and four feet high. We put our trustee prisoners on this platform on the inside and the men who were not on sentry would lie on the outside if there was room. We always had very strong coffee to drink.[46]

The small compound at Fort Macleod was also confined and measured only thirteen by ten metres.

Unsanitary conditions typified the crowded guard houses. In his Health Report for 1879, Surgeon Kittson described the difficulties of caring for "an old squaw, somewhat inclined to cannibalism, completely maniacal and very difficult to manage. Her filthy habits infected the guardroom to such an extent that she had to be removed to a small building by herself."[47] But, with good food and kind treatment, Kittson recorded, the woman completely recovered her mind.

Having "lunatics" incarcerated in the prison population was disruptive. Constable A.R. Dyre, stationed at Beaver Creek in British Columbia during railway construction, described one case:

> We have a madman who is to be sent to Winnipeg next train. We have to keep him shackled and tied down in his cell, and he yells, curses and groans nearly all the time. He broke loose about an hour ago and started to batter his head against the wall. I have often heard of the strength of crazy people but never saw anything like this before. He grasped me as we were tying him down and every muscle in him appeared to be as strong as steel. As I write he is lying down growling like a dog.[48]

In Regina, aware that the ceaseless chatter and howling of six lunatics disturbed the other prisoners and the guard, Commissioner Irvine proposed that "lunatics who have been committed to custody as 'dangerous' can be provided for other than in the police guard rooms."[49]

Guard duty lasted for seven days. In general, most policemen detested this assignment. One wrote: "You took up your quarters in the guard-room and bid adieu to society for a week."[50] Constable John Donkin disliked having to sleep in his uniform on a wooden bed. No one was allowed to leave the guard house except to escort prisoners to the latrine or bring meals from the kitchen.

The prisoners shined police boots, cleaned the compound, latrines, and stables, repaired the root cellar, whitewashed buildings and fences, cut and stored large piles of firewood, and so on. Some of the prisoners worked while encumbered by an attached ball and chain. The *Manitoba Free Press* wryly commented: "No prisoners in Fort Saskatchewan now. The boys have to saw their own wood."[51]

Even under the close supervision, some prisoners managed to escape. Sandfly, an Indian, unscrewed his lock plate and walked away unobserved. Four Indians sent out to exercise undid their chain fetters and ran, safely dodging the sentry's bullets. Sergeant Frank Spicer, on horseback, captured two of the escapees. On learning that prisoners had escaped, concerned residents in Fort Macleod demanded better police protection. In a security measure, the new gaol (jail) in Regina in 1883 had iron plates placed inside the walls to prevent anyone cutting out of their cell and the barred windows were seven feet above the floor.

However escapes continued, Corporal Jarvis chased an escaping prisoner, even throwing his own revolver to knock the man down momentarily. Finally impeded by his heavy boots, Jarvis gave up after a 10 km pursuit. Still undeterred, the next day Jarvis and Sergeant Spicer went to the Peigan reserve and arrested the fugitive who they found hiding in a cellar.[52]

One dangerous situation arose when three Indians broke from their escort and ran to a Native encampment where they obtained rifles and opened fire at pursuing Constables Simons and Hooley, but without effect. Although the police constables arrested and returned two men to jail, armed Indians were seen on the hilltops above the fort. The post quickly readied the defences, including the field pieces. No attack ensued and, that night several Mounties, dressed in civilian clothing, hid near the horse herd in case the last escapee attempted to steal a horse. He never appeared.

The weather turned cold with snow. In the morning, several Mounties returning to Fort Walsh chanced upon the wanted Indian, who had earlier discarded most of his clothes to run faster. He died from exposure while they brought him to the fort.[53] For some reason, his band asked that he be buried in a police uniform. The post accommodated this unusual request by providing a worn uniform.

An attempted escape in freezing weather was hazardous. During a raging blizzard, Sub-Constable Roger Pocock recalled taking three prisoners to carry lamps from the canteen to the mess-room. He wrote: "Midway between the buildings we got lost and I drew my revolver to be ready if either of my charges tried to bolt. They chaffed me gently, knowing that the weather was so much more deadly than my marksmanship."[54]

Should a policeman be allowed to shoot an escaping prisoner? At Fort Macleod Constable R.N. Wilson watched four Indians slip their irons and run for the trees:

> As I saw them start I could have killed them all if I wanted to but I did not try to hit any of them because a policeman has no orders that could justify him in killing an escaping prisoner. I followed them to the river after alarming the post and fired several shots over their heads. Two of them were caught in the river and brought back & sentenced to three months extra imprisonment. The other two succeeded in making their escape.[55]

Other Mounties had no qualms about shooting at escaping prisoners. Constables Alexander and Parker arrested John Benton Munro on the Blood Reserve for selling whiskey. While riding to Fort Macleod, Munro attempted to escape. After an unheeded warning to stop, Alexander fired and hit Munro in the hip, and, in the words of the local press, "he did not escape any further."[56] At the post, Dr. Kennedy extracted the bullet. The *Fort Macleod Gazette* editorialized that there can be little doubt what a policeman's duty is in such a case. Moreover, when this "is carried out and understood by prisoners, there will be few attempts to escape."[57]

An unsuccessful escape added prison time for the offender. Thunder Day, a Cree Indian, had six months added to his sentence for larceny; J. St. Joe and Jozippa received three months in addition to their six-month sentence for killing cattle.[58] And a police guard held accountable for an escape could lose rank or find himself imprisoned. When two Sioux being taken to the latrine escaped "the unfortunate escort was ordered to fill the place of one of them for one month."[59]

On infrequent occasions, prison sentences were reduced. Fifteen Cree sentenced to two years imprisonment were released after ten months in jail. An Indian prisoner gained his freedom after informing the guards that his cellmates had hidden weapons. A search found knives, an old razor, and sharpened nails. The prisoners were put on bread and water. And the Governor General's visit in 1881 proved fortunate for the men in the Fort Macleod guard house when he issued a Royal edict granting their release.

A prisoner sentenced to more than one year was escorted to the Stony Mountain Penitentiary, near Winnipeg. Travel from Fort Macleod to the penitentiary was 1,100 km. Sergt.-Major Thomas Lake accompanied

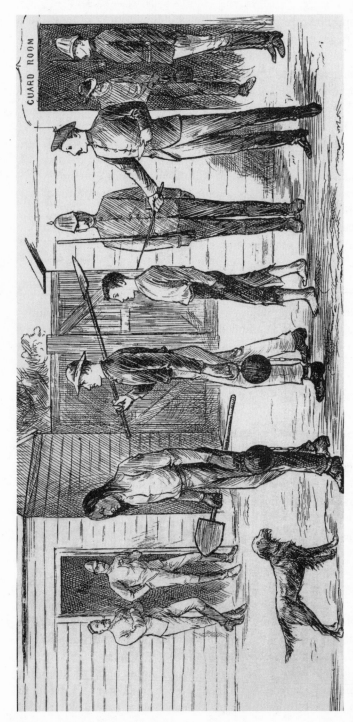

Prisoners at Fort Macleod (John Swain)

"A young Indian, son of Crow-Foot, chief of the Blackfeet, was arrested for snapping an empty pistol at a white man. He was tried, convicted and sentenced to twenty days' imprisonment, at hard labour, and at last accounts was sawing wood with gyves upon his wrists."

– *Helena Daily Independent*, 10 March 1876
   GA NA 2274 – 3

"Slim Jim" Brooks to prison with four Mounties (three of the men were leaving the Force). The group had four saddle horses and a four-horse team that was driven by "Slim Jim," a skilled driver. Two men rode in the wagon with "Slim Jim" who was dressed in a prison outfit. Each night, a chain linked the sleeping prisoner with a guard. It took twenty-one days to reach Winnipeg.[60]

Anyone who has crossed the vast Canadian prairies can only marvel at how the early policemen maintained directions, overcame or avoided slough and water obstacles, found shelter, carried provisions, managed and fed the horses, found water, food, and braved the weather. Related earlier in this book was the remarkable decision by Major Irvine's party, taking three frontiersmen charged in the Cypress Hills killings to trial in Winnipeg, to give the accused murderers rifles to hunt buffalo to sustain the party.

In winter, the transport of prisoners had dangerous risks. In February 1883, Inspector William Herchmer along with a small party escorted Snake (Ka-nah-pic-a-nahon), sentenced to five years for carnal knowledge of a girl under the age of ten, from Battleford to Winnipeg in temperatures that reached below -40°C.

Most often a single constable would take a prisoner to Stony Mountain. The prisoner rode with his feet shackled by a chain attached under the horses' belly and at night he was chained to the ground. The pair usually rode thirty to fifty kilometres a day, except when they had to travel at night to find water. The prisoner sometimes broke trail and often prepared the meals. The main food on these "hikes" was pemmican and salt-pork, along with rabbits and prairie chicken shot along the way.[61]

Sergeant F. Fitzpatrick, transporting an Indian prisoner by buckboard, kept the man's feet shackled to the crossbar of the vehicle during the day; at night, he had the prisoner lie on the far side of the wagon and shackled his feet with a chain running through the wheel spokes. Fitzpatrick slept with his revolver and shackle key within reach and felt safe. In the morning the prisoner, still wearing his shackles, hobbled about preparing breakfast.[62]

Extra precautions in the transport of prisoners were taken if Indian interference was anticipated. In the fall of 1882 a Blood Indian named Jingling Bells was sentenced to three years in prison for horse stealing. While in the Fort Macleod guardhouse, his troublesome behaviour incited his friends to keep a constant watch on the fort and to warn police that he would never be taken "out of the country." The police countered by removing Jingling Bells at night in a guarded wagon. At sunrise, they met Mounties with a wagon waiting to escort the prisoner to End of Track for rail transportation to Stony Mountain.[63] Mr. McDonald, the factor at the Fort Ellice Hudson's Bay post, foiled Indian threats to rescue "Kid"

McKeown and an Indian that Captain John French was taking to the Manitoba penitentiary. (Both prisoners were sentenced to lengthy terms— the Indian to five years for horse stealing, McKeown to three years for altering $1 bank bills to $4 to cheat Indians.) Factor McDonald warned the Indians that, if any problems ensued, he would have troublemakers go with the two prisoners to the penitentiary.[64] At Fort Ellice, Captain French and both prisoners boarded the steamer *Marquette* on its way to Winnipeg. "Kid" McKeown could be seen wandering about the boat, encumbered by a ball and chain.

A trip to Stony Mountain meant a return to "civilization." Manitoba by 1885 had 100,000 people and, in Winnipeg, the "Chicago of the North," there were merchants, street lights, horse-drawn railway trams, a university (founded in 1877), mail delivery, a roller rink, local telephone service, two daily newspapers, and, most of all—"wet" bars. Telegraph, railway, and river steamers connecting the city to the continent made Winnipeg a world apart from the isolated police posts they left.[65] Constable Francis Dobbs, taking a young Indian thief to Stony Mountain, wrote: "I was glad of the chance as I would see Winnipeg again."[66]

From a population of 3,700 in 1873, Winnipeg had increased five-fold in twelve years to almost 20,000 people. The "Manitoba Land Boom" had ended and residents could now look back at the unshakeable optimism in unfettered land speculation: between the fall of 1881 and the overnight financial collapse in April 1882, an unimaginable 300 real estate companies operated in the town.

At the end of the 1885 insurrection, ninety-seven men charged with felony or high treason were escorted from Prince Albert to Regina for trial. On one trip, there were twenty-five Mounted Police guarding a column of prisoners. Some of the leading rebels, such as Big Bear, rode encumbered by chains. Louis Riel had better service, escorted to Regina by Captain Young of the Winnipeg Field Battery on May 23. In prison, Riel was secluded and strictly guarded. The number of prisoners overwhelmed the ten-cell Regina jail capacity and forced the immediate construction of temporary prison accommodations. Superintendent Deane overrode issuing tenders and entrusted the construction to John Ross, a contractor. Sergeant Pigott alone supervised eighty-one prisoners.

Criminal Charges against Mounted Policemen.

Certainly the most bizarre criminal case involving a Mounted Policeman was that of Rishton Seymour Jones, alias "Joe Bush."[67] Jones had written Captain R. Burton Deane, with whom he had served in the Royal Navy, inquiring about employment in the NWMP. Deane advised Jones that prairie police life was probably not suitable for someone who had spent eighteen years at sea. Five months later, the Captain was taken aback when the 36-year-old Jones arrived as a recruit in Regina.

The Fort Macleod detachment had recently requested that Captain Deane provide a clandestine agent to infiltrate the local whiskey smuggling trade. And here was Jones with his long hair and disheveled appearance, a perfect agent for this undercover role. Moreover, a share of any fines would financially support his former shipmate's struggling family. Captain Deane arranged to send Jones to Fort Macleod under the alias "Joe Bush."

Deane had picked the right man. The arrest of seven whiskey traders at Fort Macleod proved "Joe Bush" had found his niche. However, his unstable nature could not cope with this success and, while he was drunk, Bush shot an Indian named Found-the-Gun-on-the-Prairie. "Joe Bush" was charged with intent to do grievous bodily harm.

Confusing evidence was featured in the trial. In his charge to the jury, Magistrate James Macleod emphasized that the evidence given by an Indian equated with that of a white man, and that the wounded Indian had submitted his testimony in a very straightforward manner. Second, Macleod declared there was no excuse for drunkenness. Although the jury found "Joe Bush" guilty on 15 December 1884 with a recommendation for leniency, Macleod sentenced the police agent to twelve months of confinement in the Fort Macleod guard-room. Captain Deane arranged to have his friend serve the sentence in Regina.

During his short stay at Fort Macleod, Rishton Seymour Jones (called "the informer") had alienated the townspeople so much that, after his trial, a mob of citizens set fire to an effigy of "Joe Bush" hanging from a tree. The "fun" all ended when a tall policeman appeared, cut down the "corpse," and dragged it to the barracks with practically the whole populace at his heels, hooting and yelling.[68]

The arrest at Battleford of Constable J.H. Wright for obtaining property by false pretenses opened a perplexing case. Wright had received a land claim, horses, property, and cash as the brother, of deceased Edmonton resident Thomas Wright. However, correspondence with the father of the deceased man disclosed that Constable Wright was not the brother but an imposter. The prosecution dropped the charge of obtaining property under false pretenses once it was disclosed that the surname Wright had applied to both the deceased man and the policeman who had mistakenly assumed the dead man was his brother in the northwest with whom he had lost contact.[69]

A number of former Mounted Police ran afoul with the law. Alcohol and gambling offences were foremost: Fred Pace, James Murray, Cecil Denny, Jean Claustre, Éphrem-A. Brisebois (the founder of Calgary), and D.J. Cochrane were convicted of alcohol offences. At Wood Mountain, after paying the $100 for illegal alcohol and completing his one-month prison sentence with hard labour, Fred Brown re-enlisted for a second term in the Force. A.H Scouten was fined $3 for punching an Indian who had been sitting on his fence. Inspector Cecil Denny faced charges for fraud, break-and-enter, and assault. Anthony Prongua, after whom the hamlet in Saskatchewan is likely named, spent five years in the penitentiary for cattle rustling. After he had left the Force, Percy Robinson secretly defrauded the Indian department.

In Calgary, an inflammatory local issue, referred to as the "Travis Case," arose when a former Mountie, Simon "Jack" Clarke, forcefully prevented policemen from searching his Castle Mountain Billiards for alcohol.[70] Personal motives quickly fueled the case. Stipendiary Magistrate Jeremiah Travis, in town only two months, seemed bent on confronting the civic administration and sentenced Clarke to six months in prison. A town meeting censured this punishment and delegated Mayor George Murdoch to travel to Ottawa to lay grievances.

Percy Neale received a lengthy prison sentence several years after he left the Force. The former Superintendent was the third man to join the Force and had a commendable seventeen-year NWMP career. He and his wife were active in theatre and the arts in Regina and counted among their close associates the prominent westerners of the day. After Neale resigned from the NWMP in 1890, he worked as a Customs Collector in Lethbridge and, in that capacity, embezzled government funds.

Neale was arrested in London, England, in 1894 carrying $1,700 cash and a passenger ticket for South America. He was returned to Western Canada and charged with defrauding the Canadian Customs Department of almost $6,000. At his trial, Neale pled guilty and asked for leniency in acknowledgement of his dedicated twenty years he spent in service to the government. Magistrate Hugh Richardson, who knew Neale well, ruled that the accused had willfully violated the law and that a legal example was in order. He sentenced Neale to seven years confinement in Stony Mountain Penitentiary.[71]

Justice had been swift: Neale was arrested on 18 September 1894 in England, returned to Canada, and imprisoned on November 1 in Stony Mountain penitentiary. It was a humiliating ordeal for a man who had contributed so much to the early NWMP.

Civil Cases Involving the NWMP

One offshoot of the bizarre "Joe Bush" affair was a lawsuit for criminal libel by plaintiffs Superintendent John Cotton and Surgeon George Kennedy against the *Fort Macleod Gazette* for having called the two NWMP officers "North American Chinamen." The two police officers lost their litigation when defence lawyer H.M. Bleeker successfully argued that the newspaper associating the police officers with a civilization capable of producing a sage like Confucius was not denigrating.[72]

Civil actions cost Inspector William Herchmer $190 in damages to Thomas Ryan, a local farmer. In his decision, Magistrate Hugh Richardson berated "the defendant's [Herchmer's] unwarranted conduct in connection with the eviction and arrest of the plaintiff."[73]

As the evidence disclosed, Herchmer had highhandedly torn down the tents belonging to Ryan and using police wagons deposited the contents on the prairie about 1 km away. Herchmer then arrested Ryan and brought him to the Shoal Lake detachment where he unsuccessfully tried to coerce his prisoner to sign a declaration affirming that he would not reoccupy the land. The affair was described by a news correspondent as a "somewhat novel incident."[74]

Trouble was nothing new for the Inspector. About four months before this eviction incident in 1880, Herchmer had three other people evicted, including another Ryan—this time, Stipendiary Magistrate Matthew Ryan—from the Shoal Lake post for using threatening language toward him.[75] In a letter to the *Winnipeg Daily Times*, the Police Superintendent defended his actions, explaining: "Matthew Ryan, Stipendiary Magistrate, was turned out of barracks by my orders for using abusive and insulting language to me in the barracks square on 20 November."[76] And, in a widely-publicized incident in November 1884 while in command at Calgary, he was knocked out by a blow to the back of his head by an unknown party. No arrests were made.[77]

The Murder of Constable Marmaduke Graburn

On 17 November 1879, five months after he was sworn in at Fort Walsh, Constable Marmaduke Graburn became the first Mounted Policeman to be murdered. The 18-year-old recruit had returned to a pasture west of the fort to retrieve an axe and a picket rope. When he failed to return to Fort Walsh, scout Louis Léveille led a search party to the location.

They found Graburn's body with a bullet (shot from close range) in his back. Both the Mountie's knife and new Winchester rifle were missing. Tracks in the snow of one shod horse and several Indian ponies pointed to Indian murderers.[78] Graburn's dead horse was found wedged between two trees with the bridle and saddle still on. Four mounties stood guarded over the corpse that night.

The next day, the detail brought Graburn's body to Fort Walsh. His comrades were shocked. One wrote: "His body was a terrible sight to see … his face was one mass of blood … little did Marmaduke think when he left Ottawa that he would be murdered by Indians."[79] A second companion recorded his thoughts: "Poor little fellow. So young, so full of life and happiness. What a prospect of advancement there was before you, had it not been for the will of God that this year should be your last."[80]

The post went on high alert. All men were issued side arms and ordered not to leave the base alone. Constable Holmes, who had studied medicine for three years, examined the body. He determined that a bullet from a Winchester rifle had hit Graburn's back and passed through the shoulder blade to penetrate the lungs. Constable McEntyre expressed the feeling of the post: "The resentment against any and all Indians was overwhelming."[81] A letter described the funeral:

> Every man in the Fort turned out, and it was really a grand solemn sight. A firing party of twelve men marched with reversed arms in front. The band playing the mournful "Dead March" came next. Then the gun-carriage bearing the corpse. The coffin, covered with the Union Jack, and with his arms and helmet on it, was followed by his troop horse with his boots in stirrups, and bridle decked with crepe, led by two of his comrades. The pall-bearers walked on each side of the corpse. Then came B troop, then F troop, every man in full uniform; the civilians brought up the rear.[82]

At the gravesite, Church of England rites were read and, as earth covered the coffin, a firing party fired three volleys over the grave.

It took two weeks after the funeral before a telegram from Comptroller Fred White to notify Graburn's parents in Ottawa of their son's death. As compensation, his mother received a land grant and $500 gratuity. In his official report, Commissioner Macleod attributed the atrocious crime to revenge against whites and not specifically the police. He added, "all his comrades mourned the sad fate of poor Graburn deeply, as he was a great favorite amongst us all."[83]

Two imprisoned Blood Indians provided a lead in the killing when they alleged that an Indian youth, Star Child, had boasted of the murder. Several Mounties at the post recalled that Graburn had been involved

Star Child

"It required more courage to acquit Star Child than to convict him."

– Edward Maunsell, GA, Elizabeth Price, M 1002, f. 1
  GA NA 451 – 1

in a confrontation with Star Child, who was scrounging for food and ordered him to leave, calling him a miserable dog. All attempts to locate Star Child failed and it was believed that the suspect was south of the border.

In May 1881, eighteen months after the murder, information came that Star Child was on the Blood reserve near Fort Macleod. A four-man police party under Sergeant Ashe went to the location where they found Star Child sleeping with a rifle and revolver hanging above his head. Ashe told his companions, Constables R.N. Wilson, Ralph Sleigh, and DaRenzie, to "riddle him" if he reached for his firearms. Star Child was awakened but, in Wilson's words, "was too wise to do anything rash and after the warrant was read to him, got up and came with us to Standoff."[84]

At the trial in October 1881, a six-man jury (that included five former Mounted Policemen), after twenty-four hours of deliberation, found Star Child not guilty.[85] White settlers scorned this verdict. An outsider wrote, "and I have it from witnesses that everyone considers him guilty."[86] The prevailing view, expressed by Inspector Steele, was that the "jurymen were afraid that the conviction would bring on an Indian war."[87]

This perception persisted. Forty years later, juryman Edward Maunsell wrote a letter explaining that the jury had doubted Star Child's guilt. William Gladstone, a prominent westerner, with an understanding of the "Indian character," convinced his fellow jurymen that young Indians routinely bragged, often without proof, of brave exploits which made the evidence flimsy. Moreover, Maunsell maintained that, since the whole country was crying out for vengeance, "it required more courage to acquit Star Child than to convict him."[88]

Capital Crimes

In the spring of 1879, an Indian named Swift Runner (Kakisikutchin) told the clergy at St. Albert that his family had starved to death during the winter. The priests were suspicious: Swift Runner looked well-nourished, unlike someone who had experienced such a horrific tragedy. The clerics notified the Fort Saskatchewan detachment.

Swift Runner was known to the police. He had worked as a police guide until problems with alcohol made him unreliable. After losing his employment, he had stolen furs and then gone on a prolonged drinking spree. In late 1878, after Swift Runner attempted to shoot a trader, the police confined him until he recovered from delirium tremens.

Superintendent W.D. Jarvis sent Sergeant Richard (Dick) Steele out to interview Swift Runner. The Mountie disbelieved the suspect's story and had him brought in irons to Fort Saskatchewan. After questioning, Jarvis had a party under Captain Sévère Gagnon take Swift Runner to the scene of the deaths, 120 km north of St. Albert. At this location, after Swift Runner's false leads made no headway, Gagnon plied him with strong tea laced with tobacco. In his inebriated state, Swift Runner became talkative and led the party to the winter camp where a search located scattered human bones. Although Swift Runner claimed that bears had eaten the bodies, no visible claw or teeth marks were evident. Gagnon suspected that the bones had been boiled. The discovery of needlework stuffed in the baby's eye socket suggested murder.

Upon the return to Fort Saskatchewan, under Superintendent Jarvis' interrogation, Swift Runner admitted his guilt. Putting his fingers into the eye socket of a skull, one of six placed on a table, Swift Runner held it up and casually commented "this was my wife."[89] After further prodding, he confessed to having killed and eaten his wife and five children; in his words, "he made beef of them." A later, more detailed confession to Father Hippolyte Leduc (LeDuc) was published in several papers. Its contents were graphic: "I took the bodies of my little girls and cut them up. I did the same with the corpse of my wife. I broke the skulls and took out the brains, and I broke up the bones in order to get to the marrow."[90]

The police guards regarded Swift Runner as being indifferent to his fate. He often was joking. Fred Bagley recalled:

> "Frenchy" a huge and particularly well-nourished member of our troop, was a constant source of merriment to the prisoner. Each time the constable entered the guard-room the Indian's saucer-like eyes gloated over the corpulent form, his lips parted in a broad grin. "Wah! Wah! You would make fine eating; there must be that much (holding up three fingers) fat on your ribs."[91]

Bagley mused that Swift Runner took a liking to him, perhaps because the young Mountie spoke Cree to the prisoner or, in Bagley's words, "because I was young and tender."[92]

At his trial on 16 August 1879, a six-man jury quickly returned a verdict of guilty of the murder of his wife and their five children. Magistrate Hugh Richardson sentenced Swift Runner to be hanged on 20 December 1879. The prisoner's request to be shot was refused.

Edouard Richard, Sheriff of the NWT, supervised the execution scheduled for Fort Saskatchewan.[93] Before he left Battleford on December 9, he telegraphed Colonel Jarvis to build the scaffold (which, Richard later praised, "would stand as a model of the kind."[94]) and second, to oversee the hanging should Richard's arrival be delayed by snow or cold weather.

The news of the public execution attracted a number of Indians to Fort Saskatchewan. On the night before the scheduled hanging, they camped outside the barracks and, in the bitterly cold weather, kept fires burning for warmth. Included in the wood burned was the trap door of the scaffold. This delayed the execution in the morning for about an hour while a replacement door was readied.

On the fated day, Swift Runner attended mass with Father Leduc and then the two men had breakfast. At 10 a.m., Inspector Jarvis led the police who were escorting Swift Runner to the scaffold. A black flag was hoisted while Swift Runner prayed alongside Father H. Leduc on the platform. The condemned man thanked the priest and police for their kindness and implored the Indian spectators to heed his fate. The trap door was sprung and the large man then dropped six feet to an instant death. His body was buried in the snow.[95]

The hangman was an old English soldier who refused to wear a mask, explaining that everyone in the small community knew him anyway. At the police barracks, trader Jim Read, a former forty-niner, exclaimed: "Byes, oh byes the purtiest hanging I've saw, an' I've seen thirty wan iv them." A Police Sergeant then countered, "Well, Jim, you may have seen thirty-one or 131 in the old days, but never before did you see a man and his whole family drop all together at the end of a single rope."[96]

Not all hangings offered an instant death, likely because the hangmen (who applied for the job) were not trained for this gruesome task. A Winnipeg newspaper described the hanging of Angus McIvor as a "bungled job." The hangman—"Jack Ketch"—had improperly tied the rope and, on the drop, the noose slipped under McIvor's chin. McIvor struggled for almost three minutes before strangulation caused his death.[97] At the hanging in Calgary of Jess Williams, the fall failed to break his neck and he convulsed for seven minutes. Police Surgeon Augustus Jukes, attending the hanging of John Connors at the Regina barracks, could still detect a pulse after nine minutes. A news reporter overheard policemen discussing whether the drop was deep enough and why wasn't the knot under the left ear rather than the chin? The columnist added that the hanging "was a ghastly sight which sickened strong men."[98] Five months later, in November 1885, in preparation for the hanging of eight Indians in Battleford, members of the detachment repeatedly tested the ropes by attaching and dropping 200-lb. sacks of bacon.

At the Battleford hangings following the North-West Rebellion, the hangman was Robert Hodson, described as a small, stocky, pock-marked, cross-eyed Englishman who was employed as a cook for the Hudson's Bay factor at Fort Pitt. During the North-West Rebellion, Robert Hodson was a prisoner in Big Bear's camp for ten weeks and had been constantly abused. One of his companion hostages wrote: "The Indians regarded him as some new variety of grub, and I know they would have liked to kill him out of mere idle curiosity to see him squirm."[99] Not unlikely, it was his perilous hostage ordeal that prompted Hodson's application to be the hangman.

The NWMP dealt with four murders before the tragic Swift Runner killings. The first murder in April 1875, at a Sheep Creek post (near High River), resulted from a drunken argument that ended with Fred Wachter killing Joseph "Castilian Joe" Arana with an iron bar. His body was brought to Fort Macleod for Surgeon Nevitt to examine. An inquest ruled the death a case of self-defence. Arana was buried beside the graves of Sub-Constables Wilson and Baxter, who froze to death three months earlier. The token inquest appears possibly to have pitted an outsider against an area resident. Fred "Dutch" Wachter, a native of Germany, had served in the Confederate army and, although a whiskey trader, had the support of the community.[100]

The murder of Po-ka-ke was unexpected and gruesome. Several hours after midnight, the woman was dancing with a young Indian inside a teepee when someone cut a hole in the tent and fired at her. The bullet entered her left ear and passed through her right eye, popping out the eye onto her cheek. She fell into the fire, smashing the pots and kettles.

In the turmoil her dancing partner was accused of the shooting but he exonerated himself by pointing out that his revolver was still fully loaded. Everyone remained in the tent for fear of being shot, allowing the killer to escape. The next day, Surgeon Nevitt prepared to examine the body but the woman had already been buried. He wrote in his diary of the ghastly murder: "After all this is a pretty wild country."[101]

The suspect was her husband, At-che-moon-e-kiss (Otsemoonee; It see moon-e-pis), a Blackfoot Indian, aged 64, who was said to have her kiss other men for gifts, which he kept. It was believed that he had shot his wife in a jealous rage. At-che-moon-e-kiss had a murderous reputation of killing thirteen people. Three victims were said to have been in an immigrant train of twelve settlers killed in the Porcupine Hills (northwest of Fort Macleod) in 1867. Once At-che-moon-e-kiss was taken into custody and scheduled to be taken to Winnipeg for trial, a second Aboriginal was arrested and brought to Fort Macleod.

Charles Gaudin (Godin), or Kiss-kah-wass-iss (Day Child), a Peigan half-breed, brutally murdered his young wife in 1872, two years before the arrival of the NWMP. She had sought safety in a river but, as she stood waist-deep in the water, Gaudin stabbed her eighteen times. He paid nine horses to the girl's relatives as compensation for her murder. The North-West Mounted Police, however, held a different view of "blood money" and he was arrested in 1875 in Edmonton for the crime. Three Mounties escorted Gaudin to Fort Macleod.

The two charged men remained in custody for a year. Finally, in August 1876, Inspector A. Shurtliff led a party that escorted the alleged killers and four crown witnesses to Winnipeg. A jury acquitted both men (on the same day) because of the lack of witnesses and concrete evidence.[102] In the case of At-che-moon-e-kiss, the jury never left the room, and only forty-five minutes was spent to decide Gaudin's fate.

In September 1875, Angus McIvor, a twenty-four-year-old Métis trader, murdered a sleeping George Atkinson and wounded Baptiste Charette, likely for the trade goods they were taking to Fort Carlton. Charette was awakened by a bullet to his face. He pushed McIvor outside the tent and dodged around a cart as McIvor fired five shots at him. In the ensuing uproar, while McIvor shouted accusations that Americans were doing the shootings, Charette managed to seize the weapon and forced McIvor to Atkinson's tent where they found Atkinson dead. The police arrested McIvor and took him to Winnipeg for trial. In court, McIvor insisted that he knew nothing about the crime as everything that night was blank.

McIvor was hanged on 7 January 1876 in Winnipeg. A large crowd had gathered, but only eighty people with passes were allowed near the scaffold and, to the disappointment of some, a large black curtain had been drawn to prevent the spectators from witnessing the death. Once an inquest was completed, McIvor's body was given to friends for burial.[103]

The fourth murderer before the Swift Runner killings was Peno, a Blood Indian, who shot a Cree east of Fort Calgary in June 1876. There is little information on this crime.

Swift Runner's tragic killing of his family occurred in a remote northern forest and, for settlers, was not viewed as threatening. Violent crimes nearer to settlements, especially on isolated farms, called for better area police protection. Near Fort Macleod, Joseph Moss confronted an Indian in the act of robbing his house and was stabbed. He reached a neighbour's home and Surgeon Kennedy rode from the police post to attend to Moss. The police arrested Cut-lip, a Sarcee Indian. He was found guilty of stabbing with intent and received six months imprisonment with hard labour. A newspaper commented that: "Considerable excitement prevails in the neighbourhood over the affair."[104]

John McCarthy (known as "Poor Old Daddy") lived alone in a sod shanty 2 km outside Fort Qu'Appelle. His decomposed body was found in a bluff some weeks after his murder. The police suspected robbery, but money was found on his person. A second wrong lead came in Winnipeg with the arrest of Abraham Stoddart, in jail for being drunk. That Stoddart was using a false name (Walsh), had blood on his shirt, and had worked for the deceased was incriminating. Stoddart, however, proved that he was in Winnipeg at the time of the murder.

Commissioner A.G. Irvine arrived from Regina for the investigation. An examination of the body found a skull fracture and broken jaw. A missing coat and satchel were possible leads in solving the crime.

When Corporal E.W. Mutch found McCarthy's coat in a trunk owned by the brothers John and George Stevenson, guilt pointed to the two Métis. The suspects were troublemakers. George had an unprincipled reputation after his wife had died under mysterious circumstances. His obsession with using playing cards to contact evil spirits and to locate hidden objects that he claimed divined the future seemed weird.

At a three-day trial, Magistrate Hugh Richardson found the brothers guilty and sentenced them to death. A Winnipeg paper observed "feeling in town is very strong and the citizens are eager to see both prisoners hang. Rumor Indians will cause trouble and raid the town."[105] A strong police guard was placed to thwart any Indian attack. The execution was delayed five times, suggesting the authorities were hesitant to incite the non-white population. The gallows were built with little space for witnesses and with a walkway that allowed the prisoners to walk directly from their cells to the platform.

The brothers remained self-possessed until a scaffold (with twin trap doors) was built. Then accepting their fate, both men gave their written confessions to priests that they had broken into McCarthy's shack and when he threatened to inform the police they killed him with an axe. The brothers were hanged in Regina on 3 April 1883, ten months after the murder.[106]

The *Regina Leader* praised the police for "indefatigable efforts in finding the perpetrators of this foul deed."[107] Less diplomatic was a comment that, immediately before the hangings, there "was a solemn and painful hush, although only the lives of a couple of half-breeds were at stake."[108] A letter to the *Prince Albert Times* asked, "Are half-breed lives less sacred than Canadian or even Irish?"[109] The Métis writer added that the *Regina Leader* has as little regard for decency as it has for the liquor laws.

A second murder in the Assiniboia District occurred in the spring of 1885 when John Connor was accused of murdering an acquaintance, Henry Mulaski, near Moose Jaw. After Constable Alexander Henderson found the mutilated body in Moose Jaw Creek, Constable Jeremiah Fyffe searched Connor's cabin, where he found copious amounts of blood and a trail of

Non-commissioned officers at Fort Walsh, 1880

L-R, front row - Cpl. Parkes, S/Sergt. Samuel Horner, Sergt. James Colvin; middle row - Cpl. J.A. Martin, S/Sergt. George Moffat, Sergt./Major Thomas Lake, Cpl. A. Westwood; back row - S/Sergt. George Fraser, Cpl. T.C. Severne, Cpl. Wilson, Cpl. T. Aspdin, S/Sergt. George Harper.

– GA NA 919 – 9

blood leading to the stream.[110] This evidence convinced a six-man jury to find "the German Jew" guilty. Connor's eccentric behavior in prison, in Surgeon Jukes' judgment, was contrived to feign insanity.

The July hanging of Connor in the Regina prison was closed to the public so as not to incite the sixty-eight inmates waiting on North-West Rebellion charges. On the day of execution, a large squad of forty-two policemen stood guard near the scaffold. Rev. Mr. Urquhart stood nearby, hoping to get a confession. Connor was sullen and then spoke a few words in Hebrew. He was non-responsive to any questions. His death was agonizing, with convulsions lasting for nine minutes. NWMP Surgeon A. Jukes served as the coroner and, with Dr. Dodd and the jury, examined the body. Their report seems sensible—Connor had died from hanging.[111]

In February 1884, townspeople in Calgary were aghast when the body of a store clerk was found with his head almost severed. Finding a suspect for the murder of James Adams was not difficult. Blood and footprints in the snow led the police to the home of Jesse Williams, a 42-year-old American Negro with a background of unruly behaviour. The police found a blood-stained razor, $30, and a bloody glove that matched Adams' other glove. There was no doubt that they had "the black demon."[112] This conviction was supported by witnesses who had seen "Nigger Dan" arguing with Adams earlier that day over an account. With overwhelming evidence facing him, the hard-bitten Jesse Williams confessed that, while he was committing a robbery, the clerk returned and, to avoid arrest, he cut Adam's throat with a knife and then hacked the wound with an axe.[113]

Outraged citizens held a meeting, chaired by T.B. Strange (who organized area defences in the North-West Rebellion), to discuss forming a vigilance committee, after the "manner of the American West." As a precaution against citizen violence, the local NWMP detachment placed a strong detail at the guard house. The lynching threats waned when Magistrate Macleod sentenced the accused to be hanged. Under the supervision of Sheriff Nutting, the detachment constructed a scaffold west of the police barracks.

At first, Williams acted indifferently, but he soon sought spiritual guidance and, in his last days became remorseful. On the scaffold, he calmly addressed the crowd, thanking his lawyer, the citizens, the police (for their kind treatment), and bid good-bye to Father Claude. He blamed his fate on whiskey: "I am here through drink."[114] Williams execution, conducted by a hangman wearing a disguise, took place within six weeks of the murder.

In June 1884, three months after J. Williams' crime, James McManus fatally stabbed his partner, Bill Reed, alias "Buckskin Shorty." The two whiskey traders were low types, who lived under a tree, slept on the ground, and only owned beside their horses and weapons, a combination of dirty blankets and several cooking pots to prepare their paltry diet of beans, slap-jacks, and a tea-whiskey drink.

George Harvey, a witness to the stabbing, rode to a Mr. Geddes' ranch for help. Geddes took several men to hold McManus and sent Harvey to ride to the Calgary police post, 7 km west. Within the hour, Corporal W. Wilde, with a five-man posse, apprehended the still-intoxicated McManus. They brought him and "Buckskin Shorty's" corpse to the police barracks where surgeons conducted an autopsy on the bloody victim. The police imprisoned Harvey, who had earlier charges for whiskey trading and no fixed residence, as a crown witness.

Magistrate James Macleod oversaw the trial. Corporals Wilde and Robinson gave evidence of the arrest and the two doctors submitted their findings of the autopsy. Crown witness George Harvey recounted the struggle and killing. The defence had portrayed "Buckskin Shorty" as a quarrelsome Montana cowboy who always carried a six-shooter and kept everyone in fear of him. The men were, in witness Harvey's testimony,

North-West Rebellion Murders in 1885

DATE	LOCATION	MURDERED	CHARGED	PENALTY
March 30	South of Battleford	James Payne	Ikta	Hanged
March 31	South of Battleford	Bernard Tremont	Man Without Blood (Wah-wah-nitch)	Hanged
April 2	Frog Lake	John Delaney	Unknown	Unknown
April 2	Frog Lake	George Dill	Iron Body (Napace and Little Bear (Apischiskoos)	Both men hanged
April 2	Frog Lake	Rev. L.A.F. Fafard	Walking the Sky (Paypamakeesik)	Hanged
April 2	Frog Lake	Rev. Felix Marie Marchand	Unknown	Unknown
April 2	Frog Lake	William Gilchrist	Kahweechetwaymot	Killed near Frenchman's Butte
April 2	Frog Lake	Charles Gouin	Bad Arrow (Manachoos) and Miserable Man (Kittimakegin)	Both men hanged
April 2	Frog Lake	John Gowanlock	Unknown	Unknown
April 2	Frog Lake	Thomas Quinn	Wandering Spirit (Pa-pa-mah-cha-kwayo)	Hanged
April 2	Frog Lake	John Williscraft	Kahweechetwaymot	Killed near Frenchman's Butte
June	Big Bear's camp	Puskayak (She Wins)	Charles Charlebois	20 years in prison
July 29	Saskatchewan Landing	George McIver	Lucky Man's band	Escaped to USA

462

drunk when the deceased jumped on McManus and struck him with a rifle butt, saying, "You Canadian son-of-a bitch, I started in to kill you and I am going to do it now!" McManus grabbed a knife held by "Buckskin Shorty" and cut his assailant's throat. The defence attorney argued that the killing was excusable homicide in self-defence.

In his address to the jury, Magistrate James Macleod emphasized that the murder weapon had belonged to the deceased. After forty-five minutes of deliberation, the jury returned with a verdict of manslaughter and recommendation of clemency. The following morning, Macleod sentenced McManus to six months confinement in the local police guard room.[115]

The *Regina Leader* ridiculed Calgary for having two murders in the first six months of 1884: "Calgary will soon become the Chicago of the northwest in matters of criminal records."[116] The *Calgary Herald* advocated using the *Vagrant Act* to rectify the town's "unenviable notoriety."[117]

In 1884, the construction of the transcontinental railway had reached the Rocky Mountains. Inspector Samuel Steele supervised thirty-two Mounties charged with maintaining order over thousands of navvies. Many workmen were hard characters with drinking problems. In the month of October, Steele convicted thirty-one men of drunk and disorderly charges. He also had two murders to investigate.

At Kicking Horse Flats, a political argument ended in a murder. James Finn, an Irish brakeman, had gone to a barber's tent for a shave. He and the barber, an American negro named William Foster, began arguing about the forthcoming 1884 American presidential election between Grover Cleveland (Democrat) and James G. Blaine (Republican). The dispute incited the Republican barber to charge Democrat Finn, with a razor, cutting his coat. Finn who just happened to come for his shave carrying a revolver, in Sam Steele's words, "filled him [Foster] full of holes." Finn surrendered to Superintendent Steele, who acquitted him, ruling it was a case of justified homicide.[118]

Robbery was the motive for the second murder on 27 November 1884. Robert (Harold) Baird, an employee of a Missoula, Montana, firm, was returning home with $4,000 in company money when he was shot on the trail south of Golden City (now Golden). One of his companions, a youth named Drainard, fled; a second companion fought with the attacker and was badly beaten. Both men returned safely to Golden City, while the murderer had escaped.

Though the murder occurred outside the NWMP's 20-mile jurisdiction, Inspector Steele sent two men to investigate the crime scene and had police search camps in the area. A reward offer of $1,000 by the Montana firm

Murders in NWT: 1874–85

DATE	LOCATION	VICTIM	ACCUSED	RESULTS
April 1875	Sheep Creek	Joseph Arana "Castilian Joe"	Fred "Dutch" Wachter	Acquitted
March 7 1875	Fort Macleod	Po-ka-ke (wife)	*At-chee-moon-e-kiss	Acquitted
Sept. 1 1875	Near Fort Ellice	George Atkinson	Angus McIvor	Executed
June 1876	East of Fort Calgary	Cree Indian	Peno (Blood)	Unknown
Winter 1879	North of St. Albert	6 family members	Swift Runner	Hanged
Nov. 17 1879	Fort Walsh	Marmaduke Graburn	Star Child	Acquitted
June 1880	Lac la Biche	Cardinal, father	Cardinal, son	7 yrs in Penitentiary
1880 or 81	Wood Mountain	Tempt Couvert	American Indians	Unsolved
1880	Wood Mountain	Antoine Laplante	American Indians	Unsolved
1881	Roche Percée	8 Canadian Indians	American Mandan	Unsolved
1882	Fort Walsh	Ne-Mo-Ke-Cut	Blood warriors	No arrests
June 14 1883	Qu'Appelle	John McCarthy	John and George Stevenson	Hanged (4 June 1883)
Feb. 9 1884	Calgary	James Adams	Jesse Williams	Hanged

Murders in NWT: 1874–85

DATE	LOCATION	VICTIM	ACCUSED	RESULTS
May 1884	Maple Creek	Saul Pollock	American Indians	Never arrested
June 1884	Calgary	Bill Reed "Buckskin Shorty"	Jack McManus	7 months for manslaughter
Oct. 1884	Red Deer River/ S. Sask. River	Charles Paul	Big Mouth Spring	Unsolved
Oct. 1884	Kicking Horse Flats	William Foster	James Finn	Acquitted
Nov. 27 1884	Golden, BC	Robert Baird	"Bulldog" Kelly	Fled to USA
April 6 1885	Moose Jaw	Henry Mulaski	John Connor	Executed
July 9 1885	Medicine Hat	Robert Casey	Ben Hale	Fled to USA
Nov. 2 1885	Blood Reserve	Wife	Wind Bellows	Escaped to USA

* At-chee-moon-e-kiss is also known as It-se-moon-a-pis and Otsemoonee.

During these early years while the west was being developed there was no consistent body regulating and enforcing the law. Both the judical system and the police force were quickly growing and responding to the current needs. The ratio of murders per capita was very high when you consider the population of the North-West Territories in 1885 was only 50,000.

and $250 from the province stirred general interest in solving the case. A description of the killer, suspected to be "Bulldog Kelly," a redheaded American drifter, was telegraphed to stations along the rail line.

Kelly had good luck on his side. At a construction camp in the Selkirk Mountains, he slept one night in a tent along with several constables. On a second occasion, Kelly was recognized on a train carrying Commissioner Irvine and Stipendiary Magistrate J. Macleod, but he disappeared when the train stopped. Although Kelly was arrested in Dakota Territory the next year, extradition attempts failed. Kelly (his real name was McNaughton) most likely died a violent death a year later in the American West.

Information on Aboriginal murders, other than Swift Runner, is skimpy. The Mandan-Assiniboine clash in the Fort Ellice area in October 1880 killed perhaps thirteen Indians. Some killings were vaguely reported. James Walsh told a Winnipeg paper that four Indian bodies were found two miles north of the boundary line.[119] The *Fort Macleod Gazette* wrote that a Blood shot a squaw dead, held off other Indians, and believed to have left for the United States. Major Cotton took thirty men to the Blood reserve to investigate.[120] Scarlet Plume, a Sioux in Sitting Bull's camp, was killed by Blackfoot warriors near Milk River in late October 1880. Whether he was in Canada is uncertain. An Indian was killed in the Sheep Creek foothills. Apparently a Stoney Indian had stolen horses from Natushappi, a Blackfoot chief. A brother of Shapomaxika, head chief of the Blackfeet, went to the Stoney camp to demand the return of the horses. He refused to stop approaching when ordered and was shot. According to the custom of these tribes, a pardon for killing a man was made by paying an indemnity proportional to the standing of the person killed, which, in this case, would probably be fifty horses—as he ranked as an important person.[121]

Temps Couvert and Antoine Laplante, both Métis, were murdered in the Wood Mountain area by unknown assailants. Nor are the Indian killers of several murders by Canadian Indians known. Blood warriors, angered by Cree horse thefts, overran the Cree camp near Fort Walsh, killing an elderly Cree named Ne-Mo-Ke-Cut. The incident at Fort Walsh was not even reported in the 1882 Annual Commissioner's report. In November 1884, Blood Indians ran off twenty-five horses near the forks of the Red Deer River. A Métis, Charles Paul trailed the thieves and was wounded three times before being killed by an Indian named Big Mouth Springs.[122]

In the North-West Rebellion, perhaps twelve deaths were murders. Four days after the opening skirmish at Duck Lake, warriors in Poundmaker's band murdered two settlers south of Battleford. Days later, on April 2, warriors in Big Bear's band murdered nine whites at Frog Lake.[123]

In late May, soldiers in the Alberta Field Force attacked Big Bear's band several kilometres north of Frenchman's Butte. Although the skirmish was without a clear victory, the arrival of soldiers forced the band to seek refuge in the northern wilderness. The military pursued the main camp in which twenty-seven white hostages were held. While fleeing from the soldiers, the macabre execution of a woman occurred.

One morning a poor wizened female named Puskayak (She Wins) began ranting hysterically. Tradition dictated that this aberrant behaviour signified a witago (wendigo), a dangerous cannibal who, for the safety of the band, had to be killed before sundown. However, finding an assassin proved difficult as no one wanted this bloody responsibility. At last, a Métis named Charlebois (Charles Ducharme) declared himself a nonbeliever of any god and accepted the gruesome task.

The woman was carried a short distance from the camp. Charlebois, his body decorated grotesquely in war paint and soot, spoke to the assembled: "My friends, you asked everybody to kill that woman and no one would do it. After I strike her, don't say I struck an old woman and laugh at me."[124] He then clubbed and shot the demented woman. An Indian accomplice, using a sabre, decapitated the poor victim and, clutching the severed head by the braids, "tried to throw the head over a clump of willows, but the braids caught in the branches and the head stayed there with its hideous face swinging three or four feet above the ground."[125]

Everyone fled in terror. "It was," in the words of hostage Louis Goulet, "the most horrible murder I ever heard of."[126] W.J. McLean, the Hudson Bay factor at Fort Pitt, echoed his words: "The scene was indescribably horrid."[127] Prisoners Henry Quinn and Louis Goulet then cremated the wretched woman's body.

In the period 1874–85, there were at least thirty-one murders in the North-West Territories. Fourteen men were hanged. In the North-West Rebellion campaign, thirty-seven rebels and fifty-six men in government forces died in military action or associated events.[128]

With a Territorial population of 50,000 in 1885, the number of violent deaths challenges the contention that peaceful settlement characterized the first years of settlement in the Canadian North-West Territories.

NOTES

1. *FBRP,* 9 November 1881.

2. *WDT,* 17 July 1883. *TM,* 2 February 1886.

3. *RL,* 17 May 1883. *SH,* 12 January 1880 on the arrest of Alexander Cunningham who, as a token of gratitude, offered a drink to the police.

4. *RL,* 24 March 1883.

5. *RL,* 31 January 1884.

6. Sub-Constables could not make an arrest until 1879.

7. *EB,* 29 September 1883. *RL,* 16 August 1883.

8. *CH,* 3 December 1884. The paper asked: "Is it proper, in a civilized society that any boy of eighteen or twenty years of age should be given the power to intrude into the private houses without a search warrant on the pretense of looking for liquor?" Also, *PAT,* 1 March 1884: "Our Grievances against men armed with the monstrous, extraordinary and utterly unconstitutional powers of Police Officers and Civil Magistrates."

9. *RL,* 27 January 1885. *MFP,* 5 April 1883 (settler's rights) and 20 August 1880 (complaints of martial law); *MFP,* 5 February 1884.

10. *RC,* NWMP, 1880, 33.

11. Utley, *Sitting Bull,* 182. Source – Robert P. Higheagle Manuscript, 41, Box 104, folder 21, Campbell Collection, University of Oklahoma, Norman, Oklahoma.

12. *RC,* NWMP, 1884, 16. Earlier in *RC,* NWMP, 1880, 16. Irvine had suggested that both countries would benefit if crimes along the border were considered as extraditable offences.

13. Craig, *Ranching with Lords and Commons,* 97.

14. "When Horse Thieves Terrorized the West," *SG,* Eighth Annual, 54—55. The *Report of the Commissioner, NWMP, 1884* states that Hooper trailed four horse thieves from Qu'Appelle to Turtle Mountain, not into the United States.

15. *FMG,* 4 May 1883.

16. *MFP,* 14 February 1878.

17. *FMG,* 24 November 1882.

18. *MFP,* 1 June 1877.

19. *Fort Battleford Post Diary,* 12—21 February 1885.

20. The *FMG* gives the minutes of a trial in the Queen v. Kanouse and Chas. Smith, 14 August 1882. Also see 21 November 1885, *Edmonton Bulletin,* for examples of the District Court.

21. F.W. Godsal, "Old Times," *AH,* XII, No. 4, 20.

22. *WDT,* 28 July 1884.

23. *HDI,* 25 July 1877. Burnett received two years in prison.

24. *RL,* 10 March 1885.

25. *HDI,* 10 March 1876. Also Grain, "Pioneers of a Glorious Future," 79.

26. Other court cases: Insp. Steele – 32, Supt. McIllree – 30, Supt. Crozier – 24, Insp. Dowling – 27, Lt.-Col. Irvine – 20, Supt. Walsh – 16, Supt. Herchmer – 14,

Roderick G. Martin, *The North-West Mounted Police and Frontier Justice*, 1874–1898 (University of Calgary: 2005), examines trials of that period.

27. *HWH*, 6 December 1877 (whiskey arrests); *HDI*, 25 July 1877 (forgery case).

28. R.C. Macleod and Heather Rollason Driscole, "Natives, Newspapers and Crime Rates in the North-West Territories," 249–69. In Theodore Binnema, Gerhard Ens, R.C. Macleod, eds. *From Rupert's Land to Canada* (Edmonton: University of Alberta Press, 2001).

29. An exception was "The Breaker" who received two days imprisonment for assault on a Cree woman. *RC*, NWMP, 1880, 18.

30. *GA*, Simon J. Clarke, M 228.

31. *RC*, NWMP, 1878, 26.

32. *MFP*, 28 February 1881.

33. *BDM*, 19 May 1883. McKinnon was fined $3 for disorderly conduct and $2 for resisting the police.

34. *MJN*, 20 June 1884. Other examples of arrests are given in Dempsey, ed., *William Parker Mounted Policeman*, 145-6 and Aitkin, *Maintain the Right*, 204; Edward Braithwaite, "Reminiscences of a Hospital Sergeant," *AH*, XXXIX, No. 4, 16.

35. *RC*, NWMP, 1878, 26. "Slim Jim" was sentenced to five years in the Manitoba Penitentiary.

36. Dempsey, ed., *William Parker Mounted Policeman*, 44.

37. *LH*, 21 June 1924. In another example, William Parker related a three-man police party traveling 600 km in frigid February weather to arrest a Métis for beating his wife. Dempsey, ed., *William Parker Mounted Policeman*, 58.

38. Fitzpatrick, *Sergeant 331*, 85.

39. Ibid., 86.

40. *MFP*, 11 February 1881.

41. *GA*, Frederick Bagley, M 43.

42. *LH*, 21 June 1921.

43. *CH*, 30 November 1883.

44. *CH*, 6 August 1884.

45. *GA*, Edward Barnett, M 6458.

46. *GA*, Robert Patterson, M 2470.

47. *RC*, NWMP, 1879, 31.

48. Rivett-Carnac, ed., "Letters from the North-West," 16.

49. *RC*, NWMP, 1884, 20.

50. Donkin, *Trooper and Redskin*, 33.

51. *MFP*, 17 January 1881.

52. *FMG*, 14 February 1885.

53. *WDT*, 21 April 1880; WDT, 3 June 1880; See Steele, *Forty Years in Canada*, 152.

54. Pocock, *Frontiersman*, 28.

55. *NAC*, Diary of Robert N. Wilson, MG 29, E-47.

56. *FMG*, 24 November 1885.

57. Ibid.

58. *WDT*, 12 March 1883.

59. Donkin, *Trooper and Redskin*, 33.

60. Dempsey, ed., *William Parker Mounted Policeman*, has a detailed account of the trip. There are several versions of "Slim Jim's" activities after his release from prison. The *FBRP*, 6 August 1884, relates that he was a prison guard; William Parker writes that he returned to Montana Territory, got caught stealing horses, and was hanged by vigilantes. "Slim Jim's" arrest is related in this chapter under arrests.

61. *LAT*, 13 August 1933. Also in *Fort Calgary Quarterly*, VI, No. 4, 2−6. To overcome the travel problems, Commissioner Irvine continually called for the constructing a prison at a central point in the North-West Territories.

62. Fitzpatrick, *Sergeant 331*, 70.

63. *LH*, 21 June 1924.

64. *WDT*, 25 June 1881.

65. Jack Dunn, "The Biggest Day Winnipeg has ever Seen: The North-West Field Force Returns from the Front," *Manitoba History*, No. 43, 2002, 25−28.

66. *GA*, Francis Dobbs, Pam 364.971 D632r.

67. William M. Baker, "The Story of Joe Bush," *AH*, XL, No. 4, 2−15. Also *RL*, 4 December 1884.

68. Norman Macleod, "Early Days at Macleod," *SG*, Twenty-sixth Annual, 15.

69. *EB*, 3 February 1883.

70. Max Foran, "The Travis Affair," *AH*, XIX, No. 4, 1−7.

71. After his release from prison, Neale worked for the City of Winnipeg engineer's office until his death at age 54. The warden during his incarceration was former Commissioner A.G. Irvine.

72. *MG*, 4 December 1884.

73. *MFP*, 5 March 1880.

74. *WDT*, 1 December 1879.

75. *OFP*, 1 December 1879.

76. *WDT*, 10 February 1880.

77. *CN*, 18 November 1884.

78. In an interview in 1945, Gabriel Léveille (son of Louis Léveille, the NWMP scout at the scene), age 13 at the time of the 1879 murder, said his father always maintained that white horse thieves had killed Graburn because the horse tracks showed three men riding abreast; the Indians always rode in single file; second, the riders had mounted from the near side, whereas Indians always mount from the off side. *RCMP Q*, XXII, No. 4, 326−28.

79. *ODC*, 10 December 1879.

80. *WDT*, 20 December 1879.

81. *SAB*, A 110, McEntyre, J.E.

82. *WDT*, 20 December 1879. A second account, *OFP*, 19 December 1879, related: "he was buried on November 20, 1.5 miles from the fort beside one Walsh, who died this summer of mountain fever ... he was interred with military honors, the whole force attending the funeral. The coffin was placed on one of the Abyssinian guns covered by the Union Jack, and his troop horse was led behind, with his riding boots reversed in the stirrups, and a firing party fired three volleys of blank cartridges over the grave."

83. *RC*, NWMP, 1879, 6–9. Mrs. Graburn thanked Constable Robinson for sending her dead son's spurs to her. Mr. Graburn forwarded a painted picture of his son in uniform to Divisions "B and F." In his application to join the NWMP, Marmaduke Graburn had listed his occupation as a sailor.

84. *GA*, N.R. Wilson, M 4421. It is assumed that the warrant was in English.

85. Ex-policemen were Don Horan (Horne), William Parker, Edward Maunsell, Charles Ryan, and William Gladstone.

86. *FBRP*, 9 November 1881.

87. Steele, *Forty Years in Canada*, 152.

88. Maunsell's letter in *GA*, Elizabeth Price, M 1002, f. 1. Almost two years later, on 21 July 1883, Stipendiary Magistrate Lt.-Col. James Macleod sentenced Star Child to four years in Stony Mountain Penitentiary for horse stealing. In Regina, on his way to prison, the *Regina Leader* (2 August 1883) described Star Child as "a vicious looking villain, and those who have to deal with him say he is a treacherous chap." Visiting Cree Indians taunted and laughed at the Blood prisoner. In Stony Mountain, Star Child was a model prisoner and, on his early release became a NWMP scout. He died of consumption in 1889. Superintendent Deane praised Star Child as one of the best police scouts.

89. *SH*, 30 June 1879.

90. *WDT*, 6 March 1880. *SH*, 9 February 1880.

91. Bagley, "The Last of Canada's Cannibals," 58.

92. The night before his execution, Swift Runner gave Bagley a smoking pipe and a fur hat.

93. Before his appointment as Sheriff, Edouard Richard had practiced law with Wilfrid Laurier and served as a Member of Parliament from 1872–78.

94. *SH*, 12 January 1880.

95. While in confinement, Swift Runner had converted to Christianity. His skull later went "on tour." The *WDT*, 3 November 1882, informed its readers that "the skull of the Indian who was hanged at Edmonton for killing and eating his wife is on exhibition at the Turf Wine Hall."

96. Bagley, "The Last of Canada's Cannibals," 59.

97. *MFP*, 7 January 1876. Although McIvor shot his victim near Fort Ellice, NWT, the trial and execution were held in Winnipeg.

98. *RL*, 23 July 1885.

99. Cameron, *Blood Red the Sun*, (Calgary: Kenway, 1926) 139. See Chapter xxix.

100. *HWH*, 25 March 1875. In a letter to the *Toronto Globe*, 6 April 1875, Surgeon Nevitt described the blow as "making as pretty a compound fracture of the skull as you would ever wish to see." Also *HWH*, 8 April 1873.

101. Nevitt, *Frontier Life in the Mounted Police*, 52.

102. *MFP*, 23 October 1876. James Steele was one of the Mounties who escorted Gaudin to Fort Macleod. He wrote his brother, Sam Steele: "I made the distance there and back 800 miles in 15 days & rode the same horse ... there ae plenty of Yankees at McLeod & they swore like troopers ... the whiskey trade is all dun outhere and the Indians are getting rich in horses & Rifles." A, 85.448/18.

103. *MFP*, 7 January 1876. Wm. Laurie in *LDH*, 5 April 1924, relates a different account of the murder. The three men were travelling separately, but camped close together.

McIvor fired three shots at Charette and Atkinson was shot dead when he came to rescue Charette.

104. *FMG*, 14 February 1883. Chapter 9 (Horses of the Mounties) describes the murder of Saul Pollack at his ranch southwest of Maple Creek.

105. *WDT*, 14 March 1884.

106. *WDT*, 17 March 1884.

107. *RL*, 10 April 1884. This edition gives a detailed account of the crime. For praise of the police investigation, see *RL*, 11 October 1883.

108. *RL*, 11 October 1883.

109. *PAT*, 24 October 1883.

110. *RL*, 5 May 1885.

111. *RL*, 23 July 1885.

112. *WDT*, 11 February 1884. On the lynching threats, see Steele, *Forty Years in Canada*, 179.

113. *WDT*, 25 March 1884.

114. *WDT*, 29 March 1884. *RL*, 3 April 1884, gives graphic details of the crime.

115. *CN*, 3 June 1884. See also *CH*, 11 June 1884.

116. Quoted in the *FBRP*, 18 June 1884.

117. *CN*, 3 June 1884.

118. *CH*, 4 October 1884. See *FBRP*, 8 October 1884, an account relates that the argument involved a broken barber chair delivered by Finn. Steele, *Forty Years in Canada*, 193. Another account says Foster attacked two Irishmen. Foster slashed the first with his knife and was shot moving in on Finn. Foster was described as a morose man who had killed a man in Montana. This was the fourth incident in which he had drawn a knife.

119. *WDT*, 31 July 1880.

120. *FMG*, 3 November 1885.

121. *SH*, 18 November 1878.

122. *RC*, NWMP, 1884, 12; *FMG*, 7 November 1884.

123. For details see Cameron, *Blood Red the Sun*.

124. Canada, Department of Secretary of State, *Epitome of Parliamentary Documents in Connection with the North-West Rebellion*, 1885. (Ottawa: MacLean, Roger, 1886), 370.

125. Charette, ed., *Vanishing Spaces – Memoires of Louis Goulet*, 138.

126. Ibid.

127. W. J. McLean, "Tragic Events at Frog Lake and Fort Pitt during the North-West Rebellion," *Manitoba Pageant*, Whole No. 48, 24. At the Indian trials in September 1885, Charlebois and Wawasehewin (his accomplice) received the death penalty. This sentence was commuted to twenty years imprisonment for Charlebois, ten years for Wawasehewin. A second Indian accomplice, Bright Eyes, received a ten-year prison sentence.

128. Doug Light, *Footprints in the Dust*, (North Battleford: Turner-Warwick, 1987) 608–11.

RECREATIONAL
ACTIVITIES

NWMP Band, Battleford – 1884

L-R: Cst. M.H. (Matt) Meredith; Cst. W. (Billy) Williams; Cst. W.H. (Billy) Potter; Cst. J.A. (Dad) Simons; Sergt. J.H. (Harry) Storer; Sergt. Fred (The Master) Bagley; Cst. J.C. (Charlie) DeGear; Cst. C.A. Lavoie; Cst. Fred (Tough) Garton; Cst. T.J. Gibson; Trumpeter P. (Paddy) Burke; Cst. J. Davis; Cst. C. (Sandy) Grogan; Trumpeter W.T. Halbhaus.

– GA NA 2328 – 1

WHOLESOME ACTIVITIES APPEAR TO HAVE been wanting at the Pinto Horse Butte outpost, manned by a handful of Mounties. Jack Clarke recorded in his diary: "I shot a candle from a bottle on Top of C. Young Head Ten feet away. We had Nothing to do being Encamp we Started some fun with Young. He just Joined the Police a few Months ago in the

East and We were putting him through some Antics to pass the Time away Until the Next day Before we Started on a scouting Tour."[1] Whether Young enjoyed this "fun" remains unrecorded.

Many of the young men soon became dispirited by life in the remote northwest posts. Bagley remembered that the "boys sobbed out their hearts on their cots at night through sheer loneliness ... I have known them to go nearly daft from homesickness ... [it was] in the early days by no means a life of beer and skittles."[2] Winter deepened the despondency. At the end of October, one Mountie at Fort Walsh looked glumly ahead to his second winter. Already two snowstorms had blanketed the region. He mused:

> Winter is upon us in good earnest now ... you have no idea how cheerless it looks about here. Nothing but bleak hillsides and the pine trees in the valley to be seen. Everything else is covered with snow. Poets may rave of the beauties of winter and tell of the delights of sitting in front of a cheerful blaze of a log fire in the old fireplace, while old Boreas is blustering outside. They should be transferred to this country and sit in front of a log fire in one of our frontier houses.[3]

In such circumstances, he continued, these poets would only find comfort under half a dozen buffalo robes, not in spinning yarns in front of the fire.

Mail and Reading Material

The arrival of mail and reading material buoyed the men's spirits. Surgeon Barrie Nevitt was ecstatic when one delivery brought him forty-eight letters and a parcel with a pocket knife and a pair of skates. The surgeon recalled that the men read and reread their letters. And there was a long wait for a return reply. A return letter from England in 1877 took fifty-three days to reach Constable William Parker, stationed at Fort Macleod.

Adding to the frustration in the first years at Fort Macleod was that no one knew when the next mail delivery would arrive. The mail to Fort Macleod came by river steamer up the Missouri River to Fort Benton and then overland; in winter the mail was delivered by the Union Pacific Railway to a station 500 km south of Fort Macleod. A repetitive poem by Constable "Daddy" Haywood reflected the mental anxiety:

> *Waiting for the mail,*
> *Waiting for the mail,*
> *Waiting for the mail,*

Excruciating agony,
Waiting for the mail,
Waiting for the mail.[4]

At elevated points near the post, the men took turns scanning the southern horizon for signs of an approaching wagon. Almost always, the first greeting to an approaching horseman was: "Do you have any mail?"[5]

There was better mail service at the Swan River headquarters. In the first winter, a series of two-man stations every 100 km linked the base with Winnipeg. One police courier, A.H. Scouten, stationed at the Palestine post (now Gladstone), recalled: "With a horse and buckboard I delivered four to six bags of mail every two weeks, having to go seventy miles [115 km] to the Little Saskatchewan."[6] At this point, the "Red River" mail would be met and taken to Swan River where it was received with "much firing of rifles and shouting and cheering as the boys galloped with and around the mail and mail couriers."[7]

Reading was important to the men stationed at the isolated posts. A letter from Fort Saskatchewan in 1876 lamented the lack of reading material:

> The members of this Police Force are widely scattered in forts and stations from the Red River to the Rocky Mountains and during the long winter nights have no amusements, books or papers to help pass the time … the officers lend any books they have to the men, and so do the settlers: but all are not sufficient, and I can assure you the men feel lonely and disconsolate at not having anything at night to amuse or interest them.[8]

Eastern Canadians were encouraged to forward books and magazines to the policemen stationed in the far northwest. In response to an appeal by the press, the Minister of Justice agreed to allow these packages free postage.[9] The *Manitoba Free Press* informed its readers in June 1876 that "a collection of reading material, contributed by booksellers and others in Toronto, for the Mounted Police will be sent to them shortly."[10] In August 1875, the government gave the Fort Macleod detachment $200 to purchase books. The men held a meeting to select what books to buy.

Commissioner A.G. Irvine proposed having a reading and recreational room at each post. "These rooms would," he reasoned, "combine amusement with the attainment of useful knowledge and teach [the men] the value of sober, regular and moral habits."[11] With this in mind, each post would construct or assign a building for papers and books, tables for cards, and a billiard table. At Fort Macleod, the officers had leased a billiard table from Tony Lachapelle, a local trader. This somewhat compensated Lachapelle for the $500 he paid in fines in 1882 for whiskey trading.

By 1882, most posts had first-rate recreational facilities. One visitor described Fort Walsh as having a comfortable, well-furnished reading room that was entirely free for the men. It had all the best papers in Canada as well as some from England and the United States. There were a great many periodicals and about a thousand books, some bound volumes provided by Col. Irvine and Captain Cotton.[12] The Annual Commissioner's Report that year praised the comfortable recreational rooms for preventing the association of policemen frequenting billiard saloons "with many men of questionable character."[13] An order issued at Fort Walsh prohibited the detachment from visiting Casey's Pool Hall in the settlement.[14]

Hunting and Fishing

Sub-Inspector John McIllree's diaries (1874–85) record daily hunting or fishing activities—a reflection of the keen interest these pursuits held for most men.[15] At Dufferin in August and September 1874, Constable W. Parker hunted or fished every day, including Sundays. In that time, he shot 109 prairie chickens.[16] His hunting ardor continued. Parker wrote his mother in England from his new posting at Swan River the following October in 1875: "The first day I shot fourteen rabbits & one partridge; second time shot eighteen rabbits & three partridges; third time eleven rabbits, nine prairie chickens & two partridges; the last day I was out shot eleven prairie chickens, two partridges and two rabbits."[17] Parker's skill was matched by many men in the Force. There were astounding fishing and hunting accomplishments.[18]

Fish were caught in numbers that absolutely defy proverbial fishing exaggerations. In just one eight-hour outing, Constable W. Parker caught 200 fish—an incredible one fish every two minutes. To his disbelief, one line with four baits hooked four fish. Constable Alexander Dyre enjoyed amazing success fishing on the Bow River using pieces of red rag as bait. A forty-pound trout caught by Constable G. Harper in Waterton Lakes, 100 km southwest of Fort Macleod, was a lure for interested policemen to spend their leave in that area. In the autumn of 1875, three men who were stationed at Fort Macleod caught 900 trout by fly reel in three days at Waterton Lakes. Some men even "fished" with shotguns. At a water basin on the upper Oldman River, Inspector A. Bowen Perry and his companions fired shotguns into the water to first stun the fish. They then gathered up the floating fish. In winter, some men enjoyed ice fishing.

Lake in Crowsnest Pass

"The first time I threw in my flies, I had four on the line; I had a trout on each fly all at the same time."

– Dempsey, ed., *William Parker Mounted Policeman*, 131
GA NA 2252 – 4

Unlike leisurely fishing, buffalo running (called the most thrilling sport on the North American continent) was the apex of excitement and danger. Badger holes could break a horse's leg and throw the rider, wounded buffalo often turned on the horseman, and stray bullets and malfunctioning guns were a constant risk. Surgeon Nevitt arranged for a wagon to bring a young Métis 70 km to Fort Macleod. The man, injured in a buffalo run, had his thigh broken in two places and his nose pushed to one side.

Success, in the words of one Mountie, required a "good rifle and a horse who understands not only the habits of the animal … but also the nature of the country over which the hunt leads, as in many places on the prairie, the badger holes are very numerous, and these have often brought an uninitiated horse to grief."[19] But the danger of buffalo running had its rewards. In 1875, two Mounties led by Johnny Healy, an American scout and later a sheriff in Montana, killed sixty-four buffalo in two days.

Avid sportsmen organized "time on leave" for hunting trips. Surgeon Barrie Nevitt and his four companions, traveling on horseback and with a supply wagon, went on a fifteen-day hunting excursion west of Fort Macleod. Two of the men shot nothing, Nevitt only three prairie chickens and a rabbit. However, scout Jerry Potts and policeman Robinson shot three buffalo, nine deer, and an antelope.[20]

The men hunted deer in woodlands and along waterways. In winter, snow allowed them to easily follow the animal tracks. Elk were hunted in woodlands and sometimes in herds on the plains. No record of moose killing by the police was found. The speedy pronghorn easily outdistanced any horseback pursuit but could be lured into rifle range because pronghorns were, according to one Mountie, as "inquisitive as a woman."[21]

Migratory game birds descended on the prairie sloughs in enormous numbers. Hunters carved wooden decoys to attract the birds. One four-man hunting party shot 133 ducks within 6 km of their Fort Saskatchewan barracks. At Fort Calgary, ducks, geese, and prairie hens rested insolently on top of the post's buildings. One afternoon, Constable Dyre shot a dozen prairie chickens inside the compound.

A Métis police interpreter at Swan River trained young Frederick Bagley how to use snowshoes and set up a trap line. Bagley proved an adept pupil and supplied the post with fox skins that were made into winter hats for the men, with the tails hanging down at the back for effect. He proudly appraised his headwear as "both comfortable and picturesque."[22] When Commissioner French returned to the post in 1875, he held a parade of "E" troop. The men stood in tattered red tunics or deer skin jackets, makeshift trousers, and fox hat headwear. French was taken aback, exclaiming "good God," and left the square. Later he commented, "the fox fur headdresses seemed to be the only resemblance to uniform in the whole troop."[23]

One ready target for shooting and trapping was the bountiful gopher. The *Saskatchewan Herald* declared acting Constable Thomas Hardy the undisputed gopher catcher in the entire North-West after he trapped forty gophers in one hour—almost one a minute. Hardy gave his catch to the nearby Indian camp where "meat pies were the order that night."[24]

Team Sports

The Mounted Police introduced team sports in the region. Competitions included baseball, cricket, polo, football (rugby), soccer, and rifle matches. Colonel Macleod was the first president of the Fort Macleod polo club. Often the victors in a contest won a reward, such as having the losers contribute a box of cigars or pay for a team meal.

Team composition was linked to a common bond: Englishmen versus Canadians, recruits against veterans, the ranks against sergeants, and so on. The growth of towns opened another challenge. In November 1883, the local detachment played a football (rugby) game against the town of Calgary with former policeman James Walker as referee.[25] As part of Christmas Day activities in 1883, the Battleford police played the citizens a football match. The result was described as a decisive victory for the police. In the North-West Rebellion, police detachments challenged eastern military units to contests. In Regina, the police detachments competed in sporting events against the Montreal Garrison Artillery.

In one bizarre occasion, keen competition clearly overrode justice. At a cricket match between Clover Bar and the Fort Saskatchewan detachment, a shortage of players posed a problem until the Mounties released three men from the guard house, two for the visitors' side and one to complete the police team. After the game, the base commander, A.H. Griesbach, and his wife hosted a team dinner party that also invited the three prisoners who were escorted from the guard house under armed guard.[26]

A problem in this distant land was obtaining acceptable equipment for the sporting events. For his cricket team at Swan River, a constable carved two bats and a set of wickets out of birch wood which he found heavier than willow, but more durable. Baseball enthusiasts at Fort Macleod had to make the needed bats and balls. At a later date, when the detachment formed a baseball club, all equipment had to be ordered from the East, an unwanted inconvenience and time delay.

Rifle matches, either between individuals or with teams, were the most popular sporting competition. In one example at Battleford, two teams of twelve men from the Citizens' Club and the local NWMP detachment, on a firing range beside the Battle River, had each contestant fire five shots at white paper targets placed at two, three, and four hundred yards. The Citizens' Club (which included three ex-Mounties) won easily by 558 to 437 points. At the end of the match, the teams met for supper at a new café. The local paper gave details on the competition and the score of each participant.[27] In a second example at Fort Walsh, great speculation and interest preceded the rifle shooting match between two four-man NWMP sharpshooter teams in an "Old Country versus Canada" match.[28]

Holiday Celebrations

The "boys" welcomed holiday celebrations as a diversion from the daily monotonous post routines. Four celebrations were most prominent: the Queen's Birthday on May 24, Dominion Day on July 1, Christmas and New

Year's Eve. Other festivities observed include Valentine's Day, St. Patrick's Day (sometimes called "the seventeenth of Ireland"), Thanksgiving Day, Orange Order on July 12, Halloween, anniversaries, and weddings. Some men joined the celebrations for the American holidays on Independence Day and Washington's birthday.

April Fools' Day puzzled the Cree band at Frog Lake. It was, as the war chief Wandering Spirit told Indian agent Thomas Quinn, "Big Lie Day."[29] And some important historic dates then honoured, such as June 18, "the Battle of Waterloo," are not observed today.

Sporting events were always part of the Queen's birthday and Dominion Day holidays.[30] Extensive preparations were required: judges and starters had to be appointed, events chosen, equipment prepared, and course boundaries marked or roped off. Usually, the post band led a parade to open the field events. Onlookers were impressed at the sight of the waving Union Jack, hoisted by scarlet-coated Mounties who were marching or riding to the stirring band music.

Events chosen at each post varied but might include: skills in throwing (cricket ball, hammer, caper); and racing and jumping contests at selected distances (walking, running, hurdles, sack, hop-step-and-jump, three-legged, running on all fours, running long jump, running and standing high jump, and vaulting using a pole). Swimming races were only held at Battleford. Horse races and rifle-shooting skills were especially popular. A tug of war between selected teams usually ended the day's competition.

The *Saskatchewan Herald* described the 1879 celebrations for Her Majesty's Birthday at Fort Battleford.[31] A subscription list (donation) circulated in the barracks collected $130 for the Field Day. The paper listed the locations for the nineteen scheduled events and listed the prizes, ranging from $7 for the mile race to $3 for other contest winners, with second place worth $2 and $1 for third. There was a box of cigars for the winners of the tug of war and a side of bacon for the successful climber of the greased pole. The rifle competition had targets at 300 yards and a baseball game was planned. A police parade in the barracks square followed by a *feu de joie* would announce the start of events, set to begin at 1:00 p.m.

In the next weekly edition of the newspaper, under the heading "Her Majesty's Birthday and How We Spent the Day Here" described the holiday. The weather was clear and, once the Lieutenant Governor had inspected the detachment, the events began and continued on until seven o'clock in the evening. Inspector James Walker did well. He won both the caber-and-sledge-throwing events and was third in the rifle competition that had twenty contestants (fifteen policemen and five civilians). Since there was no winner in the greased pole climb, a quarter-mile race only for Indians was held the following day for the prize of bacon. The horse-race winner received $20, and a score of 18 to 15 decided the baseball game.

Canada was only in its seventh year as an independent nation when the NWMP entered the North-West Territories. Optimism abounded in a land that now stretched from "sea to sea." The Dominion Day celebrations on July 1 exuded this sense of national pride.

A correspondent from Ottawa described Dominion Day 1878 at Fort Walsh under the headline "Of How They Spend the Anniversary of the Birth of our Common Country in the Far West."[32] The writer wrote that, at ten o'clock, every member of the Force along with hundreds of Indians, "dressed in most various and gorgeous costumes," assembled on the eastern parade ground for a Field Day that had twenty-one scheduled events.

The judges were Inspector William Antrobus and Superintendent Leif Crozier, the race starters Sergt.-Major Tommie Lake and Sergeant Tim Dunne. The Indians were both fascinated and amused by the "bucket race" and a "smoking race."[33] There was a "squaw race" for the women, which was won by Nellie, with Minnie second. The highlight one-mile race was won by an Indian who showed "Indian endurance." Spectators could sense the keen rivalry between the recent recruits and the Fort Walsh regulars on the final event—a tug of war with twenty men on each side. They watched the Fort Walsh regulars "disastrously defeat" the recruits. The Field Day ended with cheers for Her Majesty. The newspaper listed the first-and-second-place winners in each event.

Celebrations at Christmas and New Year's Eve brought thoughts of family, friends, the past, and the future. The preparations emphasized decorations, food, dance, and drink.[34] Some men went to great efforts to prepare their meals. At the tiny East End Post, three men rode 120 km just to get the ingredients for plum pudding for their planned dinner. Unfortunately, adverse weather delayed their return for one week. However, they arrived in time for New Year's Day. At tiny Fort Calgary, Christmas in 1877 was celebrated with a troop dinner in a decorated mess room and a dance that invited the entire surrounding country. The celebration made the men forget their isolated lot and, in the words of an outside observer, "it was hard to believe they were dining within forty miles of the Rocky Mountains and in a country where earthen floors are the rule and where carpets, staircases, wine and beer luxuries are unknown."[35]

At Fort Macleod in 1879, Jack Clarke was concerned that only six gallons of whiskey would dampen the Christmas celebrations. His fears proved to be unfounded:

Christmas, "C" Division, NWMP, Battleford, NWT, 1880s

Prairie people enjoyed the Barracks Ball as a gala affair "when treasured frocks and dresses from far-off days and places lent a formal touch to this frontier community."

− Mrs. James McDougall, "Cypress Hills Reminiscences," *Saskatchewan History*, XXIII, No. 1, 28
  GA NA 2884 − 1

C Troop had there barrack fixed up Splendid I mostley done it all myself. We had dinner at five. All the Officers were present Also the ladies we passed a very Nice evening till about one when some of the Boys got drunk and Commenced to fight. Const. McEwan and Bob Fields and Grier and G. Willes and Battersby where the fighters. David McAuley of E Troop played the Bag pipes most of the night and marched all around the Fort with Capt Winder at the head. Col Macleod and Lady drank the health of the Police Most of Men where drunk of Jamaica Ginger All the Officers joined in with the Men til Morning. We had a good Many X Police Men and Citizens with us.[36]

Even at a Christmas celebration, wrapped with nostalgia for home and family, "Peace to the World" did not always prevail. A Winnipeg reporter had attended the Fort Macleod Christmas festivities. His lengthy column described the "savage" blizzard, guests, decorations, barrack tour by the officers, sumptuous dinner, and the after-dinner toasts, songs, and dance—but no mention was made of the brawl.[37]

Edward Barnett recalled that the ninety men at Fort Walsh contributed $5 each to pay for the Christmas celebrations in 1877. The cooks had prepared a lavish meal with fresh California apricots, plum pudding, dried apples, buffalo meat, fish, and desserts. He remembered that, "for the police it was a day of remembrance for they were far away from the society of friends and the old home, but for the Indians it was merely a feast day with lots of liquor thrown in later."[38]

The post had fed the Indians outside the palisades but allowed a number of them inside for the evening dance (which they preferred to Sitting Bull's dance in the Indian camp.) Once the barracks hall was filled, the two gates of the fort were locked and the dancing began. The Mounties and the Indians sat at opposite ends of the hall while the mixed-bloods occupied the middle of the room. The dance was a boisterous affair with rousing fiddle music, the "blood-curdling" yells of mule skinners, and available whiskey. The exhausted participants only quieted down after the late-December sunrise.

The NWMP quickly gained a reputation for their skill as hosts at New Year's Eve celebrations. The Fort Macleod newspaper commented: "The mounted police have proved themselves good men and true in their invaluable service in the north west and as they have done their duty noble and well in the entire active field of police duty, so are they unsurpassed hosts ... only fault to find ... the boys are too generous."[39] At the tiny post at Fort Calgary, built only four months earlier, the men outdid themselves preparing for 1876. A visitor was astonished at how entertainment "so grand could be got up in such an out of the way place."[40]

The annual NWMP New Year's ball was the social event of the year. Policemen would travel the countryside with invitations for the event. Mrs. James McDougall at Maple Creek recalled the Barracks Ball as a gala affair "when treasured frocks and dresses from far-off days and places lent a formal touch to this frontier community."[41] For the 1880 New Year's dance, the Battleford detachment's "indefatigable efforts" prepared the hall and supper in a room tastefully decorated with mounted animals. At midnight, to the familiar strains of "Auld Lang Syne," the banner above the main entrance was torn away and the sign "1880" burst upon the spectators. Abundant food delicacies had been prepared and the dancing continued "with vigour" until morning.[42]

That year's celebration at Fort Walsh was, likewise, a great affair. Three hundred people from the post and surrounding area crowded into a 30 by 60-foot (10 by 20 m) building decorated with blankets on the walls, evergreens, weapons, mottos, and flags. Blankets partitioned the smoking and dressing areas and the passageway to the supper room that was being ceremoniously guarded by two cannons. A five-piece orchestra composed of a clarinet, violin, cornet, guitar, and brass instrument played forty dances. A motley crowd of "half-breeds, squaws and whites" intermingled cordially and without distinction. Supper was truly "a great event and eaten in a manner only attained by those living in an uncivilized country, and knowing such food rarely but in their dreams."[43] The correspondent noted that nine white ladies were present.

Everyone intently watched as the clock ticked the final seconds of the Old Year. At Fort Macleod, exactly at twelve o'clock, twenty policemen gathered around a piano and sang "Auld Lang Syne"—which the local press commented was a "very appropriate way of bidding adieu to our old acquaintance, 1884, and ushering in a new one, 1885."[44]

The opening of a new post or the completion of major additions to a fort were celebrated. The new barracks at Fort Calgary in 1882 officially opened with a grand ball. To celebrate the completion of the barracks at Medicine Hat, the detachment invited all the townspeople and, with railway service available, visitors from Regina, Maple Creek, Swift Current, and Calgary. The military decorations were imposing, magic lanterns lit up the barracks, and dancing was resolutely kept up until four o'clock in the morning. A newspaper reported that: "It was said to have been the largest and most brilliant affair of the kind which has ever taken place between here and the foothills of the Rockies."[45]

The men observed NWMP anniversaries. Most important was the first anniversary on 13 October 1875 that honored the arrival of the police at what would become Fort Macleod. The post celebrated the occasion by erecting a large marquee, decorated with flags and mottoes, in front of the Sergeants' Mess. Two rows of tables were arranged along each side of the tent for supper. It was, in Surgeon Nevitt's words "a most sumptuous repast—ham, beef, Buffalo tongue, cakes, blanc mange & rice in beautiful forms. All kinds of fruit—Peaches, Pears, Apricots, plums & Raspberry, blackberry and strawberry tarts, Peach and apple pies & jellies & preserves. Tea, coffee, cream & milk flowed in abundance."[46] Sergeant William F. Parker, the chairman, proposed a toast to the Queen and then to Colonel Macleod. The Colonel responded with a recounting of the arrival, and the work they had accomplished. He was heartily cheered. After more toasts and replies, the tables were cleared and dancing began, with intermissions for songs. Celebrations continued until four in the morning.

Fort Macleod marked its second year with a cricket match in which Staff-Constable H. Homan's eleven whipped Sub-Constable Nedham's team 118 to 93. The horse races were cancelled after a rider was severely injured in the first race. The evening entertainment featured "feats of legerdemain" by Staff Constable T. Dunne that baffled the audience. Dunne no doubt was skilled, having performed before the Governor General. Sub-Constable Nedham followed by singing his composition, "The Fort Macleod Galop." (The entire program is described later in this chapter under "Theatre.")

The policemen celebrated children's births, baptisms, and birthdays. Constable McAuley played the bagpipes as Reverend McKay christened Colonel J. Macleod's son, Norman Torqual Macleod. For the birthday of his daughter, Cora Ann, living with her mother in Ontario, Walsh had cannon fire, sporting races, a baseball game, and an old man's race. The flag staff had both a birthday flag and a balloon with the words "God Save the Queen." Walsh sat beaming at the head table for the birthday banquet.

Those men of Irish heritage never missed celebrating St. Patrick's Day. The first March 17 at Fort Macleod was definitely a time for celebration. This detachment had endured an especially difficult and cold winter, full of discontent and mutiny. Now was a time to celebrate. The men subscribed $300 for a supper concert to "celebrate Old Ireland's day in the far wilds of the northwest."[47] Constable George Crofton wrote a sixty-line poem, "Saint Patrick's Day, 1875," that celebrated the occasion.[48]

The relatively large American population at Fort Macleod invited the local detachment to the citizen celebrations for Independence Day and George Washington's Birthday. For the President's birthday on 22 February

Poker Players Sergt. M.J. Kirk, Sergt. J.A. Martin, Cpl. C. Uniacke, Const. F. Pope

This exceptional photograph (taken c. 1878) was found in a log at Captain Jacks Bottom, near Kipp, Alberta.

– RCMP Historical Collections Unit, "Depot" Division, Regina, SK., 1941.27.8

1876, there was a grand ball in a merchant's store. The *Fort Benton Record* reported the dance and described the dresses and jewels of the eight ladies. The walls had festive trimmings and a large portrait of George Washington hung on display. As the celebrations concluded, the audience sang patriotic American ballads.[49]

For the Fourth of July Centennial Ball in 1876, tickets were sold for $3 to cover the estimated cost for supper of $120. Some Mounties received a complimentary ticket perhaps in return for the police band providing the music. On each ticket was a number which, when picked and announced, allowed the man to choose a dance partner in the crowded Billiard Hall. The Americans continued with this celebratory practice for some years. Superintendent McIllree commented that, at the 4 July in 1880 celebration, "citizens made a horrible row last midnight firing off fireworks."[50]

Often the detachment feted a comrade who was leaving the post or the Force with a gift and dinner. Such was the case when Corporal Frank Dobbs left the tiny post at Shoal Lake for Dublin. The Wood Mountain post gave Joe Francis a splendid watch on his departure and at Battleford the men honoured, departing comrades Robert Wylde, W. Armstrong, and Fred Bourke with a barracks ball.

Gambling

Poker captivated many passionate participants. At times, the play became addictive. Constable Jack Clarke's diary follows the action that began 8 June 1879 when "Sub-Const. C. Daly won one Hundred dollars." On September 7, "and the Police Boys are playing Poker ten Cent ante Fred Pope banker." Two months later ... "the Men in the Barracks room are still playing Poker." Fred Pope was still the banker, but the ante had dropped to two and a half cents.[51] The officers had their own poker game that, for some reason, gave a percentage of the winning pot to Father Constantine Scollen.

Most racing events involved a wager. In a 200-yard foot race Constable S.G. Hogg defeated a Métis from Calgary for a bet of $75 on the side—the equivalent of two month's police wages. For a lesser amount of $5, Constables A. Carlyn and W. Smith had a 100-yard footrace right outside the Fort Saskatchewan barracks. For $50 on the side, Constable Wright raced John Linklater of Prince Albert. The plucky constable ran the race twice, as Linklater never moved on first pistol shot. Undeterred, Wright won the race again.

Were some races fixed? In a one-mile race at Battleford on Dominion Day 1883, Constable W.H. Potter (who had won the earlier half-mile race) ran well until the final quarter of the race when a pain in his side slowed him to finish second. The *Saskatchewan Herald* noted that a considerable amount of money had been staked on the result.[52] The detachment in Calgary had to restore order after George Irwin, a touted Ottawa runner, lost to an Indian in an exciting three-mile race for $25 on the side. Though Irwin led throughout the contest, a final spurt propelled the Indian to win the race by a step. The *Calgary Herald* claimed that $4,000 had changed hands. A disturbance arose with some bettors (probably the losers) insisting the race was "sold and a general fight became the order of the day."[53] Sergeant Fury arrested two men for drunk and disorderly conduct.

Horse racing had an enthusiastic following and gambling was a key part of the interest. The *Fort Macleod Gazette* published a horse race challenge: "The Police boys at Fort Walsh back a horse there against any horses in "C" or "E" Troops to run a quarter of a mile for $500. Challenge open for one month. The race to take place at Macleod, Address T. McA, Fort Walsh."[54] Constable George Boswell, intent on making money, brought a fleet horse from Fort Walsh and challenged any of the horses at Fort Macleod to race for $50. One horse race in January 1880 had Wagoner, "a Citizen," outrace A. Wilson of "C" Troop for $100. Constable Jack Clarke recorded: "The boys lost quick all the money."[55]

Fort Walsh organized a Fall Race Meet in November 1877.[56] In the "great race of the day," Captain Allen's black mare Lottie won the one-mile race, by twenty lengths, and the purse of $500, by beating Mr. Sanderson's chestnut horse, Too Late. Two more "scrub races" with a $10 entrance fee completed the races. In the half-mile race Captain McIllree's Maggie finished second and Surgeon Kittson's Eddie third. Observers said that McIllree's mount would have won with a better jockey. A grand dinner, given by NWMP officers, celebrated the first race meet in the Northwest.

A billiard table was a core part of a post's recreational room. Billiards was a popular pastime that usually included a wager. Even Colonel Macleod took part, betting a pound of tobacco, that Surgeon Barrie Nevitt could beat a merchant named Kidd, an acknowledged skillful player. Constable Robinson backed Kidd. Nevitt won three straight games.

The men gambled small funds for a chance to win a raffle. Constable William Metzler happily recorded in his diary: "Took a throw in a raffle for a saddle which cost me one dollar and to my surprise, I won it."[57]

Pets

The photograph of the Maple Creek detachment includes four dogs.[58] One Mountie conceded: "No dog was ever refused admittance to the dreary barracks if he but pled with eyes of sorrow and tail reversed."[59] Dogs, unlike

"A" Division, Maple Creek, 1884

"No dog was ever refused admittance to the dreary barracks if he but pled with eyes
of sorrow and tail reversed."

– F.L. Marsh, *Where the Buffalo Roamed,* 181
Fort Macleod Museum FMP 80 153

the horses, were individually owned. Several dogs were brought on the
Western March. Sub-Constable James Johnson recalled: "On the '74 March
I always kept a hunting dog, even when I was in the Force."[60] Surgeon
Nevitt, as the column moved to the Three Buttes, went out to hunt and
got lost. He was alone and further dismayed after his little dog left him.

In the massive literature on the Custer Massacre in 1876, the fate of
George Custer's greyhound (said to be a gift from Queen Victoria) has often
been speculated.[61] Constable E. Warren, stationed at Wood Mountain, was
with the first police detail that visited Sitting Bull's camp. Years later,
he wrote to a friend, "I got Custer's greyhound and had him for years."[62]
Warren's claim has authenticity since it was not intended for publication.

Dog ownership could have drawbacks, especially when Constable W.
Parker's Spot cornered an officer and his dog. Dogs harassing the sheep were
a more serious problem. At Swan River, the large flock of sheep had to
be penned and guarded every night. Still, on one occasion, the sheep got

loose and dogs killed five of the 100 animals. That all five belonged to the Commissioner was an added problem. At his post, Inspector McIllree deemed the dogs so troublesome that he ordered all dogs to be tied up. If they were found on the loose, the owner was fined $2 or the dog shot.

Cats wandered about the stables. The kittens were often cared for in the barracks. At times, cats were in great demand. When mice destroyed goods in the merchant stores, a cat was traded for a horse from a bullwhacker (ox driver). Donald W. Davis, an employee of I.G. Baker, thought that it was a good bargain.[63] Surgeon Nevitt kept a cat to roam the hospital.

Captured young buffalo and antelope made interesting pets. Sam Steele mentions that when he was stationed at Fort Macleod, there were two yearling buffalo calves that would go out to graze on the prairie every morning and return in the evening to the corral, where they would play with the men. Some young antelope were captured. When turned loose, they would go frolic with the Indian children and the only white child at the post, circling around them like kittens. The antelope would taunt the post's dogs to chase them, allowing them within a few feet, and then, with a sudden burst of speed, distance them like a flash.[64] A fawn kept in the Fort Macleod barracks was so quiet that a policemen stepped on it and broke the animal's hind leg. Surgeon Nevitt bandaged the leg and put on splints.

Other unusual pets were two bear cubs that the detachment at Fort Saskatchewan kept for only a short time. Constable Tom Hardy's Canada goose was also a much-discussed pet. The bird had the run of Fort Walsh, appeared at all of the parades as well as target practices, but would not go to the nearby creek unless accompanied by a policeman. His roost was a large stone in front of the guard house from where he would loudly honk at the approach of anyone, giving the post sentries, it was said, periods to enjoy their forty winks. He loudly challenged any Indian dogs entering the post's square, but tolerated the police dogs. In cold weather, the bird would rap incessantly on a barrack window until he was allowed inside. In time, however, his boldness grew and he began wandering out into the nearby town. This adventure proved his demise when he was killed in a fight with Indian dogs.

Late in life, Edward Warren wrote of what he called "the menagerie."

> I often think of old Fort Walsh. We had quite a menagerie then, 3 wild geese Brants, 1 wolf, 2 fine young Buffalo Bulls. The wolf broke loose one night and killed the O.C. Pigs, he paid the penalty. The Bulls were killed by Indians, they used to go out with the horse herd every day and come back at night-time,

they used to raise Cain with the hay stacks climbing on top of them and pareing them down. The Geese I do not know what became of them. When a sentry stop walking on the beat, they made an awful noise, you could hear them all over the Fort.[65]

Music and Dance

Fred Bagley recalled "Music was our salvation in an empty land. It was the only thing that kept us sane."[66] The cost and availability of instruments proved to be a problem. For the ten-piece brass band at Battleford, Col. W. Herchmer arranged to purchase available instruments in Winnipeg and mail-order the missing pieces from Ontario.

Bagley had risen from bugle boy to conductor of the Battleford band by 1884. The band held concerts to pay for the instruments. Receipts from the concerts and a $10 donation by Indian Agent John Rae in March 1884 made the band free from debt. That summer, the band practiced twice a day and gave open-air concerts on the parade ground twice each week.

During the North-West Rebellion, the Battleford band welcomed the Fort Pitt detachment's arrival (really retreat) in Battleford. Several weeks later, on May 2, General W. Otter attacked Poundmaker's camp at Cut Knife Hill. Band member Corporal Patty Burke was one of the eight men that were killed on the government side. A second band member, Sergeant Harry Storer, was killed in action thirty-two years later (5 March 1917) while serving in France with the 8th Battalion (90th Winnipeg Rifles).

The first band organized was at Swan River. Commissioner G. French, in response to a petition for a piano, found that a good one could be purchased in Chicago or St. Paul for $400, including delivery to Winnipeg by ox team. French asked the Deputy Minister of Justice in Ottawa for an annual grant for instruments (which the Canadian militia received), but his request was unsuccessful. In turn, it was suggested that the needed money come from the defaulter's fines. Undeterred by this setback, the men ordered their instruments by mail, and they were delivered by dog teams in April. Practice began at once on free time and, on 24 May 1876, the twenty-member band debuted at daybreak at the foot of the flagstaff with their rendition of "God Save the Queen."

Four months later, while en route to Fort Carlton to perform at the signing of Treaty 6, the band stopped to play at Indian camps along the way. Band members enjoyed playing booming music that frightened the women and children to flee to the safety of their teepees.[67] The Indians prized the drum and offered a fine horse in trade. Later, at Fort Carlton, the band played the national anthem in celebration of the Treaty 6 signing.

Bandmaster Frederick Bagley

"Music was our salvation in an empty land. It was the only
thing that kept us sane."

– Frederick Bagley, *SG*, Nineteenth Annual, 10
   GA NA 3173 – 10

One year later, at the Blackfoot Crossing signing of Treaty 7, the band, led by bandmaster Sergt.-Major Thomas Lake, again played an important ceremonial role on a momentous occasion. According to T. Lake, as the Indians were approaching the Governor General's tent, he had the band play "Hold the Fort for I am Coming." In response to Commissioner James Macleod's question on why did he select that song, bandmaster Thomas Lake explained that, well, isn't there a verse starting with, "See the Mighty Host Advancing, Satan Leading on?"[68]

An observer would see an assortment of "instruments" in the early bands. The first Fort Saskatchewan band consisted of a side drum (made by young Bagley), two violins, a trumpet, bugle, two pot lids, and the wheel coulter of a plow. At one dance held at the barracks, Constable George Guernsey remembered the band members used oil cans, boilers, dish pans, and any old thing that would make a noise.

Sub-Constable Boyle assembled a band at Fort Walsh in June 1878. According to Staff-Sergeant Isaac Forbes, on one occasion the band was engaged in rowdy behaviour. During a performance, mail arrived with news of General Frederick S. Roberts' decisive defeat of an Afghan army at Kandahar in September 1880. In celebration of the glorious victory, Commissioner A.G. Irvine ordered an issue of grog for the detachment. Later that evening, the band reassembled to play patriotic British military music. The men, now in high spirits from Irvine's grog ration and their own clandestine supplies, instead started a free-for-all using the instruments as weapons. Not surprisingly, the official report for 1880 fails to corroborate Staff-Sergeant Forbes' story.[69]

Choirs were organized at many posts. Fort Walsh experienced some competition from a natural source. The fort lay in a valley, somewhat in the shape of an amphitheatre. One Mountie recalled, "what wonderful 'oratorios' we listened to at night! Wolves, Indian dogs ... and the plaintive howls of a few coyotes, all singing different parts ... on one side of the valley, then on the other, as though they had a music score to look at, till finally they would all burst in one grand chorus."[70] Fort Calgary suffered the same unwanted evening entertainment. Constable Dyre wrote that: "The prairie wolves come around every night and serenade us with their unmusical voices and if we go to shoot at them they will suddenly convey themselves away like a streak of lightning until they are out of gun-shot."[71]

Dances were especially popular. Fort Walsh, for example, in the winter of 1879—80 had a dance every two weeks. Female partners were always in great demand. Constable Alexander Dyre describes a North-West Mounted Police dance at Fort Calgary in 1882:

We gave a grand ball to the civilians last Friday night. We subscribed $250 and had the best supper ever given in this part of the country. We had the barrack room decorated with bead work, mottos made from cartridges, revolvers and rifles on the walls. The music was two violins, a flute and banjo ... there was only one woman and she was Dutch with hair like my tunic, and she had one side of her dress tacked up so as to show her white petticoat, but it showed her leg as well up to her knee.[72]

A correspondent from Toronto provides a second engaging description of a dance in a Calgary billiard hall that same year.

The dancers were made up of half-breeds, squaws, cow-boys, bull-whackers, ranchmen, farmers, surveyors, C.P.R. men, Mounted Policemen, travellers, and spectators, in fact a more motley assembly could hardly be got together in any part of the country. About midnight all adjourned to the restaurant for supper, after which they returned to the hall, where dancing was kept up till a late hour. The dances embraced almost everything, from the orthodox eight–hand-reel down to the Red River jig. Waltzing was particularly in favour with the dusky damsels ... music was furnished by an old half-breed and an ex-policeman, the former playing the violin and the latter the banjo. The master of ceremonies was an ex-American soldier who has beaten his sword into a bull whip ... and exchanged his 'faded coat of blue' for the cinnamon blouse of the 'mule Skinner.' No introductions appeared to be necessary, but when the master of ceremonies called out in a voice calculated to strike terror in the heart of the most obdurate of mules, "partners for a quadrille," the cowboys with their fringed leather overalls (schappes) and jingling Mexican spurs would sidle up to the long row of dark-skinned beauties sitting with their backs to the wall and their shawls so adjusted as to conceal head and face, and ask they came to dance, and the reply was invariably the affirmative.[73]

William Laurie remembered the first NWMP ball in Battleford as a wonderful success, even though only four white women were present and a number of languages spoken. The unwritten practice had the man stand before the woman and bow; if she were willing, she stood up and took his arm. The Métis, Laurie thought, were less refined since the man walked up to the lady of his choice, took her hand, and led her to the dance floor.

The orchestra had two players: a half-breed fiddler and a policeman with a piccolo. For supper, there was cold roast beef and boiled cold bacon, stacks of pies made from evaporated apples, bowls of apple sauce, stewed prunes, and strong black coffee. Laurie reflected fifty years later that the first boisterous dances had more pure enjoyment than the later more refined formal gatherings.

Area dances, called Citizen's Balls, were held in the police barracks, which was usually the largest structure available. In Medicine Hat, the townspeople organized a dance to return the courtesies given by the police. An open invitation brought visitors from as far as Maple Creek, who came in boxcars (a distance of 100 km) as a passenger train was unavailable. The feature dance was "the NWMP Choice," in which the citizens stepped back and the police filled the floor. A reporter commented: "The red uniform trimmed with gold showed in dazzling brilliancy as they moved up and down the well-lit room and the citizens felt proud of their protectors, and many flattering remarks were passed upon them as they walked by."[74]

The duration of the dances was legendary. Constable William Metzler attended a wedding dance in 1884 that began on January 27 and continued on until two o'clock in the morning of January 29. A dance in the Fort Saskatchewan barracks in 1882 kept up with undiminished vigor to nine o'clock in the morning, but by noon it was over. Things were slowing down. One observer reflected on this: it was the "unanimous verdict of the old timers that the glory is departing from the annual ball at the barracks. Time was when the fun went on for four nights or more."[75]

Theatre

Minstrel shows were by far the favourite attraction. These performances involved extensive preparations. For one Minstrel show and dance at the Fort Saskatchewan barracks, the police traveled the countryside with invitations for the settlers, rehearsed the script, and decorated the barracks with evergreens and flags. Chairs were set aside for the ladies. Three meals had been prepared: since many guests traveled for hours, the refreshments were served at six o'clock, after which the performance began, followed by a dance. At midnight, there was a break for a second meal and then the "vigorous" dancing resumed until daylight (which came late due to it being February), when breakfast was served. Everyone enjoyed themselves even though the crowded hall forced some of the 300 attendees to stand outside.[76]

"A" Troop (named the Zulu Minstrels) from Fort Saskatchewan gave a presentation at J.A. Macdougall's store in Edmonton that attracted 300 people who crowded the building to near-suffocation. As the curtain rose,

Jollification by Mounties

The men, in blackface and wearing female attire, portray two common stereotypes of that time. Minstrel shows were popular and, in theatre, the men played female roles.

– RCMP Historical Collections Unit, "Depot" Division, Regina, SK., 1971.42.59

a semi-circle of nine black-faced Mounties, with Colonel Jarvis as the middleman, appeared. Individuals singing twelve songs completed the first half of the performance. After intermission, more songs entertained the audience. Some of the presentations would bring frowns today. In one, Cooke gave both "a song and dance in the character of a nigger wench of large disproportions and loose habits and was vigorously applauded."[77] The performance concluded with the entire company shuffling around the makeshift stage to the tune of "Shoo Fly." Then everyone in the cast eagerly sang "God Save the Queen." The enjoyable evening was not over. There was an open invitation to the Hudson's Bay fort for dancing and feasting that lasted until morning.

The ridicule of black people (referred to as Negroes at that time) was quite commonplace and tolerated. At a Battleford minstrel show, the role of W. MacDonnell as Bones and Patty Burke as Tombo had "created no end of fun for the boys ... and Constable Whitehouse's rendition of 'Nigger on a Fence' was well received."[78] A post performance (admission-free) at Fort Macleod in 1876 commemorated the founding of the base two years earlier. The program included:[79]

PART I

Overture – Poet and Peasant: Sub-Const Nedham

Feats of Legerdemain: Staff Const Dunne

FIFTEEN MINUTE INTERVAL

PART II

Fort Macleod Galop: Sub-Const Nedham

Quartette: Staff Const Dunne & Oliver;
          Sub-Const Stone & Shepherd

Song (Comic):   Sub-Const Wilson

Reading: Staff Const Homan

Song (Comic):   Sub-Const Seymore
The Blighted Shepherd

Song: Sub-Const Stone
Rocked in the Cradle of the Deep

Song: Sub-Const Shepherd

Song (in character):   Sub-Const J. Patterson

Song: *Fifty Years Ago*   Sub-Const Adams

God Save the Queen!

In the first years, policemen played the female roles. When the NWMP Dramatic Club at Fort Macleod presented "Sarah's Young Man," Const. Shea played Mrs. Moggridge, Const. Caroll played Sarah Tibbs, and Const. Scott played the part of Nellie (the daughter). In assessing the skill of the policemen performing in female roles, one paper commented: "It would surprise a stranger to see what a charming woman a buck policeman can be transformed into for some of these plays."[80] Still, a negative aspect remained. One policeman complained that, after he played the part of Alice, his companions unduly continued to call him that name for years.[81]

Regina dominated "cultural" affairs in the Territories, especially with the relocation of the government and police administration to that town. James Davis, a former Mountie, built an entertainment centre near the

Fort Calgary, 1876 (Superintendent William Winder)

Painting was another personal activity enjoyed by the NWMP. The fort is centre-rear. The foreground buildings are I.G. Baker & Co. and HBC.

– GA NA 98 – 4

barracks in 1883. The combination of new facilities along with the arrival of Captain Richard Burton Deane that summer contributed immensely to promoting entertainment in the Territories.[82]

Social status was evident at theatre and dance events. An article in the local Regina press (describing a play in 1884 at the police barracks) included a list of the prominent citizens in attendance. And no longer did policemen play female roles. Miss Jukes, daughter of Surgeon Jukes, Mrs. Neale, and Mrs. White-Fraser, wives of policemen acted in the presentation.[83]

In another example of social status, the *Regina Leader* described a grand ballroom decorated with chains of coloured paper and spruce branches (brought from the distant Rockies) hanging from the ceiling. Two brass cannons, each guarded by two men, were placed in the front corners of the hall and, on the front platform a Mountie played a piano with the Regina Stringed Band. The sight of the red coats mingling with the citizens made it a "more brilliant scene that could hardly be imagined."[84] The newspaper listed the 218 guests and described the dresses of twenty-three women in attendance. Society was becoming refined. The policemen were a long way from dancing on dirt floors in smoky teepees.

Although theatre and concerts were popular diversions from the often-lackluster NWMP life, on one occasion the Prince Albert detachment's Dramatic Club entertainment ended in a brawl between policemen and some civilians outside the Hudson's Bay warehouse theatre. The local press commented: "We are glad to know that Capt. Perry has meted out the law to the offenders with the force."[85]

Other Activities

A popular attraction at that time was Penny Readings (named after the charge in England of one pence). In one example, at the Battleford Council Hall the audience heard fifteen songs, five recitations, five readings, a banjo and guitar duet, and violin and coronet solos. Many of the performance participants were from the police detachment. The local police band played the opening overture and music at intervals.[86]

The men enjoyed many personal activities. In his four years at Fort Macleod, Surgeon Nevitt's ink drawings and watercolours portrayed the nearby landscape and day-to-day life. Some of his art provides the only depictions we have of the first years in the West. These works included images of the Helena courtroom, policemen spilling whiskey into a river, Sitting Bull's reception of Major Irvine, and a whiskey trader at High River.[87] Superintendent William Winder also painted scenes depicting the North-West Mounted Police activities.

Some men joined activities offered in the town. Prince Albert had a curling club and skating rink; Calgary had a roller rink and skating club. Major Crozier was a master in the Masonic Lodge. The men had interests in reading, astronomy, walking, horseback riding, skating, tennis, skiing, and snowshoeing. Edmonton had its own bicycle club. Surgeon Nevitt lent his microscope and telescope to anyone who had scientific interests. Card games, dominoes, chess, checkers, and backgammon were popular. Social entertaining was an important aspect of frontier life.

Tobacco was universally used. Father C. Scollen commented in a letter: "I have not seen four men in this country who are not smokers."[88] Surgeon Nevitt enjoyed a pipe. He calculated the number of pipes smoked from his weekly consumption of tobacco and found that he averaged eighteen pipes a day—a startling 128 pipes each week. Tobacco even served as a form of early monetary exchange. When Fort Macleod was under construction, the men enjoyed playing euchre. Since the troop was still waiting for its first pay, tobacco was used as a wager.

Humour and Jokes

Humour and jokes, usually unrecorded, were a key part of daily life. A few examples are disclosed in NWMP writings.

Superintendent T. Jackson persisted in playing practical jokes, but the details are not revealed. When a recruit arrived at the Toronto training warehouse, his first assignment was to go the carpenter's shop and request to be measured for his sentry's box. The men loved mimicking Louis Léveille's French-Canadian accent and how he addressed Commissioner French: "my dear Carnell [Colonel]." The men at Swan River had to smile when Commissioner French solemnly asked a Métis sled driver, who had brought the mail 600 km from Winnipeg, why he was fifteen minutes late. The Wood Mountain detachment sang a ribald song, "Paper Collar Johnny," that mocked their Inspector (A.R. Macdonell). Charles Knowles had a harrowing experience when the Oldman River swept him with his horse and wagon two kilometres downstream. His frantic rescuers wanted to know if he was scared and what were his thoughts on the wild escapade. Charlie grinned and replied: "A life on the ocean waves and a home on the rolling deep."[89] Constable Fitzgerald, the cook at Swan River, served appetizing buns which being opened contained brown paper. The men should have known it was the first of April.

As a prank at the daily cannon firing to signal noon at Calgary, Constable Tom Clarke put a rock and an old pair of breeches in the field piece barrel. An officer arrived and signaled to fire. The rock shot across the Bow River where it stampeded a herd of horses, while the breeches could be seen smoldering on the nearby bank. Another humourous story is about one recruit who mused at how his barrack mates had tricked him. He had been sick for several days and mistook the bugle call at nine o'clock that evening for reveille. Seeing everyone around their beds, he asked Sergeant Jack Breadon if he was assigned for any duties on that day. His barrack mates immediately saw their chance and started to fold their blankets as if they were preparing for the day. The sergeant told him he was to cut some ice. The recruit made his bed, grabbed an axe, and started for the water hole. On the way, he met a stable picket who asked where he was going. He answered to "the water hole." Seeing the axe, the picket backed away. The laughter of the men righted the situation but, as the recruit later remembered, "to this day troop members josh me about cutting ice at midnight."[90]

NOTES

1. *GA*, S.J. Clarke, M 228.
2. Frederick Bagley, "Cannibalism Suppressed in N.W.T. when Police took Charge," *SG*, Nineteenth Annual, 19.
3. *FBR*, 10 November 1876.
4. Gillett, "Interview of J.H.G. Bray." 10–11.
5. Nevitt, *A Winter at Fort Macleod*, 71.
6. A.H. Scouten, "One of the Originals," *SG*, Twelfth Annual, 133.
7. *GA*, Bagley Diary 17 September 1876.
8. *MFP*, 24 March 1876.
9. *MFP*, 1 May 1876.
10. *MFP*, 10 June 1876. Also Dempsey, ed., *William Parker Mounted Policeman*, 119–120 has a letter describing Christmas at Swan River Barracks, 1876.
11. *RC*, NWMP, 1880, 10. *RC*, NWMP, 1881, 22.
12. Correspondent, *SG*, Fifth Annual, 95.
13. *RC*, NWMP, 1882, 22.
14. *Fort Walsh Post Diary*, RC 18, v.2331, 15 December 1879.
15. *GA*, John McIllree, AB McIllree #1. For example, 1 July 1880: "went fishing up Willow Creek and got ten pike and shot two curleau." In 1890, McIllree wrote an article "Fishing in Southern Alberta," AH, XXXI, No. 2, 36–37.
16. *GA*, William Parker, M 934.
17. Dempsey, ed., *William Parker Mounted Policeman*, 117.
18. *TG*, 3 August 1876.
19. *MFP*, 17 October 1877. Also *TG*, 3 August 1876; Rodney, *Kootenay Brown*, 105; McKay, *Fighting Parson*, 14–17.
20. Nevitt, *Frontier Life in the Mounted Police*, 104.
21. *TM*, 8 March 1875.
22. *GA*, Fred Bagley, M 33.
23. Bagley, "The '74 Mounties," No. 8, 26.
24. *SH*, 14 July 1879.
25. *SH*, 10 December 1881. Also *SH*, 13 September 1880.
26. W.A. Griesbach, *I Remember* (Toronto: Ryerson, 1946), 47.
27. *SH*, 10 December 1881. The Dominion Day competition at Battleford had twelve competitors firing shots at 300 yards away. Three prizes were awarded: $9, $7, and $5. *SH*, 5 July 1880.
28. *SH*, 11 April 1881. Old Country marksmen were Sergeant-Major Lake, Staff-Sergeant Norman, Corporal Kenney, and Corporal Hughes.
    Canada was represented by Colonel Irvine, Captain Cotton, Surgeon Kennedy, and Staff-Sergeant Moffat.
29. Cameron, *Blood Red the Sun*, 33.

30. For examples of celebrations—*MFP*, 26 June 1876 and 30 July 1879; *RL*, 9 July 1885; *SH*, 14 July 1879 and 5 June 1881, 31 May 1884, *TG*, 9 July 1881, and Nevitt, *Frontier Life in the Mounted Police*, 78.

31. *SH,* 19 May 1879.

32. *ODC*, 24 July 1878. The *MFP*, 30 July 1879 has a second example of Dominion Day events. Again "Indian endurance" defeated "Canadian pluck" in the featured one-mile race.

33. In the bucket race the contestant ran while balancing a full pail of water on his head; in the smoking race, each runner had three matches and a pipe that had to remain lighted while he ran.

34. The first-year celebrations were outlined in Chapter 4. For Christmas at Swan River, *MFP,* 16 January 1875. Also Robert Patterson in *LH*, 23 December 1937; *MFP*, 26 January 1877. *Great Falls Tribune,* 22 December 1937.

35. *CH*, 24 December 1982.

36. *GA*, S.J. Clarke, M 228.

37. *MFP*, 17 February 1880. A Christmas performance by the NWMP Dramatic Club at the Prince Albert Hudson's Bay Warehouse Steamboat Landing ended with a "disturbance" between members of the police force and some citizens. Captain Perry disciplined the offenders under his command.

38. *GA*, Edward Barnett, M 6142.

39. *FMG*, 2 January 1885.

40. *MFP,* 20 March 1876. The *RL*, 10 February 1885, describes a New Year's Eve celebration at Fort Pitt, a small NWMP post.

41. Mrs. James McDougall, "Cypress Hills Reminiscences," *SH*, XXIII, No. 1, 28.

42. *SH*, 12 January 1880. See also 9 January 1885.

43. *MFP*, 28 February 1881.

44. *FMG*, 2 January 1885.

45. *TM*, 4 February 1884.

46. Nevitt, *Frontier Life in the Mounted Police*, 99.

47. *HDH*, 20 May 1875.

48. *HDH*, 21 May 1875. A sample of the lines … "In this weird land where space asserts her way/ We, a mere handful, celebrate the day."

49. *FBR*, 4 March 1876.

50. *GA*, John McIllree, AB, McIllree #1.

51. *GA*, S.J. Clarke, M 228. See 7 September; 4 November 1879.

52. *SH*, 7 July 1883.

53. *CH*, 12 October 1883.

54. *FMG,* 24 February 1883.

55. *GA*, S.J. Clarke, M 228.

56. *MFP*, 24 November 1877. Also *BR*, 16 November 1877.

57. *GA*, William Metzler Diary, M 836.

58. In a second example, four dogs appear in the group photograph at RCMP "Depot" Regina, SK. 938-18-3.

59. F.L. Marsh, *Where the Buffalo Roamed* (Toronto: William Briggs, 1908), 181.

60. *Pincher Creek Echo*, 14 September 1928.

61. See for example, Evan S. Connell, *Son of Morning Star* (New York: North Point Press, 1984), 295.

62. *NAC*, Edward Warren, f. 57.

63. *LH*, 21 June 1924.

64. Steele, *Forty Years in Canada*, 114.

65. *NAC*, Edward Warren, RG 18, v. 3319, f. 57.

66. Bagley, "Cannibalism Suppressed in N.W.T. when Police took Charge," 10.

67. Parker, "Bands of the Force," *RCMP* Q, VIII, No. 2, 156.

68. Ibid.

69. Ibid., 157.

70. *CH*, 4 July 1925. Also *WDT*, 2 December 1882.

71. Rivett-Carnac, ed., "Letters from the North-West," 324.

72. Ibid., 326.

73. *LH*, 3 May 1924.

74. *WDT*, 3 March 1884.

75. *WDT*, 16 March 1882.

76. *EB*, 11 February 1882.

77. *SH*, 12 April 1880.

78. *SH*, 15 April 1882. Constable Whitehouse's performance is noted in *SH*, 10 March 1879.

79. *MFP*, 11 November 1876. Another example is NWMP Drama Club, *FMG*, 3 February 1883.

80. *MFP*, 21 April 1880.

81. Pox-o-nachie, (Little Soldier), *SG*, Ninth Annual, 71—73.

82. William M. Baker, ed., *The Mounted Police and Prairie Society, 1873—1919* (Regina: Canadian Plains Research Centre, 1998), 243–61.

83. *RL*, 20 November 1884.

84. *RL*, 24 January 1884. Other examples *FMG*, 3 February 1883; *RL*, 17 March 1885.

85. *PAT*, 25 December 1885.

86. *SH*, 30 September 1882 gives the complete program.

87. Andrew J. Oko, "The Frontier Art of R.B. Nevitt," *Canadian Collector*, 11, No. 1, 46—50.

88. *GA*, Constantine Scollen, M 1108, Letter # 7. One tobacco order for Fort Macleod was 404 lbs at a cost of $388.

89. Grain, "Pioneers of a Glorious Future," 77.

90. Rookie # 2, "Reminiscences of a Tenderfoot," 59.

La Roche Percée

A five-day rest was taken. Jean D'Artigue described his comrades as "a routed army corps. For a distance the road was strewn with broken carts and horses and oxen overcome with hunger and fatigue."

– Jean D'Artigue, *Six Years in the Canadian North-West*, 50

On the March West, 1874 (R.B. Nevitt)

"All day we tramped over the endless prairie, suffering the pangs of hunger by day, devoured by parasites by night. This was very different from what we pictured ourselves doing when we joined the Force."

– E.H. Maunsell, "Maunsell's Story," 28
  GA watercolour collection, 74.7.7

West Butte, Sweet Grass Hills

Three prominent peaks ("The Trois Buttes") rise to 2,100 metres (7,000 feet)—making them visible far out on the plains. At the summit of the West Butte, Sub-Inspector James Walker asked Commissioner French to estimate the number of buffalo in sight. Walker wrote: "After looking around for some time he said there were a million or more and I agreed with him."

– James Walker, "Police Experiences," 33

Mounted Police Encampment at Blackfoot Crossing, 1877 (R.B. Nevitt)

"It was a sight that cannot be forgotten."

– George Boswell, "Indian Treaties of 1877 and 1878," 48
  GA 74.7.76

Police Dumping Confiscated Whiskey (R.B. Nevitt)

"A guard had to be put up to prevent the Indians from sifting the muddy stuff up and drinking it."

– Nevitt, *Frontier Life in the Mounted Police*, 167
  Watercolour Collection Glenbow Museum, 74.7.11

Stand Off Coulee Site of the Skirmish, 28 May 1885

The position of the Field Force, looking up at the hidden Indian rifle pits. "My men were at a great disadvantage, being overlooked by the enemy, who could see almost every man as he lay, whereas mine could only judge of their whereabouts from the smoke of their rifles and so could produce very little effect by their upward rifle fire on men in pits."

– Strange, *Gunner Jingo's Jubilee*, 488

On the trail after Big Bear (R.W. Rutherford)

"Nothing was seen of any hostile Indians nor anything learned to lead belief in their being in the vicinity."

– Colonel G.E. Saunders, GA, 5215, f. 11
  GA R 133.30

Smudges lit to protect the tethered horses (R.W. Rutherford)

Hordes of mosquitoes and bulldogs (horseflies) plagued the advancing Field Force. They were in the words of one correspondent, "inescapable, though we kept swishing them off our horses and ourselves, with branches plucked from trees."

– Angus Howard Kennedy, "A War Correspondent of '85'," *The Cree Rebellion of 1884*, 153
  GA R 133.28

13

LOVELY PRAIRIE BELLES

Assiniboine Squaws at Fort Walsh

After the completion of his North-West Mounted Police service in 1878, George Anderton opened a photography studio at Fort Walsh. His photographs are invaluable historical records of that era.

– GA NA 4452 – 3

THREE MONTHS AFTER THE NWMP arrived in the West, William Parker recounted a lively time at a dance: "Went to a Ball at Fawcetts and Bells, danced all night and had a big time, made love to a bitch half-breed girl, got home at seven in the morning."[1] This anecdote is from his diary, not in one of his many letters to his family in England.

In one letter to his sister, he bantered about bringing a Native girl home:

> You ask me if I have met a young lady yet. This is the last place
> in the world to find one, but I still have my eye on a pretty squaw.
> Come now, wouldn't you like her for a sister? I am afraid she
> would make you all feel squeamish if I was to fetch her home,
> which there is no chance of my doing.[2]

In 1882, William Parker married Mary Margaret Calder, a Métis, beginning a relationship that lasted for sixty-three years. They raised three children.

Aboriginal Women

It was not until mid-August, five weeks out from Dufferin on the western march, that the Mounted Police contacted Indians. While "A" troop rested at Fort Ellice before continuing to Fort Edmonton, nearby Indians visited the police camp. Some of the women, in Sub-Inspector Sévère Gagnon words, were "almost pretty. All the girls have their cheeks heavily painted in red."[3] And love quickly blossomed, at least once. As the column departed for their next destination, the men watched a broken-hearted recruit sadly embracing his newly found Indian sweetheart while bidding her a fond farewell. His request to take her to Edmonton for marriage had been denied. But apparently, after a few days on the march, his love waned. It proved, reflected one worldly fellow companion, the adage "hot love is soon cold."[4]

That same week, the main column met a small, impoverished Sioux band west of Old Wives Lake. The females were described as unprepossessing. Artist Henri Julien thought even the budding girls lacked a single feminine grace, but still, "like their sisters the world over, these women put on airs. They have a certain grotesque coquetry … they cast sheep's eyes and squint to see if you are admiring them. If they catch you laughing at them … their black eyes flash fire of indignation, and they strut away."[5]

Written accounts by Mounted Police describe many young Aboriginal women as very appealing. In his report on the visit to Sitting Bull's camp in May 1877, Sub-Inspector Dalrymple Clarke commented that the Sioux women were "very graceful and pretty."[6] At a Christmas dance in 1874, Surgeon Barrie Nevitt observed that many of his dance partners "were quite handsome for squaws but all of them dirty."[7] Inspector Cecil Denny wrote that the "half-breed belles" attending a dance at Fort Calgary in 1876 were "well-dressed and some very, very good looking."[8] And seventeen-year-old Frederick Bagley's diary recorded that the Fort Saskatchewan ball was a great success, with everyone within a sixty-mile radius present including a "many very pretty Scottish and French half-breed girls."[9]

Dances were a popular association between the Mounted Police and Aboriginal women. Language barriers were only a minor problem. Surgeon Nevitt recalled having a wonderful time at a dance, even though none of his partners spoke English. It was even better at one impromptu Swan River dance. One policeman participant commented: "The girls were most of them English half-breed, which made it so much nicer as a fellow could talk to them."[10]

The adeptness at which the women learned the dances was described as amazing. A letter, written in May 1876, marveled that: "It is a wonder to us how rapidly the squaws pick up our quadrilles and cotillions, and enjoy them too, entering into the spirit of the dance with an energy really inspiring."[11] And the Indian women, eagerly sought as dancing partners, must have enjoyed their popularity. At one Fort Walsh dance, six Indian women had the attention of 150 men. They chose a new partner for each of the twenty-five dances that evening.[12] The demand for female dance partners gave the women their pick of dances. At Fort Macleod, Constable Jack Clarke wrote: "The Police Boys gave a dance at in Corpl. Martins Hall. The Citizens tried to start one down at the other Hall but they culd not get the squaws. We got them at our dance."[13] Why the two groups would hold a dance on the same night was not explained.

The dances were spirited affairs. At a boisterous NWMP St. Patrick's Day dance that ended in the morning, "a good many of the half breeds Girls were drunk and wanted to fight amongst themselves and there was a great time."[14] At other times, dances were carefully chaperoned by the mothers of Métis girls. The policemen taught the women schottisches, waltzes, and polkas, often on a beaten dirt floor. Lunch was always a part of the festivities. Constable William Grain recalled interested Aboriginal women asking him how to bake a cake.

Most policemen held values that reflected Western cultural superiority. One aspect was expressed in the negative observations of Indian females. It was a time, too, when white women in Canada were denied franchise and inheritance rights, and had limited employment, educational, legal, and economic opportunities.

The North-West Mounted Police viewed Indian women occupying a passive role—subordinate, exploited, and relegated to the burdensome tasks of camp. "I don't see much of the noble savage about them,"[15] commented Constable Tom LaNauze. Jean D'Artigue, watching the arrival of an Indian band, likened the women to loaded wild beasts of burden.[16] Surgeon Kittson wrote that the cruelty Indian women endured was incredible.[17] Recruit John Donkin watched an Indian camp moving. The men could be seen riding horses while the women shuffled along. Donkin wrote: "A squaw

Prairie Meeting

"Some of the girls were almost pretty. All of the girls have their cheeks
heavily painted in red."

– Sub-Inspector Sévère Gagnon, *GA*, R.A. McDougall, M 729
NAC C9570

very soon loses her bloom and freshness of youth and becomes wrinkled and
aged."[18] And even when a woman was given an elevated status, as when the
a squaw (The-One-that-Speaks-Once) addressed the General Terry-Sitting
Bull conference, her participation was intended to be a deliberate insult
to the American delegation. As one observer wrote: "At one stage in the
proceedings Sitting Bull offered the greatest insult to the general that an
Indian could do to a white man. He introduced a squaw in council!"[19]

Countering the perception of the female person as subordinate in their
status, Commissioner Macleod observed, "even under these disadvantages
the women appear to be happy enough in their way and take the fondest
care of their children."[20] Assistant Commissioner Irvine was also likewise
impressed during his first overnight stay in Sitting Bull's camp. He wrote:
"I never saw a happier people."[21]

Most prairie tribes practised male polygamy. Colonel James Macleod said he knew one old fellow who rejoiced in the possession of eleven dusky helpmates. There were several legal charges issued against white people for bigamy, but Indians never faced this crime. Nor was the Indian purchase of women charged in court, even though its practice was widely rebuked by many white newcomers. Constable Jack Clarke's diary entry on 30 July 1879 stated: "Joe Carr an outsider bought a squaw for three dollars today."[22] Inspector Sam Steele observed that "the Indian custom of buying wives was very much in evidence at this time; some of the younger squaws were held by their fathers at high prices, and one Saulteaux girl was valued at thirty horses, although the usual price was a rifle and one horse."[23] The *Manitoba Free Press* interviewed Sergeant-Major Joseph Francis, who was visiting Winnipeg:

Question:
How about Indian women—say at Cypress and Macleod.
Can they be bought and sold?

Answer:
Yes, any man can buy a woman for a horse at any time.[24]

One trader even boasted: "I could go out and buy a dozen girls tonight from $5 to $20 each—the price depending upon the looks of the girl."[25] Corporal William Parker wrote of the sale of Indian women: "One of the Indians wanted to sell me his sister for $50. She is sixteen years old and very pretty."[26] Whites thought it absurd when reading a Winnipeg paper report that the previous week an Indian who lived near the fort traded his mother off for a horse.[27]

The Indians often sought out police mediation to resolve their domestic disputes. One Mountie wrote that they were relied upon as great "Misters Fix-its."[28] The foremost problem, related Inspector Shurtliff, "is the stealing of one another's wives. A wife is worth from one to six horses; they do all the work, skin the buffalo, dress the hide, etc. all their dusky lord and master does is to shoot."[29] Inspector Sam Steele, after hearing from a young man whose wife had left him without returning his wooing gifts, asked to hear the woman's side. She admitted loving another. Steele pointed out that it was customary for unhappy white women to return all gifts, which she agreed to do, and this advice settled the matter amicably.

Inspector A.R. Macdonell, at the request of a Native woman who could not "abide in his tents," listened to her series of complaints, and, as a magistrate, issued her a judicial separation.[30] Still, cultural differences were causing confusion. As late as 1884, a young Indian (likely Mis-a-cha-cock) was baffled at his arrest for horse theft. He had exchanged a horse for a wife and, after she left him, he had taken back the horse. The court acquitted him, but only after he had spent months in confinement.[31]

Some Indian males resented the growing independence of their women that came with the arrival of the NWMP. An Ontario correspondent who was visiting Fort Macleod wrote that the Indian men disliked the police meddling with their "time-honored custom of beating their wives. They say the police have made the women masters, thereby reversing the order of nature and preventing them [the men] from getting as much work out of their women as they used to under the old order of things."[32]

Yes, police presence, assured Surgeon Nevitt, was uplifting the status of females. "Since our arrival," he wrote his fiancée, "the squaws have struck, refusing to work, and their husbands are in a quandary … if they followed their usual plan they would kill and mutilate the women and thus keep them in order, but the women now report this to the Commissioner."[33]

The surgeon was too congratulatory. As described earlier, at a dance in a teepee, ten days after his letter, an Indian named At-che-moon-e-kiss (Otsemoonee) cut a hole in the teepee, placed a pistol close to his wife's head, and shot her dead. Nevitt learned that the killer had forced her to kiss men at dances in order to get gifts which he kept. He had deserted her, leaving her with only one blanket, and then shot her.

Sexual intercourse between the "Riders of the Plains" and Aboriginal women was common. At one level, sex was consensual or for gifts with no commitment. On his arrival at Prince Albert, recruit John Donkin observed that "between the Hudson's Bay post and barracks were a number of Sioux lodges, which was the nightly resort for a good many of our men."[34]

On their arrival in the West, policemen at once engaged in intimate relationships with Indian females. A letter to a Montana newspaper, written less than four months after the building of Fort Macleod, depicted the officers "as fast learning the ways of the country. Most of them, if not all, have their favorite Indian women, upon whom they bestow their caresses, and thus the long dreary winter is pleasantly passed away."[35] The Fort Brisebois (Calgary) detachment, outraged when Inspector Ephram Brisebois removed the barrack stove to give to his Métis mistress, sent several men to complain at Fort Macleod. As a response, Colonel James Macleod replaced Brisebois and renamed the post Fort Calgary.

Constable James Stanford's exceptionally candid diary outlines his sexual contacts over a five week period from 9 November 1876 to 12 December 1876: "Had a go at a squaw yesterday on my bed … Had a touch off a fat

Cree squaw this evening ... Had a go at a squaw in the root house ... Had a go at a Cree squaw. Got her to mend my buckskin pants and put the blocks to her after she had finished ... Had a go at Cree on blanket."[36]

Some policemen deviously abused Aboriginal women. In a rare Indian account of that time, one elderly Native woman recalled her early years while at Wood Mountain: "There were no white ladies in those days. The policemen wanted wives so they go around and pick the ones they want. They gave the starving families groceries to get the girls."[37] At Wood Mountain in 1881, Superintendent William Jarvis was dismissed from the Force for assaulting his Aboriginal partner because she kissed her dancing companion. Jarvis had enticed the woman into an intimate relationship by providing food for her family.[38]

Vulnerable Indian women were sometimes plied with alcohol for immoral purposes. One drinking bout resulted in a fire that destroyed three buildings at the Fort Macleod post. S.J. Clarke's diary relates: "It commenced about four o'clock in the shoe Shop. Some of the Boys were drunk. Corpl. Paterson He had a bad squaw in the Shoe Shop at night and she was drunk and they nocked pipes of the stove and it caught on the wall and burned out stables."[39] Ironically, Corporal Patterson was awarded $40 for his skilful operation of the Babcock extinguisher, charging across the parade grounds, "bucking harder than a three-year-old bronco in order to mix the contents so that there would be sufficient gas generated to make the machine work with all its force."[40]

Sexual intercourse between Mounties and Native women resulted in detrimental health consequences. The 1881 medical report for Fort Walsh recorded twenty-eight policemen with venereal disease, compared to none one year earlier. Surgeon Kennedy wrote: "A feature in the medical history of the past year is the introduction of syphilis among the men. It was brought over from the other side of the line by the Cree and Assiniboine camps on their return here a year ago last fall."[41]

The sexual liaisons between the police and Indian women were not without criticism. There was the western derision of the "squaw man." Christian spokesmen condemned the casual relationships as immoral and detrimental to their missionary work.[42] Censure came from within the Force. In a letter to his wife, Commissioner James Macleod complained that, when he visited Fort Macleod, he had to sleep in Major Walsh's bed:

> I don't like staying for any length of time at Cypress. It is a miserable place ... I have the room formerly occupied by Walsh and sleep in his bed. I cannot help thinking of the queer

Indian Woman

"Most of the officers are fast learning the ways of the country and have their favorite Indian women, upon whom they bestow their caresses, and thus the long dreary winter is pleasantly passed away."

– *Helena Daily Herald* 15 March 1875
GA NA 5501 – 17

companions who must have occupied it with him. I turn from the thought with a shudder. The idea of a dirty squaw in the place of the sacred person of one's wife.[43]

Macleod further criticized Walsh for attempting to make Fred White (NWMP Comptroller) believe that, in Indian camps when squaws were offered to you, taking them to bed was the right thing to do.

The sexual affairs of James Walsh were common knowledge. A letter in November 1878 from Cypress (Fort Walsh) commented that the Major's military skills had not been evaluated as he had not fought any hostiles (Indians), but the record for his ability as a propagator of the "half-breed" race was not questioned. Moreover, the writer suggested that, if there was "a personal feeling" on the part of Col. Macleod, it was probably "owing to the licentious life that Walsh is leading here, which is a burning disgrace to the Force and deserves immediate attention from Canadian authorities."[44] The influential *Manitoba Free Press* further added to Walsh's appellations "Long Lance, White Forehead, and Sitting Bull's Boss," by reporting that "they call Walsh the squaw man."[45]

The press admonished the NWMP–Aboriginal sexual relationships. The *Regina Leader* cited the disgraceful conduct of one officer:

> It is time the Commissioner of the Mounted Police was opening his eyes to the fact that a non-commissioned officer is living in open adultery with a half-breed woman … this non-commissioned officer has been keeping this woman for nearly five years or, as rumor says, she has been keeping him. It is currently reported he takes the money she earns by hard work over her washtub and spends it on frivolous living.[46]

Settlement in the region, according to the *Toronto Mail*, brought changes in attitude: "The Mounted Police who, in the period between 1874 and 1881 lived openly with Indian girls purchased from their parents, have been compelled by the presence of settlers, if not to abandon, at all events to be more discreet in their purchase of their profligacy."[47]

Ottawa's concerns over the national image of the North-West Mounted Police appear in the Lieutenant Governor Laird's letter to Commissioner Macleod in February 1878:

> I fear from what reports are brought me, that some of your officers at Fort Walsh are making rather free with the woman around there. It is to be hoped that the good name of the Force

will not be hurt through too open indulgence of that kind. And I sincerely hope that Indian women will not be treated in a way that hereafter may give trouble.[48]

Macleod denied the insinuation that it was like a regular brothel at the post. The accusations against the police, however, continued and, in 1880, Mr. Joseph Royal created a stir in the House of Commons:

All over the North-West the Force is accused of disgraceful immortality; one of the chief traders who spent the winter at the forts, reported an open quarrel between an officer and one of the constables for the possession of a squaw. He reported also that he saw another soldier slap his officer in the face on account of a squaw.[49]

Prime Minister John A. Macdonald downplayed the North-West Mounted Police misconduct, but the portrayal of immoral conduct persisted.

Sexual relationships between policemen and Native women produced offspring, many of whom were unrecorded. It appears, though, that Assistant Surgeon Henry Dodd had a daughter with a woman from the Crooked Lakes Reserve, Constable David Grier fathered three children with Molly Tailfeathers, and Major James Walsh had a child with a Blackfoot woman.

In addition to relationships called "in the custom of the country" (à la façon du pays), the Mounties had a number of legal marriages with Aboriginal women. At least six policemen had Christian marriages with Teton women from Sitting Bull's camp. These included George Pembridge-Tahnoncoach; Thomas Aspdin-Mary Blackmoon; J.H. Thomson-Pretty Smile; Archie LeCaine-Emma Loves War; and Fred Brown-Tiopa.

In 1971 Mrs. Collins in Turner Valley wrote to the Comptroller for information of her grandfather, James Thomson (his birth, where he joined, certificate of discharge). Collins knew that he had married a Sioux girl and later worked as a telegraph operator.

On the other hand, some policemen were appalled at taking an Indian wife. The day after he attended a dance at Buffalo Lake in March 1875, Jean D'Artigue confronted an awkward situation. In response to a young "squaw's" signal to dance, the young Mountie had accepted, knowing that, by custom, a refusal was regarded as an insult. Everyone in the wigwam, he thought, enjoyed his "ludicrous motions." The following morning, an Indian chief with his daughter, the dancing partner from the night before, approached D'Artigue. After a smoke, the chief said through an interpreter that, as a pledge of his peaceful sentiments to white people, he was giving

Tahnoncoach, Sioux wife of George Pembridge, NWMP

At Fort Walsh, there were at least six formal marriages between policemen and
Sioux women in Sitting Bull's camp.

– GA NA 935 – 1. Credit Sask. Archives

his daughter to a man most worthy of the honour—namely D'Artigue. The young Mountie recoiled: "Honour indeed! I was terrified." As an alibi, D'Artigue demeaned himself as both a poor warrior and hunter. Moreover, he would need time to get friends from Edmonton to come to witness the ceremony, as was the practice of his people. This response pleased the old chief and relieved D'Artigue of an unwanted situation.[50]

Likewise, Sergeant Frank Fitzpatrick found himself in an unwanted predicament. He wrote:

Chief "Little Child" of the Saulteau [who had taken a fancy to me] urged me to marry his daughter, a rather good-looking Indian girl, with the alluring offer of twenty-two good horses to go with the bride. He specified, however, that the wedding should be in the manner of the white man, before a police officer, with signed papers. In other words, he had recognized the white man's law of marriage as being the proper protection for his daughter.[51]

The point is well taken. Chief Little Child wanted stability in his daughter's marriage.[52] Fitzpatrick deferred this offer for consideration.

Relationships with Native females could impact on NWMP staffing. Constable R.N. Wilson blamed his transfer from Fort Macleod for being at odds with White Antelope, whose daughter the Commanding Officer of "C" Division had "tender feelings." Wilson suspected White Antelope asked Superintendent Crozier to transfer him, and Crozier, who couldn't do "too much to please the Old Gentleman," followed suit.[53]

Shortly after the police arrived in the Cypress Hills and built Fort Walsh in 1875, several Mounties out for a ride were dumbfounded to discover a homestead about 15 km northwest with a family who spoke English. The Métis owner, Edward McKay, arranged to supply butter, cheese, and milk for the post. But of more interest to the policemen were McKay's five daughters.[54] His farm soon had a steady parade of police visitors.

Emma McKay married Peter O'Hare; Rachael, Jules Quesnelle; and Jemina, J.H.G. Bray. The Bray marriage produced thirteen children. Their daughter, Flo, was the first child born to a member of the Force and was the centre of attention. Bray was delighted that "my mounted police brothers made much of our little daughter."[55]

Were police associations with other than white women belittled? The Fort Benton Record, for some reason, lampooned the wedding ceremony at Fort Walsh of Miss Nancy Shagarin, "a blooming half-breed maiden," and Constable Frank Fitzgerald. Major Walsh conducted the ceremony.

The blushing bride was tastefully attired in a single blanket and a pair of new moccasins. During the ceremony she was quite composed, her jaws working violently in masticating a huge roll of chewing gum. When the critical moment arrived and the all-important question was asked: "Will you take this man to be your wedded husband?" she promptly responded "Humpa-ha," and went on chewing her gum. Frank looked remarkably well in Mr. Quesnelle's black coat, borrowed for the occasion. The garment was ... too large for him, but answered every purpose.[56]

After the nuptials, the couple (with a supply of pemmican) left in a sled for their honeymoon at the home of the bride's mother. Constable Gus Rolph, the best man, hosted a breakfast the next morning.

White Women

The arrival of white women heralded settlement and was associated with "civilization." Donald W. Davis (who later became the first elected federal Member of Parliament from the North-West Territories and had lived with Indian women during his whiskey-trading days) wrote to his mother in the eastern United States: "There is one white woman here now and several more are expected before long, officer wives of the police so you can see the country is getting civilized."[57] Surgeon Barrie Nevitt, on learning that Inspector William Winder was talking about bringing his wife from Ontario and that Colonel Macleod was considering marriage, wrote to his fiancée in Toronto that "we will have some decent civilized society."[58] Near the end of his service, Nevitt reiterated this point in a letter: "I think that we have made progress towards civilization—we have no less than six white women in the place [Fort Macleod]."[59] Constable William Metzler attended a dance that had "about eight white ladies and the rest breeds. The Whites made it seem quite like civilization."[60] Offering a moral opinion with racist overtones, the *Manitoba Free Press* pontificated: "Indian women are not so moral as their white sisters, for the simple reason that they have none of the restraining influences of civilized society to guide them."[61]

The "Riders of the Plains" preferred white women as their legal wives. Constable M. Kennedy wrote to his family in England: "I am single, and likely to remain so for the present. There is scarcely a white woman in the country—nothing but Indians and half-breeds."[62]

In the first years the NWMP spent in the region, the appearance of White women was noteworthy. Sergeant Frank Fitzpatrick commented that he had not seen a White woman for three years. Young Bagley's diary

Daughters of Edward McKay, Fort Walsh

L–R, Emma who married (Peter O'Hare), Maria (James Sanderson), Rachael (Jules Quesnelle), Jemina (J.H.G. Bray).

– GA NA 4541 – 1

mentions a minstrel show at Fort Saskatchewan that was attended by 110 people including a Miss Hodgins, a white girl. He wrote: "How the deuce did she get up here?"[63] A letter from Fort Macleod (May 1876) commented: "First of all, there arrived in our midst the other day a genuine white woman. She counts something of a 'coue,' being the first to open the road to these remote regions."[64] The writer (A.A.V.) did not elaborate what a "genuine white woman" was, but her arrival was auspicious. "She had," a Mountie observer recorded, "more spectators the first few days than a circus would have in a negro town. Every man was anxious to have a peep; most of us not having seen a white woman in two years. This is the place for girls in search of a husband."[65]

Some men wrote to eastern newspapers soliciting female correspondents. Sergeant Jack Breadon placed an advertisement in two Toronto papers: "Two Mounted Policemen desire to correspond with an unlimited number of young ladies with a view to mutual improvements—and possibly matrimony."[66] The words "unlimited number" and "possibly matrimony" brought sacks of mail, many of the letters with photographs. Breadon benevolently passed his extra letters to his barrack mates.

One correspondence resulted in both a marriage and a desertion. Fred D. Williams placed "a personal" in a Toronto newspaper professing that he was an exceedingly interesting young man and was anxious to correspond with young ladies. The Mountie found true love, took a leave of absence, and went to Toronto where he married his new sweetheart. But, after his leave expired, Williams remained in the city and was arrested as a deserter. The court agreed to withdraw the charges if Williams returned to the North-West and reported to the NWMP authorities.[67]

It was a rigorous undertaking for a woman to travel to the Northwest Territories. And it was certainly traumatic if there was no one to meet her upon arrival. According to the Fort Macleod druggist, one police officer took a precautionary measure and viewed the arrival of a prospective bride from a distance with binoculars before deciding not to proceed with the marriage and then arranged her return to Eastern Canada.[68]

The wives of policemen always had a NWMP escort when traveling any distance. In August 1876, Mrs. Tabor and her child left with a police detail (returning witnesses from the Cypress Hills Massacre trial in Winnipeg) to join her husband at Fort Edmonton. After Dalrymple Clarke died of mountain fever at Fort Walsh, policemen escorted the young officer's wife to Winnipeg for transport connections to Ottawa.

After 1882, railway connections brought an increasing number of white women to the region. In the 1885 census, 21,249 females (which included Aboriginal women) made up 44 per cent of the total NWT population of 48,363. For women living on isolated ranches, the arrival of other women was a blessing. The nearest neighbour to Mary Inderwick, an early settler living northwest of Pincher Creek, was 30 km away. Mary craved company: "I simply long to talk to a woman."[69] The arrival of white women abruptly ended some intimate relationships involving Mounties and Indian women. Constable Grier left Molly Tailfeathers and their three children to marry a white schoolteacher. He was mayor of Fort Macleod in 1877.

The early NWMP policy discouraged the enlistment of married men. Comptroller Fred White cited the inconvenience and expense of families at the posts and he suggested "that in the future married men will not be engaged for service, and should men marry during their term of service, their wives will not be recognized either as to the quarters, rations, or transport."[70] The Force remained overwhelmingly single men. It was not until 1974 that women were accepted for regular police duties.

Few Mounties were married. The family of Commissioner G. French lived in Winnipeg where his two children studied at St. John's College. Policemen escorted the family to the Swan River headquarters in 1875. James Macleod was married just shortly after he became Commissioner; he fathered five children. Veterinarian Poett and Supt. Deane also had large families. Walsh's wife stayed in Ontario. Three of the Mounties' wives— Julia Winder, Julia Shurtliff, and Mary Macleod—signed Treaty Seven.

The rapid influx of white women added a sense of "balance" to the unsophisticated pioneer lifestyle. White females involved themselves in community events and promoted education, religious, and health issues. Mrs. Macleod and Mrs. Winder raised $360 to open a school. Women in Prince Albert organized a funding drive to buy an organ for the church. In February 1885, a police concert was held to raise funds for the new church organ and three of the women performed as part of the program. Dr. Nevitt liked new refinements, such as the curtains on Mary Macleod's windows. The local ladies organized a picnic to which he was invited, the strongest beverage being coffee. During the North-West Rebellion, a Ladies Committee from Regina provided comforts for the NWMP.

While the Mounted Police handled most Indian domestic discord by persuasion and negotiation, several disputes that involved white women ended in court. One incident, related by Constable Jack Clarke, must have been the gossip of the small Fort Macleod community.

> Capt. Winder and Sergt. And myself went down to Capt. Jack's house and took Mrs. O'Neal back to her husband, she was in bed with Capt. Jack when we went into the house. On febr 4 trial jack o'neal's proper name is john carines. Jack o'neal sued Capt. Jack for five hundred dollars for taking his wife away and keeping her. The case came before Col. Macleod. Mr. Boys, an X Policeman, defended Capt. Jack and Jack O'Neal pleaded his own case. The jury fetched damages one hundred and twenty-five dollars. I was a witness, so was sergt. Ryan. It was the first seduction case that was done in this part of Territory.[71]

Another "scandalous" criminal case involved Inspector Cecil Denny's affair with Victoria McKay, the Métis wife of policeman Percy Robinson. A lawsuit for $10,000 by Robinson was lost when a key witness never

Col. A.G. Irvine's home, Regina

L–R, on horses – Inspector and Mrs. M.H. Fraser-White; on verandah – Miss Jukes (first daughter), Claude Hamilton (with child) and Miss Jukes (possible sister); seated on sofa – Mrs. R. Burton Deane, Mrs. Marshall (wife of a visiting doctor), Mrs. W.H. Herchmer; at back – Mrs. P.R. Neale, Col. Irvine, Surgeon Jukes.

– GA NA 659 – 34

appeared in court. Negative publicity, however, forced Denny's resignation. Racial and economic tensions elevated as the white female population increased. White women in the towns complained that Indian women loitered, begged for food, sat on doorsteps, and peered intrusively through windows into their homes.

Two accounts that describe the NWMP New Year's Dance indicate the growing social distance. At Battleford, a reporter wrote:

> In previous years the dancers were of the half-breed element, but on this occasion, however, that race was scantily represented owing to the increase of our white population. A marked contrast too was observed in the costumes. White ball dresses superseded the gay coloured shawls and tinted dresses of the jolly half-breed girls.[72]

Since the arrival of the NWMP at Fort Macleod, the premier social event of the year was the NWMP New Year's Dance. In often hazardous weather, the Mounted Police rode hundreds of kilometres with invitations to the area residents. Arrangements had been made for distant families to stay with the local residents. Everyone anticipated a special evening, renewing acquaintances and celebrating. For 31 December 1884, the invitation list was altered. Constable William Cox remembered: "There were a lot of white ladies in the country who objected to dance with squaws, so a cut was made."[73] Such offending attitudes were not very helpful when the North-West Rebellion erupted three months later.

In the 100-day North-West Rebellion, the safety of women and children was paramount. Every settlement signaled, usually with the ringing of a church bell, for the women and children to assemble at a designated centre, such as the police barracks or at a fortified church. Fort Macleod evacuated the women and children to Calgary. Of utmost concern was the fate of Theresa Gowanlock and Theresa Delaney, whose husbands were brutally murdered at Frog Lake. The two women were among the twenty-two white prisoners in Big Bear's camp, a situation that was abhorrent to most Westerners. The far western military column, the Alberta Field Force, was directed to attack Big Bear's band and safely release the hostages.

When sensational, but unfound rumors about the mistreatment of the women reached the column as it advanced eastward along the North Saskatchewan River, the troops felt an exalted sense of duty to uphold the honour of the two imperiled females, even though no one personally knew the women. One officer wrote that "had Big Bear and his band fallen into our hands while these reports were credited, I do not think man, women, or child would have been spared."[74] In the aftermath of the Field Force's skirmish near Frenchman's Butte, both women escaped unharmed.

There were almost no females outside of the white and Aboriginal populations. The ten Chinese enumerated in the 1885 census probably were males. There were two or three females counted among the eleven "Africans" enumerated. The most well-known Negro woman was Annie "Auntie" Sanderson, who was a housekeeper for the Macleod family and later owned a laundry in Pincher Creek. She spoke of herself and Mrs. Macleod as the first white women in the region.

Women "de mauvaise réputation"

During the three-week camp at Dufferin prior to the '74 March in June 1874, saloons and brothels attracted many men across the American border to Pembina, Dakota Territory. Six months later, both Divisions "D and E" returned to garrison the Dufferin post for the winter. The attractions at Pembina apparently had not waned as the Health Report noted an increased number of men with venereal infections. The Divisions moved to Swan River in June 1875.

Prostitution increased noticeably during the early 1880s when railway construction brought almost five thousand workmen into the region. White eastern women followed and opened brothels that apparently operated independent of male procurers. The first criminal case for prostitution was in March 1884 in Calgary, when Inspector Sam Steele found Nina Dow and Nellie Swift guilty of keeping a "house of ill fame." His sentence gave the women an option: six months in jail (gaol) with hard labour or to leave Calgary on the first train—which they did. One frequenter was fined $10 and sentenced to ten days imprisonment with hard labour.

A larger raid followed on Dominion Day, 1884, at Laggan (now Lake Louise), when five women were charged with prostitution. Three women were fined $50 and costs or two months in jail, two women $25 and costs or one month. Five frequenters received fines of $10, with an option of imprisonment for one month. Two months later, one of the women, Maud Lewis, was again charged with keeping a house of ill fame and released on condition that she leave Calgary for the East within two days.[75]

Street prostitution by Indian women was first reported in 1885, but the individuals were never charged. The *Calgary Tribune* had complained: "It is a notorious fact that this town has been infested with a number of squaw prostitutes, who brazenly solicit citizens as they pass up and down the streets. The police do not appear to trouble their heads about the matter."[76]

The North-West Mounted Police handled prostitution involving their policemen outside of the court system. At Beaver Creek in the Rocky Mountains, Constable Oscar Dubreuil received a police fine of $10 for being in a house of ill fame at 6 a.m. on the morning of 7 January 1885, when not on duty therein. Dubreuil apparently was annoyed, and three weeks later, he was confined to barracks for two months for making a false statement that implicated Sergeant William Fury of sleeping in a house of ill repute.

Infrequent arrests for prostitution suggest that western frontier society tolerated this vice. In fact, the brothels had police visitors: "The red coat of the Mounted Policemen," observed the *Regina Leader*, "is seen flashing in and out of these dens at all hours. As no arrests have been made the character of these visits may easily be surmised."[77] In an editorial, "Where are the Police," the editor of the newspaper, Nicholas F. Davin, interviewed Major James Walsh (of all people) on the problem of women of bad character parading the streets and warned him the newspaper would censure the local detachment if this nuisance was allowed to continue.[78]

Saloon at Donald, British Columbia, 1884-85

Arthur Potvin, a young Quebec City medical student, described the women at Donald as *"de mauvaises réputations."*

– George F.G. Stanley, ed., "Le journal d'un militaire au nord-ouest canadien,"
Revue d'Histoire de l'Amérique française, X, No. 2, 425

GA NA 782 – 2

A letter to the *Fort Qu'Appelle Vidette* supports the contention that the North-West Mounted Police tolerated "well-behaved" prostitution:

Sir: Can you inform me whose duty it is to rid the town of its present harlot [indecipherable]! The matter was urged on the NWMP officer in charge here, and his reply was that Supt. Deane had instructed that those "unfortunate" women were not to be molested "so long as they behaved themselves," in other words, the people of the Fort were to suffer for a little penchant of Mr. Supt. Deane.

Now, sir, I ask, are our women folk to continue to be daily shocked by the flaunting of their prostitution, be it on horseback or on foot! Where are those respectable church-going citizens, who are supposed to voice public opposition, that such a living disgrace to our hitherto fair town, as a "house of ill fame" is permitted under their very noses. A fine of five dollars is no deterrent to their horrible traffic, as may be inferred from the arrival of two more of their sisters-in-sin. [signed] Qu'Appelle.[79]

Many "sisters-in-sin" were not really "well-behaved," but hard characters. In the spring of 1885, during labour agitation in eastern British Columbia over unpaid wages, a vociferous rabble-rouser was a woman (described by Steele as "the woman in red") who incited striking rail workers to defy the police. She was arrested, fined, and transported eastward.

That summer in 1885, at the First Crossing of the Columbia, Donald had mushroomed into a "boom town" with 1,200 men working in railway construction. At that location, "whiskey galore is to be had for fifty cents per drink and gambling is a natural pastime."[80] Also attracted to Donald were about thirty women, described by Arthur Potvin, a young Quebec City medical student, as "*de mauvaises réputations.*" Potvin was with his unit, the 9th Quebec Voltigeurs, on a short rail excursion to visit the Rocky Mountains as compensation for the battalion's dull garrison duties while stationed in southern Alberta during the North-West Rebellion. The conduct of the women—smoking, card playing, drinking, and even street brawls—shocked the young private. Never in his hometown in Quebec City had he seen such flagrant behaviour.[81]

NOTES

1. *GA*, William Parker, M 934.

2. Dempsey, ed., *William Parker: Mounted Policeman*, 129.

3. *GA*, R.A. McDougall, M 729.

4. D'Artigue, *Six Years in the Canadian North-West*, 71. See also Chapter 3 – The '74 March: "A" Troop to Fort Edmonton.

5. Julien, "Expedition to the North-West," 22. Constable John Donkin, *Trooper and Redskin*, 243, wrote: "They are very coquettish damsels. One of our scouts married a Sioux and brought her to Regina. She was not long in taking to oriental vanities, and shone forth in all the splendor of high-heeled boots and silk costume, dress improver, and an immense hat of brilliant plumage."

6. *RL*, 17 March 1885. Also in E. Dalrymple Clark, "In the North-West with Sitting Bull," *Rose-Belfords Canadian Monthly and National Review*, V, (1880), 66–73.

7. Nevitt, *Frontier Life in the Mounted Police*, 31.

8. Denny, *The Riders of the Plains*, 89.

9. *GA*, Fred Bagley, M 43.

10. Dempsey, ed., *William Parker: Mounted Policeman*, 157.

11. *TG*, 10 May 1876.

12. *MFP*, 21 April 1880.

13. *GA*, S.J. Clarke, M 228.

14. Ibid.

15. LaNauze, "Echoes and Letters from Fort Walsh," 38.

16. D'Artigue, *Six Years in the Canadian North-West*, 124.

17. *RC*, NWMP, 1874, 23.

18. Donkin, *Trooper and Redskin*, 243.

19. James Fullwood, "An Echo of the Past," *SG*, Seventeenth Annual, 51. Also F.A.D. Bourke, "Recollections and Reminiscences," *SH*, XXXV, No. 2, 56.

20. *MFP*, 1 June 1877.

21. *RC*, NWMP, 1877, 37.

22. *GA*, Simon J. Clarke, M 228. Also 24 May 1879.

23. Steele, *Forty Years in Canada*, 144. See William Butler, in *The Great Lone Land*, 267, observed that Indians value the possession of a horse before that of a wife: … a horse is valued at ten guns; a woman is worth only one gun.

24. *MFP*, 25 May 1880.

25. *MFP*, 31 March 1880.

26. *GA*, William Parker, M 934.

27. *WDT*, 22 August 1882.

28. Fitzpatrick, *Sergeant 331*, 89.

29. *MFP*, 3 October 1876.

30. *RL*, 12 November 1885.

31. *SH*, 5 April 1884.

32. *MFP*, 1 June 1877. Henry Halpin, a prisoner in Big Bear's camp during the North-West Rebellion in 1885, wrote: "There was one thing that struck me very soon and that was the bearing of the Native women towards their husbands. I asked Lone Man's wife the reason for it. She told me that as there was no law now, the Indian could murder or beat his wife to his heart's content without fear of the police. At other times, such was not the case, as when a Native man did anything of that sort the law would arrest him." David R. Elliott, *Adventures in the West* (Toronto: Dundurn Press, 2008), 145.

33. *GA*, Barrie Nevitt, M 892.

34. Donkin, *Trooper and Redskin*, 162, described spying on the women swimming: "It was great fun to watch their antics. They could swim like musk rats, and seemed intensely fond of splashing each other, and indulging in all sorts of rough play… it was a decided comfort to know that these dusky beauties did bathe sometimes."

35. *HDH*, 15 March 1875. HWH, 18 March 1875.

36. *UMSA*, *Missoula*, James Stanford Diary.

37. C. Frank Turner, "Custer and the Canadian Connections," *The Beaver*, Outfit 307, 1976, 10.

38. Superintendent Jarvis had a troubled marriage and was separated. His wife contacted the NWMP comptroller and had part of his salary garnisheed each month.

39. *GA*, S.J. Clarke, M 228.

40. *FBRP*, 29 December 1880.

41. *RC*, NWMP, 1881, 28.

42. *FMG*, 23 March 1886.

43. *GA*, James F. Macleod, M 339.

44. *FBR*, 22 November 1878.

45. *MFP*, 14 June 1878.

46. *RL*, 19 July 1883.

47. *TM*, 2 February 1886. *FMG*, 23 March 1886 for Samuel Trivett on church attitudes.

48. *SAB*, Laird Letterbook, 128–30. See Morgan, "The North-West Mounted Police: Internal Problems and Public Criticism, 1874–83," 56.

49. *DHC*, 1880, 21 April, 1638. See Morgan, "The North-West Mounted Police: Internal Problems and Public Criticism, 1874–83," 58–61.

50. D'Artigue, *Six Years in the Canadian North-West*, 90.

51. Fitzpatrick, *Sergeant 331*, 75.

52. John Macoun, a prominent field naturalist and Dominion botanist, contended that Indian parents were always glad to get white husbands for their daughters as an assurance of economic security. *MFP*, 1 June 1877.

53. *NAC*, R.N. Wilson, MG 29, E-47.

54. Another daughter, Clara McKay, committed suicide with strychnine following a dispute with her mother over the man her family expected her to marry. *WDT*, 3 June 1880.

55. Gillett, "Interview of J.H.G. Bray," 16. Some of the NWMP-Métis marriages include: Paddy Burke, Joseph Butlin-Angelique Roselle, William Parker-Margaret Calder and Frank Fitzgerald-Nancy Shagarin.

56. *FBR*, 16 March 1877.

57. Saum, "From Vermont to Whoop-Up Country," 68.

58. Nevitt, Dempsey, ed., *A Winter at Fort Macleod*, 80.

59. Ibid., 158. One week later, Nevitt discovered a second link with "civilization": "For dessert tonight ice cream! Is it not wonderful that way out here in this heathenish part of the world the evidences civilization should be gradually creeping in."

60. *GA*, William Metzler, M 836.

61. *MFP*, 10 June 1880.

62. *NAC*, M. Kennedy, f. 35.

63. *GA*, Fred Bagley, M 43.

64. *HDI*, 13 May 1876.

65. *MFP*, 22 June 1876.

66. Rookie # 2, "Remembrances of a Tenderfoot," 59. The article also appears in *SG*, Thirty-Second Annual, 109.

67. *RL*, 8 May 1884.

68. John Higinbotham, *When the West was Young* (Lethbridge: Herald Printers, 1978), 89. The year was not given.

69. Mary Inderwick, "The Lady and Her Ranch," *AH*, XV, No. 4, 4.

70. *RC*, NWMP, 31877, 22. Comptroller White informed Inspector William Herchmer to engage Leonard Bailey as a Constable, provided he signed a paper to the effect that his wife would not be in any way recognized. *NAC*, Leonard Bailey, f. 509.

71. *GA*, S.J. Clarke, M 228. One infrequent Indian conviction occurred in 1884 when Flint (a Sarcee) received two months in prison for kicking Hiccup (a Cree woman) and cutting off her hair.

72. *TG*, 22 January 1884.

73. *LH*, 11 July 1935.

74. John Pennefather, *Thirteen Years on the Prairies* (London: Kegan Paul, Trench, Trubner), 51.

75. *RC*, NWMP, 1884, 54−60. In the two-month period between the two arrests of Maud Lewis, four men were fined as frequenters of a bawdy house but no charges for prostitution were laid. There were no charges for prostitution in 1885.

76. *Calgary Tribune*, 16 September 1885.

77. *RL*, 17 May 1883.

78. Ibid.

79. *Qu'Appelle Vignette*, 18 June 1885.

80. *EB*, 26 September 1885.

81. George F.G. Stanley, ed., "Le journal d'un militaire au nord-ouest canadien," *Revue d'Histoire de l'Amérique française* X, No. 2 (september 1956), 425.

14

SICK PARADE AND
HEALTHCARE

Sick Parade in Police Camp (Henri Julien)

"The general health of the force at this post [Fort Walsh] during the year has not
been good. The average number on the sick list has been twelve, which would make
an average sickness about eight per cent."

– Surgeon George Kennedy, NWMP, *Report of the Commissioner*, 1880, 44
  GA NA 361 – 16

SERGEANT FREDERICK D. SHAW, a native of Nova Scotia, had taken
basic dental training in Maine. This knowledge helped on the journey west
when he ran out of money in Fort Benton. Shaw borrowed a chair, posted
a sign with his fee, and, on the main street of the frontier town, pulled teeth.
Sometimes his services were free: at Fort Walsh, he extracted seven teeth

for Sitting Bull, thereby winning the medicine man's thanks and friendship. Constable William Metzler relied on whiskey as a painkiller for his trips to the "dentist." His diary recorded: "February 10, 1884—got a bottle of whiskey from Capt. Cotton and Sergt. Shaw hauled my teeth out of me ... February 11, 1884—got some more whiskey and had the roots taken out ... April 9, 1884—got a set of teeth for $30.00."[1]

Medical Staff

Prior to 1885, the NWMP never had more than four medical doctors at one time, with one physician assigned to a post.[2] This shortcoming in medical services and facilities was a major drawback to the region. Constable A.H. Lynch-Staunton, stationed at the police horse breeding ranch near Pincher Creek, recalled: "We had no doctor, the nearest being Doc Kennedy in Macleod; people thought twice before they decided to be sick."[3]

Five NWMP medical doctors, John Kittson, Barrie Nevitt, Robert Miller, George Kennedy, and Augustus Jukes, were especially influential in the first years of the Force. John Kittson, born in St. Paul, Minnesota, to a leading business family, had studied medicine at McGill University. He participated in the '74 March and served for eight years in the Force. In 1884, at age thirty-eight, Dr. Kittson died in St. Paul under puzzling circumstances that most likely related to an overdose from his addiction to opium and morphine. One account related: "For days previous to his death he complained of his head and his memory seemed impaired."[4] A medical assistant, Teddy Warren, commented: "Kittson was a great friend of mine ... but drink got the best of him.[5]

Richard Barrington Nevitt left war torn Georgia at the end of the American Civil War and trained at the University of Toronto. He also participated in the western march. Nevitt's letters to his fiancée (Elizabeth Eleanor Beaty) in Toronto and his drawings are invaluable records of the first years of the NWMP. Some of his illustrations are the only documents available, such as Sitting Bull meeting Major Irvine, the Treaty Seven encampment, and the extradition trials at Helena. Nevitt drew pictures of the Cypress Hills Massacre site for the prosecution to exhibit at the court trial in Helena. At the request of friends of Constable Godfrey Parks, who died shortly after the Force reached Fort Macleod, Nevitt drew a sketch of the gravesite and mailed it to them. At the end of his NWMP term, Nevitt returned to Toronto, married, and had a prominent medical career.

Information on Doctor R. Miller is sparse. He joined the NWMP in 1875, served at Fort Walsh in the Battleford area, and was at the Duck Lake skirmish. In 1887, Miller shot himself in the Battleford barracks.

Surgeon John Kittson (Henri Julien)

"Kittson was a great friend of mine … but drink got the best of him."

– Constable Teddy Warren, *NAC*, E. Warren, f. 57
GA NA 361 – 15

George Allan Kennedy, who replaced Barrie Nevitt, studied medicine at the University of Toronto. Kennedy was only twenty years of age (too young to legally write a medical prescription) when he arrived in the West. After his nine-year career in the NWMP, Kennedy was instrumental in the formation of the North West Territories Medical Association and the founding of the University of Alberta. His literary contributions are very interesting. He wrote an article describing the climate of Alberta in the *American Medical Association Journal* in 1889 and an account in 1890 of the bloody Cree-Blood skirmish near Lethbridge in 1870, in which he actually interviewed some of the participants.[6]

Augustus Jukes was fifty-nine when he joined the NWMP as the Chief Surgeon in 1882. Superintendent Richard Burton Deane thought Jukes a fine old gentleman and very competent practitioner. At the end of the North-West Rebellion, Jukes observed Louis Riel in prison, testified at the trial that in his view Riel was sane, and was the medical doctor present at the hanging of the Métis leader in November 1885. Several days later, as a member of an appointed panel, he examined Riel's body to dispel rumours that the corpse had been mutilated. His final duty relating to this military conflict was serving on a medical board that had to review compensation claims from men who had suffered from wounds, disease or disabilities while on active service with the NWMP.[7]

As there were no female nurses, Hospital Sergeants or Stewards helped the overworked physicians and supervised record-keeping and medical supplies. Some of these assistants had only basic medical training. Ernest Braithwaite worked at the Medical School in London, England, and later became provincial coroner for Alberta. John Lauder had three years of medical training in Dublin; and hospital steward J.C. Holmes studied medicine, but had not obtained a diploma.

Still when his assistant fainted while he was amputating the finger of a Native woman, Surgeon Nevitt had reason to suspect his attendant's skill. Moreover, Nevitt's kicks failed to revive his helper, leaving the surgeon to complete the operation unaided. Stitching Frederick Bagley's foot (which he cut chopping wood) was interrupted when Hospital Steward George Elliot fainted and rolled over on the floor. Sergeant Fitzpatrick took on an unfamiliar assignment when Holmes, Staff Sergeant of the Qu'Appelle hospital, left to testify at a Fort Macleod trial. Fitzpatrick had accepted Superintendent Steele's request to take charge but asked to be exempt from administering medicines.

Fitzpatrick later reneged on this restriction when he suspected that a Constable was malingering and concocted a drink so effective that the Mountie chose never to report in sick again. Before Holmes' return, Fitzpatrick's confidence had grown to the point where he even performed two operations—one on a horse, a second on an Indian prisoner.[8]

The medical practitioners faced a challenging schedule. In the fall of 1880, Dr. George Kennedy cared for seventy Indians in an Assiniboine camp, then moved to a large Cree camp of 1,500 where almost everyone suffered from dysentery. On one day he treated 150 patients. Upon his return to Fort Walsh, he visited a nearby Indian camp ravaged by scarlet fever and provided care for eighty-six Native people. Tragically 12 children died. The following year at Fort Walsh, Doctor Kennedy administered to 447 Indians who were suffering from whooping cough and colds. After the Duck Lake skirmish, Hospital Sergt. Edward Braithwaite was so occupied attending the wounded men that he slept in his clothing for three days.

Injuries in the field received immediate medical attention. On the '74 March, when a gun explosion damaged a man's finger, Nevitt immediately amputated the finger—"My first operation,"[9] he recorded. Shortly after,

Nevitt left the column to return with several sick men to the Dufferin base. En route, in what must have been a remarkable operation, he removed one man's appendix. Later at Fort Macleod, upon hearing (incorrectly) that Father Constantine Scollen was critically injured in a fall from a bronco, Nevitt traveled in a wagon 8 km to bring the priest to the fort. In another example, after a horse broke Constable Francis Dobbs' leg, his companions sent for a doctor at Portage la Prairie, 125 km distance. Upon his arrival, the doctor treated Dobbs by soaking bandages in starch and wrapping them around the injured leg. Stones were heated and placed beside the leg. In three days, the bandages were as hard as a plaster cast. At Humboldt, after twenty-two men in a police column traveling from Regina to Prince Albert became snow blind, Hospital-Sergeant Edward Braithwaite asked Commissioner Irvine to sleep in a tent so that he could treat the men in the only house at the site.

Distances were only an inconvenience to the pioneer medical men. On hearing of a typhoid fever outbreak at the Morley Mission west of Calgary, Dr. L.G. DeVeber, then obtained Fort Macleod commander Leif Crozier's approval to leave immediately and, accompanied by Reverend John Maclean, left by buckboard for the Mission. The two men crossed rivers, exchanged horses, skirted a roaring prairie fire near High River, greased the vehicle, ate meals, and still reached Morley, a distance of 300 km, within twenty-three hours.[10]

At Fort Calgary, Dr. Nevitt responded to a message from Fort Macleod that a man was desperately ill by sending a driver and team ahead with supplies. Nevitt left at daybreak and joined the team for the night 60 km south at High River. In the morning, Nevitt rode ahead. The weather was stormy and a cold-blowing wind reduced visibility, making directions difficult to follow. Twice his horse stepped in badger holes, throwing Nevitt over its head. At the Oldman River, drift ice blocked the ford, and Nevitt crossed the waterway on his horse until he reached water shallow enough to wade through. Nevitt wrote: "I finally got to the Fort about 8 p.m. so tired and wet and cold that I could hardly stand up."[11]

Hospital Facilities

The first hospital buildings were rough log structures, chinked with mud, with rough plank floors and roofs of logs covered by sod. A visitor to the Fort Macleod hospital in 1876 measured a drift of dirt a metre wide and five centimetres deep. A thunderstorm washed away the dirt, leaving thirty gallons (135 L) of water to be drained from the floor. Dr. Nevitt kept a cat to prowl the building for mice.

Interior of NWMP Hospital, Calgary

Chief Surgeon Augustus Jukes described the "facilities at Calgary and everything related to it, in a most dilapidated and unsatisfactory condition."

– *RC*, NWMP, 1884, 27
  GA NB 13 – 3

Little improvement in the hospital facilities was first evident. In 1879, Dr. Kennedy complained that the Fort Macleod building was unfit for habitation. He reported in warm weather the wind deposited a layer of dust half an inch thick (1.27 cm) and in winter it was impossible to keep the building warm; moreover, rain and melting snow water continually dripped on the beds.[12] In Surgeon A. Jukes' opinion, three beds hardly warranted the name of the "pestiferous hut known as the Hospital."[13]

Hospital conditions were not much better at the other posts. On an inspection tour, Chief Surgeon Jukes described the facilities at Calgary as being "in a most dilapidated and unsatisfactory condition."[14] The Post Commander, Superintendent W. Herchmer, even proposed abandoning the buildings. As late as 1881, the territorial capital at Battleford lacked a hospital. When one man contacted measles, very cold weather prevented his isolation in a tent and he remained in the barracks. The other men, conceded Dr. R. Miller, "grumbled about having the measles represented by one of their number sleeping with them in the same room."[15]

After 1880, the construction of new facilities significantly updated some police hospitals. Dr. G. Kennedy described a new hospital building at Fort Walsh as cheerful, airy, commodious, in all a great help in treatment of the sick. The Annual Report in 1883 praised the new hospital at Fort Macleod as being a vast improvement, having fourteen beds, a waiting room at the entrance, a surgery room, kitchen, and washroom. Surgeon Jukes, in 1884, reported that the hospital at the new post at Maple Creek was in respectable order and provided with six beds. A Winnipeg newspaper commended the hospital built at the new Regina detachment as a "model of neatness and completeness."[16]

Annual Medical Reports

Each police surgeon forwarded an annual medical report that assessed the general health at the post and gave both the type and number of illnesses. Surgeon John Kittson concluded that the overall health at Fort Macleod was unacceptable. He wrote "a retrospective view of the past year (1878), from a medical standpoint, is anything but satisfactory."[17] At times, one-third of the detachment was unfit for duty.

In 1881, Surgeon George Kennedy listed forty-seven diseases of 419 patients at Fort Walsh under nine headings: general diseases, nervous system, respiratory system, digestive system, cutaneous system, glandular system, special sense, genitor-urinary system, and surgery. In a one-year reporting period following December 1883, Dr. Augustus Jukes identified fifty-eight illnesses at his Regina post. Below is a sampling of some of the entries he included in his Sick Report:

Disease	Cases	Days	Average	Surgeon's Remarks
Bronchitis	44	111	2.5	Con. Brady invalided
Syphilis	33	376	11.4	Recovered
Contusions	32	260	8.1	Principally injuries from horses
Diarrhea	25	41	1.6	Recovered
Fever	22	–	–	
Gonorrhea	18	–	–	
Constipation	13	18	1.4	Recovered
Epilepsy	2	68	34.0	Con. McCutcheon invalided
Ingrown toenail	1	2	2.0	Recovered
Frost bite	3	11	3.7	Recovered
Mental imbecility	1	1	1.0	Const. Chandler invalided

The dates of the illnesses are not given, but it would be expected that many ailments followed a seasonal pattern with, for example, respiratory illness prevalent in cold weather and during base confinement. Physical injuries were more likely to occur throughout the year.

The numbers of some illnesses varied decidedly from year to year. There were 38 cases of the dreaded typhoid fever at Fort Walsh in 1879 and not one in 1881. Venereal infections (gonorrhea and syphilis) among policemen at Fort Walsh had increased from 2 cases in 1879 to 28 in 1881. Surgeon Kennedy reported: "A feature in the medical history in the past year, and one that is very much regretted is the introduction of syphilis among the men."[18] "Syphilis," one medical report disclosed, "caused us more troubles, vexation and loss of time than any other disease."[19]

Health conditions could contrast markedly between the posts. Dr. Robert Miller reported that the general health of the men at Battleford and Fort Saskatchewan in 1882 had been excellent. The same year, Doctor George Kennedy reported: "Fort Walsh does not present many features for congratulation."[20] Fort Walsh, with its outbreaks of typhoid fever, had been regarded as an unhealthy post and its outpost at Wood Mountain an equally unwholesome place. The report for 1880 noted the average number of men on the sick list had been twelve which was 8 per cent of the detachment.[21] In addition, Kennedy regarded this number excessive in light of the fact that the Force selected healthy young men.

Pulmonary afflictions were the most prevalent illness.[22] In 1880, coughs and colds made up 25 per cent of the 422 diseases treated at Fort Walsh and the following year 144 of the 419 cases (34 per cent). Dr. G. Kennedy recorded coughs and colds counted for 21 per cent of the illnesses at Fort Macleod in 1884. Crowded living quarters and poor ventilation certainly contributed to the incidence of the illness. Chief Surgeon Augustus Jukes recommended the barracks be large enough to provide each man 300 cubic feet of air. Dr. J. Kittson correlated sound lungs with the expansion of the chest. Kittson measured the men for the elasticity of their chest expansion and then concluded "good" lungs needed a minimum increase in chest circumference of three inches (7.5 cm).

Aboriginal and Community Care

A medical doctor received an annual salary of $1,000, a rate of pay only exceeded by the Commissioner. The Department of the Interior (later Department of Indian Affairs) paid a portion of the salary for serving the Aboriginal population. In 1879, they paid $700 to John Kittson, $500 to R. Miller, and $375 to G.A. Kennedy (for nine months' service).

The Indians eagerly sought the "white man's medicine." At Old Wives Lake, on the western march, eight adult Indians approached Dr. Kittson with ailments. Kittson found respiratory and eye problems prevalent, which he attributed to poor ventilation in teepees. Dr. George Kennedy's observations several years later concurred: "It is rare to find a native woman over thirty with sound lungs."[23]

At Fort Macleod, the Indians besieged Dr. Nevitt with their ailments. He wrote:

> Busy all day long—such a number of Indians required medicine and attention ... it is very strange to see how quickly these Indians find out where I live altho' I move around so much ... at present I have no less than five Indians now in my tent talking to me through the interpreter relative to some sick people they have.[24]

The doctor then added: "The confidence the Indians place in me is very gratifying but exceedingly onerous."[25]

Nevitt prided himself on his success: "and I think too they all like me, for I am gentle and thoughtful of their feelings just as tho' they were white civilized people."[26] And ignoring his fellow officers taunting him as a fool, Dr. Nevitt gave free service to the Indians. In turn, some appreciative Indians gave Nevitt small gifts. One family presented the doctor with a pair of new moccasins.

The police surgeons applied advanced medical skills. Nevitt excised the eye of an Indian boy and amputated the leg of a second youth wounded by the Sioux south of the line. He treated Chief Crowfoot for neuralgia. Crowfoot's earlier treatment was by "an old hag" who burnt holes in his leg to drive away pain and deaden the Cree "medicine"—to which Crowfoot attributed his disease. At Wood Mountain, Nevitt delivered a baby for a fifteen-year-old mother.

An injured person's consent was required before treatment. Doctor Robert Miller wanted to amputate the arm of an Indian who was wounded while duck hunting, but the man and his companions opposed this advice. The man died the following afternoon.

The Indians were suspicious of inoculations. It took persistent coaxing by Dr. H. Dodd to convince a wary Pi-a-pot of its efficacy. However, once he was vaccinated, the chief proved a great supporter, going to each teepee to advise band members of its benefits. Over the next seventeen days, Dodd traveled in frigid weather through deep snow to five reserves where he vaccinated 732 Indians.[27] In an attempt to reduce travel and improve on efficiency, medical treatment for the Indians was arranged for Treaty payment dates. At one payment site in 1882, Dr. George Kennedy vaccinated 300 Indian children for smallpox. The treatment of Indians had a positive outcome. Inspector Edmund Frechette was quoted in a New York paper, "it may be said that the doctors help a great deal in cementing friendship between Indians and white men."[28]

In turn, the policemen sometimes availed themselves of Indian medicine. Jean D'Artigue felt an immediate soothing after a medicine man applied a chewed root to his frozen ears.

When a companion mishandled a revolver and accidentally wounded Constable "Shack" Murray in the hip, a rider was dispatched for a doctor at Fort Walsh, about 70 km away. During the wait, Murray turned to a medicine man for help. The medicine man spit a mixture of chewed roots and leaves into the wound. In response to the skepticism of his comrades, Murray then retorted: "Let him be; they have lots of practice on gunshot wounds."[29] When Dr. Kennedy arrived, he found Murray had vomited about half a litre of blood and was in extreme shock. Constable Murray was transported to Fort Walsh where he made a good recovery, although Dr. Jukes was unable to remove the bullet.

Constable George Guernsey, in the article "Red Man's Magic," credited Indian medicine men as capable of performing the most extraordinary feats.[30] A second Mountie, Cecil Denny, was likewise impressed: "These Medicine-Men had, to my own knowledge, great powers of their own, and some of the feats they accomplished, were to say the least extraordinary, and certainly those which came under my own observation, I could in no wise account for."[31]

An added responsibility for the police medical staff was to provide community care. At Battleford, Dr. Miller amputated Mr. Forget's arm that had been caught in a threshing machine; in Calgary, both of Joseph Phelin's frozen feet were amputated; Dr. Kennedy amputated the frozen foot of an American army deserter.[32] A former Mountie, Edward Maunsel, was cared for in the Fort Macleod post hospital for frozen feet. Police surgeons also offered dental services. Dr. Nevitt's first medical order to Fort Benton included dental instruments. He then extracted a tooth for Father Constantine Scollen.

Injuries and Somatic Illnesses

The daily physical work had expected injuries. There was always frostbite, sprains, cuts, gun accidents, and injuries related to the care, breaking, and riding of horses. In the Sick Report for 1885, seven cases of contusions from horse kicks caused men to lose eighty-eight work days. Surgeon Jukes

Richard Barrington Nevitt, M.D.

"Very busy all day long—such a number of Indians required medicine and attention
… it is very strange to see how quickly these Indians find out where I live altho'
I move around so much."

– R.B. Nevitt, *Frontier Life in the Mounted Police*, 186–87
  GA NA 2859 – 1

reported one man hospitalized two days from a horse bite, one man three days from a dog bite, and one man thirteen days from a bite by a man. One can only speculate of the circumstances of the last case.

Three deaths resulted from work injuries. Robert Sherlock Tetu died in Winnipeg in January 1875. The postmortem linked his death to a blow on the back of his head from a fall. There are no personal files for John Nash and Tom Hall and few details of their deaths are known. Nash's death in March 1876 near Fort Macleod apparently occurred while hauling logs to the post. Supt. John McIllree's diary in 1880 commented on Hall:

> 29 February – poor Hall is much worse. Kittson had painful duty to warn him to settle up his earthly affairs … 3 March – Hall rallied again and is quite bright but poor fellow, his disease is incurable … 9 March – Hall sinking very fast.[33]

Hall was buried at Fort Macleod. A small token made from an American silver dollar with his name, age, and date was placed in the coffin.

Careless gunfire killed two men and wounded others. On the '74 March, P.G. Robinson in "F" Division lost a finger when his shotgun burst; later, Const. Bleevor's gun burst, cutting his hand. Among the seriously wounded were Const. Murray, Staff Sergt. Ferland and Sergt. H.A. Fletcher. Const. Abram shot himself in the hand when he tripped and his gun discharged. Const. Hart suffered a severe leg wound when a comrade shot him while cleaning a revolver; Hart spent fifty-six days in hospital. Upon his release, he took sick leave, deserted, was captured, and imprisoned with hard labour.

Medical treatment and care were rudimentary by today's standards. Tea leaves and confinement in dark quarters was used to treat snow blindness; opium for diarrhea ("Prairie Cholera"); quinine for Mountain Fever. Dr. Kittson experimented and treated with "Trinitrate of Bismuth" in more than double the recommended dosage, with one grain of opium powder added. Liquid ammonia diluted in ten parts water was applied on mosquito bites. Wind, dust particles, and prairie ash caused inflamed lips that were treated with cold water and lip salves. Oil of Jupiter was used to kill lice. Chloroform lessened pain while Const. Peasnell had a finger amputated. Drugs sent to Fort Macleod were redistributed to other posts.

Mental Illness

Violent or bizarre behaviour characterized the perception of mental illness more than a depressive bearing. Court records list twelve cases (one female) where a magistrate or justice of the peace, likely with minimal psychiatric expertise, ruled a person a dangerous lunatic committed to the care of the NWMP. Some individuals convicted as lunatics remained in local police custody while others were taken to Stony Mountain Penitentiary. Inspector Sévère Gagnon had enough insight to dismiss the charge of a dangerous lunatic against "Paul" upon learning that he was an epileptic.

Two well-known incidents of mental illness involved prominent NWMP officers. In February 1876, Métis hunters reported that Inspector Crozier was wandering aimlessly alone on the winter prairie. Assistant Comm. Irvine, traveling south from Edmonton, found Crozier near the Tail Creek post, north of the Red Deer River. Irvine reported to Comm. French: "He was in a very nervous state and far from well; both Colonel Macleod and I thought it would not be safe for him to return across the prairie in the state of health he was in, so I brought him here [Fort Macleod] where he is now and I am happy to say almost quite well."[34]

An eye-catching headline in the local press—"Dr. Robert Miller Blows Head Off"—announced the tragic death of the police doctor. A twelve-year member of the Force, Miller committed suicide in 1887 in the Battleford barracks. He had methodically prepared his death by connecting twine tied from one big toe to the trigger of his rifle, placed the barrel end in his mouth, and pushed his foot away, blowing his brains all over the room.[35] His comrades recalled that he had appeared despondent for some time.

Earlier written accounts adumbrated signs of mental instability in both officers. A year previous to Crozier's desultory wandering, Dr. R.B. Nevitt had written that "poor Crozier has had the blues all winter long ... the poor chap is quite sick and so nervous he can neither eat, sleep nor keep quiet."[36] And, eleven years before Miller's suicide, Colonel Macleod had observed: "The reports I have received of Doctor Miller from Cypress Hills have me think that he is not well fitted for his position."[37] Nevitt also expressed doubts about his fellow physician: "I have no confidence whatever in Dr. Miller and I think with reason."[38]

Several documented cases of mental illness appeared among the ranks. Surgeon Augustus Jukes reported that Constable H.B. Griffith died by his own hand (gunshot), probably in a state of temporary insanity. There is little information on his condition other than a newspaper reference that he had family troubles before joining the police. Griffith had enlisted in the NWMP less than three months earlier and was said to be despondent about the loss of his wife. One man, Frank Lawton, was certified insane and committed to the Selkirk asylum. He then engaged in a series of bizarre letters to Commissioner Irvine and threats against Surgeon Miller. His only wish, Lawton wrote, was to die facing his many enemies.

A former policeman, Frank Pennock, charged as "a dangerous lunatic," died in police custody while being escorted from Fort Macleod to Calgary. The circumstances of his death were suspicious. The police had bound him in a straightjacket and placed in the back of a buckboard without shade from the hot August sun. The *Calgary Herald* commented that "those who saw the manner in which the poor man was used consider the treatment brutal to the extreme."[39] In their rebuttal, Constable Schofield and Sergeant Spicer insisted they tied up an old comrade to prevent him from injuring himself.[40] The incident seems to have been deliberately downplayed and little information followed.

Invalids

Men unable to perform daily tasks were designated as invalids. If the condition persisted, a discharge from the NWMP followed. In some years a significant number of men were released as invalids: twenty-five men in 1883 and twenty-six in 1884—nearly 8 per cent of the ranks each year.

Medical infirmities or injuries were the main reasons for discharge. James Stuart was invalided after his broken leg (injured while tobogganing at Battleford) failed to heal. Thomas Atkinson was discharged for incurable deafness. Dr. George Kennedy declared constitutional syphilis had made Staff-Sergeant A. Ferland unfit for further service. Malcolm MacKenzie was determined an invalid due to deafness. O. Payette was designated an invalid because blindness precluded him from night duty. Surgeon Jukes recommended T. McCutcheon be declared an invalid "the sooner the better" after three epileptic seizures in one month made him possibly dangerous with a loaded carbine. In 1890, McCutcheon asked for a pension, claiming injuries in the Force made him unable to work.

The attending doctor wrote the Medical Discharge:

Fort Walsh, 11 May 1880

This is to certify that Reg. No. 333 Const Fitzpatrick,
T.B. of B Division is unfit for duties as a member of the
N.W.M. Police. His disease Phthesis [tuberculosis of the lungs]
was contracted while on duty December 1875.
He also suffers from chronic Rheumatism.

George Kennedy, Surgeon N.W.M.P.[41]

Whether the disease was contracted on duty was important as it provided Fitzpatrick with free transportation home. Surgeon Jukes had diagnosed Constable J. Barkley's inflammation of the lumbar region as the result of an injury received prior to joining the Force. Macleod wrote that: "Charles Zivack's constitution was sapped by a disease of his own contracting. I therefore determined not to pay his way down [home]."[42]

An unexpected large number of men later diagnosed as invalids had entered the Force with prior afflictions. Dr. Kennedy concluded that, of the nine invalids who joined in 1880, "five were utterly unfit for the force in every way, and three of them had diseases which should have prevented their being passed by the examining surgeon. One man [James Livingstone] was driven to the hospital on his arrival here, and never left it until he was driven away to Benton."[43] Senior Surgeon Augustus Jukes' examination of seven men confirmed Kennedy's findings. Jukes diagnosed three men with long-standing diseases and a fourth man with epileptic seizures related to an earlier penetrating wound of the cranium.[44]

There were men unsuitable for the arduous work of "Policing the Plains." Andrew Jones was designated an invalid after 500 days, in the opinion of the surgeon as "a confirmed hypochondriac."[45] Dr. Robert Miller judged Sutherland Staynor "physically incapable of the various duties required from a member of the Mounted Police. He never should have been enlisted and I further recommend that he be discharged forthwith."[46] James Clarke was invalided for medical reasons and "general uselessness." Why William Wanless, who stood only 5'5" tall and weighed 115 lbs., was taken on is surprising. He served seventy-one days before prostration from the sun resulted in his being declared an invalid.

Henry Garrett was invalided after twenty months service because of eye afflictions. He admitted to having concealed his handicap at his examination by memorizing the eye chart. An angry Surgeon Jukes recommended that he "is not entitled for to passage [return] money."[47]

Jukes' comments for invaliding W. Fisher as unfit for service in February 1884 were terse:

> He is one of those men who will never do a day's work if he can help it … since he entered the Force in April 1882 he has never been one entire month free from Gonorrhea or its complications—which has enabled him to evade the greater part of his duties … he is no sooner cured of one attack than he deliberately contracts another … which resulted in his being confined to Hospital.[48]

On the other hand, in a five-page letter, Jukes recommended free passage to Ontario for Constable Fraser who suffered acute ophthalmia (inflammation of the eye) while coming by river steamer up the Missouri.

Wind and, dust had aggravated his condition and with no prospect of improvement, Fraser was declared an invalid. Jukes praised his exemplary character that won the respect and affection of all about him: "He likes the Force and regrets leaving it."[49]

Monetary compensation was given to invalids who had a justifiable reason for leaving the Police Force. Staff-Sergeant William Fury, shot in the right lung at Loon Lake in 1885, was ruled permanently impaired for any service and awarded the maximum pension of sixty cents daily for the term of his natural life.

Many compensation claims had frustrating bureaucratic delays. It took until January 1888, thirty-four months after he was wounded in the thigh at the Duck Lake skirmish, before Constable S.F. Gordon was awarded pension of twenty-three cents per diem. John H. Ward, critically wounded at the Cut Knife skirmish in 1885, had his request for monetary assistance to Comptroller White unduly delayed. One year after the shooting, Surgeon Jukes wrote Ottawa that the bullet remained in Ward's abdomen, that Ward had spent ten weeks in recovery, and was now limited to light office work. This ten-year veteran, Jukes insisted, had "done his duty gallantly and well & has sacrificed his heath and usefulness—and nearly his life in the service of his country—his care demands the most favourable consideration of the Government."[50] Comm. L. Herchmer and the Mounted Police Association, District Calgary sent letters supporting Ward's claim. Finally, in 1887, Ottawa arranged for Ward to travel to Regina to be examined by a medical board of three doctors. They certified Ex-Sergeant John Ward's incapacity and, on 2 May 1888, exactly three years after his gunshot wound, a pension of ninety cents per diem was approved.

Most discharged men returned East—"to Canada," as they called their destination. In the first years, this often meant waiting for the opening of navigation on the Missouri River or joining a police troop traveling east to Manitoba. The first man discharged as an invalid, P. Brooks, had been critically ill since the column's arrival at Fort Macleod eleven months earlier and everyone thought that he was too weak for the trip. Inspector William Winder, going to Ontario to bring his wife to Fort Macleod, was assigned to escort Brooks. Winder's departing words asked for instructions in the event of Brooks' death. Dr. Nevitt acknowledged that he was taking "a fearful responsibility" should anything happen to Brooks. Nevitt was pleased, then, when he received a letter sent by Brooks from Ontario.

Some allowances were reduced. Constable John Hayes was discharged in 1884 with a broken leg and claimed compensation of $5,000, an amount that Superintendent John Cotton declared was "preposterous." Hayes was awarded an allowance of sixty cents per day, but, in two years, this amount was cut to thirty cents per day based on a medical board ruling that he had a good and useful limb.

There were bogus claims for compensation to obtain money. Malcolm McMurchy wanted compensation for a riding injury. Surgeon A. Jukes countered that the injury existed before McMurchy joined the Force and the claimant suffered more from venereal disease.

Preventive Medical Measures

An uppermost concern was to improve the overall general health of the men. Dr. Kittson advocated quarantine and field hospitals noting their success in the American Civil War. The remarkable recovery of the invalids left at Cripple Camp on the '74 March confirmed the benefits of rest and fresh air. The value of recreational rooms for health, comfort, morale, and general efficiency was recognized. Dr. Kittson had recommended an improved diet with a daily issue of vegetables and lime juice. He further advocated a daily beer allowance as a healthful beverage.

Prevention of typhoid fever was a foremost medical concern. In 1879, 8 per cent of the Fort Walsh garrison contracted this disease. That year, typhoid fever (called "mountain fever" by western miners) took a terrible toll in the nearby village and Indian camps. Nine adults in the community died and infant mortality was staggering. One victim was trader William Walsh, a former member of the Force and nephew of the post commander James Walsh. He was buried in the police cemetery. Dr. Kennedy calculated the death rate at Fort Walsh was 90 in 1000, six times that of Ontario.

Heavy spring rains followed by hot weather was linked to a typhoid fever outbreak. Dr. Kittson observed typhoid cases never occurred in camps where they used spring water for drinking and he correctly identified the water in Battle Creek as the typhoid vector. His inspection of the creek westward discovered the waterway bordered swamps having a thick top covering of decomposing vegetable matter along with the carcasses of horses and buffalo. Heavy rains caused the swamps to overflow into the creek and shortly after mountain fever appeared. Kittson recommended that the post and Indians refrain from throwing wastes into the stream, that a well be dug inside the fort, and, at the first sign of mountain fever, the detachment relocate to tent camps near a fine spring on the East Hill.

In spite of these precautions, this disease claimed the lives of two Mounties at Fort Walsh. In October 1880, Captain E. Dalrymple Clark, a nephew of Prime Minister John A. Macdonald and a highly regarded young officer, died. He was one of the few married men in the Force.

George Kennedy, M.D.

When he arrived at Fort Macleod at age twenty, George Kennedy was too young to write a legal medical prescription.

– GA NA 2227 – 1

After his burial a police detail escorted his wife to Winnipeg. Two years later, A.E.C. Tonkin succumbed after a seven-week illness and in spite of careful nursing and large doses of quinine, then used as a remedy.

Each summer, at Fort Walsh while the men went "under canvas" (a mode which they preferred), a concerted effort was made to upgrade their accommodations. The single-storey buildings were built from logs chinked with clay, roofs of split poles overlaid with sod, and dirt floors that, in some buildings, sloped as much as half a metre. The living quarters were cleaned, washed, whitewashed, and disinfected with the fumes from burning sulfur. Added windows were installed for ventilation and clay was smeared between the logs to stop drafts. The blankets were washed, bedding aired, stable yard drainage improved, and lavatories built in each barrack. Iron cots were recommended to replace the wooden bed slats and a straw palliasse (mattress) was provided. Winter precautions included buffalo coats, gloves, and green goggles for snow glare. Frostbite was always a danger. Andrew Elliot of "B" troop had all his toes amputated.

The hygiene of many men was poor. Henri Julien, the artist, had observed on the '74 March: "There is no use washing while on the march, which, I am afraid, was a great relief to many of the men, who were not too fond of water in any case."[51] Superintendent J. Walsh had Dr. Robert Miller (on his arrival at Fort Walsh in November 1875) inspect the detachment. Miller reported that he found it necessary to recommend that all men of the detachment wash themselves all over at least once a week using plenty of soap and water. Nonetheless, the lack of such basic facilities hampered cleanliness. Dr. Kennedy noted there were only three wash basins in a Fort Walsh barrack room that held thirty men (in summer, the men washed in the creek). He recommended the men wash once a week, toilets be available for night use, and a large latrine be built outside of the fort for day use.

There was a general improvement in health conditions. After 1880, regular bathing was enforced and the men were given a medical inspection every two weeks. In addition, an orderly officer inspected the barracks and kitchens for unsanitary conditions on a weekly basis.

Medical Examinations

All candidates for the NWMP had a medical inspection. Too often, these examinations were cursory. Dr. Robert Miller at the Swan River Barracks in February 1877 wrote: "This is to certify that I have examined Ramsay and Robertson and find them fit for service."[52] A more detailed example is that of Frank Whitla:

Toronto, 30th May, 1877 ... I have examined Frank R Whitla, age 25 years, who has had service (in army) & find his height 5 ft 10½ in, weight 165 lbs, excellent physique & good muscular development, lungs healthy, heart sound, girth of chest 38 inches, expansive power 1 inch; no blemishes, good nerve condition. I consider him a very fit candidate for the service ... John P King, M.C.P.S.[53]

The Force unwisely accepted men with known medical problems. In the case of John Wilson, his Ontario doctor had written, "I am of the opinion he has used an excess of stimulants." Before his first year of service, Dr. Kittson wrote that Wilson "appears on daily sick list reports as suffering from chorea [St. Vitus Dance] with muscular spasms, declined debilitating and is unfit to undergo slightest fatigue."[54] Many other cases of incorrect diagnoses appear. The information for Herbert Gilman read:

Height: 5ft. 7in.
Weight: 170 lbs.
Chest: 39½ in.

Heart & lungs healthy.
No blemishes of any kind.
Good Physical development.
Capable of hard work.

I consider him fit for service.
F.L.M. Graselt, 8th July 1877.[55]

At Fort Walsh, Kittson diagnosed Gilman as being in a tubercular and debilitated condition. He noted that the previous fall the recruit had suffered a severe attack of inflammation of the lungs.

In June 1877, the medical report of William Weir in Montreal affirmed "a sound and robust constitution."[56] However, Kittson's examination found a traumatic structure of the urethra which would require surgery in Canada. William Stephens was discharged as an invalid after six months service for the "want of proper stamina to withstand fatigue of any kind."[57] Within nine months of joining, Samuel Cook was declared an invalid for symptoms of heart affliction. Recruits coming west in 1881, for fear of infection, were reluctant to share accommodations with Robert Walsh, said to have syphilis. At Fort Walsh, Dr. George Kennedy diagnosed Walsh as having secondary syphilis, and yet Walsh was taken on. Surgeon Augustus Jukes discharged Fred Pickering with the comment: "He never has been fit for service or capable of any exertion since he entered the Force and never should have been admitted."[58] A dissatisfied former policeman later informed a Winnipeg paper: "I know one man against whose swearing in Doctor Kennedy sent a strong protest, saying he was totally unfit for duty. He was very far gone with a venereal disease, but he was sworn in, and when I left was acting as cook at Fort Walsh."[59]

Dr. George Kennedy deplored having an Eastern examining physician approving Constable E.J. Zwicker for service based on the assumption that a dry western climate would improve his asthma. Kennedy observed Zwick's disease was perceptibly worse since his arrival. He tersely wrote: "I do not regard this country as a sanitarium for asthmatics and caution examining physicians of this point."[60] Nor was Kennedy pleased to find that Robert Bradley was declared an invalid after only eight months of service. The examining physician in Ontario was in actual fact Bradley's uncle. Moreover, the examiner falsely recorded his underage nephew's age as eighteen and, although aware of the youth's infirmities, believed that a change of air and with exercise would prove beneficial. Kennedy asserted that the boy should never have been enlisted.[61]

The Annual Report in 1881 recommended stricter medical examinations and rejection of candidates with poor eyesight. Surgeon Augustus Jukes citing "the unsatisfactory manner in which some of the examining surgeons have performed their duty," examined 570 recruits once they reached the west in 1885.[62]

In 1880, Kennedy concluded from his examination of 100 recruits that, although the "large majority of them were splendid specimens of Canadian manhood," about one-fourth were still developing and lacked both the stamina and endurance necessary for the manual task of policing. Dr. Kennedy recommended that the minimum enlistment age be twenty-one.[63] Commissioner A.G. Irvine agreed with the proposed entry age. Surgeon Jukes advocated a minimum age of twenty-three.

By 1882, the consistency of evaluating recruits improved with the introduction of a standardized printed medical form. The "Memorandum for Medical Examiners" included the date and place of the examination, age, height, weight, chest girth (with expiration and expansion), muscular development, previous occupation, intelligence, temperament, hair and eye colour, complexion, sight, feet, heart, lungs, hernia, hemorrhoids, body marks, vaccination and a comment by the examining physician.

The assessment of intelligence was a rather subjective observation. One wonders how E. Beaucairn was evaluated at medium intelligence; Abbott – above; Barry – good; Patrick Fitzgerald – medium (not educated); F.O. Elliot

– good; William Fury – a fair amount of intelligence; Sanford Jones – fair; W.S. Jones – moderately good; Andrew McKinnon – very intelligent; John Clisby – average; William Cooper – ordinary; Henry Keenan – above the average;. The intelligence of Oscar Dubriel was assessed in Montreal as good; six weeks later at Fort Walsh, Kennedy rated Dubriel ordinary.

A tally of the weight of 116 recruits (based on the NWMP personnel files) found the average weight was 157.5 lbs. (71.6 kg) with the heaviest man weighing 187 lbs. (85 kg) and the lightest weighing 130 lbs. (59 kg). A second tally found the average height of 180 recruits was almost 5 feet nine inches (175 cm) with the tallest man standing 6 feet 1.5 inches (187 cm). Only twenty of the men (one in 9) was taller than 6 feet. None of the men in the NWMP was notably tall or heavy—but many of them were likely strong from engaging in physical work.

North-West Mounted Police Deaths

In the years 1874–85, thirty-eight NWMP died. Typhoid fever and military action, with eight deaths each, were the leading causes of death. Drowning claimed six lives.[64] The attending surgeon would forward a death certificate. In the death of W. Armstrong, Surgeon Jukes handwrote:

> I hereby certify that Regnt No 843 Const Armstrong
> died at the Hospital here about eight-o-clock on
> Thursday evening, February 28,
> of Typho Malarial Fever.
>
> Augustus Jukes Sen. Surgeon.[65]

Three of the eight typhoid fever deaths were related to the '74 March. A. McIntosh died in camp at Dufferin. William C. Brown, marching west with the column, was returned on 30 July 1874 to Dufferin where he died. Godfrey Parks died shortly after the column reached Fort Macleod.

The unsanitary water at Fort Walsh took the lives of Superintendent E. Dalrymple Clark in 1880 and Constable A.E.C. Tonkin in November 1882. A nephew of Prime Minister Macdonald, Clark was regarded as a promising officer.[66] He was one of the few married men in the Force and, after his death his wife, received two months' salary and was escorted to Winnipeg. Tonkin was in the Force for 197 days, six weeks of which he spent in hospital. Both men were buried in the Fort Walsh cemetery.[67]

A sixth death from typhoid fever was W. Armstrong, who died in Regina in February 1884. Constables Richard Rutledge and A.R. Dyre died in Battleford in the fall of 1885. Both men had lingering colds from their

Senior Surgeon Augustus Jukes

"The medical duties at headquarters during the last twelve months (1885) have been more than ordinarily severe and have taxed my powers to the utmost."

– Augustus Jukes, *RC*, NWMP, 1885, 84
 GA NA 2788 – 94

trip in a leaky scow down the ice-choked North Saskatchewan River when the Mounted Police abandoned Fort Pitt in mid-April. Rutledge died after a six-day illness. An attendant wrote: "He was moved into the hospital only five days ago and it is an extraordinary fever that will carry off a man of his constitution ... what dreadful disease is this?"[68] Alexander Dyre succumbed on the evening of 31 October 1885 after losing a months' struggle with typhoid malaria. The twenty-two-year-old was interred in the cemetery behind Battleford Catholic Church with military honours. Three days later, an auction sale of his kit netted $30.35. Dyre wrote letters that are of historical interest.[69] A Death Report was filed by Widmar Rolph (Assistant Surgeon) and Leif Crozier (Post Commander).

Division ... D

Reg. No. ... 663

Rank and Name ... Cnst. Dyre, A.R.

Estimated Hour of Death ... Ten o'clock
on the evening 31st Oct 1885

Disease ... Typhoid fever complicated with pneumonia
and inflammation of liver and stomach

Constable George Hillier died at Fort Calgary in 1883 from septicemia that developed from an open wound caused by a horse kick two months earlier. (See Chapter 9)

Henry Glendenning's death had been well-documented because of the extensive communication between his family, Ottawa, and the officers at Fort Macleod. The constable had taken a leave of absence to work as a butcher for a rancher who had a NWMP meat contract. Inspector John McIllree reported that, on 3 August 1883, 18 km west of Fort Calgary, as Glendenning prepared to shoot a steer, his horse swerved, turning the Mountie's leg into an unsheathed knife tied to his saddle. An artery was severed and Glendenning bled to death.[70] His body was brought to Calgary and buried beside Constable George Hillier. A Board of Officers at the end of August verified Glendenning's service record and arranged a kit sale that collected $24.35.

Comptroller White notified Glendenning's parents in St. Catharines, Ont., that their son had died. They requested details of his death and the status of his belongings and assets. In complying with these requests, White's contact with officers at Fort Macleod disclosed that Glendenning was receiving his police salary while on a leave of absence. White wrote to Irvine that he was at a loss to understand how Glendenning could have been entitled to full police pay and, second, to list the Constable's private effects to be sent east.

In his reply two months later, Commissioner A.G. Irvine acknowledged Superintendent Leif Crozier had been wrong in the salary payment and that Glendenning's belongings had been gathered and sent to his parents. The incident hinted of corruption or illegal activity.

Superintendent Alexander Mackenzie died of a heart attack in May 1882 while supervising a contingent of recruits coming west. He was treated on the vessel while crossing Lake Superior, but died shortly after reaching Prince Arthur's Landing.

One man died two months before the '74 March began. On 8 May 1874, Superintendent W.D. Jarvis informed Commissioner George French that Sub-Constable S. G. Marshall had died of asthma. He was interred in a Church of England graveyard the following day.

After seven days in the Maple Creek hospital, E.H. Partridge died. He seemed to be recovering, and Staff-Sergeant J.C. Holmes expected that Partridge would be up in a couple of days. However, he suffered a sudden severe attack of dysentery, sank quickly and died, leaving the medical staff taken back.

Two interpreter guides died while in service to the NWMP. At Fort Saskatchewan, while he talked to his wife and mother, George Washington Brazeau dropped his rifle, which discharged. The bullet hit him in the eye and passed through his skull, "bespattering the apartment with blood and brains."[71] Joseph Lariviere froze to death in 1880. He had been educated in Montreal and spoke five languages. Lariviere had left the Wood Mountain post during a blizzard for his home 2 km away, where he lived with two Indian women. He stopped at a house about half way, left, and was never seen again. A search by the detachment and twenty hired Indians failed to find Lariviere. It was not until spring that his decomposed and half-eaten body was found and immediately buried.

NWMP Deaths: 1873–85

GUNSHOT (accidental)

Johnston, George	82 – 05 – 03	Fort Walsh
Coulson, A.	85 – 08 – 26	Long Lake

ASTHMA

Marshall, S.G.	74 – 05 – 08	Toronto or Dufferin

DROWNING

Mahoney, G.	77 – 06 – 19	South Saskatchewan
Hooley, Claudius	80 – 07 – 24	Belly River
Wahl, Adam	82 – 05 – 24	Missouri River
Rice, Matthew	82 – –	Assiniboine River
D'Arcy, N.J.	82 – 05 – 05	Qu'Appelle Lakes
Gilroy, W.E.	85 – 07 – 01	Assiniboine River

HYPOTHERMIA

Wilson, T.D.	74 – 12 – 31	Fort Macleod
Baxter, Frank	74 – 12 – 31	Fort Macleod
Ross, W. M.	84 – 12 – 31	Kicking Horse Pass

HEMORRAGE

Glendenning, Henry	83 – 03 – 08	Cochrane Ranche

MILITARY ACTION

Gibson, Thomas	85 – 03 – 26	Duck Lake
Garrett, George	85 – 03 – 27	Duck Lake
Arnold, G.P.	85 – 03 – 27	Duck Lake
Cowan, David	85 – 04 – 13	Fort Pitt
Sleigh, Ralph	85 – 05 – 02	Cut Knife Hill
Lowry, William H.T.	85 – 05 – 02	Cut Knife Hill
Burke, Patrick	85 – 05 – 03	Cut Knife Hill
Elliot, Frank	85 – 05 – 14	Near Battleford

NATURAL

Mackenzie, A.	85 – 05 – 18	Prince Arthur's Landing
Gilchrist, T. ★	85 – 12 – 10	Regina

MURDER

Graburn, M.	79 – 11 – 17	Fort Walsh

NWMP Deaths: 1873-85

SEPTICEMIA		
Hillier, W.G.	83 – 05 – 14	Fort Calgary

SUICIDE		
Griffin, H.B.	85 – 10 – 01	Regina
Gautier, A. ★★	85 – 12 – 29	Winnipeg

TYPHOID FEVER		
McIntosh, A.	74 – 07 – 20	Dufferin Camp
Brown, W.C.	74 – 07 – 21	Dufferin Camp
Parks, Godfrey	74 – 10 - 26	Fort Macleod
Clark, E.D.	80 – 10 – 02	Fort Walsh
Tonkin, A.E.C.	82 – 11 – 06	Fort Walsh
Armstrong, William	84 – 02 – 28	Regina
Rutledge, Richard	85 – 09 – 09	Battleford
Dyre, A.R.	85 – 10 – 30	Battleford

DYSENTERY		
Partridge, E.H.	83 – 11 – 17	Maple Creek

WORK RELATED		
Tetu, Robert S.	75 – 01 – 12	Winnipeg
Nash, J.	76 – 03 – 11	Near Fort Macleod
Hall, Thomas	80 – 03 – 10	Fort Macleod

★   Thomas Gilchrist, shot in the thigh at Duck Lake, had his leg broken the same night during the evacuation of Fort Carlton. Gilchrist was thirty-five when he died of heart failure just nine months later. A blood clot resulting from the earlier injuries may have been a factor in his death.

★★   The son of F.E. Gauthier, Consul-General for France in Canada. Inspector Gauthier, aged 36, was born in India and served in the Franco-Prussian War where he was awarded the military medal for personal valor.

There are vague references to two other deaths. McCrum was said to die from drink. The McIllree diary of 3 April 1877 states, "No news of George Green;" 26 April 1877: "Heard a report some Piegan Indians have found poor Green's body."

NOTES

1. *GA*, William Metzler, M 836.

2. Robert Lampard, *Five Celebrated Early Surgeons of Southern Alberta: 1874–1913* (Lethbridge: Lethbridge Historical Society), 2006.

3. *RCMP Q*, XV, No. 4, 330.

4. *SH*, 31 May 1884; Heber Jamieson, *Early Medicine in Alberta*, (Edmonton: Douglas Printing, 1947), 20.

5. *NAC*, E. Warren, f. 57. Kittson had substance-abuse problems. As early as 1875, Dr. Nevitt was informed that Kittson had been ill all winter because of whiskey problems and that he would be dismissed. Also *MFP*, 15 April 1879. Opium pills could be purchased in Fort Benton for $1 each.

6. *LN*, 30 April 1890. At age twenty, Kennedy's medical training must have been basic.

7. Other surgeons associated with the Force include: H. Dodds, J. Widmar Rolph, Henry Baldwin, Andrew Henderson, Leverett G. DeVeber, Hugh Bain, Edward Rouleau, John Lauder, J.C. Holmes.

8. Fitzpatrick, *Sergeant 331*, 101.

9. Nevitt, *Frontier Life in the Mounted Police*, 16.

10. *LH*, 21 June 1924.

11. *GA*, R.B. Nevitt, M 893.

12. *RC*, NWMP, 1879, 34.

13. *RCMP Q*, XVI, No. 3, 280.

14. *RC*, NWMP, 1884, 27. Also in *RC*, NWMP, 1884, 38, a report by Andrew Henderson, M.D. from Fort Calgary cited the unsuitableness of the buildings, the want of proper appliances, the unsuited beds (for hospital purposes), lack of proper instruments, and shortage of medicines.

15. *RC*, NWMP, 1881, 27.

16. *WDT*, 25 July 1883.

17. *RC*, NWMP, 1879, 27.

18. *RC*, NWMP, 1882, 29.

19. *Chronicle of the Canadian West*, 1875, 28.

20. *RC*, NWMP, 1882, 32.

21. *RC*, NWMP, 1880, 44.

22. *RC*, NWMP, 1880, 49; 1881, 31; 1884, 36.

23. *RC*, NWMP, 1879, 34.

24. Nevitt, *Frontier Life in the Mounted Police*, 186–87.

25. Ibid.

26. Ibid., 52.

27. *RL*, 12 November 1885.

28. *MFP*, 28 February 1881.

29. George Guernsey recalled Murray liked to have people feel the slug in his back. Guernsey, *The Great Lone Land*, 33. Also *LH*, 11, July, 1935.

30. George Guernsey, "Red Man's Magic," *SG*, Twentieth Annual, 21.

31. Captain Sir C.E. Denny, "Medicine Men's Magic," *SG*, Thirteenth Annual, 29.

32. *Fort Walsh Daily Journal*, 29 April 1880.

33. *GA*, John McIllree, AB McIllree # 1. Also *GA*, Simon J. Clarke, M 228.
   (Diary 10 March 1880): "Constable Thomas Hall died ... 10 months sickness
   of tumors of the lungs ... buried 11 March."

34. *NAC*, L.N.F. Crozier, f.10. Commissioner French informed the Minister of Justice:
   "Crozier is not at present accountable for his actions; this officer I understand is
   occasionally subject to fits of depression." Crozier's father also contacted the
   Minister of Justice, complaining that his son's duties had been most arduous.
   His son had written that he hardly was out of the saddle and too much hard
   work and too many responsibilities had undermined his constitution.
   He hoped for leave to go to Ontario to rest and restore his health.

35. *SH*, 10 September 1887.

36. Nevitt, *Frontier Life in the Mounted Police*, 63.

37. *NAC*, RG 18, Series A-1, Volume 8, f. 23 D-76. Macleod added, "I am in hopes
   that experience will improve him."

38. Nevitt, *Frontier Life in the Mounted Police*, 120.

39. *CH*, 13 August 1884. The paper stated that an investigation was pending.
   No further information in this case was found. For Spicer and Schofield's
   account, see *FMG*, 29 August 1884.

40. *FMG*, 29 August 1884. The final outcome of this incident is unclear.

41. *NAC*, T.B. Fitzpatrick, f. 330. Surgeon Kittson provides another example (*NAC*,
   George Bell, f. 415.): "I certify that Sub Constable George Bell of "C" Troop
   is unfit for further service in the Mounted Police for the following reason.
   He contacted constitutional Syphilis about two and a half years ago, which so
   reduced his constitution that he cannot stand prolonged fatigue without
   completing playing out."

42. *NAC*, Charles Zivack, f. 397.

43. *RC*, NWMP, 1880, 28.

44. *RC*, NWMP, 1884, 25. Dr. Jukes observed sixteen invalids the following year
   and concluded that five men were unfit for service and that two had concealed
   forms of insanity.

45. *NAC*, A. Jones, f. 698.

46. *NAC*, Sutherland Stayner, f. 777. Also *NAC*, William Johnson, f. 696;
   James Clarke, f. 519.

47. *NAC*, Henry James Garrett f. 852. Also *NAC* James Barkley, 510,
   NAC, T. McCutcheon, f. 965.

48. *NAC*, W. Fisher, f. 666. T.H. Hoyland (*NAC*, f. 981) badgered Headquarters
   for years with letters claiming injuries and demanding compensation.

49. *RCMP Q*, XVI, No. 1, 280.

50. *NAC*, John Ward, f. 36. Ward later was employed with British Columbia telephones.
   He died at age eighty-one.

51. Julien, "Expedition to the North-West," 13.

52. *NAC*, W.C. Ramsay, f. 294.

53. *NAC*, F. Whitla, f. 52. NAC, John Lyon, f. o.s. 224.

54. *NAC*, John Wilson, f. o.s. 105.

55. *NAC*, Herbert Gilman, f. o.s. 286.

56. *NAC*, William Weir, f. o.s. 285.

57. *NAC*, William Stephens, f. o.s. 108.

58. *NAC*, Fred Pickering, f. 844. Fourteen years later, Pickering wrote from Massachusetts inquiring about re-enlistment.

59. *MFP*, 20 July 1880.

60. *RC*, NWMP, 1879, 34.

61. *NAC*, Robert Bradley, f. 991.

62. *RC*, NWMP, 1885, 84.

63. *RC*, NWMP, 1880, 46. For Irvine, *RC*, NWMP, 1881, 29.

64. Drowning deaths are in Chapter 2; military deaths in Chapter 21.

65. *NAC*, W. Armstrong, f. 843.

66. *RC*, NWMP, 1880, 17. Commissioner A.G. Irvine commented: "I cannot refrain from mentioning the serious loss the Force has sustained from the death of this promising young officer, nor is it possible to overrate the high esteem in which Captain Clark was deservedly held by his comrades of all ranks throughout the force." Surgeon George Kennedy stated in the same annual report, page 46: "His untimely death will mark 1880 as the saddest year in the history of the force."

67. The cemetery was neglected. This caused a problem when Prime Minister John A. Macdonald crossed Canada on the newly completed Canadian Pacific Railway. At Maple Creek, Lady Macdonald decided to visit the gravesite of her nephew, Dalrymple Clark. While she traveled south by wagon, the men at the post were busily tidying, making the gravesite attractive. *RCMP Q*, XXVIII, No. 4, 287–88.

68. *Fort Battleford Post Journal*, 9 September 1885.

69. Rivett-Carnac, ed., "Letters from the North-West," 321–27; XVIII, No. 1, 13–18. Dyre's brother in Ontario corresponded with the Battleford post inspector for details on Dyre's death. He was informed that Dyre died in the hospital, "quite conscious up to the time of his death and seemed quite resigned to meet the worst ... he had been an excellent soldier, always ready to perform any duty assigned to him by day or night without a murmur. All his possessions (money, letters, photographs, Indian artifacts) had been forwarded to Regina, from where, with proof of next of kin, would be sent to you." *RCMP Q*, XVIII, No. 1, 18.

70. *NAC*, Henry Glendenning, f. 673.

71. *SH*, 21 June 1880. Brazeau was the NWMP guide and interpreter in the arrest and trial of Swift Runner who had murdered and eaten several of his family members.

15

GROWING ABORIGINAL DESPAIR

Assiniboine Indians, 1878

"The Indians have been selling their horses for a mere song and after eating almost all their dogs, reduced to gophers and mice."

– Lieutenant Governor Edward Dewdney, Blackfoot Crossing, July, 1879,
Canada Sessional Papers, 1880, XIII, No. 4, 78

GA NA 2003 – 50

FOR YEARS, THERE HAD BEEN WARNINGS that the enormous herds of buffalo would someday only be a memory. Peter Erasmus, traveling with the Palliser expedition in 1858, recalled that it seems "almost unbelievable when I looked and counted thousands of buffalo scattered over the plain as far as my eyes could see. Was it any wonder that I was doubtful?"[1]

Yet, each following year, the Métis buffalo hunt from Red River had to travel even farther west to reach the *"buffles sauvages."* At the signing of Treaty 4 in 1874, Lieutenant Governor Alexander Morris had foretold the disappearance of the great herds. Still, Morris estimated that ten years of hunting remained. His successor, David Laird, at the Blackfoot Treaty signing three years later, repeated Morris' concerns. That year, the Northwest Council enacted the *Buffalo Preservation Law*. In this ten-point ordinance, among the restrictions was a prohibition against driving buffalo into pits, pounds, and over precipices. Buffalo were not to be killed for amusement, choice parts, or if younger than two years of age. Buffalo cows could only be shot in September and October. The law was impossible to enforce and it was repealed the following year.

Disappearance of the Buffalo

When the NWMP entered the plains, the vast buffalo herds appeared without end. In the first winter at Fort Macleod (1874–75), the men shot buffalo from the stockade. One careless individual was even chased into the fort by a buffalo bull. On an eastward journey across the plains in the fall of 1875, Colonel A.G. Irvine found "it necessary sometimes at night, to fire guns to keep them away from the camp."[2] The following summer, when Major Walsh rode with a small troop from Fort Walsh to Fort Benton, the men had great difficulty in controlling their horses as they moved through herds that, "in some places were wedged so closely together that the plain itself appeared to be swaying to and fro."[3]

While the number of buffalo appeared to be countless, at the same time enormous numbers of the animals were being killed. In June 1876, it was estimated that 120,000 buffalo were slaughtered in Canada during the past winter. As early as 1875, one account from Fort Macleod portended the disappearance of the buffalo, noting the Indians were complaining about the complete disappearance of buffalo from their usual ranges.[4] A letter from the post in 1876 predicted "in a few more years, at the present rate of slaughter, they [the buffalo] will be a thing of the past. Something should be done to protect them."[5] Nevertheless, the buffalo slaughter continued. At Fort Walsh, traders bought a good robe for $4.

The last herds of buffalo remained in the southeastern North-West Territories—a region held by the American Sioux. However, they forcefully prevented Canadian tribes from hunting there. This intransigence had serious repercussions. The *Saskatchewan Herald* commented: "Wholesale slaughter and the exclusion of our Indians from their hunting grounds are undoubtedly the cause of the distress that prevailed last summer."[6] A letter from Fort Macleod related: "The old Indians here blame Sitting Bull's people for the disappearance of buffalo. They say they have stopped them from coming into the country, and I do not think they are far from wrong."[7]

In response to the uncompromising Sioux, Blackfoot Chief Crowfoot asked Indian Commissioner Edgar Dewdney to "drive away the Sioux and make a hole for the buffalo to come in and we won't bother you about grub."[8] It was a potentially dangerous situation. The Canadian bands, one reporter asserted, "all have a lively fear and hatred of the Sioux, whom they know to be superior fighters."[9] A large number of Canadian bands chose to hunt in Montana Territory where large herds of buffalo still roamed.

It seemed incredible that by 1879, only five years after the arrival of the Mounted Police, few buffalo remained on the Canadian prairies. Constable F.A.D. Bourke witnessed the unbelievable change: "It was in the year 1877 that the buffalo were so plentiful, and after that they disappeared. No one would believe how plentiful they were and how suddenly and quickly they disappeared. I have seen the prairie black with them and in places where a large band had passed over the grass was eaten down to the earth."[10] Their disappearance abruptly fractured the traditional lifestyle of prairie Natives. A letter from Fort Macleod in 1879 related "There is nothing but accounts of suffering and starvation coming in from the plains and the hunters agree in saying that there are no buffalo between here and the Cypress Hills."[11]

In the summer of 1881, a buffalo herd of an estimated 20,000 animals migrated northward into the Wood Mountain area. It was like old times. An American correspondent reported the animals were "as thick as bees at swarming time."[12] After this date, there were only scattered buffalo hunts. In November 1881, a five-man hunting party from Portage la Prairie shot fourteen buffalo in a herd, a "sight not often seen on our northern plains."[13] Buffalo sightings had become a newspaper item. In July 1883, the *Regina Leader* reported that three men watched the chase of four buffalo that "the Indians ran down magnificently."[14]

South to Montana Territory

By 1879, while few buffalo remained in Canadian territory, large herds still roamed in Montana Territory. In September 1879, United States Captain Eli Huggins, after crossing the Missouri on his way south to Fort Keogh, rode through an immense herd of buffalo:

> I think we must have seen 1,000,000 buffaloes without [any] exaggeration. For four days we passed through great herds of them, very tame too. Sometimes they seemed hardly willing to

get out of our way. Some of them are very large. They would lie in our path till we were within 30 or 40 yards, then get up, stretch themselves, twist their ridiculous little tails and canter away a little piece, then stop and look at us again … several times I galloped up onto them almost near enough to touch them with my hand, just for amusement.[15]

Four thousand Canadian Plains Indians and groups of Métis hunters, facing starvation, journeyed that year to hunt the "northern range" in Montana Territory. These "hordes of northern marauders" were unwanted.[16]

The American Indians resented this incursion of the Canadian Indians (derisively calling them "bone pickers") as they were endangering their own meager existence. One Crow woman, watching 2,000 Cree arrive, wanted the American soldiers "to drive them back to their bush swamps rather than allow them to kill buffalo and other game belonging to our people."[17] The *Fort Benton Record* branded Chief Crowfoot as "the leader of murderers … a red butcher."[18] Settlers loathed the appearance of Canadian Indians:

Added to the troubles with our own Indians was that with British Indians … each autumn after their annual payments at Forts Macleod and Walsh, these tribes swoop down upon us … robbing ranches, frightening women, stealing horses and subsisting on our cattle.[19]

Montana ranchers estimated that, in two northern border counties, 3,000 head of cattle had been "butchered" by Indians in the winter of 1880–81. The *Fort Benton Press* warned that, if "John Bull's Indians" continued to encroach into the area, desperate settlers would take matters into their own hands."[20] In response to local concerns, American soldiers forcefully returned Canadian Indians and Métis hunters to the border.[21]

The American military's reputation for harsh treatment of Indians was evident when an army company contacted forty-four Canadian Indian lodges camped along Milk River. They ordered the Indians to take down their teepees and start for the boundary line. The temperature was minus-forty degrees. One account asked: "What must the sufferings of the Indians have been, compelled to move their women and children in such weather over the open plains, without provisions themselves and with starving horses? No wonder the Indian has no love for the Yankee."[22]

Ottawa showed indifference to the southward movement of Canadian Indians. In response to American protests over the influx of "British" Indians, Prime Minister John A. Macdonald rationalized that, "you might as well try to check a flight of locusts."[23] His appointed Indian Commissioner of the North-West Territories, however, provided an honest rationale for Ottawa's motives. Edgar Dewdney reported:

> I advised them strongly to go and gave them some provisions to take off. They continued to follow the buffalo further and further south until they reached the main herd and there they remained ... I consider their remaining away saved the government $100,000 at least.[24]

And the police posts were happy to be rid of loitering Indians. Inspector Leif Crozier reported from Fort Walsh that he made "every possible effort to induce them to leave for the buffalo country before the season became too far advanced."[25] He refused the sale of ammunition to the Indians; telling them ammunition was available at Fort Belknap, south of Milk River. The 1880 Annual Report from Edgar Dewdney estimated there were seven to eight thousand Canadian Prairie Indians—25 per cent of their numbers—south of the line.

Thousands of white skinners and hostile Indian bands made Montana Territory a volatile region. Inordinate hunting soon wiped out the great buffalo herds. The Indians had suffered terribly. One account graphically describes a Canadian Cree camp near Fort Assiniboine:

> Demoralization was everywhere evident. The men were weak and emaciated from hunger; the women and children were sick and covered with rags and filth. The prostitution of the squaws had brought the foulest diseases into the camp ... the country is entirely destitute of game.[26]

Hunger compelled the Canadian bands to return north of the border. They were destitute. While on patrol, Sergeant Frank Fitzpatrick met a small band of thirty Indians that he likened to "a delegation from a graveyard."[27] When he and his partner threw biscuits to the starving Indians, the men seized any biscuits the children gathered in the scramble. To ensure that the children received their share, Fitzpatrick distributed the remaining food at gunpoint. Starving Blackfoot returned to Canada on foot, their horses eaten or sold. Inspector Cecil Denny recorded their abject misery:

> It was pitiable to see parties of the less impoverished bringing their weakened fellows, some mere skeletons, to Fort Calgary for food. Some even ate grass along the road. I have seen them

when a steer was shot, rush on the animal with their knives before it had ceased kicking, cut away the flesh and maddened by hunger, devour it raw.[28]

It is estimated that, between 1879 and 1881, at least one thousand Canadian Blackfoot died from hunger.[29]

Starvation

The disappearance of the buffalo brought unspeakable suffering to the Indians. One English sportsman, traveling on the Canadian plains in July 1878, wrote that every Indian camp complained of the scarcity of buffalo. He detailed the want:

> We passed some Indian women and children traveling, all their worldly possessions drawn by two dogs, harnessed in travails. The women said they were only living on the Navaux, the root of the wild turnip. They looked thin, and in want, so we left them a supply of pemmican.[30]

In another touching incident, a correspondent from the *Toronto Globe* chanced on a party of Indians who had been traveling for five days without food. He wrote, "The poor creatures were almost famished and suffered terribly from the cold."[31] North of present-day Lethbridge, a trader met two lodges of Cree headed for Fort Edmonton with only two porcupines on which to subsist during the 500-km journey. They wanted to trade their only gun for a horse. Under the circumstances, he told them, they had better keep the gun and he declined the offer.[32]

Starvation racked the Indian camps. The first thing noted was the absence of dogs. At one Indian camp, Professor John Macoun, a member of the Geological Survey, observed all the poplar trees had been stripped of their bark for food. The band was utterly desperate. "During my stay," he wrote, "some women came to my tent and asked permission to lick the plates off which we had been eating. They were allowed to do so … and they did lick them clean of every particle of grease and then they washed them."[33] Most commendable, the starving band left his unguarded carts alone. John Macoun wryly commented his property only needed guards when white men were around.

Hungry Indians clustered around the police posts and Indian agencies. In June 1879, the Mounted Police at Fort Macleod were feeding 1,500 Indians. The detachment did its best to help, but supplies were limited.

Blackfoot (Siksika) Family Migrating

In the late 1870s, the disappearance of the great buffalo herds brought unimaginable
suffering to the Plains Indians. An annual annuity of $5 for each Indian
provided few comforts.

– GA NA 4967 – 57

On one occasion, Superintendent Winder had only six bags of flour on
hand.[34] Cecil Denny (the former North-West Mounted Police officer)
watched the women "literally in rags fight over the old cotton flour sacks,
of which they make dresses."[35]

A letter in August 1879 described Indian children crying from hunger
after being without any food for four days. Their parents pleaded for help:
"We do not care so much for ourselves but we do not like to see our
children die." The writer commented: "It is hard to resist such pleadings
as the police are doing everything possible but their means are necessarily
restricted."[36] Desperate living conditions led to Indian children being sold.
In Calgary, a cowboy named "Shorty" told a correspondent from Toronto
that yesterday he had bought a six-year-old Blackfoot girl for $35. Just
then, the girl, attired in new clothes and appearing very happy, came up.
"Shorty" said he planned to have his mother raise the child, giving the
youngster an opportunity of a better life.[37]

At Fort Calgary, a Blackfoot Indian begged Indian Agent Denny for help: "Our people are starving, do help us, for some of us have nothing to eat ... too many other people eat our buffalo."[38] Denny gave his limited supplies to the band. The police posts and Indian agencies simply had inadequate resources for the begging Indians. An Ottawa newspaper correspondent wrote: "The swill-barrels around the soldier's camp are daily besieged by starving Indians, who will eat anything."[39] This food included police horses stricken with glanders that had been shot. One Mountie remembered that the Indians ate the carcasses before he could burn them. The meal whistle at the Wood Mountain post signaled the Indian children to run to the barrack windows to watch the policemen eat, knowing that they would be thrown hardtack biscuits and meal scraps.

The situation was desperate. Indians at Fort Macleod were outraged when informed only a limited amount of ammunition could be purchased with treaty money. Then, as a safety precaution, the police collected all the ammunition in the town to store in the fort's magazine. Constable David Grier wrote to his father in Ontario:

> Times out here are pretty stirring just now. The Indians are getting very troublesome. There are eighty men at Fort McLeod [sic], and they were all under arms last night. The men were all downtown in the evening, when the bugle sounded for them to return to the Fort. When they got there they were placed under arms all night, the Indians having declared their intention of attacking the Fort during the night. They were in their war paint, and all had rifles which they kept firing off all night.[40]

The writer warned: "Indians here are all stirring. There are no buffalo, as they have all gone south. The Government will either have to feed or fight them this winter."[41]

Father Constantine Scollen, a veteran of more than a decade on the plains, recalled when the Blackfoot had double the warriors and "when they were entire masters of the immense prairies from Benton to Edmonton and the terror of their enemies."[42] Now the tribe was depressed and helpless. Strong men were so weak, they could barely walk. The priest had seen a Blackfoot leave his lodge so that he might not listen to his children crying for food. Scollen informed Assistant Commissioner Irvine that starving Indians were eating dead wolves that had been poisoned with strychnine.

Only those bands with food sources to augment their rations remained relatively well off. The northern lakes supplied some of the needs. In the first months of the winter of 1879–80, Indians had caught over 70,000 fish at Turtle Lake. The Stoney tribe at Morley could hunt deer and mountain sheep. A news account noted that a small Stoney band in the foothills west of Edmonton had not suffered from hunger during the 1882 winter, having killed more than forty moose.[43]

In the summer of 1879, newly appointed Indian Commissioner Edgar Dewdney, accompanied by Commissioner J. Macleod, made an extensive tour of police posts and Indian reserves in the North-West Territories.[44] Their observations confirmed the misery on the plains.

At Fort Walsh on July 1, the post's sports day, Macleod introduced Dewdney to Cree, Assiniboine, and Blackfoot bands, some carrying Treaty flags. Dewdney thought the Indians were awful beggars, but there was no question of their hunger. Negotiations led the non-treaty bands of Little Pine and Lucky Man to sign treaty adhesions. Dewdney interviewed Big Bear. The talks initially seemed promising, but ended without an agreement. A reporter commented: "Of course he wanted more than any other chief; he argued and talked a good deal, and finally said he would see about signing the treaty when he saw the money."[45]

At all points they visited, hunger was evident. Commissioner Edgar Dewdney recorded at Fort Macleod on 14 July 1879: "Saw some Indians & gave them some food, numbers here very hungry. They told me they had sold their horses & pawned their guns to get food and now had nothing. There is no doubt great hardship among them."[46] Lovisa McDougall, the wife of an Edmonton trader, described the Indians who met Dewdney on July 7 at Battleford:

> They are the Miserables lot of Indians I ever saw. They have sold nearly all their horses for flour ... 2 bags of flour for a horse. Some of them came in here that had not tasted food for 7 days. They have hardly any amonition & know nothing about catching fish.[47]

Captain W. Winder had forewarned Dewdney and Macleod that the Indians at Blackfoot Crossing were on the verge of starvation. Upon their reaching the site, Jean L'Heureux, the self-appointed priest, informed them that many Indians had died, principally old people who had no means of making their own living, and who, in times of stress, were neglected by others. At once six head of cattle were slaughtered and fifteen sacks of flour issued to the 1,300 Indians who were "happy for a time." But this allotment was only temporary relief and the crisis persisted. One woman pleaded, "If I can't get food for my two children I must kill myself. I live only for them and can't bear to see them starve."[48] Commissioner Macleod wrote of the Indian reception: "We went through their camp and received a perfect ovation ... the women brought their children on their backs, to shake hands and held out tiny skeletal hands for me to shake."[49]

While hunger was the overriding immediate concern, anxiety about an uncertain future remained. Dewdney's report cited this uneasiness. "At interviews with the different bands of Indians, almost all expressed a wish to have schools erected on their reserves, to educate the children, and I should be glad to receive explicit instructions on this matter."[50]

The prairie excursion finished at Fort Walsh, where Dewdney sat in a large marquee erected inside the fort. Here he was besieged "day after day, from morning to night, to listen to the red man's wants."[51] Dewdney, however, could offer little more than encouragement for a new agrarian lifestyle and relate accounts of the success some British Columbia bands had achieved.

Even though the starvation among the Native people was shocking (one Indian had died when they visited Blackfoot Crossing), Dewdney and Macleod adhered to the government policy that required services or work for any provisions. Dewdney wrote: "We agreed that the greatest care should be taken so as not to lead the Indians to believe they would be fed regular rations whether they worked or not."[52]

Dr. Kittson's communication with Commissioner Macleod (1 July 1880) exemplifies the deplorable plight of the Plains Indians:

> Morning and evening many of them would come to me and beg for the very bones left by the dogs in my yard. When I tell you that the mortality exceeds the birth rate it may help you to realize the amount of suffering and privation existing among them. The only surprise is that they remain so patient and well disposed ... but human suffering must have its limits.[53]

The sight of Indians "hanging around" the posts and towns became commonplace. Most whites loathed their presence, especially the Indians annoying intrusiveness of peering in windows. One resident in Calgary bitterly complained:

> Why is it that our citizens must be pestered by Indians? They are everywhere apparently except on their reserves. You cannot open your door but a couple of squaws are sitting on the doorsteps; they beg grub and tobacco from you on the streets; they are a nuisance generally, dirty and disgusting, and their presence is thoroughly demoralizing to the community.[54]

The *Calgary Herald* warned: "if these Indians and their dogs are not kept on their reserves there is liable to be trouble with them."[55] The paper advised the citizens against giving any assistance (such as money for chores), thereby discouraging their visits to the town. Townspeople in Battleford faulted Indians for raiding gardens and when Indian dogs killed chickens. Everyone was disgusted at the sight of a dead "old Stoney squaw" whose friends, to save the trouble of digging a grave in the frozen ground, had placed her in a tree on the outskirts of town.[56] Residents were intimidated by the Indians lurking around the houses, chanting weird and monotonous songs, and firing their guns. Henriette Forget, wife of Amédée Forget (the secretary to Territorial Governor Laird), was both shocked and alarmed upon returning to her kitchen to find five Blackfoot men squatting on the floor eating the breakfast she had just prepared.[57] The *Brandon Sun* censured "squaws" ("the braves lie in the shade") for continually foraging through slop buckets for food. The paper cruelly condemned the Indians: "What a Magnificent Race—it cost the Dominion Government half a million a year to keep the Northwest Indians sufficiently alive to go around and empty our swill barrels."[58] At all settlements, it became the burdensome duty for the police detachment to escort the Indians back to the reserves.

As a solution to the complaints from the prairie towns, Ottawa and Indian agents proposed that Indians require a permit to leave their reserve. However, Commissioner A.G. Irvine objected, stating in his Annual Report that such a policy "would be tantamount to a breach of confidence with the Indians as they have been led to believe that compulsory residence would not be required of them."[59]

Some towns tried to ameliorate the Indian destitution. Soup kitchens were opened at Fort Saskatchewan and Fort Edmonton and, at Battleford, a committee was organized for the distribution of Native relief supplies. Superintendent Crozier provided nets for a band to fish.

A rancher at Fort Macleod denigrated the impoverished Indians for "constantly hovering around the corners and the stores, and a more lazy, filthy race can scarcely be imagined. Many have nothing on but a rag of a blanket."[60] In spite of this scathing accusation, he acknowledged, unless the government fed them regularly, these poor people would find it very hard to refrain from killing cattle. One Mountie described the Indians "as cheeky enough sometimes and kick up a great row if they don't get what they want, but I believe they have a wholesome respect for the police."[61]

The ranching community accused the Indians for killing cattle. The losses were serious. Edward Maunsell, an ex-policeman, claimed in June 1879 that he lost a hundred cows and three bulls, leaving him with only fifty-six head.

Blood Indians, Fort Whoop-Up, 1881

"They constantly hover around the corners and the stores, and a more lazy, filthy race can scarcely be imagined. Many have nothing on but a rag of a blanket."

– Duncan McEachran, *GA* M 736
GA NA 302 – 2

J. McFarland had half his herd, ninety animals, allegedly stolen by Indians. That fall, ranchers in southern Alberta petitioned the Minister of the Interior for compensation for the loss of 400 cattle. Many ranchers chose to winter their herds of cattle in Montana Territory. In turn, Dewdney admitted that a few cattle had been killed by the Indians, but did not credit the reports that actually range cattle had been killed by the hundreds.[62]

Ranchers blamed the NWMP for not protecting their herds and further criticized the judiciary for being too lax in punishing Indian offenders. Thomas B. Strange, owner of the Military Colonisation Ranche east of Calgary, wrote that the usual verdict was "not guilty but don't do it again."[63] John Glenn, a rancher near Calgary, told the Reverend A. Sutherland (who was on a tour of the west): "We have no protection from the police. The Indians may steal our cattle … but we get no redress. In that respect we would be better off if there were no police in the country at all."[64]

To the relief of the police and settlers, the starving Indians remained peaceful. Commissioner Macleod acknowledged their good behaviour in his Annual Report: "Hungry men are dangerous whether they be Indians or Whites, and I think it is wonderful how well the Indian has behaved."[65] Superintendent William Herchmer penalized an Indian band near Fort Ellice for killing four head of cattle by deducting the value from their annual annuities. Still, he sympathized with the band's plight and was quite pleased when they turned in a wanted Indian horse thief.

With the buffalo gone and farming a challenge even for experienced white settlers, the Indians looked at life with little hope or satisfaction. At Fort Macleod in 1879, chiefs of the Blackfoot Nation welcomed Indian Commissioner Dewdney and NWMP Commissioner Macleod (on their prairie tour) and presented a letter, signed by ten chiefs stating that, in their dire calamity of want, they offered "hearty cooperation for all your orders and advice."[66] Direct appeals were made to the government authorities. In June 1879, a number of chiefs and head men from the Qu'Appelle area rode to Winnipeg to lay grievances before the Lieutenant Governor over unfulfilled promises and hunger. In February 1883, chiefs at Battle River (in the Ponoka area) sent a letter to the Minister of the Interior outlining their destitution and the white policy that had "doomed us to annihilation little by little."[67] For the most part, the Indian petitions were ineffective.

The Indians complained about the substitution of bacon for beef, the substandard flour provided, and the white distributors' belittling attitude. Chief Crowfoot's assertion that some white men treated Indians like "dogs" is substantiated in a report written by the Department of Indian Affairs that described the government agents as "a rough class of men ...who had the habit of abusing Indians."[68]

Some of the Indian agents (paid $700 annually) lacked skills and appeared indifferent to their employment. Delays in receiving supplies and farming equipment impeded their efforts to launch an agrarian Indian lifestyle. Using cross ploughs rather than the breaking plows needed for the virgin prairie sod revealed a want of awareness. One chief, upset with the wild Montana milk cows provided for his band, complained: "We expected they would be tame animals that could be handled. We know why these Montana cattle were given us, because they were cheaper and the government thinking us simple people thought we would take them."[69]

A policeman agreed that: "The cattle given to the Indians are all wild Montana beasts, which even the white men are afraid to approach."[70] Constable W. Parker commented: "They were dangerous brutes, having horns two or three feet long & wilder than the buffalo. They cannot be approached on foot, always have to be herded on horseback."[71] He recounted his narrow escape when his horse bounded away after a cow struck its horns between Parker's leg and the saddle.

The Indians now reassessed their signing the treaties. As early as 1878, bands complained that they were much poorer than they were before treaties were made and, when they left their hunting grounds to attend the annual payments, non-treaty Indians came and killed the game.[72] Father Joseph Jean-Marie Lestanc wrote from Red Deer Forks:

> Traders who have visited their camps along the river report the Indians consider the treaties concluded with the Government are of no value, and that Indians should not be imprisoned for offences against the law. They also seem desirous of securing Sitting Bull's assistance to obtain another and better treaty.[73]

A petition by the Battleford representatives in 1883 warned: "If attention is not paid to our case now we shall concluded that the treaty made with us six years ago was a meaningless matter of form."[74]

An annual annuity of $5 for each Indian provided few comforts. Yet, the cost of providing relief payments for the Indians under Treaty 7 alone was $455,000 in 1885.[75] Some members of the Federal Parliament regarded this expenditure lavish in light of a total government budget of less than $35 million. It was a time, moreover, when the government was reluctant to support charities and welfare, leaving these services to the family and church. The daily ration for each Indian of one pound of both beef and flour seemed generous.

It must be kept in historical context that life for most Canadians at that time was difficult and demanding. Women were disenfranchised and had limited opportunities. Non-whites were not welcomed to Canada and the *Immigration Act* in 1885 imposed a Head Tax on Chinese. The economy underwent a severe downturn in 1875.

The nation was prominently rural. For 80 per cent of the population, daily life was a continual backbreaking struggle to make a living in an often-isolated setting. In urban centres, working conditions were harsh. Everyone worked long hours, often seventy hours each week, and there were few benefits. In Quebec City, bloody clashes erupted between Irish immigrants and French-Canadian labourers over working opportunities.

The employment of children was especially deplorable. A survey in Toronto in 1881 had reported that children made up 11 per cent of the workforce. A Federal Commission in 1882 interviewed illiterate children working in factories at ages (thought to be eight and nine) who did not even know their age. An Ontario report in 1884 detailed children who received $2 to $4 for a sixty-hour week.[76] By 1870, the first of 80,000 "Home Children"—many of them street waifs who were living in the slums of English cities—began arriving in Canada.

British Columbia passed legislation in 1877 making it illegal to employ boys under twelve years. In 1873, Nova Scotia prohibited the employment of boys under ten years at the mines and restricted the work week for boys under thirteen years to sixty hours. Workman's compensation, old-age pensions, universal medical care, unemployment benefits, an eight-hour day, and safety regulations were future concepts. Criminal laws were severe. In Brandon, Manitoba fourteen-year-old Phillip Hill was sentenced in 1893 to be hanged for poisoning former Mountie Albert Greaves.

Health conditions throughout Canada were appalling. In April 1885, the tiny Edmonton community was stunned when diphtheria tragically took the lives of five young children in the Leon Harnois family.[77] Infant mortality in Montreal among French-Canadian Catholics was a tragic 409 out of 1,000 in 1885—almost a hundredfold greater than Canada's present infant mortality rate of 4.9 out of 1,000. In October that same year, a smallpox outbreak in the city of 167,000 resulted in 3,234 deaths.

Rapidly-growing cities were crowded and lacked the proper water and sewage systems. Garbage and animal wastes left in the streets emitted an awful stench. Crowded conditions encouraged disease and were prone to terrible fires. In Saint John, New Brunswick, one of the nation's largest cities with 30,000 residents, a fire in 1877 left 16,000 people homeless.

Life in the young nation was certainly a challenge, but few areas in Canada had conditions as desperate as on Indian Reserves. Population numbers in 1884 confirm the wretched plight of the Canadian Plains Indians. The 2,278 residents on the Blood reserve recorded eight births while eighty-two adults and forty-four children had died![78] This death rate was a staggering 5.5 per cent of the tribe's population. It appeared that the "Indian Question" would be resolved within a generation.[79]

The Indians contrasted their degrading poverty, misery, tragic death rate, and living restrictions with the unfettered lifestyle they enjoyed just a few years earlier. They recalled few whites and millions of buffalo. Growing unrest was evident. Chief Pia-a-pot complained that his people, on a land which once was all their own, were denied privileges granted to foreign immigrants and hinted that there was mischief ahead if his people were not more justly treated.[80] A Roman Catholic priest, Father Louis Cochin, ministering to Cree Indians on the Poundmaker Reserve near Battleford, spoke for all Indians in the Three Provisional Districts when he wrote: "They attribute all their evils to the whites."[81]

NOTES

1. Erasmus, *Buffalo Days and Nights*, 72.
2. *MFP*, 11 September 1875.
3. *HDI*, 10 July 1877.
4. *HDH*, 9 September 1875.
5. *MFP*, 3 October 1876. On the killing of buffalo, see Denny, *Riders of the Plains*, 62.
6. *SH*, 10 February 1879.
7. *NNW*, 13 June 1879.
8. Hugh A. Dempsey, "The Starvation Year: Edgar Dewdney's Diary for 1879," *AH*, XXXI, Part 1, 9.
9. *MFP*, 2 June 1880.
10. F.A.D. Bourke, NWMP, *Sask. H.* XXXV, No. 2, 56.
11. *WDT*, 5 September 1879. The *SH*, 8 September 1879, reported Fort Walsh exported 16,900 buffalo robes in 1878; 8,300 in 1879.
12. *FBRP*, 9 November 1881. Also *SH*, 12 November 1881.
13. *SH*, 12 November 1881.
14. *RL*, 12 July 1883.
15. Francis Haines, ed., "Letters of an Army Captain on the Sioux Campaign of 1879-1880," *PNQ*, XXXIX, No. 1, 46.
16. *MFP*, 26 April 1883.
17. J.W. Schultz, *My Life as an Indian* (Greenwich, CN: Fawcett, 1935), 185.
18. *FBR*, 12 December 1879.
19. Granville Stuart, *Forty Years on the Frontier* (Cleveland, OH: Arthur H. Clark, 1925), 154.
20. *FBRP*, 18 April 1883. See also 28 March 1883.
21. Michel Hogue, "Disputing the Medicine Line," *Mont H*, LII, No. 4, 2-17.
22. *EB*, 21 April 1883. See *MFP*, 31 July 1882.
23. Atkin, *Maintain the Right*, 148.
24. Dempsey, *Crowfoot*, 115.
25. *CSP*, 1880, XIV, No. 3, 30. Also *RC*, NWMP, 1880, 31.
26. *FBR*, 7 May 1880.
27. Fitzpatrick, *Sergeant 331*, 72-73.
28. Denny, *The Law Marches West*, 143-44.
29. Hana Samek, *The Blackfoot Confederacy 1880-1920* (Albuquerque, NM: University of New Mexico Press, 1987), 40.
30. Percy, *Journal of Two Excursions in the British North West Territory of North America*, 20.
31. *MFP*, 9 April 1880.
32. *NNW*, 19 March 1880.
33. *MFP*, 21 November 1879.

34. *RC*, NWMP, 1879, 9.

35. *CSP*, IV, No. 5, Annual Report Department of Indian Affairs Year Ending 1882, 176.

36. *SH*, 3 November 1879. In Calgary, a "squaw" unsuccessfully offered to sell her baby for $1. *PAT*, 2 May 1884.

37. *TG*, 11 December 1882.

38. *WDT*, 26 May 1879.

39. *MFP*, 25 May 1880. *OFP*, 20 May 1880. *RL*, 22 November 1883. *WDT*, 4 May 1880.

40. *MFP*, 1 December 1879.

41. Ibid.

42. *GA*, M 8038, 65 f. 1.

43. *MFP*, 14 July 1882.

44. Hugh Dempsey, ed., "The Starvation Year: Edgar Dewdney's Diary for 1879," *AH*, XXXI, No. 1, 1-12; *AH*, XXXI, No. 2, 1-16. Also *CSP*, 3-4, 13:3 1880, 79-103.

45. *MFP*, 19 August 1879.

46. Dempsey, ed., "The Starvation Year: Edgar Dewdney's Diary for 1879," Part 1, 8.

47. Elizabeth M. McCrum, ed., *Letters of Lovisa McDougall, 1878-1887* (Edmonton, AB: Provincial Archives of Alberta, 1978), 20-21.

48. Dempsey, ed., "The Starvation Year: Edgar Dewdney's Diary for 1879," Part 1, 9.

49. Crauford-Lewis, *Macleod of the Mounties*, 270.

50. *CSP*, 111, No. 4, Annual Report Department of Indian Affairs Year Ending 31st December, 1879, 102.

51. *ODC*, 14 August 1879.

52. Dempsey, ed., "The Starvation Year: Edgar Dewdney's Diary for 1879," Part 1, 11.

53. *NAC*, RG 10, v. 3726, f. 24, 811.

54. *CH*, 2 May 1884.

55. *CH*, 29 January 1885. see also 6 March 1885. The *Regina Leader*, 16 July 1885, called Indian Camps near the towns as an "unmitigated nuisance."

56. *MFP*, 19 May 1882.

57. Amédée Forget became the Lieutenant Governor of the North-West Territories in 1898.

58. *WDT*, 27 June 1883.

59. *RC*, NWMP, 1884, 6.

60. *GA*, Duncan McEachran, M 736.

61. LaNauze, "Echoes and Letters from Fort Walsh," 169.

62. *CSP*, 111, No. 4, 89.

63. Strange, *Gunner Jingo's Jubilee*, 391. See *MFP*, 24 August 1879 ... "no effort has been made to protect stock or punish desperadoes."

64. Sutherland, *A Summer in Prairie Land*, 52.

65. *RC*, NWMP, 1879, 22.

66. *CSP*, 111, No. 4, 79.

67. *EB*, 3 February 1883. The petition was signed by Ermineskin, Bobtail, Sampson, and six other chiefs.

68. *CSP*, IV, No. 5, 168. Dempsey, *Crowfoot*, 143. Also see *London* (Ontario) *Free Press*, 23 November 1879.

69. *TG*, 6 October 1879.

70. *London* (Ontario) *Free Press*, 23 November 1878.

71. Dempsey, ed., *William Parker Mounted Policeman*, 148.

72. *SH*, 18 November 1878.

73. *SH*, 24 March 1879.

74. *EB*, 3 February 1883.

75. *CSP*, 1885, 111, No. 3, 158. The *Moose Jaw News*, 16 May 1884, estimated the prairie Natives—"the wards of the nation"—cost Canada $1.5 million per annum, a stupendous $43 per person. See also *Regina Leader*, 19 May 1885.

76. Gregory Kealey, "Hogtown: Working Class Toronto," 175-195. *Readings in Canadian History (Post Confederation)*, R. Douglas Francis and Donald B. Smith (Holt, Rinehart, and Winston, 1982).

77. *EB*, 2 May 1885. Mrs. Harnois was the sister of Father Albert Lacombe, who was accompanying the Alberta Field Force on its march to attack Big Bear's band at Frenchman's Butte. The tragedy certainly resulted in his leaving the military column in Edmonton.

78. *CSP*, 1885, 111, No. 3, 88.

79. "Indian Question" was a common reference to the many problems associated with the prairie Indians. For example, *MFP*, 23 August 1877; 30 December 1878; *WDT*, 4 May 1880.

80. *MFP*, 2 August 1884.

81. *The Reminiscences of Louis Cochin, O.M.I.* (Battleford: Battleford Historical Publications, 1927), 26-27. *GA*, Constantine Scollen, M 8038 b f. 1. Scollen wrote to Assistant Commissioner Irvine (April 1879): "The Indians being very superstitious, often attribute to the white man any misfortunes that may have befallen them. ...so the death of three of the chiefs during the first year, alarmed them considerably, and was looked upon as a very bad omen for the future."

16

SOLVING LINGERING PROBLEMS

Bear Shield and Blackfoot Warrior

"We hope we have heard the last of him [Sitting Bull]."

– *Saskatchewan Herald*, 15 August 1881
 GA NA 790 – 2

As the year 1882 ended, the NWMP enjoyed the satisfaction that two ongoing problems had been resolved in the past eighteen months. First, in July 1881, Sitting Bull had returned to the United States and, second, in December 1882, Big Bear finally signed his adhesion to Treaty 6, bringing all major prairie Indian bands under treaty.

The American Sioux

The Western Sioux (Tetons) entered Canada in December 1876.[1] By the spring of 1878, one traveler estimated 700 lodges, or 4,000 men, women and children, were north of the border.[2] Another count gave 506 lodges in Canada with a population of 3,000.[3] Regardless of the exact number of Sioux, there was no doubt that the warrior element far outnumbered the 150 redcoats at Fort Walsh.

The Tetons brought an unsettling presence. Had they not wiped out Custer's 7th Cavalry? Second, Sitting Bull's Hunkpapa camp was a magnet for disaffected Indians. After the bayonet death of Crazy Horse at an American army base in September 1877, 240 lodges from his band sought sanctuary in Canada. International relations would be tested if Canada became a base for Sioux incursions into the United States. The policy fourteen years earlier granting Sioux refugees from the Minnesota Massacre sanctuary and several small reserves in Canada was not to be repeated.

The Sioux, too, were long-standing enemies of the Canadian Cree and Blackfoot. In his Commissioner's report, Colonel Irvine apprised readers: "Not only were the fears of our natural and intending settlers aroused, but our own Indians and Half-breeds looked with marked disfavor upon the presence of so powerful and savage a nation (for such it really was) in their midst."[4] The last thing the hard-pressed North-West Mounted Police needed was inter-tribal warfare.

The NWMP attentively monitored the Tetons. Commissioner Macleod hired a trader, André La Rivière (who was trusted in their camps), to provide information on the whereabouts and demeanor of the American Sioux.[5] This surveillance continued. A.G. Irvine, Macleod's replacement, reported four years later: "every movement of the Sioux was carefully noted and reported upon."[6] Irvine forwarded relevant information to Comptroller White in Ottawa. One report from Fort Walsh on 15 March 1879 stated:

> Sir: I have the honour to report for the information of the Honble Minister of the Interior that about 180 lodges of Oglalas, Minniconjous, and Uncapapas (Hunkpapa) are in the neighbourhood of our post at Wood Mountain – 100 lodges of Uncapapas and Oglalas are at the Forks of the Porcupine, 35 miles south of the line – "Spotted Eagle" and "Four Horns" with about 150 lodges are near our post at the East end of those hills – "Sitting Bull" with a small camp of about five lodges and "White Bird" with about ten lodges of Nez Percés are at a place called the "Mud House" 15 miles south of the line from Wood Mountain.[7]

In all, the report accounted for 445 Teton lodges. For the most part, the Western Sioux, knowing that their return to the United States would invite inevitable American military attacks, maintained tolerable conduct. However, their five years in Canada were not without fearful incidents.

Two dangerous encounters with white people are noted. In the first, at Wood Mountain in 1879, Teton warriors, angered that a trader named Allen (Allan?) charged excessive prices and displayed a dismissive manner toward Indians, threatened one night to break into the trading store. "Peaches" Davis, an ex-Mountie who was employed by Allen (at double his police salary), and two other employees quickly built a barricade inside the building for protection.

When he went to the trader's nearby cabin, Davis found Mrs. Allen bordering on collapse. Indian gunfire endangered his return, so he decided to remain there with Mrs. Allen and her young son for the night. On his return to the trading post in the morning, Davis met 250 frenzied Indians, wearing war paint, accusing Allen of cheating them. In the uproar, an Indian burst in carrying Allen's son. It was bedlam: the agitated Indians, Davis pointing his rifle at the Indian who was holding a tomahawk above the child, and Mrs. Allen screaming hysterically. Her husband appeared stupefied before shouting at Davis not to shoot, "for if they hurt the child there would be the biggest mixture of canned goods and dead Indians ever known in the West!"[8] Allen had his rifle pointed at a keg of gunpowder. While everyone stood transfixed, Davis ran past the stunned Indians to the nearby police post for help. Major Walsh immediately sent five men to the trading post with a message that, if the Indians didn't come to the police fort within fifteen minutes, he would come and blow them up.

The crisis eased once the Allen family safely reached the police post. Walsh reprimanded Allen for his crooked dealings, but there would be no further problems. The harrowing incident had proved too traumatic and the trader left at once with his family for Cypress (Fort Walsh).[9]

A second ominous incident came in June 1880. Sitting Bull had sent his nephew, One Bull, to Fort Buford to probe the terms of the Teton surrender to the Americans.[10] On his return, One Bull stole a horse at Wood Mountain and, at Sitting Bull's camp, he evaded arrest by two policemen. An angered Walsh sent five redcoats with strict orders not to return without the accused man. They completed this task but were followed by 100 Indians bent on freeing their tribesman. Walsh attempted to contact the Wood Mountain trader Jean-Louis Légaré to come to the fort, but Sitting Bull prevented the messenger from leaving by holding the horse's reins. Walsh stepped in, pushed Sitting Bull aside, and warned him that he would be shot if he touched the horse again. The rider then rode away. Trouble erupted anew when Indians attempted to block four Mounties from escorting One Bull into the fort. Major Walsh and twelve policemen with rifles aimed at the whooping mob quickly formed a barrier between the Indians and the prisoner allowing One Bull to enter the post. After the gate was closed, Walsh shouted that he was in command and the Indians had one minute to disperse or the police would open fire. This threat was effective and the Indians left. Shortly after, Légaré arrived and, as justice of the peace, convened court and surprisingly dismissed One Bull.[11]

Major Walsh explained to a visiting newspaper correspondent that, when he told Sitting Bull not to touch the messenger's horse again, he knew that the time had come when he either completely cowed Sitting Bull or lost control of the Sioux on this side of the line. He had made up his mind to arrest Sitting Bull if he attempted to touch the horse. This might have led to killing Sitting Bull, and he was well aware that the police would in all probability have been wiped out, as the odds were terribly against them. Walsh then added: "We might as well be killed at once as to let the Tetons think we fear them."[12]

At a Hunkpapa council that discussed the confrontation, Sitting Bull said that this humiliating incident was the narrowest escape of his life. He knew he would have been shot had he touched the horse. Another spokesman told the assembly that, if the Sioux wanted to live in this country, they must obey the White Mother's laws. "Long Lance" Walsh was like Crazy Horse, not afraid to die to have his way.

Wood Mountain
Throughout their five-year refuge in Canada, the Tetons remained in the Wood Mountain region. The police post, 35 km north of the American border, was little more than a miserable collection of huts. Sergeant-Major Joseph Francis referred to the outpost as "a disgrace, being little better than a pigsty."[13] The men slept on buffalo-hide hammocks tied between the log walls and log posts driven into the dirt floor. When water leaked through the sod roof onto the buffalo-hide hammocks, the stench was unbearable. In the five years between 1877 and 1881, between seventeen and thirty Mounties manned the isolated outpost.

Rival Indian bands stealing horses was a persistent problem. Even the police herd was not immune. In one incident, Tetons stole a dozen horses from a police herd guarded by a single constable. He reported the theft and Edward "Buffalo" Allen rode with ten Mounties to the Indian camp. Sitting Bull came forward, only to be manhandled by a Mountie and the troop returned with the horses to the Wood Mountain post. Some Indians trailed them and, although they made vociferous threats, no fighting took place. This danger of retaliation was always a concern. In May 1880, the Tetons threatened to shoot the first Indian found with any of the sixteen horses stolen from their camp.[14]

Each year, life for the Western Sioux in Canada became more distressing and, by the spring of 1880, living conditions were abysmal. The horses were so debilitated, hunters were unable to reach buffalo herds 100 km distant, leaving the starving Indians to eat dying horses and carcasses strewn over the prairies from the previous year. Disease compounded the Sioux misery, and Mounted Policemen observed a growing number of graves. The detachment and Métis traders gave leftover scraps to the women and children. Walsh doubted that one ounce of food was wasted during six weeks of acute distress. He admired the "conduct of those starving and destitute people, their patient endurance, their sympathy, and the extent to which they assisted each other, and their strict observance of the law and order, [which] would reflect credit upon the most civilized community."[15]

Hunting South of the Boundary Line

In their pursuit of buffalo, Teton hunters sometimes crossed into the United States. In July 1879 at the Frenchman River, Lieutenant William Clark, with two mounted American companies, attacked a camp of 120 lodges and pushed the Indians northward. Fighting with Clark were eighty Crow and Cheyenne scouts wearing red handkerchiefs on their carbines to clearly identify themselves as allies. The return of sixty Teton warriors from their hunt stalled the American attack.

A remarkable personal engagement highlighted the skirmish. A Crow Indian, waving a white flag, approached the Tetons with a challenge from Magpie, a prominent Crow warrior, for Sitting Bull to engage in personal combat. Sitting Bull accepted. As the two horsemen raced toward each other, Magpie fired first, but his rifle misfired. Sitting Bull responded with a direct shot to his adversary's head. He dismounted, scalped his fallen foe, mounted Magpie's prized horse and returned to his party.[16] Indian warriors highly valued the capture of an enemy's horse. A report commented: "Thus Sitting Bull added as much luster of his name by the capture of the horse, as by the death of his opponent."[17]

The arrival of Colonel Nelson Miles with a 700-man task force equipped with howitzers forced the Tetons, in Miles' words, "to make a precipitate retreat and, abandoning their property, fled north until they reached the forty-ninth parallel, which provided the only safe barrier that they had found during the last three years against the soldiers."[18] Although only five

Teton Indians were killed, Miles heralded a great victory at the "Battle of Milk River." In the next weeks, Major Walsh visited "Bear Coat" Miles on two occasions to discuss the border problems. At the second meeting, Walsh brought Long Dog, a Hunkpapa, who delighted the attending American journalists with his version of the attack by Miles: "Heap shoot! Bad Medicine! God damn!"[19] In answer to Miles' question on which side of the boundary he intended to live, Long Dog turned to Walsh and replied: "We intend to remain with him."[20]

American Indians

American Indian incursions into Canada compounded the difficult NWMP policing. For the most part, these raids involved a handful of Indians stealing horses and racing with them to the safety of the Medicine Line.

Violence was ever-present. In May 1878, after the Crows rejected a proposed alliance by Tetons and Nez Percé to attack the Americans, they raided Teton camps. Sitting Bull complained bitterly that the war party had crossed into Canada and killed one man, wounded another, and stole 100 horses. He said his hands were tied as he had promised not to go into American territory.[21]

In late January 1879, Major Walsh attended an assembly organized by Sitting Bull to gauge the Crow menace. The Indians grilled Walsh over the lack of the promised police protection and what police were planning to do about the Crow intrusions. Major Walsh dodged the questions by blaming the Nez Percé for interference with the Crow tribe. He advised caution in retaliation against the Crows.

American Indian response to a Cree incursion resulted in a bloody skirmish on the eastern Canadian prairies. In July 1880, at Fort Qu'Appelle, although refused rations by the Indian agent and warned not to leave by Superintendent Sam Steele, the Cree Chief Pasque (The Prairie) took warriors 400 km south into Dakota Territory. Near the Missouri River, his war party attacked a Mandan camp where they killed several women and the horse guard. The Cree fled back to Canada with the stolen horses.

Thirty Mandan and Gros Ventres warriors followed the trail to Roche Percée, but then took the wrong track to an innocent Assiniboine-Saulteau camp of thirty Indians. The American Indians opened fire with repeating rifles in a skirmish that continued for hours.

At darkness, the Mandans left carrying five dead and driving all of the horses from the besieged camp. The firefight had been deadly. Five woman and children were among the eight dead Assiniboines, and twelve Indians were wounded. One two-year-old child had two bullets in his buttocks and a finger shot off. With their horse herd taken, the dispirited Assiniboines walked to Fort Ellice for assistance.[22] The North-West Mounted Police took no action against the American Indians.

Canadian Indian Conflicts

The NWMP needed both tact and forcefulness to resolve the continuing Canadian inter-tribal disputes. It was, in Commissioner Irvine's words, only "timely interferences" by the NWMP that prevented trouble. One example was in 1881 when Blackfoot under Chief Crowfoot camped near Fort Walsh on their return to Blackfoot Crossing. During the short stay, the police detachment was busy mediating quarrels between Crowfoot's band and the Crees, that chiefly concerned stolen horses.

In one case at Fort Walsh, Cree Indians threatened to murder a Blackfoot whom they accused of stealing their horses south of the line. Irvine took two constables and an interpreter to the Cree camp only to meet mounted warriors intent on killing the Blackfoot. Irvine forewarned the Cree that police would not allow a man to be killed in the territory and ordered the Indians back to their camp. Most warriors, however, ignored this advice and rode about, recklessly firing their rifles. In the meantime, the police had located the Blackfoot Indian and took him to Fort Walsh where he was "well satisfied at being delivered from his infuriated enemies."[23]

A more serious confrontation between Canadian Indian tribes occurred in June of 1882 when 200 Blood Indians from Fort Macleod, all armed with Winchester rifles, arrived at Fort Walsh "like a regiment of cavalry, pounding tin cups and singing a war song."[24] The detachment gave them food and bell tents that they set up on the cricket ground in front of the fort. They told Commissioner A.G. Irvine they had come to Fort Walsh to retrieve forty horses stolen by the Cree Indians. Irvine sent Inspector Edmund Frechette with six Bloods to inspect the Cree herd and reclaim any stolen Blood horses. They found five of the Blood horses and Irvine suspected that American Indians had stolen the other missing animals. The Bloods were unhappy at finding so few horses but, at a meeting with Irvine, they professed friendship and promised to leave the next day.

That night, the Bloods held a war dance. When Colonel Irvine and Supt. Cotton rode to the site, they found fires left burning, scattered utensils, and candles still lit in the tents—indications of a hurried departure. Eight nearby Cree lodges had been destroyed, but no one was injured as the occupants had taken refuge in the Fort Walsh settlement. Julia LaRoque (who had been abducted as a child and knew Blackfoot) had boldly crept near the Blood camp, overheard their plans, and warned the Cree of the danger.

The Blood warriors rode through the settlement and Cree camp. It was a hectic scene. Constable George Guernsey related:

> About midnight after a particularly wild dance they jumped on their horses and rode up and down the bottom firing volleys into every Cree tepee and half-breed shack they came across. Everyone had hidden in bushes except one old half-blind Cree [Ne-Mo-Ke-Cut] who came out of his lodge to see what was the matter and was instantly riddled with bullets, scalped and his ears cut off. [25]

For several nights after the raid, North-West Mounted Police guarded the Cree camp and the home of police scout Léveille whom the Bloods had threatened to kill. Four sentries were placed on each side of Fort Walsh with orders to fire if any Indians approached. There was a false alarm when a sentry fired at Inspector Jack French, who was carrying a lantern to inspect the defences. In their nervousness, the other sentries also began firing as they ran to the fort.

In his review of the bloody Indian murder, Commissioner A.G Irvine speculated that excitable young Blood men, humiliated if they returned home without the horses, reacted irrationally. Irvine added that problems always arise whenever Indians left their reserve in large numbers. The alleviation of inter-tribal conflict, he maintained, hinged on keeping Natives on their reserves—which, he admitted, was difficult.

During the North-West Rebellion in 1885, the government fostered the historic enmity between the Cree and Blackfoot Confederacy to thwart an Indian alliance. Although two Cree bands joined the rebel forces, the overwhelming number of prairie Indians remained outside the conflict.[26] In fact, the Blood band offered to fight the Cree rebels. Bull Shield asked his Indian agent to "give us ammunition and grub and we'll show you how soon we can set the Crees afoot and lick them."[27] Leading Blood Chief Red Crow told the police to "give the word and they would be ready at any time to fight the Crees."[28]

On two occasions, Lieutenant Governor Edgar Dewdney suggested arming Blackfoot warriors to fight the rebellious Cree bands, but Major General Frederick Middleton (commander of the Canadian militia), based on his earlier negative experience with Maori auxiliaries in New Zealand, overruled the use of Indian allies. North-West Mounted Police doctor George Kennedy attributed the long-standing Cree–Blackfoot animosity as "unquestionably why the rebellion of 1885 was so quickly and easily put down."[29]

The Western Sioux return to the United States

The unwanted Sioux presence in Canada remained in limbo. After the failed Terry–Sitting Bull conference in October 1877, although diplomatic discussions continued over the status of the Tetons, no agreement ensued on their repatriation. Individual attempts to encourage the Sioux return to the United States, however, continued.

Abbot Martin Marty had arrived in Sitting Bull's camp shortly after the band entered Canada in 1876 and, although his efforts to affect their return to the United States failed, he again visited the Sioux camp in the fall of 1879, without success in winning the band's return.[30] Another visitor to Sitting Bull's camp was Stanley Huntley, a reporter for the *Chicago Daily Tribune*. On 5 July 1879, the newspaper carried a full front-page account of Huntley's celebrated interview with Sitting Bull. Some skepticism arose whether this interview was genuine.[31]

It was Edwin H. "Fish" Allison, a Civil War veteran, interpreter, army scout, and experienced frontiersman who convinced a large segment of Sitting Bull's camp to return south.[32] In the summer of 1880, Allison was in an outfit of seventeen cowboys driving a herd of 1,200 steers eastward from Montana to Dakota Territory. Near the mouth of Frenchman Creek, they suddenly found themselves surrounded by 350 "savages." Some of the cowboys wanted to shoot at the Indians, which to Allison was "worse than madness." He advised his companions to act nonchalant while he rode ahead to meet the Indians. Allison was married to a Teton Brulé and spoke Lakota fluently. He also knew Gall, a prominent chief and a leading warrior at the Battle of the Little Big Horn, and invited him to bring twelve Indian headmen to share a meal.

At the supper, Allison lied to Gall that Queen Victoria had purchased the cattle for her army. This ruse worked and the Indians allowed the herding party to continue eastward. It was this contact with Gall, that Allison "conceived the idea of visiting Sitting Bull's camp, with a view of bringing about his surrender to U.S. authorities."[33] At Fort Buford, the commanding officer, Major D. Brotherton, approved Allison's somewhat unorthodox and quixotic mission.

Allison rode alone for four days to the Teton camp near Wood Mountain. He was at once struck by the absence of dogs. In his journal, he wrote: "There were not more than twenty dogs in camp, the rest having been killed and eaten last winter ... an Indian camp without its swarm of dogs is rather strange to think of."[34]

Sitting Bull ignored Allison's three-day presence in camp, but the scout gained Chief Gall's attention. Allison wrote on 1 August 1880:

I fully succeeded in persuading Chief Gall to come in and surrender with his entire following, which was nearly two thirds of the whole tribe, and he sealed the compact by presenting me with a fine horse, and when I started on my return, he accompanied me for nearly twenty miles, and when we parted, he promised to meet me on the Missouri River, with all his following in twenty-two days.[35]

This promised departure ruptured the Teton solidarity and power. In late October, again with the approval of military officials, Allison made a second visit to the "hostiles." Private Day of Company E, 7th Infantry wearing civilian clothes, agreed to drive a wagon carrying provisions. The two men met the Tetons near the junction of Milk and Frenchman rivers in the United States. Sitting Bull invited them to stay in his lodge.

The Teton camp was in disarray. Blackfoot warriors had attacked the previous night and stolen twenty-six horses. When another Blackfoot raid came that night, Allison and Day aggressively defended the camp, thereby winning the admiration and trust of the Tetons. Allison then arranged a council where he outlined the terms of surrender and the advantages of becoming wards of the American government. Sitting Bull agreed that the time had come for a peaceable understanding, but objected to the use of the word "surrender," declaring that his followers were only defending themselves. Sitting Bull was uncommitted to Allison's entreaties, but the frontiersman convinced Chief Gall to send twenty lodges to Fort Buford, an American fort located on the north bank of the Yellowstone and Missouri river confluence.

Allison saw his efforts undermined by Charles Thompson, a white man who was living in the Hunkpapa camp. This individual, Allison wrote, "represented himself to the chief as an agent and interpreter for Maj. Walsh ... his presence in the camp at this time is certainly undesirable."[36] Incredibly, Thompson was a Mounted Police deserter.

Thompson had a pivotal influence on Sitting Bull. One Canadian source claimed that: "Sitting Bull's refusal to surrender is directly traceable to the influence of one Thompson ... whose livelihood is dependent upon influencing Sitting Bull to remain hostile."[37] U.S. Brigadier-General Alfred Terry suggested that the conduct of this man, "who lives in Sitting Bull's camp and who has adopted Indian habits, even to the extent of wearing a breech-clout and paint, should be made known to the British authorities."[38] However, no action was taken, and Thompson remained in the Teton camp until he was imprisoned for forging a cheque to a trader, probably in April, just five months later.

Gall, Teton Chief

On his surrender, "he came riding out on his pony with his blanket wrapped around him
and arms folded and looked around him as like an old Roman as any man I ever saw."

– Utley, *The Lance and the Shield*, 220
  State Historical Society of North Dakota, 0123 – 08

After a five-day stay on his return to Fort Buford, Allison left with
interpreter George Mulligan on November 20 for his third trip to the
Teton camp. At Poplar River, 100 km west of Fort Buford, they met Gall
camped with seventy lodges. Gall promised to stay at Poplar River until
Allison returned from Wood Mountain.

The NWMP now actively supported Allison's initiative. Superintendent Crozier arranged for Sitting Bull to meet Allison at the Wood Mountain trading post. Allison purchased provisions for the Indians and provided a "sumptuous feast." Over the next ten days, the scout courted the Indian camp and, through his continued entreaties, the Tetons agreed to return with him to Fort Buford for an unconditional surrender. During this time, recently-appointed (1 November) Commissioner "Big Bull" A.G. Irvine, Captain Cotton, and two officers from Fort Walsh arrived, pleased that the Indians were at Wood Mountain and saving them the trouble of locating the camp. Irvine met Sitting Bull on November 23, without the presence of Allison. The Commissioner stressed the need for the Sioux return to the United States to avoid starvation once the buffalo were gone. Second, he confirmed that Walsh, on leave in Ontario, had been transferred to Fort Qu'Appelle. Sitting Bull was stunned:

> I was like a bird on the fence, not knowing on which side to hop ... I was inclined to surrender to the United States. He told me to wait here in Canada until he returned, and he would advise me what to do.[39]

Sitting Bull told Irvine his band needed three days to discuss alternatives and left for his camp, 30 km southeast. In turn, Irvine returned to Fort Walsh, convinced that Sitting Bull would at last leave Canada.

By the time they returned to Fort Walsh, Irvine's party had ridden over 600 km in frigid weather. Deep snowdrifts disabled the wagons, and the men rode the horses bareback the final 50 km. The only shelters on the trail between Fort Walsh and Wood Mountain were three stopping stations with a cabin and stables at distances from Fort Walsh of 60, 115, and 250 km. A *Toronto Globe* correspondent traveling with the police party related: "It would be hard to describe the misery which must be endured on a trip such as we had to Wood Mountain and back. The temperature registered 30° to 40° below zero the whole time we were out, and the snow was particularly heavy for this time of the year."[40] As a result of his ordeal, the writer questioned that attacks made against the NWMP by some Eastern papers and individuals were unjust.

On 10 December 1880, Allison led a hundred lodges of ragged and hungry Teton south toward the Missouri River. The weather was bitterly cold and the food supply short. After seven days of travel, near the confluence of Milk River and Porcupine Creek, the hungry Indians stopped to hunt a large buffalo herd estimated at 35,000 animals. Allison, with three companions, continued to Fort Buford, a distance of 185 km.

While traveling on their route, the trio found Gall still camped at the Poplar River agency. The band was at odds with the American military and no longer planned to surrender at Fort Buford. Brigadier-General Alfred Terry, the military commander of Dakota Territory, was angered over the "arrogant and threatening attitude" of Gall's band, and reinforced the nearby Camp Poplar River garrison. A council between the two parties ended with disagreement and talk of war.

The crisis escalated. On 2 January 1881, Major Guido Ilges demanded the unconditional surrender of the Indians. When no answer came, Ilges led a 300-man attack force and shelled the Indian camp with his artillery pieces. Although Gall had waved a white flag and restrained his followers from firing, the soldiers overran the camp, destroyed teepees and supplies, and seized 162 horses. Eight Indians died in the skirmish known as the Battle of Poplar River. The soldiers suffered no casualties.

The Indians were beaten and divided. Soldiers escorted Crow King (Petriarch Crow) with fifty-one lodges eastward to surrender, while perhaps forty lodges joined Sitting Bull, who remained camped hunting buffalo, 70 km to the west. Receiving information that 200 American soldiers had left Fort Assiniboine (about 270 km west in Montana) to block any escape to Canada, Sitting Bull fled at once for Wood Mountain. The ragged Indians reached this post without food and had to barter both their horses and buffalo robes for flour.

Inspector Leif Crozier had taken command of Wood Mountain on 13 July 1880, the same summer that Allison embarked on his mission to return the Sioux to the United States. Fred Cadd, a trader at Wood Mountain, estimated that the Indian camp held 200 lodges in the fall of 1880. Striking, noted Cadd, was the absence of "young bucks," who had left the starving band. The Indians, the trader had observed, were very concerned about the new police superintendent. He wrote: "I was greatly amused at the cross-examination I had to undergo as to what kind of man Crozier was."[41]

The Tetons quickly found that Crozier was uncompromising. After his first interview with Sitting Bull, Crozier concluded the Hunkpapa medicine man had only wanted to delay the surrender of the "hostiles." He then set to weaken Sitting Bull's authority. Crozier reported:

Consequently, on subsequent occasions instead of treating him with exceptional deference and addressing myself especially to him in council, I spoke to the people generally, telling them not to allow one or any set of men to prevent them from accepting the American terms of surrender.[42]

This tactic proved effective. Within weeks, Crozier persuaded Spotted Eagle, a Sans Arc Sioux with sixty-five lodges and Rain-in-the-Face with eighty lodges to surrender at Fort Keogh (located 325 km south of Wood Mountain). This departure was a critical loss to the refugee Sioux both in numbers and strength.

Crozier dissuaded Sitting Bull from securing a home in Canada. He wrote: "I explained to him that it would be a waste of labour on my part to undertake any such task, and a waste of time on his part to await the results."[43] Sitting Bull said he didn't want to be forced into the hands of people he knew were waiting, like hungry wolves, to take his life. Nevertheless, he hinted to Crozier that he was going to surrender in the spring, but as this was a critical decision, he was not going to be hurried.

Crozier was not a man to trifle with. In February 1881, when Sitting Bull said he didn't believe a promise from American military authorities that, if the Sioux surrendered, they would not be mistreated, Crozier shouted out: "I have had far too much trouble with you already. You can go to hell."[44] A second argument ended when Crozier threw Sitting Bull bodily out of the fort.

In March 1881, Sitting Bull indicated that he would not interfere with any band members who wanted to surrender. Commissioner Irvine had just visited the camp and, although he failed to gain a general surrender, twenty lodges under Low Dog left on April 11 for Fort Buford. In turn, Sitting Bull remained adamant on his personal preference, stating: "I am looking north for my life."[45]

At the same time, Sitting Bull was probing a future under the Americans. On 3 April 1881, he asked Crozier if representatives could visit Fort Buford to observe what treatment they would receive upon their surrender. Crozier agreed to this request and had Inspector Archibald Macdonell escort One Bull and three other Indians to the American post. They carried a letter from Crozier with an attached message from Sitting Bull to "tell the Americans they will see me soon."[46] The police concluded this statement was a commitment to surrender.

Major David Brotherton, commander at Fort Buford, fed the delegation and let them mingle with 1,100 Indians who were awaiting transportation for resettlement. Macdonell thought his charges had been well-received and was astounded on the return to Wood Mountain on April 17 that the four-man Indian delegation gave a decidedly negative account of their experience. Macdonell questioned whether their minds were decided not to surrender before their trip. The day after the return of the delegation, a Cree raiding party ran off with twenty-five horses. The Tetons cornered one Cree in the bush, but he safely reached the fort. Sitting Bull's demand for the man was refused. The enraged Tetons withdrew in a resentful and belligerent mood. In turn, Crozier was annoyed at the delegation's report and felt Sitting Bull had broken his promise to surrender. Later at a council, Crozier told Indian leaders they could go elsewhere as he would have nothing to do with them.

The next day, Sitting Bull left for Willow Bunch, 60 km east of Wood Mountain. Fear may have motivated this move. Now that few young warriors remained in the camp, the Cree raid confirmed how vulnerable the Tetons had become. Inspector Crozier wrote: "The Cree say they will kill Sitting Bull if they have the chance ... the Sioux are in terrible fear of the Canadian Indians."[47]

At the tiny Willow Bunch settlement, Jean-Louis Légaré, a French-Canadian from Quebec, operated a trading post. He was a generous man who provided the destitute Indians with food at his own expense. Légaré urged the Tetons to return to the United States. As a goodwill gesture, he provided supplies and carts for sixteen band members to surrender at Fort Buford, Dakota Territory. However, Sitting Bull was not interested in this offer and, after one week there, he left with thirty-eight lodges for Fort Qu'Appelle. There he hoped to consult with Major James Walsh. Three ex-Mounties related: "He wants to see Major Walsh badly, as he thinks he cannot believe anyone in the Northwest but that officer."[48] Although Major Walsh was still in Ontario, he was not out of touch with the complex Sioux situation. In an interview with an Ontario paper, the Major clearly assessed the state of affairs:

> I know Bull ... and am satisfied he has no intention of returning
> to U.S. territory until he sees me ... and although my command
> is 200 miles distance from his camp, I do not think very many
> days will elapse before Bull makes an appearance there.[49]

At Fort Qu'Appelle, the residents dismissed Sitting Bull's Hunkpapa as no longer a threat. One observer counted only thirty lodges and 125 horses in the Indian camp.[50] He noted the warrior element were nearly all old men.

A Minister of the Interior memorandum two years earlier (28 June 1879) had directed the NWMP to avoid encouragement of any kind to the Western Sioux and to press for their return to the United States. Now the pressure on the weakened Tetons was becoming petty to the point, in the words of one policemen of being prevented from sharing, "even a biscuit with him."[51] Another policeman complained:

He [Sitting Bull] always treated us square after he got to know us, and many a time helped us with his braves in recovering stolen horses, cattle, &, and we did not think it fair ... that we should now be ordered, under severe penalty, not to give him or one of his tribe or children, so much as a biscuit, or, even speak to them.[52]

The Tetons subsisted on fish and ducks. They visited the Lebret Mission on the north shore to ask Father Joseph Hugonard for food. Through an interpreter, Sitting Bull expressed his anxiety: "I have never been afraid of our enemy, but I cannot stand the sight of our children crying with hunger."[53] The priest traded flour for jewelry, mostly ear pendants made from watch parts taken from Custer's dead at the Little Big Horn.

About this time a reporter for the *New York Herald* interviewed Sitting Bull. He thought the medicine man offset his unimpressive appearance through tact. The news correspondent wrote: "His following has decreased gradually and steadily, until now but a handful of warriors and a horde of squaws, papooses, and old men remain. But of these he is king—his word law."[54] In response to the question: "Would you go back to the States?" Sitting Bull was adamant: "No! The Big Knives would scalp me. I would rather stay and starve because the Big Knives are not true to their word."[55]

Canadian authorities held two meetings with Sitting Bull. In the first conference, Indian Commissioner Edgar Dewdney reproached Sitting Bull for backtracking on his promise to surrender to which Sitting Bull replied that he had changed his mind. Dewdney then proposed that the Western Sioux return to the United States through Pembina (Dufferin). Food and good treatment were promised on this move. After the meeting, Sitting Bull told a Mounted Policeman that Dewdney might own the country, but he did not think he had any right to order him out of it. At a second council the following day, Commissioner Irvine repeated Dewdney's offer. No agreement was reached. Sitting Bull had expressed his suspicions to Dewdney: "I shake hands with the white men on this side and I feel safe. I shake hands with the Americans and I am afraid of them."[56] On June 16, the small band returned to Willow Bunch.

Légaré had ignored Sitting Bull's request to wait until he returned from Fort Qu'Appelle and taken thirty-two Indians to Fort Buford. Notable in this group was Sitting Bull's seventeen-year-old daughter, Shook-na-o-ta (The Woman with Many Horses), who was attempting to elope with her lover, unhappy that his offer of horses for her hand had been refused by her father. Légaré placed his cost of escorting this group at $1,024.

Superintendent William Winder

Superintendent Winder helped launch the ranching frontier by encouraging his brother-in-law, Fred Stemson, to finance the Northwest Cattle Company—the historic Bar U.

– GA NA 1385 – 2

At Willow Bunch, Sitting Bull's demoralized and starving followers were prepared to surrender but, when asked to join a second caravan Légaré was organizing for Fort Buford, Sitting Bull said he was not ready to move and wanted to rest. Unaffected by this response, on 12 July 1881, Légaré headed south to Fort Buford with thirty-seven carts and wagons. Seventeen carts were left behind for others to join and, in a short time, Sitting Bull and

Sitting Bull's Surrender at Fort Buford, 19 July 1881

"Nothing but nakedness and starvation has driven this man to submission and that not on his own account but for the sake of his children, of whom he is very fond."

– Captain Walter Clifford in Utley, *The Lance and the Shield*, 230
State Historical Society of North Dakota B1036

his disgruntled followers caught up to the train. Sitting Bull was sulky and declared they would go south and west to Poplar River, not to Fort Buford. On the first night, ungrateful Indians plundered the food supply. One unruly individual threw a sack of flour near Légaré's feet and fired two bullets into it. Other Indians sat silent and surly for hours. Légaré remained undeterred by the ill-disposed behaviour and, in the morning, continued the 210-km trip, knowing the Indians had no choice other than to stay with the scanty rations.

Before he left Willow Bunch, Legaré had sent a scout, Johnny Chartrand, with a letter informing Major David Brotherton at Fort Buford that he was bringing leaders Sitting Bull, Four Horns, Red Thunder, and almost 200 Indians, but only had provisions for two or three days. The courier returned with a reply that Captain Walter Clifford would meet the advance, followed by Brotherton with supplies.[57]

Captain Clifford described the on-coming Indians as being dirty and threadbare. Sitting Bull told Clifford: "I come to yield to the wishes of the government, not on my own account, but because my women and children are starving."[58] The distraught Hunkpapa leader wanted to know why the Americans had put his daughter in irons. Clifford needed time to calm Sitting Bull and convince him that Shook-na-o-ta was not held in chains.

On July 19, after seven days' travel, the bedraggled column reached Fort Buford. The townspeople were captivated by the arrival of the fifty-year-old medicine man, and Sitting Bull found himself a "tourist" attraction. He did not speak English, but could write his name and, for $1, signed autographs. The brisk demand made him raise his price to $5 that afternoon.

The surrender of Sitting Bull was compelling national news. Charles Diehl of the *Chicago Tribune* observed that, "although Sitting Bull was not a fighting Indian, was never in battle action and was known among his people as a medicine man 'this savage' had a mystical art of keeping on the first page of American newspapers."[59]

At the assembly the next day, Sitting Bull wore shabby dirty clothing and sat with a "sullen, bull dog expression." After Major Brotherton outlined his government's surrender policy, Sitting Bull sat silent for five minutes before briefly addressing the officials and the thirty-two Indians present. He then handed his rifle to his young son, Crowfoot (named after the Blackfoot chief), to give to Major Brotherton, saying: "I surrender this rifle to you through my young son ... I wish him to learn the habits of the whites and to be educated as their sons are educated."[60] Sitting Bull spoke of a new life for the band and asked to be reunited with his daughter. He spoke warmly of his years in Canada:

My heart is very sad at having to leave the Great Mother's country. She has been a friend to me ... and I also wish to visit two of my friends on the other side of the line—Major Walsh and Captain Macdonell.[61]

Sitting Bull had kind words for Jean-Louis Légaré: "I would like to trade with Louis Légaré, as he has always been a friend for me ... I hope he is to be rewarded for his services in bringing me and my people in here."[62]

Jean-Louis Légaré's initiative was recognized. The *St. Paul Pioneer Press* acknowledged: "Much credit is given here to Mr. Légaré for his faithful service to the Government in finally inducing Sitting Bull to come in."[63] In addition, the trader deserved compensation for his time and money in helping the destitute Western Sioux in their final months in Canada.

Légaré visited Washington in 1882 but was not reimbursed for his expenses. The Canadian Department of the Interior gave him $2,000 —hardly enough for his expenses. Légaré, out of care and compassion, estimated that, since the arrival of the band on 11 July 1881, he had spent $6,000. His claim in 1882 for $13,500 in compensation from the United States government was later approved by the American Congress, but the Court of Claims stalled the payment for years.[64] It was not until 1905— twenty-three years afterwards—that the United States government paid Légaré, now aged sixty-four, $5,000.[65]

The return of the Sioux to the United States ended a five-year stay north of the border. In Ottawa there was a sense of both satisfaction and relief. At Fort Walsh, Commissioner Irvine wrote of the NWMP success:

It is ... a matter of utmost congratulations that the Dominion Government has thus peacefully effected the surrender of a warlike and powerful nation of Indians, whose presence in our country has been a source of perpetual anxiety. In connection with this surrender I trust the Government has every reason to be gratified with the manner in which this policy has been carried into effect by the force under my command.[66]

Const. E. Barnett, in the police escort to Fort Bufort, commented:

We were satisfied to see the last of him because he was a constant source of trouble around Fort Walsh ... very few people understand the dangers there was at every turn, night and day, to convince those blood-thirsty savages to keep to the right road which they had very little knowledge of.[67]

William Laurie, editor of the *Saskatchewan Herald* expressed the prevailing western Canadian opinion of Sitting Bull, leader of the Teton Sioux: "We hope we have heard the last of him."[68]

Walsh and Sitting Bull

The close bond between Walsh and Sitting Bull compromised attempts to return the Teton to the United States. Walsh was the one white man he trusted. Walsh, in turn, spoke highly of the Indian medicine man:

> Sitting Bull is the shrewdest and most intelligent Indian living, has the ambition of Napoleon and is brave to a fault; he is respected as well as feared by every Indian on the plains. In war he has no equal, in council he is superior to all. Every word said by him carries weight, is quoted and passed ... camp to camp.[69]

In a Police-Indian confrontation, Walsh always asserted himself. After a Métis buffalo hunter named Poitras had seventy horses stolen, the victim followed the trail to the Teton camp, only to be told that the horses would not be returned unless he gave them ten of the best animals. Poitras refused this demand and reported the theft to the Police post. Major Walsh, one constable, and several interpreters rode to the Indian camp where Walsh, through forceful talk with Sitting Bull, had all the horses released. Louis Goulet, employed by the police as a mail carrier, was impressed: "Major Walsh! Boy, that's a brave man. I never see man so brave as that. The Sioux are not going to do much with Major Walsh, I think."[70]

A self-serving individual, Walsh elevated his authority in his dealings with the Tetons. He vaguely promised a reserve in Canada, wrote letters to American newspapers and, in one fanciful promise, spoke of going to Washington to confer on behalf of the band with none other than the American president. Clearly, in Ottawa's view, Superintendent J. Walsh was impeding Canadian dealings with the Western Sioux. In a letter Prime Minister John A. Macdonald confided to the Governor General, Lord Lorne, that Walsh deserved dismissal but, if he were cashiered, he would at once create an imbroglio "for he is a bold, desperate fellow."[71] In a later letter, Macdonald suggested:

> Walsh undoubtedly has influence with Bull which he tried to monopolize in order to make himself of importance and is, primarily, responsible for the Indians' unwillingness to leave Canada ... when this is over we must dispense with Major Walsh's service to the Mounted Police.[72]

Walsh had taken leave to visit Ontario in the spring of 1880. Ottawa used his absence from the North-West Territories to limit his influence over the Tetons. The Department of the Interior, under Macdonald, extended Walsh's leave two months and then transferred his command to Fort Qu'Appelle, 235 km northeast of Wood Mountain. The removal of Major Walsh was not unexpected. A letter from Fort Macleod—a town the writer described as the next thing to the North Pole—stated: "It is rumored in these parts that Major Walsh, of Sitting Bull fame, is to get the 'bounce' this spring."[73]

Pia-a-pot and Big Bear

In 1881, Ottawa proposed the relocation of all Indians in the Cypress Hills to reserves north of the rail line. There was some initial success. Chiefs Jack and Long Lodge accepted reserves near Qu'Appelle and, on August 1881, young "Peaches" Davis had singlehandedly escorted 1,100 Indians under Bear's Head and Poor Man to Battleford.

Some Indian bands, however, were reluctant to accept living on a reserve. Commissioner Irvine addressed this concern by holding daily councils at Fort Walsh throughout April 1882. His report stated: "Obstacles placed in way very innumerable. I had considerable difficulty in inducing them to accept a new and northern reserve ... the Indians were wretchedly poor and without horses."[74]

Countering the government plan to impose a regimented Indian lifestyle remained the lure of the free, nomadic ways. Chiefs Pia-a-pot and Big Bear were foremost in continuing to follow the traditional ways. But this life became increasingly difficult with the disappearance of the buffalo.

Pia-a-pot agreed to move to a reserve in July 1882, on condition that he receive a team of horses and a wagon for himself and for each head man. However, the assigned reserve displeased his followers and Pia-a-pot led them back to the Cypress Hills in September. There they passed a winter of extreme hardship.

After further negotiations, in May 1883, the 800 Indians under Pia-a-pot accepted a second reserve near Fort Qu'Appelle. Ten railway boxcars were allocated to facilitate the movement of the band and their horses from Maple Creek to the new location.

The departing train unexpectedly derailed on the poorly ballasted track, and two cars slid down a three-metre embankment. One car held band members, some of whom suffered minor injuries. "A Council of War" called by Pia-a-pot accused the rail workers of deliberately derailing the train. Several Indians, with drawn knives, threatened to kill the engineer who

Pia-a-pot (Payipwat)

Pia-a-pot complained, "his people, on a land that was once all their own, were denied privileges granted to foreign immigrants and hinted that there was mischief ahead if his people were not more justly treated."

– *Manitoba Free Press*, 2 August 1884
  GA NA 532 – 1

started running down the track, pursued by "a mob of yelling Indians." It took food, tobacco, and an explanation by an interpreter on the cause of the accident to appease their anger. The engineer was coaxed to return, and the train departed without the two derailed boxcars. Some shaken Indians chose to ride on horseback to Qu'Appelle. Being very mindful of those Indians who returned to the train, the engineer decided that, "for the balance of the run he could not be induced to progress faster than about six miles an hour."[75]

Big Bear (Mistahimaskwa) had refused to sign Treaty 6. He had attended the Treaty payments at Sounding Lake in 1877 and discussed his adhesion to the Treaty with Lieutenant Governor David Laird, but no agreement was reached. On the final night of the meetings, some of his Indians began firing bullets above the government tents. Superintendent James Walker went to Big Bear's teepee and warned him that he would be arrested if any more shots were fired.

A far more serious confrontation arose when his band obstructed some government surveyors near present-day Medicine Hat. On news of the band's interference, Colonel Irvine assembled the Fort Walsh detachment and asked for volunteers to step forward. Every man available responded. Irvine selected twenty-six men, all armed with Winchester rifles, and left for the scene. On their way, the column spent one night in a Blood camp where they watched half-naked warriors work themselves into a state of delirium as they danced around a fire of buffalo chips. There was profound disappointment in the morning when Irvine selected only one Blood chief and one warrior to accompany the police to Big Bear's camp.

At the Indian camp, all the women and children were absent—always an indication of possible trouble. Still, as one trooper noted, the Indians were poorly armed, with only one repeating rifle.[76] Irvine bluntly told Big Bear that he would be arrested and locked up at Fort Walsh if his band interfered with the surveyors. At that moment, a Blackfoot courier arrived with letters for the surveyors. Big Bear, thought Irvine, assumed that there was collusion with the Bloods, Blackfoot, and police to attack him, and he submissively agreed not to bother the surveyors. Irvine wrote: "If it had not been for these fortunate co-incidents, my having a couple of Bloods with me, and the Blackfoot dispatch carrier arriving in the nick of time, that we might have had some fighting."[77]

Perhaps for his alleged stubbornness, independence, and his refusal to accept Ottawa's dictates, Big Bear was held in contempt by many White people. An eastern newspaper labelled him "a bad Indian ... a nuisance for some time [who] wanted more than any other chief."[78] His unprepossessing appearance was belittled. One writer described him as a "most miserable specimen of the red man; small puny and—well they are all dirty—but with a low cunning countenance ... which western men would describe as a mean countenance."[79]

Persistent demands by Big Bear exasperated the police at Fort Walsh. One day, Inspector L. Crozier, tired of his begging, brought him into the kitchen and told Constable McEntyre, the cook, to feed "this old duffer. We want to keep him in as good humor as possible."[80] As McEntyre reluctantly prepared the meal, he was upset that Big Bear helped himself to dried apples. McEntyre decided to "fix" the chief by giving him cups of tea. The resulting excruciating stomach ache got rid of the chief—much to McEntyre's smug delight. The Cree chief was, in the opinion of one North-West Mounted Policeman, a "bad egg," and the "sooner he had a bullet in him the better."[81]

In contrast to the prevailing negative opinion of Big Bear, Lieutenant Governor E. Dewdney gave a positive assessment of the maligned chief. Dewdney wrote: "I have not formed such a poor opinion of 'Big Bear' as some others have done. He is a very independent character, self-reliant, and appears to know how to make his own living without begging from the Government."[82] Further, Big Bear was anxious to observe whether the reserve land and money proved satisfactory.

Big Bear was far from an isolated Indian. The *Saskatchewan Herald* noted: "Although it is not generally known, it is nevertheless true, that the Indians on the plains keep themselves well posted as to what the newspapers say about them."[83] When a letter to the paper accused Big Bear of fomenting trouble at Indian secret meetings, Big Bear forwarded a message to the newspaper denying secret meetings and stating that although he had not received treaty money, he was a true friend of the white men and always returned stolen horses to police. His delayed treaty vow had hinged on him observing for a period of time whether the government would honor its promises to the Indians.

In the six years Big Bear remained outside the treaty, his band followed a nomadic lifestyle both in Canada and Montana Territory. While south of the line in Montana, he met Louis Riel.

As the buffalo numbers declined, conditions for Big Bear's followers became increasingly desperate. In the spring of 1882, American troops barred his band from entering into Montana. In May 1882, Big Bear visited Fort Walsh, ahead of his 130 lodges. Commissioner A.G. Irvine bluntly told him the band could not camp in the vicinity of the fort and instead they were to go to Cypress Lake, 50 km southeast, where they could fish. Big Bear accepted this ultimatum. Several weeks later, rumours had reached the police that the Indians planned to come to the fort with

Fort Walsh, 1878

"Every day the Indians would ride down in front of the fort and fire shots over it. Some of the young bucks would back their horses against the stockades and knock some of the logs over that had rotted in the earth."

– Ex-NWMP, "A Night Alarm," *Scarlet and Gold*, Tenth Annual, 94
  GA NA 1060 – 1

exorbitant demands for food and if refused they would help themselves. Commissioner Irvine immediately took precautionary steps. All supplies were moved inside the fort and ammunition in the hands of traders was collected and placed inside the police magazine. The detachment was also confined to barracks and the 7-pr. mountain guns readied.

On May 14, Big Bear arrived along with 150 armed "bucks." After the Indians were disarmed before entering Fort Walsh, Irvine held a council at which the Natives conducted themselves in an orderly manner and made civil speeches. For his part, Irvine "distinctly impressed upon them, that, as non-treaty Indians that they had no claims whatever from the government."[84] He refused their requests for ammunition.

Irvine congratulated himself: "My treatment of Big Bear at this time had a most satisfactory effect, showing him, that he as a non-treaty Indian would not obtain assistance from the Government, and any attempt of his to obtain such by force must prove entirely futile."[85]

Big Bear's band returned to Cypress Lake. Shortly after, news reached Fort Walsh that the Indians for "one week were entirely without food with the exception of a few gophers ... and had to boil and eat grass to keep themselves alive."[86] Living conditions were dreadful. A Mountie wrote:

> I began to wonder how they managed to eke out an existence, for beyond some suckers they caught in the creek leading out of the lake, and a few antelope and gophers there was nothing, and the nearest trading stores were at Fort Walsh ... to this day it is a mystery to me.[87]

The band's lifestyle was beyond hope On 8 December 1882, six years after the signing of Treaty 6, Big Bear, representing about 250 followers, signed his adhesion and accepted a reserve in the Fort Pitt region.[88] Starvation more than government policy had brought what the *Manitoba Free Press* called "the contumacious chief" to heel.[89]

The Closure of Fort Walsh

By the end of 1882, Fort Walsh had lost its strategic importance. The Tetons had returned to the United States and, with the Canadian bands moved to reserves north of the projected rail line, for the first time in memory there were no Indians in the Cypress Hills. In addition, the Cypress Hills at an altitude that reaches 1,392 m (4,567 feet), made growing gardens and crops unreliable. The Commissioner certainly had misgivings about the post. Irvine contacted Lieutenant Governor Dewdney: "I wish we were out of this hole. It is a bad situation in every way. From a military point of view the situation could not be worse, the place invites attack … we are surrounded and commanded by hills on all sides. It is a most unhealthy place and the buildings are in a wretched state."[90]

In late 1882, Fort Walsh and its outposts were closed and, in May 1883, after all the salvageable timber was transported to a new base at Maple Creek, the post's buildings were demolished. Now the most important North-West Mounted Police post for seven years was only a memory.

For the men who had served at this isolated post, Fort Walsh had for a moment, attracted international attention as the site of the historic Brigadier-General Terry—Sitting Bull conference. And who could forget the murder of young Marmaduke Graburn? Or Pia-a-pot throwing his treaty flag and threatening to make the men suffer because they had refused his entry into the post? And how, on one occasion, the oats stored in the bastions had to be hastily removed to position the field guns in the event of an Indian attack. McQuarrie recalled awakening one night with bullets flying over the police tents. A bugle sounded to fall in and fifty men went to where the firing came from but not an Indian was seen; in fact, the Mounties did not know if it was Blackfoot or Cree firing. There was always anxiety when antagonistic tribes camped nearby and the Indians often harassed the detachment. One Constable recalled: "Every day the Indians would ride down in front of the fort and fire shots over it. Some of the young bucks would back their horses against the stockades and knock some of the logs over that had rotted in the earth."[91] The men repaired the damage that night. Some years, mountain fever (typhoid) made Fort Walsh, the least desirable fort in the West.

It was here that they learned drill and horsemanship skills. The post introduced the arduous routine that would govern their lives for the next years. The *Saskatchewan Herald* commented:

> Fort Walsh will be long remembered by the hundreds of young men who served within its walls as a protective force, as a place where the romance of a free life on the plains was rudely dispelled, and where they first learned the value of the comforts and advantages of a home which they had formerly so lightly prized.[92]

Fort Walsh was the first posting for most recruits. Robert Patterson would always remember his first night at the fort when a group of Blood warriors ran down and killed an old Cree Indian. For Patterson, it was a jarring introduction to his new occupation.[93]

NOTES

1. The Sioux tribal structure had three geographical divisions: Eastern (Santee), Middle (Yankton), and Western (Teton). The Tetons had seven sub-tribes: the Hunkpapa (Uncapapa), Minneconjou, Sans Arc, Oglala, Brulé, Two Kettle, and Sioux Blackfeet (Sihasapa). Collectively these bands called themselves Lakota. The NWMP reports and the Montana press referred to Sitting Bull's refugees in Canada as Teton Sioux or Tetons.

2. *MFP*, 23 May 1878. One account exaggerated the number of Sioux at 9,000. *NAC*, RG 7, G 21, Vol. 319, 38.

3. David McCrady, *Living with Strangers: Nineteenth-Century Sioux and the Canadian-American Borderlands* (Lincoln: Univ. of Nebraska, 2006), 74. Although the Hunkpapa were the largest sub-tribe, they numbered less than half of the American Sioux Indians living in Canada.

4. *RC*, NWMP, 1881, 3.

5. *GA*, RCMP Fonds, M 8380.

6. *RC*, NWMP, 1881, 4. *MFP*, 3 May 1878: "Whites carefully knew where all the Indian bands were located."

7. *NAC*, RG 7, G 21, Vol. 320, f. 2001, Pt. 4b. Also *NAC*, RG 7, G 21, Vol. 119, 118–19, 121, 125, 146–47.

8. "Peaches" Davis, "Trading with the Indians at Wood Mountain," *SG*, Sixteenth Annual, 59–60.

9. *NYT*, date c. February 1881 for Frechette's letter on the incident. Also in *MFP*, 28 February 1881.

10. One Bull reported that Colonel B. Hazen, in command of the American post, insisted that any agreement reached hinged upon the Sioux relinquishing their arms and horses.

11. *MFP*, 26 June 1880.

12. Ibid.

13. *MFP*, 25 May 1880.

14. *MFP*, 2 June 1880.

15. *RC*, NWMP, 1880, 27.

16. *MFP*, 20 September 1879. *BT,* 31 October 1879.

17. Ibid.

18. Nelson A. Miles, *Personal Recollections and Observations* (Chicago: Werner, 1897), 309. Also BT, 31 October 1879.

19. *CT*, 9 August 1879. Also Robert Utley, *The Lance and the Shield* (New York: Henry Holt, 1993), 209. Colonel Miles advocated aggressive military actions against the Western Sioux, even attacking their camps in Canada. He regarded hostile Indians near the border as a menace to the peace and welfare of Americans living on the northwestern frontier and even suggested the Canadian government intern and remove the "hostiles" north.

20. Utley, *The Lance and the Shield*, (New York: Henry Holt, 1993), 209.

21. *MFP*, 23 May 1878.

22. *TM*, 8 November 1880. Steele, *Forty Years in Canada*, 155. *WDT*, 6 October 1880 gives a different account of the incident. Also see *WDT* 25 October 1880 and 2 November 1880.

23. *RC*, NWMP, 1881, 23—24.

24. *LH*, 11 July 1935. Diary of a Mountie, from 1880 to '85.

25. Waseecha Hoska (George Guernsey), "The Passing of 'The Great Lone Land'," *SG*, Ninth Annual, 32. In addition to the mutilations, the Assistant Surgeon found eight gunshot wounds and three stabbing cuts. *TG*, 28 October 1882.

26. Blair Stonechild and Bill Waiser, *Loyal to Death* (Calgary: Fifth House, 1997).

27. Hugh Dempsey, *Indian Tribes of Alberta* (Calgary: Glenbow-Archives Institute, 1978), 24.

28. Ibid., *Red Crow* (Saskatoon: Western Producer Prairie Books, 1980), 152.

29. *LN*, 30 April 1890. Also Mike Mountain Horse, *My People the Bloods* (Calgary: Glenbow-Alberta Institute, 1979), 49–51.

30. *NAC*, RG 7, G 21, Vol. 320, F. 2001, 286–91.

31. Lewis O. Saum, "Stanley Huntley interviews Sitting Bull: Event, Pseudo-Event or Fabrication?" *Montana the Magazine of History*, XXXII, No. 2. Saum accepts the validity of the interview. Also *BT*, 28 June 1879.

32. E.H. Allison, "Surrender of Sitting Bull," *South Dakota Historical Collections*, VI, 1912, 235. Allison's Indian name was Hogahu (Fish). *BT*, 19 November 1880.

33. Ibid. 235.

34. *MFP*, 27 November 1880.

35. Allison, "Surrender of Sitting Bull," 240. See also *MFP*, 27 November 1880. The statement by Allison that Gall's following made up two-thirds of the camp is exaggerated. See Walsh in *WDT*, 26 October 1880.

36. *MFP*, 27 November 1880. *WDT*, 4 April 1881. *FBRP*, 26 January 1881, *WDT*, 10 May 1881.

37. *MFP*, 22 January 1881. Also *SH*, 5 June 1881.

38. *FBRP*, 26 January 1881. No arrest was made even though Thompson visited Wood Mountain at least twice. One diary notes that he was at the post on 10 December 1880 and 26 January 1881. *Royal BC Museum*, J.W.W. (Jonathan Wolfrid Wurtele), Daily Diary, Wd Mountain, E C W96A.

39. Utley, *The Lance and the Shield*, 217.

40. *MFP*, 21 January 1881. A letter, signed "Tenderfoot," responded that the perils of this route were unduly exaggerated by the correspondent. *MFP*, 22 January 1881.

41. *TG*, 26 September 1880. Also *MFP*, 1 November 1880.

42. *RC*, NWMP, 1880, 32.

43. *RC*, NWMP, 1880, 28.

44. *Dictionary of Canadian Biography, 1901—10*, vol. XIII (Toronto: University of Toronto Press, 1994), 233.

45. Utley, *The Lance and the Shield*, 206.

46. Ibid., 222.

47. Ibid., 223.

48. *SPPP*, 25 June 1881. The ex-Mounties were George Mowat, David Craig, and George Wencraft. Also *TG*, 24 August 1885.

49. Robert Utley, *The Lance and the Shield*, 226.

50. *WDT*, 15 June 1881.

51. *WDT*, 13 July 1881.

52. *GA*, Stuart Z. Wood, M 8065, Box 2, f. 11.

53. *RL*, 27 May 1916.

54. *TG*, 5 July 1881.

55. *SPPP*, 13 July 1881. Also *TG*, 5 July 1881; *WDT*, 15 July 1881; *MFP*, 11 June 1881.

56. Gary Pennanen, "Sitting Bull: Indian without a Country," *Canadian Historical Review*, L1, No. 2, 139.

57. G.D. Cameron, "Departure Time for Sitting Bull," *SG*, Fifty-first Annual, 85–93. *WDT*, 20 July 1881.

58. *SPPP*, 7 August 1881.

59. Charles S. Diehl, *The Staff Correspondent* (San Antonio, Texas: Clegg, 1931), 132.

60. *BT*, 29 July 1881.

61. *SPPP*, 21 July 1881. *Bismarck Tribune* details the surrender, 29 July 1881.

62. Ibid.

63. Ibid., 20 July 1881.

64. Expenses ranged from $15 for a revolver for Sitting Bull to $6,400 for supplies and travel. See Grant MacEwan, *Sitting Bull – The Years in Canada* (Edmonton: Hurtig, 1973), 199.

65. *RC*, NWMP, 1882, 8–9. In April 1882, ten months after Sitting Bull's surrender, thirty-two Cree warriors abducted J.L. Légaré and two helpers while they were returning with trade goods from the United States. That night, Légaré overheard Indian plans to kill him and his workers and in the morning Légaré expected any moment to die. Two shots were fired at the trader but, fortunately, the guns misfired and, in the confusion, Légaré was able to bargain for their lives.

Légaré reported the harrowing incident to Inspector A.R. Macdonell at Wood Mountain. Macdonell sent messengers to area camps to warn of the war party and, learning the Indians were on foot with lariats (indicating horse stealing), the Inspector led his detachment and Légaré to a camp of forty-five lodges. The Indians remained sulky until Macdonell covered the leading agitator with his revolver. This cowed the Indians and the police arrested eight men (or eleven) who were taken to Wood Mountain. At a trial at Fort Qu'Appelle, Stipendiary Magistrate Inspector Macdonell (who had arrested them) found them guilty of bringing horses to Canada and sentenced each man to twenty days imprisonment with hard labour.

66. *RC*, NWMP, 1881, 3.

67. *GA*, Edward Barnett, M 58.

68. *SH*, 15 August 1881.

69. *NAC*, RG 10, f. 13893.

70. Camp Crier, "Taming Sitting Bull," *SG*, Twelfth Annual, 99–100.

71. *NAC*, RG 10, F. 13893.

72. *NAC*, Lorne Papers, MG 27, IB4. Also Pennanen, "Sitting Bull: Indian without a Country," 136.

73. *FBRP*, 9 March 1881.

74. *RC*, NWMP, 1882, 3. *TG*, 10 September 1883. *TG*, 28 October 1882.

75. *MFP*, 5 May 1883. Also *LH*, 11 July 1935. A second version of the incident, in the *Saskatchewan Herald*, 21 July 1883, relates that the Indians blamed the derailment on the brakeman who, while walking on top of the car, had somehow purposely caused the car to tip. And it was the brakeman, not the engineer, who the Indians had chased. Pia-a-pot's concerns over a reserve had justification. The following year, after the deaths of six children and five adults in one week, Pia-a-pot bitterly complained that the reserve was unhealthy. *MJN*, 16 May 1884. Also *RL*, 2 August 1883 for expected treatment for performing a dance.

One account described Pia-a-pot: "We were much struck with his appearance, for he was very tall, and a fine, bold looking fellow. W. Henry Barneby, *Life and Labour in the Far, Far West* (London: Cassell, 1884), 234. TG, 10 September 1883 – Steele reported the Indians were peaceable as ever, except grumbling from Pia-a-pot, "who is hard to please, and does not know what he really wants."

76. *LH*, 31 December 1937. Irvine also contacted the survey party, which agreed to leave. It was October and most of their work had been completed.

77. *LH*, 7 January 1909. A.G. Irvine, "A Parley with Big Bear," *AHR*, 11, No. 4, 19.

78. *TG*, 15 August 1879.

79. *NNW*, 1 August 1879. The writer added: "He talked and talked. Wanted twice as much as any other chief." The *Toronto Globe*, 15 August 1879, described Big Bear as "a wretched specimen of an Indian—small and cadaverous looking, with the reputation of being a first-class liar." Also *ODC*, 14 August 1879. Staveley Hill observed: "he is certainly not a very distinguished-looking man, and about as plain-headed an Indian as it is possible to see amongst this not very handsome race." 143.

80. *SAB*, A 110, McEntyre, J.E.

81. Alex. Staveley Hill, *From Home to Home* (London: Sampson Low), 143.

82. *CSP*, 1880, 111, No. 4, 77.

83. *MFP*, 24 August 1882.

84. *RC*, NWMP, 1882, 8.

85. Ibid.

86. *MFP*, 2 June 1882.

87. Waseecha Hoska (George Guernsey), "The Passing of the Great Lone Land," *SG*, 33. See also *MFP*, 2 June 1882.

88. *RL*, 11 October 1883. Even after accepting a reserve, Big Bear and "the obstructionist" Pia-a-pot were "collecting so many desperadoes, as well as lazy and worthless ones together, and thus becoming a cause of constant anxiety to our authorities."

89. *MFP*, 28 February 1885.

90. *GA*, Edgar Dewdney M 320. Atkin, *Maintain the Right*, 165.

91. Ex-NWMP, "A Night Alarm," *SG*, Tenth Annual, 94.

92. *SH*, 21 July 1883.

93. Pox-o-Nackie (Little Soldier), "When the West was Young," *SG*, 71.

17

TROOPS IN RED
AND BLUE

Constable Daniel "Peaches" Davis

"A Canadian fighting under the British flag, considers himself equal to three or four Yankees."

– Constable Jean D'Artigue, *Six Years in the Canadian Northwest*, 25
  RCMP Historical Collections Unit, "Depot" Division, Regina, SK.

IN A LETTER WRITTEN TO HIS MOTHER in Ontario, James Stanford affirmed: "The Indians have more respect for one red coat than they have for 100 blue ones."[1] The young Mountie was referring to the forthcoming Brigadier-General Alfred H. Terry–Sitting Bull conference to be held at Fort Walsh. The colour designations, meaning "red coat or boys in red" for the Mounted Police and "blue coat or boys in blue" for the American cavalry, were a common reference that distinguished the two military forces on the northwestern frontier.[2] Stanford added in his letter that: "Colonel Macleod was now in Sitting Bull's camp with 19 men while General Crook was coming to meet him with an escort of 1,100."[3]

The Fort Walsh conference was scheduled three weeks after the Treaty 7 negotiations set for Blackfoot Crossing on 19 September 1877. It was anticipated in Montana Territory that the Blackfoot Confederacy meeting would fail. The *Fort Benton Record* speculated: "The police are entirely too weak to control the number of Indians and disastrous consequences are not unlikely in the coming treaty."[4]

"The boys in red" cast aside such pessimism. In response to an American trader's warning that his detachment would never return to Fort Macleod from the "gigantic" Indian encampment at Blackfoot Crossing, Constable A. Nedham countered that, "they forgot that we knew how to treat Indians with tact, and because of that accomplishment the dire fear of outsiders proved unwarranted."[5] And were not the Mounted Police superior to their American counterparts?

An Eastern Canadian correspondent, visiting Wood Mountain, observed that the American scouts were greatly surprised at the freedom with which the NWMP moved about the Teton camp. "They said," he wrote, "one of your men go where we dare not send a hundred ... and it is perfectly true that the police are held in the greatest respect by these Indians who have played such havoc with the American troops."[6] In 1874, at St. Paul, Minnesota, on the NWMP journey west and even before he had seen one Indian, former French schoolteacher Sub-Constable D'Artigue rebutted a warning that the Indians fearlessly attacked strong American fortifications, by enjoining his questioner not to forget "that a Canadian fighting under the British flag, considers himself equal to three or four Yankees."[7]

Canadians prided themselves with the perception that a handful of North-West Mounted Policemen routinely controlled situations that taxed their more numerous American military counterparts. Supporting this conviction was the well-known story of Sub-Constable Daniel "Peaches" Davis who single-handedly supervised 1,000 Indians that were escorted to the border by the American cavalry. One version relates:

Davis introduced himself to the cavalry major.
"I've come for the Indians," said Constable Davis simply.

The cavalry major looked at him in astonishment.
"Where's your squad of police?" he enquired.

Davis hesitated for a moment and then said, "He's down at the creek washing the dishes," and before the major could ask any questions, Constable Davis was among them and ordering them to prepare for the journey.[8]

The two mounted policemen moved the band to Fort Walsh. At that NWMP post, nineteen-year-old Davis was detailed to independently conduct the Indians north to the Fort Battleford area, a 400-km journey. The hungry Indians had little choice but to remain with the food rations, loaded in twenty-five Red River carts. At each meal, Davis personally distributed the rations.

The young Mountie suspected Blackfoot warriors were trailing his plodding column. After crossing the South Saskatchewan River, Davis recalled, "We made camp and the Indians declined to corral the horses in spite of my pleadings, and sure enough in the middle of the night a war party of Blackfeet crossed the river and ran off every horse in camp. That put us in a nice fix."[9] Davis commandeered a horse from a nearby Métis camp and sent a rider to Fort Walsh for assistance. By the next afternoon, Sergeant John Ward arrived with horses and the trek resumed.

After overseeing the band to their assigned reserve in the Eagle Hills, Davis reported back to Colonel William Herchmer at nearby Battleford. He recalled, "I'll never forget Colonel Herchmer's face when he read the dispatches. He looked at me full in the face without speaking for at least two minutes and then said: 'Did you do it, Davis? By gad, you did damn well.'"[10] For his return to Fort Walsh, Davis requested a new uniform and then burned his lice-infested clothes.[11]

Most police assignments were considered routine and are unrecorded. Only scattered references to Davis' accomplishment have been found. The *Saskatchewan Herald* noted the arrival of the Indians at Battleford and that "Constable Davis took charge of the first lot of provisions and had general management of the pilgrims."[12] Second, the Annual North-West Mounted Police Report of the Commissioner stated that, when "Bear's Head" and "Poor Man" (Assiniboine Indians) left Fort Walsh on May 23 for Battleford, they were accompanied by a constable of the force who issued rations while en route.[13]

The facts of the undertaking aside, the legend grew. On the death of Daniel "Peaches" Davis in March 1937, the *Calgary Herald* carried a front-page column titled the "Lone Mountie of 1881" who "chaperoned" 1,100 Indians from the line where American soldiers were flabbergasted to see one man singlehandedly setting out with his "child-like" Indians on an eighteen-day journey.[14]

Constable Charles Webster (horse), Constable William Osler, Corporal G.B. Moffatt at Fort Walsh

"A Canadian fighting under the British flag, considers himself equal to three or four Yankees."

– Jean D'Artigue, *Six Years in the Canadian North-West*, 25
  Maple Creek Oldtimers Museum

A number of accounts relate how a handful of Mounties mastered Indian movements that challenged large American cavalry units. When Constable William H. Cox and Sergeant Sam Horner arrived at the border with a four-horse supply team to meet Indians escorted by American soldiers, Cox recalled that "the Major was surprised that we didn't have a complete battalion to meet the Indians. There were several battalions escorting them."[15] Publisher William Laurie described an incident in 1882 when American soldiers rounded up Canadian Indians in Montana Territory and accompanied them to the international border north of Fort Assiniboine. They were met by Sergt.-Major John Kirk and one constable:

> The officer commanding the United States cavalry was very much surprised upon asking the Sergeant-Major where his party was, to be told that it consisted of himself and one constable. These men brought about four hundred Indians north to Battleford.[16]

Constable Jim Connell, in a newspaper interview written fifty-seven years after Sitting Bull's Indians were guided to the U.S. border, recalled (incorrectly) being met by two detachments of American cavalry. This incident was hardly noteworthy as arrangements for the surrender of the destitute Teton band were in place.[17]

Books reinforced the image of the "brave lone Mountie." A.L. Haydon's *The Riders of the Plains*, published in 1910, narrated how a handful of Mounties supervised Indians while the clumsy Americans watched in awe. Haydon wrote:

> In due course 200 very dissatisfied and wild-eyed Crees, with 450 horses, were rounded up and started northwards, with a strong force of United States cavalry in attendance. They were met at the Boundary Line by three Mounted Policemen, one corporal and two troopers. The American commanding officer looked at them with a surprised air.
>
> "Where's your escort for these Indians?" he asked.
>
> "We're here," answered the corporal.
>
> "Yes, yes, I see. But where is your regiment?"
>
> "I guess it's here all right." said the corporal.
> "The other fellow's looking after the breakfast things."
>
> "But then there are only four of you then?"
>
> "That's so, Colonel, but you see we wear the
> Queen's scarlet."[18]

Author Howard Angus Kennedy, in *The Book of the West*, echoed the perception of Mounted Police mastery over the Indians, in contrast to the ineptitude of their American counterparts. He described the meeting of a whole troop of United States cavalry with one Mounted Policeman. The United States officer was puzzled. "Who is in command?" he asked. "Myself," said the Canadian corporal. "But where's your troop?" said the officer. "Here they are," replied the corporal, as he pointed to his solitary constable. Astonished, the officer asked what the corporal would do if the Indians turned sulky—there were more than a hundred of them and only two of you. "They won't," said the Canadian corporal promptly; "We shall have no trouble with them."[19]

Canadian Success

Canadians lauded their "Riders of the Plains" as a superior frontier force. The *Toronto Globe* boasted: "300 Mounted Police are doing the same work that ten or fifteen thousand American soldiers are doing and scattered over a larger territory."[20] A letter to Eastern Canada, written nine months after the arrival of the NWMP, extolled the Force:

> Surely Canada owes a debt of gratitude to her sons in red who thousands of miles away from kith and kin, patiently toiling in the wilds of this "Great Lone Land." have accomplished more substantial good to the Indian race under their control in one short year than our American Cousins with all their frontier cavalry, daring scouts and fraudulent agencies, have succeeded in effecting in ten.[21]

The *Manitoba Free Press* belittled American newspapers for exalting Brigadier-General Alfred Terry's campaign against the Sioux while, at the same time, ignoring the operations north of the border where a handful of Mounties successfully controlled the situation. While A. Terry had a force of 4,300 men, Colonel Irvine, with only 10 men, had entered an Indian camp of 150 lodges in the Cypress Hills and peacefully recovered a large number of stolen horses.[22]

Second, the NWMP was a far more economical body. The Report of the Commissioner in 1877 listed NWMP expenditures at $1,000 for each policeman, one-third less than that spent on a United States cavalryman.[23] The far superior accommodations and added amenities at the American posts, however, far offset differences in this monetary comparison. Outside observers wondered how the North-West Mounted Police could achieve such good results in light of their shabby accommodations and the vast territory they had to administer.

Canadians insisted that the NWMP provided better security than their American counterparts. John McDougall, the Methodist minister, wrote on crossing from Montana Territory into Canada: "We began to feel safer; the police were behind us. They represented the British Government. This was much to us."[24] A Winnipeg newspaper boasted:

> The force has rendered most excellent service. It has, indeed, greatly distinguished itself by its energy, activity and skill. The result is a peace and a sense of security for life and property in those remote regions in striking contrast with the condition of things along the southern side of the boundary.[25]

Americans living in the rapidly growing Montana frontier praised the NWMP for its success in handling Indians. A merchant in Fort Benton commented to a Canadian newspaper: "The police are doing good work out north, and by another year will make the North-West Territories one of the most desirable to live in north of the Missouri river. By the strictness with which they enforce the law, property, life and everything else will be more secure under your Government than ours."[26] An American visitor to Canada affirmed this comparison: "Here [in Canada] are 400 mounted police who do the work that 15,000 of ours cannot, or, at least do not, do." He concluded, "the British management of the Indian question is so far superior to our own, that I can but make the comparison with a feeling of shame."[27] One paper contended: "it is strange that we have any Indians left in this Territory since their treatment by the Government and the agents is not only unjust, but inhuman, while on the other side of the line they may enjoy all the rights and privileges accorded to the whites."[28]

John F. Stevens, an American engineer working on the construction of the C.P.R. through the Rocky Mountains, was quoted: "They were a wonderfully efficient body of men … one member of that much respected [and feared] force could police an extent of territory where we, south of the 49th parallel, would need 100 of our police force."[29] In this regard, a Fort Benton paper advocated: "If Major Walsh could be permitted to lead one company of his trusty British troopers against the hostiles, he would accomplish more satisfactory results in a single day than Miles could do in a season's campaign."[30] The well-known saying the Mounties, "got their man" may have had its source in the *Fort Benton Record* in 1877: "The M.P.'s are worse than bloodhounds when they scent the track of a smuggler, and they fetch their man every time."[31]

The bravery of the NWMP was undeniable. A Montana newspaper acknowledged: "The Mounted Police don't scare worth a cent."[32] A detailed account of Major Walsh entering an Indian camp and rescuing a ravaged woman bolstered this belief. In the aftermath of the Battle of Bear Paw (5 October 1877), several hundred Nez Percé fled to Canada. Assiniboine and Gros Ventre warriors, responding to a reward offered by Colonel N. Miles, killed or captured fleeing Nez Percé. On news that one woman was held captive by the Gros Ventre, Major James Walsh, Captain Edwin Allen, and one constable rode to the Indian camp and, at gunpoint, boldly rescued the abused woman. The *Benton Record* detailed this "dangerous errand" and added, "too much credit cannot be given Major Walsh and Capt. Allen for their prompt and determined action in this matter, which shows that as long as the Canadian Government employs such officers there is little danger of the law being trifled with on Canadian territory."[33]

Was the praise heaped on the NWMP by the Montana press only ridicule of the American frontier army?[34] On the ongoing problem of stolen horses, the *Fort Benton River Press* commented: "The conduct of the mounted police in this matter is to be commended and is in marked contrast with our own troops. While the mounted police will turn out to recover horses stolen from American citizens, the military on this side of the line will not even protect our own people."[35] One Montana resident, in a letter to a New York paper, mocked: "There is nothing so little thought of in this part of the country as a soldier. There are only two creatures who look upon a soldier here without scorn and contempt, and they are little children and dogs."[36]

Canadians rebuked the American army for its harsh treatment of the Indians. The *Edmonton Bulletin* denounced the forced expulsion of a band of Canadian Indians in temperatures as bitterly cold as -40°C.[37] North-West Mounted Police Sub-Inspector Dalrymple Clark declared, "The American Indian policy was rotten to the core."[38] A Toronto paper commented: "the United States have had Indian wars innumerable, costing millions upon millions of dollars. What is the predominant feeling in the breast of the United States soldier? Simply that the Indian must be exterminated."[39] The *Manitoba Free Press* supported the negative perception of the American soldier, by stating "The United States soldier despises the Indian, and treats him with undisguised contempt and too often with brutality."[40]

Factors Contributing to the Early NWMP Success
The first Mounties encountered conditions that contrasted sharply from the northwestern American experience. Most important, the Mounted Police had entered Western Canada before there was white settlement. Commissioner A.G. Irvine recognized this reality:

> The experience of our neighbors to the south of the international boundary cannot be without a lesson to us. In their case the military had no trouble with the Indians until settlers appeared on the scene. These settlers, unaccustomed to the Indian manner and habits, do not make due allowances and exhibit that tact and patience necessary to successfully deal with Indians.[41]

A Helena paper agreed with Irvine's assessment: "The Canadians have not had much difficulty with their Indians, because the development of the country has been so slow that the settlements have not pressed on the Indian hunting grounds."[42]

Sitting Bull in Canada (Henri Julien)

U.S. Soldier: Send him over to our side of the line and we'll take care of him.

NWMP Officer: So long as he behaves himself, the British right of asylum is as sacred for this poor Indian as for any royal refugee.

– GA NA 4809 – 2

At the Sitting Bull–Terry Conference, Colonel J. Macleod pinpointed the frontier clashes south of the line to White miners searching for minerals in "Indian country." Macleod wrote: "These men always look upon the Indians as their natural enemies, and it is their rule to shoot at them if they approach after being warned off."[43] Macleod added that the other day an American settler had asked him if Canada had the same rule.

There were predictions that settlement in Canada would bring conflict not unlike the American experience. As early as September 1875, Johnny Healy, who had built Fort Whoop-Up, forewarned: "As soon as settlers and gold prospectors arrive in the territory in considerable numbers, petty collisions with Indians must frequently occur and a much larger force will then be necessary."[44] The United States Interior Secretary Carl Schurz (1881) foresaw the same future problem:

When in the British possessions agriculture and mining enterprise spreads with the same energy and eagerness as in the United States, when railroads penetrate their Indian country, when all that is valuable in it becomes thus accessible and tempting to the greed of white men, when game becomes scarce and ceases to furnish sufficient sustenance to the Indians, the Canadian authorities in their management of Indian affairs will find themselves confronted with the same difficulties.[45]

This foresight by Healy and Schurz proved correct. Within ten years, the escalating Indian "problems" and serious military confrontations forced the NWMP to increase its numbers three-fold to 1,000 men.

Second, an established legal system bolstered the early Canadian police experience. The *Ottawa Citizen* commented that when "the settler appeared on the scene, he found that already a firm bulwark of British law had been constructed, so framed and maintained as to free him from all dangers of savage raids from Indians."[46]

In addition, Canadian jurisprudence gave the NWMP the authority to both arrest and adjudicate the suspect—jurisdiction their American counterparts lacked. An Eastern Canadian reporter mocked this privilege: "The Saulteaux chief in this case comes before Major Walsh, magistrate, to lay an information. Major Walsh issues a warrant which has to be executed by Mr. Walsh, policeman. Major Walsh, as a policeman, arrests the parties, and carries them before Major Walsh, the magistrate."[47] As white settlement grew, the police powers became increasingly challenged. A number of town hall meetings vociferously objected to the Mounted Police's heavy-handed tactics when making arrests and the fact that a policeman received half the fine.

Canadian prairie Indian population numbered less than 30,000—one person for each 25 km^2 of prairie land. (Montreal, Canada's largest city, had a population of 200,000 in 1876). Moreover, the Canadian bands followed a nomadic lifestyle that ranged over the broad Canadian prairies and northern United States. A traveler could cross this land for weeks without encountering a single Indian. On his famous reconnaissance from Fort Garry to Rocky Mountain House in the winter of 1870–71, William Butler met only two individual travelers (both white) on the 6,000-km return journey. By 1885, only eleven years after the arrival of the police in 1874, the Indians were a minority population.

In addition to limited numbers, the Canadian Aboriginal population was impoverished and poorly armed. An appalling smallpox epidemic in 1870, only four years before the arrival of the NWMP, had killed one fourth of the Aboriginal population, crippling their morale and military strength. This tragedy was followed by American whiskey traders entering the southern fringe of western prairies and further destabilizing Native society. Estimates placed the total adult male numbers (1885) of the Sarcee at 50 and the Blood-Blackfoot a total of 600.[48]

Unlike Montana, where many Indian bands had long-standing hostile contact with advancing white settlement, the Indians in Western Canada welcomed the NWMP with the hope that the whiskey trade would end. Reverend George McDougall observed: "On the American side the Indian looks upon the American soldier as an enemy, and avoids him in every possible way; not so in this country—the redcoat was received as a friend, and the wild Blackfoot at this hour regards him as such."[49]

The Mounted Police benefited from that historic Cree and Blackfoot antagonism negated a common Indian front against encroaching Canadian settlement. A point was made to keep the tribes apart to avoid conflict, but horse stealing continued as a major problem. During the North-West Rebellion, government authorities fostered this tribal animosity to fragment any Indian alliance. In fact, the Bloods were eager to fight the rebellious Cree in Saskatchewan.

The arrival of 4,000 American Sioux in 1876–77 destabilized the region and accelerated the destruction of the buffalo herds. Although the Teton Sioux were enemies of the Canadian bands, they avoided trouble for most of their four years in Canada. In his 1879 report, Major Walsh stressed that the good conduct of the Sioux, "is only reached by their fear of being sent back to the United States by the Canadians."[50] Their presence, however, "changed everything." Almost half the Force was deployed to administer the area under Sioux control.

Lastly, the presence of a relatively large Métis community acted as an important buffer between the settlement and the Indians. This element (commonly called half-breeds at that time) numbered almost one quarter of the Indian population. Through the fur trade, white people had a long association with this society. That the Métis were often at odds with the Indians made them an important buffer between white settlement and Indians. The North-West Rebellion of 1885 was primarily a Métis clash, with relatively little Indian involvement.

"Red and Blue" Interaction

The NWMP and the American army enjoyed friendly relations and fully cooperated on policing matters. Both frontier forces struggled in the same climate, geography, and isolation to contain what was called the "Indian Problem." The *Fort Benton Record* used the term "entente cordiale" (hearty understanding) to characterize the cooperation between the two policing bodies. Commissioner Macleod related: "South of the line the United States army officers have invariably shown the greatest courtesy and attention to the members of the force whenever they came in contact with them, and the best of feeling exists between the members of both services."[51]

Official military reports attested to the collaboration. Commissioner Irvine stated in 1882:

> United States military authorities have in all cases aided us as far as lay in their power. General Sheridan, United States Army, in his annual report, mentions the amicable relations which exist between the United States troops and this force, which, he says, go far in ensuring quiet along the boundary line.[52]

In their report of the Sitting Bull–Terry conference at Fort Walsh of 17 October 1877, American Commissioners A. Terry and A.G. Lawrence had expressed their grateful thanks for the courtesy with which they were received by senior NWMP officers.[53] In turn, Superintendent Sam Steele remarked that Terry and his officers were smart soldiers, very punctilious in their bearing toward them.

American uneasiness that the Teton Sioux refuge in Canada endangered their northwestern frontier heightened the collaboration between the two frontier forces. Couriers regularly exchanged intelligence across Canadian and American military posts. When Walsh received reports that Sitting Bull was proposing raids on Fort Peck and Fort Belknap, he "very kindly dispatched couriers to each fort."[54]

In one dispatch, Major Guido Ilges at Fort Assiniboine alerted Major Albert Shurtliff at Fort Walsh on 7 May 1883 that, twenty-five miles east of Fort Walsh, 300 lodges of Crees under Big Bear and Little Pine were having nightly war dances preparatory to crossing the line into American Territory to attack Gros Ventres and Assiniboine camps near Milk River.

He also pointed out that, the previous week, small Cree parties had entered American territory and stolen thirty-three horses. What could be done to prevent these raids?

Superintendent Shurtliff responded that his daily information from the large Cree camp indicated any trouble was not forthcoming as the band could not procure sufficient ammunition. The excitement in the Indian camp, an informant had related, involved a war party returning from the Sweet Grass Hills with two Piegan scalps. In regard to small raiding parties, Shurtliff acknowledged these movements were hard to detect as individual men left quietly at night and met at an appointed location. Still, Canada was determined to end these horse theft raids. Shurtliff informed Major Ilges that, recently, Commissioner Irvine had sentenced four Indians to five years in the Manitoba Penitentiary and another eleven Indians each had received sentences of two years' imprisonment.[55]

The two frontier forces always accommodated each other.[56] In one case, Colonel Miles sent Lieutenant Tillson to Wood Mountain to arrest five Indians suspected of murder near the Yellowstone River and thought to be in Canada. Tillson brought a witness along named Sturms (wearing a disguise) to identify the suspects. Commissioner Irvine accompanied the two Americans 50 km to the Teton camp but Sturms was unable to recognize the murderers among the warriors. Although no arrests were made, the fact that the Commissioner had ridden 100 km demonstrated the NWMP willingness to assist the American military.

Sometimes, information was shared first-hand. An American officer, Eli Huggins, in camp one mile from the "British line," wrote on 25 July 1879: "Major Walsh came over the line yesterday and had a long talk with [Colonel] Miles ... four Mounted Police in red coats came to escort Walsh. They say Sitting Bull was with the party we met a week earlier. Eight Indians were killed. They say the Indians will be forced to hunt on this side of the line again before winter as they have very little."[57]

The American military assisted the North-West Mounted Police in matters of both health and safety. In the first winter the NWMP spent on the plains, American military doctors at Fort Pembina attended to the Mounted Police detachment stationed across the border at Fort Dufferin. Inspector Walker recounted that "Colonel Wheaton and his officers made our stay at Fort Dufferin that winter very pleasant."[58] That same winter, an American cavalry troop rescued the Macleod party, trapped for days in a blizzard on a trip south to Fort Benton. One member, Cecil Denny, wrote: "These were the first American troops we had met ... they were most kind and hospitable, and we always found the American frontier troops

North-West Mounted Police Drill at Fort Walsh, 1877

"The sentiments of the Force were always military."

− Superintendent Sam Steele, GA, Steele, M 3462
  Bruce Peel Special Collections & Archives, University of Alberta

the same way."[59] At Fort Shaw, the officers' wives cared for the half-frozen Canadian troop. In 1883, a lost Corp. Pringle wandered into an American infantry camp, "where he was treated like a prince ... the United States soldiers and officers were overwhelming in their kindness."[60]

The NWMP used Montana Territory as a supply base and telegraph link with headquarters in Ottawa. On a personal and social level, Canadian policemen enjoyed Montana, where beer was readily available in the towns and at the military posts. Prominent families in Helena and Fort Benton invited NWMP officers to dine. The local press regularly reported the visits of the Mounted Police officers: "Major Walsh left yesterday for his post of duty in the Whoop-Up Country. During this, his second visit, the Major added largely to his list of personal friends here, all of whom will be glad to welcome him back."[61]

Both frontier forces honoured their counterparts. The Mounties eagerly participated in American celebrations at Fort Macleod on Independence Day and George Washington's Birthday. Upon news of the assassination of President James Garfield in 1881, the Canadian police posts flew the Union Jack at half-mast. That same year, North-West Mounted Police troops escorted the Governor General, the Marquis of Lorne, from Fort Macleod to Fort Shaw, Montana Territory. The troops were met by the American commanding officer 30 km from the post and, as they neared Fort Shaw, the band greeted their arrival by playing Rule Britannia and other British airs.

The boys relished their short stay at the American Fort. "We left for home again," wrote Constable William Metzler, "having had a good time and plenty of whiskey."[62] Trooper George Guernsey enjoyed the reception at Fort Shaw: "Nothing could exceed the kindness and hospitality of our hosts and after all these years it remains a pleasant memory."[63]

Fading "Legend"

Only five years after the arrival of the North-West Mounted Police in 1874, few buffalo now remained in Canada. Their disappearance brought deplorable destitution to the Indian people. In desperation, 4,000 of the Canadian Indians (encouraged by the NWMP) went to Montana Territory to hunt the last great herds.

The northern Indians were unwanted, and despised. Their presence only heightened the already volatile unrest in the region. In several years, the Montana herds were gone and the Indians returned to Canada where they lingered around food depots, police posts, and settlements. Starvation became widespread.

NWMP–Indian conflicts escalated dramatically. At Fort Walsh, the murder of Constable Marmaduke Graburn in 1879 shocked westerners. Townspeople loathed the presence of Indians, and it became an unwanted police task to return the Indians to their reserves. At the Blackfoot reserve near Gleichen, two disturbing incidents, the Bull Elk (1882) and the Bear's Head (1884) confrontations, featured Indian resistance, gunfire, and arrests. By 1884, challenges arose in Saskatchewan. In February, starving Indians swarmed a ration house at Quill Lakes, overpowered the Indian agent, and seized supplies. Police arriving at the scene were met by armed Indians in what was known as the Yellow Calf incident. In the summer, in what was called the Poundmaker Racket, Indians obstructed the arrest of a band member and, with their weapons, openly faced the police. It was the most dangerous encounter between police and Indians to date. Everyone realized one rash shot would have launched widespread gunfire.

The 1885 North-West Rebellion brought bloodshed. At Duck Lake, Métis sharpshooters killed twelve white people and, within days, Cree Indians at Frog Lake murdered nine white men. Soon after, three more white men were killed near Battleford. All western settlements prepared for Indian attacks.

Although the 5,000 government troops focused on suppressing Louis Riel and his Batoche base, there were three attacks on Indian bands. At Cut Knife Hill (west of Battleford), Colonel William Otter's Queens Own Rifles (including fifty NWMP auxiliaries) attacked Poundmaker's camp. The government casualties count of eight dead and fourteen men wounded were high compared to the five Indian deaths. On May 28, at Standoff Coulee, a three-hour skirmish by the Alberta Field Force had resulted in the killing of one Indian and the wounding of five other men. The Field Force suffered three men wounded. A sixty-man contingent of police (Steele's Scouts) and cowboys arduously pursued the fleeing Indians and, one week later, at Loon Lake, attacked and killed six Indians while suffering three casualties.

Even though a decisive victory had eluded the attacking forces, the assaults had killed fourteen Indians and demoralized the Indian camps. Flight into inhospitable northern wilderness was the only option. There was no respite. In the final weeks of the campaign, Colonel Irvine led 136 Mounties as part of a futile, but harassing search for the starving Indians.

In trials in the aftermath of the 100-day rebellion, eight Indians were sentenced to death and forty-two others received prison terms exceeding two years. The Prairie Cree were left leaderless, weary, and dependent on Ottawa for subsistence. Clearly, the NWMP–Indian honeymoon was over.

The spectacular early success of the "boys in red," although extremely important, lasted barely five years. Yet, the press and written accounts embellished many incidents in order to create a lasting glowing legacy of the North-West Mounted Police. In the long run, the living conditions of Indians on the northwestern American frontier and Canadian West were similar. Problems in both countries of Indian poverty, health, life expectancy, unemployment, inadequate education, and crime plagued each following generation. For well over a century, the former lords of the land remained on the fringe of mainstream society, and any distinction between the "boys in red or blue" became increasingly blurred.

NOTES

1. Montana State Archives, Missoula, James Stanford, Letter, 10 October 1877.

2. For example, *FBRP*, 9 November 1881: "The boys in red are in hopes that someone will come along soon again, as the boys in blue used them so well at Fort Shaw."

3. Ibid.

4. *FBR*, 24 August 1877; *MFP*, 18 September 1877. The newspaper added: "If hostilities should occur, the Indians will have everything their way." Also *FBR*, 26 October 1877.

5. *LH*, 11 July 1935.

6. *MFP*, 21 January 1881. The Wood Mountain post was located 275 km east of Fort Walsh and 35 km north of the 49th parallel.

7. D'Artigue, *Six Years in the Canadian North-West*, 25.

8. Scribe, "!,000 Hostile Indians," *SG*, Seventh Annual, 72. *CH*, 18 November 1933 and 29 March 1937, relate this episode.

9. *RC*, NWMP, 1882, 1.

10. Scribe, "1,000 Hostile Indians," 73.

11. W.R. Abbott, "Old Days Recalled," *SG*, Eighth Annual, 39. Forty-five years later, ex-Sergeant-Major Abbott reminded "Peaches" Davis of the demanding task: "It was," wrote Abbott, "things being done like yours that helped make the old NWMP the Force it was."

12. *SH*, 24 June 1882.

13. *RC*, NWMP, 1882, 3. "Peaches" Davis passed his final years, as did many early Mounted Policemen, living in abject poverty. In 1934, he wrote the Commissioner of RCMP that he was seventy-seven and trying to support himself, his wife, and a grandchild on a pension of only $20 a month. He asked for compensation for his service in escorting the band northward. Commissioner J.H. MacBrien later responded that no further recognition could be recommended. Davis' service of six years was not sufficient for a pension and he had received the recent North-West Rebellion scrip payment of $300. In further correspondence, Commissioner J.H. MacBrien suggested that the well-publicized escort of the Indian band was overly exaggerated and none of the men at Fort Walsh regarded it as anything extraordinary as the Indians would go with the grub wagons. (*NAC*, D. Davis, f. 74.)

14. *CH*, 29 March 1937. The Herald added: "by means of his wits and dare-devil courage, he made a heroic trip."

15. *LH*, 11 July 1935.

16. *LH*, 3 May 1924.

17. *NAC*, Jim Connell, f. 812.

18. A.L. Haydon, *The Riders of the Plains* (Edmonton: Hurtig, 1971), 85.

19. Howard Angus Kennedy, *The Book of the West* (Toronto: Ryerson 1925), 96–97.

20. *MFP*, 10 June 1880. Also Alexander Staveley Hill, *From Home to Home* (London: Sampson, Low, Marston, Searle & Rivington, 1885), 424.

21. *SN*, 29 July 1875.

22. *MFP*, 31 July 1876.

23. *RC*, NWMP, 1877, 22. Also *GA*, Wood, Box 2 f.11.

24. John McDougall, *On Western Trails in the Early Seventies*, 273.

25. *MFP*, 1 June 1876. The population of Montana increased from 20,600 in 1870 to 143,000 in 1890.

26. *MFP*, 4 June 1875.

27. F.W. Warner, *Montana and the northwest territory* (Chicago: Blakely, Brown, & Marsh, 1879), 8–9.

28. John F. Stevens, *An Engineer's Recollections*. Reprint News-Record McGraw-Hill, 1936, 3.

29. *FBR*, 22 November 1878.

30. *FBR*, 13 April 1877.

31. *FBR*, 13 October 1876.

32. *FBR*, 17 December 1877.

33. At the same time the Montana Territory press acknowledged and praised the NWMP for its mastery of Indian affairs, the papers delivered trenchant criticism of the Force for pressing the extradition trials and supporting HBC economic intrusion into the southern NWT.

34. *FBRP*, 8 July 1885.

35. *NYH*, 10 May, 1878. Sharp, *Whoop-Up Country*, 127.

36. *EB*, 21 April 1883.

37. *RL*, 17 March 1885.

38. *TM*, 31 July 1879.

39. *MFP*, 23 January 1879. Canadian officials routinely defended Canadian Indian problems by referring to the horrendous American situation.

40. *FBRP*, 21 September 1877.

41. *RC*, NWMP, 1880, 6.

42. *HDI*, 20 August 1879.

43. *RC*, NWMP, 1877, 46.

44. *MFP*, 4 September 1875.

45. Robert Utley, *The Indian Frontier of the American West, 1846–90* (Albuquerque: University of New Mexico Press, 1984), 270–71.

46. *OC*, 29 March 1884.

47. *TM*, 31 July 1877. Reprinted in the *FBR*, 7 September 1877.

48. *CH*, 9 April 1885. The actual warrior number would be much lower.

49. *MFP*, 2 May 1876. Letter written 23 December 1875.

50. *RC*, NWMP, 1879, 16.

51. *MFP*, 1 June 1877. *LH*, 21 June 1924.

52. *RC*, NWMP, 1882, 11.

53. Report of the Sitting Bull Indian Commission (Washington: Government Printing Office: 1877), 12.

54. *FBR*, 29 September 1876. Also *MFP*, 9 November 1876. *HDI*, 4 October 1876.

55. *GA*, RCMP fonds, M 8380. Also *FBR*, 26 April 1883; *WDT*, 24 July 1883.

56. *RC*, NWMP, 1883, 19.

57. Francis Haines, ed., "Letters of an Army Captain on the Sioux Campaign of 1879–1880," *Pacific Northwest Quarterly*, XXXIX, No. 1, 44.

58. Colonel James Walker, "Police Experiences," *SG*, First Annual, 33.

59. *LH*, 21 June 1924.

60. *FMG*, 14 August 1883. *FBRP*, 29 August 1883.

61. *HDN*, 11 January 1875. Also *HDI*, 1 April 1876; 15 January 1878; 19 September 1879.

62. *GA*, William Metzler, M 836.

63. Waseecha Hoska (G.W. Guernsey), "Wheels, Wagons, Whitewater," *SG*, Tenth Annual, 17–21.

18

RAPID PRAIRIE
SETTLEMENT

Station Platform, Calgary, 1884

"The North-West was turning into a white man's country. The buffalo were scarce, about gone you might say. The Government was shutting the Indians up on Reserves, and everything was getting rather tame."

– Norbert Welsh, *The Last Buffalo Hunter*, 116
  GA NA 660 – 2

THE EXPANDING WESTERN SETTLEMENT brought many benefits for the North-West Mounted Police: telegraphic communication, reliable mail service, rail travel, improved diet and amenities, added social activities, far less isolation, and new detachments built at points along the rail line. Daily life had increasing variety and enjoyment. In turn, there were added police responsibilities. The monthly Canadian Pacific pay car required six police guards. And court cases now included the non-payment of wages, highway robbery, counterfeit railway passes, deserting employment, and concealing a birth—criminal charges that the men of '74 never faced.

One incident involved a dispute over a body. Doctors at End of Track (the farthest point of railway construction west) had ordered an immigrant worker east for medical attention but when the man was caught without a passenger ticket, the train conductor put him off at the Fourth Siding west of Medicine Hat. As the train began to depart, the navvy attempted to climb aboard but fell under the wheels, crushing his thighs "almost to jelly." The engineer stopped the train and the crew boarded the injured man for medical treatment in Medicine Hat.

At that station the dying man (who had no identification) refused to give a Hungarian interpreter his name or family contacts and soon died in terrible agony. In light of the heartrending circumstances, the Mounted Police determined that an inquest was unnecessary. A dispute then arose concerning the burial: the police maintained that as the deceased was a C.P.R. employee and was killed by their train, this undertaking was now the responsibility of the railway; rail authorities countered that since the NWMP had possession of the body and personal effects ($8), this relieved them of all obligations. The police finally buried the poor man.[1]

Population

The population of the North-West Territories in 1885 was 48,362, a two-fold increase in ten years.[2] White arrivals accounted almost entirely for this growth. By 1885 almost one-half (48 per cent) of the population was born outside the Territories.[3] Aboriginal numbers had in fact decreased.

In only eleven years after the arrival of the NWMP in the West, the racial composition of the region had undergone a marked change. Whites were now the largest ethnic group with almost one-half of the Territorial population. The 793 North-West Mounted Policemen (7 per cent of the white adult population) formed a highly visible presence. Below is a breakdown of the population in 1885.

District/Population		White	Indian	Métis
Assiniboia	22,083	16,567 (75)	4,492 (20)	1,017 (5)
Saskatchewan	10,746	1,892 (18)	6,260 (58)	2,594 (24)
Alberta	15,533	4,864 (31)	9,418 (61)	1,237 (8)
Total	48,362*	23,323 (48%)	20,170 (42%)	4,848 (10%)

*including 11 Africans and 10 Chinese

Racial groups were pocketed within the Territories. The District of Assiniboia, for example, had largely a white population, while Indian numbers still dominated the Districts of Alberta and Saskatchewan. One-half the Métis population lived in Saskatchewan, a concentration that became Louis Riel's base at Batoche in the North-West Rebellion. And within a district, ethnic groups often were concentrated. While the Métis in southern Alberta numbered only 233 in a population of 10,000, this group made up approximately 20 per cent of the Edmonton area population. Together with the French-Canadian White population (36 per cent of the area's White numbers), the French-speaking element totalled almost 60 per cent of the Edmonton-area non-Indian population. This French language and Roman Catholic influence contrasted sharply from southern Alberta.

The rapidly growing frontier had a young population. Census numbers in 1885 list 46 per cent of the population was under twenty-one and only 178 people (less than 1 per cent) were over seventy years of age.[4] Another characteristic of the region included a strong male component in the 19–30 age group. Numbers in the 1–18 age range, as expected, males made up 51 per cent of the total population. This balance shifted in the 19–30 age group where males represented 69 per cent (7,050 to 3,113) of the population. The ratio certainly reflects the 800-man Mounted Police contingent and young white men in the region—men capable of bearing arms.[5]

An Evolving Land

Remarkable economic developments accompanied the rapid population growth. It could be called a "changed land" with towns, farms and ranches, bridges spanning waterways, the prairie now surveyed, and a railway crossing the region. Planted trees and telegraph poles now dotted the landscape. When Colonel Macleod visited Winnipeg in 1882 after a six-year absence, he was astounded at the visible changes in the landscape. He was quoted: "No one can appreciate it without personally seeing it."[6]

The great buffalo herds were gone, bringing terrible suffering to the nomadic Indian bands now confined to reserves. In turn, regional agrarian growth was spectacular: the 1885 census recorded a Territorial harvest of more than one million bushels of both wheat and oats and almost half a million bushels of potatoes. Livestock numbered 18,500 working horses, 6,000 working oxen, 330 mules, 11,000 milch cows, 20,000 sheep, 22,500 swine, and 70,000 range cattle. Annual butter production had exceeded 500,000 lbs. and cheese 11,000 lbs. By 1885, the C.P.R. had opened ten experimental farms near the rail line. Western produce was exhibited in the Toronto Fall Fair in 1883 to promote the region and settlement.

The police posts raised chickens and planted crops. Gardens sometimes included individual plots. In 1879, Superintendent J. Walker reported that his Battleford detachment harvested 16,742 lbs. of oats, 5,237 lbs. barley, 36,117 lbs. of potatoes, 1,060 lbs. of beets, 3,850 lbs. turnips, 200 lbs. carrots, and 200 heads of cabbage.[7] One newspaper complained that the Mounted Police commitment to farming supplanted their policing responsibilities.[8]

Beginning in the late 1870s, the Dominion Land Survey had mapped most of the western plains by 1885, in the most extensive land survey in history. In the peak year (1883), 119 field parties subdivided 27 million acres of prairie into 170,000 farm units of 160 acres each. These quarter sections were sold as homesteads for $10 and had a three-year residency commitment. Members of the NWMP, however, were ineligible for the homesteads. Men who joined the NWMP in the first years could, upon completion of a three-year term with good conduct, receive a 160-acre land warrant (grant) which, in effect, was a homestead.

Other policemen entered the nascent ranching frontier, stocked with cattle driven northward from the United States. Constable R. Whitney was the first rancher, taking up land in the Porcupine Hills. Other early ranchers with NWMP experience were J. Daley, J. Bruneau, and the Maunsell brothers.[9] The first three brands issued in Alberta were to former policemen. Among the sixteen cowboys on the first round-up in Alberta in August 1879 were five former Mounties—Albert Shurtliff, William Winder, Fred Parker, Robert Patterson, and John Miller.

Several members of the Force promoted land leases that could reach 100,000 acres. While on a visit to Ottawa, Superintendent James Walker apprised Senator M.H. Cochrane of the western ranching opportunities. Walker left the Force to manage what became the Cochrane Ranche, west of Calgary. Superintendent William Winder, on leave in Quebec in 1879, had his brother-in-law, Fred Stemson, raise financing to launch the North-West Cattle Company—the historic Bar U. Where once there had been the sight of buffalo, the residents of Fort Macleod witnessed a herd of 3,000 head of cattle driven up from Idaho to stock the ranch. The ranching frontier had burgeoned after the Federal government issued twenty-one-year ranching leases in 1881 for an annual cost of one cent per acre. By the fall of 1882, the success of ranching in southern Alberta could be seen when the first large herds of cattle were driven to End of Track (then west of Old Wives Lake) for shipment to Winnipeg.

Most demanding, now that the buffalo herds were gone, was preventing starving Indians from killing cattle. The ranching community pressed for police protection, but it was difficult to apprehend poachers across this vast region. The news in 1884 that marauding American Indians had murdered Saul Pollock in his corral near Maple Creek heightened fears about safety on isolated ranches.

A pivotal decision by the C.P.R. to build a southern route reshaped the direction of settlement. In the early 1880s, both the Territorial capital and the NWMP headquarters were transferred to Regina. New North-West Mounted Police detachments opened along the rail line at Medicine Hat, Maple Creek, Broadway, and Moosomin. But one historic settlement was gone: the Fort Walsh police post, built in 1875, was abandoned in 1883.

The arrival of the first train was a red-letter day for a community. Construction spiraled overnight. In the spring of 1884, three hundred buildings were constructed in Calgary. A man, it was said, could go to bed at night and awake to a mansion, the creation of the night, staring him in the face. One observer commented on Regina: "Less than four months ago this place was unknown; now there are about 200 houses with a population of 1,500 ... never in the annals of any other city, even the famous Chicago, has such miraculous growth been known."[10] Where the visitors once saw straggly tents and half wooden canvas buildings squatting with no regard for position or regularity, the streets were bordered by wooden sidewalks and construction paint adorned the once-uncouth buildings.[11] In June 1883, Medicine Hat mushroomed from 200 to 800 inhabitants. Police Surgeon George Kennedy even envisioned the town as the "future capital of the northwest and as the headquarters of the Mounted Police force."[12] Residents in Maple Creek may have disputed the police surgeon's optimism. One account talked of Maple Creek "as the future capital of the NWT and a second Winnipeg is a possibility."[13]

An unbridled "boosterism" characterized the booming western towns —an optimism that overlooked the short-lived Winnipeg "Boom and Bust" growth a few years earlier. Superintendent Crozier told a Toronto reporter in 1884: "Three years ago at what was called Moose Jaw Creek there was not even an Indian dog, while today it is a large and thriving town."[14] Moose Jaw interests advertised a large business directory in the *Manitoba Free Press*. Businessmen in tiny Calgary published a ninety-four-page booklet extolling the area and cited Calgary, population 800, as the "Canadian Denver," comparing it to a city of nearly 100,000 inhabitants. Prince Albert styled itself "the Chicago of the North-West." The press in Fort Macleod foresaw the tiny town as the hub of a north-south railway connecting the Peace River with Mexico.[15] This concept was a far cry from a visitor's description that Fort Macleod was just emerging from barbarism with an uncouth appearance that could not even be compared to a Hottentot village, as the latter was cleaner.[16]

Medicine Hat, June 1883

"From three tents on the first of May by mid-July sixty wooden buildings and over 200 tents now form the town."

– *Toronto Globe*, 21 July 1883
GA NA 2622 – 8

The emerging West's economy was predominately agrarian and resource-based. As outlined, the agrarian component had expanded enormously. The 8,000 farmers made up the largest single occupational group. More than 3,200 individuals listed their occupation as hunter in the 1885 census. Although the buffalo hide trade had diminished markedly after 1880 (only thirty-six buffalo hides were traded in 1885), a substantial number of furs from northern areas were marketed at North Saskatchewan HBC posts.[17]

Coal was the primary natural resource, with production of 5,583 tons in 1885. The mines at Coal Banks (near Lethbridge) employed 300 men. Prices of coal varied considerably: at the pit mouth, coal sold for $4 a ton, $15 at Fort Macleod, and $35 at Fort Benton. The steamboat, *The Baroness*, and river barges delivered coal from Coal Banks to Medicine Hat where local mines also operated. By 1884, coal was transported daily by rail to Winnipeg. That same year, a well drilled for water by the C.P.R. near Medicine Hat struck natural gas at a depth of 355 metres.

Lumber was a leading industry with sawmills employing 218 men. Another 1,350 labourers and carpenters worked in the rapidly growing settlements. Occupational opportunities developed with the completion of the railway and telegraph lines, opening 315 positions.[18] Federal presence was conspicuous with 800 NWMP and 110 government employees.

Employment disputes encumbered the already-overburdened courts. In 1884, the North-West Mounted Police in Medicine Hat heard a total of forty-eight charges for non-payment of wages against the Saskatchewan Coal Mining and Transport company. Inspector J.P. Dowling in Calgary handled fifteen cases involving unpaid wages.

Education was poorly served, with thirty-six teachers instructing 1,300 of the 6,680 (including Indians) children in the six to sixteen age group. The one Edmonton school had to close for one week due to the illness of the teacher, Mr. Harris; there were no substitute teachers. The first Indian Industrial schools opened in 1883.

Under vigorous leadership, Christianity decidedly influenced area society. Church membership was growing rapidly. The 1885 census numbered 9,976 Church of England adherents, 9,301 Roman Catholics, 7,712 Presbyterians, and 6,910 Methodists. Pagan numbers were given at 7,893.

Government

In October 1875, the Dominion Parliament passed the *North-West Territories Act*. This legislation established a territorial government directed by a resident Lieutenant Governor, assisted by a North-West Council of five appointed members.[19] A provision in the Act allowed an electoral district of 1,000 square miles with a population of more than 1,000 residents (excluding Indians) to elect a representative to the Council. By 1884, Lieutenant Governor Edgar Dewdney supervised a North-West Council composed of five appointed and six elected members.

Having the North-West Mounted Police Commissioner as one of five appointed Council members assured Mounted Police input into decision making. The appointment of former Commissioner James Macleod (then a Stipendiary Magistrate) increased police influence in the legislative body.

The Council considered petitions from residents leading to a diverse number of bills and regulations enacted. These included tax rates, control of animals affected with contagious diseases, prevention of prairie fires, registration of business associations and partnerships, relief of indigent children, Lord's Day restrictions on commercial sales, running horse races, seasonal hunting restrictions from February to September, construction of chimneys, auctioneer licences, control of dangerous lunatics, licensing of ferries, landowner's responsibility to destroy the noxious weeds and to repair fences, encouragement of tree-planting, fees on both billiard and gaming tables, and timber regulations. Inadequate revenue limited the Council's effectiveness. Receipts from May 1881 to September 1883 totalled $2,674. Expenditures were minimal, only $54.[20]

Although Battleford was selected as the capital of the NWT, Swan River (Fort Livingstone) remained the temporary capital until the summer of 1877. David Laird, Lieutenant Governor from 1876 to 1881, resided and conducted meetings in the building used by former Commissioner French.

To attend the first Council meeting in March 1877, Commissioner James Macleod undertook an arduous journey. He rode south from Fort Macleod to take American railway connections to Winnipeg where his wife joined him for the final leg of the journey to Swan River, 550 km northwest. The couple traveled by dog team in bitterly cold temperatures. The post was thrilled to see Macleod. One sub-constable recalled: "I am sure none of the men who were stationed at Fort Livingstone ever forgot the morning the commissioner and his esteemed wife arrived by dog train—there were five trains of four dogs to each sleigh."[21]

The Council consisted of Lieut. Governor (David Laird), Stipendiary Magistrates Hugh Richardson and James Macleod, and Matthew Ryan. Macleod wryly explained: "The Great Council of the mighty Territory met this afternoon ... there are three members, Richardson, Ryan and myself. The first two do not speak to each other and Ryan does not speak to me. I have proposed a triangular duel to settle the matter."[22] Inspite of the problems, the council approved twelve ordinances in a week.

In the summer of 1877, the Territorial government moved to Battleford where it remained for six years. In March 1883, the Federal government, transferred the Territorial capital to Regina. The town was located on the railway line, but widely considered an unattractive physical site. A cloud of controversy arose over speculative land deals linked to the new capital. One syndicate included Frederick White, Comptroller of the NWMP, and Lieutenant Governor Edgar Dewdney. The C.P.R., in turn, protected its economic interests by constructing its station on company land.

Prime Minister John A. Macdonald compromised these conflicting economic positions by building the Government House and the NWMP barracks on Dewdney's land near Wascana Creek and then constructing the Government Land Office, Post Office, and Custom House near the C.P.R. station. As a result of these competing interests, Regina grew as a disjointed community strung along the rail line.

Each western settlement organized a town council. In Calgary, for example, Mayor George Murdoch and four Councillors wrestled with the problems of a rapidly growing town. In 1885, the council's budget detailed digging numerous wells to provide better protection from fires, hiring a dog pound keeper, allotting land for a cemetery, constructing a new town hall (estimated cost: $750), and soliciting federal financial assistance to build a bridge across the Bow River. Relief for the poor was budgeted at $20. A municipal budget of $6,000 limited the council's options.

The North-West Mounted Police detachments assisted with political activities. The Fort Qu'Appelle post supervised the 1885 local census. At an election to organize the Edmonton school district, Sergeant John Geldert stood by to ensure order while Captain Griesbach supervised the counting of the ballots that were printed in French, English, and Gaelic. Former Mountie James Walker chaired a meeting in Calgary in 1884 that discussed the formation of a federal electoral district.

Federal jurisdiction enacted important territorial boundary changes. The first, in 1881, extended the Manitoba boundary 256 km northward and 150 km to the west, bringing Brandon into the province's jurisdiction. The small Shoal Lake North-West Mounted Police detachment, opened in 1874 and now no longer in Manitoba, was closed. Second, in May 1882, a federal Order-in-Council formed the Provisional Districts of Assiniboia, Alberta, Saskatchewan, and Athabasca.

Other Federal government policies that impacted on the region related to development of the Canadian Pacific Railway, land surveys, homesteads, ranching leases, and the establishment of Banff National Park in 1884. A Federal representative for the Territories was elected in 1886.

Town–Police Interaction

An assault on Superintendent William Herchmer in Calgary was certainly the talk of the town in November 1884. The *Calgary Nor'Wester* reported that "Last week Colonel W. Herchmer while proceeding home and when near the bridge was violently assaulted by two or three unknown parties. The Colonel was struck a blow on the back of the neck from an unknown opponent, and felled."[23] The assault was never solved.

Another noteworthy confrontation took place at Fort Macleod between the police and citizens. Constable Jack Clarke described the brawl: "We got orders to clean the house out and we put them out pretty quick. It commenced by a Citizen calling Constable J. Daley a bad name and we went for them. Most of the boys were drunk ... Captain Winder came down and stopped it but he said as much as to go for them."[24]

Often-trying relations prevailed between the police detachment and the town. The *Calgary Tribune* editorialized, "For some time there has been a sad want of harmony between our municipal heads and the commandant in charge of this post."[25] Inspector Richard Burton Deane's restriction against townspeople walking through the barrack grounds certainly annoyed the residents of Regina. The local press commented: "If Deane is popular about the barracks, he is quite the reverse about the town."[26] A police officer's arrogance angered citizens in Medicine Hat. In question was a horse, stolen three years earlier from a man named Ross and found later with a contractor named Muirhead. Although Ross was able to prove his case, the North-West Mounted Police officer let Muirhead keep the horse. He dismissed Ross' protests by saying: "there is no use in protesting, sir ... what I have done I have done." A local barrister named Lougheed remonstrated: "Is it not time this paternal justice should cease. Is this Russia?"[27]

In turn, the police blamed the local merchants for charging exorbitant prices on meals and personal items.[28] Eggs, for example, were priced at $1 per dozen at Fort Macleod in April 1883. North-West Mounted Police officers accused the town of exerting negative influences on "the boys." As an alternative to the lure of the nearby town, Colonel A.G. Irvine recommended activity and reading rooms at the barracks.

Cooperative activities helped to mitigate the sometimes testy relations between the police and residents of the town. The police were an important segment of the community and, when river ice threatened to carry away the bridge on the Battle River, the detachment dismantled the structure and rebuilt the bridge once the ice danger cleared. In Medicine Hat, members of the Force helped set up tents and swings for the Presbyterian Sabbath School party. In thanks, the church ladies gave the policemen a three-tiered cake. At Moose Jaw, Constable J.W. Fyffe sold a policeman's kit to purchase thirty books for the local school. Men at the Fort Macleod post helped move a log church for Pastor John Maclean. After a hailstorm destroyed Edmonton-area crops in 1876, the police detachment organized a committee for community relief and distributed surplus North-West Mounted Police supplies. The police barracks, as the largest building in the community, was available for local theatre and dances.

A keen, healthy rivalry between the town and the police garrison in shooting matches and competitive sports encouraged goodwill. The local press published results of the competitions. Readers of the *Fort Macleod Gazette* were informed that the civilians defeated the garrison 213 to 189 in a shooting match. Each four-man team fired five shots at targets placed at 100, 200, and 300 yards. At Battleford, after a cricket match, someone commented, "That was a surprise indeed." The citizen team had defeated the police eleven. The day was fine and there was considerable interest taken in the game by a large number of spectators.[29]

A town with a police detachment enjoyed significant economic benefits. Merchants sold the men personal items and local produce of milk, eggs, butter, and vegetables all had a ready market. The NWMP detachment required extensive supplies. The police contract awarded at Battleford for one year involved a number of local contractors.[30] In June 1884, Supt. Leif Crozier issued tenders for 50,000 lbs. of beef, 200,000 lbs. of oats, 15,000 lbs. of potatoes, 3,000 lbs. of bran, 300 tons of hay, 50 tons of straw, 100 tons of coal, and 200 cords of wood. Supt. Percy Neale advertised in the local Regina press for tenders for 1,500 square yards of paint (two coats) for the police barracks. Ottawa issued tenders for 1,500 tons of coal to be delivered to five police posts for the winter of 1884–85.

During the North-West Rebellion, the 100 Mounted Policemen who were stationed in Calgary became a prominent one-tenth of the town's population. When rumours surfaced that the detachment was to relocate, a town hall meeting approved sending a petition to Ottawa that "the people of Calgary are against the contemplated removal of the Mounted Police as vital importance to safety."[31] This document contained the names of 100 businessmen, many, no doubt, with economic interests in mind.

NWMP Communications – Mail, Telegraph, and Newspapers
In the first winter in the West, dog teams brought the mail from Winnipeg to the NWMP headquarters at Swan River once every ten days. The Fort Macleod post had its mail delivered by bull teams or any willing rider traveling between the post and Fort Benton. Fort Edmonton was the most

isolated police post, having mail delivery coming overland from Winnipeg. In April 1883, a delivery from Winnipeg arrived in twenty-one days, said to be the fastest time yet made. Fort Walsh received its mail from Fort Macleod and Fort Benton.

There was a never-ending demand for quick and reliable mail service. In 1879, the Dominion Postal Organization replaced the previous police delivery service. Some routes were contracted: North-West Mounted Police scout Pierre Léveille won the delivery contract between Fort Walsh and Battleford. The American merchant company I.G. Baker contracted the Fort Benton-Calgary route for $6,000 a year. In January 1883, Comm. Irvine was appointed Post Office Commissioner. Once its rail line crossed the prairies, Canadian Pacific Railway became the main mail courier.

By 1883, there was regular mail service between Calgary and Winnipeg. Because of mail theft on trains, postal authorities placed the North-West Mounted Police in charge of security and the police barracks often served as the town post office. Sergeant Turner in Calgary used the rear of the orderly room for mail service.

On 2 April 1875, the headquarters at Swan River learned of the deaths of Constables Frank Baxter and T.D. Wilson, frozen while on patrol near Fort Kipp on New Year's Day. Sub-Constable Frederick Bagley lamented over this news "That was three months ago, yet this is the first word we had of it. This gives us some real idea of our complete isolation from even our own comrades in the N.W.M.P."[32]

After leaving Dufferin on the '74 March, there was limited contact with what the men called "Canada." It was not until the column reached the Sweet Grass Hills after seventy-three days of travel that Commissioner G. French was able to telegraph Ottawa from Fort Benton for information and instructions. Six months later, Col. James Macleod rode in late winter from Fort Macleod to Helena to wire Ottawa for a bank draft to pay his dispirited troops their first cheque. Clearly, a direct telegraph link to Canada was essential. The route would follow the first proposed C.P.R. railway line.

Work began in the summer of 1875 on a telegraph line from Winnipeg to Fort Pelly, near the NWMP headquarters at Swan River. This was the beginning of a 1,350-km undertaking from Winnipeg to Edmonton that crossed swamp, forest, and prairie. The shortage of timber for poles in the prairie areas made this a challenging undertaking. Ten thousand poles, at $2 each, were needed to link Edmonton and Battleford.

In spite of the many construction obstacles, in April 1876, the first telegram was sent from Battleford to Winnipeg. Then, by November of the following year, Inspector William Jarvis at Fort Saskatchewan was able to send messages to Colonel James Walker in Battleford, completing the line. Telegraph poles and wires now marked the landscape and served as a directional landmark. In one remarkable case, a lost, blind Indian was able to follow the line to reach Battleford.

Maintenance of the lengthy line was difficult. The poles rotted in water, buffalo rubbed against the poles, prairie fires were always a threat, and wet weather affected transmission. In the fall of 1880, the line was down for seventy-three consecutive days. The station's telegraph flag at half-mast informed the townspeople when the line was not operational.

It was expensive to send a telegram. A message from Edmonton to Winnipeg cost $1 for the first ten words and seven cents for each additional word. A portion of this money (twenty-five cents on the first ten words and two cents on each additional word) was allocated for line maintenance. On New Year's Day in 1880, Inspector Jarvis received a telegram from Toronto that cost $3.50. This expense was rationalized that this contact otherwise would have taken weeks. News now crossed the prairies in minutes. On 16 May 1884, the *Winnipeg Daily Times*, using the new telegraph line built beside the C.P.R. tracks, printed a brief article "The Further West," relating incidents that happened earlier in Calgary that same day!

Every community lobbied for telegraph communication. In Prince Albert in 1883, townspeople purchased and placed the poles along a planned branch line. There was a "great fracas" in the town when the government, claiming there was not a good site available in Prince Albert, connected the service to the HBC post at Goshen, about 6 km away.[33] At an angry public meeting in Prince Albert, townspeople agreed to dig up the poles and take them to a town lot purchased that day. In the disorder, the police arrested ten citizens and the situation quickly got out of hand. Irate residents rushed the courtroom and forced the magistrate to flee while the eight-man police detachment stood helplessly aside. At a second general meeting, citizens prepared to tar and feather the Dominion Inspector of the telegraph lines, who had wisely left for Battleford. However, at the next court hearing, all the charges were dropped and the dissent faded when Ottawa promised a second station would be built at Prince Albert.

Telegraph communication significantly enhanced North-West Mounted Police effectiveness. Information was rapidly accessible. In October 1876, a telegram from Prime Minister Macdonald granted Inspector Sévère Gagnon at Fort Saskatchewan three months leave. A telegraph message from NWMP authorities informed the Battleford detachment to watch the river for a skiff carrying three deserters. The three constables were apprehended and sentenced immediately to twelve months in prison. In October 1884, near the Red Deer-South Saskatchewan confluence, Indians murdered Charles Paul and stole twenty-five horses. Finding that the horse thieves were headed toward the Macleod district, Superintendent J. McIllree at Maple Creek telegraphed Calgary to inform the Fort Macleod detachment to watch for the suspects.

On news that a war party of Bloods had returned home with stolen horses, Superintendent Cotton took a strong police troop to the reserve where they recovered ten horses and made several arrests. On information that Peigan Indians were also involved, John Cotton was able to recover twenty-two of twenty-five stolen horses. Superintendent Cotton (who made the arrests) tried Wolf Pawing and The-Man-Eating for stealing horses and sentenced each to two years in prison. The murderer of Charles Paul was not arrested. Information later pointed to an American Piegan.

Telegrams increasingly played a part in police activities. In one example in Calgary in 1885, a series of telegrams involved the case of C. Gilbert. Inspector T. Dowling responded to a telegram from Chief Constable McMillan in Brandon and arrested Gilbert for horse stealing. A return telegram informed McMillan that an arrest had been made and to come collect the prisoner. However, Gilbert escaped before McMillan reached Calgary. The case then took an unusual twist.[34]

Gilbert was really wanted for murder in Dakota, and there was a $500 reward for his arrest—a fact that McMillan, probably hoping to benefit personally, had concealed from the Calgary North-West Mounted Police. A week later C. Gilbert was recaptured and, with the facts now known (through a telegram to Dakota), charged with murder. McMillan came to Calgary for the prisoner, but Dowling and the mayor denied him access to Gilbert. McMillan then traveled to Regina where he had Superintendent Deane telegraph to Dowling to hand over the prisoner. The mayor, in turn, contacted Lieutenant Governor Dewdney on the matter. Dewdney had supported Inspector R. Deane. The mayor then telegraphed the Minister of Justice, who replied to hold the prisoner in Calgary for extradition. The final outcome of this confusing situation is poorly documented.

Thousands of telegrams sent during the 100-day North-West campaign gave the Canadian militia an overwhelming military advantage over the insurgents.[35] The need for immediate information was evident early in the insurrection when the telegraph line to Edmonton was cut. A town hall meeting agreed to dispatch a mounted courier to Calgary for news. Rider James Mowatt rode the 300 km in a remarkable thirty-six hours. Within weeks, construction was underway to build a telegraph line to Calgary, giving Edmonton a second outside contact.

Since the police post at Fort Macleod lacked a telegraphic link, the Mounted Police posted relay riders at stations every 30 km to deliver information to and from Calgary. This service proved very effective, with Fort Macleod, on one occasion, receiving a message sent from Montreal twelve hours earlier. Yet, white people at Fort Macleod were astounded that Indian prairie communication ("the moccasin telegraph") consistently relayed rebellion news faster than telegraph courier service.[36]

The 1885 military conflict spurred construction of railway and telegraph lines from Dunsmore (Medicine Hat) to Lethbridge. A police detachment protected the workers and their campsites. Alexander Galt, manager of the North-West Coal and Navigation Company, thanked Superintendent Cotton at Fort Macleod: "The presence of your men among our workmen along the line in the late rebellion inspired them with confidence without which it might have been a difficult manner to keep them at their work."[37]

The North-West Mounted Police sent key telegrams in cipher. In one example, Commissioner L. Herchmer wired Frederick White, comptroller of the Force. The first example below is in cipher, the second is decoded:

> Sergt Major Lake congo territory
> cataclysm smarken this morning
> at Golden. Have ordered Steele to
> hold kimbo as there is no
> cuckhold in District.

> Sergt Major Lake committed suicide
> by shooting this morning
> at Golden. Have ordered Steele to
> hold investigation as there is no
> coroner in District.[38]

The policeman in question, Sergt.-Major Thomas Lake, had a prominent career in the NWMP from March 1874 until his suicide on 7 July 1887.

Telephone service began in 1884 when a line connected Edmonton to St. Albert at fifteen cents a call. The following year, Lieutenant Governor Dewdney had his residence in Regina connected by telephone to the Canadian Pacific Railway station and the North-West Mounted Police barracks. That year, telephone construction began on a line connecting Regina with Moose Jaw and Wood Mountain.

In the first winter at Dufferin, two policemen, R. Wyld and C. Gilkinson, published a weekly bulletin with police news. It was not, however, until 1878 that the first newspaper appeared in the North-West Territories.

First NWMP detachment at Golden City, B.C.

L–R, standing – Cst. Peter Kerr, William Ross, Charles Knight, Cpl. W.R. McMinn, F.W. Fane(?); lying down – Cst. Albert McDonell and Richards. Ross froze to death 1 January 1885.

– GA NA 498 – 7

That year, P.G. Laurie loaded his printing press in an ox cart in Winnipeg and headed west to a place he had never seen. Seventy-two days later, he arrived in Battleford and, within months launched the *Saskatchewan Herald*.[39]

Almost every settlement had a local newspaper. Prominent spokesmen for western political affairs appeared when Frank Oliver published the *Edmonton Bulletin* and Nicholas F. Davin opened the *Regina Leader*. Davin was an outspoken opponent of prohibition and his ongoing disputes with the NWMP were legendary. At Fort Macleod, two former Mounties, Charles E.D. Dudley Wood (who was invalided after a fall from his horse) and Elias "Si" Saunders, borrowed $150 from the I.G. Baker Company to establish the *Macleod Gazette* in 1882. Until an engine was installed for their cylinder printing press, Wood and Saunders employed Blood Indians to rotate the handle of the press for the 250 weekly copies. Customers paid $3 a year, payable in advance.

T.B. Braden and printer Armour started the *Calgary Herald* in August 1883, with 100 subscribers at ten cents a weekly copy. Inspector Sam Steele, in command of the local detachment, "lent" Constable Tom Clarke, who had printing experience, to assist with the first few issues. By 1885, twelve English weekly newspapers and several French papers were providing news and information for the prairie population.

The forthright editor-owners spouted opinions that would make today's advocates of political correctness cringe. A headline in the *Regina Leader* referred to a Chinese delegation in Victoria as "Pigtail on the Pacific." The *Saskatchewan Herald* commented that an incident "gives weight to the old adage that the only good Indians are dead Indians."[40] The *Calgary Herald* labelled the presence of Indians in town "as generally a nuisance."[41] The *Regina Leader*, in its crusade against prostitution, had berated the local detachment for its inaction and named "a man who stands high in one of our religious bodies, Mr. Johnston, who has a stationer's shop, has been seen in broad daylight to visit one of these dens."[42]

The early prairie newspapers promoted regional growth, influenced public opinion, and fought negative images of the West. For historical researchers, the candid comments of the editors, even though often biased, offer penetrating insights into frontier society.

The police used the local press as a constructive communication vehicle. Tenders were posted in the paper for construction and supplies. Horses held in police possession were described with the date of sale given, and rewards were offered (like $10 for a dark bay Canadian mare that strayed from the Battleford barracks). On a personal level, Constable W. Parker placed an advertisement in the *Edmonton Bulletin* for his lost dog.

The newspapers contained frequent references to the Mounted Police. Police theatrical presentations were detailed and reviewed. The *Fort Macleod Gazette* congratulated Major Leif Crozier on his promotion: "The force is pre-eminently a Canadian one, and as such they should be given the first opportunity."[43] Some papers included a special police column, such as "Barrack Notes" in the *Calgary Herald* or "Police News" in the *Prince Albert Times*.[44] The "Police Items" column in the *Fort Macleod Gazette* on 15 July 1882 included staffing information.[45] The *Calgary Herald* kept its readers informed: "We notice an additional stripe on Corporal Wilde's sleeve raising him to the rank of sergeant while T. Gilchrist has been made a corporal. We congratulate both on their promotion."[46] The *Regina Leader* printed a career biography of Inspector Richard Deane, just appointed to the base. The paper added: "Judging by results and efficiency, Captain Deane is the most capable officer we have had in the police."[47]

Comments in the *Prince Albert Times* referring to the transfer of Corp. O'Brien must have impressed the policeman: "Many of our citizens will view his departure with regret ... he has been a useful member of our community, having turned his talents in the theatrical line to good account in helping raise money for public purposes, as well as taking a lively interest and prominent part in social matters."[48]

The press took sides on controversial NWMP matters. The *Macleod Gazette* supported policemen applying for homesteads, pointing out that they would make needed and desirable settlers. Most noteworthy was the staunch newspaper support of Comm. A.G. Irvine who was roundly ridiculed by the Eastern press for the NWMP indecisiveness at Prince Albert during the North-West Rebellion.

The press praised the local detachment for positive impressions. The *Regina Leader* commented that the police, who had nothing to do but feed themselves and grumble about that, "now march through the streets and make a fine soldierly appearance."[49] The *Prince Albert Times* complimented the police detachment: "The men looked remarkably well in their helmets, tunics and cross belts, and went through their drill with excellent precision. Altogether the detachment here is second to none in the country."[50]

On the other hand, there was quick criticism of the Force when deemed necessary. The *Manitoba Free Press* had reported that, in a case of discipline, Captain John French had strapped Constable Daley's wrist to a stirrup, breaking his collarbone. A "Sufferer," one of the men posted at Swan River, thanked the paper: "If it had not been for the public press we might very likely be worse treated than we are."[51] The *Regina Leader* condemned the vulgar behaviour of two Mounted Police while in the dining room of the Commercial Hotel that was so ribald, "that the paper would not even indicate by dashes the foul language."[52] The *Fort Macleod Gazette* disapproved NWMP management for the frequent transfers of officers.

A letter printed in the *Regina Leader* berated Superintendent Deane for confining Arthur "Blizzard" Des Barres to three days' solitary confinement with only a little food for refusing to shovel coal on a Sunday. The writer questioned Deane's "villainy" and authority since the superintendent was not a Stipendiary Magistrate or even justice of the peace, "nor has he brains enough to become one."[53] But criticism could be beneficial, according to N.F. Davin in his Regina newspaper: "The mounted police are not like the same body they were six months ago, and the improvement is striking proof of the advantage of public criticism."[54]

Transportation

In 1874, people and goods in the West moved by barge, horse, dog team, Red River cart, and lumbering bull team. Stage coach service was limited. By 1882, the I.G. Baker stage line connected Fort Benton to Fort Macleod three times each month, with connections to Calgary and Edmonton.

The steamer *Northcote's* arrival in Edmonton in the summer of 1875, opened a new entry to the region. Included in its cargo were supplies and mail for Troop "A" who were building Fort Saskatchewan. By 1883, four steamers—(*Saskatchewan, Marquis, Northwest,* and *Northcote*)— operated on the North Saskatchewan River. In the North-West Rebellion, these vessels were used for transporting troops. The *Northcote* even ineptly engaged in the attack on Batoche.

Passenger travel by steamer was expensive. Travel from Fort Garry to Edmonton cost $70 in 1880. Merchandise between the same two points in 1882 were six and a quarter cents a pound. Meals were priced at fifty cents each and the passengers paid $55 for a cabin, $35 for the open deck.

River transportation never drastically involved nor improved NWMP policing. On one trip, Commissioner A.G. Irvine traveled by steamer from Edmonton to Fort Saskatchewan and then rode horseback to Winnipeg. However, waterway travel was seasonal and often unreliable. On one trip from Medicine Hat to Batoche, sand bars stranded the *Northcote* eleven times. The completion of the transcontinental railway in November 1885 abruptly ended river transportation.

Ferry service facilitated major river crossings. The ferry fare on the Oldman River at Fort Macleod was fifty cents each way. In spring of 1883, the local police detachment operated a ferry crossing the Bow River for a few months until the C.P.R. reached Calgary.

North-West Mounted Police post at Golden City, British Columbia, 1884

The NWMP stationed men in small camps that moved with construction as it proceeded westward.

– GA NA 5656 – 4

On his march to Batoche during the North-West Rebellion, General Frederick Middleton transferred one-half of his command of 800 men across the South Saskatchewan by ferry at Clarke's Crossing, an important telegraph and land route to the northwest. This movement across took four days. The skirmish at Fish Creek one day later forced the troops on the west bank to re-cross the river to rejoin the main column. Overall, the limited ferry crossings curtailed travel and commerce in the region. Even in 1885, there was no ferry service on the Red Deer River.

Some farmers charged a toll for crossing their land. This did not go over well when Sergeant William Parker was conveying a prisoner to Stony Mountain Penitentiary. Parker's companion, Sergeant Tommy Lake, pointed his revolver at the settler's head and ordered the prisoner, who was driving the buckboard, to continue.

The Canadian Pacific Railway significantly shortened the time spent in traveling. Superintendent Crozier, visiting his brother in Toronto, told a reporter, "It took me as long to go from Macleod to Fort Shaw [Montana Territory] five years ago as from Calgary to Toronto. I was just one week on my journey to Toronto."[55] Crozier must have recalled the '74 March when the Force took almost 100 days from Toronto to reach Fort Macleod.

Whole troops now could be transported effectively. In 1885, Troop "H" traveled by rail from Regina to Lethbridge in thirty-four hours. The men loaded the horses in boxcars at 4:30 a.m. and boarded the train five hours later. They ate their lunch at Moose Jaw, supper at Swift Current, and, by 1:30 a.m., arrived at Dunmore station, near Medicine Hat. That night, the men slept in a boxcar and the officers in a freight shed. In the morning, the troops and horses were transferred to boxcars on the narrow-gauge Galt line. The policemen sat on benches in their car and kept a fire going in a stove for warmth. The train reached Lethbridge by 7:30 p.m. that night. This journey on horseback would have taken longer than a week.[56]

The railway facilitated policing tasks. Commissioner Irvine inspected NWMP posts along the rail line. Two Mounties escorted a lunatic from Frog Lake overland to Swift Current and, from there, traveled with the prisoner by train to Stony Mountain Prison. After 1882, the Saskatchewan treaty money arrived by rail at Fort Qu'Appelle and was taken by the police north to Battleford and Fort Carlton. At the outset of the North-West Rebellion, the Calgary detachment was moved by train to reinforce Swift Current. In another move, Inspector Herchmer had the cumbersome baggage for a thirty-two-man detail riding from Calgary to Blackfoot Crossing delivered by train.[57] On a personal level, William Herchmer and his wife traveled by rail from Calgary to Winnipeg to visit their moribund son who was attending college there.

Completion of the C.P.R. redirected settlement and trade. Most goods now came west by rail, ending the need for the Montana bull train service. Rail excursions were arranged to promote both tourism and investment in the region. One special train in late 1883 took 300 passengers to Calgary. West of Medicine Hat, the engineer sped the train at 100 km an hour.

One Mountie recalled both good and rough times during his year at Fort Walsh. He reflected, saying these times would never come back, "as the C.P. Railway changed everything as far as the real old West was concerned."[58] Now there were events once thought unimaginable. In August 1884, a two-day circus entertained large crowds at Fort Qu'Appelle. It was a changed land. Where yesterday a policeman, using his saddle for a pillow, listened at night to the howling of wolves—today the whistle of the locomotive at the Regina station was a welcome sound on stormy nights.

Policing the C.P.R.

A well-known anecdote recounted Corporal William Wilde toppling Chief Pia-a-pot's teepee that was blocking the railway track. According to the standard version, Wilde had given Pia-a-pot fifteen minutes to move his teepee from the track. In the interval, although warriors fired shots in the air and backed their horses against Wilde, he remained unperturbed and, once the allotted time passed, kicked the centre pole, crashing the teepee to the ground.[59] There is no official documentation of this incident and its authenticity has been questioned.[60]

There is one documented account of Pia-a-pot blocking the railway, not during construction, but in 1886. In response to a report of the chief's obstruction, Constable Phil Williams and Sergt.-Major Douglas, stationed at Maple Creek, investigated the complaint. Douglas told Pia-a-pot that he had twenty minutes to remove his teepee from the railway. Once the time passed, Douglas kicked down the centre pole and the structure collapsed. "Pia-a-pot was bluffing," recalled Williams, "but I have an idea Douglas was too, at the start."[61]

Many Indians resented the *Pewabiskmuskenew* (Iron Road) crossing the land. In January 1882, Front-man demanded provisions from a work gang cutting railway ties in the Cypress Hills. The "thoroughly frightened" men immediately left for Maple Creek to report the threat. Superintendent A. Shurtliff met Front-man and convinced him to stop interfering with railway construction. There were concerns that disgruntled Indians would sabotage the rail line and a strong deterrent was necessary. When the line was obstructed west of Moose Jaw, Sergeant Blight arrested three Indians and, on flimsy evidence, Buffalo Calf received a two-year prison sentence.

NWMP at C.P.R. Construction Camp, Winter 1882–83

"Without the assistance of the officers and men of your splendid force under
your command, it would have been impossible to have accomplished as much
work as we did. On no great work, within my knowledge, where so many men
have been employed, has such perfect order prevailed."

– William Van Horne, General Superintendent, C.P.R., *RC*, NWMP, 1882, 14
  GA NA 1315 – 1 (credit PAM)

Trouble was expected once construction reached the Blackfoot reserve
in 1883. Chief Crowfoot allegedly had sent tobacco to Pia-a-pot with a
proposal to have council discussions to oppose the rail line. The rumour that
Blackfoot tore up the tracks at night seems unlikely. Indian bitterness did
materialize, according to Surveyor C.A. Shaw, when they "defecated upon
the top of every available survey stake, which added nothing to the amenities
of the job."[62] Father Albert Lacombe acted as an intermediary, visiting the
tribe with gifts and food. He obtained the band's approval for construction.

Construction of the C.P.R. was a pivotal economic boost to the Canadian
economy. In July 1883, eighteen to twenty carloads of steel rails and up to
forty-eight carloads of railway ties were required each day. There was a daily
issue of 1,600 bushels of oats for the horses. One horse died each day and
had to be replaced. The 4,200 workers consumed an immense amount of
food. Three hundred 100-lb. sacks of flour were needed each week to make
the bread required. Everything arrived on a massive scale: sugar by the barrel
and carloads of canned peaches and canned corn. It was estimated that 1,000
head of beef would be butchered that year.[63] In 1884, in addition to the
timber needed for bridges, 400,000 railway ties were cut.

In view of the large number of construction workers, many men with alcoholic problems and an unregimented life style, the relative absence of trouble was considered remarkable. This sense of "order" was attributed to the NWMP control of alcohol. Policemen traveled with the graders and track layers and monitored the work camps. A newspaper reporter noted the men received $2.25 for ten hours of work and paid board of $4.50 a week, leaving ready cash at hand, but with no ready source of alcohol. He watched a large crowd of men around a bonfire and in their midst the red coat of the mounted policeman, there to guard against drink. A Winnipeg newspaper had quoted Doctor Brett, medical supervisor for the C.P.R., as being "surprised at the good order which prevailed among the men on construction. This is due, he thinks, to the absence of whiskey."[64]

The workmen constructed the railway tracks at a spectacular pace—some days completing 7 km of track. In 1882, from Moosomin, the first station inside the Territories, 700 km were laid and grading brought the line past Medicine Hat. The first train reached Calgary in August 1883. The pace of construction, however, was not without critics. The running of trains on Sunday led Reverend Fortin in Winnipeg to admonish: "It is better to ride to Heaven in a Red River ox cart than go to hell in a palace sleeper."[65]

Two serious labour disputes marred the railway construction. In both cases, the NWMP supported management, provided security, and, on one occasion, Constable Walter R. Johnson even operated a locomotive.

The first confrontation began on 11 December 1883, when members of the Brotherhood of Locomotive Engineers, supported by union firemen, refused to report to work, halting travel on the main line and on several branch lines in Manitoba. The grievances focused on the C.P.R.'s proposed $6 monthly reduction in the engineer's salaries and a demand that each engineer sign a statement that endorsed the company. Other factors causing dispute were simmering concerns over the long working hours, inadequate sleeping quarters at the divisional points, and the unreasonable cost of the company meals.[66]

Railway officials, fearing sabotage to company property, arranged for special trains to transport Mounted Police to trouble spots at Broadview and Moose Jaw. At Moose Jaw, 400 striking workmen appeared intent on stopping what they thought was a mail train. Sergeant Frank Fitzpatrick recorded: "Their astonishment was unbounded when they saw our men emerge with revolvers and Winchesters, ready for business."[67] The two officers and thirty-five Mounties quickly cleared the C.P.R. grounds.

Superintendent William Herchmer took nineteen men with him by train to Broadview. He reported:

On arrival there, I took charge of all railway property. There was a good deal of excitement among the strikers, and I have no hesitation in saying that if it had not been for our men there would have been serious trouble ... beside guarding the roundhouse, every engine which left the yard was guarded.[68]

As a security measure during the strike, constables took charge of the mail on the railway trains.

When the negotiations between the workers and management became deadlocked, railway General Manager William Van Horne hired twenty-two replacement workers (in the union's words "strikebreakers") from Chicago. Other than scattered incidents of vandalism, within one week the strike ended and, on 19 December 1883, union leader James Slavin signed the Canadian Pacific Railway document.

C.P.R. management appreciated the NWMP support during the strike. Superintendent J. M. Egan wrote to Commissioner Irvine: "The service of your men during the recent trouble among a certain class of our employees, prevented destruction of property, and preserved obedience to law and order in a manner highly commendable."[69] The *Regina Leader* also agreed: "The mounted police have progressed in efficiency, and on several occasions ... especially in connection with the late railway strike ... have shown how admirably adapted they are to meet the needs of the country in the position of the North-West."[70]

A second serious labour dispute arose in the winter of 1884–85. In this situation Inspector Samuel Steele policed the railway construction between Revelstoke and Laggan (now Lake Louise). His entire command held only twenty-five men with thirteen horses, posted at a number of camps.[71]

It was a difficult assignment with avalanche dangers, two murders to solve, and no prohibition restrictions in British Columbia. Near the work camps, gamblers and toughs built rudimentary log saloons, dance-halls, and disorderly houses to attract the workforce. One ongoing problem was toughs "rolling" drunken workers. To prevent this crime, Steele had patrols place drunken men in crowded police cells. In the morning, Steele would often adjudicate up to thirty men.

In March 1885, 1,200 navvies struck over unpaid wages. Steele met a delegation of workers and counselled patience, but affirmed that he would uphold the law. Several hundred workers accepted Sam Steele's advice and returned to their camps but about 700 men remained at Beaver River where they obstructed construction and incited other men to quit working. Steele had only eight policemen in his camp.

Sam Steele and detachment at Beavermouth, B.C.

"We had a great deal of trouble with gamblers and toughs of every description, who had concentrated first at Donald, and had built log-houses, saloons and dens of all sorts."

– Steele, *Forty Years in Canada*, 194
GA NA 294 – 1

When Constables Pete Kerr and Oscar Dubreuil attempted to arrest sub-contractor Hughie Behan for being drunk and disorderly, a boisterous mob forced the two Mounties to release Behan. Sergeant Bill Fury and two constables returned and located Behan (who was alleged to have killed three men the previous winter in Arkansas) drinking in a makeshift building. They escorted Behan outside, but a mob of some 200 men forced them to release their captive and return to the police post. Fury threatened to shoot anyone who crossed over the footbridge leading to the police cabin. This warning intimidated the strikers from further unruliness.

Fury, his face bleeding and his tunic torn, returned to the police post for instructions. Inspector Sam Steele, sick with mountain fever (typhoid), ordered Fury to take four armed men to arrest Behan and, if necessary, shoot anyone who interfered with their assignment. Fury led constables F. W. Fane, Thomas Craig, and John Walters to the ramshackle settlement. The noise of a shot aroused Steele from his bed. He saw constables Craig and

Walters dragging one man, shot in the shoulder, across the footbridge while Fane and Fury pointed their revolvers at 500 strikers, led by a woman dressed "in scarlet" who was inciting the mob to free the wounded Behan. Steele grabbed a rifle from Constable Oscar Dubreuil and, with George H. Johnson, a Justice of the Peace, ran to the footbridge where he addressed the mob in words, Magistrate Johnson recounted, "for strength of diction, I have rarely heard surpassed."[72] While he stood holding a copy of the *Riot Act*, Johnson described the wild scene:

> Hold on for God's sake, Sam [Steele], till I read the Riot Act. Although the crowd looked very ugly no one had the temerity to take a chance on [William] Fury's deadly revolver, and I read the proclamation. I hope the crowd heard it, I know I didn't. This was, however, quickly remedied by the worthy County Down man who spoke thusly—'now min, ye have heard what the magistrate has read, and if there are twelve of you found together, after this, ye are able to be fired upon and may God have mercy on yer sowls.'[73]

In the melee, Walters knocked the prisoner senseless. The strikers, though verbally abusive, obeyed Steele's threat to shoot anyone who stepped on the footbridge. The critical moment passed. Behan was carried to the police cabin and the "woman in scarlet" arrested. That night, a train took the two prisoners 100 km east and, in the morning the detachment arrested other ringleaders without incident. Hughie Behan and several leading agitators were given $100 fines or six months' imprisonment with hard labour.

On April 7, payment of the delayed wages eased the discord. Steele, with some of his men, then left for Calgary where he organized a mounted troop—Steele's Scouts—for military service in the North-West Rebellion.

NOTES

1. *CH*, 9 July 1884. The *CN*, 8 July 1884, suggested that the victim, identified as Joseph Mozinsky, committed suicide by throwing himself under the boxcar's wheels.

2. *Canada, Census of the Three Provisional Districts of the North-West Territories, 1884–1885* (Ottawa: Maclean Roger, 1886).

3. Birthplace: NWT 25,619; Canada 14,218; British Isles 7,158; United States 1,007, Germany 124; Scandinavia 111; Russia/Poland 97; France 93. Not given 385.

4. The Census statistics in *Ages of the People* do not identify race and are incomplete, giving the ages only for two-thirds of the population (31,990 out of 48,362). The unknown numbers most likely are Indian populations.

5. Ibid. A White population in Manitoba that numbered 95,000 made Louis Riel's vision of a military victory in 1885 fanciful.

6. *WDT*, 27 September 1882.

7. *RC*, NWMP, 1879, 25.

8. *MG*, 27 September 1879.

9. D.H. Breen, "The Mounted Police and the Ranching Frontier," Hugh A. Dempsey, *Men in Scarlet* (McClelland and Stewart West, Calgary), 1974.

10. *WDT*, 12 December 1882. *MFP*, 14 July 1883.

11. *WDT*, 25 July 1883.

12. *HWH*, 3 August 1882.

13. *FBR*, 20 July 1882.

14. *FBRP*, 20 February 1884.

15. *FMG*, 2 January 1885.

16. *EB*, 1 November 1884. Nor did Fort Macleod compare favourably with a Chinese mud village that was built with regular streets.

17. Muskrat pelts (144,000) were by far the most traded fur. Others furs included: mink (16,000), skunk (7,900), beaver (5,800), deer/antelope/moose (5,300), fox (4,940), lynx (2,270), bear (810), and wolf (600).

18. Other leading occupations in the census were servants (371), teamsters/freighters (309), clergymen (108), butchers (36), lawyers (36), bakers (24), and ranchers (16).

19. This act replaced the territorial government of 1872, which had a Lieutenant Governor (also serving Manitoba) and an appointed council of eleven members.

20. Receipts included: Notary public fees – $42, Fines under ordinances – $1,212, Ferry licences – $416, Billiard licences – $846, Marriage licences – $158. Expenditures included: W.G. Scott, (registering marriage certificates) – $20, A. Spoat, (registering marriage certificates) – $29, W.C.G. Montgomery, (acting orderly at session of council) – $5.

21. Black, *History of Saskatchewan and the North West Territories*, 315.

22. Klaus, "Fort Livingstone," 107–108.

23. *CN*, 18 November 1884. The incident is also outlined in Chapter 11.

24. *GA*, S.J. Clarke, M 228.

25. *CT*, 16 December 1885.

26. *RL*, 16 June 1885.

27. *RL*, 12 July 1883. *MFP*, 20 October 1880, gives settler complaints on martial law. Regional grievances against the NWMP are found in *MFP* 20 August 1880; 10 September 1883; 19 September 1883. Also *Calgary Tribune*, 16 December 1885. The Oxarart case in December 1884 involved custom charges and stolen horses.

28. During the North-West Rebellion, the Canadian Militia bitterly complained about price-gouging by Alberta merchants. See Jack F. Dunn, "Ripping off the Soldiers in Alberta," *AH*, XLI, No. 2, 12–15.

29. *FMG*, 24 November 1885; for Battleford game, see *WDT*, 7 July 1881. Also *Calgary Nor'wester*, 17 June 1884.

30. *SH*, 9 June 1883. Hay – $10 a ton (Mr. Prince), Oats – $0.90 bu., Potatoes – $0.57 bu. (MacFarland Bros), Beef – $0.18 lb. (Wyld and Beurke), Cordwood – $3.50 a cord (Jos. Ducharme), Bran – $3.50 per 100 lbs. (HBC). Other examples are *EB*, 19 May 1883 and 10 October 1885.

31. *CT*, 16 December 1885. *EB*, 14 October 1882, lauded the news that a sixteen-man detachment would be established in the town. Prince Albert petitioned Ottawa not to move the local detachment. *TDM*, 10 November 1881.

32. *GA*, Frederick Bagley, M 43.

33. Hawkes, *The Story of Saskatchewan and its People*, vol. 2, 1012–13.

34. *CH*, 1 July 1885.

35. D.P. Morton and R.H. Roy, eds., *Telegrams of the North-West Campaign, 1885* (Toronto: The Champlain Society, 1972).

36. Jack F. Dunn, "The Moccasin Telegraph during the North-West Rebellion," *AH*, XLV, No. 2, 9–14.

37. F.M. Kerr, "Steel Rails and Scarlet Tunics," *RCMP Q*, XXX, No. 4, 26. The work was completed by August.

38. *NAC*, T.H. Lake, f.13.

39. There was no Territorial press until the publication of the *Saskatchewan Herald* in 1878. Valuable information on the early NWMP was provided by correspondents posted in Fort Macleod and Fort Walsh by newspapers in Helena and Fort Benton.

40. *SH*, 23 April 1885.

41. *CH*, 5 March 1885. The *EB*, 27 October 1883 informs that Rosenthal, a Jew, has been caught selling whiskey.

42. *RL*, 17 May 1883.

43. *FMG*, 7 November 1884.

44. *PAT*, 13 February 1885, items under "Police News" included: "Finger posts have been erected by the Police on different trails in this district, which have proved a great boon to the travelling public. We understand it was the idea of Sergt.-Major Dann", "Const. T.C. Craigie met with a severe accident, a hay fork having been run through his foot", and "Const. C.E. Helmer was kicked on the head by a horse and is confined to his room." The *CH*, under *Barrack Notes*, 19 October 1883, has nine items related to the local detachment.

45. *FMG*, 15 July 1882. One example: "Staff-Sergt. Horner arrived in charge of a four horse team. We hope that the sergeant will be stationed at Macleod." For promotions and transfers, see *EB*, 2 February 1882, *RL*, 26 July 1884, *FMG*, 14 August 1882.

46. *CH*, 6 August 1884.

47. *RL,* 15 October 1885. Also *RL,* 26 July 1883.

48. *PAT,* 25 July 1884. Also *MFP,* 7 August 1884; *RL,* 26 July 1883, with respect to Corporal Norris, "if ever a man deserves a promotion it is he."

49. *RL,* 18 October 1883. Also *RL,* 25 October 1883.

50. *PAT,* 26 September 1884.

51. *MFP,* 6 November 1875.

52. *RL,* 23 August 1883.

53. *RL,* 15 October 1885. Arthur Des Barres was serving five months' imprisonment for illegally importing liquor into the North-West Territories.

54. *RL,* 18 October 1883. Also *RL,* 25 October 1883.

55. *TM,* 2 February 1884. In 1884, it took Sandford Fleming fifty-six hours by train to reach the Rocky Mountains from Winnipeg; eleven years earlier, on his trip across the continent, he had taken thirty-six days to travel this distance.

56. *GA,* Sanders Diary, M 1093 f. 38.

57. *PAT,* 28 August 1885.

58. *NAC,* William McQuarrie, f. 724.

59. This version is given in A.L. Haydon, *The Riders of the Plains* (Edmonton: Hurtig, 1971), 105–6; R.C. Fetherstonhauge, *The Royal Canadian Mounted Police* (New York: Carrick & Evans, 1938), 50–51; R.G. MacBeth, *Policing the Plains* (Toronto: Holder and Stoughton, 1921), 96–97, *EJ,* 11 April 1925; John Peter Turner, *The North West Mounted Police,* 11 (Ottawa: King's Printer, 1950), 5–6; Pierre Burton, *The Last Spike* (Toronto: McClelland and Stewart, 1971), 234.

60. David Lee, "Piapot: Man and Myth," *Canadian Plains Studies,* XVII, No. 2, 251–62.

61. *GA,* DeGear Jessie, M 314, f. 27. The *EJ,* 11 April 1925, stated that it was Sergeant Davis, west of Maple Creek in 1882, who gave the Indians ten minutes and then kicked the pole down.

62. Raymond Hull, ed., *Charles Shaw: Tales of a Pioneer Surveyor* (Don Mills, Ontario, Longmans, 1970), 105.

63. *WDT,* 20 July 1883.

64. *MFP,* 18 July 1884.

65. *FBRP,* 21 February 1883.

66. *WDT,* 11 December 1883.

67. Fitzpatrick, *Sergeant 331,* 111.

68. *RC,* NWMP, 1883, 11.

69. *RC,* NWMP, 1883, 14. Irvine added: "I shall only add that prompt and I trust effectual, quelling of what at one time appeared to be a universal railway strike is ... a matter of utmost congratulations."

70. *RL,* 3 January 1884.

71. Golden City, First Crossing of the Columbia, Beaver Crossing, Summit of the Selkirks, Second Crossing of the Columbia (Revelstoke), and Third Siding.

72. *CH,* 4 July 1925. A companion described Steele as "an officer of magnificent physique, mounted on a steed worthy of the rider in appearance ... he was a rigid disciplinarian, but a lovable and fearless commander, whom the men would have followed anywhere. " Fitzpatrick, *Sergeant 331,* 14–15.

73. Ibid.

19

THE VICE-REGAL
TOURS

Escort for the Governor General at Cluny, 1885

"We were astonished and delighted at the manner in which you have performed your arduous duties and at your great efficiency your Force is often spoken of in Canada as one which Canada is justly proud."

– Ian Campbell, Marquis of Lorne, Governor General, *Calgary Herald*, 4 July 1925
  RCMP Historical Collections Unit, "Depot" Division, Regina, SK.: 1935. 29.10.

IN THE 1880S, TOURS OF THE NORTH-WEST Territories were made by two Canadian Governor Generals. The first tour in 1881 promoted opportunities for economic and regional growth; the second tour in 1885 was a response to the North-West Rebellion and the trials now underway. Different modes of transportation used reflected the incredible changes occurring in the region. In 1881, the Marquis (or Marquess) of Lorne covered a wide loop of the open prairies by stage coach. Only four years later, Lord Lansdowne primarily used rail travel on his excursion through the western land.

Marquis of Lorne: Tour of 1881

The region bubbled with excitement in 1881 with word that none other than the Governor General of Canada, Ian Campbell, Marquis of Lorne and son-in-law of Queen Victoria, planned a late summer tour of the North-West Territories.[1] The scheduled travel route was from Fort Ellice to Battleford, then southwest (with stops at Blackfoot Crossing, Calgary, and Fort Macleod) to Fort Shaw, Montana Territory. From this American military post, the Governor General would continue south to make his American railway connections for Winnipeg while the NWMP escort returned to Canada. Everyone eagerly anticipated the coming event.

In June of 1881, the NWMP Comptroller Frederick White contacted Commissioner A.G. Irvine to organize the taxing logistics of the 2,000 km excursion. An uppermost concern was the sole comfort of His Excellency. Difficulties had to be minimized. A water wagon was constructed: at no time would His Excellency have to drink slough water. And, throughout his journey in this isolated region, he would be updated on world news. When the entourage arrived at Calgary, for example, the mail was waiting for him, delivered by a young constable who had ridden a remarkable 175 km in twelve hours. One stipulation on the journey remained in effect: the Governor General's party had to adhere to the Territorial prohibition law. A reporter observed: "The Governor General cannot drink his own glass of claret, without having obtained the Lieutenant Governor's permission."[2]

Fort Qu'Appelle was the prairie organizational point for the grand tour. Inspector Percy Neale purchased thirty-four horses in Winnipeg, three army ambulances at St. Paul, Minnesota, and hired local men to train the horses for pulling wagons. At key points, oats had to be cached and replacement horses waiting for the cavalcade. In this regard, 3,600 lbs. of oats (1,640 kg) was delivered to Fort Calgary. The escort had to be readied. Superintendent W. Herchmer arrived with seven men from Battleford, and Sergt.-Major Thomas Lake brought twenty-two Mounties and three wagons from Fort Walsh. When this troop returned to Fort Walsh two months later, the men had ridden an amazing 3,500 km.

Problems arose from the beginning. A thunderstorm stampeded the horses, necessitating the purchase of fifteen replacements. The oats to be stored at Fort Carlton were sent to Fort Battleford. The contact point was then changed. After William Herchmer's forty-man column left Fort Qu'Appelle to greet the Governor General on his arrival by steamer at Fort Ellice, a messenger overtook the troop with revised orders to meet the vice-regal party at End of Track, located at that time west of Portage la Prairie, an added 200-km ride.

The vice-regal party arrived by train at End of Track on 8 August 1881.[3] After consultations between Herchmer and F. DeWinton (the military secretary), it was agreed that, as planned, the regal party would travel by steamer up the Assiniboine River to Fort Ellice while Herchmer's troops, with ninety-six horses, twenty-one tents, seventeen vehicles, and gifts for the Indians, would return to Fort Ellice, hopefully in time to greet the Governor General.

Herchmer was at the landing dock when the steamer arrived. It was an impressive moment. One correspondent wrote: "The sight of the police horses in prime condition, bright sunshine glinted on horses, the bright scarlet tunics of the police against green prairie scene was a striking and beautiful one."[4] After official greetings, the thirty-six-year-old Governor General visited the Hudson's Bay post (Fort Ellice) where, on August 13, he held a council and gave gifts to the attending Indians.

The tour was widely publicized by five newspaper correspondents who accompanied the fifty-day vice-regal journey.[5] Sydney Hall of the *London Graphic* and the Marquis of Lorne himself drew illustrations of the journey for publication. The correspondents related to their readership in Canada and Great Britain the vastness of the land, the indescribable beauty of the setting sun on the distant Rocky Mountains, the fury of thunderstorms, the scattered buffalo bones lying about, wolves howling outside the tents, and two lonely female homesteaders.

James MacGregor thought there was "nothing is more characteristic of these immense rolling plains than their utter solitariness, their almost absence of life, except near water, even of bird and insect life. The silence and loneliness of the prairie is awful."[6] Well, what could one expect in a land where, one settler told the reporters, there are four months of mosquitoes and eight months of winter?

The reporters paid extra attention to the Indians and the police—often with contrasting impressions. While they highlighted "colourful" Indian names, the frenzied Indian sham battles at Blackfoot Crossing and Fort Macleod, and the Indian explanations of the origin of place names such as Sounding Lake, too often, the Indians were denigrated as "little more than grownup children."[7] Correspondent M. Austin wrote on this topic in the *London Times*:

It is certainly disenchanting to find the Indian dressing as no decent scarecrow would ever voluntarily submit to be dressed, and it is positively painful to find that he never opens his mouth except to beg that something may be put into it.[8]

Native language "eloquence," he continued, "was little more than incessant begging and whining whenever a Government official appears in sight."[9]

The Mounted Police were praised and admired. They had, in the view of correspondents, secured the confidence and goodwill of the Indians:

The red men are not only afraid to come into forcible contact with the red-coats, but they feel that their best interest lies in assisting the police in their discharge of their duties. They have confidence in the justice of the administration of the police and feel that the Indian rights will be protected as well as those of the white men.[10]

In the event of trouble, the police acted quickly and forcefully: "If a crime was committed out on the prairie, a handful of mounted police seized the criminal, a chief it may be, surrounded by his tribe, and carry him off to the nearest fort as coolly as a policeman would take up a pickpocket in Cheapside."[11]

Throughout the five weeks of travel, there was unqualified admiration of the police escort. The *Toronto Mail* quoted one of the Governor General's party professing the police "combine the discipline of the regular soldiers with the handiness of sailors."[12] Reporter Austin of the *Times* described "our escort of mounted police as always cheery, most willing, hard-working fellows."[13] The daily travel, management of horses, and the campsite duties were very demanding and, at times, unsafe. Constable Lemay's crushed finger had to be amputated. An eastern paper summarized the overall opinion: "The conduct and exertions of the mounted police escorts and drivers, under Lieut.-Col. Herchmer, have been beyond praise."[14]

The first leg took the tour west from Fort Ellice to Fort Qu'Appelle. The daily routine throughout the prairie journey followed a set pattern. Each morning, reveille sounded at 3:30 a.m. and the horses were watered, groomed, and harnessed. Tents were taken down and the baggage loaded preparatory to the 6 a.m. start. Usually, there were three stops—a halt by 10 a.m. for breakfast, a stop at 2 p.m. for lunch, and the final stop for supper and camp in the early evening. At night, guards were posted in four hour shifts. Two sentries guarded the Governor General's tent. On an average day the entourage traveled 40 km.

View of Blackfoot Crossing, Marquis of Lorne Sketch, 1881

One of the many sketches the Governor General drew while on his 1881 excursion across the western plains.

– GA NA 1269 – 12

On August, 19 the cavalcade of forty-six men with eighty-four horses left Fort Qu'Appelle for Battleford. A scow ferried the men, supplies, and nineteen wagons across the South Saskatchewan River while the horses were forced to swim the waterway. The current swept many of the animals downriver, making the crossing take five hours. At Fort Carlton, located on the south bank of the North Saskatchewan River 30 km north, the party separated, with the Mounted Police riding westward to Battleford while the Governor General's entourage boarded the steamer *Northcote* for a downriver trip to Prince Albert. After a brief visit, the delegation traveled upstream on the steamer *Lily* to rejoin Inspector Herchmer's mounted troop and wagons at Battleford, the Territorial capital.

The vice-regal party reached Battleford on August 30, one day after Herchmer's arrival. The town had attached banners of welcome and a large portrait of Queen Victoria to an arch made of grain sheaves. With what appeared to be the entire town on hand and before a police honour guard, Lieutenant Governor David Laird greeted their guests, followed by school children singing "God Save the Queen." A dance by Stoney Indians added to the ceremonies.

In one of his official duties during the three-day stay, the Governor General inspected the police barracks where, to his surprise, he encountered his cousin, Corporal J. MacNeil. As a gift to the detachment, Lord Lorne presented the non-commissioned officers with two pounds of tobacco and the constables with one pound.

From Battleford, a seventy-two-man column including Herchmer with forty-five Mounties, eighty-two horses, twenty-one wagons, nineteen tents, and a boat headed southwest for Calgary. Scouts Johnny Longmore (Johnny Saskatchewan), Louis Laronde, and Cree Chief Poundmaker were each paid $1 a day to guide the column.

Two spellbinding incidents highlighted the 500-km trek. First, there was the now-rare sight of a small herd of ten buffalo near the Red Deer River. A spectacular chase followed where three animals were killed.[15] Reporters watched in astonishment when Poundmaker cut a kidney from one of the slain animals and ate it raw, "slicing it with his knife as a schoolboy slices an apple."[16] Second, a huge gathering of 2,500 Blackfoot and Sarcee Indians was waiting at Blackfoot Crossing on the Bow River, where Treaty 7 had been signed four years earlier. To celebrate the Governor General's arrival, the Indians performed a wild sham battle featuring adroit horsemanship and reckless gunfire.

While at Blackfoot Crossing, Lord Lorne and his staff, dressed in official uniforms and with a NWMP guard of honour standing at hand, heard leading chiefs appeal for aid. One chief, Loud Voice, gave an hour-and-a-half speech which scout Jerry Potts translated: "he say grub."[17]

Commissioner A.G. Irvine met the oncoming official party with fresh horses and a supply of oats to help facilitate their journey on to Calgary. On September 12, at Calgary, rested horses, a supply of oats, and mail awaited them. During his three-day stay, Lord Lorne enjoyed the excellent fishing. A distant mountain was named in his honour, but the place name was never given permanent status.

A large group of settlers and Indians eagerly awaited the arrival of His Excellency at Fort Macleod. Mounted Policemen (including seventeen men from Fort Walsh to bolster the reception) lined the road from the Oldman River Crossing to the post on an island. In the distance, two 9-pr. guns boomed a salute. An honour guard under Inspector Francis Dickens stood at the entrance of the fort.

The arrival of Canada's Head of State was a memorable day for the region. Every effort was made to please the visitors. Part of the pageantry highlighted hundreds of Indian horsemen demonstrating yet another breathtaking sham battle which was followed by a powwow.[18]

At this stop, the post's Commander, L. Crozier, replaced Superintendent William Herchmer as the NWMP liaison. In a letter to Herchmer, His Excellency praised the admirable way the police had performed their duties in the seven-week journey across the plains. It was noted that, on this arduous journey, only two horses had died.

The Governor General's arrival proved timely for five inmates held in the barrack jail. In response to a petition from the Rev. Samuel Trivett, Lord Lorne exercised Royal Clemency by pardoning the four Mounted Policemen imprisoned four months earlier for desertion and one Indian charged with stealing horses.[19] A second Indian, Starchild, awaiting trial for the murder of Const. Marmaduke Graburn, remained in custody.

To date, the tour had proceeded remarkably well, but now a possible problem arose. Jerry Potts, the police scout, was drunk (apparently nothing unusual) and he had been threatening to settle a score with an Indian. The detachment had a solution: scout Potts was bound, placed in a wagon box, and left for the night.

Superintendent Crozier guided the vice-regal party to the North-West Mounted Police horse ranch at Pincher Creek, 50 km directly west. At the same time, contact was made with Fort Shaw, Montana Territory, 250 km south, to expect the coming entourage.

Americans at Fort Shaw warmly welcomed the Canadian Governor General. Constable J.R. Royce recalled that, "as we came close to the fort, the band marched out, played our national anthem, "Rule Britannia," and other British airs, which greatly pleased the marquis and the men."[20] A large arch decorated the main gate and the men could hear the beginning of a seventeen-gun salute. Once the troop reached the fort's square, the band began playing "God Save the Queen." Frances Roe, an American officer's wife, observed that "instantly every head of Englishmen and Canadian was uncovered."[21] In the evening, the post's commander, Colonel J. Kent, hosted a superb banquet for the Canadian visitors.

On the following morning, Governor General Lorne departed with an American cavalry escort for Helena. Before leaving, he shook hands with each policeman and then addressed the North-West Mounted Police escort, saying that he, along with his staff, "were astonished and delighted at the manner in which you have performed your arduous duties and at your great efficiency ... your Force is often spoken of in Canada as one which Canada is justly proud."[22]

The police escort enjoyed a carefree three-day stay at Fort Shaw where, unlike the Canadian posts, the army canteen supplied inexpensive beer and cigars. The reception possibly was too good. When the troop returned

Officers and Escort to the Governor General at Regina, 1885

L–R, front row – Insp. Howe, Insp. Irwin, Insp. Gilpin-Brown, Comm. Irvine, Insp. Cartwright, Surgeon G.B. Bell; sitting in carriage – the Governor General and Inspector Baker (seated behind); on horseback – Sergt.-Major Hooper (far right); back row – Mounted Police escorts
★ J.H. McIllree's team of greys are pulling carriage

– RCMP Historical Collections Unit, "Depot" Division, Regina, SK.: 1935.29.8

to Canada, two men had deserted.[23] In his report, Superintendent Leif Crozier stated that the troop remained at Fort Shaw for two days after Lord Lorne's departure to purchase some horses. Francis Roe suggested otherwise: "I suspect that is because their commander is having such a pleasant time driving and dining with his hostess, who is one of our most lovely and fascinating women."[24]

Mounties could not help but contrast the superior accommodations they had experienced at the American base with their shabby posts. In addition to beer, the barracks at Fort Shaw had verandahs, shade trees, and irrigation ditches. To one Mountie, "It looked like the acme of comfort as compared to the log shacks and mud roofs we were accustomed to."[25] Both the Governor General and the press reporters had commented on the rudimentary accommodations and the extraordinarily difficult duties that the Mounted Police undertook. One newspaper reporter wrote: "They are ludicrously underhanded for the ground they have to cover and the number of Indians and white men, often more unmanageable than the Indians, whom they are expected to keep in order."[26]

On his return to Winnipeg, at a civic reception being held in his honour, Lord Lorne praised the North-West Mounted Police as "a corps of whose services it would be impossible to speak too highly." His speech continued:

A mere handful in that vast wilderness, they have at all times shown themselves ready to go anywhere and do anything. They have often had to act on occasions demanding the combined individual pluck and prudence rarely to be found amongst any soldiery, and there has not be a single case in which any member of the force has lost his temper under trying circumstances, or has not fulfilled his mission as a guardian of the peace ... I am glad of this opportunity to name these men as well worthy of Canada's regard, as sons who have well maintained her name and fame.[27]

In the words of Lord Lorne, the North-West Mounted Police were "as fine a troop as he ever saw."[28]

Marquis of Lansdowne: Tour of 1885

In September 1885, Henry Petty-Fitzmaurice, 5th Marquis of Lansdowne and fifth Governor General of Canada from 1883 to 1888, undertook the second official tour of the North-West Territories. The purpose of this expedition related to the North-West Rebellion and the trials that

NWMP Honour Guard at Lethbridge, 1885

"Their duty is always performed cheerfully and vigorously and it is quite safe to say that there are no other troops in the world who could do the same amount or variety of work as that done by the police."

– *Fort Macleod Gazette*, 29 September 1885
PAA A-11294

were underway against the accused. The NWMP played a prominent role in the guidance and safety of the tour. Rail travel made the logistics for the police easier than in 1881. The one-week tour (compared with the fifty-two days taken by Lord Lorne) and the absence of traveling news correspondents meant this visit received far less publicity than the earlier tour.

The Landsdowne party arrived in Winnipeg by rail and, after several side excursions in Manitoba, entered the Territories on a special train with an engine and six cars, one of which held the North-West Mounted Police escort under Inspector Montague White-Fraser. Also on board was Lord Melgund, who had served in the recent North-West Rebellion as General Middleton's Chief of Staff. Melgund (as Lord Minto) later served as Canada's Governor General from 1898 to 1904.

At Indian Head, Sergeant Thomas Kempston, with sixteen Mounties, escorted Lord Landsdowne north to Fort Qu'Appelle. Here they visited the police post and Catholic Mission, where children entertained them with songs. By the time they returned to the train, the party had ridden a total of 70 km that day.

On September 23, Edgar Dewdney, Lieutenant Governor of the NWT, met the train in Regina. The visit of the Governor General was of immense importance and a number of committees had worked diligently to arrange the reception, banquet, program of activities, and accommodation.[29] Fifty Mounties, from Fort Qu'Appelle, the police guard, and men from the local North-West Mounted Police headquarters were all part of the ceremonies. The small town was crammed with excited citizens and area settlers who were not going to forego this spectacle. An upscale hotel that had opened several days earlier was suitably named the Landsdowne.

At Dunsmore (near Medicine Hat), His Excellency switched from the main C.P.R. line to a train on the newly constructed rail line to Lethbridge, a narrow-gauged track referred to as the "Turkey Trail." At the same time, his private rail coach was taken to Calgary.

An enthusiastic crowd had assembled at the Lethbridge station platform, now covered with carpet for the occasion, to greet the Governor General. Forming the receiving line were Mounties from Fort Macleod and the distant Fort Qu'Appelle. It was no doubt a red letter day as it marked both the arrival of Canada's Head of State and the official grand opening of the new railway link.[30] Again there were official greetings, responses, tours, and an evening banquet.

The next morning, the vice-regal party rode to Fort Macleod. On their way, just east of Kipp (the former whiskey post), cowboys entertained the visitors with a dazzling exhibition of roping, branding, and herding a great herd of 4,000 cattle. The picturesque scene—the bellowing mass of cattle, the mountain backdrop, and the cowboy expertise—was described as a sight that could be witnessed in no other part of the world. Later that day, on the Blood Reserve, Indians greeted the party enthusiastically. Lord Landsdowne gave gifts to prominent Indians and applauded the band's loyalty and duty to the Queen during the recent rebellion. Red Crow led a number of the Indian speakers voicing their concerns over inadequate food rations.

The ride to Calgary took two days. Even though the party's arrival was hours later than expected, anticipation was such that "every eye remained fixed on the Macleod Trail."[31] Finally, at 7 p.m., Lord Landsdowne, who was now accompanied by Lord Melgund and Superintendent Cotton, led the delegation into the town. They were met by a group of enthusiastic citizens, a NWMP guard of honour, and a brass band. After a welcome from Mayor George Murdoch and the conventional response, His Excellency retired to his private rail car.

The following day, Lord Lansdowne and his police escort traveled by train east to Cluny. A 5-km ride south took the mounted party to Chief Crowfoot's camp where Indians displayed a rousing welcome of gunfire, making the site look like a terrible battlefield. The Governor General praised the Blackfoot for remaining neutral during the recent rebellion and gave gifts to the leading chiefs. Crowfoot was anxious to know what the government intended to do with Louis Riel.

At four o'clock in the afternoon, Lord Landsdowne returned to Calgary. In the two-hour stop before the train left for Banff, His Excellency visited the Roman Catholic mission and, prior to departing, he presented each member of the North-West Mounted Police escort on the journey from Lethbridge with a meerschaum pipe and gold sleeve links.

The vice-regal train continued westward to End of the Track, which was now in the Purcell Range, British Columbia. Lord Landsdowne and his staff then traveled by boat and horseback to Vancouver and Victoria.

The vice-regal tours gathered information and elevated interest in this empty land. Everyone recognized the potential of the region. Positive reports on the NWMP helped counter both the unpopular authoritarian image held by many settlers and the tarnished military reputation of the Force in the North-West Rebellion. The *Fort Macleod Gazette* praised the NWMP: "It is quite safe to say that there are no other troops in the world who could do the same amount and variety of work as that done by the police."[32]

NOTES

1. Governor General from 25 November 1878 to 21 October 1883.

2. *London Times*, 1 November 1881.

3. Members of the regal party included the Governor General, John Douglas Sutherland "Ian" Campbell, Assistant Indian Commissioner Elliot Galt, Chaplain Dr. James MacGregor, Surgeon Dr. Sewell, Military Secretary F. DeWinton, Aides-de-Camp Major Chater, Captain Bagot, Captain Percival, Private Secretary Mr. Campbell, a French chef, and five servants. The Marquis' wife, Princess Louise, Queen Victoria's daughter, was visiting England at this date. Rumours held that their marriage was having difficulties because of Lord Lorne's alleged homosexuality. DeWinton, Alberta is named after the Military Secretary.

4. Williams, *Manitoba and the Northwest*, 46.

5. Sydney Hall, artist (*London Graphic*); W.H. Williams (*Toronto Globe*); James MacGregor (*Edinburgh Courant and Edinburgh Scotsman*); M. Austin (*London Times*); C.H. Roche (*London Telegraph*).

6. James MacGregor, "Canada and the North-West as an Emigration Field," *The Contemporary Review*, XLII, August, 1882, 229. Also, James G. MacGregor, "Lord Lorne in Alberta," *AHR*, XII, No. 1, 1-14.

7. *London Times*, 21 October 1881.

8. Ibid.

9. Ibid.

10. Williams, *Manitoba and the Northwest*, 135.

11. *London Times*, 21 October 1881.

12. *TM*, 4 November 1881.

13. *FMG*, 2 November 1881.

14. *TDM*, 3 October 1881.

15. *London Times*, 9 November 1882.

16. Ibid., 1 November 1882.

17. Fitzpatrick, *Sergeant 331*, 78.

18. MacGregor, "Lord Lorne in Alberta," 13.

19. The NWMP prisoners were: R.M. Morton, G.J. Convery, George Scott, and W.A. Cooper. The Sarcee Indian was named Travel Out.

20. *WDT*, 10 October 1881.

21. Frances Roe, *Army Letters from an Officer's Wife* (New York and London: D. Appleton, 1909), 280. She thought the Mounted Police were gorgeously dressed with their jaunty, side-tilted caps, but were mounted on small, inferior horses.

22. *CH*, 4 July 1925.

23. The two deserters were Leonard Bailey and Alexander Duffy. Bailey had served only 116 days in the NWMP. His kit was auctioned and, with his forthcoming pay, a total of $31.75 was forwarded to the Receiver General of Canada. Bailey had a wife in Ontario. Duffy had served in the NWMP for 15 months. He previously was a member of the Irish Constabulary.

24. Roe, *Army Letters from an Officer's Wife*, 283.

25. Guernsey, "Wheels, Wagons, Whitewater 1," *SG*, Tenth Annual, 21.

26. *London Times,* 21 October 1881.

27. The Dominion Annual Register and Review, 1880-1881 (Montreal: John Lovell, 1882), 461.

28. *WDT*, 17 November 1881. *TG*, 19 December 1883.

29. *RL*, 15 October 1885.

30. *FMG*, 29 September 1885.

31. *CH*, 7 October 1885.

32. *FMG*, 29 September 1885.

20

CONFRONTATIONS AND UNREST

Bull Head, Sarcee (Tsuu T'ina) Chief

"I strongly recommend that this chief be deposed ... he is a very bad man and exercises a most pernicious influence over his people."

– Superintendent John McIllree, *Dictionary of Canadian Biography*, XIV, University of Toronto Press, 1998, 214

GA NA 583 – 1

THE RAPIDLY DETERIORATING INDIAN LIFESTYLE had brought increasing friction between the Indians and North-West Mounted Police. Many minor incidents resulted and several serious confrontations narrowly averted bloodshed. No longer did the NWMP command the prestige and unchallenged authority of the first years.

Treaty 7 had assigned the small Sarcee (now Tsuu T'ina) tribe to a reservation in the present-day Gleichen area, but, because of continuing difficulties with the nearby Blackfoot, Chief Bull Head (called Chula by his followers) negotiated with Ottawa to have the Sarcee relocated 20 km southwest of Fort Calgary. The 400-member tribe had a reputation for being unaccommodating. Inspector Cecil Denny called the Sarcee "by far the most troublesome Indians in the west."[1] In the Cypress Hills, Inspector Crozier persuaded the Sarcee band to return to the reserve near Calgary. They departed as promised, but took with them a number of horses from an Assiniboine camp. A six-man police pursuit was sent to retrieve the stolen horses. Inspector Steele at Fort Walsh wrote: "We were very glad to be rid of the Sarcee, the most unprepossessing of the plain Indians."[2]

Before relocating near Calgary, wandering Sarcee came to the four-man post and demanded food or they would burn the fort down. The Indian Agent and Sergeant Johnstone were unable to fulfill the food demands, but persuaded the Indians to go to Fort Macleod for rations. The eleven-day trip in bitterly cold weather was a terrible ordeal and the hungry Indians suffered dreadfully. About 30 km north of Fort Macleod, the band, unable to continue in the cold, camped in a coulee for three days. A policeman went on ahead and returned with food. It was realized that the Calgary garrison was understaffed and twenty-five men were deployed to return the Sarcee north, in Corporal LaNauze's words, "to Fort Kill-Garry."[3]

The Sarcee moved to their new reserve in 1882. The tribe's interaction with the nearby town was often fractious. Most dealings were trivial, but annoying. One theft involved a washtub that the band had wanted to make into a drum. When the NWMP sought its return, Chief Bull Head refused, saying that the tribe needed a drum more than anyone in Calgary needed a washtub. The police dropped the matter.

In May 1883, a serious encounter arose over the reduction of Indian rations. To show his displeasure, a brave named Crow Collar broke into the reserve ration house and damaged the weigh scale. Bull Head obstructed Sergeant Ward's search for the offender and armed Indians forced the police to leave. Superintendent John McIllree responded by taking ten men to the reserve and, when band members refused to surrender Crow Collar, McIllree ordered the arrest of Bull Head. McIllree reported:

> He resisted violently and called on the young men who were in the Soldiers' Lodge to assist him. They burst all around and were in a most excited state. As I saw the arrest could not be made at that moment without bloodshed, and as it was fast getting dark, I ordered the men to the Agent's house.[4]

A trooper was sent to alert Fort Calgary of the situation and the men slept that night in the agent's house. Reinforcements from Calgary arrived in the morning and both Crow Collar and Bull Head were arrested and taken to the Fort Calgary guard room.

Angry Sarcee appeared in the town singing war songs, brandishing their guns, and threatening bloodshed. An officer's explanation that Bull Head was only a witness against the other prisoner and would be released when a hearing was held only temporarily mollified the Indians. They returned the next morning wearing war paint and carrying weapons. Under these threatening circumstances, the police released Bull Head. At his trial, Crow Collar was charged with malicious injury to property and received ten days' imprisonment with hard labour. The charge against Bull Head of creating a disturbance was dismissed with a caution. He had spent three days in jail.

Another serious confrontation happened in January 1884 when Whitecap interfered with Constable Fury's attempt to arrest an Indian. Inspector Sam Steele took a large police detail to the Sarcee reserve where he explained the consequences of obstructing an arrest. Several days later, Whitecap was arrested and, after a magistrate's warning, set free. For all their difficulties, the Sarcees were regarded more of a nuisance than a danger, having, at most, fifty warriors. Still, any dispute was unwanted.

Chief Beardy (Kamiyistowesit)

Chief Beardy came to NWMP attention in 1876 when he threatened to obstruct Lieutenant Governor Morris's entourage from crossing the South Saskatchewan River, preventing the signing of Treaty 6 at Fort Carlton. Settlers felt the chief was a troublemaker. The *Saskatchewan Herald* implied Beardy was "synonymous with everything that is base and dishonest."[5]

In the spring of 1880 at Duck Lake (site of the future 1885 skirmish), Indians in his Cree band had shot four cows provided by the government. In response, Superintendent William Herchmer rode to Duck Lake with an interpreter, eighteen men, and set up a camp beside the police post manned by Constable William Ramsay.

Superintendent Herchmer, Captain Antrobus, and six men, carrying only side arms, walked 3 km to the Indian camp to arrest the suspects. They were met by Indians who threatened them with knives and fired bullets over their heads. The police remained firm in this tense situation. Antrobus put his revolver in the face of one brave who had thrust a knife towards him. Constable Ramsay pointed out chiefs Beardy and One Arrow, who were seized and handcuffed by the police. Chief Beardy yelled to his unarmed warriors to get their guns.

The encounter became menacing. A Mountie wrote: "Soon they began shooting, not point blank at us, for we were in a small way protected by the two prisoners, but unpleasantly near us to hear the ping of the bullets."[6] Herchmer had interpreter Louis Laronde warn the Indians that, if any policemen were injured, the two chiefs would be shot. This threat proved effective and the gunfire stopped, allowing the police to arrest Cut Nose who, while held by two policemen, implored others to die now and not in a white man's prison. However, once the uproar had subsided, it was agreed to go to the Duck Lake trading store and nearby police cabin. The police took the three prisoners (followed by the entire Indian camp, not forgetting the dogs) to the police post. Indian spokesmen, along with police, went inside the store while, outside, 200 armed Indians stood intently listening and unaware that twelve policemen had surrounded them.

Once the police presence was noticed, the surprised Indians left for their camp. This allowed the police to arrest a fourth wanted Indian and, within an hour, three teams transporting the four prisoners were on the road to Prince Albert. At that settlement, the prisoners were held for several months before a jury trial acquitted Chief Beardy, One Arrow and Cut Nose. The fourth Indian, Omenakaw, was found guilty and ordered to pay the costs of the government cattle shot. For Beardy it had been a puzzling and trying ordeal. A witness at the trial observed:

> The spoken word was not necessary to understand how keenly the old Chief felt the indignity of his position. The grim and stern visage, the flashing eye, told all present how deeply he felt, what to him anyway was the injustice of the white man in arraigning him before this J.P. Court—for what? For fulfilling a law of necessity in the wild, the necessity of feeding his hungry people.[7]

NWMP–Blackfoot Troubles

Two very troublesome NWMP–Indian confrontations occurred on the Blackfoot reserve near Gleichen. The first, in January 1882, resulted from a misunderstanding over the purchase of a steer. The Indian agent, John Lauder (a former Mountie), accused Bull Elk, a minor Blackfoot Chief, of stealing the head of a butchered steer and demanded its return. Excited Indians came to the ration house and fired bullets in all directions. Bull Elk fired two shots at the ration house, almost hitting Const. Charles Daley. Lauder sent for assistance from the NWMP detachment, located on the other side of the frozen Bow River.

Superintendent William M. Herchmer, NWMP

"Everyone who knew 'Billy' Herchmer knew that, whatever his failings were, lack of courage was not one of them."

– Deane, *Mounted Police Life in Canada*, 146
 GA NA 2520 – 48

On their arrival, a four-man party under Inspector Dickens saw Bull Elk running and pursued him. Bull Elk climbed a small hill, where he waited with a readied gun. Sergeant Joseph Howe continued to advance until Eagle Shoe ran up and offered to help. Bull Elk surrendered and was marched off.

The party hadn't walked twenty paces when thirty young Indians, in the words of one Mounted Policeman, "began to gather around us, howling and whooping, with shouts of 'don't let them take him; they are not many.'"[8] Further trouble followed on the river ice when Indian women carrying axes and knives and Indian youths with carbines joined the angry mob. Howe remembered:

> An Indian caught me by the right arm, another came behind me and tripped me up; the constable on the left was treated in the same manner; as soon as I fell an old squaw ran at me and snatched the prisoner's gun out of my hand before I could recover myself. I still held the prisoner with my left hand, while Inspector Dickens kept the Indians back in the rear with his revolver.[9]

After a bullet whistled over their heads, Howe fired his revolver three times into the air. His shots intimidated the Indians and the prisoner was taken to the police post.

Seven hundred milling Indians surrounded the police, who were now confined in the store room and a stable. Large fires were started, around which the Indians would shout, whoop, and dance. Several warriors, with axes, climbed on the roof as if they planned to chop into the buildings. The situation was chaotic. One policeman had the hot muzzle of a rifle just fired placed against his face. Lauder thought "anything might happen" when he saw an Indian pointing the barrel of a rifle into a Mountie's mouth, while other warriors disarmed the Mountie's companion.[10] In the uproar, Dickens approached Blackfoot leaders for intervention.

However, assistance for the police was not forthcoming. Chief Crowfoot berated the Indian Department and refused to allow Bull Elk to be removed from the reserve. Inspector Dickens had no choice but to hand over Bull Elk to Crowfoot. Unrestrained yelling and a rampant discharge of firearms accompanied his release. As soon as the Indians left for their camp, Dickens sent a messenger to Fort Macleod for assistance and ordered his twelve-man garrison to fortify the police buildings.

It took four days before Superintendent Leif Crozier arrived with twenty reinforcements, all being armed with repeating rifles. After he completed additional defensive fortifications, Crozier opened forceful negotiations with the Indians, telling Crowfoot that, if Bull Elk was not given up the next day, the police would take him by force. This threat proved effective and Bull Elk was taken into custody and escorted to Fort Macleod where he received a fourteen-day sentence for using a weapon in a threatening manner. A former Mountie said that this was "the first serious resistance shown toward the police since they have been in the country."[11] Stipendiary Magistrate J. Macleod described the incident as "a very nasty business."[12]

Two years later, in the spring of 1884, Bear's Head, an alleged Métis agent, was arrested for disturbing the peace. The accused, however, made a daring escape when he slipped his handcuffs, grabbed Sergeant Dann's rifle, and jumped off the train going to Calgary. He returned to the Indian camp where the annual Sun Dance was in progress.

Several days later, Inspector Sam Steele, along with Constables Walters and Kerr, arrested Bear's Head at gunpoint inside Chief Crowfoot's teepee. Although Indian protesters became extremely defiant, Steele succeeded in taking Bear's Head from the camp. On 3 April 1884, Steele convicted Bear's Head of vagrancy and sentenced the "Half-Breed" to fourteen days' hard labour.[13] To the Indians, this case had exposed police harassment of a guest in their camp.

In response to the two very disturbing Blackfoot incidents, Lieutenant Governor Edgar Dewdney arranged a train excursion to Winnipeg in 1884 for Blackfoot chiefs Crowfoot and Three Bulls, Red Crow of the Bloods, and Eagle Tail of the Peigans. His intention was to awe the chiefs with the exposure to white power and technology.

Winnipeg, in July 1884, with a population of 20,000, a university, newspapers, government buildings, street lights, telegraph and railway connections, a street railway, and river steamers, visibly demonstrated the technology and strength of the newcomers. The *Calgary Herald* reported that Crowfoot returned "greatly impressed with the power of the whites, and said they could produce as many soldiers as blades of grass."[14] Any defiance to the Canadian encroachment took on added awareness. When the North-West Rebellion erupted eight months later, all the Indian bands in southern Alberta remained outside the conflict.

Turmoil in Saskatchewan

In 1884, the same year as the Bear's Head incident, two serious clashes between police and Indians erupted in Saskatchewan. In February 1884, in what was called the "Yellow Calf Incident," hungry Saulteaux Indians on the Crooked Lakes reserve in the lower Qu'Appelle Valley seized flour and bacon from stores belonging to the Indian Department.[15]

Chiefs – Eagle Tail (Peigan), Three Bulls and Crowfoot (Blackfoot), Red Crow (Blood)

Lieutenant Governor Edgar Dewdney arranged a trip to Winnipeg for the four chiefs. Chief Crowfoot returned "greatly impressed with the power of the whites, and said they could produce as many soldiers as blades of grass."

– *Calgary Herald*, 7 May 1884
  GA NA 3432 – 1

The winter had been severe and game was scarce. Living conditions were tragic. A Hudson's Bay trader recalled that "in some cases children died of starvation, their mothers not being able to suckle them from their weakened condition."[16] Urgent appeals to the Indian Department asking for aid went unheeded. In December, James Setter, a popular and helpful farm instructor, was dismissed for his laxity in following rigid government work policies.

Hayter Reed, the Assistant Indian Commissioner, visited the Crooked Lake reserve to assess the need for food and the government's "work for rations" policy. He upheld his Indian name, "Iron Heart," by ordering a reduction in the already inadequate supplies. Hilton Keith, the replacement farm instructor, was to enforce the regulations.

At an interview requested by Yellow Calf, Keith rejected requests for food, saying his instructions were only to give rations to elderly people. He offered a minimum supply of ammunition. Frustrated band members, uttering war whoops and carrying scalping knives, rushed the storehouse, knocked Keith down and pressed knives across his leather coat. According to Keith's report, they "all swarmed in like bees into a hive and stole right before my eyes, about sixty sacks of Flour and twelve of Bacon."[17] In the midst of the uproar, Keith suffered an epileptic seizure and became unconscious for an hour.

Upon notification of the incident, Inspector Burton Deane at Regina took ten men and horses in freight cars east to Broadview. The next day, February 21, they rode 15 km north to the reserve. At several homes that were visited, the police noted the absence of men, a sign of possible trouble. A leading band member named O'Soup directed the Mounties, Keith, and an interpreter to a building packed with sixty young men who were in a state of frenzy after dancing without intermission for at least a week.

With the assistance of an interpreter, Deane spoke for "two weary hours." The Indians insisted that it was hunger which had forced their theft of government supplies. From the discussions, Deane concluded the Indians were respectful and friendly from first to last, but added that "the Red Man's song is always grub, grub, more grub. Moreover, these rascals had been dancing for thirteen days straight on end, and had neglected even to go and draw their rations."[18] He suggested the Indians would win sympathy and understanding for their theft if the raid leaders had been tried by the judiciary. The Indians agreed to discuss the matter.

On the following day, Superintendent William Herchmer, in response to a telegram, arrived with reinforcements, giving the police a total of twenty men. When this contingent approached the Indian dance building, every Indian visible held a firearm. This was an ominous sign. One policeman had observed: "Indians seldom resort to violence at this time of year, preferring to wait until spring ... and for this reason they must be in a bad condition and feeling hunger pretty bad."[19] Indian agent Colonel Allan McDonald asked to talk to the band, but a rash Herchmer refused his suggestion and McDonald angrily left the scene.

Deane wrote in his journal: "Everyone who knew 'Billy' Herchmer knew that, whatever his failings were, lack of courage was not one of them, and he presumed that bluff would carry the day."[20] Herchmer walked boldly into the conference building, only to have a double-barrel shotgun pointed in his face. Within seconds, Indian arms aimed at the policemen who were encumbered by heavy buffalo coats and carrying only revolvers. Moreover, Hayter Reed had instructed the police to avoid any shedding of blood.

Deane realized, "we were, in effect, provoking the Indians to commit willful murder by threatening to thrust ourselves into premises which we had no right to force our way without the Queen's Warrant."[21] All of the policemen knew that one wrong move would bring bloodshed. Yellow Calf, at Herchmer's request, persuaded the Indian to drop his shotgun. The tension eased and with the return of the Indian agent, a meeting was arranged. A request was sent for Hayter Reed, the Assistant Indian Administrator, to attend.

The Indians' appearance at the meeting with weapons and wearing war paint created a tense atmosphere. Yellow Calf insisted the seizure of the provisions was because of the band's hunger and that the Indians might as well die fighting in battle than be starved by the government. Discussions continued for eight hours before an agreement was arranged for police to escort Yellow Calf and three Indians by train to Regina for a trial. In the end, the court chose to drop the case against Yellow Calf and gave his companions suspended sentences. "It was," commented Deane, "practically understood from the first that this was to be the outcome of the trial."[22]

It was west of Battleford, four months later (June 1884), where the most volatile North-West Mounted Police–Cree conflict occurred prior to the North-West Rebellion. In what was to be known as the "Poundmaker Racket," a large gathering of Cree had assembled at the adjoining Little Pine-Poundmaker reserves for a Thirst (Sun) Dance.[23]

Trouble started when Kahweechetwaymot (Cow-itch-it-e-Wanat), a follower of Big Bear, asked John Craig, the Indian agent, for provisions for a sick child. When Craig insisted no rations would be given without due work and shoved him, Kahweechetwaymot allegedly struck Craig three times with an axe handle. Craig reported the assault to the Battleford detachment. Superintendent Crozier sent Constable Ralph Sleigh to arrest Kahweechetwaymot. The Indian resisted arrest, much to the admiration of many young braves. Sleigh dutifully notified Crozier of his unsuccessful arrest attempt.

The next day, Crozier rode to the reserve with twenty-five policemen, an interpreter, and Indian agent John Rae. Once they had set up a base, Crozier took several troopers, Rae, and interpreter Louis Laronde to the Thirst Dance to identify and arrest Kahweechetwaymot. However, the accused remained evasive. The Indian chiefs temporized and offered no information or assistance. On the advice of Rae, Crozier decided to delay any arrests until the Thirst Dance ended.

During the wait, the police constructed a breastwork of logs and earth at an old agency building about 5 km from the dance site. As an added precaution, Crozier sent a courier to Battleford, 50 km away, with orders for Inspector William Antrobus to bring reinforcements. Further, a police party went 10 km west to remove government supplies from a warehouse

Blackfoot Indian carrying rifle

A letter from a mounted policemen described the Blackfoot as "a warlike, dangerous lot of fellows, armed *cap a pie* with the most improved weapons ... they are a fine intelligent race of men, tall and slight, but wiry and muscular."

– *Ottawa Daily Citizen*, 7 April 1875
   GA NA 354 – 26

on the Little Pine reserve. On their return, although the four ox teams had carefully skirted the Indian camp, the police had been seen. More than a hundred mounted Indians charged the wagon train, circling and firing over the Mounties' heads. The teams continued on to the improvised forts.

Negotiations began once the Thirst Dance ended. Crozier assessed that, the leading chiefs did all in their power to have Kahweechetwaymot arrested, but, they lacked influence over the "young bucks." Crozier was by now thoroughly aggravated and refused offers from Poundmaker and Big Bear to become a replacement prisoner.

The two chiefs agreed to deliver the prisoner to the police fort and, although Big Bear and Poundmaker returned with Crozier to the makeshift outpost, the other Indians stopped on a small hill 1 km away. Exasperated, Crozier realized that the surrender of Kahweechetwaymot was not going to be forthcoming and ordered a mixed force of men on horseback and foot to advance on the Indians.

Crozier went ahead with Craig, but the Indian agent was unable to pinpoint his assaulter, who had again remained hidden. Their presence in the Indian ranks was agitating and now, at the sight of the approaching police force, the younger warriors shouted threats of violence while, at the same time, older Indians pressed for calm. In the uproar, Crozier demanded: "Bring me the prisoner, or I shall arrest you all."[24]

A leading Indian named Lucky Man now brought Kahweechetwaymot forward. Crozier reported: "When I was about to put my hand on him to arrest him, he stepped aside and said 'don't touch me.'"[25] Nor would he accept HBC Factor William McKay's suggestion to surrender.

The situation was out of control. Poundmaker threatened Antrobus with a hideous club that held three attached butcher knives. In turn, Constable F.E. Prior put his rifle barrel against the chief's head. Sergeant-Major Kirk, faced by Indian guns, never wavered under threats of death. In the melee, Kahweechetwaymot was identified and later seized by Constable Warren "Slingo" Kerr, saying in his Irish brogue: "Come on ye haythen, the kernel wants ye."[26] Crozier grabbed a second wanted Indian. Guarded by a protective semi-circle of thirty-five mounted policemen, the Mounties on foot moved the prisoners toward the improvised stockade.

Infuriated Indians charged the retreating ranks, stabbing the police horses and spitting at the men. Constable William McQuarrie had recounted that: "One young buck put his heels to his pony and made the pony rear then he reached over and hit me a nice crack in the face with his whip I put my rifle to his head when someone shouted don't shoot me Well I did not intend to shoot me as I knew that would start the fireworks."[27] One policeman who became separated from his companions had his tunic and rifle seized. Warriors carried off interpreter Louis Laronde, whose life was in jeopardy. Amazingly, in the madness, no one fired a shot.

The police escorted Kahweechetwaymot inside the makeshift stockade. At that moment, HBC Factor McKay told Crozier to throw bacon and flour sacks (part of their defensive breastworks) at the raging Indians. The effect was described as magical. The Indians were so famished that they stopped their rampage to gather the food. In the turmoil, Laronde safely reached the bastion and Factor McKay asked and got the interpreter's rifle returned.

The clash ended with a desired result for the police. It had been an extremely dangerous incident. Crozier concluded: "I unhesitatingly state that never since the occupation of the Country by the Police was there anything like such a determination shown by any Indians anywhere in the Territory."[28]

Superintendent Leif Crozier

"If there ever was a cool officer and a brave man it was Supt. Crozier that day."

– William McQuarrie, *NAC*, f. 724
  GA NA 343 – 1

Everyone had realized how one shot could have started a bloodbath. McQuarrie wrote that: "All it kneded that day was a shot to be fired and it would have been every man for himself as those Mounted men would have been useless as those Bronchos would have stamped [stampeded]."[29] A western newspaper reflected: "Too much praise cannot be accorded the police for their control of temper displayed under great provocation, as it needed but the accidental discharge of a revolver to precipitate an Indian war."[30] It was not mentioned that the Indians also held their fire. And, for the citizens in Battleford, the peaceful resolution of the confrontation came as a great relief. For several days, the suspense of not knowing what was happening had been harrowing.

Ten weeks later, on 29 August 1884, Judge Charles-Borromée Rouleau sentenced Kahweechetwaymot to one week's imprisonment for assault. Nine months later, at the Frenchman's Butte skirmish on 28 May 1885, shrapnel fired from the "Macleod Gun" wounded Kahweechetwaymot and he died after a night of terrible agony.

By the end of 1884, NWMP–Indian relations were extremely strained. There had been three serious confrontations during that year and, most troublesome, in July, Louis Riel returned to the North-West Territories. Although Riel professed a moderate agenda, the North-West Mounted Police showed concerns over his arrival and the earlier "Poundmaker Racket" by assigning an additional 122 men to police the Prince Albert and the Fort Carlton-Battleford region. As events turned out, an open rebellion erupted in late March 1885.

NOTES

1. Denny, *The Riders of the Plains*, 144.

2. Steele, *Forty Years in Canada*, 153.

3. LaNauze, "Echoes and Letters from Fort Walsh," XI, No. 2, 75.

4. *RC*, NWMP, 1883, 15.

5. *SH*, 16 August 1880. In a further indictment of Beardy, on 27 January 1879, the paper called Beardy's "rights of labour and property are such as would not disgrace the most extreme communist leader, and not only does he refuse to work himself, but will not permit any of his young men either to work or hunt."

6. Cow Oxy Coo Cha Set (Harry Ross), "Daring Arrest of Indian Chiefs in Armed Camp," *SG*, Eighth Annual, 59. Also Wm.B. Cameron, "Gentlemen Unafraid," *SG*, Thirteenth Annual, 69-73. *WDT*, 10 September 1880.

7. *The Voices of the People* (Prince Albert Historical Society, 1985), 126. *MFP*, 10 September 1880.

8. *MFP*, 13 April 1882.

9. *RC*, NWMP, 1882, 53. See also Crozier's report, 53-55.

10. *CH*, Magazine section, 25 October 1930.

11. Denny, The *Riders of the Plains*, 159-160.

12. Turner, *The North-West Mounted Police, 1873-93*, I, 631.

13. *RC*, NWMP, 1884, 54.

14. *CH*, 7 May 1884. McKay, *Fighting Parson*, 145, relates: "Upon their return home, the lodges of the Blackfeet echoed for months with the tales of the wonders of the East and the cities of the white man."

15. Isabel Andrews, "Indian Protest against Starvation: the Yellow Calf Incident of 1884," *Sask Hist*, XXXVIII, No. 2, 41-51; Captain Burton Deane, *Mounted Police Life in Canada* (Toronto: Cassell, 1916), Chapter XIV.

16. Deane, *Mounted Police Life in Canada*, 151.

17. *NAC*, RG 10, Black, File 10, 181. Andrews, "Indian Protest against Starvation: the Yellow Calf Incident of 1884," 43.

18. Deane, *Mounted Police Life in Canada*, 144.

19. *WDT*, 23 February 1884.

20. Deane, *Mounted Police Life in Canada*, 146.

21. Ibid., 147.

22. Ibid., 149. The defence counsel was A.E. Forget, the future Lieutenant Governor of Saskatchewan. Yellow Calf's band proved resourceful. That summer in 1884, the band won a contract to construct the local Indian agency with 75,000 feet of lumber, 54,000 shingles, and 150 barrels of lime. Noting that the band had also broken 30 acres, the *Regina Leader*, 23 October 1884, acknowledged, "This is a very acceptable practical demonstration of how the Red Man can be self-supporting, not withstanding the diminution of buffalo." Questions continued to plague the Yellow Calf Incident. The *Edmonton Bulletin*, in October 1887, reported Stipendiary Judge H. Richardson inquired whether Supt. Deane had acted without a warrant and why there were hushed-up references to Indian starvation.

23. For details of the "Poundmaker Racket" see Cameron, *Blood Red the Sun*, 9-25. *LH*, 17 May 1924. For the trial, see *SH*, 12 July 1884.

24. *RC*, NWMP, 1884, 11.

25. Ibid.

26. *LH*, 17 May 1924.

27. *NAC*, William McQuarrie, f. 724.

28. *GA*, Dewdney Papers, Box 4, f. 69, 1493-96.

29. *NAC*, William McQuarrie, f. 724.

30. *WDT*, 23 June 1884.

21

GOPHERS IN THE
REBELLION?

Richardson Ground Squirrel

"An animal of the ground-squirrel type, who burrows on the prairie, and who retreats
to its hole on any approach of danger."

– Constable John Donkin, *Trooper and Redskin in the Far Northwest*, 149

FOR FOUR DAYS, FROM 9 - 12 MAY 1885, militia troops under the
leadership of Major-General Frederick Middleton, Commander-in-Chief
of the Canadian militia, attacked the rebel base at Batoche. After their
victory, when asked what his next move would be, the General replied:
"We will go to Prince Albert and drive those gophers out of their holes."[1]

By "those gophers," Middleton was referring to Commissioner A.G. Irvine's 225-man North-West Mounted Police contingent, snug in their camp at Prince Albert, only 60 km north. Newspaper reporters at the scene recorded his comment and the derisive term "gophers" at once had become a widely applied slur for the evasive combat role of the NWMP during the North-West Rebellion.

In his book, *Trooper and Redskin in the Far Northwest*, Constable John G. Donkin explained to his British readers that a gopher is "an animal of the ground-squirrel type, who burrows on the prairie, and who retreats to its hole on any approach of danger."[2] During the North-West Rebellion, many questionable police actions certainly tarnished the reputation of the NWMP, but did the red-coated "Riders of the Plains" deserve this demeaning sobriquet?

Duck Lake

On 26 March 1885, Superintendent Leif Crozier at Fort Carlton ordered Sergeant Alfred Stewart, four scouts, and seventeen constables to retrieve goods seized from a store by supporters of Louis Riel. Near Duck Lake, a Métis force under Gabriel Dumont blocked their path. What happened is not clear. According to the official NWMP report, scout Thomas McKay went forward to meet the rebels who, he claimed, were both overbearing and threatening. Dumont prodded a loaded rifle into McKay's ribs and demanded the surrender of the police.[3] In his version, Dumont recorded:

> I took my carbine and advanced toward the police to harass them ... a sergeant in a second sleigh yelled "if you don't stop, I will kill you." ... "Don't try it," I yelled at him, "I will kill you first." I shouldered my gun and aimed at the sergeant. He put his rifle across his knees ... and in two or three jumps, I was at the sleigh and on top of the sergeant. I hit him in the chest with the barrel of my rifle, and he fell back in the sleigh, his rifle pointed straight up in the air. Because he had his gloves on, it went off by mistake.[4]

The conflict ended with the police detail withdrawing to Fort Carlton. Sergeant Stewart sent a dispatch rider ahead to inform base commander Crozier of the incident.

This clash, to Crozier, again had challenged police authority. Only one week earlier, Riel had demanded the surrender of Fort Carlton. In his report on the disturbance, Crozier recorded that he foresaw "if the Indians see that a party of half-breeds can contemptuously drive back and prevent officers of the Government from doing their duty, thus defiantly seizing property with impunity, they [the Métis] would then be able to gain firm allegiance of the wavering Indian tribes."[5]

Crozier immediately organized a company of almost 100 men, fifty-six Mounties, and forty-three Prince Albert Volunteers. As Stewart's returning party neared the fort, they joined forces with Crozier's column that was just moving out.

Horse-drawn sleighs quickly conveyed a 7-pr. field piece while most of the troops marched along the snow-covered trail. Near the point of the earlier disturbance, a Métis force turned back four advance scouts and, with war-whooping yells, chased them on horseback at full speed.

North-West Mounted Police Volunteer Alex Stewart recalled: "I could see them coming over the hills like bees, and all shouting. The Indians were all painted up like demons, as were the French half-breeds."[6]

As a defensive measure, Crozier positioned skirmishers at the sides of the trail while other men took cover behind the overturned sleighs that were extended in a line across the trail. After the horses were taken to the rear, Crozier, along with translator "Gentleman Joe" McKay, moved in front to talk with Isidore Dumont (a brother of Gabriel Dumont) and an Indian who held a white flag. The talk became quite heated and suddenly, McKay shot both opposing negotiators. According to one witness, Leif Crozier turned quickly, waved his sword above his head, and then shouted "commence firing."[7] Sweeping gunfire followed.

From natural cover on the flanks and shielded by several buildings, the rebel marksmen held the upper hand, firing at the police force protected only by sleighs. The field piece proved ineffective, firing only four shots and, with the deep crusted snow hindering its movement, Crozier had little choice but to withdraw from the costly firing exchange. In the disordered retreat, the column left behind nine dead combatants in the snow, the field piece, two sleighs, twelve rifles, ammunition, and stores. Five police horses were killed or disabled. The skirmish had lasted less than thirty minutes.

Crozier's contention that the bravery and coolness of his force was simply astonishing in facing murderous fire downplays the military costs of the skirmish. Twelve deaths and twelve wounded men in the police column was extremely high—twenty-five per cent of the troop. Second, the equal proportion of wounded to dead indicated excellent Métis marksmanship as the expected ratio was five to one in skirmishes at that time. In fact, a number of policemen had been shot in the head.[8] Third, the field piece was near the front of the column and exposed to rifle fire. The proper position for the weapon should have been at the rear of the advancing column.

NWMP Detachment, Fort Carlton, 1884–85

L–R, front row – Cst. T.C. Fleming, G. Pook, (dog), J.H. Wilmot, R. Carter, unknown; middle row – Waite, W.A. Manners-Smith, unknown, Surgeon Robert Miller, Supt. S. Gagnon [beard], unknown, Cst. D.H. MacPherson; back row – Frederick G. Dann, Consts. J.J. Roberts, G.S. Oliver, E. Littlefield, J.H. Doyle, unknown, H. Des Barres, J. Pringle, unknown.

– RCMP Historical Collections Unit, "Depot" Division, Regina, SK., 1946 .3.12

Who could have envisioned the tragic consequences of this advance to Duck Lake? Other than the Corporal Charles Chassé, a veteran of the Franco-Prussian War, no one else had ever experienced military combat. One volunteer reflected: "Little did any of us think as we drove out of Fort Carlton this morning amidst the hearty cheers of our comrades who were not permitted to accompany us, that the cold hand of death would be laid upon any of us ere the sun set."[9]

Seventeen men died in the bloody skirmish.[10] The rebel side lost five men, including their two negotiators. For the Prince Albert Volunteers, it had been a tragic clash: nine men were killed and five others wounded. That the dead had been left on the field only compounded the anguish. In the assessment of Sergeant Wilson of the Prince Albert Volunteers: "but worst of all, we were conscious of defeat and our enemy elated."[11]

Three Mounted Policemen had been counted among the twelve deaths in the government force: Constable Thomas James Gibson, the driver of an ammunition sleigh, was shot through the heart. Alex Stewart recalled "he threw up his hands, gave a sigh and fell out on his shoulder, striking my feet."[12] Two of the policemen died of their wounds the following day: Constable George Garrett, hit by bullets in the neck and left lung, and Constable George P. Arnold, only seven months in the Force.

Garrett had fervently wanted to join the NWMP. He had written to the Canadian Governor General requesting a position in the Force as there were few employment opportunities in Ireland. Irvine sent Comptroller White a parcel by registered post containing eleven items belonging to the deceased to forward to his father in Ireland. Irvine added a letter telling the grieving father that his son's record in the police force was without a blot.

Arnold was a Canadian-born trooper who had served as a scout in the United States cavalry during the Indian Wars. His North-West Mounted Police medical exam noted three bullet scars—two on his body and one on his right leg—as evidence of combat. As soon as he finished his picket duty, Constable William Patrick Lynch went to the makeshift hospital to see his friend, Arnold:

He was lying on his cot theire was no men in at the time he called me and told me to tell constable Meferson [D.H. McPherson] Doil [J.H. Doyle]. And crat [O. Cratt] to come in he wanted to see them When they came in he said to them the Red S of got me good tell Bella good by that was a half breed girl that lived down towards the Saskatchewan River then he died With a Smile on his face.[13]

Arnold's last words were, "Tell the boys I died game."[14] At sunset on March 27, the day after the skirmish, Commissioner A.G. Irvine read a burial service by the light of lanterns. The three Mounted Policemen were buried in one grave outside Fort Carlton.[15]

Seven Mounted Policemen were wounded.[16] And there were many "close calls." Surgeon Robert Miller found a bullet embedded in the field surgical case carried in his breast pocket; Const. August "Dutchy" Miller's hat had a hole in it; and Const. A.H. McMillan was knocked senseless by a spent bullet. Inspector J. Howe's horse had been hit by five bullets.

Had Crozier reacted rashly to the Métis obstruction of Sergeant Stewart's detail? In an explanation of his actions, Crozier stated that there had been no fighting as of yet and a show of force might settle the matter without bloodshed. He admittedly had underestimated the numbers of Métis, but rationalized that his actions forestalled the rebels from an attack on Fort Carlton. Nonetheless, he knew through the couriers that Irvine's force of almost 100 men had arrived at Prince Albert. These reinforcements reached Fort Carlton less than an hour after the return of Crozier's force. In his official report, Commissioner A.G. Irvine, while acknowledging the troop's gallantry under heavy fire, expressed a "belief that this officer's better judgment was overruled by the impetuousness displayed by both the police and the volunteers to go and take the stores and, if necessary, fight for them."[17] And although "Paddy" Crozier was promoted to Assistant Commissioner the following week, his North-West Mounted Police career was now ruined. Government officials scuttled his application to become Commissioner Irvine's replacement in 1886 and, shortly after, he resigned from the Force.

The news of the outbreak of fighting was not a complete surprise in the prairie region. John Donkin, a Mounted Police recruit stationed in Regina, later recollected: "We in the rank and file used to talk in quite a familiar way, in the barrack room, of the coming rebellion as a matter of course. We even had the date fixed."[18] Recruit Roger Pocock recalled hearing men wager on whether hostilities would begin within a month, or by June when the Nitchie's horses were ready.[19] Inspector Francis Dickens at Fort Pitt wrote in his diary on March 23: "Rumors abroad to the effect that the halfbreeds are in arms against the Government."[20] And the day right before the outbreak, on March 25, the *Fort Benton River Press* in Montana Territory carried a column titled "Saskatchewan Special: The half-breed population here is on the verge of an incipient rebellion."[21] Prior troop movements, too, forewarned impending hostilities. "Riel and his Friends are on the move and so are the Police," observed the *Saskatchewan Herald* on March 13. Two 7-pr. guns had been transported to Regina from Calgary and, eight days before the Duck Lake skirmish, Irvine had left Regina with a column to reinforce the newly occupied post at Fort Carlton, located 35 km west of Riel's base at Batoche. Superintendent W. Herchmer took thirty Mounties and twenty-four horses from Calgary to replace the men who went north with Irvine. But, most significant as the crisis loomed, Major-General Middleton, Commander-in-Chief of the Canadian Militia, was westward bound on American railways.

The column under Irvine that left Regina to reinforce Fort Carlton included four officers and eighty-six men, sixty-six horses, and sleighs. The weather was extremely cold and traveling conditions were hazardous on the 500-km route to Prince Albert. Many streams were frozen solid, leaving no water available for the men and horses. Twenty-two men had become snow-blind from the bright glare of the sun on the snow-swept landscape. Hospital-Sergeant Edward Braithwaite arranged these men in a row, one man's hand on the advanced man's shoulder, to continue along the trail, at times, singing the favourite marching song of the column —"The Spanish Cavalier."

Recruit Roger Pocock foolishly chose to ignore advice to occasionally run beside his sleigh in order to stimulate circulation and froze his feet; a doctor at Prince Albert had to amputate all the toes on his right foot. Irvine, in his report on this seven-day journey (in which the column had averaged 70 km each day), describes the conditions: "The hardships experienced on such a march can only be understood ... by those who have resided in the Territories, and so become familiar with the severity of the North-West winter."[22]

The police column skirted the rebel base at Batoche and, on the evening of March 24, entered Prince Albert to an enthusiastic welcome. The town, a disjointed collection of buildings strung along the North Saskatchewan for 7 km had doubled its population to 1,500 as area settlers sought safety. After a one-day rest, Irvine's troops left on the morning of March 26 for Fort Carlton, 85 km to the southwest.

The North-West Mounted Police had rented this old Hudson's Bay post for only a few months. From a military standpoint, its location on a river flat that was open to enemy fire from nearby wooded elevations was a poor defensive position. One Prince Albert volunteer wrote: "It is the worst place I ever saw for a fort; 25 men could keep 500 men in Carlton."[23]

In light of the Duck Lake debacle, Commissioner Irvine met with the officers to weigh the military alternatives. His force had 225 policemen and volunteers. Twelve men were wounded at Duck Lake and required care.

Overriding the discussion were urgent concerns by the Prince Albert volunteers to protect their families. The decision reached was to abandon Fort Carlton and return to Prince Albert.

To deny the rebels Fort Carlton's stores, the men destroyed what they could. They soaked coal oil and spread manure over the flour sacks. In the heat of this general disorder, widespread looting began. Constable John Donkin watched men seizing suits of clothing, blankets, underclothing, tobacco, pipes, and even perfume. He recorded seeing "tins of preserves, of lobsters, of sardines, and boxes of fancy biscuits were carried off to the rooms, and there was a general picnic on the beds."[24]

The looting, loading of supplies, care for the wounded men, and burial of the three Mounties delayed the withdrawal from Fort Carlton until the early morning of March 28. The departure became hectic when a lantern accidentally ignited some hay, setting off an uncontrollable fire that rapidly spread, lighting the early morning sky. Concerned that flames would alert the rebel force at Duck Lake, Irvine deployed a line of skirmishers to guard their withdrawal from the fort. It took more than two hours before the last sleigh reached the top of the steep hill to the upper plain. From there, the force moved on to reach Prince Albert about 4 p.m.

Residents in Prince Albert, staggered by the news of the deaths of nine townsmen, were outraged to learn that Irvine (thinking it was a trap) had refused Louis Riel's offer for the safe recovery of the dead bodies at Duck Lake and instead interned Tom Sanderson, the rebel negotiator.

The uppermost urgency was to retrieve the remains. Irvine released Sanderson, who left with three men to collect the corpses which they found piled in a shed. They also gained the release of an injured prisoner, Charles Newett, a Prince Albert Volunteer. He had been wounded in the knee and his hand was broken as he lay on the ground warding off bayonet thrusts. For the residents of Prince Albert, it was a wretched sight to see a wagon arrive carrying Newett on top of a pile of frozen corpses.[25]

News of the Duck Lake skirmish spurred outlying prairie settlers to seek safety at the nearest fort. About 700 area settlers took refuge in Prince Albert. The entire Red Deer community fled to Calgary. All women and children at Fort Macleod, except for one female, were evacuated to Calgary.

Every western settlement organized its defences. The ringing of the church bell signaled women and children to seek safety in that structure. At Fort Saskatchewan, the twenty-man detachment repaired the decaying fort, dug a well, and enrolled a Home Guard. In Calgary, former Mountie James Walker directed a 100-man volunteer unit. The Police at Battleford provided arms for a forty-two Rifle Volunteer Company. The men elected their officers, took an oath of allegiance, and began drilling. The post now sent military messages in cipher, stationed extra guards, and organized police patrols east of town. Earlier, the deployment of Mounties to Fort Carlton had left Inspector W.S. Morris with a detachment of only eighteen men.

Rebel Ascendancy

Within days of the Duck Lake hostilities, the violence escalated. In the Eagle Hills, 150 km west of Duck Lake, Assiniboines murdered their farm instructor and a settler. This band then joined Poundmaker's Cree to approach Battleford, now swollen with more than 500 settlers seeking safety. The Indians burnt several outlying buildings, but never chose to attack the town's barricades.

Even more startling news came from Frog Lake, 180 km northwest of Battleford. On April 2, Cree Indians under Big Bear murdered nine white men. When news reached the North-West Mounted Police post at Fort Pitt, 50 km southwest, civilians and the police detachment under Inspector Francis Dickens, a son of the renowned novelist, Charles Dickens, prepared for an expected Indian attack. The so-called fort was a small Hudson's Bay depot and several buildings, but without barricades or even a well. The defenders organized supplies, constructed barricades, and repaired a scow.

After twelve days passed with no sign of the expected Indians, Dickens detailed Henry Quinn, a Métis scout, and two policemen to reconnoiter west toward the Frog Lake area. The trio had just left when Big Bear's warriors arrived at Fort Pitt, killed several cattle, and set up camp a short distance north of the post. The Indians sent messages requesting specific goods and asked for a meeting. Hudson's Bay Factor W.J. McLean went to the Indian camp where it was agreed to begin talks the next morning.

The negotiations were underway when shouts of "Redcoats! They are coming to shoot us" interrupted the meeting.[26] The returning scouting party had inadvertently ridden into the Indian camp.

A hectic chase followed. Scout Henry Quinn escaped on foot into the brush, but both policemen were shot as they rode frantically towards Fort Pitt. Constable Clarence Loasby recalled:

> Lone Man was right behind me when a young buck shot my horse and Lone Man's horse smashed into my wounded mount and we all went down together. I got to my feet and lit out for the fort. I had not gone far until one of those bullets drilled me. I kept going until Lone Man nailed me with a second slug. I went down for the count and while out Lone Man snaked

NWMP at Fort Pitt

"Tuesday, April 14. Mr. McLean still parleying with Indians. During the parley the three scouts out yesterday rode through the camp. Constable Cowan was shot dead and Loasby wounded. Quinn got away. Indians were fired upon."

– Vernon LaChance, ed., *Diary of Francis Dickens*, 17
 NAC PA 118770

through the grass, rolled me over, cut my gun belt off and slithered away. A minute later I woke up and started for the fort again. The police poured in heavy covering fire … when I got close, Stan Simpson jumped the barricade and hauled me to safety.[27]

At a later date, Loasby had the bullets extracted and then made into a "souvenir" ring.

The second Mountie, eighteen-year-old Const. David Latimer Cowan, was thrown off his horse and shot as he ran for the fort. As he lay wounded, Louison Mongrain approached. Cowan raised his hands and begged, "Don't brother, don't!" Mongrain fired two bullets into his head.[28]

The Indians mocked and barbarically mutilated Cowan's body. They had bound the young policeman's hands with his handcuffs, cut out his heart and placed it on a stake. A hostage, trader Louis Goulet, watched several Indians eating Cowan's heart. "Take a look at this," Goulet was told, "an Indian can eat the heart of a white man, but a white man can't eat an Indian's."[29] Cowan's body was left to decompose.

That afternoon, Factor McLean, now a prisoner, made a proposal to the Indians that allowed the twenty-four-man police detachment to leave undisturbed by the scow for Battleford, while forty civilians voluntarily entered the Indian camp as hostages. Even though this band had murdered Cowan and nine men at Frog Lake, McLean, an experienced Hudson's Bay factor, thought this agreement was the safest course of action for his large family that included his wife and nine children.

The police abandoned their supplies and horses and, in the words of a constable, "gracefully retired across river."[30] The diary of Corporal Ralph Sleigh, who died in action at Cut Knife Hill sixteen days later, related:

April 16 – Up at 4:30, after passing a wretched night. Snowing fast and very windy. Moving slow. Several men frost-bitten. Clothing frozen to our backs. Had some narrow escapes in ice jams. Camped at nine for dinner. Resumed trip at noon.[31]

As soon as the police left Fort Pitt, the Indians began a frenzied pillage of the Hudson's Bay stores that lasted all night. The hostages prudently kept out of their sight.

It took the police six days to reach Battleford. The scow had to be maneuvered through icy waters and the wounded Loasby required special care. On the fifth day, a three-man police patrol, carrying dispatches for Fort Pitt, hailed the scow with news that Battleford was safe and a relief column was expected soon. On the morning of April 22, the Fort Pitt detachment reached Battleford. Sleigh wrote: "Garrison turned out and presented arms. Police band played us into fort. Enthusiastic greeting. Ladies gave us a grand dinner."[32]

The Canadian press and military authorities portrayed the North-West Mounted Police retreat from Fort Pitt and the hazardous river trip as a courageous and gallant exploit. This "heroic" escape by the police, however, quickly became controversial. Why would the police leave twenty-seven whites and up to sixty Métis as hostages with a murderous Indian band? Did the police regard their personal safety paramount? The surrender of Fort Pitt had become one of the many questionable NWMP tactics that further smeared the Force's reputation. Most likely, the Fort Pitt episode and his failure to take command at Battleford, even though he was the most senior officer, contributed to the resignation of Inspector Dickens the following year.[33]

Major-General Frederick Dobson Middleton

Fifty-nine-year-old Major-General Frederick Dobson Middleton arrived in Winnipeg the morning after the Duck Lake skirmish and, by 6 p.m. that same day, departed by train with 260 men of the 90th Winnipeg Rifles for Troy Station (Fort Qu'Appelle). Military action against the insurgents, however, had to wait until the campaign logistics were addressed.[34]

Although Ottawa had been accused of delay and indecision on many Territorial issues, the government resolutely responded to this military challenge to its western hegemony. Within days of the Duck Lake skirmish, almost every Canadian militia battalion was under mobilization.

In his second confrontation with Canada, Louis Riel ineptly failed to comprehend the technological advancements made since the Red River Rebellion fifteen years earlier. While the Red River Expeditionary Force under General Garnet Wolseley took three months to reach Winnipeg from Prince Arthur's Landing (the Lakehead) in 1870, eastern troops, who even had to walk four gaps totaling 140 km of uncompleted railway north of Lake Superior, reached Western Canada within one week. Three thousand eastern soldiers campaigned on the prairies that spring.

Second, telegraph communication had now given Middleton's forces an overwhelming military advantage. Adolphe Caron, the Canadian Minister of Militia and Defence, attended to as many as 165 telegrams a day. Men under Middleton's command received a congratulatory telegram from Ottawa only three days after their victory at Batoche. It was from none other than Wolseley, who at this point was commanding Imperial forces in Egypt.[35]

Constable Clarence Loasby, NWMP

"I got to my feet and lit out for the fort. I had not gone far until one of those bullets drilled me. I kept going until Lone Man nailed me with a second slug."

– Constable Clarence Loasby, NWMP
  RCMP Historical Collections Unit, "Depot" Division, Regina, SK., 41-8-7

Most important, the demographical composition of the region had decidedly changed. White people now made up the largest group in the North-West Territories and, with the "Manitoba Boom" having increased the white population in that nearby province to almost 100,000 people (more than twice the North-West Territories population) whites totalled four times the prairie Aboriginal numbers.

Until the troops and supplies were in place, it was imperative for the government to localize the insurrection. In southern Alberta, the Blackfoot Confederacy received additional food rations, and influential individuals like Father Albert Lacombe and Canon George McKay visited the tribes. Lieutenant Governor Edgar Dewdney offered the former Mountie, Cecil Denny, charge of the Indians under Treaty 7. Denny, whose resignation in 1884 as an Indian agent had stemmed from his frustration over the inept bureaucratic administration, accepted with a proviso that gave him supreme authority in dealing with the five tribes. At Wood Mountain, Jean-Louis Légaré contacted Dewdney to have forty local Métis, all living in dire conditions, employed as scouts.[36]

The Saskatchewan crisis had enormous military implications for the young nation of 4.5 million people. In 1871, Britain had withdrawn its garrisons from Canada. This meant that, for the first time, Canada would independently confront a military threat. Here was an opportunity for the eighteen-year old Dominion, with a permanent force of only 750 men, to prove itself as a nation.

Adolphe Caron, Canada's Minister of Militia and Defence, supervised the complicated campaign logistics and acted as the government spokesman in Parliament. In spite of his lack of military experience, Caron proved to be a tireless and capable master of detail, whether distributing 10,000 free cigars to "the boys", purchasing 10,000 rifles from England, or sending a routine congratulatory note.

In a remarkably short time, over 3,000 militia had been mobilized and transported to western Canada to join 2,000 men and teamsters organized in the West. General Middleton began the attack on Batoche only forty-two days after the opening clash at Duck Lake. This was a truly incredible accomplishment.[37] With his troops were two gatling guns (ordered "rush") and sent along with instructor A.L. Howard from Hartford, Connecticut. These prototype machine guns, capable of firing an amazing 1,200 rounds a minute, were used for the first time in warfare.

The response to a telegram from Batoche on May 12 demonstrated Canada's resolve in this conflict. Middleton had informed Caron: "Force can succeed in holding but no more—want more troops."[38] Caron then

Major-General Frederick Dobson Middleton, Commander-in-Chief of the Canadian Militia

"He [Middleton] took good care to up the impression that the Mounted Police was an inefficient, useless body …we say he came west with full determination to dislike the police force."

– *Saskatchewan Herald*, 18 January 1886
NAC PA 12197

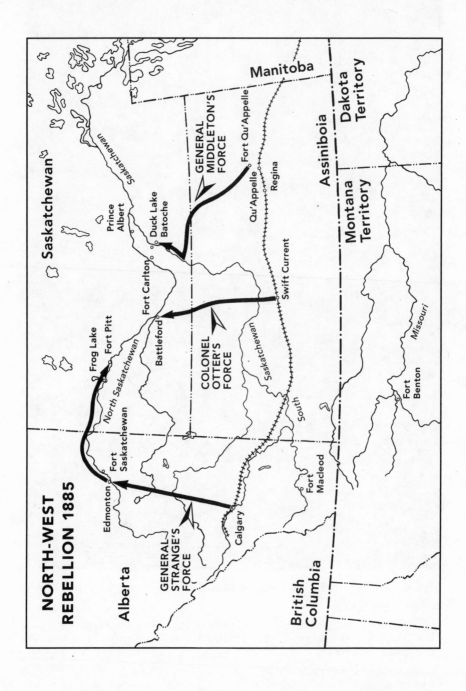

NORTH-WEST REBELLION 1885

Manitoba

Dakota Territory

Assiniboia

Montana Territory

British Columbia

Alberta

Saskatchewan

GENERAL MIDDLETON'S FORCE

COLONEL OTTER'S FORCE

GENERAL STRANGE'S FORCE

Fort Qu'Appelle
Qu'Appelle
Regina
Swift Current
Duck Lake
Batoche
Prince Albert
Fort Carlton
Battleford
Fort Pitt
Frog Lake
North Saskatchewan
Saskatchewan
South
Fort Saskatchewan
Edmonton
Calgary
Fort Macleod
Fort Benton
Missouri

mobilized four battalions. More than 1,000 men were gathered. Canada's grand concept of a nation "from sea to sea" was not to be thwarted by a handful of prairie rebels.

Middleton's revised campaign strategy, that used the C.P.R. line as a springboard, had authorized a three-pronged military offensive northward, with each against a point of insurgency. He correctly identified Batoche as the primary campaign objective. Victory here would decide the entire conflict. Middleton would lead this advance. There were no Mounted Policemen attached to this column.

On April 6, only eleven days after the Duck Lake skirmish, Middleton's force left Fort Qu'Appelle for Batoche, 280 km to the northwest. Freezing temperatures slowed the advance, but enabled reinforcements and supply wagons to overtake the column. At Humboldt, the Force turned west to Clarke's Crossing on the South Saskatchewan River. Here, on April 17, in a questionable tactic, Middleton divided his force to approach Batoche (located on the east side of the river) on both sides of the river. Each column contained 400 men and a field piece. Flag signals and a scow served as communication between the advancing columns.

Gabriel Dumont, the Métis military commander, concealed 200 men in a ravine called Fish Creek (Tourond's Coulee), near the east bank of the river. On the morning of April 24, rebel marksmen prematurely fired at advance scouts, alerting the column of the ambush. In the fighting that raged until early afternoon, the Métis combatants held the wooded ravine while, for the most part, the Canadian troops remained prostrate and fired at the hidden enemy. Several probing attacks by the soldiers proved costly and failed to dislodge the rebels from their concealed positions.

Other than long-range fire (that killed fifty-five tethered rebel horses), the soldiers underwent an unusual baptism of fire. In the early afternoon, three companies crossed by scow from the west bank to reinforce the government combatants. Middleton chose to withdraw from fighting once the dead and wounded had been removed from the field.

The skirmish was bloody: eleven soldiers dead and forty wounded. This casualty rate of almost fifteen per cent of the force in one day was unusually high. Métis losses were six dead and an unknown number of wounded. Middleton telegraphed Caron the Minister of Militia and Defence: "The troops behaved well in this their first affair, but owing to their inexperience the killed and wounded are I deeply regret to say numerous."[39]

On May 7, two weeks after reuniting their troops on the east bank, the 900-man contingency of infantry, two scouting units, a gatling gun, four artillery guns, and 150 wagons, resumed the march northward for Batoche.[40]

Their 22-km route was unopposed and, in two days, Middleton opened an assault on the rebel base. Although the determined rebel defenders had laboriously constructed a strong network of defensive rifle pits, they faced a pressing force with overwhelming numbers, munitions, and reserves.

There was no avenue of retreat, and an attack on the rear from the police force in Prince Albert remained a possibility. Ammunition was critically short and concerns for their families in the nearby village were uppermost. Moreover, the rebel strategy lacked co-ordination with the two rebel Cree bands to the west. The fanciful suggestion (by some writers) that the Métis use their mobility and knowledge of the country to harass the advancing columns in guerrilla warfare ignores the fact that the rebel horses were not grain fed and unable to travel effectively until green grass became available. Waiting at Batoche for an eventual assault by overwhelming numbers with superior weapons made defeat inevitable.

Middleton's attack at Batoche, shaken by his Fish Creek setback, lacked determination. Each day, the soldiers moved from the rear zareba (campsite) to launch cautious probing assaults on enemy rifle pits. Rebel sharpshooters repelled these advances and, in three days, killed three men and wounded eighteen soldiers. Middleton's field pieces randomly shelled buildings in the village, and the gatling gun spectacularly, but ineffectively, raked the concealed enemy positions. The probes, however, depleted the ammunition of those in the rifle pits and many demoralized defenders left to join their families in the village. On the fourth day, the rebel trenches held only sixty men with forty rifles.

A quixotic aspect of the battle at Batoche was the appearance of a river steamer sent downstream from Medicine Hat to attack the rebel base. On the first day of attack (May 9), the *Northcote*, fortified with timber and sacks of flour, arrived with a thirty-five man Infantry Corps to participate in the assault on the settlement. The steamer's whistle, however, alerted the rebels, who strung a cable across the river that knocked down the steamer's mast and smokestacks. The disabled vessel helplessly drifted downstream and far away from a naval victory on the broad Saskatchewan prairies.

The fourth day, however, May 12, brought a convincing government military victory. That morning, the Canadian lines advanced toward the rebel positions in what appeared to be another day of indifferent fighting. At about noon, the Midland Battalion surged forward from its far left placement near the river and, followed by the 10th Royal Grenadiers, made a general charge on the rifle pits. Middleton, at lunch in the zareba, heard the cheering and asked what was happening. Before he was able to act, the soldiers had overrun the rifle pits and village. His official report lied: "So I pressed on until I saw my chance and ordered a general advance."[41]

Lieutenant-Colonel Arthur Williams, member of the House of Commons and the Conservative party whip, directed the attack and victory. His tragic death from fever and sunstroke two months later disheartened the troops, but added to his acclaim as the hero of Batoche. To the militia, Williams symbolized young Canada's vitality and a refreshing contrast to the disliked General Middleton and his stodgy British officer staff.

The Battle of Batoche was the only decisive military action in the entire campaign. Thirteen rebels were killed in the four-day battle, far fewer than Middleton's exaggerated report of 51 dead and 173 wounded. Eleven soldiers were killed: three in the first three days and eight on the final day. Forty-three men in the military column had been wounded.

Among the dead was John French, brother of the first North-West Mounted Police Commissioner. French, described by Middleton as full of pluck and energy and a first rate rider and scout, had served in the NWMP as an officer from 1874 to 1883. At the start of the Rebellion, he left his farm in the Qu'Appelle area to raise a thirty-five-man troop of scouts called French's Scouts. After Batoche was overrun, a bullet fired from the other side of the river hit French, who was standing in a doorway of a house.[42]

Several days later, the capture of Louis Riel by scouts sealed the victory. Riel was a danger in name only, a figurehead who had never fired a shot in the rebellion and, if anything, interfered with Gabriel Dumont's tactics. Dumont escaped to Montana Territory, where he was immediately arrested, then released after several days. He returned to Canada eleven years later. In a bizarre twist, the Canadian 1985 commemorative postage stamp of the North-West Rebellion bears his picture, and not of Middleton nor the forgotten dedicated militia who had returned home to ecstatic greetings.[43]

Since the Duck Lake skirmish eighty days earlier, North-West Mounted Police Commissioner Irvine oversaw an inadequately armed force of 308 Mounties and volunteers at Prince Albert. Campaign strategy clearly directed him to secure the town. He had police patrols (the men dressed in brown and wearing slouched hats to disguise their conspicuous scarlet tunics) circle the town and scour the immediate area. On one occasion, on April 19, Irvine took 200 mounted men toward Batoche, but retired when scouts reported the rebel base was not being attacked as believed. Military communication to Prince Albert was decidedly inadequate. Still, as one Mountie wrote: "Why we did not march out and attack the rebels was a constant topic of conversation."[44]

That the Prince Albert force remained in camp while the four-day battle at Batoche raged immediately became a serious campaign issue. General Frederick Middleton's response to a reporter that his "next move was to go to Prince Albert and drive those gophers out of their holes" publicized

Gabriel Dumont

"After Batoche, Father Andre said to the police 'you are looking for Gabriel? Well, you are wasting your time, there isn't a blade of grass on the prairie he does not know.'"

– Michael Barnholden, ed., *Gabriel Dumont Speaks*, 23
    GA NA 1063 – 1

an unwanted appellation.[45] And, when his soldiers found out that while they attacked Batoche, the police were holding garrison sports and competing for money prizes upwards of $300 offered by the Hudson's Bay Company, one soldier commented, "The police have rightly been named by our troops, who cordially despise them, 'Gophers.'"[46]

With Batoche overrun, Middleton marched his column 60 km north to Prince Albert. They were met by Irvine and his troops "dressed in their cleanest and brightest uniforms, with shining faces and trim appearance, on their fat and prancing steeds."[47] This contrasted sharply with the Batoche column's travel-stained dingy purple apparel, a colour that was matched by Middleton's face when he saw the police. Middleton further denigrated the NWMP when he exclaimed to Irvine: "Look at my men, sir, they are dirty, sir, and ragged sir, but I am proud of them."[48]

Soldiers in the militia treated members of the North-West Mounted Police with contempt. A news reporter for the *Winnipeg Sun* wrote: "Feeling against the mounted police amongst the troops ran very high, and the appellation of 'The Gophers' was freely applied to them to commemorate the business like manner in which they stuck to their hole whilst there was any fighting to be done."[49] The Midland Battalion from Ontario, known for their unruly conduct, thought the term "gopher" the "very highest order of wit," and even challenged Mounties to fisticuffs. Lieut. R.S.Cassels, in the Governor General's Foot Guards stationed in Battleford wrote: "Two of their officers [Midland Battalion)] yesterday had the bad taste to visit the mounted police camp and accuse the Prince Albert police of cowardice. Very soon they found it too hot and had to depart; today they have been ordered to make a public apology."[50] The NWMP practice of not saluting the military officers was another point of contention.

Irvine justified his garrison duty in Prince Albert by stating that he had "received no orders to join General Middleton, which rather surprised me, as I am sure, from my long service in this country, and my knowledge of Indian and half-breed ways, would have been of great service to him."[51] Even before the skirmish at Duck Lake, Prime Minister John A. Macdonald had informed Irvine that, when acting with the militia, he was "to take orders from General Middleton on the latter's arrival."[52]

In Regina, Inspector R. Burton Deane defended his fellow comrades: "The whole North-West knows ... that the General Officer Commanding the Militia has so far forgotten himself as to apply the term 'gopher' to our comrades in the north."[53] However, the widespread image of "gophers" clearly attributed to the shake-up of the Force and the removal in early 1886 of Commissioner Irvine.

The Relief of Battleford

On April 24, three weeks before Middleton overran Batoche, a relief force, commonly called "Otter's Flying Column," had entered Battleford to a delirious welcome.

Understandable fears had still gripped the isolated town. The Custer Massacre, only nine years earlier, was in everyone's memory. Two local men were murdered by Indians and many people personally knew the nine murdered men at Frog Lake. That Big Bear's camp held hostages filled everyone with apprehension. Tensions ran high: the previous summer, a volatile Police-versus-Indian confrontation at Poundmaker's reserve compelled townspeople to prepare against an Indian attack. The lack of communication and distant Indian signal fires added to their anxiety.

NWMP Inspector William Morris saw his first duty was to ensure the safety of the fort with its 500 women and children. The police detachment strengthened the stockade, enrolled fifty civilians in the Home Guard, and conducted daily patrols. Three policemen imprisoned for desertion, P.H. Hawkins, J. Wright, and E.F. Davies, were released from jail and returned to duty.[54] On the morning of April 22, the arrival of the twenty-five-man Fort Pitt detachment bolstered morale. Nothing was done to prevent the Indians from looting and burning several homes in the abandoned "Old Town," south of the Battle River.

The downing of the telegraph line forced Morris to use riders to relay messages to Swift Current. This carried dangers: Morris reported that "plucky" Constable John H. Storer, the only volunteer in the Battleford detachment, was chased by Indians for 100 km while on this assignment. The young constable also went unscathed at the Cut Knife Hill skirmish but, thirty-two years later, on another continent, he was not so fortunate. While serving with the Canadian Expeditionary Force, Lieutenant John Henry Storer, age fifty-three, was killed in action in 1917.

The night of the arrival of the Fort Pitt detachment, Indians had fired on a two-man patrol that was checking for weapons left at a nearby farm, hitting civilian Frank Smart and his horse. Smart's companion, Constable Thomas White, rode up but, not hearing an answer from Smart, returned to the barracks. The next day Sergt.-Major M.J. Kirk took thirty-five men about 5 km to retrieve Smart's body.

As the military funeral for Smart ended the following day, Constable Charlie Ross arrived with the news he was with a relief column that was approaching town. The somber funeral mood turned to joy. For four long weeks, the settlers had been restricted to living in the overcrowded fort. Merchant James Clinkskill recalled "It is impossible for me to describe the joy with which this news was received. Women were crying and embracing each other, men went about with a brisk jaunty air, every eye was brightened, the long suspense was broken at last."[55]

The tiny rail station at Swift Current served as the supply base for the middle column. The initial campaign strategy had troops move from this point downstream in barges to join the attack on Batoche. Exaggerated rumors of danger (called "Nor'Westers" by Middleton) and urgent appeals to aid Battleford prompted Middleton to revise this strategy and direct a column north to relieve Battleford.

Lieutenant-Colonel William Otter, a forty-one-year-old Canadian militia officer in the Queen's Own Rifles, led the advance from Swift Current in what was called "the Relief of Battleford." His "Flying Column" included 200 teamsters, 450 horses, and 550 men, of which 50 were Mounted Police under Superintendent William Herchmer.[56] The barren land meant the column had to carry food, forage, oats, and firewood.

A broken ferry cable delayed the troops for four days at Saskatchewan Landing until the arrival of a river steamer, *Northcote*, facilitated the river crossing. On April 18, the march northward resumed in a heavy snow squall. For most of the 220 km, the column crossed over empty prairie that was described as dreary and dull. The North-West Mounted Police rode as the advance guard and, according to their commander, "were universally praised by the officers of the brigade."[57]

Other than the Indians firing several shots at the advanced scouts, most of the trail was uneventful. The men found and confiscated the supplies in a storehouse on a nearby abandoned reserve. When the column was only 5 km south of Battleford, Otter chose to camp rather than advance through thick woods in the growing darkness. This decision surprised and disappointed many of the men. They had seen the town from a high hill and, earlier that day, Constable Charlie Ross had ridden to the town to announce their presence. That evening, the men faintly heard Constable Patrick Burke sound Last Post in Battleford. One week later, Burke was killed in action at Cut Knife Hill.

A fire was seen coming from the distant town. Ross led six men on foot to investigate. His party met and exchanged shots with the Indians; Ross thought one Indian had been wounded. The gunfire alerted the camp, and Herchmer took thirty dismounted police in the direction of the shooting. No contact with Indians was made, but the nighttime patrol was harrowing. The Mounties returned to their camp, in one participant's words, "all worn out, as our nerves had been strung to the highest pitch in anticipation of volley from a concealed foe."[58]

At 8 a.m. on April 24, the relief column marched into Battleford. The destruction of buildings and still-smoldering home of Judge C.B. Rouleau (the fire seen from the camp) confirmed the troops' disappointment at not reaching the town the previous night. One soldier commented: "I never saw such havoc as has been done and it is galling to think how stupidly we missed them last night by not coming right on."[59] The men established a tent camp, appropriately named Camp Otter, beside the fort.

Otter contacted Middleton and Lieutenant Governor Dewdney as to the course of action. Middleton advocated vigilance, to hold Battleford and patrol the countryside. At this time in the campaign, Middleton had just had a setback at Fish Creek and was cautious. However, one of Dewdney's telegrams, recommended an active military role. Dewdney suggested: "Think you cannot act too decisively or the Indians will collect in large numbers."[60]

Military glory, for Otter, had to be more than just marching across the empty prairie and guarding a town. On April 29, a scouting patrol sighted Poundmaker's camp at Cut Knife Hill, 60 km west of Battleford.

Cut Knife Hill

Two days later, Battleford was abuzz as Otter assembled his striking force. There were the Queen's Own in their dark green uniforms, "B" Battery in blue with red facings, Governor General's Foot Guards resplendent in scarlet, the local volunteer Battleford Rifles, and fifty North-West Mounted Police dressed in brown field service uniforms and carrying Winchester carbines. In total, the assembled force had 325 men, two 7-pr. guns, a gatling gun, and 48 transport wagons.[61]

Halfway to Cut Knife Hill, the column stopped to water the horses and wait for the full moon to rise. The men sang songs and were in high spirits at the prospect of a brush with the enemy. At 11 p.m., the advance resumed. Superintendent Herchmer's Police rode about one kilometre in advance and several hundred paces on each side of the column. The night was chilly and, at daybreak, the troops, stiff from the cramped wagon ride, warmed themselves with exercises.

The column found the Indian campsite abandoned, the band having moved the day before. The sight, however, of cattle grazing on a hillside indicated the presence of nearby Indians. "We hurried on," wrote a Toronto reporter, "as everyone was anxious for the fray."[62]

After a laborious crossing of Cut Knife Creek, the column ascended Cut Knife Hill. From this elevation, the men spotted and fired at distant Indian teepees, forcing the occupants to run for cover. The Indians, however, knew of the approaching column. An old man who had risen to see the sun rise spotted the advancing wagons and alerted the camp. Warriors had waited hidden in the wooden ravines surrounding three sides of the hill. "We were somewhat surprised," recalled Sergeant George Cooper, Queen's Own Rifles, "to find bullets coming from our rear and left ... evident that the Red Devils had surrounded us."[63] Other than one assault on the two artillery guns, the Indians remained in hidden positions. Captain Robert Rutherford in "A" Battery wrote in his diary: "The Indians came on with war whoops and jumping up and tossing their blankets up above them to misdirect our aim, then fell on the ground and fired at us."[64] Police fire forced the Indians back into the ravines. One account credited the Mounties for bearing the "brunt of the fight ... and were admirably handled by Colonel Herchmer, a dashing and brilliant officer."[65]

Fine Day oversaw the Indian side, using a mirror to signal. His warriors were remarkably mobile. R. Cassels in the Queen's Own evaluated the Indian tactics: "They fought in a way that surprised the police, who have been accustomed to look upon them as arrant cowards. They are the beau ideal of skirmishers, expose themselves but little and move with marvelous quickness."[66] At any given time, there were never more than fifty Indian fighters, as many men checked on their families. Media and soldiers wildly exaggerated the opposing numbers between 400 and 700 warriors.

Throughout the skirmish, Otter's forces remained pinned in a small depression on the hilltop. The wagons were circled into a defensive corral formation, with a makeshift field hospital operating within. "We realized," recorded one Mountie, "that our very existence depended upon defending this position."[67] The gatling gun had ineffectively raked the hidden Indian positions and, as the fight continued, both of the aged 7-pr. guns became inoperable. Soldiers, steady in their baptism of fire, soon refrained from firing at distracting tactics as when the Indians threw blankets in the air.

In the six hours of firing, the Indians held the upper hand, remaining hidden and cleverly using natural obstacles to their advantage. Frank Elliot, who was killed ten days later, wrote to a friend that, "they were in so strong position that we could not dislodge them ... they fought like born Devils."[68] Matthew Envoy assessed the skirmish: "It was a battle of sharpshooting. No one distinguished himself more than Constable Charlie Ross."[69]

A teamster caught in steady fire on the hilltop evaluated the combatants: "The troops behaved very well; their fire may have been a little wild, but they were steady ... the Indians were very brave and did not flinch a bit."[70] Shortly before noon, after six hours of constant firing, Otter ordered a retreat. The troops were exhausted, the wounded needed better care, and the hilltop position held no advantages. And they were very hungry. Private C. Fraser, handicapped by a leg wound, wrote: "What was most trying was that we had no breakfast and nothing but tea and hard tack the previous day. When you consider we drove all night in a cold atmosphere you can see an appetite was worked up."[71]

Head scout Charlie Ross, along with a party of Mounties and Battleford Rifles, cleared a line through the creek and then set fire to the prairie to cover the retreat. Charles Ffolliott (?) wrote: "It was a ticklish time crossing the creek in a ravine, teams getting stuck, redskins yelling and coming down the hill like devils; but our fire kept them off until we got over. If the Indians had got possession of the ravine, not one of us would have escaped."[72]

Poundmaker contained his warriors from harassing the column as they retreated. "Had they done so," Otter reflected, "much delay and loss of life might have entailed upon us, as the country was favourable to them."[73] It took ten hours for the extremely exhausted column to reach Battleford. One Mountie remembered:

> Our wounded were in a most pitiable condition, as we were ill prepared for such an emergency. The dead were placed side by side in a wagon and the wounded rested on top of the corpses. Thus we marched from about two o'clock p.m. until midnight, when we reached Battleford.[74]

The body of Private William Osgoode, a member of the Governor General's Foot Guards, had been left in the field. On the following day, Father Louis Cochin, a hostage from the Indian camp, found and buried his mutilated body. At the end of the rebellion, Osgoode's remains were exhumed and transported to Ottawa for reburial.

Cut Knife Hill had been an exhausting and harrowing experience. In thirty-six hours, the men had traveled 135 km and fought a six-hour battle. Who would have imagined when they left Battleford that, on their return, wounded men would lie on top of corpses?

Otter reported that thirty to fifty Indians had been killed. This was incorrect. Cochin counted only five Indian bodies on the battlefield. The government casualty numbers were precise: eight men were killed. Three of the dead were Mounted Policemen. A bullet in the mouth killed Constable Sleigh. Two Mounties died in Battleford the next day: Corporal W.H.T. Lowry, a native of Ireland (and schoolmate of Sleigh), succumbed to a head wound, and Trumpeter Paddy Burke died from his wounds. Burke (age thirty-two) also was born in Ireland, served at Red River, and was nine years with the NWMP. He left a Métis wife and six young children. His family was destitute: the sale of Burke's kit collected only $7.25, and his pension benefits were a meager $12 a month for his wife. His comrades collected $100 to help the family.[75] The three men were buried May 4, with military honours.

Of the fourteen men wounded at Cut Knife Hill, Sergeant John Ward, seriously wounded in the abdomen, was the only Mounted Policeman. At the end of the Rebellion, the Privy Council provided Ward a pension of ninety cents per diem for life for his fourteen years of service.

Otter, in a telegram to Adolphe Caron, the Minister of Militia and Defence, downplayed his abysmal attack:

> Fought Poundmaker and five hundred men yesterday. Our men behaved admirably; loss seven killed and fourteen wounded, enemy from thirty to fifty killed; silenced his fire—both our guns broke down and had to withdraw.[76]

Otter further justified that his (unauthorized) attack had prevented Big Bear and Poundmaker from joining their camps, even though there is no evidence that the two rebel Indian bands even had this intent.

General Middleton was annoyed that Otter overstepped his mandate. He contacted Caron: "This is contrary to my orders to him. I am uneasy: he is as inexperienced as his troops."[77]

After the disastrous Cut Knife battle on May 2, the troops remained in camp. Fatigue parties built a bridge across the Battle River, dug trenches, built barricades, and cleaned the daily litter deposited by settler refugees. The supply line to Swift Current was maintained and, each day, mounted scouting parties scoured the nearby countryside.

One Mounted Policeman was killed during an encounter with Indians. Sergeant John C. Gordon was leading an eight-man police detail to retrieve two buried guns in a settler's yard, 12 km south of Battleford. The troop followed a rough trail through brush and unexpectedly met Indians when they rode over a hill:

> For a moment they were as startled as we ... our only hope was to make a run for it. Rifles barked—theirs and ours—and the Indians made a concerted rush forward, yelling like fiends. We emptied a few off their saddles, then turned and rode for cover. To our dismay we saw a large party of Indians bearing down on us from the crest of a hill on our right. To think of stopping and making a stand was out of the question, so we rode like mad.[78]

For the next ninety minutes, the Mounties would retreat, stop, fire to check their pursuers, and then mount to ride farther. During the exchange of gunfire, Constable F.O. Elliot was shot on his horse, but his comrades were unable to help him. Constable William Spencer spurred his horse and, as his companions cursed him, raced ahead of the party. After a time the Indians quit the pursuit, allowing the patrol, including Elliot's horse, to reach Battleford. Spencer was in the field hospital, which explained his sudden departure. A bullet deflected by a cartridge in his belt had entered his body and, unable to control his horse, he had let it run.

A larger troop under Sergeant-Major Thomas Wattam was immediately organized and, as E.F. Racey recalled, it was "almost before we could get our cartridge belts replenished, saddle fresh horses, and get a mouthful of food, we were off again with the view of recovering Elliot's body at all costs."[79] The police found Indian tracks leading from where he had been shot to his corpse. Markings indicated that the wounded Elliot crawled into the bush where spent cartridges showed he had made a last stand. There were bullets in his spine and head. The men were enraged at the sight of Elliot's body covered with dirt from a badger mound, with his head sticking out, and left to the "mercy of any wild beast that chanced by."[80] However, the patrol thought it too difficult to carry the body over the rough ground to place in the wagon and, wary of an ambush in the gathering darkness, the police returned to Battleford with the intention of returning in the morning.

Early the next morning, twenty-five mounted policemen (with a four-horse team) returned to collect the body. The corpse was undisturbed and, as they placed it in the wagon, Indians were seen running through the bush. Gunfire quickly followed.

The police detail rode away, returning gunfire in what became a wild ride. As the wagon descended a rocky hill, the corpse became dislodged and the extra driver (the off man) threw himself into the wagon box and gripped Elliot's hand to hold his body in the wagon. At the foot of the hill, the Mounties took cover to retie Elliot in the wagon box. It was a menacing moment. Racey recalled, "the Indians seemed to be advancing over a fairly wide front, tom toms were being beaten from the top of the hill, whoops and yells were resounding from all sides accompanied by continuous fire on our position."[81] However, the police held firm and, with steady fire, they forced the Indians to withdraw. With Elliot's corpse firmly secured, the patrol returned to Battleford without further incident. Constable Elliot was buried with military honours in the North-West Mounted Police cemetery. When he died, Elliot was thirty-seven years old and had served seven years with the American cavalry.

An absorbing aftermath of his death came two weeks later when D.T. Elliot, a clergyman, contacted the Minister of Militia and Defence, that he had read that Frank Elliot was the son of a minister in Troy, New York:

> I am the only minister of that name located in Troy and I have a son who has not been home for eleven years but I am still in doubt for the last I heard of him he was in the U.S. Cavalry in Montana Ter. Asking information.[82]

In the extensive correspondence that followed between Comptroller Fred White and interested parties, it was indeed clear that Frank Elliot was the minister's son. Surprisingly, too, Elliot was married and had a child. Shortly after the birth, his wife had tragically died. Elliot had left the baby with her maternal grandmother and went to Montana to join the United States cavalry. He had never contacted his family, or had his comrades ever heard him say he had been married or was a father. The eleven-year-old daughter was eligible for a NWMP pension. The Privy Council awarded her aunt a gratuity of $66.90 and daughter, Minnie, an orphan's pension of 13½ cents a day until she married or reached age twenty-one.

Ten days after the Cut Knife fight, Poundmaker's band began moving toward Batoche, unaware that General Middleton had just overrun the rebel base. Two days later, warriors captured a supply wagon train from Swift Current about 20 km south of Battleford. Twenty-one teamsters placed the thirty wagons in a defensive circle with oxen inside. Each man had a Snider rifle, but only twelve bullets. A Métis negotiator approached and convinced the men to surrender. The Indians took supplies, money, watches, and rings. For the next twelve days, the teamsters were prisoners.[83]

When news came that Batoche had been taken, hostage Robert Jefferson, a teacher on the Indian reserve, was sent to open the negotiations with Middleton. He returned to the Indian camp with Middleton's ultimatum for the Indians surrender to him unconditionally on May 26 in Battleford. There was no alternative. The hostages were then released and the band prepared for the meeting with Middleton.

The Alberta Field Force
In southern Alberta, Major-General Thomas B. Strange, a retired Imperial officer and now an area rancher, had energetically organized the defence forces. His initiative, key political connections, lengthy Imperial military experience, and being bilingual in French and English, earned Strange his appointment as commander of military operations in southern Alberta.

From a small nucleus of forty cowboys, his command quickly expanded to include prominent missionaries Albert Lacombe and George McKay, two French-speaking Quebec battalions (65th Mount Royal Rifles, 9th Battalion Voltigeurs), the Winnipeg Light Infantry (led by Osborne Smith, who briefly served as the North-West Mounted Police Commissioner in 1874), and two NWMP units: "Steele's Scouts," twenty-five Mounties from End of Track led by Inspector Sam Steele, and Inspector A. Bowen Perry with twenty-two men and a 9-pr. field piece from Fort Macleod.

The orders for this far-western column—The Alberta Field Force— were to "over-awe" the area Indians and then march to Edmonton. From there, the troops would proceed eastward along the North Saskatchewan River to the Indian-controlled Frog Lake area. While the 9th Battalion Voltigeurs from Quebec City would remain to garrison southern Alberta, helped by a 150-man scouting troop, the Rocky Mountain Rangers. This troop, led by the legendary frontiersman, Kootenai Brown, was to patrol between High River, Fort Macleod, and Medicine Hat.[84] Included in its ranks were thirteen former Mounties.

On April 20, fifty-four-year-old T.B. Strange, who referred to himself as "Gunner Jingo," led the first of three echelons (that totalled 1,000 men) north to Edmonton. Steele's Scouts served as the vanguard of this ten-day march through an almost empty land. The soldiers called themselves "alligators" in view of their ordeal through the spring mud and flooded waterways. Everyone recognized the potential development held by this empty, but fertile land.

At the end of their military service, their first-hand observations of the prairies drew some soldiers back to Western Canada. Twenty-year-old Cortlandt Starnes, a member of the 65th Mount Royal Rifles, returned the following year to join the North-West Mounted Police. He rose in rank to become the Commissioner of the Royal Canadian Mounted Police from 1923 to 1931. Starnes succeeded A. Bowen Perry, Commissioner of the Force from 1900 to 1922. That spring in 1885, the two men marched together, Starnes with his Montreal unit and NWMP Inspector Perry in command of the second echelon of the Field Force.

Halfway between Red Deer and Edmonton, 800 Indians resided in five adjoining reserves at Battle River. Early in the rebellion, the warriors plundered the trading posts and threatened reserve missionaries. Upon reaching the site, Strange met with the chiefs and warned that strong measures would follow should further troubles ensue. When he learned that the Indians were not impressed with the green-uniformed Montreal battalion who spoke like the "half-breeds," Strange had the following echelon, the red-coated Winnipeg Light Infantry, march past with the band playing and every soldier armed. The visual presence of the 1000-man Alberta Field Force proved effective, and Indian unrest at Battle River subsided. To secure his line of communication with Calgary, Strange garrisoned sixty soldiers in three small forts constructed between Red Deer and Edmonton.

In Edmonton, the three Field Force echelons regrouped and prepared for the eastward movement to Frog Lake. The horses were accustomed to the field piece firing and to soldiers shooting a rifle placed on their backs. Local volunteers (including Sam Steele's three brothers) joined the column, and six scows were built to transport the field piece and one-half of the men downriver. Steele's Scouts led the troops marching near the north bank of the North Saskatchewan River.

After a cold and wet ten-day march, the Field Force reached Frog Lake on May 25. A fatigue party of the Winnipeg Light Infantry buried the nine still-exposed victims of the massacre two months earlier. The burnt settlement, brutal murders, and extensive vandalism outraged the soldiers. That two of the murdered men's wives were hostages in the Indian camp aroused an irrational sense of rage. That same day, scouts reached Fort Pitt, the post Inspector Francis Dickens had abandoned.

A foul smell coming from nearby poplars led them to the decomposed body of Constable David Cowan, only eighteen years old when he was killed by the Indians on April 13. Near Cowan's body, the uneaten portion of his heart was impaled on a stick. The scouts at once dug a grave and buried his remains, "the rattle of musketry his only funeral requiem."[85]

In the search for the Indian trail, and perhaps in a misunderstanding of his orders, Perry took a troop of seventeen Mounties, five scouts, and missionaries John McDougall and George McKay to Battleford, a 150-km journey that they completed in only thirty-six hours. The absence of this scouting detail, all mounted, came at a critical time in the campaign. First, with more than half the Montreal 65th remaining at garrison stations along the Calgary–Edmonton trail, the striking force now numbered 515 scouts and soldiers, along with 160 teamsters. Second, the departure of Perry's Mounted Police entailed training an artillery crew for the "Macleod gun."

Once the Indian trail was located, Inspector Sam Steele led ninety-two men in that direction. As the troop prepared to bivouac for the night, an Indian suddenly jumped up from the grass and ran. Scout Joe Butlin fired and the Indian returned two shots, which passed between Steele and Butlin. The Indian then moved toward scout Tim McClelland, who shot him dead. A wild shooting scene followed. Steele recounted:

> We were in the midst of a yelling, whooping band ... the hot
> flashes of the Winchesters of the Indians almost singed our faces,
> and several times we had to pause lest we shoot each other.
> This lasted a minute, when the Indians departed to the eastward,
> exchanging shots with my rear party as they passed by.[86]

The Indian party contained twenty men. After a cursory search in the dark underbrush for warriors, Steele ordered his men to lie on the ground and prepare for an attack. It started to rain and two miserable, uneventful hours passed before the light of dawn allowed the men to return.

In the unforeseen encounter, an Indian named Meeminook was killed. He was cruelly defiled. Scouts stripped and mutilated his body leaving the corpse to rot in the sun. One teamster carried one ear in his waistcoat pocket. Someone pulled the body in circles through the tall grass with a rope attached to his saddle pommel. E. A. Hayes, a civilian scout in the Field Force, wrote, "one of the boys scalped Meeminook. This scalp hung for a long time in a billiard hall which was on the corner of First Street East and Ninth Avenue [Calgary]."[87]

At daylight, May 27, Steele led his scouts on the Indian trail. A count of nearly two hundred campfires gave the approximate size of Big Bear's camp. Steele directed a small detail under Scout Whitford to move ahead. Within half an hour, they returned "riding for dear life," pursued by a large party of yelling warriors. Steele's men dismounted and prepared for the onslaught. Steele recalled, "as soon as the savages caught sight of us they halted at a respectful distance and galloped away."[88]

Shortly after this incident, the main column arrived. Once the wagons were corralled, and left with the teamsters to guard, the Field Force began moving through difficult country. After advancing about 5-km, the men reached the base of a prominent elevation called Frenchman's Butte (now Frenchman Butte). As a detail of eight men began ascending a trail toward the summit, Indians appeared between them and the main column about 200 m to the rear. Gunfire drove the Indians away.

The shooting forced the men to take cover. As they intently watched up at the bald summit of Frenchman's Butte, Indians suddenly appeared. Trooper Hicks remembered: "They had gathered in considerable numbers, both mounted and on foot. They were yelling Astom Schmognus, Asum Pugumawa, in Cree—Come on white man and fight."[89]

This was the first sighting of hostile Indians for the rank and file, and the setting had accentuated their impressions. In his memoirs, Steele wrote of the absorbing scene:

A fine-looking band of Indians appeared on the summit of a large round butte, about 1,500 yards distant. They were galloping in a circle to warn their camp, their excellent horsemanship and wild appearance making a remarkable picture as they were silhouetted against the blue sky.[90]

Strange was not one to watch. He ordered shrapnel shells to clear the hilltop. The first shot fell low, but a second blast scattered the riders. On foot, the column advanced to reach the summit. Not an Indian was in sight.

It had been thirty-eight days since the column left Calgary and the men were gung-ho to fight Indians. "The Crees under Big Bear have captured Pitt and we are going to get it back or lose our hair," wrote one young Mountie to his mother in Ontario.[91] Notwithstanding their ardor, only "Gunner Jingo" and two other men had experienced combat. Moreover, there was no urgency for action. All communication with the Field Force followed the long line of advance from Calgary. The distance and rugged country delayed information. Still, ten days earlier, a messenger brought news that Batoche had fallen, Riel was a prisoner, and Dumont had fled to the United States. In effect, the campaign was over.

After a cold night without rations, on the morning of May 28, the column moved several kilometres north to a valley where the sluggish Little Red Deer Creek flowed into a swamp. To the north, at the summit of a steep, barren hill, warriors waited in concealed rifle pits. The Indians, with the forced help of prisoners, had spent all night digging trenches. Henry Halpin dug a hole seven feet long and four feet deep using a knife and pan. The Cree defensive position appeared formidable.

General Strange suspected an ambush. He and his scouts were certain the Indians were hidden on the hilltop. That morning, despite the Indians' strategic advantage, his sparse rations, danger to the white hostages held in the Cree camp, orders from Middleton not to advance beyond Fort Pitt, and possible inferior numbers, Strange chose to attack. For ten years (1872–82), "Gunner Jingo" commanded "B" Battery Canadian Artillery in Quebec City. Not surprisingly, he opened the skirmish with an artillery barrage on the wooded hilltop. A shower of bullets responded.

It was shortly after 6 a.m. and, for the next three hours, scattered firing continued. The conflict on the morning of May 28 has been incorrectly called the Battle of Frenchman's Butte. It was actually on the summit of Frenchman's Butte, 2 km south, where the Indians had circled on horseback until driven off by shelling the previous day. Strange and his force referred to the skirmish site as "Stand Off Coulee."

Big Bear and General Strange

"The Crees under Big Bear have captured [Fort Pitt] from the Police and we are going to get it back or lose our hair."

– C.E. Rivett-Carnac, ed., "Letters from the North-West," *RCMP Quarterly*, XVII, 17 GA NA 1353 – 16 (*Illustrated War News*, 6 June 1885)

The 400 men under Strange faced a distinct disadvantage in terrain and natural cover. There was little the soldiers could do other than lie prone behind improvised timber barricades. The Montreal soldiers were eager to charge up the steep glacis, a move that Strange wisely rejected. Other than one unsuccessful attempt by troopers with Sam Steele to flank the enemy, the Field Force remained immobile. It was an unusual baptism of fire.

The Indian camp had 150 warriors, far fewer than the number estimated by the Field Force. Some of the men guarded the main camp, located 2 km north, and, throughout the skirmish, others left the rifle pits to go check on their families in the Indian camp. During the fighting, the warriors would crawl from their hilltop rifle pits to the edge of the hill, fire, and then retreat to safety. For the most part, they had remained invisible to the soldiers lying in the valley below.

In three hours of firing, the number of casualties was remarkably light. A young Mountie, A.R. Dyre, who survived this day (only to succumb to typhoid fever four months later while on garrison duty in Battleford) vividly described the firing:

> A bullet grazed so close to the hand I was holding my rifle with as almost to burn it, while others struck the ground between my long legs and whistled around my head like devils let loose. McRae was shot in the leg not two feet from me.[92]

The shelling wounded five Indians. Kahweechetwaymot, the instigator of trouble a year earlier at the "Poundmaker Racket," died the next day from shrapnel wounds. Three men in the Alberta Field Force suffered wounds: Private Joseph Lemay, 65th Mount Royal Rifles, shot through a lung; Private Joseph Marcotte, 65th, shoulder wound; and NWMP Const. Donald McRae, shot in the leg. McRae had to be moved from the field under arrest as he refused to quit firing until his fifty rounds were gone.

In Montreal, the parents of Private Joseph Marcotte were notified that their son was killed in action. A Toronto newspaper reported:

> Joseph Marcotte, No. 3 Co. 65th, was a printer by trade and was working on the *Herald* when ordered to the Northwest with his battalion. He was unmarried and was looked upon as a steady young fellow. His father and mother were informed of their son's death in the fight by Bishop Fabre.[93]

On June 3 in Montreal, at a special church service (to bless a banner made by ladies for the 65th), Reverend Father Hanson declared that the unit, "Was now consecrated in fire and blood."[94] Research fails to reveal when Marcotte's anguished family learned that, far from dead, their son had been recuperating in the fresh air of the great northwest.

With the skirmish going nowhere, General Strange decided it was inadvisable to sacrifice men for doubtful results. Moreover, the Field Force (on half rations) needed supplies, the field piece had only twenty-two shells left, and the horse teams had remained harnessed throughout the fight. Before the withdrawal, Strange asked about the condition of the casualties. He was astounded to hear one officer say that Private Joseph Lemay, 65th

Battalion—who "would die anyway"—remained badly wounded in an advance position. When ordered to command a stretcher party to assist the wounded private, the officer replied to an incredulous Major-General T.B. Strange he had "been shot at quite enough today, and I am damned if I go down there again."[95]

Strange would never leave a fallen comrade on a battlefield. He ordered the field piece to open fire and, with Surgeon Paré, a stretcher party, and Father Prevost, began a search for Joseph Lemay. They found the wounded man and, after Strange urged Father Prevost to hastily administer the last rites, placed Lemay on a stretcher. As the party moved through rebel fire, the rear man dropped his end of the stretcher and Strange relieved him. With a sense of pride, "Gunner Jingo" was the last man off the battlefield.[96]

Fighting ended with both sides retreating in opposite directions. The Alberta Field Force returned 20 km to Fort Pitt where, to the amazement of everyone, Lemay was walking about before the camp broke up. The Indians moved northward into inhospitable brush and muskeg country. In the confusion of the Indian retreat, twenty Chipewyan families led by Father Laurent Legoff left for their settlement at Beaver River. For three weeks, the band had given the Cree gifts (including forty head of cattle) for permission to leave the Indian camp, but some excuse, delay, or false promise always ensued. Six white hostages escaped, including the wives of two men who had been murdered at Frog Lake. However, twenty-seven white hostages remained in the Indian camp, including the McLean family.

Although, from a military standpoint, the clash was inconclusive, it was a decided psychological victory for the Field Force. Indian communication surprisingly had not detected a large approaching military column. Its arrival had abruptly ended a Thirst Dance arranged to appease the tenuous Plains –Woodland Cree alliance.[97] To the Cree, the termination of a dance already in progress was an especially disheartening omen. Throughout the skirmish, explosions from the field piece could be heard in the Indian camp, each reverberation a disquieting reminder of the presence of soldiers who were determined to kill Indians.

"The cannon frightened the Indians very much,"[98] observed hostage George Mann. Demoralized Indian warriors acknowledged the superior firepower and realized their families restricted movement and fighting, while the soldiers "traveled without women and children."[99] Most serious, the band knew the soldiers would follow the American army strategy of unrelenting total warfare. Military harassment was deemed certain. While the dispirited Indian camp faced a dismal future, the soldiers were now more determined than ever before. They were encouraged the next day by the arrival of supplies.

One soldier, in the Winnipeg Light Infantry, now with only three hours battle experience, confidently predicted: "We expect to attack them again in a week or so, and then we will wipe them out entirely."[100]

Foray to Loon Lake

Inspector Sam Steele was determined to badger the fleeing Indians. At 2 a.m. on the morning of June 2 (five days after the skirmish), he loudly roused his cavalry troops in the pre-dawn light, ordered them to get eight days' half-rations, ammunition, and follow him. As the men groped for their supplies, Steele raced his horse down the trail. Quickly, his troopers followed. Steele described his urgency:

> We could not wait for either pack-animals or pack-saddles. The supply of ammunition was small, but there was no help for it, as no time was to be lost ... Strange informed as I moved off that General Middleton had landed, and would be sure to send mounted troops in support.[101]

Steele commanded forty Mounties and twenty-two Alberta Mounted Rifles. The troopers were eager for action as it was "generally believed that once Middleton came all chance for other fights would be lost."[102]

The Indians had retreated through a lightly timbered region interspersed with sloughs, muskeg, and waterways. They burned or discarded unwanted articles along the trail and at key points, felled trees to obstruct any pursuit. "They did," wrote trooper Hicks, "the very things they could to make us trouble."[103] The troopers found the trail extremely difficult. Mosquitoes and horseflies tormented the horses, and forage was mainly tough slough grass. As a measure of the horses' torment, only twenty-six of the seventy-five animals that began the pursuit survived the ordeal. Once a man's horse was disabled, the trooper walked back to Fort Pitt.

At noon on the first day, Steele's force contacted several Indian rear scouts and exchanged shots. Canon George McKay dropped one Indian with a scalp wound, and then fired a few shots over his head "to see if he could increase his speed."[104] In turn, Indian fire had wounded one scout, Thomas "Jumbo" Fisk. Steele's troop proceeded quickly, hoping to reach the main Indian camp before warning arrived of the pursuit. To conceal their presence, the scouts had no fires that evening, supper was without tea, and the men slept on the wet, cold ground.

On the morning of June 3, Steele's Scouts reached the Indian camp. The riders had only two hours of sleep that night. Trooper R.L. Barber recalled that "We took up Big Bear's trail at daylight, which was about

Steele's Scouts

L–R, front row, reclining – Frederick Richardson, W.R. McMinn, Donald McRae, J. McCarthy; middle row, seated – Alexander L. Davidson, John Robinson, Oscar Dubreuil, John Bunt; back row, standing – Peter Kerr, John Walters, F. Fane, Thomas Waring, Alexander Davidson, Robert Morton, Samuel Hetherington, James Whipps, Ernest Percival.

– R.C.M.P. Museum, Regina

two o'clock in the morning and came upon him about 10 o'clock."[105] It had been a determined pursuit. In thirty-one hours, the scouts, had ridden 85 km over difficult terrain.

The Indian camp straddled both sides of a ford between two lakes (Loon Lake was not mapped at that time). A count of seventy-five campfires at the band's last camp indicated that Steele's force would be outnumbered. From a high ridge, the troopers could see Indians crossing the ford.

Steele had planned to have McKay call in Cree for the Indian surrender. However, gunfire from an Indian sentry served, in Steele's words, as "a signal for us to attack and we rushed to the front with Indian yells."[106] The men, on foot, charged to the brow of a steep hill southwest of the ford. The retreating Indians, mistakenly thinking only six men were attacking, were exhorted by a chief to retake the position. To their surprise, they moved into a waiting police ambush. One Indian died three paces from Constable William Fielders, two others as they ran from the scouts. A lively exchange of gunfire continued on from concealed positions in the brush. The scouts fired at distant teepees, killing a fourth Indian. This shooting endangered the hostages in the Indian camp. Sixteen-year-old Kitty McLean had a bullet pass between her head and an Indian child she was carrying.

The police pressed the attack. The men, numbered odd or even, raced down the ridge. At the bottom, the odd-numbered men turned left and up a hill; the even-numbered men moved to the right along the lake toward the camp and ford. Both charges forced the Indians to retreat. The skirmish continued with long-range firing from hidden positions.

Steele had McKay make a second attempt to contact the Indians. He quickly withdrew when a bullet cut his sweater. Ironically, in the confusion of battle, the Indians had also attempted to open negotiations with the help of prisoner Hudson's Bay Factor, W.J McLean. While waving a white cloth on a long pole, McLean called loudly in French and English but only received rifle fire. To see the soldiers and yet not gain their freedom disheartened the hostages.

In contrast to the skirmish near Frenchman's Butte one week earlier, the clash at Loon Lake involved quick movements and close-range fire. Scout E.A. Hayes recalled: "This was a battle of action. The Scouts' rifles got so hot that they had to be dropped to the ground to cool."[107] Scout Joseph Hicks remembered: "I had Indians run by me within ten feet and we were all busy attending to them."[108] There were many close calls. One Mountie with his back to a tree later found a bullet lodged in the centre of that tree.

Sporadic shooting continued for three hours. An attack across the ford (today called Steele Narrows) would have been too costly in lives. Retreat appeared the best decision. Both the men and horses were played out and there was only one day's food ration and fifteen rounds of ammunition for each man. "The worst of the situation," Steele evaluated, "was that there was no sign of the promised support [from Middleton] which should have been with me earlier in the day."[109] Before leaving the battle site, Steele's men seized six Indian ponies and set fire to the teepees on the south side of the ford. A barrage of bullets directed at the unseen enemy covered the withdrawal. Combatant Thomas Wilson summed up the morning attack: "A good time was had by all."[110]

Steele's surprise attack at Loon Lake had killed five Indians, with no deaths to the police. One Indian victim was Cut Arm a Wood Cree who was friendly to the hostages. Two troopers were wounded in the fighting. Both men recovered, but a bullet through Sergeant-Major William Fury's right lung invalided him from the North-West Mounted Police. "Long and meritorious service" entitled Fury to receive the maximum pension of sixty cents daily for the term of his natural life.[111] The other wounded man, scout Billy West of Edmonton, had a bullet in his thigh.

The skirmish at Loon Lake proved that determined troops, with superior firepower, could easily pursue and harass the band. According to the hostage witnesses, the Indians were completely surprised by the attack, even though police scouts fired at them just several days earlier. Other than surrendering, the demoralized band saw no possibility of a military victory. A retreat into the inhospitable northern wilderness was the only option.

The Indians now moved northeastward around Upper Loon Lake, while Steele's Scouts retreated toward Fort Pitt where, early on the morning of June 6, they met Middleton's large advancing force. On the orders of the General, they joined his column moving to Loon Lake, where they found three mounds with Indian dead. Another sight was a crippled old woman hanging from a tree, a victim of suicide.

Thawing muskeg north of the lake prevented any further pursuit. After camping for several days (spent mainly catching immense numbers of fish in nets placed in the channel between the lakes), the column headed south. One soldier recorded General Middleton's return to Fort Pitt on the night of June 11: "We gave him three hearty cheers. Then the band struck up 'See the Conquering Hero Come'!"[112] The tune was ill-chosen; Middleton had spent eight days on the trail of the Indians. Little had been accomplished.

The Loon Lake skirmish severed the tenuous Indian alliance between Big Bear's Plains Cree who forcefully dominated the larger Wood Cree band. Within days, the Wood Cree left the camp and the Plains Cree broke into small groups. No longer were the Indians a danger to the region. For the next month, all their energies were concentrated on avoiding police and military patrols and merely surviving in the harsh wilderness.

Skirmish at Loon Lake

"This was a battle of action. The Scouts' rifles got so hot that they had to be dropped to the ground to cool."

– Scout E.A. Hayes, *Calgary Herald*, 20 April 1935
   GA NA 1353 – 33 (*Illustrated War News*, 11 July 1885)

The Indians realized the importance of having unharmed hostages should the soldiers appear for a third time. W. J. McLean wrote: "The only reason the Indians kept us was to protect themselves in case they were cornered."[113] The hostages treatment improved as the Indians now valued them as a bargaining tool. Factor McLean was even given a rifle to hunt rabbits for his family.

After Big Bear (Mistahimaskwa)

One week after the Batoche victory on May 12, Major-General Middleton's troops entered Prince Albert, 60 km north, to a very enthusiastic welcome. On May 22, again with great fanfare from the townspeople, Middleton, with 1,500 men, left for Battleford by steamer or on horseback. His contempt for the Mounted Police as "gophers." left no doubt as to what would be their next assignment. He dismissed Colonel A.G. Irvine's offer to contribute 175 Mounted Policemen for the search and, much to their annoyance, the NWMP still remained "gophered" in Prince Albert.[114]

On May 26, at Battleford, Middleton haughtily accepted the surrender of Poundmaker's band and arrested several men on charges of murder.[115] This left Big Bear's followers as the only remaining rebel group. Information on this band came with the arrival of Inspector Perry's wayward troop from the Alberta Field Force and two scouts Strange sent downriver by canoe.

Middleton, in his usual arrogant manner, dismissed NWMP Sergeant George Borradaile's request to replace a revolver (lost traveling downriver), commenting: "It was not necessary, as he himself would go through the country with a stick."[116] Upon his return to the Field Force, a note pinned to Borradaile's hat—"I was not at Fish Creek; I was not at Batoche"[117]— clearly informed his comrades that Middleton did not have any respect for their contribution to the military campaign. As for him walking through the country with a stick, a sarcastic Thomas B. Strange noted that "when he did come, he arrived with steamers, carrying a Battalion of Infantry, Gatling guns, and Cavalry."[118]

Following the surrender of Poundmaker's band, Middleton moved his column (which had fifty Mounties under Superintendent W. Herchmer) northwest to Fort Pitt. Left behind in Battleford was the 245-man Queen's Own Rifles who had garrisoned the fort since their inglorious attack on Cut Knife Hill just four weeks earlier. This forced inactivity, the troops believed, was Middleton's retribution for their unauthorized assault on the Indians. "Otter was," wrote one diarist, "being punished for his drive on Cut Knife Hill."[119] Charles Dunning of the Queen's Own Rifles wrote: "We all take it as a big slight."[120] Middleton's troops, observed one soldier, "seems to be imbued with nothing but the sense of their own importance and valor after the Fish Creek and Batoche fights. We are nobody at all."[121] As his force broke camp on May 30, the Queen's Own Rifles stayed in their tents, ignoring the customary three cheers for departing troops.

At Fort Pitt, Middleton had a brief acrimonious meeting with Strange and then led his column along Steele's trail to Loon Lake.[122] As stated previously, thawing muskeg prevented the soldiers from pursuing Big Bear's band and Middleton returned his force to Fort Pitt.

Strange was gone. During Middleton's absence, he had taken the Field Force more than 100 km northwest to Cold Lake. Perhaps "Gunner Jingo" knew Headquarters planned to remove him from his command. In recent weeks, Middleton and Minister of Militia and Defence Adolphe Caron had exchanged a series of cryptic telegrams that criticized Strange's alleged ill-treatment of Indians and his liberal promotion of subordinates which upset the militia ranking system. Geography, however, effectively foiled the removal of Strange from command of the Alberta Field Force.

With the Alberta Field Force at Cold Lake cutting off any Indian escape to the west and the main base at Fort Pitt blocking the south, Middleton ordered the Queens Own Rifles at Battleford and Irvine's Prince Albert North-West Mounted Police detachment to pursue the elusive band on the east flank. This gave the two contingents an opportunity to rectify their earlier controversial military actions. Their men rejoiced at this chance to finally prove themselves.

Otter moved 385 soldiers in the Queen's Own Rifles from Battleford north to Turtle Lake. From this camp, patrols scoured the nearby area, but captured only a handful of Indians, now scattered about in small groups. The anticipated excitement of fighting Indians quickly faded. Mundane camp routines, hot weather, and mosquitoes added to their disillusionment. What had begun as a spirited assignment was now, in the words of one officer, "a goose chase with less satisfaction than before starting out."[123]

Irvine's Mounted Police column of 136 men, 127 horses, and 19 wagons was detailed as the far-eastern search column. From Prince Albert, the contingent moved southwest to Fort Carlton where the steamer *Baroness* transported the men across the North Saskatchewan, opening the way north to Green Lake, a distance of 160 km. As a mounted patrol, the police were the most far-ranging column in the search for Big Bear.

It took five days to reach Green Lake. From this base camp, Irvine had patrols search the countryside. One group scouted westward to Loon Lake, a difficult 100-km trip to find "news" of Big Bear. Other patrols searched the nearby countryside. They had found several caches of food but, as one Mountie observed, "nothing was seen of any hostile Indians nor anything learned to lead belief in their being in the vicinity."[124]

The camp discomforts and monotonous daily routine quickly soured the NWMP assignment. With only four tents for the entire column, most men had to sleep under wagons or tarpaulins. The horseflies and mosquitoes were troublesome, and a food shortage arose. By June 18, the men had only a scanty breakfast. Later that day, teams arrived with supplies, oats, and a steer that was immediately butchered. Within two days, these supplies were consumed and the rations reduced to tea and hardtack. At Pelican Lake,

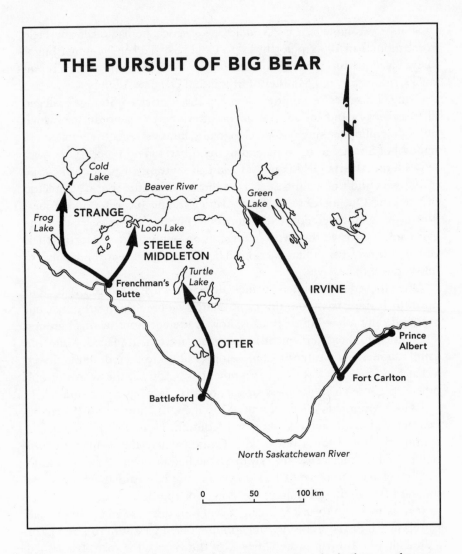

THE PURSUIT OF BIG BEAR

following a trying trip through dust, intense heat, and a hailstorm, the men expressed their frustration in what was called "a buck" in police parlance. A delegation of men approached Commissioner Irvine with an ultimatum: unless the food improved, there would be no further patrols. In response, Irvine ordered the slaughter of an ox.

Recognizing his troops' disillusionment with the Green Lake assignment, Irvine sought to bolster the morale of his force. At a general parade on June 23, he reminded the assembled group that the NWMP had surmounted all previous difficulties and, therefore, until the surrender of the Indians, they had to endure more hardships and food shortages.

Another inactive week passed before news came of Big Bear's capture. The police column quickly departed south, reaching Fort Carlton in two days. After arresting some Indians near this charred trading post, the column headed to Prince Albert. As they rode slowly down the street in a driving rain, a Mountie stationed in the town recorded his thoughts on the futility of the Green Lake assignment:

> The men certainly looked haggard and worn. Their long blue cloaks were muddy and torn, their slouched hats out of shape, their spurs red with rust, and the boots indescribable ... thin, bronzed, and with beards of scrubby growth, they were a grim, hard lot to graze on ... each man armed to the teeth.[125]

Three weeks earlier, companies under Otter and Irvine had rejoiced at their opportunity to redeem themselves. In spite of their arduous efforts, however, the assignment had devolved into little more than fruitless patrols, based around dull camp routines. By now, the scattered Indians, starving and unable to withstand the constant harassment, had conceded defeat. On June 18, the band released the hostages, without supplies, into the northern wilderness, leaving them to walk 230 km to Fort Pitt.

It took eight days for the twenty-eight hostages to reach the fort. Along the way, they shot rabbits for food. The journey was difficult, but spirits remained elevated now that they had their freedom after forty days of captivity. On June 26, news of the hostages' arrival at Fort Pitt brought the recall of the searching columns. The rebellion was considered to be over and Middleton prepared to demobilize the force.

The "capture" of Big Bear on July 2 concluded the military campaign. The sixty-year-old chief arrived at Fort Carlton along with Horse Child, his twelve-year-old son. Since the skirmish at Loon Lake four weeks earlier, Big Bear had walked hundreds of kilometres and easily avoided the four columns of more than 1,200 troops. Ironically, it was NWMP Sergeant William Smart, in charge of a four-man detachment left to guard the ferry at the burned-out fort, who arrested the most wanted Indian in the North West. In the words of a cynical General Strange, "Smart was about the only man on the Force who had never gone after him."[126]

The Rebellion Trials

Over the months that followed, it took a major effort by the North-West Mounted Police to identify and arrest Indians and Métis they believed implicated in the rebellion. A routine report from Battleford reads:

Big Bear (in chains) with his police captors

Sergt. W. Smart, Const. C. Colebrook (or Const. W. Kerr), Const. F. Nichols, Const. A. Sullivan. "Big Bear was in a pitiable condition of filth and hunger. He was given a good scrubbing in a tub at the barracks, though this was anything but pleasing to him."

– Donkin, *Trooper and Redskin in the far North-West*, 156
NAC C17491C

> Corpl. Chassé & Const. Hawkins left at 12:30 for Poundmaker's to bring witness "One-that-shot-the-eagle." Corpl. McConnell & Const. Meredith left at 12:30 for Sweetgrass to bring in "The Conjuror" – returned at 8:30.[127]

Most of the suspects were escorted to Regina for trial. In all, there were seventy-two rebellion trials. In late July, national attention focused on the trial of Louis Riel in Regina. The state of his mental health, being unstable in the past, was critical to determining his guilt. Three mounted policemen testified at the trial. Dr. Augustus Jukes, Senior Surgeon of the NWMP, contacted Riel daily and, although admitting not having a background on insanity, stated that his observations of the prisoner never gave him the impression that he was insane. Gaol (jail) warden Captain Richard Deane testified that his contact with Riel related to prison discipline and following regulations. In answer to a question on Riel's excitement or irritability, Deane replied that he remained polite, suave, and appeared shrewd. Prison guard Corporal Joseph Piggott never conversed with the prisoner, but observed Riel several times each day and considered him of sound mind.[128]

In October, appeasing discord in Quebec, Prime Minister Macdonald appointed a three-man Medical Commission to examine Riel's sanity. Jukes, as a member in the Commission, upheld his earlier opinion and agreed with it's decision that, although Riel had some unorthodox beliefs, he was legally accountable for his actions. On 16 November 1885, the North-West Mounted Police oversaw the hanging of Riel. Jukes, as coroner, examined his body and declared Riel dead.

Rumours circulated several days later that a brutal policeman, to the accompaniment of a blasphemous oath, had stamped his booted foot into the dead man's face.[129] To investigate this charge, Commissioner Irvine opened the casket in the presence of witnesses that also included NWMP officers Deane, Jukes, and Gagnon. Although no trace of disfigurement was evident, to insure security, a police detail guarded the casket on the rail transport to Winnipeg for burial.

Most of the Indian and Métis trials were cursory. When required, the police gave their evidence, and Constable Louis Napoleon Blache served as a court French interpreter when needed. Eleven men were sentenced to death. Three of these sentences were later commuted to life in prison. Prominent chiefs Big Bear and Poundmaker received three-year sentences and fifty Indian and Métis rebels were given prison sentences. Forty-two Indians were incarcerated for more than two years. These severe prison sentences, and the flight of Big Bear's son, Imasees, to Montana, left the rebel Cree bands leaderless.

At Battleford, on an overcast and bitterly cold day in late November 1885, a large force of 350 police and militia stood guard at the public execution of eight Indians. The scaffold in an open square, seven metres above the ground, gave an unobstructed view for thirty area Indians and a number of settlers to watch what was Canada's last public hanging. At 8 a.m., each prisoner, handcuffed and wearing black capes and face veils, was escorted by two policemen from the cells to the execution platform. The *Battleford Post Diary* described the hangings:

> All ascended the scaffold with comparatively firm step, some silent—while nooses were being adjusted, others singing war songs. Pères Cochin & Bigonesse on scaffold with them to the last. Nooses fixed, lever pulled and all were in eternity in a second. They died without a struggle and were cut down 10 minutes later, coffined, and buried within half an hour.[130]

A young Mountie in the burial detail, C. Whitehead, recalled:

> The bodies were duly placed in the boxes and we escorted them to a trench that had been excavated in the frozen ground with some difficulty. To our dismay, we found they would not fit in the grave, and we had no tools or dynamite to blast a bigger hole, so it was necessary to put them in sideways.[131]

Ottawa's assertion of authority was clear-cut.

Aftermath of the Rebellion

In 100 days, the North-West campaign concluded with Canada firmly in control of its vast prairie lands. More than 5,000 soldiers had marched against the rebels. Their presence proudly demonstrated that Canada, in its first independent military action as a new nation, could overcome complicated logistics and field a potent force thousands of kilometres from its centre of population. In response to this military crisis, the government, although on the verge of bankruptcy, had exigently raised $5 million for the campaign. Moreover, the defeat of the insurgents had unquestionably proved that the transcontinental railway justified its enormous costs.

At the beginning of the conflict, both the English and French-speaking Canadians responded patriotically to the news of an insurrection. Recruits raced to militia drill sheds and special recruiting locations to enlist, and enthusiastic crowds cheered their westward departure. At that moment, it was unthinkable that, within three months, the rebellion would fracture the very foundation of the young nation, leaving the country divided along religious and language lines for generations.

The end of the North-West Rebellion brought pivotal changes in the North-West Mounted Police. Most important was a shake-up in command. Ottawa now wanted new leadership. Even before the end of the campaign, newspapers were suggesting replacements for Commissioner A.G. Irvine. In November, Prime Minister Macdonald contacted Lieutenant Governor Dewdney to "get rid of Irvine as soon as possible."[132]

On 1 April 1886, Lawrence Herchmer, an outsider who had no police experience, became the fourth Commissioner of the NWMP. He had served on the Boundary Commission in 1874 and was also the brother of Superintendent William Herchmer. Perhaps being a Kingston neighbour of Prime Minister Macdonald factored in his selection.

The appointment of Lawrence Herchmer overlooked many long-serving superintendents. Nor did the resentment ease when he appointed his own brother, "Colonel Billy" Herchmer, to replace Superintendent Leif Crozier as the Assistant Commissioner. Second, the rebellion signaled the need for greater regional protection. Four new Divisions—"G-H-K and Depot"— were formed, giving the Force ten Divisions and over 1,000 men.

There was a memento of the campaign issued—the North West 1885 Canada medal. Ironically, for a campaign that prided itself on being distinctively Canadian, it was the Imperial government that assumed the responsibility and cost of minting the 5,250 medals.

Members of the NWMP were ruled ineligible for a medal. The outcry was immediate. Superintendent Frances Dickens, whose actions at Fort Pitt and Battleford met widespread criticism, wrote:

> These medals however, are not meant as pecuniary compensation, but as badges of honor earned by sterling soldier qualities, and this being the case, I should think that the police who fought under Crozier at Duck Lake, Herchmer at Cut Knife and Steele in the Fort Pitt country, as fairly entitled to them as volunteers.[133]

The furor from the press and police continued and, on 10 July 1886, an Order-in-Council recommended medals for those Mounted Policemen who had faced rebel gunfire. However, it was not until August 1900 that another Order-in-Council recommended medals for all members of the North-West Mounted Police who were part of the Force in 1885, with exception of those men who had chosen to desert.

A lingering negative aspect of the campaign was the "gopher" label pinned on the North-West Mounted Police. Certainly, there were police actions that warranted censure. Was Crozier too hasty in confronting the rebels at Duck Lake? That the Fort Pitt detachment had fled, allowing the civilians to become hostages of an Indian band responsible for nine murders, was questioned. Inspector W.S. Morris watched idly while Indian warriors pillaged the "Old Town" at Battleford. And had not the NWMP remained inactive while the fighting at Batoche raged?

On May 16, four days after the capture of Batoche, Minister of Militia Adolphe Caron telegraphed to General Middleton: "I want you to make a searching enquiry into the conduct of Irvine, Morris, Crozier and the Colonel of 65th Battalion. I want you to give these matters your personal attention."[134] After the campaign, Middleton further downplayed the role of the Force, recommending that a military unit replace the North-West Mounted Police who, he informed Caron, had "completely lost all prestige with whites, breeds and Indians."[135]

Irvine's leadership during the conflict was controversial. In his ten-year NWMP career, Irvine unwaveringly confronted every challenge. In 1885, he and his force were keen to fight the insurgents. Moreover, they could offer valuable skills:

> We were able to travel twice as fast as the militia troops General
> Middleton had with him ... we not only knew the country, and
> the habits of the Indians, but even the men in the ranks knew,
> and could recognize at a glace, the chief, head men and others
> against whom operations were being conducted.[136]

Irvine stressed that the safety of Prince Albert was his prime concern. His official report states: "Prince Albert was the key to the whole position, and the falling of it into the hands of the rebels would have been disastrous to the Dominion, and involved great loss, in lives and property."[137] Lord Melgund, Chief of Staff in the Batoche column (also Governor General of Canada, 1898–1904), agreed that the defence of Prince Albert was of uppermost importance:

> The fact of Col. Irvine's forces in Prince Albert afforded a safe
> refuge to many outlying settlers, and, if it had not been there,
> the task General Middleton had to solve would have been quite
> a different one. Hampered, as Colonel Irvine was, by the civilian
> population of the settlement and the difficult country, the

possibility of successful junction with Middleton must always have been doubtful, whilst the moral effect of the force at Prince Albert was certain.[138]

Father Alexis André, who attended Louis Riel in prison, agreed to the assessment of the NWMP garrison duties in Prince Albert "as preventing an attack on that settlement and extending rebel regional control."[139]

Opinion in Western Canada supported the Mounted Police against both Middleton and the eastern "Grit" press. The *Saskatchewan Herald* had commented: "He [Middleton] took good care to keep up the impression that the Mounted Police was an inefficient, useless body ... we say he came west with full determination to dislike the police force."[140] Bertie Antrobus, wife of a North-West Mounted Police officer at Fort Macleod, wrote that: "Gophers in their holes the newspapers dubbed them, but we knew better, and that they were merely obeying orders like good soldiers."[141] The *Edmonton Bulletin* described Middleton as being "petulant to the verge of overbearing insolence, variable as a weathercock and obstinate as a Scotch boatswain."[142]

A town meeting in Prince Albert sincerely thanked Irvine for his very thoughtful manner in conducting affairs during the crisis and offered support to "our old friends of the NWMP from attacks that were unjust and ungenerous."[143] Shortly after the campaign ended, Fort Macleod gave a banquet for the Commissioner. An enthusiastic audience applauded the speaker's contention that "we in the west have always been ready to give credit where it was due, and that it seems strange that the eastern press should have ignored the gallant conduct of the police."[144] In his reply, Irvine spoke of slanderous attacks from the Eastern press. Residents in Calgary shunned Middleton's visit to the town by remaining inside while Lieutenant Governor Dewdney (also unpopular) and Middleton rode about town in a carriage. The visitors, aware of the snub, quickly left for Banff.

On his return to Eastern Canada, Middleton enjoyed an appreciative response in Ottawa. Parliament made him a Knight Commander of the Order of St. Michael and St. George, and they awarded him $20,000 for suppressing the insurrection. These honours found little support with Westerners. One Mounted Policeman in Battleford thought otherwise, describing his commander as "simply an egotistical, lying old hog, no more worthy to be knighted than I am."[145]

The North-West Rebellion cost the lives of eight Mounties. Eleven men were wounded. In every military engagement, the police were bold and brave. Colonel Otter referred to Lieutenant-Colonel W. Herchmer as my "most valuable assistant ... he displayed the most sterling qualities of a soldier, while the men in his command have time and time again proved themselves invaluable to my force."[146] Thirty-six-year-old Inspector Sam Steele even won respect from dour General Middleton, who conceded that, "Steele and his men were useful to Strange and they did excellent service for me."[147] Near the end of the campaign, General Strange acknowledged Steele's contribution. To a friend in Quebec, Strange wrote: "Things are drawing to a close ... I look back and think why we were not destroyed 100 times over? Why? Simply because I was fortunate in having a most splendid body of Scout cowboy cavalry—under Steele, a rare combination of caution and daring."[148]

Newspaper correspondent Fred Harris aptly summed up the military campaign:

> The war is over. It has been a small affair ... and yet it has served to show that Canada can, when necessary, put a formidable force in the field, arm, equip, transport and provide for her soldiers in a manner not surpassed by older countries with ten times her experience in warlike affairs. It has shown also that the volunteers may be depended upon ... men who are willing to bear hardship and privation and to confront danger at the call of their country.[149]

In the final analysis, although there were several incidents to justly criticize, the North-West Mounted Police served loyally and arduously throughout the rebellion. In his log book, Inspector A.B. Perry recorded his police troop from Fort Macleod had ridden an incredible 2,100 km. (1,308 miles). To remain saddled with the disparaging image of a gopher, quick to flee to safety, does not reflect the overall contribution made by the vast majority of men.

NOTES

1. *MFP*, 16 July 1885; *SH*, 18 January 1886.

2. Donkin, *Trooper and Redskin*, 149.

3. *RC*, NWMP, 1885, 25.

4. Michael Barnholden, ed., Gabriel Dumont, *Gabriel Dumont Speaks* (Vancouver: Talonbooks, 1993), 54.

5. *CSP*, 1885, XIII, No. 153, "Report of the Commissioner of the North-West Mounted Police, 1885," 44.

6. *MG*, 12 May 1885.

7. William Laurie, "What I Saw of the North-West Rebellion," *SG*, Seventeenth Annual, 20. Both sides accused the other of firing first. Even on McKay's death fifty-three years later, a headline in the *RL* (21 December 1938) asked: "Question Again – Who Fired First Rebellion Shot?"

8. W.A. Griesbach, *I Remember* (Toronto: Ryerson, 1946), 66.

9. *SH*, 23 April 1885.

10. Rebel deaths included: Isadore Dumont, Jean-Baptiste Montour, Joseph Montour, Augustine Laframboise, and Assiyiwan (Charlie Cree). Prince Albert Volunteers deaths included: Captain John Morton; Corporal William Napier; Constables Joseph Anderson, James Bakie, Skeffington Elliot, Alexander Fisher, Robert Middleton, Daniel McKenzie, Daniel McPhail. Prince Albert wounded: Captain Henry Stewart Moore; Sergeant Alexander McNabb; Constables—A. Markley, George Duck, Charles Newett, and Alexander Stewart.

11. Griesbach, *I Remember*, 62.

12. *WDS*, Rebellion Number, 3 July 1885.

13. *NAC*, Wm. Patrick Lynch, f. 1105.

14. Laurie, "What I Saw of the North-West Rebellion," 22.

15. Two years later, a four-man detail under Sergeant William Parker exhumed the bodies and had them interred in a Prince Albert cemetery. Parker wrote: "We found them buried in one deep grave, one on top of the other. The first two were fairly easy to get out, but the third, a very heavy man, was eight feet down and gave us a lot of trouble. The bodies were in a wonderful state of preservation." Dempsey, *William Parker, Mounted Policeman*, 79. Garrett's father wrote from Ireland that receiving his son's North-West Rebellion medal is "dearly prized by myself and his sorrowing mother." Robert Knuckle, *In the Line of Duty: The Honour Roll of the RCMP since 1876* (Burnstown, Ontario: General Store Publishing, 1994), 40.

16. Superintendent Leif Crozier (flesh wound, cheek), Inspector Joseph Howe (flesh wound, leg), Corporal Thomas Gilchrist (left thigh shattered), Constable August Miller (scalp wound), Constable Stanley Gordon, (flesh wound, leg), Constable J.J. Wood (flesh wound, arm), Constable Alfred Manners-Smith (bullet passed through upper chest). Gilchrist's broken hip was injured while being carried out of Fort Carlton. He died nine months later, possibly from the effects of his wound.

17. *CSP*, "Report of the Commissioner," XIII, No. 153, 36.

18. Donkin, *Trooper and Redskin*, 103.

19. Pocock, *Frontiersman*, 31. "Nitchie" was a derogatory term for Indians.

20. Vernon LaChance, ed., *Diary of Francis Dickens* (Kingston, Ontario: Bulletin of the Department of History and Political and Economic Science in Queen's University, 1930), No. 59, 12.

21. *FBRP*, 25 March 1885.

22. *CSP*, 1885, XIII, No. 153, "Report of the Commissioner of the North-West Mounted Police, 1885," 23.

23. Alexander Stewart, *WDS*, Rebellion Number, 3 July 1885.

24. Donkin, *Trooper and Redskin*, 128–29.

25. *GA*, RCMP Fonds. Newett (sometimes Newitt) was on crutches for two months and afterwards needed a cane. His knee and hand injuries prevented his work as a plaster. He sought compensation and was examined by NWMP doctors on 18 November 1887. The results were not found.

26. W.J. McLean, "Tragic Events at Frog Lake and Fort Pitt during the North West Rebellion," *MP*, Whole No. 47, 7.

27. Donald J. Klancher, *The North West Mounted Police and the North West Rebellion* (Kamloops: Mounted Police Research and Consulting, 1997), 23.

28. *CSP*, 1886, XXX, No. 13. Queen vs. Louison Mongrain, 11. Mongrain was sentenced to hang. Shortly before his execution, his sentence was commuted to life imprisonment.

29. Charette, ed., *Vanishing Spaces – Memoirs of Louis Goulet*, 133.

30. Charles Boulton, *Reminiscences of the North-West Rebellions* (Toronto: Grip, 1886), 338.

31. Ibid.

32. Ibid., 339.

33. Inspector Francis Dickens died suddenly in Illinois in June 1886. Before joining the NWMP, he had served with the Bengal Mounted Police for seven years. His NWMP career was uneventful and handicapped by alcohol problems and an increasing loss of hearing.

34. Middleton, born in Belfast, was an Imperial officer with combat experience in the Maori Wars and the Indian Mutiny. He had come to Canada in 1884 to command the Canadian Militia.

35. Alexander Laidlaw, *From the St. Lawrence to the North Saskatchewan* (Halifax, N.S.:Bowes, 1885), 36.

36. Superintendent Percy Neale hired five Sioux from Moose Jaw under ex-policeman LaQuesne to watch Indian activities.

37. During the European War, a German commander who had studied military science with the German General Staff, called the performance of Government forces in the North-West Rebellion unique in military history. Upon no other occasion had a detachment been sent such a distance, with so few facilities for movement and supply, and the objective accomplished in such short time. See W.C. Pollard, *Pioneering in the Prairie West* (Uxbridge, Ontario: Cave, 1924), 32.

38. D.P. Morton and R.H. Roy, eds., *Telegrams of the North-West Campaign, 1885* (Toronto: The Champlain Society, 1972), 268.

39. Ibid. 207.

40. Units with number of men included: "A" Battery, Quebec (86); Winnipeg Field Battery (40); 10th Royal Grenadiers, Toronto (210); Midland Battalion, Ontario (81);

90th Battalion, Winnipeg (254); Boulton's Mounted Infantry, Russell and Birtle, Manitoba (65); "C" Company Detachment, Toronto (48), French's Scouts (35), and, on May 10, Dominion Land Surveyors' Intelligent Corps, Ottawa (50).

41. Morton and Roy, eds., *Telegrams of the North-West Campaign, 1885*, 271. On the battle, Allan Cameron, *CH*, 17 May 1922.

42. *Dictionary of Canadian Biography*, vol. XI (Toronto: University of Toronto Press, 1982), 326. French left a wife and four children. Two sons would serve in the NWMP.

43. Dumont certainly would have been imprisoned, if not executed.

44. Donkin, *Trooper and Redskin*, 133.

45. *MFP*, 16 July 1885.

46. *RL*, 9 June 1885.

47. Ibid.

48. Ibid.

49. *PAM*, George A. Flinn, MG3, C13.

50. *GA*, Diary of Lieut. R.S. Cassels, BG 3. Q. 3. Also Donkin, *Trooper and Redskin*, 149.

51. *CSP*, 1885, "Report of the Commissioner," 42.

52. Morton and Roy, eds., *Telegrams of the North-West Campaign 1885*, 3.

53. R. Burton Deane, *Mounted Police Life in Canada*, 24–25.

54. Hawkins continued to complete his five-year term. He was awarded the NWR medal and, in the 1930s, a $300 government grant. Wright purchased his discharge in 1886.

55. Bob Beal and Rod Macleod, *Prairie Fire* (Edmonton: Hurtig, 1985), 240.

56. The column had 50 NWMP; 113 men "B" Battery; 275 Queen's Own Rifles; 50 Governor General's Foot Guards; 47 "C" Company Infantry School Corps.

57. *RC*, NWMP, 1885, 51.

58. A.H. Rumball, "The Relief of Battleford," *SG*, Third Annual, 47.

59. *GA*, Diary of R.W. Rutherford, M 4843, Box 44.

60. Beal and Macleod, *Prairie Fire*, 242.

61. The force contained 75 NWMP (Superintendent P.R. Neale); 80 "B" Battery, Royal Canadian Artillery (Major C.J. Short); 45 "C" Company Infantry School Corps (Lieutenant R.L. Wadmore); 20 Governor General's Foot Guards (Lieutenant H.H.O. Gray); 50 Queen's Own Rifles (Captain Thomas Brown); 50 Battleford Rifles (Captain E.A. Nash). See Robert H. Caldwell, "Cut Knife Hill," in Donald Graves, ed., *More Fighting for Canada* (Toronto: Robin Brass Studio, 2004), 73–146.

62. *TM*, 19 May 1885.

63. *TW*, 2 June 1885.

64. *GA*, Diary of R.W. Rutherford, M 4843, Box 44. Other battle accounts are J. Elton Prower, "With Otter's Column in the North-West," *United Services Magazine*, Vol. XI, 493–509, and *PAM*, J.S. Chisholm Fraser, P517–2.

65. *TM*, 7 May 1885.

66. *GA*, Diary of Lieut. R.G. Cassels, BG. 3. Q.3.

67. Rumball, "The Relief of Battleford," 49.

68. *RL*, 19 May 1885.

69. *RL*, 12 May 1885. Charlie Ross, born in Australia, had a remarkable adventurous life. See Neil Speed, *Born to Fight* (Melbourne: Caps and Flints, 2002).

70. *GA*, Gower, M 6480.

71. *PAM*, J.S. Chisholm Fraser, P 517 – 2.

72. Ibid.

73. *CSP*, 1886,Vol,. 5, No. 6a, Department of Militia and Defence, "Report upon the Suppression of the North-West Rebellion in the North-West Territories, in 1885," 25.

74. Rumball, "The Relief of Battleford," 50.

75. In 1887, Burke's widow was awarded a grant of $274 and a pension of one-half the daily pay of her husband, for the term of her natural life, provided she remain a widow; the children received four months of their father's pay and seven and a half cents daily until age 18; the daughter until marriage, or age twenty-one. Burke's sons would later join the Mounted Police.

76. Morton and Roy, eds., *Telegrams*, 242.

77. Ibid., 243.

78. E.F. Racey, "A Police Patrol Skirmishes with Indians," *RCMP Quarterly*, XII, 313.

79. *NAC*, E.F. Racey, f. 969.

80. Racey, "A Police Patrol Skirmishes with Indians," 314.

81. *NAC*, E.F. Racey, f. 969.

82. *NAC*, Frank Elliot, f. 973. Superintendent William Herchmer wrote that Elliot was a brave man and did his duty well. His effects were auctioned for $3.10.

83. Neil Brodie, *Twelve Days with the Indians* (Battleford: *Saskatchewan Herald*, 1932). John W. Shera, "Poundmaker's Capture of the Wagon Team in the Eagle Hills, 1885," *AHR*, 1, No. 1, 16–20.

84. Gordon Tolton, *The Cowboy Cavalry* (Vancouver: Heritage House, 2011).

85. R.G. MacBeth, *The Making of the Canadian West* (Toronto: William Briggs, 1898, 175.

86. Steele, *Forty Years in Canada*, 221.

87. E.A. Hayes, "Okotoks Old-Timer," *CH*, 20 April 1935.

88. Steele, *Forty Years in Canada*, 221.

89. Joseph Hicks, "With Hatton's Scouts in Pursuit of Big Bear," *AHR*, XVIII, No. 3, 17.

90. Steele, *Forty Years in Canada*, 222.

91. Rivett-Carnac, ed., "Letters from the North-West," 17.

92. Ibid.

93. *TG*, 1 June 1885.

94. *MFP*, 4 June 1885. Fellow employees at the Montreal newspaper celebrated Marcotte's return with a grand party.

95. Strange, *Gunner Jingo's Jubilee*, 492.

96. Charles R. Daoust, *Cent-Vingt Jours de Service Actif* (Montreal: Eusèbe Senécal & Fils, Imprimeurs-Éditeurs, 1886). An English copy was published by the City of Wetaskiwin, Alberta. See 76–84.

97. The Cree camp contained Wood and Plains Cree and twenty Chipewyan lodges. The Plains Cree forcefully exerted control over the camp. They were responsible for the Frog Lake killings.

98. George Mann, *The Fort Pitt Trail*, comp. Dorcas Alma Hewitt (n.p., 1968), 7.

99. Duncan McLean, "The Last Hostage," *The Albertan Weekend Magazine*, 17 August 1968, 8.

100. *Winnipeg Daily Sun*, Rebellion Number, 3 July 1885.

101. Steele, *Forty Years in Canada*, 224.

102. Hicks, "With Hatton's Scouts in Pursuit of Big Bear," 19.

103. Ibid.

104. George McKay, *Fighting Parson* (Kelowna: Privately Printed, 1968), 226–27.

105. F.C. Jamieson, *The Alberta Field Force of 1885* (Battleford: Canadian North-West Historical Society, 1931), 46.

106. Steele, *Forty Years in Canada*, 225.

107. Hayes, "Okotoks Old-Timer," *CH*, 20 April 1935.

108. Hicks, "With Hatton's Scouts," 22.

109. Steele, *Forty Years in Canada*, 224.

110. Thomas E. Wilson, *Trail Blazer of the Canadian Rockies* (Calgary: Glenbow Alberta Institute, 1972), 51.

111. J.R. Henry, "Sergeant Fury," *RCMP Quarterly*, XVII, 45. *NAC*, William Fury, f. 333. It was three years before a medical board of three doctors declared Fury suffered from the effects of a bullet received in action at Loon Lake. He lived for forty-nine more years, until age ninety-five.

112. Iris Allan, ed., "A Riel Rebellion Diary," *AHR*, XII, No. 3, 22.

113. *TG*, 17 July 1885.

114. *RL*, 9 June 1885.

115. C.F. Winter, "The Surrender of Poundmaker," *Canadian Magazine*, XXXVI, No. 5, 411–19.

116. Strange, *Gunner Jingo's Jubilee*, 468.

117. Ibid.

118. Ibid.

119. R.H. Roy (ed.), "Rifleman Forin in the Riel Rebellion," *SH*, XXI, No. 3, 106.

120. *Archives of Ontario*, Charles Dunning Diary, 1885, 12843.

121. *GA*, Diary of R.W. Rutherford, M 4843, Box 44.

122. Strange resented Middleton's arrogance, stating in a letter to a friend that his superior was "so puffed up over Riel's surrender ... that he thinks that there is but one Middleton." *GA*, Strange–Lotbinière Correspondence, M 692, Reel 2.

123. *Archives of Ontario*, Charles Dunning Diary, 1885, 12843.

124. *GA*, Col. G.E. Saunders, 5215 f.11.

125. Laurie, "What I Saw of the North-West Rebellion," 29.

126. Strange, *Gunner Jingo's Jubilee*, 506.

127. *Fort Battleford Post Diary 1885*, 6 October 1885.

128. *The Queen vs Louis Riel*, (Toronto: Univ. Toronto Press, 1974), Jukes' testimony, 269–74; Joseph Piggott, 284; Richard Deane, 283–84.

129. Deane, *Mounted Police Life in Canada*, 232.

130. *Fort Battleford Post Diary 1885*, 27 November 1885.

131. C. Whitehead, "A Day in Battleford," *SG*, Fifth Annual, 91.

132. *GA*, Dewdney Papers, 587.

133. Donald J. Klancher, *The North West Mounted Police and the North West Rebellion*, 81–82.

134. Morton and Roy eds., *Telegrams*, p. 287. *FMG*, 29 December 1885.

135. Desmond Morton, *The Last War Drum* (Toronto: A.M. Hakkert, 1972), 145.

136. *RC*, NWMP, 1885, 31.

137. *RC*, NWMP, 1885, 26.

138. Rev. R.G. MacBeth, "The Story of the Royal North West Mounted Police," *SG*, First Annual, 99.

139. Edmund Morris, "L'T-Col. Irvine and the North-West Mounted Police," *Canadian Magazine*, XXXVII, No. 6, 500–501. Also George H. Ham, *Reminiscences of a Raconteur* (Toronto: Musson, 1921); *FMG*, 13 June and 4 August 1885; *FBRP*, 10 June 1885; *PAT*, 24 July 1885.

140. *SH*, 18 January 1886.

141. Bertie Antrobus, "Reminiscences of Fort Macleod in 1885," *Canadian Magazine*, VIII, No. 1, 4.

142. *EB*, 8 August 1885.

143. *PAT*, 5 June 1885.

144. *FMG*, 25 August 1885.

145. Atkin, *Maintain the Right*, 252.

146. *CSP*, 1886, Department of Militia and Defence, "Report upon the Suppression of the Rebellion in the North-West Territories, 1885," 25.

147. Frederick Middleton, *Suppression of the Rebellion in the North West Territories of Canada*, 1885, 65.

148. *GA*, Strange–Lotbinière Correspondence, M 692, Reel 2, 20 June 1885.

149. *The Trip Hammer*, August 1885, 1, No. 7.

22

BOYS OF THE OLD
BRIGADE

Mounted Police Veterans in Calgary Stampede Parade, 1925

"After sixty years on the Alberta frontier, my mind often wanders back to recall the many
events of my three years with the NWMP. Most of the men of those days have gone ...
We were young then. The pace was fast and furious, danger was ever present."

– Edward Barnett, NWMP, *GA* M 6142
   GA NA 1522 – 1

THIS ACCOUNT OF THE NORTH-WEST Mounted Police (1873–85)
covers the most momentous twelve-year period in Canadian prairie
history. And always front and centre were the scarlet-coated "Riders of
the Plains." The Mounties had entered the vast prairie land to establish
law and order, preparatory to a wave of settlement destined to come.

They were, as the sign proclaimed on their first Christmas spent at Fort Macleod, "Pioneers of a Glorious Future." Everyone was aware of their role in history. On his inspection tour of the police posts in 1875, Major-General E. Selby Smyth reported that: "Above all they have the conscious knowledge that they are pioneers in a rich and fertile territory, magnificently spacious though still strangely solitary and silent, which at no distant time will re-echo with a busy life of a numerous and prosperous population."[1] Howard Kennedy, a newspaper reporter from Toronto, recalled how, during the North-West Rebellion, he rode beside a Mountie for an hour in dead silence. Suddenly, the young man spoke for all the men serving in the campaign with the words: "We're making history, eh!"[2]

During the First World War, Constable R.G. Mathews drove Colonel Robert "Bobbie" Belcher to visit Major-General Samuel Benfield Steele, who now was the General Officer in command of the Southwestern District of England. On the square outside Steele's office, thousands of men were marching, but Mathews watched the two old comrades who were totally oblivious to the military drills as they:

> Yarned about the old days in the Northwest. They spoke of men long gone and of incidents long since history: how Paper Collar Johnnie (Inspector A.R. Macdonell) had done this and what Tommy Wattam had done there … about Billy Herchmer and Governor Dewdney, about Johnnie Cotton and Red Crow and Bull Stewart and Pat Mahoney and Charlie Ross and a host of others. They discussed the North-West Rebellion, and the C.P.R. construction through the mountains.[3]

Mathews felt ignored (and truly was)—"but to hear them roam from Fort Benton to Batoche, and from Fort Walsh to Battleford and to listen to their chuckles as they recalled when a buck-board upset in the St. Mary River and they lost their bed-rolls and had to swim for their lives, was something worth while. Forty years ago—and here they were, still 'in the saddle.'"[4]

For most Mounted Policemen, until their final moments, the years on the plains remained an indelible part of their lives. Inspector Frank Norman had signed Treaty 7 and, for thirteen years, played a leading role in the NWMP. Though dismissed for incompetence, his thoughts remained with those years on the Force. His wife agonized: "My husband was not conscious for several days before he died and it was pathetic to hear him going over in his mind the old life on the plains, calling out words of command and asking to have his score on the rifle range read out … we buried him in his uniform as he had asked and the British flag was folded over his coffin."[5]

My Proudest Boast

The "boys," as they called themselves, experienced sights and adventures now gone forever. While riding alone, William Parker came upon a buffalo bull aggressively keeping six wolves away from a dead buffalo calf. It was a compelling sight, a captivating moment.

John "Jack" Herron rode with the NWMP escort on Major-General Smyth's inspection tour of police posts in 1875. At points en route, men were released and, when the troop entered Washington Territory, Herron was the only remaining Mountie. With winter approaching, mindful that it was unwise for the young trooper to return alone through the mountains, Smyth gave Herron $300 in gold pieces to pay for his return to Fort Calgary.

Herron traveled by stagecoach and the Union Pacific to Salt Lake City, where he purchased two horses and some supplies, and struck north alone for Fort Calgary, a direct distance of 1,140 km. He recollected: "Going north I encountered great herds of buffalo and many bands of roving Indians, but I made good time."[6] After an amazing ride and unforgettable adventure, Herron reached his destination on Christmas Day, 1875.

T.B. Boys intently watched several daring companions chase and kill a prairie grizzly bear. He later wrote in his diary: "It is not often that a white man sees a grizzly killed ... some of the men ate the bear meat which was excellent, especially with a little fat of pork."[7] In the summer of 1876, Sub-Inspector Cecil Denny was part of a patrol camped near a 60-metre cliff that overlooked the Bow River near present-day Gleichen. That night, a prairie fire driven by a strong wind soon had the grass ablaze as far as the eye could see. Denny wrote:

> An immense herd of buffalo were running for their lives along the parallel to the line of the fire. It was an awe-inspiring sight. The roaring of the fire driven by the wind, the thunder of the hoofs and the bellowing of the great herd made a pandemonium not easily forgotten. Our situation was by no means a safe one, and all turned out to set back fires around the camp. By good luck and the continual firing of our rifles we managed to turn the buffalo away. However, a large number were driven in the blind rush away from the fire right over the cutbank west of our camp and plunged in a bellowing mass down some hundreds of feet onto the rocky shores of the river.[8]

In the morning, the Indians began a ghastly slaughter of the moaning animals, many immobilized with broken legs. At one great pile of more than a hundred animals, they laboriously dragged the animals aside to reach a prized white buffalo that had been supposedly seen the previous year. The animal, however, turned out to be only a white Texas steer that had been running along with the herd.

At the isolated Pinto Horse Butte post, Jack Clarke talked with Sitting Bull. His mother, the Hunkpapa leader told Clarke, had said that he was going to be a brave man and a war fighter. Edward Barnett saw his first buffalo hunt west of Qu'Appelle where, "Naked Indians riding cayuses bareback with bows and arrows was a sight never to be forgotten."[9]

Being chased by a buffalo certainly was hair-raising. John "Doc" Lauder remembered walking west of Battleford in 1877 when "an old buffalo charged at me and chased me to camp, where one of our party shot him down."[10] On his journey westward, recruit James Fullwood recalled it took the sternwheeler almost half an hour to pass through tens of thousands of migrating buffalo swimming the Missouri River. Fullwood recorded in his journal:

> The noise was like pandemonium let loose. The lowing of buffalo cows, calling for lost calves, the roaring of the young and old ... thousands in the water swimming for the opposite side, and hundreds carried past us by the rapid current. Cows, within two feet of the boat, sweeping by, with wide open, staring, anguished eyes, crying pitifully for their lost calves.[11]

Until the sternwheeler's captain intervened, passengers from the East (called "Pilgrims") took pot shots at the helpless beasts.

Had not Edward "Buffalo" Allan boasted that he could catch a buffalo? His opportunity to silence the barracks' jibes came when a small buffalo herd began moving down a nearby coulee to cross the Frenchman River. Allan and a volunteer, "Peaches" Davis, hid themselves ahead of the herd, and soon the animals began passing by the men. When a young bull was crowded to the side, Allan grabbed it by the tail, jerked it sideways, and held its head. His partner stuck a knife into their quarry, but when this attempt failed to kill the young animal, Allan pithed the buffalo, earning his nickname "Buffalo."[12]

The first Mounties felt themselves fortunate to have observed and interacted with prairie Indian tribes in their last days of a nomadic lifestyle. The men observed Indian customs and dress, attended their Sun Dances, visited their camps, dodged fierce camp dogs, and, in some instances married their "squaws." An Indian camp on the move with it's teepees, horses, innumerable dogs, people walking and riding, and paraphernalia was a fascinating sight.

Danger was always present. At Fort Walsh, after Blackfoot riders had overrun the Cree camp, killing one old man, 110 Mounted Police guarded Cree tents that night to forestall further trouble. The next morning, the Blackfoot paraded in stunning apparel, war paint, and feathers. "It was," said one Mountie, "a wonderful sight and nothing like it has been repeated."[13]

The fascinating landscape left unshakeable memories in the minds of those men. While on late-night guard duty, George Guernsey looked west to see the Rocky Mountains gloriously lit up by the rising sun. It was his first sight of the storied mountain range and a moment to be forever remembered. Two members of the Force witnessed the historic driving of the last spike at Craigellachie in November 1885.

Most men valued their years in the NWMP. Constable Scott recalled, "the experiences of patrol work, the privilege of working with mighty fine men, the lessons of obedience and perseverance have been invaluable to me in after life, and my recollections of the traditions and associations of the Force are my most valued possession."[14] On his return to Montreal, Frank Fitzpatrick, "found myself again, after six years of absence, glad of the interesting and wonderful experiences which seldom come to a young man between the ages of eighteen and twenty-four. I was a hundred times healthier than when I left, and I hope wiser, as well."[15]

A.H. Scouten kept North-West Mounted Police mementoes—his scarlet tunic, rifles, cartridge belt—displayed on a wall in his home. Each time he looked at his finger ring, Clarence Loasby must have thought of the morning outside Fort Pitt when he was shot by Indians. His companion, Constable David Cowan, was killed and scout Henry Quinn had been captured. After he recovered from his wound, Loasby had the two bullets extracted and made into a ring.

The "boys" were proud of their years of police service. Const. Scouten declared: "I am proud that I was a member of the Force that is honored for its wonderful service rendered to the Dominion of Canada, particularly in the Wild North West in the early seventies."[16] Teddy Warren recalled, "the best years of my life were spent in the old force."[17] In 1973, Marjorie Frizzell remembered that her Grandpa Sutherland was very proud of his North-West Mounted Police career.[18] Sixty years after he joined the Force, Alfred Nedham told a news reporter in Victoria, B.C., that his discharge papers, signed by Commissioner James Macleod, embodied all the memories of his service and were "my most cherished possession today."[19]

The Great Lone Land had captured their youth, Const. F.A.D. Bourke arrived at Fort Walsh on his twenty-first birthday and was assigned to whitewash the barracks. "I thought," recalled Bourke, "it rather tough on the day I came of age."[20] Yet, upon taking his discharge, Bourke never regretted having joined the North-West Mounted Police, even though there were some very rough times. Edward Maunsell reflected that, "while have the honor of being a pioneer rancher, my proudest boast is that I was a pioneer Mounted Policeman."[21]

One eighteen-year-old recruit prized his three-week trip traveling from Fort Walsh to Fort Macleod: "What could be more splendid than this, especially for young red blooded men who were seeking adventure in a land practically unknown to white men."[22] Robert Patterson also spoke fondly of his Mounted Police career "as the only years I have ever lived and long for the old days, old friends, trackless prairie, mountains, rivers and lakes, and the comradeship of the finest men who ever collected in one organization."[23] In his final years, Harry Keenan lamented that, "I miss the old friends my companions in the force."[24] James Fullerton bewailed the passage of time: "It is a strange feeling being the last of a lot of good fellows but not one of those who came up to Lower Fort Garry with me are left."[25]

Late in life, William Grain, blind from an accident, dictated his NWMP adventures to his granddaughter. Grain proudly reflected:

> That seventy years later, it is the most wonderful feeling in the world to review the march of progress which has steadily developed our country into the great nation that it is today, and to know that I had the privilege of playing even so small a part in its early history."[26]

While he reminisced, Grain, at ninety-six, and one of the last '74 men, foresaw Canada's "vast potentialities as yet unfolded, and the heights to which she can rise as a nation ...we can look back to that old motto which hung on a roughly hewn wall in Fort Macleod and realize that we, as Canadians, are still the 'Pioneers of a Glorious Future.'"[27]

The bravery of the North-West Mounted Police was beyond reproach.[28] Being outnumbered meant nothing. Commissioner A.G. Irvine wrote:

> I think it is perfectly marvelous when I look back to the time, some thirty years ago, that a mere handful of police could keep peace and order among thousands of wild Indians, ranging from the Rocky Mountains to the border of Manitoba, and from the United States boundary to the North Saskatchewan ... Sometimes a dozen men would go to a camp of two hundred lodges and arrest horse thieves.[29]

Irvine could have spoken of himself. In the summer of 1876, a great gathering of Indian tribes had camped in the Cypress Hills. When reports implicated the Sioux, in Canada only three months, with inciting unrest among the 3,000 lodges, Major Irvine rode with eleven men from Fort Macleod to the Cypress Hills.

In a bold encounter, Irvine led his troop into the centre of a troublesome camp where they threw "hand grenades" made from missiles of biscuits, tea, coffee, sugar, and tobacco at the Indians. On the following day, one man returned to the Indian camp where he recovered a number of stolen horses. Irvine later mused: "How about the moral influence of the Police Force in this country?"[30]

That a handful of Mounted Police could keep order among thousands of Indians had become legendary. Inspector Cecil Denny wrote: "On many occasions officers, accompanied by two or three men, went into Indian camps of several hundred lodges and made arrests for a crime, or put a stop to drunken orgies, without encountering opposition or resistance, although the tribes had it in their power to wipe out the whole force had they felt so inclined."[31]

And, while the NWMP took forceful action when necessary, they were also adept negotiators. A reporter for the *Fort Benton Record* noted that, whenever the large Cree and Assiniboine camp at Fort Walsh had a grievance, "they come at once to Colonel Irvine, who at once sets matters all right."[32] A Winnipeg paper agreed: "Colonel Irvine is a great favorite among the Indians. They speak of him as the Big Thunderer."[33]

In the spring of 1879, uneasy that American refugee Sioux and Nez Percé Indians were in Canada, a Montana paper, *The New North-West*, employed frontiersman Duncan McDonald to live as a spy in the Indian camps. And, for six weeks, McDonald sent letters to the newspaper. In one letter, he evaluated: "I never saw an officer with better 'Indian way' than Col. Irvine. He seemed to understand the Indian nature, and at once impressed the Indians favourably toward him."[34]

Acheson Gosford Irvine: Third Commissioner

Colonel Acheson Gosford Irvine, the first Canadian-born Commissioner of the North-West Mounted Police, commanded the Police Force from 1 November 1880 until 31 March 1886—five years and four months in total. Irvine, nicknamed "old sorrel-head," was a compassionate man, well-liked, and engrossed in an extraordinary taxing work routine that is evident in his Annual Reports. A confidential assessment written by Commissioner James F. Macleod stated:

The Assistant Commissioner is an active and conscientious officer in the discharge of duties. He is a good disciplinarian, well up in drill and interior economy. His only faults are indecision and a tendency to be governed by the opinions of junior officers, who happen to be his intimates. His age is 43.[35]

A second evaluation commented: "I look back with pleasure on the two years I had under Colonel Irvine. He knew how to do things nicely, and he was always so nice and polite, genial, fair and anxious to learn."[36] Constable Tom LaNauze wrote to his parents in Ireland saying: "Irvine is always good to us."[37]

Irvine was an acclaimed figure throughout his forty-six years in Western Canada. It is ridiculous that the *Dictionary of Canadian Biography 1911–20* omits a biography of Irvine. The volume that listed deaths in Canada in the years 1911–20 includes unimportant Indians (called First Nations—a label that didn't exist at that time), minor Mounties, and criminals.[38] This exclusion of the third Commissioner of the NWMP can only be ascribed to silly revisionism of Canadian history or academic ineptitude.

Irvine was born into a prominent Quebec City family in 1837.[39] Once he had completed his formal education, Irvine entered commercial work. After service in several militia companies, Irvine joined the Second Battalion Quebec Rifles as a Major in the Red River Expeditionary Force of 1870. When this military column downsized the following year, Irvine became the commanding officer of the Fort Garry Provisional Battalion of Rifles, a position he held until he joined the North-West Mounted Police in November of 1875.

The citizens of Winnipeg appreciated his administration. On the news that he would leave his military command, a committee on behalf of the mayor and city council expressed "their deepest regret that we hear of your intended departure from us … but appreciation for conduct that at all times merited our warmest approval and admiration."[40] The city gave Irvine a farewell dinner. The *Winnipeg Standard* commented: "He has succeeded in gaining the good will of every living creature who knows him."[41]

Lord Lorne, Governor General of Canada, on his tour of western Canada in 1881, described Irvine as "able and indefatigable."[42] This assessment of Irvine appears often. The *Regina Leader* called Irvine, "the indefatigable commissioner of the force, in whom every man in the Territories has the most implicit confidence."[43] An early Alberta rancher, Duncan McEachran, observed that: "This officer is said by those who know him best to be most efficient and energetic, and very desirous of seeing the force raised to a high state of efficiency."[44]

Acheson Gosford Irvine: Third Commissioner

"I never saw an officer with better 'Indian way' than Col. Irvine. He seemed to understand the Indian nature, and at once impressed the Indians favourably toward him."

– Duncan McDonald, *The New North West*, 28 March 1879
GA NA 1353 – 37

Irvine's close relationship with James Macleod began when they were cadets in the Quebec school of infantry. Their friendship continued in the 10th Huzzars stationed in Toronto and as officers on the Red River Expedition. Both men were stationed the winter of 1873–74 in Winnipeg: Macleod as the NWMP commander of Divisions "A-B-C" and Irvine in command of the Manitoba militia.

Irvine joined the NWMP in November 1875. The following spring, his first assignment took him by sternwheeler to Montana to assist Macleod in the arrest and trial of seven frontiersmen charged with the Cypress Hills Massacre. Their subsequent acquittal in Helena failed to curb Canadian efforts to apprehend other suspects. When three men were arrested in Canada, Irvine escorted them for trial in Winnipeg. Incredibly, as outlined earlier, Irvine's troop, being inexperienced in running buffalo, provided the alleged murderers rifles to hunt buffalo for the company's food supply. Irvine was congratulated by the *Manitoba Free Press* "for his decisive and energetic manner in which he brought these three criminals to justice."[45]

On 1 January 1876, Irvine became the Assistant Commissioner of the North-West Mounted Police when Macleod left the Force to become a Stipendiary Magistrate. The resignation of Commissioner French six months later returned Macleod to the North-West Mounted Police as its new Commissioner, a position he held until 31 October 1880. Macleod's resignation in 1880 elevated Irvine to the top position. He prepared for this responsibility by taking a winter leave to visit Dublin Castle where he studied the operations of the Royal Irish Constabulary, the model for the North-West Mounted Police.

In his six years as Commissioner of the NWMP, Irvine introduced major policing policies. The Force was strengthened to 1,000 men and their armaments updated with Winchester repeating rifles. The American Sioux had returned to the United States, Canadian Indians were moved from the Cypress Hills to reserves north of the railway, and Fort Walsh was closed.[46] New police detachments were opened at Maple Creek, Medicine Hat, Moose Jaw, and Moosomin. The North-West Mounted Police headquarters relocated to Regina, where a training depot was established. Mounted Policemen monitored thousands of railway construction workers and kept order during a C.P.R. strike. Several serious Indian confrontations had been resolved without bloodshed. White settlement added new police responsibilities. The court duties increased significantly. Within a few years, the Force had undergone significant changes and adjustment.

The successful return of the Sioux to the United States was Irvine's most heralded achievement. The *Saskatchewan Herald* commented that: "It is well-known that Colonel Irvine has labored most ably and zealously to bring about this desired state of affairs."[47] A Montana newspaper agreed: "There is no doubt whatever that Sitting Bull's surrender is attributable to the great exertion shown by Col. Irvine. The old warrior found himself completely checkmated."[48]

Commissioner Irvine was forty-eight at the time of the North-West Rebellion. His command was controversial and the North-West Mounted Police administrative shake-up that followed the military campaign ended his police career. His resignation in April 1886 was regretted. Inspector Steele wrote: "The resignation of Lt.-Col. Irvine, our commissioner, came as a great shock to all who knew him. He was a great favourite throughout the west, a hard-working, conscientious officer who had served his country faithfully for many years."[49]

After leaving the Force, Irvine worked as an Indian agent for the Blood band for the next six years. He then became warden of Stony Mountain Penitentiary near Winnipeg, a position he held until shortly before his death in 1916 in Quebec City. Irvine never married.

Later Lives of "The Boys"

Only a handful of the early Mounties had made policing a lifetime career. Those men with trades applied themselves to their skill. Other men chose to enter business. H.W.C. Jackson owned a newspaper in Rossland, B.C. D.J. Grier was a partner in three hotels, and Jean D'Artigue became a real-estate developer. The land grant available until 1879 attracted some men, on the completion of their term, into ranching where they were prominent in establishing the ranching frontier. In 1883, Superintendent A. Shurtliff had 700 head of cattle on his range near Maple Creek.

Some former Mounties entered politics. Dr. L.G. DeVeber became a senator. John "Doc" Lauder was elected to represent the Calgary district in the North West Council in 1886. Edward Maunsell and Robert Paterson became members of the Alberta legislature. "Honest John" Herron was the first president of the Northwest Territories Stock Association and later represented the Macleod constituency in Ottawa as a Conservative member of Parliament from 1904–11. Jack Clarke, a Calgary alderman, became involved in the "Travis Affair" in 1884 and spent six months in jail.[50] Sergeant A. Meneley became mayor of Maple Creek. Thomas Boys, writer of the poem, "Riders of the Plains," was the town clerk in Calgary in 1884. C.J. King, first to cross the Bow River at what later became Calgary, was elected its mayor in 1886–87 and was city postmaster for thirty-six years. G. Guernsey served as a police magistrate for twenty years in Penticton. In 1905, William Reed was the first police chief of Pincher Creek.

There was always the attraction of military service. Sam Steele played a prominent role in the Boer conflict and the Great War. Frederick Bagley served in South Africa and attended Queen Victoria's Diamond Jubilee in 1897. Inspector Gilbert E. Sanders, who also participated in the Boer War, later was Calgary's Police Magistrate from 1912–32. "Hardfaced" William Parker served in the South African war and was a recruiting officer in the First World War. Among those men in the Canadian Expeditionary Force in Europe were Jack Leader and James Workman. At age 58, Edward Drinkwater, enrolled with the 13th Mounted Rifles in the Great War and fought briefly in the trenches in France before being withdrawn because of his advanced age. In a blistering letter to the Defence Ministry in Ottawa, Drinkwater protested this order and refused to accept the pay that he was owed. John Edward Taylor fought in the North-West Rebellion, Boer War, and the First World War. J.B. Mitchell raised and commanded the 100th Battalion Winnipeg Grenadiers in the Great War.

In the summer of 1939, with another war threatening, the RCMP headquarters sent a letter to ex-members of the Force questioning whether they would be available for re-engagement. More than 650 men offered their services. Sergt. Orrin W. Evans of Keremeos, B.C., replied: "Sir: in answer to yours of 28th I am Ready & Willing to serve in any capasity in case of war or other troubles." Assistant Commissioner, G.H. Hill, in response to Evans, wrote these instructions regarding his letter: "As this ex-member must be well over 80 years of age it is thought unlikely that he would be of value in event of any crisis ... write letter of appreciation decline services."[51]

Surgeons Barrie Nevitt and George Kennedy had distinguished medical careers. James Walker left the NWMP to manage the Cochrane Ranche. He later opened a lumber company and was active in Calgary civil affairs. A committee selected Walker as Calgary's most prominent citizen in first half of the twentieth century. J. R. Royce became a probation officer and juvenile court judge in Calgary. Tom Wilson went prospecting. He was the first white man to ever see Lake Louise, Emerald Lake, and spectacular Takakkaw Falls, which, at the height of 503 m, is the second-highest waterfall in Canada.

Other retired Mounted Police chose reclusive lives. In 1938, a Calgary ambulance crew had to coax George Gamsby to leave his isolated cabin, horses, and dog at Priddis for care in a Calgary hospital. In an area where residents easily commute to Calgary for daily employment, Gamsby had not visited the city for nineteen years. Nurses described him as a restless patient until his death seven weeks later. A news reporter was told they (the nurses) had "with discouraging efficiency, foiled his attempts to leave."[52]

George Gamsby, Priddis, Alberta

"They keep telling me I'll get better, but I know I ain't gonna. Good Lord,
I'm over eighty years old."

– *NAC*, George Gamsby, f. 133
   GA NA 970 – 3

Edward "Teddy" Warren prospected from his secluded cabin near Fort Steele until his early nineties. The RCMP detachment at Cranbrook kept a watchful eye on the old bachelor, who had been one of the first Mounties in Sitting Bull's camp. Warren thwarted all attempts to have him settle in the town and stubbornly remained in his cabin that was described as no longer fit for human habitation. J. Buchanan, the detachment supervisor admitted: "As you know, Mr. Warren is not easy to handle ... and it would not do for any of us to suggest he should have a new home."[53] In spite of his stubbornness and isolation, Warren kept abreast of everyday affairs. In February 1941, he wrote to a friend: "I think we are going to come out on top in this war."[54]

There were men who, perhaps intentionally, severed their family ties. The daughter of Edward Whitehouse (who had joined the Force in 1876) wrote to the Commissioner from New Jersey in 1900 for information on her father. In 1930, the brother of Thomas Smith wrote to the NWMP that the family never had any contact with Smith since his discharge fifty years earlier. Commissioner Starnes located Smith, age eighty-six, in the Yukon and had him promise to write to his family, but unfortunately, Smith died before fulfilling his agreement.

In response to letters that requested information on mounted policemen, the Commissioner usually referred to the man's personnel file. This source varied in content, with some files having only a few pages while others encompassed several volumes. E.A.S. Day, who asked in 1963 about his great Uncle, Robert Stewart, "who journeyed west in about 1880 to join NWMP and was never heard of again," was informed that Stewart had joined the Force in 1879, listed his occupation as a carpenter, and, when discharged eleven months later at Fort Macleod, disclosed that his intended residence was Fort Benton.[55]

Most men moved with the times. After George Anderton left the Force in 1878, he opened a photographic studio at Fort Walsh. His images are invaluable records of the early years.[56] John C. Geldert went to California where he acted as Mary Pickford's father in Hollywood's silent pictures. A.H. Scouten described himself as a radio fan. James Fullerton boasted that he had learned to type. In 1940, in his late eighties, J.B. Mitchell could be seen driving his automobile in Winnipeg.

For the most part, life had become increasingly difficult for the former "Riders of the Plains." In 1913, W. Ritchie wrote Ottawa, inquiring whether there was a Fenian money grant for the 1866 campaign. Ritchie gave his return address as "Old People's Home, Vancouver." A review of the service personnel files reveals that many, if not most, of the early Mounties had spent their final years in misery and abject poverty. Canada lacked the social safety network of today, and very few men qualified for a NWMP pension that required twenty years service. The *Old Age Pension Act* of 1927 provided $20 a month for a person over 70 years of age who qualified on a means test, but this amount was hardly adequate for daily expenses.

Earlier, an Order-in-Council in 1921 had provided a maximum $75 (if it received approval by the Commissioner) from the RCMP Benefit Trust Fund for burial in a respectful manner. Local North-West Mounted Police Associations also helped with the funeral expenses, "to prevent dishonor cast on the name of the force on which we all had the honor to belong and let it not be said that an ex-member of the force was buried in a paupers plot."[57] A Headstone Benefit Grant provided a headstone costing no more than $50. When Joseph Chabot arranged to have his wife buried at his side, and he inquired whether her name could be included on the approved headstone. Headquarters responded that: "The wife's name cannot, under regulations, be included on the headstone."[58]

Poverty among the old former policemen was widespread. A merchant friend of George Harpur wrote, "Poor old George did not leave enough to bury him."[59] In 1925, George Boswell, living in Los Angeles, contacted the comptroller of the RCMP:

> On the 26 day of September we buried Stevens, an old member of the NWMP. He was a member of "F" Troop at Fort Walsh and took his discharge in 1880 ... I was informed of his death by the Manager of the Charity Board who stated that if he did not hear from me he would be buried in Potter's Field and I at once raised money from Canadians so I can state that he now lies in his own grave, buried with the British flag on his coffin ... it is a shame that so many Mounted Policemen have to go this way, in the last year we have taken care of three others, and in every case had to raise money this way.[60]

Constable George Boswell was destitute when he died five years later.

Sam Horner contacted the Commissioner in 1924, stating "His means are exhausted, and he now faced starvation or the poor house ... at age 79 a pension wouldn't extend over many years, and be no great burden to the country but a great relief to myself."[61] In a note attached to Horner's, his Member of Parliament stated that: "Mr. Horner is in extremely reduced circumstances and suffering from deprivations. There is no outlook for the future except the poor house ... a most deplorable eventuality. Can anything be done?" The Commissioner's reply was negative: Horner had only fifteen years of service and was ineligible for any benefits.

In an age before Medicare, even former Mounties with a pension were hard-pressed to meet medical costs. Arthur Dorion's medical expenses at Saskatoon and the Mayo Clinic (Minnesota), noted a Prince Albert paper, "entirely used up his savings and now his widow who is seventy-six years of age has nothing and the funeral expenses have not been paid."[62] The local Royal-Canadian Mounted Police detachment was unable to help out. Seventy-five dollars came from the NWMP Benefit Trust Fund.

The NWMP Veteran's Association in Calgary applied for the $75 funeral expenses grant on behalf of A.J. Gilmore who "died in destitute circumstances, leaving nothing to defray funeral expenses. For years he was living on his old age pension, which barely kept him in food."[63] For his last four years, he had been receiving $7.50 a month from the Sir Cecil Denny Bequest Fund.

When J. Julest died in Calgary in 1894, the attending priest wrote to the brother of the deceased: "I need not tell you, he is very poor … He owes the Sisters of the hospital about $30, to the Doctor about $8, and to the funeral about $10 or $15."[64] Richard Steele (brother of Sam Steele) wrote to Comptroller Fred White in 1907, imploring him (without success) for employment in Ottawa. When he died nineteen years later in Cochin, Saskatchewan, the local priest contacted the RCMP in Ottawa, stating that Steele's wife was unable to pay funeral and burial costs of $44. Comm. Cortlandt Starnes responded with a reference to the Benefit Trust Fund.

Some former policemen helped their less-fortunate comrades. George Allen left the Force after eighteen months to support his widowed mother in London, England. He profited in real estate and, on a visit to Calgary years later, generously donated $5,000 to support his old comrades mired in poverty. Cecil Denny, who became the Provincial Assistant Archivist, gave $3,000 in a fund to help veterans. However, Denny's problems with excessive drinking eventually left him destitute. When he died in 1928 (as Sir Cecil Denny), the Police Trust Fund paid his funeral expenses.[65]

Dire circumstances experienced by old veterans were well known. Fred Bagley reflected that his thoughts often drifted back to again see those gallant comrades of sixty-four years ago, now nearly all gone across the Great Divide, "many of whom were allowed by a grateful (?) country to end their days in poverty and want."[66] A. Mackenzie, who suffered from rheumatism he developed while working as a Mountie, received a paltry $10 monthly pension for twenty-one years of service. A Regina newspaper commented his story might fittingly be titled "Canada's Gratitude." All pension benefits, other than the amount due that month, ended with the death of the recipient.[67] Peter O'Hare's wife received a firm negative response to a letter asking if her deceased husband's pension continued.

Older Mounties welcomed the Federal Rebellion Grant in 1932 that awarded $300 for their service in the North-West Rebellion in 1885, forty-seven years earlier.[68] For most men, the need for money was urgent. Michael Regan, who qualified for the grant, wrote asking officials to hurry the payment: "I am a pretty old man and owing to the hard times I am desperately in need of funds. I am behind the taxes on my humble home for the past two years and am afraid I may loose same if not paid soon."[69] From New Westminster, J. Wilkinson expressed his dire need: "So you see i am getting to be an old Man over 70 and nobody wants an Old Man so if i have to wate many Years for the Grant it will be to late."[70]

John A. Martin, in Charlottetown, contacted the Commissioner J.H. MacBrien on 8 October 1931:

> Dear Sir,
>
> I here by make application for this grant that has been made to 1885 men. I wish to state that my services were from 1873–1898 continues services 25 year 1 month. I now hold a medal for the 1885 Rebellion for being under fire at said times. I have the honor to be
>
> Sir,
> Your Obedient Servant.
> J.A. Martin

The Commissioner acknowledged Martin's letter and sent the prescribed application form to be declared before a Justice of the Peace.[71]

The application form requested the years of service, along with a birth certificate. Many men, lacking these documents, contacted the North-West Mounted Police Headquarters for the information. J.C. Martin had his documents destroyed in a fire when he was prospecting in central British Columbia. A.H. Scouten wrote: "Owing to poor health I can't remember long ago … but there are some old comrades living who can certify to My Serving in the N.W.M. Police with them."[72]

To help verify applications, Headquarters prepared a list of questions for the claimant asking for: next of kin, where he was living at the time of engagement, what division served, the date of discharge, and so on. J.S. Nicholas' answers to the questions included: How old were you when you joined the Force? (21); previous occupation? (surveyor); tattoo mark? (G.J. underside of left forearm); officer who signed you in? (Herchmer); where signed? (Regina, N.W.T); where serving when discharge purchased? (at Wood Mountain Post, "B" Division, Supt. Jarvis in command).[73]

An applicant was ineligible for the funding if he had deserted after the North-West Rebellion or was dismissed for misconduct. The application by William Lynch was not recommended because of problems of identity. It was revealed that, under the surname Grant, Lynch had (at age 64) served six weeks in the Provincial Gaol at Lethbridge for possession of burglary tools.[74] John Albert received his $300 grant and also a second payment by fraudulently using the name of a constable who had died 25 years earlier. Albert requested the cheque be sent to General Delivery, Ottawa. When confronted by NWMP Headquarters, he blamed his behaviour on trying circumstances and was never charged with fraud.[75]

A number of claims mistakenly assumed the Rebellion Grant applied to all former Mounties. Martha Watson, daughter of H. Lewis, wrote to the commissioner:

> Dear Sir,
>
> I saw by the Paper that there is a sum of Money sat aside for the first N.W.M.P. My father. H.T. Lewis left London ont With the Police in 1874. he has lived in Canada all his life & is about 85 years of age. If there is anything for him he would be very glad of it as things are very hard with him just now.

The Commissioner replied that the funds were for living North-West Rebellion veterans and, since her father had not fought in the campaign, he was ineligible for the grant.[76] Mary Loscombe, whose husband died two weeks before the government announced the grant, was told that her claim was ineligible. Twenty years later, she wrote again for support, citing poor health and an insufficient old age pension of $40 a month.

The Sioux widow of Tommy Aspdin assumed (incorrectly) that her possession of his North-West Rebellion medal made her eligible for the funds. Her letter added that she was a good housekeeper and manager. The reply from Ottawa stated that the benefits were available for living ex-members of the Force and not for dependents. H.B. Hammond, living in Australia and unware of the grant until 1938, was informed that the deadline for application had passed.[77]

Ottawa requested acknowledgement of the Rebellion grant. H. Banham wrote from Essondale, B.C. to the Commissioner on 14 October 1931: "Sir: I beg to acknowledge receipt of Cheque for $300.00 in lieu of Script for Veterans of the North West Mounted Police who served in the Rebellion of 1885 with many thanks Yours Respectfully H. Banham."[78] J.P. Bunt wrote: "Thanks for $300 and also wish the Dear old Force every success."[79]

NWMP Camp near Fort Walsh

Robert Patterson recalled his NWMP service "as the only years I have ever lived and long for the old days, old friends, trackless prairie, mountains, rivers and lakes, and the comradeship of the finest men who ever collected in one organization."

– GA, Robert Patterson, M 2470
  GA PD 339 – 6

The NWMP Headquarters adhered to rigid bureaucratic policies. Peter Coutts, who had an indifferent career, was dismissed because of drinking problems after nineteen years and 252 days of service. His many letters of appeal for a pension were summarily rejected. Was he not three months short of twenty years service? Jack Leader wrote in 1922 to Commissioner Perry that his age limited manual work and he had no visible means of support. Leader had forty-one years of continuous employment with the government in the NWMP, Fisheries, and Canadian Expeditionary Force. Comm. Perry responded there was no pension as he had served only seven years in the NWMP.[80] Service time for pensions was not transferable.

There were a few infrequent cases that overrode the rigid bureaucratic regulations. W. Cowls, paralyzed from a stroke eight years earlier, had his wife apply for his grant. Unfortunately, he died while the cheque was in the mail. His wife returned the cheque and inquired that, since he was alive when the money was issued, could a cheque be sent to her? Headquarters informed her that if she provided a death and a marriage certificate, the money would be sent to her. George Service's eligibility for a pension in 1899 was jeopardized by a conduct mark of "indifferent." Three earlier evaluations had been positive. Superintendent McIllree "saved the day" when he decided to cross out the word "indifferent" and wrote "good" on the discharge certificate, granting Service 40 cents per diem for life.

When Frederick Bagley applied for his land grant in 1900, he had been informed that, although he served the required number of years before the grant expired, he was only 18 years and 7 months in 1879—under the legal age of 21 and, therefore ineligible for this benefit. Bagley vigorously persisted with his claim and, within a year, received a land grant.

A government war pension enacted during the Second World War applied to earlier military service and included wives. In 1945, Chrissie Craig was very pleased to receive $30 monthly stipend since her husband had fought in the North-West Rebellion, sixty years earlier. Alexander Wyndham's service in the Rebellion provided a War Veterans' Allowance of $30.41 per month, effective 5 December 1944.

Many of the early Mounties died in tragic circumstances. Only five years after his promotion to Inspector for outstanding bravery at Cut Knife Hill, Thomas Wattam was confined in Kingston Asylum with an incurable mental disorder, shortly after, he suffered a terminal paralytic stroke. Two prominent Mounties, Surgeon Robert Miller and Sergeant Major Tommy Lake, shot themselves. Frank Hyles committed suicide by drowning. Alfred Wilson accidentally drowned in Pincher Creek and J. Dunbar in Willow Creek. Constable Welland Brooks died in quicksand at the mouth of the Red Deer River.

Three hunters found the missing body of George Frederick "Skinny" Adams who, while wandering in the forest near Vancouver, apparently tripped and drowned in a ditch. John Donkin, who published his adventures in *Trooper and Redskin in the Far Northwest* in 1889, died from inflammation of the lungs in a poorhouse in England the following year. He was only thirty-six, penniless, and addicted to alcohol. In 1907, Albert Cudlip, stationed at Dawson, Yukon Territory, fell from a bridge while he was returning to the barracks at night. Cudlip had been dismissed in 1898 because of alcohol problems, but was re-engaged three years later. Colin Colebrook, engaged in 1881, was later killed in the noted "Almighty Voice" affair in 1895. George Alexander "Grizzly" Adams died tragically in a Maple Creek hospital fire in 1945.

Eighty-four-year-old Philias Brunette dropped dead while cashing his Old Age cheque in a downtown Edmonton bank. The city police searched his residence and concluded that he died without any living relations or financial assets beyond his old age pension. The local Veteran's Association submitted an application with seven supporting letters to the Commissioner for the Benefit Grant to defray funeral expenses. During the service preparations (which included six red-coated pallbearers), two telegrams arrived from granddaughters, completely altering all arrangements.[81]

Lightning killed both Staff Sergeant George Bossange and his mount near Spirit River in 1919. The long-serving Mountie had just questioned a farmer, Ivan Yaremko (an alleged Bolshevik agitator), clearly demonstrating the changing duties Bossange undertook since he joined the Mounted Police thirty-six years earlier. His body was returned from the Peace River area by train to Calgary in a hermetically sealed casket, since there were no embalming facilities in the northern town. Pension benefits were offered to his wife, provided she didn't remarry.[82]

At least two men were murdered. George Purches died in Alaska in a domestic dispute in 1909. Albert Greaves died from poison in Brandon in 1893. The trial attracted widespread attention. Apparently, the motive was the theft of Greaves' watch by a thirteen-year-old troubled youth, Phillip Hill. The case involved both the exhumation of the victim and a medical examination of his stomach, where doctors analyzed there was strychnine in the porridge he had eaten.

A former policeman named Edward McDonald (or MacDonald) was lynched in Montana. Inspector Steele gives a vague account: "Another innocent man was a freighter from Canada who had been a sergeant in the force and who, with several others, was lynched through the treachery of a British subject."[83] The Fort Macleod Gazette news article "Lynched in Montana" relates that McDonald, an ex-policeman, took the "hemp line home to the Great Hereafter."[84] A sheriff had arrested McDonald and an associate with stolen mules from Canada and was proceeding with the men to Fort Benton when they met a group of cowboys, who "relieved" the sheriff of his charges and took the men over to the nearest tree. While it deplored lynch law, the paper suggested that this punishment in Montana "doubtless will have a wholesome effect in checking the crime of horse stealing here."[85] Dutchy Koerner, who allegedly joined the North-West

Mounted Police to escape justice in the United States, deserted the Force and was hanged south of the line by a vigilante committee who found him in possession of a stolen horse.[86]

Some former Mounted Policemen requested an RCMP presence for their funeral. Thomas Banbury had wanted six police pallbearers. James Fullerton, living in Port Townsend, Washington, arranged to be "planted" in Victoria, British Columbia:

> When I go on the long journey, it will be a great satisfaction to me to know that my old bones will lie under the Union Jack that I have always loved. I am British to the back-bone and would like to see the dear old flag over my box and the fine fellows of the Force helping to put me away.[87]

When John Johnson died at age 81 in Spokane, an attachment to the death certificate stated that he was senile and had been living in destitute circumstances. His request to have his body sent to Coleman, Alberta, to rest beside his wife, was eventually arranged. Six RCMP pallbearers attended the burial.

The local detachment assigned to a police funeral and burial submitted a statement of their service to Headquarters in Ottawa. At the funeral of Harry Keenan in January 1935 in Prince Albert, the statement included the time, date, place, the officials, clergy, relatives attending, a list of uniformed police officers as pallbearers, other police attending, the last post, expenses, police cars used, newspaper clippings, and whether the deceased had funds to cover the expenses. The city's detachment contributed a wreath and flag for the casket. After the funeral of William Fury, the local detachment had "investigated" his widow's age, her living conditions, and estate.[88] In some cases, local organizations, such as the fire brigade, participated at funerals. In Penticton, a Canadian Legion squad fired a salute for George Guernsey.

Newspapers reported Mountie deaths and often recounted their lives. "Another Mountie Dies," headlined the *Calgary Herald* on the death of "Peaches" Davis. Readers were informed that Robert McCutcheon was in the search party that found murdered Constable Graburn, the oldest member of the Alberta Oldtimers' Association, and the first white man to shake Sitting Bull's hand in Canada.[89] The papers embellished their lives calling James Sutherland, who supervised the Cripple Camp on the '74 March and bought his discharge the following year, "an Indian fighter."[90]

In July 1935, 10,000 people in Calgary watched the funeral procession and then attended the graveside service of George Cliff King. He was the first Mounted Policeman in Calgary, its postmaster, and a mayor. On his career, the *Albertan* commented: "He saw the country before it opened up and took part in its subsequent development."[91] King was buried in the red uniform he had donned sixty years earlier.

Old age brought recognition for the role the men had played in early settlement history. Townspeople in Banff pointed out Fred Bagley as an "icon" as he daily walked about town. By 1945, widespread interest now focused on those four remaining men who participated in the '74 March, seventy-one years earlier. All four men—Frederick Bagley (#247), J.B. Mitchell (#50), William Parker (#28), and W. Grain (#52)—died that year. The *RCMP Quarterly* lamented: "Since the Quarterly began twelve years ago the number of those grand old troopers has dwindled one by one … they rode out into the great beyond on their last patrol … Now all are gone. Last Post has sounded for the originals of '74."[92]

Reunions

An urge to reunite with old comrades always found a warm response. The organizers of Calgary's first Stampede in 1912 attracted twenty-two members of the '74 March to the event. With a population of 40,000 and undergoing a staggering building boom, the city provided the men with accommodations and arranged a dinner.

Edward Maunsell wrote: "This was the most pleasant reunion. Most of us had not met for some thirty-five years. All conversation referred to the good old days. Needless to say, we also discussed prohibition."[93] And no reporters were allowed. City postmaster G.C. King related: "We had a real talkfest and we didn't have to care who heard us. We were able to tell stories on each other that couldn't have been told if reporters were there."[94]

The "boys" laughed about how General Selby Smyth, on his inspection tour in 1875, had stood on a box, stamped his feet, and ranted at the troops after a "medicinal" keg of whiskey had disappeared. After Smyth left, the men removed a two-gallon keg of "special" hidden inside the box. Later that night, the General had failed to notice that the lights in Troop "D" barracks were on late into the night.[95] Among the stories former Mountie Frederick Bagley may have recounted:

> Nowadays each time I pass via the C.P.R. yard through the prosperous town of Moose Jaw, I indulge in a quiet chuckle as I recall that on the 13th of October sixty-four years ago the boy Bagley was placed under arrest charged with "conduct to the prejudice of good order and military discipline in that he was five minutes late in sounding Reveille."[96]

And as they narrated their past adventures, no doubt the first Mounties marveled at the incredible changes underway on the Canadian plains. By 1931, 1.6 million people lived in the former North-West Territories —16 per cent of Canada's 10.4 million people and a larger percentage of Canada's population than today.[97] Edward Maunsell, a '74 man, reflected:

> Few people have seen our vast country change from a wilderness into what it is now. When I visit Calgary and stay at the Palliser Hotel I feel like a second Rip Van Winkle. To one who has not had my experience, it would require a vivid imagination to see Indian teepees on the ground now occupied by the hotel and envisage large herds of buffalo on the town site of Calgary.[98]

Four decades after he had left the Force, looking out from his railway car at Regina, Frank Fitzpatrick observed large trees where once he slept on the barren ground. John Herron remembered Lethbridge and Calgary "when they were not."[99]

Few men envisioned how quickly this wilderness would be transformed into a modern society. Cecil Denny, in 1934, commented on this: "We little imagined, when we hunted buffalo or did dangerous duty among the Indian tribes, that our opening up the country to settlement and bringing law and order should result in such rapid growth and building such fine cities and great railway lines."[100] James McEntyre regretted the opportunity he had missed in 1881. He had just left the Force and was now surveying for the Department of Indian Affairs when Father Constantine Scollen encouraged him to take up a homestead adjoining the Catholic mission in Calgary. McEntyre recalled:

> I laughed at the idea and replied "I guess not Father, you are too far from the centre of things." "My boy," he retorted, "the ground we are on will one day be the centre of Canada." Nearly prophetic words as events have shown; today the city of Calgary covers the old mission land. What a chance I let go by. I could not visualize the changes a decade could make.[101]

Unlike James McEntyre, Father Constantine Scollen foresaw the potential opportunities in the region.

The great prairie land was now known as "The Breadbasket of the Empire." The buffalo grass had been ploughed under and the prairie wolf, prairie grizzly, and the buffalo had long disappeared. Some police posts were also gone. A visitor to Fort Walsh found only foundations, half-filled root cellars, and the graveyard. For eight years, Fort Walsh had been the largest and most important settlement on the Canadian plains. And, at Swan River, the first headquarters of the North-West Mounted Police, only rotten timber outlined the post.

The fiftieth anniversary commemorating the arrival of the North-West Mounted Police in Alberta was observed in 1924. On July 1–3, Macleod (no longer called "Fort" and not officially reached by the '74 column until October 13) celebrated the Jubilee. An estimated 27,000 visitors, many arriving in trains from Calgary and Lethbridge, attended. Premier Herbert Greenfield was there with a military band from Calgary. Most important, fourteen '74 men had attended.[102] John Martin came from distant Prince Edward Island. The '74 men, in the words of the *Macleod Times*, were not just "Oldtimers," but "Real Oldtimers."[103] Local members of the RCMP (as the NWMP was renamed in 1905) accommodated their retired forerunners.

Commissioner Cortlandt Starnes had come from Ottawa. Thirty-nine years earlier, as a lieutenant with the 65th Battalion, Mount Royal Rifles in the North-West Rebellion, he had marched north alongside the Alberta Field Force to attack Big Bear's band. Starnes was so enthralled with the land that he joined the NWMP the following year, rose in rank, and, in 1922 was appointed Commissioner.

The Macleod anniversary preparations were extensive. The town, in the words of the *Lethbridge Daily Herald*, "refuses to let the old west vanish."[104] There was a Dominion Day parade that included decorated automobiles. One vehicle carried a sign depicting a whiskey trader with lettering: "Two barrels of the Curse of Canada." A rodeo was held, only to be tragically marred by the death of a bronco rider. It was estimated that 15,000 people watched the famous musical ride (which began in 1887). For fifty cents, interested parties could attend an illustrated lecture at the town hall that told the story of the early days of the West and ended with the singing of Auld Lang Syne. Ideal weather buoyed the celebrations.

Alberta had changed. It had been a province for almost twenty years. Beer was now sold and even advertised. The local theatre was screening a motion picture—Hoot Gibson in *The Thrill Chaser*. And the town was anticipating the production of a local film—*Policing the Plains*—a portrayal of Sir Sam Steele. A carload of trained motion-picture horses was en route to Macleod, along with photographic equipment. Norman Evans, a very popular film star in England, would portray the hero, Steele. J.G. Boyd, the provincial cowboy champion of British Columbia, would play the role of an easterner named "Bud," who came west with the Mounties and made good. "He contributes much of the comedy," commented the *Lethbridge Daily Herald*.[105]

Newspaper reporters sought out the veteran Mounties for stories of interest. Peter O'Hare said the Jubilee was all right for "youngsters" of '77 and '80, but the lads of '74 were getting too old for this kind of stuff. Jack Herron of Pincher Creek, the newspaper reported, tried to find some of his old '74 wrestling rivals to take him on for a throw or two, "but John still is, and looks too husky."[106].

The first week in July 1925, in what was called Jubilee Week, Calgary celebrated the fiftieth anniversary of "F" troop founding Fort Brisebois. More than 100 Mounties registered, including thirteen veterans from the '74 March. The city provided accommodation for the old policemen at the upscale Palliser Hotel, out-of-pocket money, as well as distinctive badges for complimentary use of the streetcar and entry into the Exhibition Grounds. Colonel G.E. Sanders, head of the local veterans' organization, arranged a luncheon at the Elks Hall, a smoker at the Great War Veterans' Hall, and participation in the Stampede Parade.

Dignitaries unveiled a rock cairn in Central Memorial Park marking the anniversary. Attendees included Mary Macleod (widow of Colonel James Macleod), Cecil Denny, G.C. King, and Fred Pope. Indian representatives were Big Plume (Sarcee) and Drunken Chief (Blackfoot). A flagstaff was erected at the gravesite of Colonel James Macleod in Union Cemetery.

In 1935, a sixtieth reunion was organized in Calgary. George Guernsey relished reuniting with comrades he hadn't seen for fifty years. The men were now in their eighties, with many in poor health. They visited a dying George King in an emotional gathering. William Grain had come. He was now blind, but attentively listened to all conversation. James Walker, Fred Bagley, and J.B. Mitchell rode in an open automobile in the Stampede Parade—a mode of travel that was inconceivable when they came West.

All of the '74 men were dead by the time Macleod celebrated its 75th anniversary in 1949. It was, nevertheless, a valued historic event. Inquisitive onlookers approached police veterans for anecdotes. Someone had asked William H. "The Colonel" Cox how he kept in such good shape. The nearby rancher, who arrived sixty-nine years earlier at Fort Walsh as a youthful eighteen-year-old, had sage advice: "I make it a point only to drink with friends and strangers and before and after meals."[107]

Reminders of the Early Mounties

Western Canada abounds with reminders of the early Mounties. Headstone inscriptions marked their presence. Constables George Johnston and E.C. Tonkin and Captain Dalrymple Clarke rest in the isolated Fort Walsh graveyard. West of this cemetery, at the side of a gravel road, a small cement

NWMP veterans in 1925, at the fiftieth anniversary of the founding of Fort Calgary

L−R, front row − Thomas LaBelle, John Stuttaford, Fred Pope, Sir Cecil Denny, James McKernan, Joe Marion; middle row − William Parker, Robert McCutcheon, Fred Bagley, G.C. King, John Herron, T. Danbury; back row − Dick Steele, Godfrey Steele, Col. J.B. Mitchell, Ed Larkin, Walter Boss.

− GA ND 8 − 385

pillar informs travelers that Constable Marmaduke Graburn was murdered nearby. There is an impressive monument to Colonel James F. Macleod in the Union Cemetery in Calgary. William Metzler is buried at Pincher Creek. Scout Jerry Potts is buried in the Fort Macleod police cemetery. The Old Banff cemetery has the remains of Frederick Bagley, Tom Wilson, and "Grizzly" Adams.

Other markers are found throughout the world. Sam Steele is buried in Winnipeg. The headstone for Francis Dickens stands in Moline, Illinois, for George Guernsey in Penticton, for James Fullwood in England, and for James Boswell in Los Angeles.

Many communities in Western Canada have preserved their memory in their very names. Fort Macleod, Fort Steele, and Fort Walsh are now well known. On the Trans-Canada Highway, just east of Medicine Hat are the tiny hamlets of Irvine (now population 326,)and Walsh, (now population 69). While other less-known places are Prongua, after Saskatchewan (John Prongua), Millarville, Alberta (Malcolm Tanner Millar), and Osborne, Manitoba (Osborne Smith, the interim Commissioner in 1874).

Some place names have now disappeared: Fort Brisebois became Calgary; Herronton, after John Herron, and Hollis Coulee in the Porcupine Hills no longer exist. Commissioner's Lake, named after A.G. French on the '74 March, is probably Grassy Lake. The men themselves named some geographical features. Other than the well-known forts are East End (or Chimney Coulee), 8 km north of Eastend, Saskatchewan, and Wapella village, named by James Walsh from the Sioux, "Water Under Ground."

The names of the early Mounted Police are commemorated in many geographical sites.[108] There is Kittson Butte, "Grizzly" Adams Creek, McIllree River, Macleod Island, Nicolle Flats, MacKay Hill, Pott's Bottom, Dickens Lake, Léveillé Provincial Park, Winder Ranch, Jarvis Park, and Bray Lake. Mountains in Kananaskis are named for Cecil Denny, Jerry Potts, and L.G. De Veber. A narrows, fort, glacier, and mountain carry Sam Steele's name. Marmaduke Graburn is remembered in a campsite, coulee, gap, creek, road, walk, and abandoned church.

Municipal roadways carry the names of the NWMP. Examples include Macleod Trail, Walsh Avenue, King Close, Bray Crescent, Brisebois Drive, Claustre Avenue, McCutcheon Place, and Maunsell Street. A railway stop in Lacombe is named Barnett. South of Fort Saskatchewan, the name of Yorkeville School District honours James Yorke.

Buildings bear their names. Calgary has schools named after Colonel Macleod, Colonel Irvine, James Walker, Milton Williams, Fred Parker, Jerry Potts, and Colonel Sanders. In Edmonton, there are schools named Macleod, Griesbach, and McKernan. J.B. Mitchell Junior High School in Winnipeg is named after the last living '74 man. Calgary has the Colonel Belcher Care Centre, and the Deane House Historic Site (a restaurant). In Fort Macleod, there is Macleod Manor; Steele Heights is a subdivision in Edmonton; in Calgary, a downtown roof park is named after James Walker and there is also the Fort Calgary Museum.

Depot Division in Regina honours the men killed in the North-West Rebellion. There is Arnold Mews, Sleigh Square, Lowry Place, and Elliot Avenue. Burke Lake, just 20 km east of Saskatoon, is named after Patrick "Paddy" Burke, who was killed at Cut Knife Hill. Members of the Battleford detachment took up a subscription for a memorial plaque and bell placed in the Cathedral Church of the Redeemer in Calgary for comrade William Lowry, killed in the Cut Knife Hill skirmish in 1885.

Tourism promotes the heritage of the North-West Mounted Police. Provincial roadmaps label the connected highways from Fort Macleod to the Manitoba border the Red Coat Trail. Historic cairns remind travelers of the earlier presence of the Mounted Police. A marker placed at Gravelbourg, Saskatchewan, points to the Cripple Camp where, on the '74 March, Commissioner George French posted five sick troopers and twenty-eight weak horses to recuperate.

In 2005, Fort Calgary erected a statue of a mounted Colonel Macleod on its grounds. Fort Saskatchewan, Fort Macleod, Fort Battleford, and Calgary have constructed replica forts as tourist attractions. Regina Depot has recently renovated it's Royal Canadian Mounted Police museum and archives. In 2000, the Edmonton military garrison named it's new barracks after Sam Steele. Fort Walsh has been rebuilt as a National Historic Site, complete with museum displays, guides, lunch room, and a shuttle bus to the nearby Cypress Hills Massacre site. Hired student guides wear Mountie uniforms and, the day that I visited, free lemonade was available.

The Federal government has issued postage stamps to commemorate Sam Steele, Jerry Potts, Colonel Macleod, Fort Walsh, and the RCMP Centennial. For years, the $50 bill portrayed the musical ride. Steele's Scouts, a Calgary volunteer troop, re-enacts the early troop marches. A commemorative book, *The Astonishing Cavalcade*, describes the re-enacted '74 March West across Manitoba 120 years earlier. Hollywood has long romanticized the strong, clean-cut, incorruptible, still-romantic Mountie. Books in "Sergeant Preston" mode number in the hundreds.

The early men left behind their own legacy. Fort Macleod veterans had an association as early as 1886. Calgary organized a NWMP Veterans' Association in 1901 headed by Colonel James Walker. Young Constable Frederick Bagley and several of his companions carved their names on the sandstone walls of a cave at Three Buttes. Some men donated their personal articles to museums. Cora Walsh gave artifacts, given to her by her father. The LaQuesne family donated twenty-one Indian artifacts to the Regina RCMP museum in 1957.

The magazine *Scarlet and Gold* published its First Annual in 1919. Many of the first articles were written by the early policemen. George Guernsey, under his Indian name, Waseecha Hoska (Long White Man), found time to contribute twenty-four articles. A second magazine, still available, the *Royal Canadian Mounted Police Quarterly*, began publication in 1933.

Colonel James Walker leading NWMP veterans at the 1912 Calgary Stampede Parade

L–R, Colonel James Walker, Superintendent J.H. McIllree, Sgt.– Major J.H.G. Bray, Sergt. Hall, Capt. Parker.

– GA NA 335 – 6

There are many fascinating accounts of personal police experiences in manuscripts, letters, and diaries. Poems by Thomas B. Boys, "The Riders of the Plains," and Sam Carruthers, "Pass the Tea," are well-known. George Crofton wrote a number of poems about daily experiences.[109] Late in life, John Herron reminisced in a seven-verse poem:

> *Fifty years on the prairie*
> *(Boys but the thought is grand)*
> *To have helped make this province*
> *From the wild, lone prairie land*
> *Still my heart yearns for the old days,*
> *With the 'Riders of the Plains'.*
> *And I like to be back in the saddle*
> *With the 'Scarlet and Gold', again.*[110]

Frank Spicer recorded several Indian legends. William Grain dictated his memoirs. The press interviewed many of the "Originals" for stories. Charles Orr gave a "vivid" account of his police experiences to a reporter from *The Evening Times-Globe*, St. John, New Brunswick, not mentioning that he had deserted after 157 days. Captain Frechette wrote letters to the *New York Tribune*. Colonel Macleod had to censure Major Walsh for his self-serving news correspondence. One unnamed recruit had his engaging letter home (that described a "diabolical" Indian dance) published in the *Sherbrooke News*.[111] Surgeon Barry Nevitt and Superintendent William Winder depicted the NWMP in their sketches and paintings.

Their legacy continued in their children. A.R. Moody had six sons and three daughters to help him farm near Vilna, Alberta. J.H.G. Bray had seven sons and six daughters. J.R. McMaster could boast of seventeen grandchildren. Many men (such as Paddy Burke, Tom Clarke, W.D. Jarvis) had sons who would grow up to join the Force.

Boys of the Old Brigade

At the first Calgary Stampede in 1912, twenty-two former Mounties were outfitted in police uniforms in the style of '74 and given horses to ride in the downtown parade. At the end of the parade, arrangements called for the men to ride to the Stampede Grounds.

At the main entrance to the Exhibition Park, Frederick Bagley, the boy trumpeter of the '74 March (now fifty-four), conducted a waiting band. When he saw James Walker leading the approaching horsemen, Bagley motioned the band to stop playing.

Bagley and Walker were old friends. Thirty-eight years earlier, when the column neared Roche Percée on the westward march, Bagley's foot blisters had made walking difficult and the broad-shouldered Walker had carried the fifteen-year-old youth piggyback into the camp. In later years, Bagley recalled, "Colonel Walker often reminded me of this incident."[112] This was one memory—there were so many.

Then, as the old troop began riding through the entrance gate, Bagley signaled the musicians to play a stirring and nostalgic military air. It was: "Where are the Boys of the Old Brigade." One citizen bystander, Anthony Weatherup, recalled "feeling a lump in my throat and moisture in my eyes for a few seconds."[113]

NOTES

1. *CSP,* 1876 (No. 7), Annual Report on the State of Militia for 1875, XXXV, 110.

2. Howard Angus Kennedy, "Memories of '85," *Canadian Geographical Journal,* LXX, May, 1965, 55.

3. R.G. Mathews, "A Memory of World War Days — Yarns of the Old Force," *SG,* Sixteenth Annual, 57–58.

4. Ibid.

5. *NAC,* Frank Norman, f. 5.

6. *LH,* 21 June 1924. Major-General Smyth continued westward to San Francisco. Having $300 in gold pieces, Herron "thought I would never see a poor day again."

7. *UMM,* Thomas B. Boys, Diary, 9 October 1876.

8. Cecil Denny, "Animals of the Early West," *AHR,* IV, No. 2, 24. Also Maunsell, *SG,* Second Annual, 58.

9. *GA,* Edward Barnett, M 6450.

10. *CH,* 25 October 1930.

11. James Fullwood, "When the Buffalo Swam the Missouri," *SG,* Seventh Annual, 91.

12. Wood Mountain Historical Society, *They Came to Wood Mountain,* 24.

13. Pox-o-nachie, "When the West was Young," 71.

14. J.W. Scott, "Recollections of Half a Century Ago," *SG,* Ninth Annual, 61.

15. Fitzpatrick, *Sergeant 331,* 126.

16. A.H. Scouten, "One of the Originals," *SG,* Twelfth Annual, 40.

17. *NAC,* T. Warren, f. 57.

18. *GA,* Tom Moore, M 3627.

19. *LH,* 11 July 1935. Colonel Macleod had written: "Conduct, very good."

20. F.A.D. Bourke, "Recollections and Reminiscences," *Sask H.* XXXV, No. 2, 55.

21. Maunsell, "With the North West Mounted Police from 1874 to 1877," 59.

22. Pox-o-nachie (Little Soldier), "When the West was Young," 71.

23. *GA,* Robert Patterson, M 2470.

24. *NAC,* Harry Keenan, f. 301.

25. *NAC,* James Fullerton, f. o.s. 66.

26. Grain, "Pioneers of a Glorious Future," 82.

27. Ibid.

28. Oka, "A Blood Indian's Story," 13–16.

29. *LH,* 7 January 1909.

30. *TG,* 24 July 1876. Fort Walsh was under construction at this time.

31. Denny, *The Law Marches West,* 58.

32. *FBR,* 9 June 1881.

33. *WDT,* 1 August 1883.

34. *NNW,* Deer Lodge, Montana Territory, 28 March 1879. *WDT,* 24 May 1879. *MJN,* 12 December 1884.

35. *Fort Macleod Archives*, 79–1–5. James F. Macleod, Confidential Report of the Officers of the Force. In a letter to his wife, Macleod foresaw a problem: "I know Irvine very well but he is not the man to tackle a serious difficulty although I dare say he is a good soldier." Craufurd-Lewis, *Macleod of the Mounties*, 262.

36. *RCMP* Q, II, No. 2, 9.

37. LaNauze, "Echoes and Letters from Fort Walsh," 170.

38. *Dictionary of Canadian Biography*, XIV, 1911–20 (Toronto: University of Toronto Press, 1998). References include Inukjuarjuk, an Inuit camp leader (two pages); Paul Splintlum, a Lillooet labourer and convicted murder.

39. His father, Colonel John George Irvine, was ADC to the Governor General; his mother, Anne, was the daughter of the Honourable Matthew Bell, an influential industrialist and politician in Quebec. A.G. Irvine, was awarded the Imperial Service Order in 1903.

40. *MFP*, 24 November 1874.

41. *WS*, 28 November 1874. The *EB*, 24 May 1884, wrote of his service in the Provisional Battalion: "No man was more deservedly respected or liked in the whole force."

42. MacGregor, "Lord Lorne in Alberta," 8.

43. *RL*, 22 November 1883.

44. *GA*, Duncan McEachran, Notes on a Trip to Bow River, North-West Territories, 971.23 M141.

45. *MFP*, 18 September 1875. The three men were acquitted.

46. *SH*, 27 May 1882.

47. *SH*, 11 April 1881.

48. *FBR*, 28 July 1881.

49. Steele, *Forty Years in Canada*, 240. The *Lethbridge News*, 9 April 1886, commented: "Perhaps no prominent officer ever left public service in the North-West Territories who carried with him more universal respect than Colonel Irvine."

50. Max Foran, "The Travis Affair," *AH*, XIX, No. 4, 1–7.

51. *NAC*, O.W. Evans, f. 328.

52. *NAC*, George Gamsby, f. 133.

53. *NAC*, Edward Warren, f. 57.

54. Ibid.

55. *NAC*, Robert Stewart, f. 386. *NAC*, Robert McKay, f. 368. *NAC*, Francis Fane, f. 664. *NAC*, Otto Wilkie, f. 1089.

56. Brock Silversides, "The Face Puller," *The Beaver*, October/November, 1991, 23–31.

57. *NAC*, C. Grogan, f. 679. His family was financially supported by the city of Toronto.

58. *NAC*, Joseph Chabot, f. 474.

59. *NAC*, George Harpur, f. 10. Harpur had written earlier requesting compensation.

60. *NAC*, George Boswell, f. 168. *NAC*, G. Stevens, f. 206.

61. *NAC*, Sam Horner, f. 6.

62. *NAC*, A. Dorion, f. 324. Dorion's wife was left to live on charity and a meagre Old Age Pension. When she died eleven years after her husband's death, the Benefit Fund also provided $75 for her funeral.

63. *NAC*, A.G. Gilmore, f. 131. For the local detachment supporting a destitute family, see Albert Thom, f. 569.

64. *NAC*, J. Julest, f. 985. Also *NAC*, Alfred Manners-Smith, f. 1045; Charles Grogan, f. 679.

65. In 1921, Denny succeeded his half-brother as baronet of Tralee Castle in County Kerry, Republic of Ireland giving him the title, Sir Cecil Denny.

66. Bagley, "The '74 Mounties," No. 8, 27.

67. *Regina Daily Post*, 3 March 1925. *NAC*, A. Mackenzie, f. 370. The local RCMP Superintendent angrily responded to the paper over it's comments on the pension.

68. In one group of 79 recipients, 34 still lived in the former NWT. Other locations included BC (20); Ontario (13); U.S.A (5); England (4); New Zealand, Ireland, and Quebec (1).

69. *NAC*, Michael Regan, f. 499.

70. *NAC*, Joseph Wilkinson, f. 1106.

71. *NAC*, John Martin, f. 41. Martin responded "I wish to thank you for the check I received, with many thanks." Many men had problems regarding documents for the Old Age Pension Act of 1927.

72. Scouten, *NAC*, f. o.s. 349.

73. *NAC*, J.S. Nicholas, f. 977.

74. *NAC*, William P. Lynch, f. 1105.

75. *NAC*, John Albert, f. 1023. His two desertions before the Rebellion did not make him ineligible for the grant. Albert led a life of deceit. He joined the Force and soon deserted and fled across the border. Two years later, he rejoined the NWMP under the name James Anderson and was soon recognized and sentenced to six months in the guardhouse. He was a skilful carpenter and was taken on again, only to desert to the United States with a young lady in a bizarre romance. Six years later, he returned to Canada and was given nine months in prison and dismissed from the Force. Later, in Ottawa, he was committed to a mental institution, under the name Jean Baptiste Albert, for extortion of money from prominent residents with threats of kidnapping, torture, and torching their summer homes.

76. *NAC*, H. Lewis, f. 289. Also *NAC*, John Murphy, f. 426.

77. *NAC*, H.B. Hammond, f. 1099.

78. *NAC* H. Banham, f. 1206.

79. *NAC*, J.P. Bunt, f. 975.

80. *NAC*, Jack Leader, f. 358.

81. *NAC*, P.B. Brunette, f. 249.

82. *NAC*, George Bossange, f. 979.

83. Steele, *Forty Years in Canada*.

84. *FMG*, 11 April 1885.

85. Ibid.

86. Pocock, *Frontiersman*, 25.

87. *NAC*, James Fullerton, f. o.s. 66.

88. See *NAC*, Peter McEwan, f. 233.

89. *CH*, 29 September 1943.

90. *NAC*, James Sutherland, f. 297. Sutherland's final years were miserable. He blamed his ineligibility for service in the First World War because of the loss of an eye rather than his age of sixty-five. At age eighty-two, Sutherland applied for the position of caretaker at an armoury. Also *CH*, 3 September 1912.

91. *Albertan*, 24 April 1931. Also *CH*, 4 July 1925.

92. *RCMP* Q, VIII, Nos. 2 and 3, 85. They all died within seven months: Parker (16 May); Bagley (8 October); Grain (25 October); Mitchell (14 November).

93. *CH*, 11 October 1912.

94. *Calgary News-Telegram*, 7 September 1912.

95. Maunsell in *CH*, 13 October 1923.

96. Bagley, "The '74 Mounties," No. 7, 18.

97. Population 1931 in thousands:

Sask. Alta. Canada
922 732 10,377

Alberta and Saskatchewan 15.9 per cent.
In June 2015, Alberta and Saskatchewan
had 14.8 per cent of Canada's population.

98. Maunsell, "Maunsell's story," 26.

99. *LH*, 11 July 1935.

100. Cecil Denny, "Building Fort Calgary," *SG*, Fifteenth Annual, 27.

101. *SAB*, McEntyre Diary, A 110.

102. Among the men were Cecil Denny, John Martin, John Herron, James Walker, James McKernan, James Stanford, Ike Forbes, "Paper Collar Johnny" (A.R. Macdonell), John McIllree, and William Parker.

103. *MT*, 10 July 1924.

104. *LH*, 2 July 1924.

105. *LH*, 24 July 1924.

106. *FMT*, 10 July 1924.

107. *RCMP* Q, XV, No. 2, 156.

108. See William J. Hulgaard and John W. White, *Honoured in Places* (Surrey, BC, Heritage House, 2002).

109. "A Poet in Scarlet," *AHR*, XV, No. 3, 17–23.

110. *Ottawa Evening Citizen*, 2 June 1937.

111. *SN*, 29 July 1875.

112. Bagley, "The '74 Mounties," *CC*, XIII, No. 4, 27.

113. *NAC*, James Fullwood, f. o.s. 444.

SELECT
BIBLIOGRAPHY

BOOKS

Aitkin, Ronald. *Maintain the Right*. Toronto: MacMillan, Canada, 1973.

Beal, Bob and Robert Macleod. *Prairie Fire*. Edmonton: Hurtig, 1984.

Brown, Wayne. *Steele's Scouts*. Surrey: Heritage House, 2001.

Charette, Guillaume, ed. *Vanishing Spaces*. Translation, Ray Ellenwood. Winnipeg: Editions Bois-Brules, 1980.

Clipperton, Robert. *The Cypress Hills Massacre*. Saskatoon: Saskatchewan Archaeological Society, 2015.

Craufurd-Lewis, M. *Macleod of the Mounties*. Kemptville, Ontario: The Golden Dog, 1999.

D'Artigue, Jean. *Six Years in the Canadian North-west*. Toronto: Hunter, Rose, 1882.

Deane, R. Burton. *Mounted Police Life in Canada*. Toronto: Cassell, 1916.

Dempsey, Hugh. *Firewater*. Calgary: Fifth House, 2002.

Dempsey, Hugh, ed. *William Parker Mounted Policeman*. Edmonton: Hurtig, 1973.

Ibid, ed. *Men in Scarlet*. Calgary: McClelland and Stewart West, 1973.

Ibid, ed. *A Winter at Fort Macleod*. Calgary: Glenbow-Alberta Institute, 1974.

Ibid, ed. *Frontier Life in the Mounted Police*. Calgary: Historical Society of Alberta, X, 2010.

Denny, Cecil. *The Law Marches West*. Toronto: J.M. Dent and Sons, 1939.

Ibid. *The Riders of the Plains*. Calgary: The Herald Company, 1905.

Donkin, John G. *Trooper and Redskin in the Far Northwest*. London: Sampson Low, Marston, Searle & Rivington, 1889.

Finerty, John F. *War-Path and Bivouac or Conquest of the Sioux*. Chicago: Donahue and Henneberry, 1890.

Fitzpatrick, Frank. *Sergeant 331*. New York: Published by the author, 1921.

Goldring, Philip. *The First Contingent: The North-West Mounted Police, 1873–1874*. Ottawa: Parks Canada, 1979.

Griesbach, W.A. *I Remember*. Toronto: Ryerson, 1946.

Hildebrandt, Walter and Brian Hubner. *The Cypress Hills*. Saskatoon: Purich, 1994.

Loew, Franklin and Edward Wood. *Vet in the Saddle*. Saskatoon: Western Producer Prairie Books, 1978.

Macleod, R.C. *The NWMP and Law Enforcement 1873–1905*. Toronto: University of Toronto Press, 1976.

McCrady, David. *Living with Strangers*. Lincoln, NE: University of Nebraska Press, 2006.

McDougall, John. *On Western Trails in the Early Seventies*. Toronto: William Briggs, 1911.

Manzione, Joseph. *I am Looking North for My Life*. Salt Lake City: University of Utah Press, 1990.

McCullough, A.B. *Papers Relating to the North-West Mounted Police and Fort Walsh*. Parks Canada, 1977.

Official Reports of the North-West Mounted Police, 1874–1881. *Opening Up the West*. Toronto: Coles Canadiana Collection, 1973.

Official Reports of the North-West Mounted Police, 1882–1885. *Settlers and Rebels*. Toronto: Coles Canadiana Collection, 1973.

Pocock, Roger. *A Frontiersman*. London: Metheun, 1903.

Pocock, Geoffrey. *Outrider of Empire*. Edmonton: University of Alberta, 2007.

Sharp, Paul F. *Whoop-Up Country*. Helena: Historic Society of Montana, 1960.

Steele, Samuel. *Forty Years in Canada*. Toronto: McClelland, Goodchild & Stewart, 1915.

Turner, J.P. *The North-West Mounted Police, 1873–1893*. 2 vols. Ottawa: King's Printer, 1950.

Utley, Robert. *The Lance and the Shield*. New York: Henry Holt, 1993.

Waiser, Bill and Blair Stonechild. *Loyal to Death*. Calgary: Fifth House, 1997.

Wilkins, Charles. *The Wild Ride.* Vancouver: Stanton Atkins & Dosil, 2010.

Wilson, Garrett. *Frontier Farewell.* Regina: Canadian Plains Research Centre, 2007.

Wallace, Jim. *A Double Duty.* Winnipeg: Bunker to Bunker Books, 1997.

Ibid. *A Trying Time.* Winnipeg: Bunker to Bunker Books, 1998.

ARTICLES, DOCUMENTS, NEWSPAPERS

Antrobus, William. "A Mountie's Diary," *The Early West.* Historical Society of Alberta.

A Tribute to the Mounted Police. *Alberta Historical Review*, XV, No. 3

Bagley, Fred. *Glenbow Archives*, M 2111, f.1.

Ibid. "The '74 Mounties," *Canadian Cattlemen*, XIII.

Barnett, Edward. *Glenbow Archives*, M 6142, M 6458 [diary].

Boswell, George. "Indian Treaties of 1877 and 1878," *Scarlet and Gold*, Seventh Annual.

Bourke, F.A.D. "Recollections and Reminiscences," *Saskatchewan History*, XXXV, No. 2.

Brathwaite, Edward. "Reminiscences of a Hospital Surgeon," *Alberta History*, XXXIX, No. 1.

Carscadden, Joseph. *Glenbow Archives*, M 6608.

Clarke, S.J. *Glenbow Archives*, M 228.

Clarke, Dalrymple. "In the North-West with Sitting Bull," *Rose-Belford's Canadian Monthly and National Review*, V.

Cox, W.H. "Diary of a Mountie," *Lethbridge Herald*, 11 July 1935.

Dempsey, Hugh, ed., "The West of Edward Maunsell," *Alberta History*, XXXIV, No. 4; XXXV, No.1.

Dobbs, Francis. *Glenbow Archives*, Pam 364.971 D 632r.

Dunn, Jack F. "James Fullwood, NWMP," *Prairie Forum*, XXXI, No.1.

Finlayson, Jas. *National Archives Canada*, MG 29, E-58 [Diary].

Francis, Sergeant-Major. "Fort Walsh to Winnipeg." *Manitoba Free Press*, 25 August 1876.

Fullerton, James. "Toronto to Fort Garry." *Scarlet and Gold*, Seventeenth Annual.

Fullwood, James. "Hazardous Trails in 1875," *Scarlet and Gold*, Seventh Annual.

Ibid. *News of the World*. 23, 30 April; 7, 14, 21, 28 May 1939.

Gillett, Earl. "Life of the Late Ex-Sergeant Major J.H.G. Bray," Kootenai Pioneer Village, Pincher Creek, 998.88.1 PG 322 m 1 Drawer No. 8.

Grain, William. "Pioneers of a Glorious Future," *Scarlet and Gold*, Twenty-ninth Annual.

Historical Society of Alberta. *A Chronicle of the Canadian West*. Calgary, 1975.

Horrall, S.W. "Sir John A. Macdonald and the Mounted Police Force for the Northwest Territories," *Canadian Historical Review*, LIII, No. 2, 1972.

Ibid. "The (Royal) North-West Mounted Police and Prostitution on the Canadian Prairies," *Prairie Forum*, X, No. 1.

Irvine, A.G. *Diary 1885* [in *Glenbow Archives*, Sanders, M 1093].

Jukes, Augustus. *Glenbow Archives*, M 607 [Diary].

Julien, Henri. "Expedition to the North-West," *Alberta Historical Review*, IX, No. 1.

LaNauze, C.D. "From the Pampas to the Prairies, 1872–1885." *Canadian Cattlemen*, December 1947.

MacDonell, Archibald. "How Sitting Bull came to Canada: Recollections of an Old Royal Mounted Police Officer." *Saskatchewan Historical Society*, File Number 205, Siouan Indians.

Maunsell, E.H. "Maunsell's Story." *RCMP Quarterly*, XLVIII, No. 1.

Ibid. "With the North West Mounted Police from 1874 to 1877." *Scarlet and Gold*, Second Annual.

Mansfield, Maureen and Mike. Library, University of Montana, Missoula. Thomas B. Boys [Diary]; James Stanford [Diary].

McDougall, R.A. *Glenbow Archives*, M 729. "A Troop – An Eyewitness Account of the March West" [Sévère Gagnon Diary].

McEntyre, J.E. *Saskatchewan Archives Board*, A 110.

McIllree, John. *Glenbow Archives*, AB McIllree #1.

McKernan, James. *Athabasca Library and Archives* [Diary].

Ibid. "Expeditions Made in 1873." *Scarlet and Gold*, Second Annual.

McQuarrie, William. *National Archives Canada*, RG 18, v. 3335, f. 724.

Metzler, William. *Glenbow Archives*, M 836.

Mitchell, Col. J.B. *Winnipeg Tribune*. 30 November and 7 December 1940.

Morgan, E.C. "The North-West Mounted Police: Internal Problems and Public Criticism, 1874–1883," *Saskatchewan History*, XXVI, Spring, 1973.

Parker, William. *Glenbow Archives*, M 934.

Patterson, Robert. *Glenbow Archives*, M 2470.

Pox-o-nachie (Little Soldier). "When the West was Young," *Scarlet and Gold*, Ninth Annual.

Rivett-Carnac, C.E. ed., "Letters from the North-West," [A.R. Dyre], *RCMP Quarterly* XVII.

Rookie #2. "Remembrances of a Tenderfoot." *Scarlet and Gold*, Third and Thirty-second Annual.

Walker, James. "Police Experiences," *Scarlet and Gold*, First Annual.

Ibid. "My Life in the North-West Mounted Police." *Alberta Historical Review*, VIII, No. 1.

Walsh, James. *Provincial Archives Manitoba*, MG 6, A-1.

Warren, Edward. *RCMP Quarterly*, VIII, No. 2.

Wilson, R.N. *National Archives Canada*, MG 29, E-47.

Wurtele, J.W.L. Daily Diary, Wood Mountain, 1880, *Archives of British Columbia*, M 1400.

INDEX OF
NAMES

[B] INDIANS

[C] MÉTIS

[D] OTHER INDIVIDUALS

GLOSSARY OF TERMS

[bc] boundary commission
[cpr] Canadian Pacific Railway
[c] crime
[g] government
[hbc] Hudson's Bay Co.
[ia] Indian agent
[j] judiciary
[m] military
[nwr] North-West Rebellion
[r] religious figures

[s] scout
[st] settler
[sur] surveyor
[t/sb] Terry-Sitting Bull Commission
[t] trader
[US] United States
[wt] whiskey trader

Adshead, W. [c]   436
Adams, James [c]   460-61
Adams, William [c]   436
Akers, David [t]   8, 129
Alexander, S. [c/t]   438
Allison "Fish", Edwin [t]   585-88
Allen, __ [t]   578
Amyot, Guillaume [m]   414
Anderson, Samuel [sur]   [2: fns 17, 72]
Andre, Alex [r]   739
Arana, Joseph [c/t]   457
Archibald, Adam George [Lt. Gov.]
  15
Armour, Samuel   46, 282, 397, 645
Arnold, __ [c/t]   438
Atkinson, George   458
Austin, M. [*London Times*]   661-62
  [19: fns 2, 5, 8, 9, 11, 16, 26]

Baird, Robert [m]   260, 463
Beaudouin, J. [wt]   318
Beaupre, Victor   415
Behan, Hughie [c]   653-55
Bell, Charles [t]   [1: fn 23]
Bell, George [t]   180
Bell, Robert [s]   48

Bernard, Hewitt [g]   19, 173, 190, 310
Berry, Dick [wt]   164-65
Berry, William [t]   188
Biggs, S.C. [j]   181
Blake, Edward [g]   29
Bleecker, H.M. [j]   433, 451
Bond, William [t]   161-162
Boulton, Charles [m]   [21: fn 30]
Brady, J.H.   405
Brennan, __   413
Brett, Dr.   652
Bridges, John [hbc]   [7: fn 26]
Brodie, Neil   [21: fn 83]
Brooks "Slim Jim" [wt]   405, 438,
  440, 446
Brotherton, David [m]   585, 590, 595
Brown, John "Kootenay" [t]   10, 718
Burke, McKinney   432
Burnett, Freeman [wt]   436
Bunn, John [hbc]   188
Butler, William Francis   6, 15-17, 21,
  49, 58-59, 84, 619

Cadd, Fred [t]   589
Cameron, Alan [m]   [21: fn 41]
Cameron, Donald R. [bc]   14, 27, 142

ABOUT THE
AUTHOR

JACK F. DUNN, a native of Turner Valley, received his BEd, BA, and MA (major: Western Canadian History) from the University of Calgary. Dunn is a long-time member of the Champlain Society, the Canadian Historical Association and the Historical Society of Alberta.

He has published *The Alberta Field Force of 1885* as well as a number of articles in historical magazines. Jack Dunn lives in Calgary with his wife, Maureen.